# A WORLD SAFE FOR COMMERCE

PRINCETON STUDIES IN INTERNATIONAL
HISTORY AND POLITICS

*Tanisha M. Fazal, G. John Ikenberry, William C. Wohlforth,
and Keren Yarhi-Milo, Series Editors*

For a full list of titles in the series, go to https://press.princeton.edu/series
/princeton-studies-in-international-history-and-politics

*The Geopolitics of Shaming: When Human Rights Pressure Works—and
When It Backfires,* Rochelle Terman

*Violent Victors: Why Bloodstained Parties Win Postwar Elections,*
Sarah Zukerman Daly

*An Unwritten Future: Realism and Uncertainty in World Politics,*
Jonathan Kirshner

*Undesirable Immigrants: Why Racism Persists in International Migration,*
Andrew S. Rosenberg

*Human Rights for Pragmatists: Social Power in Modern Times,* Jack L. Snyder

*Seeking the Bomb: Strategies of Nuclear Proliferation,* Vipin Narang

*The Spectre of War: International Communism and the Origins of World War II,*
Jonathan Haslam

*Strategic Instincts: The Adaptive Advantages of Cognitive Biases in International
Politics,* Dominic D. P. Johnson

*Divided Armies: Inequality and Battlefield Performance in Modern War,* Jason Lyall

*Active Defense: China's Military Strategy since 1949,* M. Taylor Fravel

*After Victory: Institutions, Strategic Restraint, and the Rebuilding of Order after
Major Wars, New Edition,* G. John Ikenberry

*Cult of the Irrelevant: The Waning Influence of Social Science on National Security,*
Michael C. Desch

*Secret Wars: Covert Conflict in International Politics,* Austin Carson

*Who Fights for Reputation: The Psychology of Leaders in International Conflict,*
Keren Yarhi-Milo

*Aftershocks: Great Powers and Domestic Reforms in the Twentieth Century,*
Seva Gunitsky

# A World Safe for Commerce

AMERICAN FOREIGN POLICY FROM THE
REVOLUTION TO THE RISE OF CHINA

DALE C. COPELAND

PRINCETON UNIVERSITY PRESS
PRINCETON & OXFORD

Published by Princeton University Press
41 William Street, Princeton, New Jersey 08540
99 Banbury Road, Oxford OX2 6JX

press.princeton.edu

All Rights Reserved

Library of Congress Cataloging-in-Publication Data

Names: Copeland, Dale C., author.
Title: A world safe for commerce : American foreign policy from the
    revolution to the rise of China / Dale C. Copeland.
Description: Princeton : Princeton University Press, [2024] | Includes
    bibliographical references and index.
Identifiers: LCCN 2023018406 (print) | LCCN 2023018407 (ebook) |
    ISBN 9780691172552 (hardback) | ISBN 9780691228488 (ebook)
Subjects: LCSH: United States—Economic policy. | United States—
    Foreign economic relations. | United States—Foreign relations—China. |
    China—Foreign relations—United States. | BISAC: POLITICAL SCIENCE /
    Political Economy | HISTORY / Asia / China
Classification: LCC HC103 .C76 2024 (print) | LCC HC103 (ebook) | DDC
    330.973—dc23/eng/20230606
LC record available at https://lccn.loc.gov/2023018406
LC ebook record available at https://lccn.loc.gov/2023018407

British Library Cataloging-in-Publication Data is available

Editorial: Bridget Flannery-McCoy, Alena Chekanov
Jacket: Katie Osborne
Production: Erin Suydam
Publicity: Kate Hensley (US); Kathryn Stevens (UK)
Copyeditor: Alison S. Britton

Jacket Credit: Hong Kong and Victoria Peak circa 1855 / Wikimedia Commons

This book has been composed in Arno Pro

Printed on acid-free paper. ∞

Printed in the United States of America

10 9 8 7 6 5 4 3 2 1

# CONTENTS

*Preface*   vii

*Acknowledgments*   xi

*Abbreviations for Primary Documents and Source Material*   xv

|     |                                                                        |     |
| --- | ---------------------------------------------------------------------- | --- |
|     | Introduction                                                           | 1   |
| 1   | Foundations of Dynamic Realist Theory                                  | 12  |
| 2   | Character Type, Feedback Loops, and Systemic Pressures                 | 33  |
| 3   | The Origins of the War for Colonial Independence                       | 63  |
| 4   | The United States and the World, 1790–1848                             | 94  |
| 5   | American Foreign Policy from 1850 to the Spanish-American War of 1898  | 142 |
| 6   | The U.S. Entry into the First World War                                | 189 |
| 7   | The Second World War and the Origins of the Cold War                   | 232 |
| 8   | The Crises and Conflicts of the Early Cold War, 1946–56                | 286 |
| 9   | Trade Expectations and the Struggles to End the Cold War, 1957–91      | 319 |
| 10  | Economic Interdependence and the Future of U.S.-China Relations        | 354 |

*Notes*   395

*References*   447

*Index*   469

PREFACE

THE TITLE of this book, *A World Safe for Commerce*, has within it both light and dark undertones, swirling in tension like the two halves of the "yin-yang" symbol in Chinese Daoism. On the one hand, by playing off of Woodrow Wilson's inspiring statement to Congress on April 2, 1917, that the United States had to enter the European war to "make the world safe for democracy," I wish to evoke the idea that commerce has been and can still be a force for peace, and thus a worthy end of any state's foreign policy. Yet by shifting the phrase to its commercial equivalent, I want to stress the dark and calculating side of power politics that the vast majority of American leaders since the eighteenth century have so effectively practiced. And this includes that great liberal internationalist, Woodrow Wilson himself. For more than two and half centuries, American policy makers have typically conceived of "world" as meaning not the planet, but *their* world, the places on the earth that most determine their interests and concerns. And when they conceive of keeping that world "safe," they are almost always thinking of how to ensure continued access to the goods and markets that will keep the economy strong and national security intact. If other powers help to promote and secure the expansion of this commercial world, great. Peace can prevail. But if others challenge America's access to this world, watch out! Conflict and war may have to be chosen, even when other powers want a peaceful status quo. This book represents a sustained exploration of this and other such fundamental tensions, and the trade-offs in policy that go with them.

The book represents the third in an unplanned trilogy of books that seeks to offer a more dynamic view of international politics. When I was a second-year grad student, a professor of mine made an offhand comment that Kenneth Waltz's famous *Theory of International Politics* had already shown us how great powers respond to outside forces (the "systemic" level in Waltz's language), and that all interesting work in international relations would now come from the study of domestic politics and leaders (the "unit" level). Since I had already taken to heart critiques of Waltz's book which underscored, above all, that it provided a far too static picture of the international system, I remember approaching him after class and stating that I thought there was still a lot more to be done at the systemic level. Most important, we needed to show how trends in systemic-level factors such as relative power and trade dependence force great powers to alter, often radically, their foreign policy behaviors. I recall he looked rather bemused, said something like "Good luck!" and walked off.

At the time, it was commonly believed that systemic or "neorealist" theories of power politics could only explain broad recurring patterns in great power relations, and that for any purchase on the specific behavior of states, one had to "dip down to the unit level" (to use a popular phrase from those days). I resisted this view then and have resisted it ever since. Great powers don't simply face general and largely fixed systemic factors such as bipolarity (two large states) and multipolarity (many large states), as Waltz claimed. They also must deal with their specific relative positions within those polarities and how those positions are expected to change over time. They must answer questions such as: Who is bigger than whom, and by how much? Are we rising or declining in our level of power and economic dependence compared to other states in the pecking order? How have past decisions shaped current trends not just in military power, but also in economic and technological power? And perhaps most important of all, what do we expect will happen in the future, independent of current trends, that might affect our ability to access the materials and markets we need to sustain our economic power base and thus our long-term national security?

The first book, *The Origins of Major War*, focused mostly on how dynamic trends in a state's relative military power position caused it to act either moderately in foreign policy—when it was inferior but rising in relative power and wished to buy time for future growth—or aggressively, given beliefs that it was declining from a strong current position and would be vulnerable to attack or coercion later. The second book, *Economic Interdependence and War*, took one step back in the causal chain. It showed how changes in a great power's dependence on trade and financial flows, combined with expectations of the future commercial environment, could lead those in power to believe that the state was either rising or declining in long-term power. If expectations of future trade were positive, leaders could expect the state to grow in power, and would thus have more reason for moderate foreign policies. But if expectations turned sour and leaders came to see that others were either cutting the state off from trade and investment, or were likely to do in the future, then they could anticipate decline and be more inclined to hard-line policies to rectify the situation. In short, both books, drawing from the preventive war literature, demonstrated that anticipated decline is a major reason for great powers to turn to policies that lead to risky crises or war, with the second book also showing one very important reason for why leaders come to believe their states are indeed in significant decline.

This book builds on the theoretical arguments of the first two books, but also adds three new elements to help complete the larger dynamic argument I am developing. First, drawing from offensive realism but going beyond it, I argue that in any situation of anarchy where there is no central authority to protect states from the threatening actions of others, great powers have an incentive not only to seize opportunities to expand their territorial-military positions as a hedge against potential attacks down the road. They also have an incentive to grab opportunities to expand their economic power spheres—the realms of trade and commerce they rely upon for continued growth—to reduce the chances that others will cut them off from future access to vital goods and markets. The fact that the United States and China today share this age-old drive to expand and protect their commercial realms goes a long way to explaining why in 2013 Beijing created the Belt and Road Initiative (BRI) to continue its "going out" policies from the 1990s and 2000s, and why Washington is so keen to ensure that the BRI does not hurt U.S. trade ties in Asia, Africa, and Latin America. Indeed, the reason underlying China's expansion outward parallels one of the foundational drives propelling American expansion after 1790—namely, the need for a larger sphere that could ensure continued access to raw materials, investments, and markets.

Yet the United States in its past, as with China over the last forty years, could not seize opportunities to increase its economic sphere without also considering the risk that this might upset other major powers. Smart great powers understand that overly hard-line behavior can cause a spiral of mistrust and hostility that may lead other states to reduce trade or even to engage in military actions to protect their own economic spheres. This is the second way that I extend past work. I seek to build a dynamic realist theory that integrates offensive realist insights on the need to expand as a hedge against the future with defensive realist insights on the need to worry that one might acquire a reputation for being a state with an aggressive, even pathological, character. Rational leaders will take into account both needs simultaneously as they make difficult decisions about the level of moderation or assertiveness in their foreign policies. And they will assess these needs in light of the severity of external changes in power and commerce, shifting to more hard-line policies either when they have reason to fear deep decline, or when they are rising but believe that without stronger policies, they will start to peak and decline in the near future (for the latter, think of the United States after 1895 and China after 2007).

The third new element is the book's analysis of exactly how rational leaders interested in security go about making assessments of the other's character—assessments that, in conjunction with power trends, shape the way such leaders estimate the level of future threat arising from the external environment. Since these leaders are focused on the external environment—the other state's character, and whether it is, like their state, rational and security-seeking, or something else altogether—this is not a "dipping down to the unit level" to explain why these leaders make the decisions they do. Rather, it is simply an unpacking of the various forces that shape the behavior of potential adversaries and that must go into any rational security-maximizing leader's evaluation of the other's future willingness to trade and to trade at high levels. This leader's commercial expectations for the future, in short, come from somewhere, and in chapter 2 I unpack "the where," using the assumption that *nothing from within this leader's state* is shaping his or her expectations. The expectations are shaped only by factors outside of the state. This assumption preserves the core assertion of all systemic realist arguments: namely, that rational leaders focused on national security are driven only by changes in the external situation the state faces, not by domestic pressures bubbling up "from below." So while I later add complexity to my initial barebones argument, the book also bounds its argument in a way that gives the theory a strong measure of parsimony, and most importantly, allows it to be tested against the many theories that *do* start from unit-level domestic pressures to explain a state's behavior.

The empirical focus of the book is on the main cases of American foreign policy over the last two and a half centuries. These cases, from the War for Independence to the Cold War, reveal something important. They show that American policy makers, far from simply responding to pressures from below or personal impulses, have regularly operated from a logic that I claim is a universal and overhanging "force from above" for all great powers, or at least for those in the post-1660 age of modern globalized commerce. American leaders, in sum, are not naïve, nor are they all that different from the leaders of the European and Asian states explored in my first two books. In fact, they understand the commerce of power politics better than perhaps any other single group of state leaders over the last three centuries. Even if they cloak their policies in the warm and fuzzy language of liberal individualism and freedom, and occasionally find themselves shaped (and trapped) by this language, they prove themselves to be, first and foremost, careful calculators of national security through the lens of economic and commercial power. And for the most part, the world is a better place for it.

ACKNOWLEDGMENTS

THIS BOOK has a long history, and there are many people to thank for their help along the way. I first presented some of my initial and largely inchoate ideas on economic interdependence and international conflict back in my last year of graduate school at the University of Chicago, and I had a chance to return a quarter century later to present what I hoped was a much improved and better supported version of those ideas at the University of Chicago's Program on International Politics, Economics, and Security (PIPES). John Mearsheimer and Charles Lipson were there on both occasions to offer direct and insightful comments on my overall logic and evidence. The dynamic realist theory that I present in this book may ultimately show that offensive realism should be best thought of as what physicists call a "special case" within a larger theoretical framework. But it was John's version of offensive realism that convinced me that all great powers are forced by their uncertainty about the future to seek to expand their realms of power—in the military-territorial sense for John; and in the commercial-economic sense for me. And it was Charles's graduate seminar on international political economy, which opened with Waltz's seminal book, that pushed me to consider how the issues of the IPE and security subfields might be brought together within a single framework.

The rigor of the critiques offered that day at the PIPES seminar decisively shifted the direction of this book, and for that I want to also thank Paul Poast and Marc Trachtenberg and the graduate student participants who were there that day. Around the same time, I also greatly benefited from a seminar at MIT, where many of the case studies in the book were discussed. In particular, I wish to thank Frank Gavin, Ken Oye, Roger Peterson, Barry Posen, Dick Samuels, and Stephen Van Evera for their great comments on that day. Also significant to the development of the argument were two presentations over two years I did at workshops on trade and conflict at the University of California, Irvine, organized by Michelle Garfinkel and Stergios Skaperdes of Irvine's economics department. Feedback from Michelle and Stergios, as well as from Tommaso Sonno, helped me see more clearly how economists might go about formalizing my expectations-based argument. I've held off publishing the formal model that I developed out of those sessions for my next book. But the exercise itself served to hone the deductive logic behind my argument. I also want to thank Mike Beckley and Pat MacDonald for comments on my theoretical argument and the First World War chapter at the online 2020 APSA convention, Michael Mastanduno for his astute critique of the final draft, and Chris Carter, Gary Goertz, Stephan Haggard, and David Waldner for valuable discussions on the book's methodological approach.

As the book was nearing completion, I had a chance to present chapters from the manuscript in three quite distinct venues. The theory chapters were presented to the Institute for Security and Conflict Studies seminar on international security at George Washington University. For suggestions that helped me refine many aspects of the final argument, I thank Alex Downes, Charlie Glaser, and Joanna Spear, as well as the attending GWU grad students. At Haifa University's workshop on the future of the world order, sponsored by Israel Science Foundation, I received great feedback on my chapter on the future of U.S.-China relations from an amazing group of scholars, including Lars-Erik Cederman, Tom Christensen, Andrew Hurrell, John Ikenberry, Arie Kacowicz, Deborah Larson, Jack Snyder, and the workshop's organizer, Benny Miller. The same chapter was also presented at a conference on the future of the U.S. dollar and the global economic order at Credit Suisse Bank in Zurich. I was surprised and delighted to have John Major, former prime minister of Britain, as my discussant. Sir John offered trenchant comments about the practical implications of my trade expectations logic that significantly shaped the way I think about China's ability to use the global system for its advantage.

At the University of Virginia I benefited greatly from a scrub session on the book and two later discussions organized through the Miller Center and the program on Democratic Statecraft. Will Hitchcock, David Leblang, Jeff Legro, Melvyn Leffler, Allen Lynch, John Owen, Len Schoppa, Todd Sechser, and Mark Schwartz provided incisive comments on specific chapters. I was also fortunate to receive feedback from a number of smart graduate students who directly shaped the book's ultimate form: Josh Cheatham, Ghita Chraibi, Justin Gorkowski, James Kwoun, Yuji Maeda, Sowon Park, Sunggun Park, Angela Ro, John Robinson, Melle Scholten, Luke Schumacher, and Chen Wang. Six terrific undergrad students also offered great comments on the overall argument: Sam Brewbaker, Jenny Glaser, Lily Lin, Adrian Mamaril, Dao Tran, and Nick Wells. I'm also very grateful to four of my former grad students who took time away from their own busy academic careers to read the near-finished manuscript and help me hone the final product: Kyle Haynes, David Kearn, Mike Poznansky, and Brandon Yoder. And, of course, I need to thank four anonymous reviewers for their insightful comments and my wonderful editors at Princeton University Press: Bridget Flannery-McCoy, who guided the book through the challenges of the review process and the crafting of the final product; and Eric Crahan, who first inspired me to write a book on American foreign policy building on the ideas from my previous book for Princeton.

Finally, I dedicate this book to my family: V. Natasha Copeland and my two amazing children Liam and Katya. They kept my spirit up through the long and winding road that was this book project: tolerating long hours in my room going through documents when I could have been playing more soccer, volleyball, or Clue with them; and helping me relax with Seinfeld, Harry Potter movies, and Beatles albums when I seemed just a bit too stressed out. Couldn't have done it without you!

CDJD     *The Cabinet Diaries of Josephus Daniels, 1913–1921*, ed. E. David Cronon (Lincoln: University of Nebraska Press, 1963).

CIA (CWE)     *At Cold War's End: U.S. Intelligence on the Soviet Union and Eastern Europe, 1989–1991*, ed. Benjamin B. Fischer (Washington, DC: Central Intelligence Agency, 1999).

CIA (HT)     *CIA Cold War Records: The CIA under Harry Truman*, ed. Michael Warner (Washington, DC: Central Intelligence Agency, 1994).

CR     *Churchill and Roosevelt: The Complete Correspondence*, 3 vols, ed. Warren F. Kimball (Princeton, NJ: Princeton University Press, 1984).

CWIHP     Cold War in International History Project. Washington, DC.

CWIHPB     *Cold War in International History Project Bulletin*, Issues 1–11 (Washington, DC, 1992–1998).

DAPS     *Containment: Documents on American Policy and Strategy*, eds. Thomas Etzold and John Lewis Gaddis (New York: Columbia University Press, 1978).

DDEL     Dwight D. Eisenhower Library, Abilene, Kansas.

DS     *Dimitrov and Stalin 1934–1943: Letters from the Soviet Archives*, ed. Alexander Dallin and F. I. Firsov (New Haven, CT: Yale University Press, 2000).

DSB     Department of State Bulletin (Washington, DC, various years).

ED     *The Eisenhower Diaries*, ed. Robert H. Ferrell (New York: Norton, 1981).

FCY     Department of Commerce, *Foreign Commerce Yearbook* (Washington, DC, various years).

FD     *The Forrestal Diaries*, eds. Walter Millis and E. S. Duffield (New York: Viking, 1951).

FDRL    Franklin D. Roosevelt Library, Hyde Park, New York.

FP    *Federalist Papers.*

FRUS    *Foreign Relations of the United States* (Washington, DC: U.S. GPO, various years).

FTP    *For the President, Personal and Secret: Correspondence between Franklin D. Roosevelt and William C. Bullitt,* ed. Orville H. Bullitt (Boston: Houghton Mifflin, 1972).

GOC    *The Governance of China: Xi Jinping Speeches,* 4 vols. Beijing: Foreign Language Press.

HD    Edward House Diaries, Yale University Library.

HSTL    Harry S. Truman Library, Independence, Missouri.

IAFP    *Ideas and American Foreign Policy: A Reader,* ed. Andrew Bacevich. Oxford: Oxford University Press.

IPCH    *Intimate Papers of Colonel House,* 2 vols., ed. Charles Seymour (Boston: Houghton Mifflin, 1926).

JFKL    John F. Kennedy Library, Boston, Massachusetts.

JFKL NSF    John F. Kennedy Library, National Security Files.

KR    *Khrushchev Remembers,* trans. and ed. Strobe Talbott (New York: Little, Brown, 1972).

KR: LT    *Khrushchev Remembers: The Last Testament,* trans. and ed. Strobe Talbott (Boston: Little, Brown, 1974).

KT    *The Kissinger Transcripts: The Top-Secret Talks with Beijing and Moscow,* ed. William Burr (New York: New Press, 1998).

LC    Library of Congress.

LLWP    *The Life and Letter of Walter H. Page,* 3 vols., ed. Burton Hendrick (Garden City, NY: Doubleday, Page, 1926).

LTT    *The Letters and Times of the Tylers,* 2 vols., ed. Lyon G. Tyler (New York: De Capo, 1970).

LWES    *Life of William, Earl of Shelburne,* ed. Lord Fitzmaurice, 2 vols., 2nd rev. ed. (London: MacMillan, 1912).

MH    *Masterpieces of History: The Peaceful End of the Cold War in Europe,* eds. Svetlana Savranskaya, Thomas Blanton, and Vladislav Zubok (Budapest: Central European University Press, 2010).

MJQA    *Memoirs of John Quincy Adams,* ed. Charles Francis Adams. 12 vols. (New York: Lippincott, 1875).

MP      *Papers of James Madison, Presidential Series*, 11 vols. (Charlottesville: University of Virginia Press, various dates).

MPWW    *The Message and Papers of Woodrow Wilson*, 2 vols., ed. Albert Shaw (New York: Review of Reviews Co., 1924).

NA      United States National Archives.

NPD     *Polk: The Diary of a President, 1845–1849*, ed. Allan Nevins (New York: Longmans, Green, 1952).

NSA (BC)    National Security Archive, *The Berlin Crisis, 1958–1962* (Alexandria: Chadwyck-Healey, 1991, microfiche).

NSA (SE)    National Security Archive, *The Soviet Estimate: U.S. Analysis of the Soviet Union, 1947–1991* (Alexandria, VA: Chadwyck-Healey, 1995, microfiche).

NYT     *New York Times*, various years.

PD      *The Diary of James K. Polk During His Presidency, 1845–1849* (Chicago: McClurg, 1910).

PTBF    *The Political Thought of Benjamin Franklin*, ed. Ralph Ketcham (Indianapolis, IN: Bobbs-Merrill, 1965).

PV      *The Price of Vision: The Diary of Henry A. Wallace, 1946–1949*, ed. John Morton Blum (New York: Houghton Mifflin, 1973).

PWW     *The Papers of Woodrow Wilson*, 68 vols., ed. Arthur S. Link (Princeton, NY: Princeton University Press, various years).

TJW     *Thomas Jefferson: Writings*, ed. Merrill Peterson (Library of America).

TP      *The Tiananmen Papers*, eds. Andrew J. Nathan and Perry Link (New York: Public Affairs).

UECW    *Understanding the End of the Cold War: The Reagan/Gorbachev Years*, briefing book prepared by the National Security Archive for an oral history conference, Brown University, 7–10 May, 1998.

WWLL    *Woodrow Wilson: Life and Letters*, 8 vols., ed. Ray Stannard Baker (Garden City, NY: Doubleday, Doran, 1935).

WR      *Wilson and Revolutions, 1913–1921*, ed. Lloyd C. Gardner (Lanham, MD: University Press of America, 1982).

WSA     *The Writings of Samuel Adams*, 3 vols., ed. Harry Alonzo Cushing (New York: G. P. Putnam's).

YCY     Department of Commerce Statistics, various years.

# Introduction

THE WORLD has changed. Over the past decade, we have witnessed a distinct shift toward a renewed competition between the great powers. The green light that China seems to have given to Russia's brutal invasion of Ukraine in February 2022 and its subsequent saber-rattling over Taiwan six months later only served to reinforce concerns that have been building within the American foreign policy community since at least 2010. Just how intense this great power competition will become is uncertain. But what seems clear is that the optimism of the 1990s—when pundits and politicians alike saw growing economic interdependence and a rules-based international order as fostering long-term prosperity and peace between the United States, China, and Russia—is gone. In its place is talk of new cold wars and even military conflict. A rising China now seems willing to flex its muscles not just in its region but around the globe. Leaders in Beijing have not only challenged the U.S. navy for dominance in the South China Sea and the Pacific but also have signaled that they intend to extend China's economic and political influence not just to Eurasia and Africa, but to an area Americans have always considered their backyard: Latin America. Russia, with a GDP the size of Italy, may have been reduced to the status of a middle power within the larger Sino-American competition. Yet its leaders' very resentment of this fact, combined with Russia's vast energy resources and the willingness to take military actions against neighbors—Georgia in 2008, Ukraine in 2014 and again in 2022—make Russia a continued threat to the global economic and political system. Even if Russian leaders cannot contribute to this system, they can undermine it, thereby interfering with the plans of both the United States and China as they struggle for more influence and control around the world.

Russia's continued ability to play the role of spoiler, however, should not distract us from a larger geopolitical fact: it is the bipolar struggle between the United States and China that is the new Great Game of the twenty-first century. Because both sides have nuclear weapons, we can expect leaders in Washington and Beijing to be inherently reluctant to engage in behavior that might raise the risk of actual war. And we can be thankful that at least one key lesson came out of the Cold War: that neither side can afford to push the system to anything that looks remotely like the Cuban Missile Crisis of 1962. This is the good news.

Yet as this book shows, there is also bad, or at least concerning, news. Great powers need continued economic prosperity to support their militaries and to ensure that they can maintain stability at home in the face of other states' possible efforts to subvert it. They thus have an ongoing drive to expand their economic and commercial power spheres beyond their borders, and to support these spheres with strong navies and offensive power-projection capability. The American ongoing military presence in the Middle East and the Indo-Pacific regions since World War II and China's growing naval support for its Belt and Road Initiative are only two obvious examples from recent history. This means that even in the nuclear age, great powers will struggle to improve their geoeconomic positions around the world. They will worry that their adversaries might decide to cut them off from access to vital raw materials, investments, and markets ("RIM"). In short, *commercial struggles* for prosperity and position remain an essential element of great power grand strategy, and these struggles can end up leading to crises that increase the probability of devastating war between the powers.

To see the inherent dangers, we need only remember that the Second World War in the Pacific came directly out of the tightening of an economic noose around Japan beginning in the early 1930s and ending with a total allied embargo on oil exports to Japan in 1941. Chinese leaders are very much aware that the scenario of 1941, even more than that of 1914, is the one to avoid. Yet like Japanese leaders after 1880, they also know that China must work hard to extend its commercial presence, even at the risk of a spiral of hostility, if it is to sustain the growth that has made it the stable and secure superpower that it is today. This tension between needing to expand one's economic sphere of influence and wanting to avoid an escalatory spiral that might restrict access to vital goods and markets is baked into the DNA of modern great power politics. It is a tension, as we will see, that the United States has faced repeatedly since the founding of the American republic.

When it comes to explaining how competitions over commerce affect the likely behavior of great powers, there are two big questions that need to be examined in depth. What exactly is the role that commerce plays in driving states *either* toward more accommodating soft-line actions *or* toward more assertive hard-line postures, including the initiation of military containment and war against adversaries? And how significant is this role compared to the many other causes of cooperation and conflict that scholars have identified? This book seeks to answer these questions through a study of American

foreign policy from the eighteenth century to contemporary U.S.-China relations. Yet this is not simply a book that explores the fascinating changes in
American behavior toward the outside world since 1750 and then applies historical lessons to twenty-first century geopolitics. More than that, it represents
a test of the relative explanatory power of the key theories of international relations (IR) for one very important country over time and across highly varied
circumstances. These theories can be divided into two main groups: "realist"
theories that focus on *how threats external to a state* will force almost any type
of leader or elite group toward similar policies; and "liberal" theories that emphasize *how forces internal to a state* shape and constrain its behavior
independent of the effects of the external factors. It is clear to nearly all IR
scholars that the United States, due to its strong liberal democratic foundations, poses a hard case for any realist theory, including the one offered here.
We just expect American leaders to "think differently" about global affairs, and
to be guided more by a sense of moral values, domestic pressures, and ideological ends than by traditional European notions of *Realpolitik*. So as that
great philosopher (and sometime singer) Frank Sinatra might have said, if realist theory can make it here, it should be able to make it anywhere.

This book has three specific goals. The first is the building of a better, more
dynamic realist theory of international relations, one that can resolve some of
the problems with the two main versions of systemic realism in the field—
namely, offensive realism and defensive realism. Systemic realists start with
the common assumption that in anarchy, with no central authority to protect
them, great powers will be primarily driven by factors that transcend domestic
issues: factors such as differentials in relative power and uncertainty about the
economic and military threats that other states pose, now and into the future.
Yet offensive and defensive realists remain divided over the role of such systemic forces. By bringing together the insights of both forms of realism, the
book establishes a stronger foundation for thinking about how states grapple
with trade-offs presented by their external situations. Great powers do worry
about building power positions that can handle problems that may arise in the
future, as offensive realists stress. But they are also concerned that being overly
assertive in the pursuit of this position can lead them into undesired spirals of
hostility and conflict, as defensive realists emphasize.

By fusing these insights and then extending them into the realm of commercial geopolitics, this book goes beyond the limitations of current realist
theory. It reveals the importance of two crucial variables to the decision-
making process of any great power: the intensity of a state's drive to extend and
protect its economic power sphere to ensure a base-line level of access to key
raw materials, investments, and markets; and leader expectations about how
willing adversaries are to allow the state future access to areas of trade and

finance beyond its immediate power sphere. Modern realist theories tend to focus primarily on the military and territorial aspects of the great power security competition, downplaying the economic. These former aspects are important, to be sure. But by tying drives for *commercial* spheres of influence to *expectations of trade beyond those spheres*, I show that the overall trade environment and the way leaders anticipate changes in that environment regularly play an even more fundamental role in driving the foreign policies of great powers.

The second main goal of the book is to show that this new more dynamic and commercial approach to systemic realism can more than hold its own with the very case that has always proved problematic for realism: the United States and its foreign policies over the last two and a half centuries. Contemporary realists often buy into the liberal premise that America is exceptional, that it is founded in an ideology that rejected "Old World" aristocratic power politics in favor of the liberal pursuit of individual happiness, and that this outlook often leads the United States to act in ways that are contrary to realist predictions. Such realists are inclined to accept traditional arguments that the perceived need to spread democracy or protect liberal institutions abroad have been driving forces for why American leaders moved to a more globalist strategy after 1916 and why Washington continues to promote "liberal hegemony" long after the end of the Cold War. This starting assumption can lead offensive and defensive realists to give too much away to domestic-level explanations for American foreign policy behavior. To be sure, U.S. leaders and officials have at times sought to extend American liberalism's reach when they could do so at low cost or when having liberal states in one's sphere was seen as essential to countering the extension of an opponent's sphere, as during the Cold War. And at certain points in U.S. history, as I show, bottom-up domestic pressures within a pluralist American state did indeed play important roles in shaping policy. This book's empirical chapters demonstrate, however, that the importance of commercial and power-political factors on American foreign policy behavior over the last two and a half centuries has been significantly underplayed, at least by political scientists if not always by neo-Marxist revisionist historians. From the formation of the republic to the current era, U.S. leaders, concerned about long-term national security, have been driven by a combination of commercial factors and relative power trends that have often overshadowed the ideological and domestic determinants of foreign policy. Americans, it turns out, are extremely smart and savvy realists, precisely because they have intuitively understood from the get-go the importance of dynamically fusing offensive and defensive realist insights with commercial power politics.

In the testing of its dynamic realist approach, this book does something unusual. Almost every book of historically based political science tries to set its theory against "competing arguments" in order to show that the causal factors posited by other theories are less useful in explaining the empirical cases of conflict and war than the pet theory of the book in question. This leads to endless cycles of debate as to which scholar's factors were most critical to the understanding of controversial cases. My method is different. By recognizing that almost every case involves numerous key causal factors, I seek to identify the *causal role* that these factors are playing in a particular case, such as Woodrow Wilson's decision to enter World War I or Franklin Roosevelt's and Harry Truman's policies that helped establish the post–World War II global order. Specifically, I ask questions such as: To what extent was a factor *propelling* the leader to act, rather than acting as a *facilitating* factor for that action, or perhaps as a *constraining factor* that forced the postponement of the action? Was the factor merely *accelerating* the leader's timetable for action or perhaps only *reinforcing* the original decision by giving added reasons to act, rather than being the factor that propelled the leader to act in the first place? As I discuss in chapter 2, by analyzing the various roles different causal factors play within any particular "bundle" of factors leading to an important event in world history, we can provide nuanced understandings of history while at the same time isolating "what was really driving the event" as opposed to simply helping bring it on or change the manner in which it occurred.

This book examines almost all the cases of American foreign policy history after 1760 where there was a significant shift toward conflict or away from conflict with other states. Although this makes for a longer book, covering so many cases avoids biasing the research toward events that support one's theory, while helping scholars and practitioners understand the full scope of causal forces that are at work across time and for very different sets of both domestic and international conditions. There are cases that do not work for my theory, such as the 1835–42 disputes with Britain over Canada, the inward turn from 1865 to 1885, and important aspects of America's twenty-five-year involvement in Vietnam. Finding such problematic cases is a *good* thing. Since no theory in social science can (or should try to) explain everything, such negative cases serve to highlight—for both theorists and policy makers—the conditions under which a theory likely will and *will not* be useful.

This caveat notwithstanding, the broad sweep of cases covered in this book reveals an important pattern. From the get-go, American leaders were very concerned about maintaining and enhancing a core economic power sphere that would ensure access to key trading partners, initially in the neighborhood and then around the world. When these leaders were confident about future commerce and believed that trade was helping to build a strong and growing base of economic power, they were inclined to maintain peaceful relations with European and Asian great powers, even when ideological and domestic variables were pushing for conflict. When, however, their expectations of future trade turned sour and they saw others trying to restrict American access to the vital goods and markets needed for economic growth, these leaders almost invariably turned nasty—and for national security reasons, not for fear of the loss of elite power and wealth as left-leaning revisionist scholars typically argue. American decision-makers knew that without a forceful response to the other states' policies, the long-term security of the nation would be put at risk. A weakened economy at home would have reduced the nation's ability to protect its interests and might even leave the homeland vulnerable to attack or outside efforts to subvert the social order. Commercial ties, therefore, proved critical in pushing American leaders either toward peace or toward war, depending on whether their expectations of the future were optimistic or pessimistic and whether American and foreign diplomacy was seen as able to overcome mistrust and foster positive expectations into the future.

The empirical chapters begin with the War for Colonial Independence by adding a commercial explanation of the origins of the war to the ideological and domestic-political ones of traditional historiography. I seek to answer a puzzle that historians often ignore or downplay: why were the British North American colonies from 1763 to 1773 so reluctant to begin a war with the mother country, Britain, and yet why did they ultimately, and as a cohesive group, choose to undertake such a risky move? I argue that the war for independence was initiated not only to defend the concept of personal liberty—a taken-for-granted notion since Britain's Glorious Revolution of 1688—but to safeguard American commercial and economic growth in the face of London's determined efforts to restrict the rise of an increasingly vibrant British North America. The continuation of the liberties and society that the colonists had come to value were seen as intimately tied to the continued development of trade; without the latter, the local power structures that protected the former would decline over the long term.

The subsequent conflicts of the young republic were also driven by fears for long-term commercial access and the economic growth needed to protect the unique American republican experiment. The War of 1812 may have been about the safeguarding of republicanism in a general sense, as some historians suggest. But it was not a war chosen to protect the power of certain parties or to give western and southern "war hawks" more land for territorial expansion. Rather, President Madison reluctantly moved to war as a response to British policies that had shut U.S. products out of the European continent, policies that would have hurt the nation's viability as a republic into the future. Similarly, President Polk did not initiate the war against Mexico in 1846 to extend slavery westward or to make his Democratic Party more popular, but to preempt an expected British move to acquire California and then use its ports to dominate the burgeoning trade with China and the Far East. If he could not secure this future trade, the nation itself would be more vulnerable to the economic and political predations of European powers.

By the late nineteenth century, the United States had become what it was not in 1812 or 1846—namely, a real player in the great power game. But its position was still vulnerable, albeit in a different way. To continue its industrial growth and to protect its increasing overseas trade—the growth of which was set in motion by the policies of the 1840s—U.S. leaders had come to see the importance of securing the American commercial position in the Caribbean and the Far East against the increasingly expansionistic powers of Britain and Germany. When a humanitarian crisis arose in Cuba after 1896, President McKinley was initially reluctant to act. By early 1898, however, with China being carved up by the European powers and a Central American canal needed to complete Alfred Thayer Mahan's vision of the United States as a secure naval and commercial power, McKinley shifted gears. He became convinced that a war with Spain over Cuba would kill two birds with one stone: it would not only solve the humanitarian crisis but would allow the taking of Spanish territories needed to counter British and German commercial expansionism in the Far East and the Caribbean.

Perhaps the most surprising case of the book is the 1917 U.S. intervention into World War I. Almost every historian of this intervention suggests that Woodrow Wilson was reluctant to enter the war but felt forced to do so in order to have a say at the peace table and to help to reshape the world according to his liberal ideological vision—a vision that included promoting democracy and collective security as alternatives to traditional balance of power politics. The truth is much more complex and interesting. Wilson did harbor thoughts from his first days in office that the world would be a better place if it had more liberal democracies, especially ones trading freely with each other. But he also understood that global politics was about trade-offs. And if he had to choose between spreading democracy and protecting U.S. trade access, the latter would have to come first. It was only later in the war, with an allied victory on the horizon, that Wilson gave free rein to his more idealistic fantasy of remaking the world in the American image. Up until that point, his primary goal was to protect America's economic power position in the western hemisphere and in Asia from threats of great power encroachment.

This broader objective was in place from his first month in office in March 1913 and it continually shaped his willingness to contain civil conflicts in Central America and the Caribbean prior to and during the European war. Wilson's liberal mindset shaped his perception of which states were seen as the greatest threats to U.S. commerce through the Panama Canal and in the Far East: namely, the great rising neo-mercantilist nations of Germany and Japan. Spreading liberal democracy was at best an occasional means to his larger geopolitical ends. That the nation's commercial security was foremost in his mind is shown by his great concern in mid to late 1916 that *Britain* had perhaps become the greatest threat to U.S. trade in the western hemisphere. Germany's shift to unrestricted submarine warfare and its encouraging of a Mexican attack on the United States in early 1917 made it clear that war to ensure a British-French victory would be necessary. But when he told Congress on April 2 that the world must be made "safe for democracy," his main goal remained Germany's defeat and the denial of its penetration into the western hemisphere, not the more expansive objective of consolidating global democracy that would show itself at Versailles two years later. Until the end of 1917, for example, he worked hard to pull Austria-Hungary out of the war by promising Vienna that it could keep its oppressive multiethnic empire. As in the War of 1812, a war whose parallels Wilson keenly understood, ensuring trade access and U.S. economic security proved to be the primary motivating reason for war.

I have covered the decision-making of Franklin Delano Roosevelt that led to the U.S. entry into the Second World War in a previous book, so I only briefly discuss those decisions as part of a larger consideration of the U.S. turn to "globalism" after 1940. I show that Roosevelt's concerns for Hitler's Germany after 1935 initially resembled Woodrow Wilson's regarding Germany from 1913 to 1917. He worried that if Hitler were ever able to defeat the other European great powers, Germany could then directly threaten the strong U.S. commercial and geopolitical position in the western hemisphere. But after France's defeat in June 1940, FDR realized he had to go much further than Wilson. He saw that the increasingly complex U.S. economy needed access to Eurasia and Southeast Asia, and that if Germany proved able to eliminate its adversaries in continental Europe, it posed a direct threat to America's long-term power position. He thus adopted a strategy of holding Germany to Europe and North Africa as he consolidated a "Grand Area" that would contain German growth in the short term and hopefully lead to an eventual American victory over Nazism in the long term. Once Hitler attacked the Soviet Union in late June 1941, however, FDR immediately saw that he needed to supply Stalin with the military equipment and resources he needed to stop Germany from controlling Eurasia. He feared that Japan would take advantage of Hitler's action and go north, splitting Russian forces in two and allowing Germany to win control of the Eurasian heartland, giving it an impenetrable base for future expansion of its closed economic sphere. He thus cut Japan off from access to oil and raw materials, forcing it to launch a war south rather than going north, and saving Stalin from a two-front war. The strategy worked, and by mid-1943, German forces were in retreat. Yet the larger strategy for a Grand Area of trade and bases led by the United States was kept in place. By late 1943, the United States was already preparing for the coming struggle over economic and military power spheres with a victorious Russia—a struggle that would see America emerge in a dominant position by 1945.

For most realist and liberal scholars, the ensuing Cold War between the United States and the Soviet Union, with its numerous crises and war scares, seems to be the kind of conflict that cannot be explained by commercial factors. After all, with little trade between the two superpowers after 1945, we should expect commerce to drop out as a potentially important cause of either conflict or cooperation. But to think in this way is to think only in terms of snapshots of trade at any point in time. I show that expectations of future trade were critical in many of the key Cold War crises, and in the start of the Cold War itself. In 1945, both sides sought to stabilize the peace through commercial means that would maintain the high level of cooperation they had realized during the war. But extraneous factors, particularly the economic chaos in Europe after the war, made it impossible for either side to believe that trade and financial flows between their spheres could be maintained. The ideological divide made things worse, since the Americans worried that states in western Europe that fell to Communism would quickly join the closed economic realm of the Soviet Union. With each side fearing that the other was trying to improve its economic position at its own expense, a Cold War struggle for economic power spheres in Europe and Asia became inevitable.

For the next four decades, the ups and downs of American-Soviet relations had much to do with perceptions of threats to commerce and with perceptions that trade expectations could be improved by diplomatic negotiations and détente. While many of the key superpower standoffs of the 1950s and 1960s were shaped by trade expectations, two in particular were not: the Berlin Crisis of 1948 and the Korean War of 1950–53. Here, I briefly explore the noncommercial forces behind these conflicts. I also consider the case of Vietnam, 1948 to 1965, which partly works for my argument and partly does not. From 1948 through the 1950s, the Truman and Eisenhower administrations saw Vietnam as critical to helping Japan rebuild economically and play its key role in the U.S.-led alliance structure. By the early 1960s, however, with Japan's economy having rebounded, a more purely geopolitical fear—the fear of falling dominos—took over and led to the disastrous U.S. policy from 1963 to 1972. I then turn to the economic diplomacy of efforts to reduce superpower tensions after 1955. On two main occasions, in 1971–73 and in 1987–90, Americans held out the carrot of future trade deals to help secure the agreements that initially moderated the intensity of the Cold War and then ended it for good. I also show, perhaps surprisingly, that there was an opportunity for a commerce-based détente in the late 1950s and early 1960s, when presidents Eisenhower and Kennedy seriously contemplated offering the prospect of increased trade in return for promises of more moderate Soviet behavior in the Cold War, including in the now-decolonizing Global South (the "Third World"). Unfortunately, the conditions for a peace deal in the late 1950s and early 1960s were not yet in place—in particular, neither side yet had a secure nuclear second-strike to deter attacks on the homeland. Once they were in place, expectations of future trade shaped by astute diplomacy could play a key role in the eventual ending of the Cold War.

The final chapter fulfills the third goal of the book—namely, to use the theoretical and historical insights of the first ten chapters to analyze the implications of different scenarios for the future stability of U.S.-China relations. Notwithstanding Russia's continued ability to disrupt the system, at least on its own immediate periphery, in larger grand strategic terms it is the geopolitical competition between the United States and the new Chinese superpower that matters. No one can predict whether China will keep growing or will peak in relative power before overtaking the United States, nor can one predict the nature of the Chinese state and its goals in another ten or twenty years. But we *can* use well-developed international relations theories such as the dynamic realist theory of this book to predict how and why the United States will likely *respond* to the different scenarios that could arise, depending on combinations of these power and domestic regime-type variables. If U.S. leaders and officials can properly understand what these scenarios entail, and how they can best deal with the dangers and opportunities in each, we may be able to avoid the mistakes of the past that have led to unnecessary wars and the devastation of societies.

To conclude this introduction, let me suggest that different audiences will want to read this book in different ways. I have designed the chapters so the general reader interested mostly in the historical cases can read just the introductory chapter and parts of chapter 1 and then jump to the historical analyses of chapters 3 to 9 and the evaluation of the future of U.S.-China relations in chapter 10. Scholars of international relations and political science will want to examine the full explication of the theory of this book in chapters 1 and 2. Chapter 1 sets down the foundations of the dynamic realist theory of the book. It accepts the offensive realist insight that great powers are driven to expand their spheres of influence to hedge against future problems. Yet I show that this insight is even more relevant to economic and commercial spheres than to the military and territorial ones typically stressed by offensive realists.

Chapter 2 extends the initial analysis by bringing in defensive realist insights on the character type of the adversary as well as on the security dilemma and the related reality of feedback loops between hard-line behavior and spirals of hostility and commercial restrictions. Rational security-driven leaders will understand that they must calibrate the severity of their policies based on variations in character type. They will also know that they will have to balance their desires to expand their nations' economic power spheres with the risks of provoking increasing restrictions on their global trade. Chapter 2 also lays out the alternative method of "doing" historical case analysis, one which focuses on identifying the causal roles of the different factors involved in a case, rather than trying to disconfirm competing explanations for specific cases. It thus provides a way to help both international relations scholars and historians avoid talking at cross-purposes, and to see the value of debating not *whether* specific factors were important to explaining changes in state behavior over time but rather *how* such factors were operating in the cases—whether they were propelling leaders to act as opposed to, say, facilitating, constraining, or accelerating their actions. If done properly, this approach to history can help decision-makers understand the conditions under which certain policies will lead to a stable peace or to destabilizing conflicts. And, of course, we can all hope that as the subtlety of their understanding grows over time, better policies will emerge.

# 1

# Foundations of Dynamic Realist Theory

THE THEORETICAL WORK of this book is animated by two puzzles. First, what explains why American foreign policy often shifts dramatically from peaceful engagement with other states to assertive or even aggressive policies designed to achieve policy goals through either threats to use force or the actual initiation of war? In the 1761 to 1776 period, this was a switch from seeking cooperation with Great Britain to a war for independence. In 1795 to 1812, we saw a move from economic engagement to the U.S. initiation of war against British Canada. In the 1824 to 1846 period, the United States moved from the avoidance of conflict to a near-war with Britain and an actual war with Mexico. After turning inward to deal with slavery, this pattern was again repeated from 1865 to 1898, with a largely isolationist America ultimately shifting to a program of intense naval buildup, war with Spain, and the creation of an overseas empire by force.

In the early twentieth century, it might seem that the United States was again seeking to avoid military adventures outside of its immediate sphere of influence on the continent of North America. Yet from 1898 to 1928, the country's leaders felt compelled to intervene militarily over twenty-five times in the Caribbean and Central America to, among other things, build and protect a Panama Canal, formalize the hold on Hawaii, and develop a naval base in its Philippine colony, and of course to enter World War I to help defeat Germany before it was too late. By the mid-1930s, isolationist sentiment was in the ascendant, and individuals such as Franklin Delano Roosevelt, who did see major overseas threats emerging, were having a hard time creating the naval power and alliance structures needed to counter them. Yet from 1940–41 on, the United States embarked on a deliberate policy of military power projection designed to deter or fight any great power that might seek to control Eurasia. This policy turned into a forty-five-year Cold War struggle over the Eurasian "periphery" and the western hemisphere that almost led to thermonuclear war on more than one occasion. The end of the Cold War seemed to provide a permanent respite from this historical pattern of peaceful engagement and subsequent conflict—indeed, a possible "end of history," as Francis Fukuyama's popular phrase went.[1] Yet today we are seeing the United States and China apparently moving closer and closer to a new cold war, despite calls by leaders and officials on both sides for measured calm and a sustaining of economic engagement.

This book will help to explain these ups and downs of American foreign policy beginning in the mid-eighteenth century and continuing until the present era. Yet there is a second, more theoretical, puzzle lurking in the background here: Why do there seem to be so few theories of international relations that purport to explain more than a few specific events or time periods in American foreign policy history?

It is perhaps understandable that theories about bureaucratic politics or the impact on state behavior of new technologies such as nuclear weapons and strategic missiles are only really applied to the period after 1941, given that prior to that time the U.S. leaders minimized the size of even military bureaucracies, and the nation was not yet vulnerable to quick and devastating attacks from the homelands of other great powers. Yet those theories specifying more general causal variables such as relative power, social conflict, and the role of democratic institutions are almost never applied across the full spectrum of American foreign policies cases from 1750 to the present era. To be sure, John Mearsheimer does briefly note that American expansion in the western hemisphere in the nineteenth century is consistent with his argument that states seek regional hegemony. But he offers no documentary evidence to support his argument.[2] We also have left-of-center "revisionist" interpretations of United States history that presume that pressures caused by capitalism—the needs firms have for profitable markets, cheap raw materials, and places to invest surplus capital—have been driving forces behind important shifts in U.S. policy, including the building of a colonial empire after 1898 and the countering of communism after 1918.[3] But these interpretations, aside from assuming capitalist elite greed rather than national security as the core propelling motive, focus mostly on the period after 1888, presumably because this was the time when the United States was indeed beginning to exhaust its potential for continental expansion and a modern navy and overseas trade were seen as essential to continued economic growth.[4] The pre-1888 period is largely ignored or treated separately from the twentieth century.

Historians, of course, have written textbooks providing survey narratives of American foreign policy history from the time of the War for Colonial Independence.[5] But such textbooks do not set out to test alternative theories of international relations, let alone provide new ones to challenge the accepted views. And there are numerous books that lay out the different ways U.S. leaders over time have conceptualized the problems of American foreign policy and the best strategies for dealing with them, perhaps most influentially Walter Russell Mead's description of the Hamiltonian, Jeffersonian, Jacksonian, and Wilsonian schools of thought and Henry Nau's separation of American foreign policy traditions by whether they have conservative or liberal orientations and by their level of "internationalism."[6] Yet such books are interesting more as typologies that describe alternative forms of policy and the particular leaders that use them than as theories that explain and predict when leaders will shift their behavior from soft-line to hard-line policies and even initiate costly wars.

Perhaps most surprising is the fact that scholars with potentially generalizable arguments—in particular, realists who focus on relative power and liberals who emphasize the nature of democratic institutions and ideological mindsets—do not seek to use their theories across the sweep of American foreign policy history from the eighteenth century to the present day. For realists, this is due to the perception that in the American case, realism only works as expected for certain time periods, primarily the periods of intense great power rivalry such as during the two world wars and the Cold War.[7] But I have found no good explanation for why liberals almost invariably pick only certain time periods for empirical analysis and do not test their theories of institutions and ideological drives across at least a representative sample of events from 1750 onward.[8] One obvious constraining factor, aside from simple limits on a scholar's time, is that American political culture did undergo significant shifts over time—from early minimal-state government and the North-South divide over slavery to significant urbanization after 1870 to the modern welfare state and the "conservative" backlash against it in the late twentieth century. So, while liberal scholars are more than willing to point out the "exceptional" nature of the American state and its emphasis on individualism, opportunity for advancement, and equality before the law,[9] the significant shifts in *the way* these baseline values have been manifested over time seem to have made it necessary for liberals to pick narrow time periods for the testing of specific causal arguments.[10]

This book thus sets out to do something that has not yet been successfully done and that perhaps for many scholars should not even be attempted: namely, to lay out a general theory of great power behavior that can be applied across the full range of events in American foreign policy history since the struggle to establish the republic.[11] This theory offers a new way to think about systemic realist explanations of great power politics, one that integrates the strengths of both offensive and defensive variants of systemic realism while using a dynamic understanding of the commercial realm—specifically, leaders' expectations for the future trade and investment environment and their fears that their own present behavior may *cause* this environment to turn against them—to overcome some of systemic realism's current limitations.[12]

In this chapter, I focus on the core foundational logic of my argument. The stress is on the offensive realist side of my logic, specifically the way fears of the future drive great powers to seek to expand their economic power spheres as hedges against later problems, and the way falling expectations of the future commercial environment can cause leaders to shift to more hard-line policies to avert a decline in power. Chapter 2 shows how one can extend the insights of defensive realism—in particular, the importance of an adversary's character type and the fear states have of causing a spiral of mistrust and hostility—into the realm of great power commerce and leader expectations of the future trading environment. The integration of these insights with those of chapter 1 derived from offensive realism leads to a quite different approach to great power politics, one that shows how states grapple with the tension presented by needing to reduce simultaneously the risk of spirals of misunderstanding and the risk of not doing enough to build the nation's power sphere. A decision-making logic based on trade-offs helps us predict when states will stay with more cooperative strategies and when they will start to lean toward more aggressive policies, including the initiation of crisis and war. Chapter 2 will also provide a discussion of the alternative methodology I use to examine the value of "competing theories" against the broad sweep of two and a half centuries of American and global history covered in the empirical chapters.

## The Taproot of Great Power Politics

What drives great powers to compete and sometimes go to war with each other when they seem to have good self-interested reasons to avoid such conflicts? International relations scholars are divided into two large camps on this question, camps that often go by the names "realist" and "liberal." The realist camp should perhaps be called the externalist camp, since its adherents tend to believe that it is factors and forces *outside the state* that will drive it into military struggles.[13] A state is pushed into assertive or aggressive behavior by its situation, not by its internal make-up.[14] Great powers exist within an anarchic system, meaning there is no central authority above them to keep the peace. They thus worry constantly about other great powers building up their geopolitical and geoeconomic power positions to do them harm, either by direct invasion of their territories or by actions to subvert the social cohesion and way of life of the society. Uncertainty about how much relative power other states will build up or acquire, and what they intend to do with it down the road, will play a fundamental role in shaping their present strategic plans and policy behaviors. Different types of realists will disagree on to what extent *variations in power* versus *variations in adversaries' character type and intentions* determine the level of hostility or moderation in a great power system (see chapter 2). But they agree that the policies of the great powers will be shaped more by their understanding of the external (or "systemic") pressures of forces beyond the state than by "bottom-up" pressures arising from within the state. For any state Y whose policies a realist seeks to explain, it will thus be things such as changes in Y's relative power, trends in its trade dependence, and anticipated shifts in adversary X's regime type, rather than domestic factors within Y, that will fundamentally determine its behavior.[15]

The liberal camp adopts a very different starting point, one that might best be called internalist.[16] For this camp, it is not a state's objective situation that pushes them into more hard-line postures or the initiation of wars, but rather forces from within, such as inherently aggressive leaders or factions, the inability of certain political structures to resolve domestic conflict, and the restrictions placed on inter-state bargaining by social groups and political parties that have ideological or self-interested reasons for conflict and war.[17] The systemic factors stressed by realists may still hang over state leaders as they interact with their adversaries, but they operate more as constraints on leader goals arising from below than as forces that propel leaders into action, as realists would contend. In short, the "preferences" of states as they come to any inter-state relationship are a function of the previous domestic battles that have played out within the states, and not a matter of their power situations or their worries about the future intentions of adversaries.

The approach of this book is decidedly externalist. As this and the next chapter show, it is possible to build a causally powerful theory at the systemic level that can explain a great deal of the changes in any particular great power's behavior over time without having to dip down to the domestic (or "unit") level of that state. Unfortunately, because the realists that focus on external factors remain divided amongst themselves between offensive and defensive realist versions of systemic realism, they have made systemic approaches appear as if they can explain only a small percentage of what goes on in international politics.[18]

It is the premise of this book that the limited explanatory power of contemporary systemic realist theory is not inherent to the theory but a function of the divide between offensive and defensive realists and their unwillingness to recognize the insights of the other side. Offensive realists have made an important contribution to the field by emphasizing that the fear of the future intentions of other powers leads states to struggle for power now as a hedge against what might come later. This insight is theoretically ignored in defensive realist writings. Yet offensive realists such as John Mearsheimer wrongly argue that uncertainty about the future forces great power leaders to assume "worst case" about the other's intentions to ensure they aren't taken by surprise down the road.[19] This leaves offensive realism as a theory that can only explain the more hard-line and conflictual aspects of international politics, not why great powers regularly cooperate with each other over long periods of time without the "intense security competition" that offensive realists expect.[20] Defensive realists stress something that is downplayed or ignored by offensive realism—namely, the existence of a "security dilemma" between great powers. Security dilemmas exist when the efforts by state Y to improve Y's security tend to hurt state X's perception of *its* security. State X's efforts to respond to Y's original measures will then likely cause state Y to worry about X's power and intentions, leading to a spiral of hostility and mistrust that can undermine both sides' objective security over time, either by causing actual wars or by leading to overspending on the military and the undermining of both states' economic viability.[21]

Defensive realism thus provides a useful check on the pessimism of the offensive realist approach to great power politics. If the leaders of state Y know ahead of time that overly aggressive actions will lead to arms races, counterbalancing alliances, and hard-line actions by state X and other states that now view Y as a threat, then these leaders have a self-interested reason to be more moderate in their policies. In short, the avoidance of undesired spiraling will become a major foreign policy objective of rational security-driven states. Defensive realist insights can thus help us explain why the United States and China had relatively cooperative relations between 1985 and 2010. Both sides were worried (and still are worried) about creating a spiral of hostility that might lead to war.

Yet defensive realists miss the core insight of offensive realism: that uncertainty about the future intentions of adversaries tends to push leaders to develop their states' power positions *now* as insurance against what might come *later*. Defensive realists have no explanation for why great powers do indeed constantly seem to struggle for power in world history—or at least no explanation that does not require positing an initial (erroneous) belief in the other state's non-security-driven character that then sets the security-dilemma spiral in motion. Offensive realism, on the other hand, can argue convincingly that essentially all great powers are forced to be at least partly revisionist in their foreign policies for fear of the future. This will hold even in the best-case scenario when two great powers only seek security and *each knows that the other is also a security seeker*, since both sides must worry that the other might change and become driven by non-security motives such as greed and glory down the road.[22] Because defensive realism focuses on uncertainty about the present character and intentions of other states, it misses the offensive realist point that it is uncertainty about the future character and intentions of others that drives actors to compete for better power positions in the near and medium terms.[23]

In the next chapter, I offer a more detailed analysis of how any security-seeking state Y will come to make estimates of the future character and intentions of its potential great power opponents, and how they grapple with the trade-off between trying to build power for future security and seeking to minimize the likelihood of a security-dilemma spiral to war. For now, however, I will focus on the offensive realist insight that uncertainty about the future will drive state behavior in the present.[24] There is, in other words, something we might call *the offensive realist baseline* in great power politics. Every great power has at least some desire to revise the system in its favor. None, not even the strongest, can afford just to sit back to enjoy its current power.[25] Leaders of each state will therefore seek to take advantage of opportunities to improve the power position of the state when they can do so at low cost and when the risks of an uncontrolled spiral of hostility are minimal. Perhaps the most definitive example of this is Neville Chamberlain, Britain's much maligned "softie" of the late 1930s who trusted Adolf Hitler not to go beyond the concessions on Czechoslovakia given to Germany in September 1938.[26] Chamberlain may have taken a soft line in 1938, but in 1919–20 he enthusiastically supported a League of Nations mandate system that extended Britain's empire into the Mid-East and parts of Africa formerly controlled by the Ottoman Empire and Germany. If even a Chamberlain, amidst a new peace, is willing to grab new territory that falls into the British lap at little short-term cost, then how much more inclined to revisionist behavior will most world leaders be in the face of uncertainty about the future? Offensive realism has an undeniably important insight here—that future uncertainty can drive current competitive behavior—and this insight must be incorporated into any properly specified systemic theory of international relations.

A key problem with offensive realism, even before we consider the issue of undesired spiraling (chapter 2), is that its adherents have been focused almost exclusively on the military and territorial aspects of the drive for expansion. They have placed little or no emphasis on the *economic and commercial* determinants of expansion. To be sure, John Mearsheimer mentions "latent power" as a foundation for military power in his important book, *The Tragedy of Great Power Politics* (2001). And his concept of latent power does include a state's relative GDP and such things as population size and fertile territory. But his focus is solely on what might be called a great power's "core" latent power—that is, its economic and demographic power within the confines of its own homeland. The economic power a state can build up through the creation of commercial connections with the outside world is ignored. In fact, in a later book, *The Liberal Delusion* (2018), he goes so far as to say that trade plays little role in the shaping of great power politics because, when push comes to shove, leaders of great powers will put military questions above economic and commercial questions. The reasons why a Mearsheimer and other offensive realists such as Sebastian Rosato discount the role of commerce in world history are not hard to figure out. Offensive realists believe great powers will avoid trade, at least with other great powers' spheres of influence, out of both a fear of increasing their vulnerability to cut-off from vital goods and a worry that other states will get relatively more out of the trading relationship than they do (the "relative gains" concern).[27] This means, from the offensive realist standpoint, that trade between great powers will typically be quite low and thus not terribly important to their decision-making relative to more purely military and territorial matters. Hence, for Mearsheimer, Rosato, and other offensive realists, states will struggle over territory and military power projection in order to position themselves for any wars to come in the future.

This is an incomplete view of what propels states to expand in world history. To be sure, deterring or preventing invasion, and thus the building of larger militaries and the pre-positioning of forces in foreign territories, have been critical elements of great power grand strategies for thousands of years, from ancient Roman efforts to control the Mediterranean region to counter future military threats from 300 to 31 BCE, to Spain's moves to reduce its European adversaries during the Thirty Years' War, to Prussian and German moves from 1860 to 1918 to build a consolidated imperial realm. But to say that the taproot of great power struggles through history is a function only of the fear of military invasion, and that territorial expansion is thus *the* critical means to greater national security, is to miss two fundamental realities. First, leaders who are concerned about national security, especially in the post-1685 era of nationalism and ideological standoffs, do not worry simply about invasion by foreign forces. They also worry about adversaries trying to destabilize the state and its social cohesion either through the support of factions hostile to the government or by the export of ideologies that undermine the way of life that most citizens have come to value. James II's willingness to encourage the re-Catholicization of England, backed by Louis XIV of France, led to the Glorious Revolution and the simultaneous geopolitical and ideological struggle of Britain and France through the eighteenth century. From the French Revolution of 1789 onward, as Mark Haas has shown, great power conflicts were often triggered by fears that the other constituted a threat to one's political society simply by the fact of its different ideology and its willingness to see it flourish.[28] This of course became most self-evident during the Cold War, when the United States viewed the Soviet Union and Maoist China as threats to "the free world."

The point that leaders worry about an adversary's ability to undermine social stability, and not just about its capacity to invade, leads to a second and even more important point. Great powers do indeed need large and expanding

commercial realms if they are to have the economic wherewithal to both counter the military-territorial threats that may emerge in the future and to resist
any outside efforts to undermine the state and its society from within. Commerce is critical to a growing GDP base, both for the homeland and for a great
power's military allies. Indeed, a great power that lacks a strong commercial
realm and strong trade and investment connections to states outside that
realm *cannot build a strong defense against both external invasion and subversion
by outside influences.*[29] This was again seen most clearly during the Cold War.
The United States smartly used foreign aid and trade and investment linkages
to build up Western Europe, Japan, South Korea, Latin America, and other
areas from 1945 onward to create what we now call the "liberal international
economic order" (LIEO). The Soviet Union was confined to a much more
limited commercial sphere (Eastern Europe and certain aligned states, including China until 1960, North Vietnam, and a few states in Africa and Latin
America). The vast superiority of the U.S.-led sphere in economic/commer-
cial power not only allowed it to keep pace with the Soviet Union in arms and
strategic nuclear power—at a fraction of the cost to the U.S. economy—but
it reduced communism's appeal as an alternative ideology and way of life. Not
surprisingly, the Soviets under Gorbachev recognized that they could no longer compete with the United States unless they acquired the trade and technology from the West to reenergize the Soviet-bloc economy. The Cold War
ended even before the collapse of the Soviet Union itself, once Soviet leaders
realized they must join the world economy.[30]

This leads to one of the foundational claims of this book: that the true
taproot of great power competition across the modern post-1660 period of
international relations *lies more in the commercial realm than in the territorial-
military realm per se.* Stated more precisely, because great powers need strong
and expanding economic power spheres to protect their societies from both
territorial invasion and internal subversion, they need strong and expanding
commercial ties with not only states in their immediate neighborhoods, but
around the world. Alfred Thayer Mahan saw this key insight back in the 1890s
when he advocated, in a series of seminal books and pamphlets, the expansion
of both American global commerce and a navy to protect it. Revealingly, his
first book on the subject was an examination of Britain's rise to global hegemony through commerce and its navy after 1660 and up until the wars of the
French Revolution. Even before Mahan, however, the brilliant founding father
Alexander Hamilton laid out a commercial and naval vision for the future
development of an American empire in the Federalist Papers, numbers 6–9
and 11. Hamilton, drawing like Mahan from an intimate knowledge of British
history, saw that great powers rose and fell according to their ability to build
their commercial spheres of influence and then use those spheres for the

export of manufacturing products and the import of inexpensive raw material inputs.[31] After Deng Xiaoping's ascendency in the early 1980s, China took a page directly out of Hamilton's book. Over the last two decades, it has added the Mahanian naval component as the defense of China's overseas trade became a priority. (China by 2018 had become the largest trade partner of over one hundred states, including the European Union, Russia, Japan, and the United States.)[32]

For the rest of this chapter, I will show how this claim can be expressed through a well-specified deductive theory in the realist tradition. Chapter 2 will deepen this theory, developing further its dynamic approach rooted in leader expectations of future changes and feedback effects. But the proof is in the pudding, and empirical support for the role of commerce in American foreign policy history will come in the historical chapters 3 to 9.

## Economic Power Spheres and the Protection of Commercial Access

The idea that economic and commercial power is the foundation for military and territorial power is not new, of course. Klaus Knorr and Robert Gilpin emphasize this linkage in their seminal writings in the 1970s and early 1980s, and it was the basis of mercantilist thinking in European history going back to the sixteenth and seventeenth centuries.[33] These early scholarly examinations of the role of commerce and great power conflict have two main limitations, however. First, the authors have focused largely on providing inductive insights based on a certain reading of history, rather than the setting out of a deductive theory that can predict when and under what conditions great powers are likely to push hard to extend their spheres of influence versus being relative moderate in their foreign policies. Modern offensive realism helps us to some degree here, since it provides an explanation, rooted in the universal problem of uncertainty about the future, for why great powers feel the ongoing need to expand. Yet by ignoring the true importance of commerce and economic growth to this strategic hedging against future problems, it has left a hole that needs to be filled.

The second thing missing from these early writings on commerce and security is the defensive realist insight of the security dilemma and the problem of action-reaction spirals that get states into undesired conflicts and war. If leaders are rational, and thus aware that spirals of hostility may be sparked by their own behavior, they are likely to be more moderate in their policies than they would be otherwise. In short, awareness of feedback loops between behavior and the conditions that shape behavior will tend to *offset some of the forces such as uncertainty of the future* that would, even in a more economically based offensive realism, have been expected to push states into hard-line expansionism. After all, rational security-maximizing states may need to expand to hedge against future threats, but if this expansionism ends up *creating* those future threats, then it may be self-defeating.[34] This indeed is the core defensive realist critique of offensive realism—namely, that the latter ignores the downside of expansionism, and thus ends up encouraging behavior that can hurt the security of the state, not help it.

The main problem with defensive realism as it stands, aside from its downplaying of the offensive realist baseline, is that it focuses only on the military dimensions of the security dilemma, ignoring how commercial relations have a parallel and very important dynamic—what I call the "trade security-dilemma."[35] Actions by state Y to extend and protect its trading realm, say, by increasing its projection of naval power or by occupying smaller trade partners, can lead state X to cut Y off from access to trade and investments with X's trading realms and with X itself. This can lead to action-reaction spirals that, as seen in U.S.-Japan relations in 1940–41, can lead to war. As the next chapter shows, the trade-security dilemma must be incorporated into any deductive theory of commerce and conflict. Only by assuming that rational leaders understand its basic dimensions can we explain why great powers might cooperate for long periods of time, and then shift to more hard-line and provocative policies in the face of changing external conditions.

For the rest of this chapter, however, I will put to the side the importance of feedback loops in order to lay out the basic causal framework that takes us from core commercial and economic factors to the situations that will be most likely to lead states to move from cooperative to conflictual policies, including the initiation of war. I will then supplement this framework in chapter 2 with the feedback (endogenous) aspects of a fully rationalist logic as well as the inclusion of other parameters, including the character type of the other state, that will shape a great power's sense of the threats it faces now and into the future.

Thinking in broad geostrategic terms, any modern great power—that is, any great power since the commercial and shipping revolutions from 1450 to 1660 made long-distance commerce both viable and profitable—must worry about three distinct areas or "realms" of economic connection to the outside world. The nature of these realms is captured visually in figure 1.1 below. The first or primary realm is its trade and investment with countries and regions in which it has a clear political and military advantage over other great powers. These are often states geographically close to the great power in question, as with Central American and Caribbean nations for the United States after 1890. But this first realm will also include oversea possessions, such as British overseas colonies after 1600 and the American territories of Guam and Puerto Rico

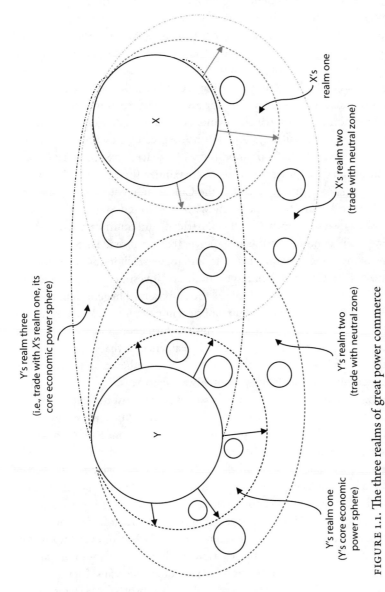

Y's realm three
(i.e., trade with X's realm one, its
core economic power sphere)

Y's realm one
(Y's core economic
power sphere)

Y's realm two
(trade with neutral zone)

X's
realm one

X's realm two
(trade with neutral zone)

FIGURE 1.1. The three realms of great power commerce

*Note:* The solid straight arrows coming out from Y's and X's homelands represent their respective inherent drives to extend their economic power spheres, discussed further below.

after 1898. Finally, areas that are militarily allied with a great power can typically be considered part of this first realm, at least if they are relatively small, since the great power can exert political influence over the ally's commercial dealings that its security dependence implies.[36] The Western European states that have been a part of the North Atlantic Treaty Organization (NATO) since 1949, for example, found it hard to ignore the United States' desires to restrict trade with the Soviet Union during the Cold War, despite clear economic interests in such trade, at least after 1953.[37]

The second realm includes states that are either politically neutral in the great power competition or which, for a variety of reasons including geographic position and resource endowments, seek to trade freely with all the great powers in a particular system. South American states after 1850, for example, sought to trade their commodities with the United States, Britain, and other European great powers in order to maximize their potentials for economic growth. Both during and after the Cold War, most African states followed this model and traded equally with the United States, Russia, and China. Today we see South American, African, and Southeast Asian states orienting their economies to the great power that can provide the "best deals" in terms of investment, export markets, and higher-tech industrial products. Many now claim China as their largest trade and investment partner, displacing the United States' historical role as the commercial hegemon in their regions, even as they continue to claim political nonalignment. Needless to say, both American and Chinese leaders aspire to turn economic ties into more concrete political ties even if not into formal alliances—that is, to push these states into the first realm—but the existence of the other superpower makes such an effort both difficult and potentially escalatory.

The third realm is the one whose existence is the most difficult to explain for most systemic realist theories of international politics, most obviously, offensive realism. It involves any great power's trade and investment ties to its adversary's homeland and the commercial partners the latter directly or indirectly controls—that is, to the *other's first realm*. An offensive realist such as Mearsheimer might accept that a great power will trade within its first realm, such as the United States trading with states in Central America and the Caribbean after 1900. After all, the great power exerts such influence over these states that they are unlikely to sever commercial relations or even impose tariffs to which the great power objects. Trade with neutral states in the second realm might also be allowed by more relaxed offensive realist logics, at least when an adversarial great power seems unlikely to absorb these states into its sphere. But why would any rational great power move to the third realm of trading extensively with another great power and its sphere if that meant increased vulnerability to a cut off in vital goods such as raw materials or an increase in the adversary's relative power through trade? Mearsheimer and other offensive realists have argued that the double whammy of worries over increased vulnerability and "relative gains concerns" should make great powers avoid almost all economic cooperation between their home countries and their primary economic realms.[38] Yet this argument confronts a series of self-evident empirical anomalies that should make us question its deductive veracity. Prior to 1914, Germany, France, Britain, and Russia traded very heavily with each other, including with those states they mistrusted the most. This trade returned by the late 1920s before it was hurt by the Great Depression. Even during the Cold War, the Soviet Union on three separate occasions—the late 1950s, the early 1970s, and the late 1980s—worked very hard to build strong trade relations with the United States and its sphere; and American leaders, at least in the latter two cases, proved willing to accommodate Russian desires. And, of course, we have the phenomenon of China's speedy integration into the world's global system after 1985, aided by extensive trade and financial connections with the United States itself.[39]

The offensive realist view of global economics suffers from two key problems. First, it misses that there is a fundamental tension between the concern for vulnerability and the concern for the other's relative gains through trade. If two great powers start up direct trade with each other's economic sphere, the state that gets any relative gain from the trade is almost certainly *also* the one that is becoming more vulnerable to a cut off. Consider Japan's decision to integrate itself into the world economy after 1880. By selling its products to acquire oil and raw materials from abroad, it made massive gains in absolute and relative power compared to states such as the United States that did not really need what Japan had to sell. But because Japan became very dependent on imported oil and other resources, its leaders knew the country would suffer what Kenneth Waltz has called "costs of adjustments" if its trade ties were ever to be severed.[40] Chinese leaders faced the same tension and trade-off when they shifted from Mao Zedong's strategy of autarchy to Deng Xiaoping's strategy of commercial engagement in the 1980s. Yet the recognition that trade with another great power's sphere may be *essential* to both absolute and relative growth and thus to the viability of the state *as* a great power can cause leaders to overcome their fears of vulnerability—and the other's concomitant increased bargaining leverage—in order to maximize their state's position over the long term.

There is a second larger point that piggybacks on the first. Even if a clear relative gain is unlikely to arise through trade with an adversary's sphere, there are at least three dimensions of modern geoeconomics that make great powers realize they might need to trade with an adversary's sphere or risk long-term decline.[41] The first is the need for *economies of scale of production*. Modern industries have huge "fixed costs" that they must pay every month largely regardless of their sales—for salaried employees, competitive research and development budgets, the maintenance and financing of gigantic high-tech factories, and the like. This means they need large markets for their goods just to make a profit. Because other great powers are wealthier than less developed countries, they have a lot of purchasing power. Leaders will thus often feel compelled to trade with other great powers just to make sure they can sustain the profitability of companies needed for long-term reinvestment in technology and for social stability. This is true even of state-owned companies, as contemporary Chinese leaders know well.

The second issue is the fear of so-called *diminishing margin returns to growth* that can set in when a state is strong in one or two dimensions of the "land, labor, capital" mix needed for the production of goods, but not necessarily in a third.[42] The United States, for example, had all three in abundance during most of the nineteenth century, but as it started to use up key raw materials its leaders felt the strong need to find them wherever they could, including in other great power spheres. Japan after 1900 and China after 1993 experienced this with their dependence on foreign resources, particularly oil imports. Without access to low-cost raw materials, an industrializing great power, even one strong in labor and capital, will simply start to fall behind compared to great powers that do have such access. When one brings in the third dimension—that the *variety of raw material inputs* for most modern industries has increased significantly over time, and that these inputs are often found only in the other great power's sphere—we can see why great powers feel compelled to trade with even their main adversaries. China today would not be the superpower it is without access to the markets and raw materials of the traditional American economic sphere of influence.[43]

We have seen from the above that great powers have good strategic reasons to increase their trade across all three distinct economic realms: their own core sphere of influence (the first realm), the "middle area" of neutral states willing to trade with all sides (the second realm), and the economic region another great power controls, either directly—its homeland and colonies/territories—or indirectly through military and political power projection (the third realm, which amounts to trade with another great power's first realm). Without a willingness to trade across all three realms, most great powers would suffer significantly over the long term. Austria-Hungary, for example, was the only great power in the half-century prior to World War I that minimized trade connections with other states, and its economy and technological base suffered greatly for it. The Soviet Union sought until 1955 to maintain trade largely within its first realm (Eastern Europe and China), until Nikita Khrushchev saw what it was doing to his country's growth rate. He thus sought to open trade ties both with the second realm (the so-called Third World) and with the United States itself. Mao never grasped the importance of trade until it was too late. Deng and his successors have pushed a simultaneous first-, second-, and third-realm strategy that has created the superpower we see today.

Yet this picture of great powers trading beyond their homelands and even beyond their most immediate economic power spheres has not yet dealt with the key question: leader uncertainty about future access to trade and investment. If the taproot of great power politics is the need to grow one's economic power sphere in order to provide the military strength to protect the nation from invasion and to counter other's efforts to undermine social order, then great powers will have the incentive to extend their economic power spheres into the second realm by both political and military means. And this can be highly destabilizing to the system. As great powers seek to grow their economic power spheres beyond the current first realm, *they will almost inevitably bump up into one another*, leading their adversaries to react. After all, any great power X that is extending its sphere into the neutral zone of nonaligned states (realm two) will be seen as a direct threat to any great power Y that had previously traded in that zone. Indeed, if state Y is highly dependent on that trade, and if it expects access to the raw materials, markets, and investments (RIM) of that zone to be increasingly restricted, it will anticipate both a relative decline in its economic power as its adversary grows its sphere, and perhaps even an absolute decline as costs of adjustment start to kick in. It may even anticipate that X intends to chip away at Y's control over its *own* sphere (its realm one). Either scenario, but particularly the latter, would constitute a direct threat to the economic viability of state Y, and would likely provoke a major upswing in its willingness to project military power against state X, both to deter further advances and to compel retreats from X's encroachments on realms of commerce Y has come to see as vital to its long-term security as a great power.

In short, even before we consider the issue of back-and-forth spiraling dynamics that can lead to undesired crises and war (chapter 2), we can make initial predictions about how the key causal forces animating the commerce of great power politics can lead to either peace or conflict. Figure 1.2 shows how three factors in particular will drive state behavior: the baseline intensity of any dependent state Y's drive to extend its economic power sphere; Y's level of dependence on trade in realms beyond that sphere (that is, in its second and third realms); and its expectations of future open access to trade and investment across all three realms.

These three factors (or independent variables) will interact to shape Y's leaders' perception of the state's future economic and military power position

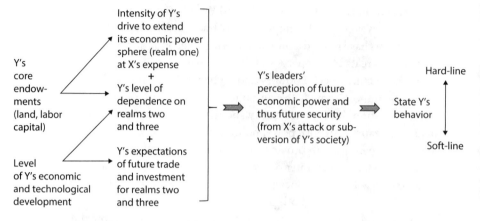

FIGURE 1.2. Three core causal factors

which in turn will drive the relative "hardline-ness" of Y's policies toward X and the outside world. The more intense Y's drive to expand its economic power sphere—a variable that will be shaped by a number of prior factors such as the nation's core endowments of land, labor, and capital, and its level of economic and technological development[44]—the more likely it will take risks to seize opportunities to grab territories in the second realm by force or political coercion. As revisionist scholars point out, the United States was much more willing to grab colonies overseas after 1890 once there was no more land in North America to occupy and once the possibility of future diminishing marginal returns became clear to political elites. The error they make is to assume that it was the greed of large corporate firms and the fear that their profits would decline that led the political elites to embark on America's first plunge into globalism. Rather, as chapter 5 shows, these political elites understood that without the plunge, the United States might be overshadowed in the great power game by states such as Britain and Germany, which were already pushing for expanded commercial spheres in East Asia and Latin America.

The core endowments of any great power will also play a big role in determining state Y's level of economic dependence on the second and third realms. Industrializing states such as Japan and Germany after 1880 started from small first-realm power spheres because of the modest size of their homelands and their initially limited colonial possessions. Both countries by 1913 thus found themselves highly dependent on other great powers and the few neutral states that existed for the vital resources critical to their continued growth. This dependence was not in itself an immediate problem as long as the leaders could be assured of continued access to trade outside their economic power spheres.

But for Germany and Japan, this trade began to be restricted after 1900 and 1930 respectively, and it led to changes in their willingness to deploy and use military power, as I have shown elsewhere.[45]

To understand how increasing levels of dependence might lead to conflict or cooperation, we need to bring in the third factor—*the expectations of the future trade and investment environment*. If a great power is growing in dependence on trade and investment in realms two and three, but its leaders have positive expectations for the future of that commerce, then the state is likely to be moderate in its behavior. After all, the state can be expected to grow from its commercial connections that bring in low-cost raw materials, provide markets to allow economies of scale, and offer places to invest surplus capital. Yet if expectations for the future turn sour, and the state is being cut off from full RIM access or anticipates increasingly harsh restrictions in the future, then the state's economic and thus military power position is likely to decline. Lack of access to raw materials can kick in both high costs of adjustment and diminishing marginal returns, while the inability to find markets or places to invest can lead to firm losses and unused capital stock. The clearest example of this dynamic is Japan's initiation of total war in the Pacific in December 1941. Japanese leaders' expectations for future trade, which were already quite pessimistic in 1940, plunged in 1941 as the United States and Britain imposed draconian sanctions on the island nation, particularly on oil and natural resources. Anticipating deep and inevitable decline in Japan's power, its leaders chose total war as the only perceived way to shore up the nation's long-term security position.[46] The empirical chapters of this book show that a similar dynamic of high dependence and falling commercial expectations has led to many crises and wars in American foreign policy history, even if none were perhaps as dramatic as Japan's attack on Pearl Harbor on December 7, 1941.

## Conclusion

This chapter has laid out the foundations of the book's dynamic realist theory. Leaders of great powers, focused on what must be done to protect their states from invasion or from efforts to undermine social order, will understand that long-term security requires high and growing levels of economic power. This economic power is itself fundamentally shaped by an ability to use external trade and investment to grow "homeland" GDP by exploiting economies of scale (EOS), avoiding diminishing marginal returns (DMR), and ensuring that the benefits of commerce accrue to the state and not to its adversaries. The first task of great power leaders, therefore, is to expand and protect the state's core economic power sphere—that is, commerce within the homeland

and with states around its region and around the world that are under the great power's political sway, either through colonization, territorial control, or military alliance. This is what the chapter has been calling the first realm of trade and investment. But because great powers need large markets to exploit EOS and because they need access to low-cost raw materials and places to invest-ment surplus capital, they will want to also create commercial linkages with countries that occupy a neutral zone (realm two) between the great powers. More than that, the great power's endowments of land, labor, and capital and its level of industrial development will shape the intensity of its drive to extend the economic power sphere—that is, to push beyond its current first realm in order to control more fully its access to the neutral zone of realm two.

A great power may be quite dependent on trade and investment with not only neutral countries but with a third realm—another great power's core economic power sphere—simply because EOS/DMR concerns and the need for cheap or otherwise unavailable raw materials make such commerce essential to its long-run position as a great power. Yet this is where leader expectations of the future trade and investment environment play an especially critical role in determining whether a dependent great power will be peaceful or hostile in its foreign poli-cies. Positive expectations will help leaders in state Y remain confident about the state's future power trajectory, and thus will foster moderate behavior and con-tinued imports and exports in and out of its own sphere. Most generally, how-ever, we can predict that when a dependent state Y's leaders have falling or nega-tive expectations for future commerce in realms two and three, they will be more inclined toward more hard-line behavior in order to compel other great powers to stop their encroachments on the neutral zone or to reverse their restrictions on commerce with their economic power spheres. Not surprisingly, if state Y's own economic power sphere, its first realm, is being targeted by state X, then this threat will be seen as existential, requiring the fiercest response Y can muster. As we will see, direct threats to the American first realm, including those that arose from European wars from 1914 to 1917 and 1939 to 1941, have led to some of the costliest foreign policy decisions in American history. They have also led to in-tense and extended crises such as with Britain over Oregon from 1840 to 1846 and with the Soviet Union during the 1959–86 period when the Soviets were able to establish outposts for communism in the western hemisphere (Cuba, and later Nicaragua).

Most of the cases in the book, however, involve struggles with other great powers with trade in realm two, the neutral zone. This is not surprising, since as the theory would expect and as I will discuss more in the next chapter, great powers are typically wary about challenging each other's first realms, knowing the kind of reaction this will engender. But the nonaligned states of the neutral zone are more easily absorbed into an expanding economic power sphere without provoking great power war. The United States did this when it began to expand its economic influence south after 1820 and into the Pacific after 1840, despite warnings from London that this threatened Britain's commerce with the states of these regions. American struggles to protect access to China's resources and markets after 1897 as the European powers and Japan struggled to establish areas of dominance, as well as American worries about Soviet encroachments into the oil-rich Middle East after World War II, are prime examples of U.S. policy becoming more hard-line as threats to the second realm grew. Today with China we see the basic problem. China needs to expand its economic power sphere further to secure cheap resources and avoid diminishing returns while it offsets the huge, fixed costs resulting from its massive investment in steel and manufacturing industries. Its Belt and Road Initiative (BRI), backed by the Chinese-controlled Asian Infrastructure and Investment Bank, are the main tools of this expansion beyond its current first realm. But this drive to "go abroad"—as the first version of the BRI logic was called— necessarily competes with the U.S. effort to sustain *its* commercial influence with nonaligned states in the Global South. In fact, with the European Union encouraging trade links that have made China the EU's number one trade partner, China bumps into U.S. efforts to develop *its* first-realm power sphere through NATO expansion and closer economic ties with the EU.

Before we turn to the historical cases (chapters 3 to 9) and to contemporary U.S.-China relations (chapter 10), we need to add two more elements to the foundations of dynamic realism outlined in this chapter. The first is state Y's assessment of not just X's economic and military power but its present and future *character and intentions*. Great powers are not all the same, and for any rational leader of Y seeking to maximize Y's security, the type of X that Y is dealing with or anticipates at any point in time will have an important impact on Y's estimates of the future trade and investment environment and the probabilities of conflict and war. The second additional element is the inclusion of feedback loops (endogeneity) to show how state Y's behavior may affect X's behavior and thus lead to changes in Y's expectations of the future commercial environment. This will allow us to see how extending defensive realist insights on the security dilemma to the realm of commerce can deepen our understanding of how rational actors grapple with the trade-off between trying to expand their economic power spheres and trying to avoid creating mistrust and hostility that leads to commercial restrictions and potential spirals into military disputes and war.

The next chapter will take up these challenges. I will show how estimates of the adversary's future character type, and the anticipation of feedback loops interact with the core variables of this chapter—the drive for an expanded economic power sphere; the dependence on foreign raw materials, markets, and investments; and the expectations of future commerce—to determine Y's perception of future economic threats and thus its behavior on the hard-line/soft-line spectrum. By assuming that great power leaders are constantly thinking about the future as they grapple with the various tensions and trade-offs inherent in responses to external stimuli, the book shows the true explanatory power of realism both for history and for the understanding of contemporary power politics.

# 2

# Character Type, Feedback Loops, and Systemic Pressures

THE PREVIOUS CHAPTER laid down a foundation for thinking about the external or "systemic" pressures on great powers from a broad commercial and economic point of view rather than simply from a territorial-military perspective. The current chapter deepens the understanding of dynamic realist theory by developing what it means to be a rational security-maximizing state trying to protect itself from invasion and subversion in the modern post-1660 age of global commerce and geopolitics. Chapter 1 showed that such states have an inherent drive to extend their economic power spheres beyond simply the smaller states and territories that they currently control (realm one) and build tighter ties with political entities in the neutral zone (realm two), even if in doing so they hurt their adversaries' commercial ties with these entities. They will likely also have a need, determined by such things as economies of scale and fears of diminishing marginal returns, to trade directly with their adversaries' spheres—what was labeled realm-three commerce—even though such trade leaves the state inherently more vulnerable to future restrictions and embargoes. Under certain circumstances and conditions, this vulnerability or "dependence" may actually lead to militarized tests of will, destabilizing crises, and even all-out war. The purpose of this chapter is to unpack more specifically what those circumstances and conditions are, and how and when they are likely to change over time. This will allow for a more precise understanding of why great powers in history remain relatively moderate in their behavior for long stretches of time, and then shift to much more hard-line policies that often lead them to clashes of arms and war.

Chapter 1 indicated that three key variables are involved in any great power Y's effort to maximize its short- and long-term security. The first is the intensity of Y's drive to extend its economic power sphere, which itself is a function of its core endowments in land, labor, and capital, tied to its level of economic and technological development. This chapter will hold the level of this drive constant in order to focus on the causal effects of the two other variables: *Y's level of dependence* on commerce with realms two and three, and its *expectations of future trade and investment* with both of these realms.[1] Y's core endowments will shape its level of dependence, and its degree of economic and technological development will likely shape both dependence and expectations for future commerce. When state Y is highly dependent on trade with realms two and three but expects that trade to continue into the future—that is, when it expects state X will not interfere with or restrict that trade—then Y is likely to remain relatively peaceful in its behavior to facilitate continued economic growth. But when Y believes X is constraining Y's access to trade, or will likely do so in the future, Y is more likely to turn to hard-line policies both to ensure current access and to deter X from intensifying its restrictions later.

Yet there are two other important dimensions of power politics that need to be included to create a full picture of how great powers will grapple with changes in their relative power positions over time. The first is *the nature of the adversary's character type* and how this affects their estimates of level of external threat posed by rising or declining adversaries. The second is the way rational actors deal with the issue of endogeneity—namely, the knowledge that their own policies can *create* increased mistrust in an adversary and thus lead to reactions that hurt the state's long-term security. Both these dimensions of statecraft have been well addressed by defensive realist scholarship, in particular the work of Stephen Walt and Mark Haas on the origins of threats and by Robert Jervis, Charles Glaser, and Andrew Kydd on the reality of security dilemmas and spirals of increasing hostility. The goal of this chapter is to extend this scholarship to an area it has not yet deeply engaged—namely, the realm of commerce—and to show how these defensive realist insights can be fused with baseline ideas drawn from offensive realism that were on display in the first chapter. This synthetic argument will allow us to develop a theory of international relations that captures *how rational leaders deal with the trade-offs that are inherent in great power politics*. In particular, we can predict that any dependent great power Y will be quite worried that if it engages in overly hard-line behavior, it will incur the wrath of other states and thus find itself increasingly cut off from access to raw materials, investments, and markets (RIM). So, while strong policies can help project power and resolve, the trade-offs created by these anticipated feedback effects give Y an incentive for more cooperative behavior to ensure continued economic growth, as long as future commerce is otherwise expected to be high. Yet when expectations are hurt by things outside the control of Y, such as by domestic changes within X, the actions of third parties, or exogenous shocks such as global recessions or depressions, then state Y can be predicted to move to more hard-line policies despite the known risks of creating further spirals of misunderstanding and commercial restrictions.

This chapter will proceed as follows. I will first discuss the importance of an adversary's character type, considering not only the core motives of the other state, but also its ability to employ the best means to its given ends—that is, its "rationality" as an actor. This mixing of actor ends with actor rationality goes beyond the defensive realist focus on the uncertainty about another's motives—namely, whether the adversary is driven primarily by security or by non-security objectives such as glory/status, ideological missions, wealth for its own sake, and elite survival in office. It allows for the possibility that a rational security-maximizing state Y (or RSM-Y) might believe that it is facing another security-seeking actor, but an actor that *does not know how to rationally achieve its goal of greater security.*

Overall, then, uncertainty in great power politics is much deeper and more complex than most defensive realists would allow. State Y may be uncertain, both *now* and *into the future*, about two main things: whether X is and will remain security-maximizing; and if security-maximizing, whether X is and will remain rational in the pursuit of its security ends. And this uncertainty can push an RSM-Y to policies that are more hard-line than they would be otherwise were Y confident it was dealing with another rational security-seeking actor, and one that would remain so into the foreseeable future.[2]

From this base, I will examine a key determinant of Y's assessment of X's character type—namely, Y's view of the *cultural differences* between itself and actor X. The notion of Y's sense of cultural difference or distance draws on Mark Haas's seminal work on ideological distance as a structural characteristic of the system. I go beyond Haas's focus on differences in political ideology to bring in three other aspects—foreign economic orientation, religious values, and ethnicity—that also help shape Y's assessment of X's character and thus Y's perception of the threat that X poses now and into the future.[3] I also show that because state Y is *assumed to be and always remain a rational security-seeking state focusing on its external environment*, its assessments of X's character in terms of cultural differences remains systemic in its focus. As with Stephen Walt's balance-of-threat version of defensive realism, one does not have to dip down to the domestic characteristics of state Y to show how *changes in X's type*—something external to Y—will shape Y's assessment of the threats that X might pose to Y in the short term and long term.[4]

The chapter then turns to a discussion of what I call *the trade-security dilemma* and the problem of endogenous spiraling due to overly hard-line behavior. The concept of the trade-security dilemma captures the idea that actions that state Y does to protect its commercial linkages abroad—such as an increased naval buildup, the placing of soldiers in small third parties, and the projection of the resolve to defend one's commercial interests—can cause state X and other states to believe Y has hostile intentions, and to then begin to restrict Y's access to trade and investments abroad. These actions in turn can reduce Y's expectations for future commerce, which leads to a further hardening of Y's policies. Since I have outlined the nature of the trade-security dilemma and the related trade-security spiral in other work,[5] the emphasis here will be on the way the combination of Y's assessment of its core endowments, its economic development, and X's character type can lead to changes in its view of future threats independent of X's current behavior, and thus to Y starting the ball rolling by increasing the "hardline-ness" of its policy, despite awareness of the risks of spiraling.

In short, I show why state Y might rationally initiate more hard-line policies without provocation—that is, without X first switching to a more assertive policy stance. Part of the problem, as we will see, is that Y's leaders might be anticipating a future peaking in Y's power trajectory (as many see happening with China today). Under such circumstances, these leaders might feel it is necessary, even though the state is currently still rising, to increase the assertiveness of their foreign policies to secure a strong position for trade into the future.[6] (This is one powerful explanation for the intensity of effort Beijing has given to its Belt and Road Initiative, as I explore in chapter 10).

The last part of this chapter deals with the literature my theory is going up against and the method I use for testing the value of the various causal variables across this literature. By examining the importance of the causal roles different variables might play in jointly bringing about changes in state behavior, we arrive at a new, more balanced way of testing theories of international relations. The competitive effort to reject certain theories as we support our own is left behind, in favor of determining whether factors are propelling the decisions of leaders or rather acting to facilitate, constrain, or perhaps accelerate and reinforce their decisions, given what is propelling them.

## The Importance of the Adversary's Character Type

Chapter 1 showed that systemic realists are divided by whether it is uncertainty about an adversary's present intentions or its future intentions that matters most to a security-seeking state, with defensive realists stressing the former and offensive realists the latter. Yet these realists are also divided by the related question of how state Y, as a rational security maximizer, will evaluate the nature of adversary X's "character" as it shapes X's intentions. Character type is of course a multifaceted concept, and it can include such attributes as another actor's willingness to accept costs (its "resolve") or its tolerance for risks in situations when both actors want to avoid war (the "crash" of a Chicken game) but have reason to fear things may get out of hand if they press too hard for concessions.[7] When it comes to the issue of intentions, however, defensive realists will stress the distinction between two types of motives that underpin an adversary's likely intended behavior: namely, whether X is driven primarily by security or by non-security ends. For defensive realists, if X is a security-seeking actor, and just wants to protect itself from invasion or the undermining by foreign states of its internal social order, then Y should be able to work with X to reduce any uncertainty about each other's types and create a stable relationship where both sides avoid measures that might trigger misunderstanding and a spiral of hostility. In particular, if both states are driven by security as the primary ultimate end of statecraft, they can use so-called costly signals to reveal to the other that they are not interested in aggressive expansion for non-security reasons such as glory, greed, or ideological mission.[8]

Offensive realists counter that because of the uncertainty about the future intentions of X, any rational state Y will be forced to treat X as a state driven by non-security ultimate ends—that is, to assume "worst case" about the other's type. After all, as John Mearsheimer emphasizes, even an X that is a nice democracy today might "backslide" into aggressive authoritarianism later, and Y can never be completely sure it will not (as the example of Weimar Germany in the 1920s teaches us).[9] Starting from a worst-case assumption about X, state Y will be compelled to compete strongly for more military and territorial power as a hedge against what might happen down the road.[10] Indeed, because X, even if it is a security-seeking actor, cannot be sure of *state Y's* future intentions, it will also have to compete for more military and territorial power. Both Y and X will be forced by their uncertainty about the future to act *as if* they are aggressive, non-security-driven revisionist states. Thus, we derive the grim picture of international life that is the offensive realist worldview.

Although both offensive and defensive realists have insights into the importance of X's character type in predicting Y's policy behavior, both are incomplete as they stand. Offensive realism's great insight is that because smart states worry not just about the present but the future intentions of adversaries, they have an interest—especially since intentions can change much faster than relative power—to build up their power positions now as a hedge against deleterious events later. The dynamic realist argument of chapter 1 extends this insight to the commercial realm: Great powers will compete to extend their control over trade routes beyond the immediate group of small states they currently control, and they will build navies to help the state respond effectively to any emerging threat to these routes. In fact, as we will see, the United States from 1790 to 1917 tended to treat all the European great powers, even the more liberal British state, as potential threats to U.S. commerce.

Yet the extreme nature of some of the states of the post–World War I period, particularly Nazi Germany and Soviet Russia, indicate that we cannot ignore the importance of character type in a rational state's assessment of future commercial and political threats. Here, two errors of reasoning show that offensive realism's dismissal of character type as a variable is both problematic and self-defeating in terms of realist theory development. First, by their very notion of "backsliding" and their emphasis that X might change later, offensive realists are acknowledging that there is indeed a clear difference in the likely intensity and scope of the desire of some states to expand beyond what they currently possess. One can accept that all great powers are "revisionist" to some degree, and that Y knows this and prepares to counter expected revisionism by any particular X with revisionism of its own. But there is a huge difference, as I noted earlier, between the revisionism of a Neville Chamberlain and the revisionism of an Adolf Hitler or a Genghis Khan. The former type of actor has clearly limited geopolitical and geoeconomic aims and is much more inclined to "stop" before the rest of the system aligns against it. The latter type has extreme or unlimited aims, and there is little Y can do to deter or stop its expansion without an all-out war. Offensive realism, in short, cannot sustain its worst-case assumption in practice, both because empirically there *are* less intense and less expansionistic revisionist actors out there, and because its advocates implicitly build this fact into the theory itself by noting how currently more moderate Xs can backslide and become highly aggressive unlimited-aims revisionists down the road.[11]

The second conceptual error that is baked into offensive realism is the assumption that *all great powers are rational actors* seeking to maximize the achievement of their ends in the best possible way, given information available to them at the time. This may be a useful starting assumption to establish certain predictions from the offensive realist argument, just as game theorists and economists of the firm start with the idea that all actors are rational in terms of means-end thinking and that they know others are rational (the so-called common knowledge assumption). But the assumption of systemwide rationality is clearly empirically wrong on many occasions in world history, as psychological approaches to international relations have stressed for more than half a century.[12] Leaders may *not* be able to see the reality in front of them because of pathologies of information processing, unconscious drives to avoid disturbing facts, bureaucratic distortions, and the like. But beyond the point that irrational actors exist lies the more important theoretical point: that the leaders of state Y would have to be quite foolish themselves to always assume that other actors are as capable of rationally processing information as they are. That is, the common knowledge assumption of offensive realism and game theory ironically requires leaders who ignore the possibility that the adversaries they face may have highly irrational dimensions to their characters, whether that involves the inability to form good beliefs about reality or the continued use of poor means-end thinking (MET) even when such MET is not creating the results one expects.

There is an important bottom-line point to the above analysis. One can only talk about a truly rational security-maximizing state Y if one builds into the theory two key points: first, that such RSM-Ys are rational only if they make probabilistic estimates of *where on the spectrum* from moderate limited-aims revisionism to extreme unlimited-aims revisionism adversary X is and will likely be in the future;[13] and second, that RSM-Ys will estimate *the degree of rationality* state X is likely to display in the pursuit of various means to its ends.[14] If both these dimensions are missing from a theory, as they are with offensive realism, then the theory is in fact starting from an assumption of *irrational* actors who so oversimplify their initial assumptions that they can't possibly do what is smart for long-term national security. In a nutshell, we see that while offensive realism is right to highlight the problem of future uncertainty, by assuming that states must assume worst case yet will be deterred from expansion when costs objectively rise, the theory can only explain the "middle" of the hard-line/soft-line spectrum of state behavior. It can only explain why great powers in history tend to compete for more relative military power and territory but then "stop" when the prospect of very costly wars is on the horizon.[15] It cannot explain why great powers cooperate for long stretches of time, such as the United States and Japan from 1880 to 1930 or the United States and China from 1985 to 2015, especially in the economic realm. And it cannot explain why these periods of relative cooperation deteriorate not just into all-out arms races and alliance buildups, but into total wars that risk the states' elimination as great powers.

Defensive realists are thus correct to stress that a security-seeking Y will generally be less worried about an X that is also security-seeking than an X that is driven by non-security ends. Even if we start from the insight that all great powers are at least to some degree revisionist, preferring to acquire more power if they can get it at low cost, we can expect that, all things being equal, adversaries that are propelled by security are likely to be less extreme (more limited) in their intentions than adversaries driven by non-security motives such as greed, glory, and ideological mission. Yet defensive realists, when they use costly signaling models to show how a state X might reveal its core motives to state Y, adopt the common knowledge premise of game theory that both X and Y are rational actors and that each knows that the other is rational. As we have just seen, this assumption is problematic both in practice (there are indeed irrational adversaries in history) and in theory (no rational Y could be truly rational were it to ignore the possibility of X being irrational either now or in the future).

To conceptualize how state Y will likely make estimates of X's character type, therefore, two separate dimensions will be key: X's motives or ultimate

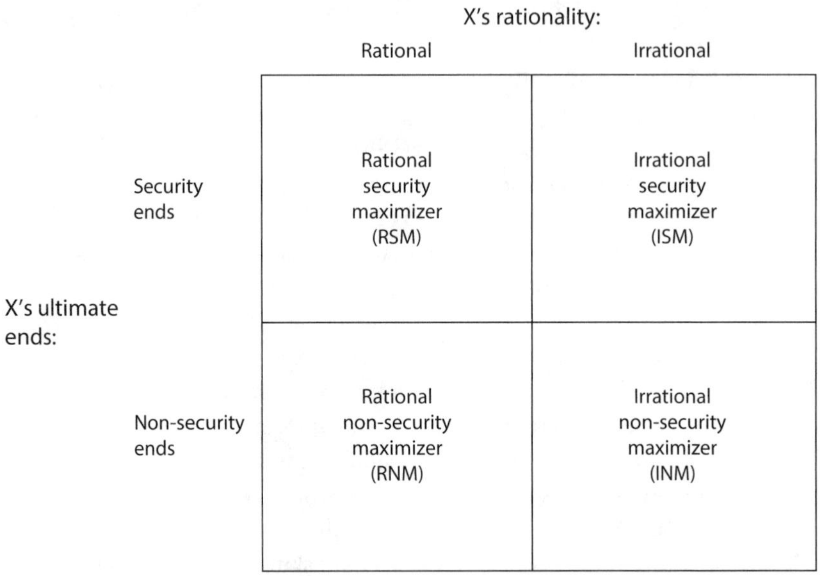

X's rationality:

|  | Rational | Irrational |
|---|---|---|
| **Security ends** | Rational security maximizer (RSM) | Irrational security maximizer (ISM) |
| **Non-security ends** | Rational non-security maximizer (RNM) | Irrational non-security maximizer (INM) |

X's ultimate ends:

FIGURE 2.1. Types of state X

ends (whether security-seeking or non-security-seeking) and X's rationality (whether rational or irrational). As figure 2.1 shows, this suggests that from Y's perspective, four different types of X may be "out there" now or into the future: X as a rational state that, like Y, also seeks to maximize its security (a "rational security maximizer" or RSM); an X that is rational but is driven by ends other than security (a "rational non-security maximizer" or RNM); a security-seeking X that is irrational in its understanding of how to maximize security (an "irrational security maximizer" or ISM); and finally, an X that is both irrational and pursuing non-security goals (an "irrational non-security maximizer" or INM). The following figure captures these four logical types.

This more complete conceptualization of state types allows us to understand why great power Y might worry as it looks around the system and calculates its relative security, or its "expected probability of survival."[16] Variations in state X's type over time, in conjunction with the trade and power factors of chapter 1, will drive Y's estimates of the level of threat X poses to Y. If X is also a rational security maximizer and is likely to stay that way, this at least tells Y that each state can work to ensure that the other sees it as "limited" in any actions it must take, given the offensive realist baseline, to expand its sphere, knowing that more extreme efforts may provoke an action-reaction spiral of hostility and mistrust given the security dilemma.[17] But if X is seen as rational but driven by non-security motives such as status and wealth for their own sake (a rational non-security maximizer or RNM), then Y will see X as more threatening than if X were a pure RSM. After all, X might be willing to attack its neighbors even when that sacrifices its own security to some degree because the non-security ends make such a trade-off "worthwhile."[18] Y would be more willing, all things being equal, to lean toward more hard-line policies in order to hedge against future aggressive behavior by X. In chapter 10, for example, I will explore the popular notion for some American political elites that Chinese leader Xi Jinping is animated not just by security concerns but by desires to restore China's place or status in the world after the "century of humiliation" from 1839 to 1949, and yet that he is also a highly rational calculator of the best means to this non-security end.

In most situations, it would be of even greater concern to Y to learn that X, although a security-seeker, was incapable of maximizing its expected probability of survival in a rational way. Leaders of X that are paranoid, or simply don't understand *how* to properly realize security—what figure 2.1 refers to as irrational security maximizers (ISMs)—can be very dangerous in world politics. They tend to overreact to the actions of others, believe that only continuous and large-scale expansion can ensure their security, and feel that only constant projection of military power will deter other great powers. Depending on how extreme X's irrationality was seen to be, Y would likely move toward increasingly hard-line policies both to deter X from extreme expansionism but also to "teach" it that its policies are indeed irrational, that unrestrained aggression does not improve X's overall security. If X is indeed capable of learning restraint—that is, to become more rational in its pursuit of security maximization—then it may well prove less threatening than the typical rational non-security maximizer (RNM). But until it does, such an irrational security maximizer (ISM) is likely to provoke Y into strong hard-line policies that can easily lead to a further spiral of hostility and cold-war politics. Such is the situation, I will suggest in chapter 10, with the Chinese state in the Indo-Pacific region: since 2008, China has resembled more and more a state obsessed with geoeconomic expansion to avoid a peaking in its power, notwithstanding the costs to its reputation as a moderate actor committed to the existing global order.

The worst possible type to face, however, is clearly an irrational non-security maximizing state (an INM). These are the states that not only are willing to trade-off security for ends such as glory and ideological mission but are irrational in their pursuit of such ends. They are the actors in history that are more likely to have unlimited aims—including the seeking of regional or global hegemony by total war—and are willing to risk the life of the state in the process. Hitler's Germany by 1940–44 or perhaps Genghis Khan's empire of the early thirteenth century can be seen as exemplars of this type of state.[19] Some might put the Soviet Union in the 1920s in this category, given its enthusiasm for spreading communism beyond its border, despite the implications for security-dilemma spiraling. Yet Stalin showed after 1935 that he would indeed settle for building "socialism in one country," at least in the short term. The Soviet Union was clearly still a threat after 1945, as chapter 7 will discuss, but not because it was an all-out INM, but rather because of its potential for growth, its ideological appeal to poor nations, and its strong belief in its own long-term ideological triumph. (As chapter 10 discusses, whether China today is closer to Stalin's Russia circa 1950 or to a more restrained version of either a rational non-security maximizer or an irrational security maximizer has direct implications for debates on what American officials "must do" to deal with the rise of China.)

The larger point here—that different types of adversaries shape different levels of threat perception and thus changes in the intensity of policy behavior—is a foundational point for all defensive realist scholarship. But by including state Y's concern about X's rationality and not just its ends, we see that Y has much more potential uncertainty about its external environment than defensive realists typically acknowledge.[20] And this is even before considering the problem of X's possible *future type* many years down the road. Because defensive realists stress that truly security-seeking states can signal their types to each other and overcome uncertainty, they tend to overlook the fact that current signaling, even if it works, can usually say little about what a state will be like later, especially if in the interim it has grown in relative economic and military power. And it is the likelihood of the other's future type being something other than RSM that will lead the state Ys in history to struggle even with Xs that they currently believe are reasonable and moderate RSMs.

## Cultural Difference as an Additional Determinant of External Threat

This section discusses the role that cultural differences play in state Y's estimates of X's type and thus in Y's calculations, as a rational security maximizer, of the best way to reduce the risks of a foreign power such as X either attacking Y or subverting its domestic order. It employs a simple causal diagram, figure 2.2, to show this state Y grapples with the interaction effects of critical factors that shape its external threat environment. Drawing from defensive realism, I argue that Y's perceived level of threat will be a function of two key variables, both involving the external situation in which Y finds itself. The first is Y's anticipation of its future economic power position as it affects its expected future military power. Future economic power will in turn be shaped by Y's level of economic dependence on the outside world (especially in realms two and three) and its expectations of future trade, with dependence and trade expectations affected by some of the factors mentioned in chapter 1, including endowments in land, labor, capital, technological development, and economies of scale (see links 1a and 1b in figure 2.2). The second variable shaping Y's sense of external threat is X's character type, defined, as above, in terms of Y's perception of X's ends and rationality, now and into the future.[21] Figure 2.2 shows the way anticipated power and character type interact to determine the level of threat Y perceives in state X. (The figure incorporates figure 2.1, but the space is now continuous; that is, the "box" of ends and rationality now shows the *degree* of X's relative emphasis on security versus non-security ends on the vertical dimension and the *degree* of X's rationality on the horizontal.)

We can predict that these two variables will reinforce each other to determine Y's perceived level of threat (from low to high) and thus the severity of its policy behavior on the hard-line/soft-line spectrum. Power changes are the core independent variable in dynamic realism, for the reason that Y must still worry about a rising X that it sees as also a rational security maximizer, simply because of its uncertainty about whether X will change its type after it has overtaken Y in relative power. Given uncertainty about the future, we can predict that the more Y anticipates a deep and inevitable decline in its power position, the more it will be likely to adopt harder-line policies even if X is currently considered a "good" actor.[22]

It is therefore Y's fear of a poor position later that is the "primary driver" of its policy. Indeed, even if Y is still rising in power, there can be a problem. If it expects that a combination of internal problems and the policies of X will soon cause it to peak and then decline unless it adopts more aggressive policies now, then we can predict that it will likely start to shift to the hard-line end of the spectrum in order to reenergize the state's growth rate and avoid an otherwise likely decline later.[23] This was, for example, how the thirteen colonies as a group saw the situation during the turmoil of 1764 to 1775. And we will see in chapter 10, this is a good explanation for China's increasingly assertive behavior in the Far East since 2010, and why the Belt and Road Initiative and a massive naval buildup were undertaken.[24]

Yet we can also predict that if any RSM-Y believes it is in decline, or soon will be, it will be *even more hard-line* the more it believes that the other state is driven by non-security ends or appears to be irrational in its ability to pursue its ends. That is, for any given level of decline Y is anticipating, a rising state X that is not a rational security maximizer (a "non-RSM," either as an RNM, ISM, or INM) will make Y worry even more about its decline, since the other will be even more likely to be aggressive later if allowed to rise at Y's expense.[25] Policies by Y to maintain its position in the system by force or coercion will start to seem more appealing, despite the risks of provoking a spiral of mistrust and hostility. And of course, the more that state Y is dependent on X for access

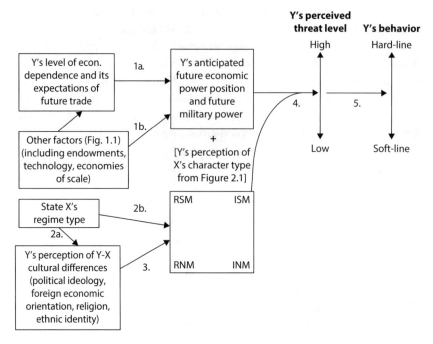

**FIGURE 2.2.** Incorporating character type into threat

Assumptions:

1. State Y remains a rational security-maximizing actor over time and is not constrained by factors within it.

2. The other core systemic variable, Y's intensity of drive to extend its economic power sphere as a function of core endowments, remains moderate but fixed over time.

to raw materials, investments, and markets (RIM) and the more Y expects that X will be trying to restrict its access to this RIM, the more Y will anticipate a peaking or decline in its economic power trajectory, and the more this will reinforce the need to shift to harder-line policies.[26]

The new element in figure 2.2 is the inclusion of factors that shape the way Y will form its estimates of X's character type. Most importantly for our purposes is something I label the cultural differences (or distance) between Y and X on four distinct dimensions: their respective political ideologies, their foreign economic orientations, their religions, and their ethnicities. These four dimensions of cultural distance will be partly shaped, of course, by Y's leaders' assessment of X's regime type—most obviously, whether it is democratic or authoritarian as well as the specific aspects such as whether it is parliamentary or presidential, liberal or illiberal, a fascist or communist authoritarian state, or perhaps a personalist dictatorship (see link 2a in figure 2.2).

But cultural distance goes beyond regime type. Even when states Y and X are the same general type—for example, both being liberal and democratic, as the United States and Britain were after 1870—there can be a strong sense of cultural differences across the four main dimensions. The first is *political ideology*. As Mark Haas summarizes, these are the principles by which a leadership group attempts to legitimate its claim to rule and its particular vision for the ordering of domestic politics.[27] This can include the extent to which the leadership group is committed to citizen rights and the rule of law, the relative freedom of economic units (e.g., free enterprise versus state control), representative institutions, and an independent decision-making role for these institutions relative to a monarch or executive branch.[28]

A related but distinct dimension is a state's *foreign economic orientation*— namely, whether the state is dedicated to principles of relatively free and open commerce or to a program of restricted commercial flows under the belief that this will grow the economy or protect the nation's unique way of life. State Y's foreign economic orientation will often be shaped by its political ideology—elites within capitalist states that believe in the value of internal free enterprise are often likely to see the value of free enterprise between national units. But as the British-American trade relationship of the nineteenth century shows, even actors founded on liberal principles can adopt very different views of the proper commercial orientation to the outside world: the British were very oriented to free trade by midcentury and the Americans were very protectionist.[29]

The third dimension of culture involves an actor's *religious beliefs and values*—in essence, their sense of how (if at all) individuals should be connected to a "higher" spiritual realm and the meaning of their lives given that realm's presumed existence (or nonexistence). The first two dimensions of cultural difference, political ideology and foreign economic orientation, are about "this world" and the pragmatic organization of political and economic life to realize secular goals. The religious dimension of culture captures the sense that human beings often need to find their place and purpose within the cosmos, and thus may fundamentally disagree on the nature of the higher realm and its significance for their lives.[30] And as the paratheses above remind us, there can also be a fundamental divide between individuals that see their countries as largely secular, at least in terms of domestic and foreign politics, and those that make their religious norms and values part and parcel of "who they are" and what goals are worth striving for. During the Cold War, for example, Americans were inclined to see Soviet and Chinese leaders as "godless Communists," and this accentuated their sense that any increase in the size of the opposing sphere would increase the threat to both the American sphere's power and its internal cohesion.

The final dimension or determinant of cultural difference is that of *ethnic identity*. Since the beginnings of great power politics in the ancient Near East, perceptions of ethnic differences have been critical to understanding the way leaders view external threats. Although the self-perceived distinctions between "Egyptians" and "Hittites" in 1300 BCE or "English" and "French" in the eighteenth century clearly incorporated aspects of the first three dimensions, the sense of ethnic difference went beyond these categories to include such things as language, facial features, family values, clothing, and even mundane things such as eating habits and manners of greeting.[31] Indeed, as modern nationalism developed since 1600 to become arguably the most powerful collective force on the planet, a people's sense of "nation" and "ingroup" often had more to do with ways of daily life than with a larger sense of political, economic, or religious differences.[32] When the Germans brought on a war in 1914 for fear of the rise of Russia, it was the vision of the uncivilized Russian "hordes" running roughshod over Europe that pushed German leaders into a preventive war. On the other dimensions of culture, the Russians were not seen as terribly threatening.[33]

Figure 2.2 suggests that Y's perception of X's character type in terms of X's ends and rationality will be a function of Y's view of both X's regime type and its sense of the cultural differences between Y and X across the above four dimensions. The figure shows that regime type—democracy versus various types of autocracies (fascism, communism, military dictatorship, etc.)—should have an effect, along with other factors, on Y's perception of cultural difference (causal link 2a in figure 2.2). Yet the institutional aspects of regime type can also have constraining and facilitating effects on X's character type independent of culture (link 2b). Even a democracy that has an illiberal leader, as John Owen notes, can be constrained from going to war because of the checks and balances built into the system.[34] Likewise, some autocracies are able to check otherwise aggressive leaders through the checks that are created by high-level institutional bodies that select and reject leaders based on performance. This allows Jessica Weeks to make predictions about the propensity of different types of authoritarian states to initiate war.[35] In terms of the theoretical set-up of this book, however, I treat Weeks's argument as if it only applies to the probability of *state X* being an aggressive actor, since I allow only X to have non-security and nonrational reasons for war, not Y.

My argument thus focuses attention on how any rational security-maximizing state Y would look at the nature of state X, including its regime type, in deciding on the "hardline-ness" of its policies. This move keeps my argument an externalist one. State X's regime type and its institutional constraints (or lack thereof) will be one such factor that Y will take into account. But in addition to regime type, state Y will need to examine cultural differences that, while partly shaped by X's regime type (link 2a), will also operate independently of it (link 3). For example, when U.S. leaders looked at the Soviet Union for the four decades after 1944, they saw strong cultural differences in political ideology (Soviet collectivism versus American individualism), in foreign economic thinking (closed versus open commercial spheres), and religious beliefs and norms (state-led atheism versus religious freedom and Christian values). Not surprisingly, then, with the possible exception of Mikhail Gorbachev, Soviet leaders during the Cold War were seen as "not like us." They were believed to be obsessed with ends other than mere security (including a sense of duty to spread communism) and they could not be automatically considered as rational in their pursuit of ends (as when Khrushchev put missiles into Cuba in 1962).

To summarize, the dynamic realist theory I am putting forward suggests that there are two main external variables that come together to determine Y's behavior as a rational security-maximizing state: Y's current and anticipated relative economic and military power position in the system and Y's perception of X's character type. Power is the primary variable, because even an RSM-Y that knows it is dealing with an X that is also a rational security maximizer must think about the probability that X will change its type later. But Y will be even more worried about any decline in power if it sees X as having non-security ends or being unable to act rationally in the pursuit of its ends. Hence, when Y believes X's foreign economic behavior is harming (or will likely later harm) its long-term position by reducing access to raw materials, investments, and markets, Y will likely increase the severity of its overall policy behavior toward X and the system. It will believe it necessary to act strongly to protect its access to the commerce that sustains its long-term economic and military power position.

We can thus predict that even when Y estimates X to have a moderate character, an anticipated decline in Y's power position due to commercial restrictions will make it worry more about X's future type and put more emphasis on averting decline. This leads to the baseline prediction for how anticipated power changes affect Y's fears of the future. Yet to the extent that X's domestic changes only make Y increasingly worried about X's type—namely, to believe X is moving closer to the bottom-right corner in figure 2.1, where non-security ends and irrationality in decision-making are more entrenched—the more Y's fears of future decline will grow. The hardline-ness of its behavior will thus likely rise.

There are a fair number of moving parts to the above argument, and this can of course make it more difficult for dynamic realism to predict which of the two main external variables (power and character type) and which of the four main determinants of character type (ideology, foreign economic policy, religious views, and ethnic differences) will have the greatest causal salience at any point in time. In 1945, for example, U.S. leaders were worried simultaneously about the ability of the Soviet Union to rebuild its economy and about the character of Soviet leaders, not just Joseph Stalin but who might replace him. Moreover, American mistrust of the character type of the Soviet Union was a combination of the liberal-communist ideological divide, Moscow's autarchic economic policies, Soviet atheism, and the European/American stereotypes of Russians as a backward, less-civilized people. Which of the different factors in such situations are going to be the most important in determining whether there will or will not be conflict, and its intensity?

The answer is that rational security-maximizing executives can be expected to do something similar to what militaries do when they make "net assessments" prior to a war. Generals know that many things come together to shape the overall ability of an army to defeat another state on the battlefield. Through wargaming and other techniques, they can make estimates about the army's probability of winning a war given the multiple factors at play in the heat of battle. Likewise, political leaders within state Y will try to figure out the "net future threat" that the other state X represents, given the likelihood of it overtaking Y later on and the probability that X will engage in coercive behavior or war to advance its interests at the expense of Y's security. The variables outlined above all go into this net threat assessment of the state's expected probability of survival given the external situation the state faces.[36] And documents will allow us to see how leaders are evaluating the mix of the different elements going into the overall threat level. If all the variables point to increasing threat over time, then the leaders will likely keep ratcheting up their own assertiveness to try to reduce decline and to project resolve. If some of the variables suggest high future threat while others temper the overall net assessment, then we should expect to see debate between officials within state Y over the extent to which X truly is a future threat, and whether Y can risk upsetting X by an overly hard-line policy. Regarding American views of China, for example, such internal debates are to be expected given the high uncertainty surrounding the differing inputs into threat (see chapter 10). Yet it will be the net threat assessment of a particular administration that can be predicted to drive the severity of its policies. And as we will see in the next section, rational officials will constantly pose their assessments of future threat against the risks that more assertive postures will lead to undesired spirals of hostility and even war.

## Feedback Loops, Trade Security Dilemmas, and Policy Trade-offs

Up to now, to simplify the analysis and to isolate the core effects of the main variables, I have avoided a detailed discussion of the issue of endogeneity. Yet the leaders of any rational security-maximizing Y will be aware that the hardline-ness of Y's behavior will shape the way other states make estimates of Y's character and thus the intensity of its intentions. Y's leaders may know that they only seek to ensure the state's security and that they are rational in the calculation of the best means to this end. But they also know, given the inherent difficulty of seeing into the heads of others, let alone figuring out their future intentions, that *other actors* may be quite uncertain about Y's motives and rationality.[37] And they know that the other great powers will spend a great deal of time and money watching for clues about Y's character and intentions, and that one of the biggest clues is Y's behavior itself. The more hard-line Y's behavior, the more Y builds up its arms, projects its military power, and uses force against smaller actors, the more other great powers will come to doubt Y's statements that it is only rationally seeking to ensure its security. This problem of growing mistrust is of course nicely captured in the defensive realist notion of the security dilemma. At its core, states Y and X face a security dilemma when the actions by Y to improve its security tend to make X feel less secure. State X's responses to Y's actions will in turn tend to make Y feel less secure, and a spiral of increasing mistrust and hostility is likely to follow, a spiral that can undermine both sides' real security by increasing the probability of actual war, causing states to spend too much on guns versus butter, and allowing third parties to exploit the Y-X conflict for their own gains.[38]

Defensive realists are right to argue that leaders aware of the security dilemma will be more moderate in their behavior than they would be otherwise.[39] These leaders will act to avoid or reduce the impression that either they have goals going beyond mere security (greed, glory, etc.) or that they do not understand the best means to security (they are irrational security maximizers) or, heaven forbid, both. For defensive realists, because overly hard-line behavior invokes "balancing" against the state that can make that behavior self-defeating, the short-term policies of rational security-maximizing actors will tend to be cautious, all things being equal.[40] This focus on the short term and not appearing to have a currently aggressive character type, however, downplays the importance of future uncertainty emphasized by offensive realists and the dynamic realist theory of this book. Rational actors not only need to prepare now for problems that might come later, but in environments where they anticipate a decline in power and the potential for the other's character type to be worse in the future, they will be inclined to hard-line behavior now to shore up their deteriorating security situations.

Defensive and offensive realists remain divided in terms of causal predictions because they only stress either the short-term risks of overly hard-line behavior (sparking security dilemma spirals) or the long-term risks of overly cautious behavior (falling behind in the great power competition for position and becoming vulnerable later). Yet to state the obvious: *both types of risk must matter* for any truly rational actor seeking security. To plow ahead with expansion, heedless of the endogeneity of spiraling, would be to get oneself into far more wars and expensive conflicts than would be necessary for survival. Yet to ignore future power and the ability of the state to deal with future problems would be irresponsible given "the problem of the future"—the problem that the other's character type can change, that relative power changes much more slowly than intentions, and that in anarchy the commitments others make to being nice later cannot be enforced or guaranteed.[41]

There is a simple theoretical move that can help us transcend this divide: *combine both sets of insights into a single model of decision-making.* Up until now, I have largely focused on the forces that can cause a rational security-maximizing state Y to shift to more hard-line policies to protect itself from future invasion or efforts by adversaries to undermine its social order. By incorporating time explicitly into the theory—namely, an actor's varying estimates of the likelihood of future restrictions in access to raw materials, investments, and markets, based in part on assessments of the other's future character type—I have sought to make systemic realist theory more truly "dynamic."[42] But there is an additional popular sense of the term dynamic that can be integrated with the first. And this is the sense of an action-reaction dynamic that over time can push all actors to a place that neither of them could have fully anticipated when they first starting to adjust their policies.[43] As Robert Jervis reminds us, security-dilemma logics can explain moves toward stable balances of power, but they can also alert us to runaway "positive feedback" effects that end up leading states into arms races and wars that neither side initially wanted.[44]

Smart leaders will be aware of both of these types of systemic pressures *simultaneously.* Knowing that any policy on the hard-line/soft-line spectrum involves trade-offs, they will try to calibrate the intensity of their policies to reflect the relative mix of factors in any specific situation. If state Y sees X as relatively similar in overall culture (a low cultural distance), stable in its regime type, and not likely to overtake Y in relative economic or military power, Y will likely want to "lean" more to the soft-line end of the spectrum. This will reduce the probability of a spiral of mistrust and hostility that leads to an undesired crisis or war. It may still be inclined to grab opportunities to expand its realm—one economic power sphere when they arise, but it will try to show X that it is a moderate rational security-maximizer with quite limited aims.[45] If, on the other hand, Y sees X as growing quickly and likely to overtake Y in overall power in the future, and as probably having a character type that would be aggressive once superior, then Y can be predicted to start to lean to the hard-line end of the spectrum, or even contemplate initiating preventive war before it is too late. The severity of Y's external situation, in short, compels it to increase the severity of its policies—to "trade-off" its reputation as a moderate character for a better future power position that can leave the state "ready" to tackle whatever comes down the pike.

This integration of defensive and offensive realist insights into a better decision-making model is still incomplete, however. It has left out the uniquely commercial aspects of endogeneity—what I call the trade-security dilemma, as opposed to the military-security dilemma of traditional defensive realist scholarship. State Y is not only concerned about X's potential to use military force to expand its territorial scope. It is also worried that X will become more willing to restrict Y's access to raw materials, investments, and markets in realms two and three, either through simply sanctions and embargos or perhaps political pressure on third parties. As we saw in chapter 1, state Y will have reason to develop RIM commerce beyond its original realm-one sphere to exploit economies of scale, avoid diminishing returns, and acquire diverse inputs. But in doing so, it will begin to feel more vulnerable to X's geoeconomic diplomacy. Leaders in Y may feel they need to increase the size of the navy to protect trade routes, or even to deploy soldiers to key third-party states to ensure domestic order and the continuation of trade. Yet such moves by Y to protect the security of its commercial interests can easily be seen by X as actions that hurt *X's commercial and political interests*. If X responds with a naval buildup, more boots on the ground abroad, and a tightening of its political ties to neutral nations in realm two, then Y will likely see this as an intensification of the commercial struggle for assured access, or worse.

X's own increasingly hard-line behavior, in short, can cause Y's leaders to have more negative expectations for future trade or to see X's character type as less moderate than it was previously. The probability of an intense trade-security spiral of mistrust would increase, leading us to predict that Y would be more willing to initiate regional crises or even start a war. The spiral of trade restrictions and military power projection that led to war between Japan and the United States in 1941 can be seen as a paradigmatic example of this unfortunate dynamic. And as the rise of China over the last fifteen years demonstrates, the more one state's growth suggests that it will overtake the other in economic power, the more the declining state will undertake actions to slow this growth, and the greater the likelihood that a back-and-forth spiral of mistrust and hostility will arise (see chapter 10).

Figure 2.3 captures the way the trade-off logic of dynamic realism works in both theory and practice. It extends figure 2.2 by now including X's likely *response* to changes in Y's behavior—particularly how X is likely to become more hard-line in its policies upon seeing more assertive policies by Y (link 6).[46] These changes in X's behavior will likely have a feedback effect on Y's estimates of the core variables from previous figures, especially Y's expectations of future trade and its perception of both the X-Y cultural distance and X's overall character type.

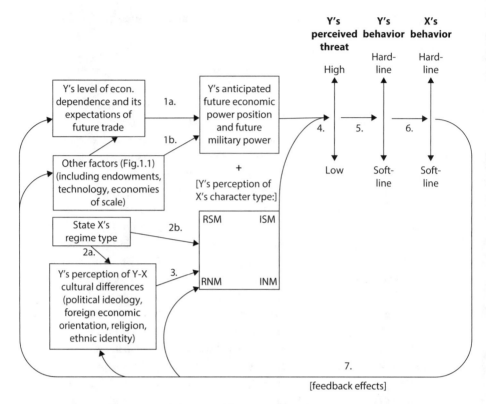

FIGURE 2.3. Summary of the causal factors and pathways
Assumptions:
1. State Y remains a rational security-maximizing actor over time and is not constrained by factors within it.
2. The other core systemic variable, Y's intensity of drive to extend its economic power sphere as a function of core endowments, remains moderate but fixed over time.
3. Other exogenous factors that may shape the hardline-ness of X's behavior, such as changes in third parties and depletion of its raw materials, are held constant.

But here's the key point: state Y, as a rational security maximizer, *knows ahead of time that X is watching Y's behavior for signs of Y's possible aggressiveness,* either in the commercial realms or the more narrowly territorial-political realms. This knowledge will act as a major constraint on Y moving toward more hard-line behavior—Y knows that to project a more assertive posture would likely cause X to restrict RIM and force Y to become even more assertive. In short, the very existence of a trade-security dilemma, along with the need for realm-two and realm-three trade to develop a strong economic base for future military spending, will make great powers likely to lean to moderate policies that seek to preserve the current positions of states without creating the kind of mistrust that can lead to a downward spiral in commercial and political relations. It can explain such anomalies for offensive realist theory such as the quarter century of relatively cooperative behavior by China after 1985, despite ongoing disputes over Taiwan and the South China Sea. Chinese leaders understood that as long as Washington was not already trying to cut China off from RIM, it had to worry about provoking U.S. leaders into such policies through overly aggressive policies around the world. Thus, they followed Deng Xiaoping's advice to not be provocative and to bide their time as China built its economic power (the so-called hide-and-bide strategy).

Yet figure 2.3 also highlights why a state Y might start to lean toward more aggressive policies over time, despite being aware of the potential spiral effects. Information may come out suggesting state X's leaders, in addition to worrying about Y's growth, have motives other than strictly security ones or are less rational than previously thought. And if this assessment and X's behavior, independent of Y's policies, start to indicate X is less willing to trade openly with Y or to allow Y access to RIM in the neutral zone, then Y has a reason to start to lean toward more severe policies to ensure its long-term commercial security.[47] It is more willing to trade-off its reputation for moderation for an improved power position in the system. The risks of falling behind in the power game and being hurt later now start to outweigh the risks of sparking a spiral of mistrust and hostility.[48]

The more complete dynamic realist picture of figure 2.3 thus shows how the defensive realist insight of the security dilemma—now expanded to include uncertainty about the other's willingness to allow open access to RIM—can be combined with offensive realist concerns about the need to hedge against future problems, including commercial ones, to understand why great powers will often cooperate for long periods of time and then switch to more aggressive policies that risk both extended and destabilizing security competitions. Neither defensive realism or offensive realism on their own can fully explain "both ends of the dependent variable"—the periods of great power cooperation and periods of intense conflict and war—nor can they understand how that cooperation or conflict is both reflected in and driven by commercial needs and concerns.[49] Dynamic realism solves these problems by specifying a trade-off logic that shows under what conditions rational decision-makers will lean one way or the other as they go about protecting their state's security over the long term.

## Summary of Propositions

We are now at a point where we can summarize the major propositions of dynamic realism. It is important to note that because the theory of this book is based on a trade-off logic where causal factors work in tension with one another, we cannot specify simple and specific "hypotheses" linking causal factor A to likely effect E in the typical way of most political science books. (Consider, for example, common hypotheses suggesting that "increasing trade will lead to less aggressive behavior" or that "the more democratic a state, the more it will be adopt cooperative policies.") A trade-off logic is not discon-firmed, as it is with A → E hypotheses, by simply showing that A was present and yet E did not occur, or that E regularly occurred even though A was not present. Instead, we must use documents to see if leaders in Y, when adjusting their behaviors on the hard-line/soft-line spectrum, were responding to the factors outlined in the theory in the way the theory anticipates they will—that is, in terms of the tensions and trade-offs *between* the factors as they shape the actors' sense of the relative risks and benefits of either becoming increasingly hard-line or soft-line.

This book offers three main sets of propositions, the first two coming di-rectly out of the theoretical logic of chapters 1 and 2, and the third involving predictions that arise when one relaxes some of the assumptions underpinning the theory as it has been developed. Each proposition can be examined in light of the documents, as I do in the empirical chapters.

*Proposition 1*: All great powers, because of their need to grow the economic foundations of their security, have a drive to extend their core economic power spheres (realm one) and to protect their access to raw materials, investments, and markets with neutral actors (realm two) and with other great powers (realm three). This drive can lead them to develop strong navies and military power projection capability to deter adversaries from restricting their future RIM access. Yet these great powers, if they are rational security maximizers, will also be wary of setting off undesired spirals of increasing commercial re-strictions and more assertive and militarized policies. They will lean to more soft-line policies when their expectations for future trade and investment are strong, when they expect that continued trade will increase their long-term economic power, and when there are few opportunities to expand their eco-nomic power spheres without increasing the risk of spiraling. They will lean to more hard-line policies when their expectations for future trade and invest-ment are negative, when they believe that current or likely restrictions in trade will cause a decline in long-term economic and thus military power, and when the risks of spiraling are overridden by the risks of decline in their long-term power positions. A great power will also be inclined to harder-line behavior when leaders expect that a rising trend in power will not last and that the state will peak and then decline in relative economic power in the absence of greater effort to expand the state's economic power sphere.

*Proposition 2*: Any rational security-maximizing state, for any given level of power and degree of change in that power, will be more likely to see a threat to its future RIM access when an adversary becomes either more inclined to non-security motives (greed, glory, ideological mission, diversionary war) or less able to think rationally about the best means to its ends. It will be more willing to trade off its reputation for moderation to ensure that its relative power position, both economically and militarily, is preserved. But to the extent that an adversary is changing internally and becoming either more security-driven or more rational in its means-end thinking, the state will again see the risks of spiraling as predominant and will be inclined to return to a more moderate posture typical of rational security-maximizing states.

*Proposition 3*: When it comes to specific historical cases, variations in key parameters will have potentially important effects on the way the predictions of the first and second propositions play out.

*Proposition 3a* (regarding *polarity*): Relaxing the assumption of two main great powers Y and X and the incorporation of additional great powers will mean that state Y must concern itself with the rise of states other than X. It will thus be more inclined to accept the economic growth X receives through trade and will even align economically and politically with X against rising state Z should Z demonstrate the potential to overtake both states.[50]

*Proposition 3b* (regarding *the offense-defense balance*): Relaxing the assumption of offense-defense neutrality, state Y will be more likely to trade off its reputation for moderation to gain a strong economic power position when offensive currently has the advantage, or is expected to have the advantage in the future, given that its own spheres of commercial influence are or will become more vulnerable to attack by state X (and in multipolarity, by state Z and other great powers).

*Proposition 3c* (regarding *domestic constraints on behavior*): Relaxing the assumption that state Y, the state whose behavior we are trying to explain, has no domestic impediments to executing the "best" policy will mean that unit-level factors may indeed constrain Y's leaders from acting as the theory predicts. Yet as long as the propelling forces of Y's behavior are coming from outside the state, then the *desired* behavior of leaders at any point in time should follow the logic of the first and second propositions. They may have to delay their desired policies until they have overcome domestic constraints, but the theory predicts that they will try to overcome them or work around them so that the best policy for the nation's security can be implemented.[51]

# The Methodological Approach to Testing "Competing Arguments"

The standard way to test any theory of international relations is to set up its hypotheses—of the form "changes in factor $A$ lead to predictable changes in event $E$"—against the hypotheses of competing arguments that predict it will be changes in factor $B$ or $C$, not $A$, that lead to changes in $E$.[52] This is not only the way large-N quantitative studies tend to work, whereby factor $A$ of the new theory is tested for its statistical and substantive significance against a host of "control variables" from alternative theories. It is also the way more qualitative and historical empirical studies have usually operated. A scholar will offer a new theory that predicts, for example, that as independent variable $A$ increases there will be an increase in dependent variable $E$, and then show that in a series of cases, variable $A$ did indeed lead to $E$ and in fact overrode the effects of the variables $B$, $C$, and $D$ of the competing arguments.

In large-N work where one is seeking to explain the average effect of individual causes on changes in $E$ across hundreds or thousands of cases, the above approach makes some sense. The goal, after all, is not to explain any specific case but see how much overall variance in $E$ is explained by adding new factors to the variables that most scholars already accept as important. Rather than trying to refute existing theories, a scholar is simply trying to show that one cannot ignore the *additional* explanatory power provided by the new theory.[53] Qualitative research, however, is typically much bolder. The goal is to show the causes of individual cases, not to reveal average effects. Hence, there is a tendency to seek to show that competing theories are simply *wrong* when it comes to case $J$ or $K$, and that only the new theory can explain the reasons that event $E$ happened or did not happen in such cases. The qualitative literature in international relations thus seems plagued by continual "knock-down-drag-'em-out" battles over controversial historical cases such as the First World War and the Cuban Missile Crisis, with scholars seeking to show that their preferred factor $A$ does a better job explaining the case than factors $B$, $C$, and $D$ of the alternative arguments.

There are two main problems with such a qualitative research agenda. First, the typical reason one will use qualitative methods over quantitative methods is that there usually are not that many event $E$s to study. Things such as the onset of great power wars or shifts in great power alliances are rare events—they are not like exchange rates or levels of industrial production that are varying on a monthly if not daily basis, and therefore lend themselves to tests of a "large number" (large-N) of data. But rare events such as war are, as the phrase goes, *rare for a reason*. Exchange rates and industrial production levels are the result of thousands of individual decisions, with most of those decisions outside the full control of state leaders. Decisions for war, however, are almost always made "at the top" by a few select policy makers. And given the huge costs and risks associated with their decisions, not only for their countries but for themselves, they are only likely to choose to initiate a war or a hard-line policy that risks a spiral to war under a bounded set of conditions. Leaders may desire to get a war or a new more expansionistic policy going but find that their state is "not ready" for this shift, perhaps because the public does not support it, the state is currently weak in military power, or the logistical and strategic plans are still incomplete. In short, because there are a whole host of necessary conditions that need to be in place before leaders can bring on the event, qualitative case-study work will often see the causal effect of factor A *not* operate as expected because the leaders are still "getting their ducks in a row."

In such situations, causality will not take the simple "if A, then E" form but rather the form of "*individually necessary, jointly sufficient*" (INJS). Factor A alone will not cause E, because factors B, C, and D *also* have to be present to create the effect. Pundits and scholars know this intuitively when they talk about there being a "recipe for war" at a certain point in time t (such as in July 1914). Just as one cannot make an omelet without at least five necessary conditions—eggs, a pan, a fire, a whisk, and a person who both wants and knows how to make it—one cannot make a war without giving attention to factors B, C, and D as well as factor A. And yet this bundle of factors A, B, C, and D may only explain a certain number of individual cases. Bundles of other factors—perhaps A, D, F, and G or D, G, and H—may explain other cases. When doing qualitative research, therefore, scholars will need to be attentive to which "INJS bundles" are operating for any specific cases over time.[54] Otherwise, they may fall prey to the self-defeating tendency of arguing only for factor A over competing factors B and C as an explanation for case J, without realizing that A, B, and C are all implicated in event E for that case.

The second issue that arises in qualitative research comes out of the first. Many qualitative scholars are aware of the INJS nature of the cases they are studying.[55] But they typically fail to address, at least self-consciously, a critical issue associated with a complex INJS approach—namely, *what causal role* is each factor in the INJS bundle playing such that event E is likely to come about? We need to know more than simply that factor A was associated with the arising of event E. We need to know whether factor A was *propelling* an actor toward a behavior that led to E, or whether it played more of a *facilitating* role for more primary propelling variables, or indeed whether it was *constraining* the actor from taking actions that might have otherwise produced E. Such terms are frequently used in historical research but rarely defined. A propelling factor is one that involves an actor's ultimate ends and desires or fears—its "reasons" for acting. A leader worried about the state's future power because of a trade cut-off, for example, is propelled by the fear of the future and a concern for security into initiating a crisis or war. A facilitating factor is one that is incidental to the actor's ends but needs to be in place before the desired action can be carried out. A leader that needs to have a certain threshold of popular support before starting a war is thinking of domestic politics as a facilitating factor: this support is not pushing the leader into war but instead must be achieved before the war can begin. A constraining factor is in some sense the flip side of a facilitating factor: if public support does not reach the threshold level, the leader is constrained from acting. More narrowly, however, a constraining factor is something that is pulling actors back from doing what they might otherwise want to do. Fear of hurting one's reputation for moderation can constrain a leader from pursuing a projection of naval power to defend a state's commercial interests, for example.

Factors can play other types of causal roles beyond these three. An *accelerating* factor is one that speeds up a plan that is already propelled by something else. Seeing other states start to form alliances in anticipation of an actor's initiation of war can make this actor go more quickly into that war, for example. A *reinforcing* factor is one that operated to make the potential effect of a key propelling factor that much more likely to occur. Leaders of state Y may be planning for a war primarily to solve the problem of long-term economic decline relative to X but believe that war will also leave Y in a stronger position relative to Z after the war is over. The latter reason would probably not drive Y into war alone, but it reinforces the importance of acting against X. Finally, a *distorting* factor is one that causes the final decision to move away from the "ideal" point on the hard-line/soft-line spectrum. The decision is still implemented, but something "gets in the way" of it being the truly best choice given the circumstances. A legislature that requires "pork barrel" spending on outdated military technology as the price for approval of the executive's desired containment strategy, or a bureaucracy that offers a less efficient means to get to the executive's desired end, simply because it aligns with its standard operating procedures, can be said to distort the leader's plan away from the ideal.

In qualitative research of the kind undertaken in this book, the integration of both the complex conjunctural causality of INJS with the examination of the causal role played by a factor in a particular INJS bundle leads to a new way to test the value of different theories of international relations. The idea that empirical work is designed to "prove" one theory better than another is abandoned. Different theories put forward different factors that *may be working together* as necessary conditions for the arising of event E. And the factors of different theories *may be operating in different ways* and *to different degrees* across time, even for same great power. For example, if factor A is "the level of economic decline" state Y is anticipating and factor B is the "level of domestic support" Y's leaders are experiencing at home, then in cases J and K both factors may be at work as necessary conditions for explaining the leaders' initiation of war. But in case *J*, economic decline may be the propelling factor (fear of future vulnerability pushing a leader to choose preventive war) and domestic support only a facilitating factor, while in case *K*, domestic support—or lack thereof—may be propelling the leaders to start a diversionary war to help them stay in power, and the fact that the state has peaked and is declining in relative power is merely facilitating the action by giving the leaders the maximum chance of a short and popular war.[56] In a third case *L*, however, it may be that neither *A* nor *B* are necessary to explaining event *E*, and that *D*, *F*, and *G* together provide the INJS bundle leading to *E*. In this way, we see that *A* and *B* are absolutely critical to explaining *E* for cases *J* and *K*, albeit with different causal roles, but are not even a part of the explanation for case *L*.

The focus of good qualitative research, therefore, must be reoriented from a desire to "beat" other theories and their factors to seeing how factors work together to explain the cases of interest, and in what ways. This is how I proceed in the empirical chapters of this book. The so-called competing theories that can be used to explain different cases across the sweep of American foreign policy history from the eighteenth century to the twenty-first century are not really "competing" at all. This book may be offering a dynamic realist theory that argues that the fundamental propelling factors pushing American leaders over the centuries are rooted in expectations about future commerce and the probability that others will try to restrict access to raw materials, investments, and markets. But this does not mean domestic-level variables such as American values, bureaucratic politics, regional tensions, legislative politics, and the like are not playing important roles in the INJS bundles that explain changes in foreign policy over time. The factors of liberal and neo-Marxist "internalist" theories can thus be brought in for every case and examined objectively to see *how often* they are causally salient and *whether they are operating as propelling, facilitating, constraining, or some other causal role* in the INJS bundles. The same can be done for the factors of other systemic theories, such as theories stressing the role of geography, weapons technology, and alliance cohesion as causes of policy behavior.

The above discussion indicates the importance of balance in research, but it does not preclude being bold. And that is what I will do in the remaining chapters. I will boldly suggest that the factors and reasoning outlined in the dynamic realist theory of this book are not only important necessary conditions for explaining a very large number of the key cases across two and a half centuries of American foreign policy, but that they generally provide the *propelling reasons* for American action—why the American leaders acted as they did. I will show that while domestic-level variables were certainly important, they rarely were the primary propelling reasons for actions taken. While they were sometimes reinforcing of the systemic reasons, most often they played facilitating, constraining, and distorting roles that either delayed the executive's response to an emerging threat (Roosevelt dealing with Hitler from 1935 to 1941, for example) or pushed U.S. leaders away from their ideal policies (as when Polk in 1846 had to provoke Mexico into a war in order to secure California ports).

In what follows over the next five chapters, I will set my dynamic realist theory against the major unit-level theories that might be able to explain the key cases of American foreign policy from 1750 to the present. My argument represents the primary systemic or "externalist" approach to these cases since, as I have shown, the insights of offensive and defensive realism can be brought together in a more powerful synthetic argument that also includes commercial and economic factors. Offensive realism and defensive realism become what physicists call "special cases" within the larger framework: the former operate as individual theories only under narrow boundary conditions specified by the latter. I will therefore refer to the explanatory value of offensive realism and defensive in particular cases only when conditions are extreme enough to allow either to shine without reference to the other.[57] Otherwise, the focus will be on setting my argument against theories that posit the importance of domestic and psychological variables operating "within state Y"—that is, within the American polity at a particular time.

There are, of course, a massive number of individual unit-level or liberal/ internalist arguments, drawing on international relations theory, that have been deployed to explain the historical cases of American foreign policy. As I have discussed, there are really no unit-level scholars that seek to use their arguments across the full sweep of cases from 1750 on. It is thus better to postpone treatment of these arguments until the individual case studies of chapters 3 to 9. Nevertheless, we can place these liberal theories into five main categories of argumentation: *ideational, domestic-institutional, bureaucratic, interest-group domestic political, and psychological.* The first camp includes those scholars who stress the exceptional nature of the American nation, at least as it manifests in more self-evident examples of ideationally driven presidents such as Thomas Jefferson, Woodrow Wilson, and Ronald Reagan. Such scholars tend to accept there is a baseline level of desire of presidents and legislature leaders to spread the benefits of liberal democracy or at least to protect existing examples of it. All presidents after 1948, for example, apparently believed that the "Western Alliance" countries in NATO and the Far East (Japan) needed to be made secure against the threat of Soviet and Chinese communism. But presidents such as Wilson and Reagan appeared to believe that benefits of American-style individualism, rule of law, and free enterprise needed to be extended to countries that were not currently liberal democratic.[58]

The domestic-institutional camp includes scholars that focus on the structural and constitutional aspects of the American polity. The most prominent arguments here are versions of democratic peace theory, the idea that American executives will be restrained by members of the legislative chambers from initiating crises and wars against other democratic states.[59] John Owen provides an important twist on this argument, one that draws insights from the first camp. He suggests that since U.S. legislators are beholden to the liberal ideas that Americans in general have internalized, these legislators will pull presidents back from war with democracies but will *push* reluctant executives into conflicts with non-liberal states that the public view as threats to liberal democracy.[60] More constitutionally focused scholars emphasize the way presidents, at least until the first half of the Cold War, often found themselves bound by the checks and balances of the U.S. legislative branch.[61]

The bureaucratic camp includes all scholars that go *within* the executive branch to show how the agencies of the U.S. government shape the way foreign policy is made. The bureaucratic politics model, in which different agencies compete for influence and bigger slices of the budgetary pie, are of course included here.[62] But so are organizational theories, especially as they relate to the military, that suggest that individual bureaucracies advocate policies that help their own agencies, thus distorting policy at the expense of the national interest.[63] Finally, there are all the more specific arguments focusing on the nature of particular organizations and their members such as the State Department, the National Security Council, and the intelligence community more broadly.[64]

The interest-group domestic politics camp goes beyond the institutional view of the second camp by looking at the pressure groups in society that seek to shape policy according to their wishes. The focus is on powerful lobbying groups that push legislators and sometime executive officials to push policy in their desired directions—industry lobby groups that want tariff restrictions on their products; arms manufacturers that press for larger slices of the defense budget; and so forth.[65] These interest groups can also include lobbying groups for regional economic issues,[66] specific political economic ways of life such as slaveholding (the southern "slave power" prior to 1861) or free enterprise (e.g., the U.S. Chamber of Commerce), and individual countries.[67] What is most notable about all of these various arguments is the presumption that these groups not only distort policy being propelled for other reasons, including Realpolitik ones, but that they can propel it directly through monetary support for politicians or threats to organize against them.

The final camp is a broad one and includes all theorists emphasizing the role of psychological predispositions and pathologies that get in the way of good rational decision-making. Two of the most well-known predispositions are the tendencies of individual leaders cognitively to close themselves off from new or dissonant information or to see information according to their desires (wishful thinking and bolstering) and to thus form distorted views of reality.[68] Leaders may also suffer from tendencies to be more risk-taking when they see themselves in the realm of future losses,[69] to make dispositional attributions toward the undesired behavior of adversaries,[70] or to allow emotions to distort their thinking.[71] The social psychology of small groups can also be brought in to show how desires to conform can lead to groupthink—the unwillingness to question what one sees as the emerging group consensus—and to overemphasize the superiority of the group.[72] Finally, there are theories that focus attention on fixed personality traits of particular leaders, such as their tendencies to stress honor over shame, or the importance of the self's position within the social setting.[73]

In the empirical chapters to follow, I will pick from the unit-level camps those theories that are relevant to the particular cases being discussed, rather than trying to cover the value of different liberal theories across the broad sweep of cases. This is for two simple reasons: first, the theorists themselves do not try to apply them beyond a few cases; and second, my methodological goal, to reiterate, is not to defeat other theories but to see when and in what way (with what causal role) the factors of the other theories work to explain particular cases of American foreign policy history. This approach is not only more balanced and interesting, but it greatly simplifies the task ahead. I do not have to make obvious points, such as the fact that bureaucratic theories did not work well before the advent of large bureaucracies in the mid-twentieth century, or that certain interest groups, such as southern slaveholders, only have potential influence on cases where the expansion of American territory might influence the domestic balance between slave and non-slave-owning states.

To summarize, in what follows, the propositions of dynamic realism discussed earlier in this chapter will be set against the unit-level propositions that fit with the cases at hand. Since I am offering a theory that does something unique—attempting to apply one theory across two hundred and fifty years of American foreign policy history, and to show that the theory provides the core *propelling* reasons for American actions—the main thing being "tested" is whether theories at the unit level offer good alternative explanations for what was propelling the leaders into changes in behavior. When these other theories offer important factors within the "individually necessary, jointly sufficient" bundles that work for individual cases, but when these factors are not playing propelling roles but some other type of role (constraining, facilitating, etc.) then I will simply acknowledge the value of these theories in identifying such factors. Yet if I can show that the theory of this book very often correctly identifies the main propelling factors of American foreign policy history, it will have made a contribution to understanding this history.

# 3

# The Origins of the War for Colonial Independence

THE WAR for American independence from Great Britain, fought from 1775 to 1783, set the foundation for much of what transpired in American foreign policy over the next two centuries. The war not only created a country whose commitment to ideals of liberty brought into question the legitimacy of the absolutist states of Europe, it also introduced to the world system a land-rich and dynamic nation that these states knew might one day challenge them in both commercial and military power. Yet surprisingly, the War for Colonial Independence is rarely studied by international relations scholars, presumably because it seems to be a case of civil strife within a political unit rather than an "inter-national" conflict. Narrowly defined, this of course is true, since the Americans were seeking to break from an imperial realm that they had been a part of for a century and a half. Yet if we look at *how* the war broke out in 1775–76, this is clearly a conflict between thirteen political units (the colonies) that had seen themselves as essentially free to run their internal affairs and a power (Britain) that sought to restrict these traditional rights. Moreover, in the 1760s each of the thirteen colonies, unlike in British Canada or East and West Florida, had its own functioning political structure and elites that made decisions for their specific colony independent of London, even if the crown often had a final say on legislation. Hence when these elites gathered in Philadelphia in September 1774 for the first Continental Congress, they were acting *as if* they already had the legal power to commit their fellow colonists to a common strategy and to use established institutional tools to enforce the colonies' agreements. And because of the long tradition of independent decision-making enforced by separate colonial bureaucracies, they were for all intents and purposes acting as sovereign actors resisting the oppression of a foreign power.

For the purposes of this book then, the fight of the colonies for formal independence can be treated using the theories of international relations before us (thus my choice of the label the "War for Colonial Independence" rather than, say, the War of American Independence).[1] Indeed, as we shall see, this case is one of the clearest cases of a war that neither side wanted, but which they fell into as a result of the spiral of mistrust and hostility that had built up over many years. As such, it represents one of the best parallel cases to how military conflict might break out between nuclear powers such as the United States and China in the contemporary environment.[2] It is therefore worth exploring this seminal case in some detail.

The origins of the war are shrouded in mystery and mythology. American high schoolers are routinely taught that this was a war fought for ideals of "liberty," the desire to break away from a repressive British political system that sought to impose increasingly high taxes on its colonial subjects without their consent. American scholars of course know that the war was much more than a fight over "taxation without representation." But they remain divided on its ultimate causes. There are two main camps in the historical literature. The domestic politics camp focuses on the internal conflicts between regional factions and between classes caused by the rise of commercial capitalism in the eighteenth century. Scholars within this camp, while diverse in their specific explanations, agree that elites across the colonies were driven by their own personal and local interests to expand those sectors of commerce and economic development in which they were most directly involved. Once the British began seeking greater economic and political control over these sectors, they put aside their differences and their worries about emboldening the lower classes to unite in opposition to the British challenge.[3]

The second main camp emphasizes the role of ideology and shared values. The seminal work of Bernard Bailyn and Gordon Wood in the 1960s led many scholars to argue that the internalized ideas and ideals of liberty and freedom were indeed primary forces uniting the colonists to fight. The issue of taxation without consent was only one part of a much larger American concern for the colonists' sense of their long-term way of life.[4] Increasing British efforts from 1761 to 1775 to arrest Americans and seize their goods without specific warrants, to limit the ability of colonial governments to issue paper money, to control the payment of governors and judges from London, to place British standing armies in their cities and not just on the frontier, and to quarter those troops at colonial expense were affronts to American conceptions of their traditional liberties, protected, as they had presumed, by British law and norms. For this latter perspective, the war was not a conflict driven by the material interests of rising elites seeking more wealth and power at home. Rather, it was driven by the ideological values that a broad swath of Americans across different classes had internalized and saw as threatened by British behavior.[5]

The purpose of this chapter is not to show that these two perspectives are wrong, but rather to supplement such domestic-level views with an argument

couched more at the systemic level of power politics and the commercial development of nations. The two established approaches do a good job identifying the factors that helped the organizers of rebel camp create a cohesive and
unified front against the British government, both during the 1774–75 negotiations to avert an all-out war and during the fighting of the war itself from 1775
to 1783. There is little question that, once the war had begun, many of those
that fought on the "Patriot" side believed or at least hoped that a victory over
the British would lead to personal and family gains in both position and
wealth. And most Patriots certainly came to internalize the idea that their
cause was morally and ideologically justified, and indeed that it might spread
republican and liberal values across the world.

The problem with the two dominant approaches, however, lies less with
their arguments and evidence and more with their completeness. The first
approach focuses on the decision-making of the British North American elite.
Yet it cannot answer a key question: Why would members of this elite risk not
just their fortunes, but also their lives and sacred honor—the famous triad
from the final line of the Declaration of Independence—for the chance to
improve their material positions within their societies? Most were already
doing well within the British empire and would likely have continued to do so
even with the additional headaches caused by British policies. The costs and
risks of all-out war with the most powerful nation on earth seemed much
greater than expected benefits, and indeed after British compromises in 1766
and especially in 1770, almost every major figure in American politics (except-
ing perhaps Sam Adams) believed that their colonies would and should remain
a part of the British empire system. So why risk it all in 1774–76 over the *continuation* of a seemingly minor tax on tea imposed in 1767 and accepted largely
without complaint during the period of détente from 1770 to 1772? What was
it about Parliament's Tea Act of May 1773 and its reaction to the dumping of
tea into Boston Harbor in December that confirmed to these elites that Sam
Adams and the Sons of Liberty had been right all along, that Britain did indeed
represent a long-term existential threat to their colonies?

The second explanation, as intuitively powerful as it is, suffers from one
main limitation. If the colonists were driven by internalized ideologies, why
did the crisis with Britain go on for more than a decade without the elites
choosing war to achieve their ideological ends? Why, even after the first Continental Congress in the fall of 1774, did almost every political and economic
elite in British North America (BNA) hope that the British would once again
compromise, allowing the colonies to exist within an empire that for them had
represented progress and liberty, especially compared to those living within
the French realm? Sam Adams was certainly one individual who saw war as an
inevitable necessity from 1770 on. But few others did. What was the causal

reasoning that allowed Sam Adams and a few others to convince the political elites of BNA to start a war they all knew would be very costly and risky? Ideological reasons for fighting were particularly powerful once the war got going—to mobilize the lower classes to fight and perhaps die in the war, and to help rationalize the elites' often brutal policies. But they did not push the elites into the war itself.

Notably, even the doyen of the ideological view, Gordon Wood, freely acknowledges that most American elites were "conservative" in that prior to the war they sought a *return* to the pre-1763 British-led order, not a new order. They saw themselves as "English gentlemen" who were both loyal to the king and great admirers of the hierarchical structure of British society that protected both their privileges and liberties. In Wood's account, the "radicalism" of the American "revolution" only became truly internalized and entrenched *after* the war got under way.[6] In short, even for Wood, radical republican ideology operated as more of a facilitating factor than as a factor that propelled the dominant political class into war. We are thus back to the puzzle of why BNA elites that had been enjoying a relative return to normalcy from 1770 and 1772 would suddenly confront King and Parliament in 1774–75 at the risk of total war. Emotions were certainly high when the British blockaded Boston and imposed martial law in June 1774. But to explain why the elites across BNA would support Massachusetts at great risk to their own colonies, we need to go beyond mere self-interest and ideological fervor.

There is a third perspective in the literature that points us in a different direction—namely, toward a more geopolitical take on both British and American actions from 1761 to 1776. Domestic politics and ideological explanations are ultimately rooted in what goes on within a polity (the "internalist" approach of chapter 1). They assume that the motives driving the key players are their desires for improved material or political position within their polities or their senses of identity and purpose. The geopolitical account of the War for Colonial Independence sees political elites on both sides looking out for what is good for their "countries" over the long term ("country" being the popular expression at the time to denote one's colony). Most importantly, they were seeking to expand their economic and political power spheres without causing spirals of mistrust that would lead to undesired wars, either with Britain or with neighboring colonies. And while these elites certainly had concerns for how peace or war would affect them and their families personally, in this account they are assumed to be more worried about their colonies as a whole and with preserving their cherished ways of life into the future. These elites thus looked to the economic and political position of their polities, and to what extent their countries were losing or gaining in economic and military-political power relative to their main internal and external threats.[7]

As I will show, elites in London were fundamentally concerned by the 1750s and 1760s with Britain's position in the global system vis-à-vis France and saw the growth of BNA through that lens. In particular, they worried that a rising BNA would be less inclined to support the British mercantile system and would in the process help France and other powers grow economically at Britain's expense. The American elites were concerned that British economic and political policies after 1761 would increasingly constrain BNA's ability to grow into its potential. The war that began in 1775 was thus fundamentally about a "struggle for power" between the two sides.[8]

In this chapter, I will seek to build on the third perspective, to show how the geopolitical explanation can supplement the first two sets of arguments by accounting for many of the anomalies that they leave unexplained. At the core of the geopolitical argument that I develop is the notion that political elites in Britain were divided by the 1760s into two very different views of how the British mercantile system should work. On one side were those that supported an emphasis on *the production of staples* from the colonies in America or on the import and reexport of Indian- and Chinese-produced goods from the Far East. Such a focus, they believed, would minimize costs by reducing the expanse of the empire while maximizing the state's income through duties on the imports of these staple goods. The other side stressed the importance of imperial expansion, both in territory and increasing population, in order to *maximize the size of markets* for British manufacturers. As we will see, this divide played a critical role in determining how the elites of Britain viewed the rise of BNA and whether this rise likely meant that BNA would break away from the British Isles once it reached a certain size. Markets-based mercantilists were less worried by BNA's growth but, unfortunately, they rarely held positions of power from 1762 on. The staples-based mercantilist elites were fundamentally worried that BNA's rise would mean it would break from the empire and offer the world a competing economic power that would destroy Britain's post-1763 commanding position in the world economy.[9]

In what follows, I will not spend much time discussing the way British North Americans understood their fundamental "liberties" as British subjects since I take their desire to preserve these liberties in the face of London's efforts to restrict them for granted. I will also not go through the details of the twelve-year crisis from 1763 to 1775 since they are so well known. Instead, I will provide an inside picture of how the British viewed the rise of BNA and the threat it posed to the long-term cohesiveness of their realm. I will also examine in detail how key American elites such as Benjamin Franklin, Sam Adams, John Adams, and others interpreted the shifts in British foreign policy after 1750 and especially after the victories over the French in 1759–60. Part of my goal here is to show that the American elites, even the most radical ones such as Sam Adams, genuinely hoped that the British would let up on their commercial and political restrictions and stop worrying about BNA's growth. Yet British policy makers were unable to do this, given their own economic concerns and their inability to trust American intentions down the road. In short, *the British felt they had to preserve control over their commercial power sphere* while the Americans understood *that this control would mean the gradual loss of their wealth and power*, thus calling into question their colonies' abilities to protect their social orders and their frontiers.[10] For the Americans, using the language of chapters 1 and 2, the economic and political life of realm one, their core power sphere, was under direct threat. The British policies were causing the rising British North Americans to start to believe that without war, their colonies would start to peak in relative power and be left in an inferior and vulnerable position to administrators in London. Since they knew war would be both risky and costly, they hoped Britain would return to a semblance of the pre-1763 arrangement that fostered BNA growth. Until the last moment, American leaders held out hope that London would offer concessions, as it had in 1766 and 1770. The unwillingness of British officials to make concessions itself proved that British intentions were malign, reinforcing the trade-security spiral that was becoming increasingly entrenched. By April 1776, war had become inevitable.

## American Concerns with British Policy Prior to the 1760s

The literature on the War for Colonial Independence tends to focus on the actions Britain took after the end of the French and Indian War (concurrent with the Seven Years' War in Europe). The common assumption is that the Americans were largely content with the pre-1763 commercial system, and it was only the increasing restrictions imposed by London after 1763 that led to resentment and protest.[11] In terms of sustained protest, it is true that the Americans did not take to the streets or begin to impose nonimportation schemes until the 1760s. But their resentment of British mercantile policies has deep roots going back a century before that. In 1651 Oliver Cromwell initiated a series of "Navigation Acts" by pushing through legislation that required all goods into and out of England be shipped on English ships. This move initially helped subjects in England's North American empire since ships made and owned by Americans were considered "English." A decade later, however, starting in the early 1660s, King Charles II began to "enumerate" certain staple products coming from BNA—in particular tobacco from Virginia and Maryland. This enumeration imposed two restrictions: enumerated goods now had to be shipped only to England, meaning the loss of key foreign markets in Europe; and the Americans had to pay an import duty on the goods sent to England. A few years later this duty had to be paid even when enumerated goods were shipped between colonies.[12]

This system of enumeration by the middle of the eighteenth century was raising a few hundred thousand pounds sterling a year for the crown, a significant sum that underwrote British imperial power. And it was seen by American elites for what it was: a form of taxation that both increased American costs and reduced their sales. Adding insult to injury, because enumerated goods had to be offloaded in England, it was *English* merchants that were in charge of reexporting the goods to continental Europe. The profits to be gained from the European market thus went to British shippers, not American. These were not insignificant losses for the BNA colonies, especially for Virginia and Maryland farmers and plantation owners perpetually in debt to British merchants. More than ninety percent of the tobacco brought from BNA, for example, was reshipped from Britain to the continent.[13]

The colonists also resented the fact that they were required to buy British manufactured goods and could not purchase often cheaper French and Dutch products. This was another indirect form of taxation on the BNA colonists, since it meant greater costs and the potential for monopoly pricing by British agents. Colonists were also forced to buy products such as tea and textiles brought from India and China by British shippers, who would have to land them in Britain first and pay import duties. Even when the shippers received most of the duties back as an incentive to reexport to America ("drawbacks"), this system raised prices by increasing transport costs and lowering competition.

Three other restrictions raised the resentment of the colonists through the eighteenth century: the laws against manufacturing in BNA; restrictions on colonial banks and the issuance of paper money; and the high duties paid on the importation of molasses. In 1699, the Woolen Act made it illegal for Americans to manufacture woolen products for export, even to a neighboring colony. The 1732 Hat Act outlawed the manufacture of beaver felt hats, meaning that in theory all beaver pelts had to be shipped to Britain before they could be turned into hats for the American market. The 1750 Iron Act was designed to stop the production of manufactured goods made of iron. The Americans were allowed to produce the basic pig and bar iron that could be later refined into specific iron products such as nails, tongs, and steel. And they were certainly encouraged to export bar and pig iron to Britain. But the Iron Act meant not only higher prices on key manufactured goods (even horseshoes in theory had to be made in Britain!) but that American technological development would be hampered by disincentives to invest in manufacturing.

Restrictions on banks and paper money hit New England particularly hard. In the 1730s, Samuel Adams's father sought with a number of other investors to open a "land bank" that would offer loans to farmers using their land as collateral. The bank was scotched by London for fear that bank notes would become a form of currency, creating inflation and undermining the ability of British merchants to acquire hard currency in their trade. New England colonial governments, particularly Massachusetts, were also prone to issuing paper money when expenses exceeded local tax revenues, such as during wartime. The Privy Council and Board of Trade allowed some issuance of paper money during wartime. After a war had ended, however, London would press the governments to withdraw the paper from circulation using new taxes. New England colonies, being on the border with New France, generally had much higher war debts and thus were more inclined to keep issuing paper after the wars were over. In 1751, Parliament passed the Currency Act, which targeted New England and made it illegal to issue new paper money and not call in old money that was in circulation. For crown colonies such as Massachusetts, this act, combined with the absence of a land bank, meant that hard currency or specie would continue to flow out, reducing the money supply and constraining commercial growth.[14]

The Molasses Act of 1733 was probably the most irritating and controversial of all the pre-1763 British commercial restrictions. It put a six pence per gallon duty on molasses imported from the French and Spanish West Indies. Molasses was the vital ingredient in the production of rum, one of the key products of New England. Rum in turn was critical to overall commerce not only within BNA, but for the triangular trade within the Atlantic system. Colonies such as Massachusetts and Rhode Island, having few staples and reliant on shipping for their income, needed rum to purchase slaves in Africa and bring them to the West Indies and the southern colonies. Yet as commerce grew in the 1700s, the British West Indies could only supply about one-fifth of the molasses needed for New England rum production. The duty on French and Spanish molasses raised the cost of molasses by somewhere between sixty and ninety percent, greatly cutting into merchant profits while hurting their relative competitiveness.[15]

Prior to the 1760s, these economic restrictions were resented but accepted, for one main reason: aside from the duties on enumerated products shipped to Britain (mainly tobacco), the restrictions were not well enforced by British authorities. Colonial agents in charge of collecting import duties in BNA could usually be bought off, while the smuggling of goods such as molasses would do the job when agents proved less corruptible. Moreover, there simply weren't enough British ships patrolling the coastal waters of BNA to monitor the inflow of goods. Beginning in 1764 with the Revenue Act, however, British officials set out to enforce the new act and previous acts in a way that took BNA by surprise. Colonial agents would now be punished severely should they not enforce the commercial acts on the books. British naval ships were brought in to assist in the identification and prosecution of smugglers (receiving a cut of the loot collected). And new admiralty courts were established away from the main cities of Boston, New York, and Newport to ensure that violators could indeed be fined and jailed for violations of the laws. These new measures not only significantly reduced short-term profits, but threatened the overall viability of BNA's involvement in the Atlantic trade—a problem that hit commercial towns such as Boston, New York, Philadelphia, and Newport, Rhode Island, particularly hard. As we will see later, American elites quickly understood that the new British policies of 1764–65, if allowed to stand, would restrict the long-term ability of BNA to continue to grow economically. Should its rapid growth come to an end, their ways of life at home would be threatened.

## British Concerns with BNA's Rise and the American Response

When the English authorized the settlement of colonies in North America, beginning with Virginia and Massachusetts, they had no idea that the colonies would become the main lever for commercial growth of what would emerge after 1707 as the British empire, centered on BNA, the Caribbean possessions, and the trade with India and China. While there had been some concern as far back as the 1680s that colonies such as Massachusetts and Virginia were growing too rapidly in population, it was really British North American growth in the eighteenth century that took everyone by surprise. Through immigration and a tradition of large families, its population grew fivefold from 1700 to 1750, and then doubled again by 1775 to approximately 2.5 million people (including 400,000 slaves across all colonies, including 5,000 in New England). Its wealth per capita by the 1760s was larger than Britain's, leading to a vast increase in demand for British manufactured goods and products shipped by English and Scottish merchants from the Far East.[16] This rapid growth in population and wealth made BNA simultaneously more of an asset within the larger British empire and also more of a long-term threat to it. In 1732, an official in London worried that with BNA manufacturing of hats now booming and New England ships now handling one-third of the trade across the Atlantic, future "independency" was "highly probable" and would have "a fatal consequence to this kingdom." In 1741, a British officer mused that it might be good to transfer colonists in BNA to Cuba so they would not be able to set up more manufacturing sites "to the prejudice of the Mother Country." Governor Shirley, the crown's appointment in Massachusetts, wrote home in 1745 that due to the surprising growth of the number of BNA inhabitants within the last century, in one or two more centuries BNA would have more people than France, a state that already had twice Britain's population.[17]

Shirley saw this as a good thing relative to the ongoing struggle with France, since it would "lay a foundation for a superiority of British power" in Europe. Others back in Britain were not so sure. In 1748, Londoner Otis Little published a pamphlet that noted the suspicion "frequently exhibited in England at the growth of the North American colonies." Some elites were insinuating that "great care ought to be taken, lest those colonies grow too powerful, and set up a government of their own." Little himself felt that this fear was probably overblown, given BNA's dependence on English manufactures. But his analysis reveals the extent to which concern was already growing about the continued advance of BNA and the possibility that once it had grown sufficiently it would break away from the mother country. Benjamin Franklin, working on his scientific pursuits in Philadelphia, was concerned enough by such talk by the early 1750s to pen a response entitled "Observations Concerning the Increase of Mankind" (written 1751, but not published until 1754). He reiterated that BNA's population was indeed doubling every two decades and that within a century its population would be bigger than Britain's. But like Shirley, he sought to show that this was generally a good thing for the empire. Because North America had abundant land, the vast majority of Americans would remain farmers who would require the products produced by Britain. And despite fears that BNA would turn to mass manufacturing to supply their needs, the low population density in cities meant wages would stay too high to make BNA manufactured goods competitive with British.[18] Franklin's analysis seems to have had an impact on a young John Adams. The twenty-year old Adams wrote in 1755 that if France could be removed from the continent,

> our people according to the exactest [sic] computations will in another century become more numerous than England itself. Should this be the case, since we have . . . all the naval stores of the nation in our hands, it will be easy to obtain the master of the seas, and then the united force of Europe will not be able to subdue us.[19]

Adams, like Franklin, was still thinking in terms of strengthening the British empire against France and continental European threats. But from the British perspective, it did not take a genius to realize that the Americans might decide to leave the empire altogether once they had achieved enough strength to do so. Such fears in London had to be downplayed in the 1740s and 1750s because of the looming possibility that France would indeed defeat Britain in the struggle for global commercial dominance. France had done well near the end of the 1740–48 war, forcing the British to hand back the valuable fortress of Louisburg on Cape Breton Island in return for the French relinquishing Madras in India. From 1749 to 1753, the French had initiated a concerted campaign of their own to contain the growth of BNA, a campaign that, if successful, would have shifted the balance of commercial and territorial power on the continent. They began the construction of a series of forts in the contested Ohio Valley country, most notably Fort Duquesne (the future Fort Pitt/Pittsburgh). French strategy was guided by the thinking of Count de Maurepas, the secretary of state for naval affairs in the 1740s, and by Marquis de la Galissoniere, a former naval officer and the governor of Canada after 1748. For Maurepas, "commerce creates riches" and consequently national power, and maritime states that control the seas and colonies dominated those commercial benefits. He hoped to "break the yoke" of Britain on trade with North America and perhaps even align the British colonies with France. Galissoniere was one of the first to convince Paris that without a series of forts joining Quebec with the Louisiana territory, the ever-growing British Americans would overwhelm the no-man's-land between the two and split France's empire in half.[20]

In the face of these French moves and the impending war for empire these moves implied, London could not undertake a major campaign to constrain BNA growth. Parliament did pass the Iron Act in 1750 to prevent the Americans from transitioning from low-level iron production (pig and bar iron) to higher-tech iron and steel manufacturing.[21] But the global war that began in 1754 in North America and then became the Seven Years' War in Europe by 1756 meant that London again had to put any strategic reforms in North America on hold until after the stunning victories over France in 1759–60.

The capture of Quebec City and then Montreal in 1759–60 changed the fundamental balance of power in Britain's favor. The main question was no longer whether Britain would win the war, but only how complete a victory it would be. While William Pitt continued to argue from 1760 until the end of the war in 1763 that Britain had to use this opportunity for destroying France's colonial empire once and for all, the huge costs of the war had made it clear by 1760 that London could not hold onto all of its acquisitions if it wanted Paris to agree to peace. The core debate was whether to retain Quebec or the French sugar island of Guadeloupe in the Caribbean. The pamphlet war that transpired from 1760 into 1761 revealed the divide between two conceptions of commercial strategy within the British political elite: namely, staples-based versus markets-based mercantilism. Those in favor of keeping Guadeloupe argued for the immediate increase in income derived from placing the island on the enumeration list and from the ability to reduce the French share of the European and North American sugar markets, a share which had been growing since Haiti's development in the 1730s. Those arguing for the retention of Quebec contended that by eliminating the French presence, Britain would enable western expansion into the Ohio Valley and the Great Lakes region. Over the long term, this would increase the population of BNA still further, building future markets for British manufactured goods.

The staples-based mercantilists, who later came to dominate British policy during the critical years of 1763 to 1776, feared that as BNA grew, Americans would be much keener on breaking away from Britain. By giving Quebec back to France, these restless Americans would feel the need for British military protection and thus be deterred from seeking independence. As a pamphlet from 1761 put it, the BNA colonies "increase daily in people and industry" and over time will seek to rely on their own labor, and "care little about the Mother Country." If, therefore, they find "no check from Canada, they will extend themselves, almost without bounds into the inland parts," allowing them to "increase infinitely." Hence by grasping at extensive territory, "we may run the risk [perhaps in the not so distant future] of losing what we now possess." Having the French control Canada would keep the Americans in "awe" and effect a useful "balance of power" check on their aspirations.[22]

A series of counters to this line of argument was spearheaded by none other than Benjamin Franklin, now in London as colonial agent for Pennsylvania. Franklin knew that he had to not only convince British elites that the Americans had no interest in independence, even over the long term, but that retaining Canada would greatly increase the markets available for British manufactured goods. Franklin wrote to statesman and philosopher Lord Kames in early January 1760 that "the foundations of the future grandeur and stability of the British empire lie [in] America." If Canada was kept, "all the country from the St. Lawrence to the Mississippi [would] in another century be filled with British people." This would lead to an "immense increase in [Britain's] commerce." Later that year he published a pamphlet making similar points and reassuring the British that the BNA colonies were too divided to ever unite against Britain.[23]

In the end, the strategic arguments for preventing future war in North America and for building long-term markets by retaining Quebec prevailed over the lure of immediate gains from Guadeloupe's profits and duties.[24] Yet those on the losing end of this debate set down the logic that would dominate the thinking of staples-based mercantilists during the postwar period and would spark the spiral of mistrust that would lead to war in 1775. One influential pamphlet by an unnamed member of Parliament argued in great detail that given the size of the North American land mass, its natural resources, and BNA's increasing population, as well as its distance from the British home islands, such an area "could never remain long subject to Britain." Without the French in Canada as a check, "we should soon find North America itself too powerful and too populous to be long governed by us at this distance." After all, as BNA increased in population so must it increase in manufactures and trade and the "less [it would] want from Britain." The sugar islands, given their political economy, would remain dependent on Britain, "but America as she rises to maturity, may endanger our trade and liberty both." He rejected as absurd Franklin's argument that even when America had a larger population than Britain, it would continue to be dependent on Britain for manufactured goods. As the American "child" reached maturity and began to develop its scientific knowledge and industry, it was simply natural that it would want independence from its "fond parents."[25]

The victory of Pitt's pro-markets faction was short-lived.[26] Pitt and his allies such as Lord Newcastle were out by 1762, and individuals such as Lords Bute and Grenville came to power. Their approach of pushing British North Americans to focus on the Atlantic trade over inland expansion would dominate British policy-making for the next four years. In the next section, I will detail how the staples-based mercantilist elites from 1763 to 1775 used restrictive policies to contain BNA economic growth and ensure the colonies' political and economic subordination within the empire.

## British Drives to Maintain Hold on BNA and Its Commerce

The British were well aware by the early 1760s that BNA had become the linchpin of the British commercial system and Britain's ability to overawe its main rival, France. BNA now consumed close to half of British exported manufactured goods, and it supplied the naval stores and masts that ensured the maintenance of its naval superiority at a relatively low cost. Once the British had eliminated the French threat in North America and expanded their control up to the Mississippi River and into Canada, they had to return to the dilemma left unresolved before 1754—how to keep a rising BNA in the empire and economically loyal to Britain. The war between 1754 and 1763 had itself reinforced the importance of preventing the Americans from violating British mercantile rules. The Americans, even as they fought French armies on land, had been increasing their illegal trade with the French West Indies. The French were having trouble supplying the islands and transporting its sugar due to the British naval blockade, and American shippers had jumped in to fill the void. When Britain was on the ropes during the terrible years from 1755 to 1758, London had allowed this trade to go unpunished. But after the capture of Quebec and Montreal, policy changed. Pitt himself was outraged by American trade with the French, blaming it for extending the war, reducing British manufacturing exports, and depriving the British treasury of additional dollars in potential duties during a very costly war. In late 1760 he imposed new tougher regulations on customs collections in North America, leading to James Otis's famous legal argument in defense of Boston merchants in February 1761 that British subjects were protected from arbitrary search and seizures of their property.[27]

In retrospect, Pitt's new policy and the Boston trial would mark the beginning of a crisis period in British-American relations that would eventually lead to war in 1775. Yet the irony here is that William Pitt was one of BNA's greatest supporters through the crisis to come. From 1764 until his death in 1777, he would viciously critique any British leader or official seeking to impose taxes and economic and political restrictions on the Americans without their consent. Indeed, he was instrumental in getting the Stamp Act repealed in 1766, which resolved the first cross-colonial organized revolt of BNA subjects in the history of the British Atlantic system. In 1774 and into early 1775, now acting as Lord Chatham, Pitt sought to get the Tea Act repealed and to have Parliament pull back from the Coercive Acts that had so outraged the Americans. In the end, of course, he could not prevent the war that began in April 1775. This leads to the obvious question: What explains the inability of such a respected statesman and his compatriots, including Lord Shelburne and Edmund Burke, to prevent a major shift of British policy that would lead to a disastrous war with the American colonists?

The usual answer given by most historians is that British policy was hijacked by political elites who either did not understand how the Americans would react to the new policies or were too concerned with their own wealth and positions to worry about the larger imperial picture. In essence, the leaders that led Britain into war were either irrational or corrupt.[28] The problem with this perspective is that it ignores the larger strategic perspective pushed by those advocating the need for change in colonial policy. Political elites favoring a staples-based mercantilism were only too happy to be back in power in 1762, since they felt that the debt that Pitt's faction had built up in pursuit of market expansion had left Britain weak financially and vulnerable to political changes in BNA. For them, an increased staples trade would bring the kind of short-term duties that were critical to paying off the war debt.[29] It also would help allow Britain to control the new territories that had more than doubled British North America's size. For Bute and Grenville, peace itself was going to be very expensive, precisely *because of* Pitt's successful expansionist policy in pursuit of future markets. It seemed reasonable to them, given that the British army in North America would have to be increased from 5,000 to 10,000, for the Americans to foot some of the bill. The two acts that so upset the Americans in 1764–65—the Revenue (or "Sugar") Act of 1764 and the Stamp Act of 1765—directly reflected the need to pay for the patrolling of the larger empire at a period when Britain's national debt, due to the war, had risen from £80,000,000 to £133,000,000. While London retreated from the Stamp Act in 1766 given pressure from the Americans and British merchants, imperial expenses on the frontier were still draining the British treasury. The result was renewed efforts to increase the revenue flowing from America, leading to the

Townshend duties of 1767 and the Tea Act of 1773. To some degree, therefore, the standard historical view for why taxes were imposed on America after 1763 is correct.

Yet what is missing from this story is the larger geostrategic logic that drove a whole slew of new policies beginning in 1763 and continuing until 1775. Most of these policies had little to do with revenue generation ("taxation without representation") per se. Rather, they were primarily designed to keep BNA from growing too fast, both in terms of the settling of the new western lands and in manufacturing. Specifically, it was seen as critical to the long-term strength of the empire that British North American colonies orient their commercial behaviors toward the British Isles and not toward themselves and the west. Most importantly, the Americans should remain, as the phrase went, largely "hewers of wood and drawers of water," selling to the home islands key raw materials and food stuffs and purchasing in return products from the Far East and British-produced goods, particularly woolen textiles and high-end household products.

The key to this strategy was to keep a ceiling on BNA growth, both in territorial size and industrial development, and to constrain the Americans' ability to organize their own imperial realm. These goals led to four interlocking policies. First, those in BNA who had a desire to cross the Appalachians had to be dissuaded from doing so. Keeping the population on or near the coast would not only ensure their trade goods, especially staples such as tobacco, rice, timber, and naval stores, would go east, but it would also reduce the incentive for the lower classes in Britain to emigrate to America in the hope of cheap land and a fresh start. Second, by increasing *enforcement* of the duties already on the books or specified in the new acts, as well as by ensuring that enumerated products were indeed sold only to Britain, London could make sure that the Americans did not help archrival France rebuild its power. The Americans had been trading illegally with France and other powers for decades—including, most distressingly for the British, during wartime. But with the French modernizing their economy and increasing their demands for staples—in France and in the Caribbean—it was even more important now to end the American trade with the French West Indies and continental Europe, or at least control it better and pocket the duties from this control.

Third, London was keen to increase the dominance of British merchants and financiers in the Atlantic trade, and thus to ensure that the Americans selling their products relied on English and Scottish shipping and loans rather than setting up their own arrangements. Thus in 1764, Parliament passed the Currency Act that extended existing restrictions on colonies issuing paper currency from New England (from the 1751 Currency Act) to all the core colonies in America.

Fourth, given that France was no longer an immediate threat that would keep the Americans "in awe" and not thinking about independence, British leaders saw the importance of more direct control of the political systems already established in the colonies. This meant most obviously a beefed-up presence of British troops in New York, the center of British command, for quick deployment to areas showing signs of rebellion, especially New England. And for crown colonies such as Massachusetts, London would seek to use revenues raised by new taxes and better enforcement to pay the salaries of the governors and judges that were appointed by the crown. Such individuals had been traditionally paid by local legislatures, which gave these legislatures, and by extension the voting public, a major stick to keep them in line.

The first move to show that British leaders had a new plan for BNA's future was the Proclamation of 1763. This was the announcement in October 1763 that Americans would not be allowed to cross a newly established line that went down the middle of the Allegheny Mountains unless they had permission from the crown. The land on the western side of the mountains now was reserved for Indian nations and for fur traders that possessed the proper licenses.[30] On the surface, this announcement simply reflected the fact that Pontiac's War, a coordinated Indian revolt that had begun in June, was not yet resolved, and that for the sake of avoiding future conflicts, Americans should stay out of the western region. Yet the logic behind the proclamation had already been set down in a report of May of that year—before Pontiac's surprise attacks—by Maurice Morgann, secretary to the young Lord Shelburne when he was president of the Board of Trade. Morgann was responding to inquiries as to the kind of military establishment needed for the new western territory. Morgann argued in his first report to Shelburne that it would be wise to copy the former French strategy and use the army to "awe the British colonies." In a second report, entitled "Plan for Securing the Future Dependence of the [BNA] Provinces," Morgann noted that by positioning troops in East Florida and Nova Scotia and by placing the British navy offshore, "the whole of the [American] provinces shall be surrounded." Under the pretense of regulating the Indian trade, Britain could encourage Indian nations to think of themselves as sovereign entities. This would mean that the BNA colonists would feel encircled by both the British and "hostile tribes," giving London the leverage formerly created by the French threat to "exact a due obedience to the just and equitable regulations of a British Parliament." As a side benefit, it would also encourage Americans seeking a better life to emigrate to unpopulated colonies of Nova Scotia and the new East Florida, which would reinforce a desired orientation to the Atlantic trade over inland trade.[31] Needless to say, the Americans quickly understood the Proclamation for what it really was: a clear effort to restrict their ability to develop the western lands that, since

Franklin's writings in the 1750s, had been seen as essential to the long-term growth of British North America.

The second new policy direction—the increased collection of revenue from the colonies—began with the 1764 Revenue Act and the 1765 Stamp Act. It is often supposed that the American revolts of 1765 were driven by what these acts represented—namely, that the British, for the first time, were moving from the simple regulation of the Atlantic commercial system to the direct raising of revenue to pay for costs incurred in BNA, thus breaking the tradition of allowing Americans to tax themselves for internal expenses. This interpretation is erroneous and was known to be so at the time. Legislative acts such as the Molasses Act of 1733 were explicitly designed to raise revenue from the importation of French West Indian sugar products, not to prevent their purchase or to stop Americans from supplying goods to the French Islands during peacetime. Moreover, in 1713 the British had set up a postal system within the colonies, using prepaid "stamps" to fund the service (Benjamin Franklin himself later being one of its postmaster generals). Most importantly, the British raised hundreds of thousands of pounds annually from the duties on the transport of enumerated staple goods from colonies such as Virginia and Maryland. There had been grumbling throughout the eighteenth century on all these items which, far from having a simple regulative effect, as would have been the case in a true customs union, were designed to raise revenue to pay for the empire.[32]

The real beef was not with legislation to raise revenue, but with *the new level of enforcement* of this legislation, which significantly raised the costs to the colonists of doing business. When Lord Grenville pushed for and secured three major acts from 1764 to 1765—the Revenue Act and the Currency Act in 1764 and the Stamp Act in 1765—he knew what he was doing. Without the French threat to keep the colonists in line, the British needed to fund a much bigger military presence in North America, both to keep the Americans down and to prevent them from starting wars with the Indians through illegal (according to the 1763 Proclamation) western expansion.

The Revenue Act was designed to do what its name implied, to *truly* raise revenue by focusing on the collection of mostly existing duties, especially on the highly lucrative molasses trade with the Caribbean. Ironically, given the protests that followed, British officials thought they could encourage the Americans to stop smuggling and actually pay the molasses duties by *reducing* the level of the duties set by the 1733 Molasses Act. That act had imposed a six pence per gallon duty on any foreign molasses imported into America, effectively doubling the cost of the product. The Revenue Act dropped this duty to three pence. So why were the Americans so outraged? The act and the discussions in Parliament made it clear that from now on these duties would indeed be collected come hell or high water. Combined with the duties on new products, the Americans could plainly see the intent of the new policy—to pay for the troops that would keep them in their place and to improve the prospects of competing English and Scottish merchants.

The most obvious impact of the new legislation was on the rum manufacturing and molasses trade centered in New England. Rum was the key product for the West Indian trade that kept the always struggling New England economies going. Rum was sold or traded to the West African leaders who supplied the slaves that were needed for the British, French, and Spanish West Indies plantations. The slaves, especially when sold to French West Indian islands, were a major source of specie (hard currency) for a cash-starved New England. New England perpetually imported more from Britain than it sold, since its only staples wanted in the British Isles were naval stores and timber. Without cheap molasses to make the rum needed for the slave trade, profits not only would fall dramatically but their rum would be less competitive on the African market relative to rum produced by English or French companies. The Americans had put up with the six pence duty on French molasses since 1733 for one simple reason: since it had not been enforced, and since customs officials could be bribed to look the other way, smuggled French molasses could do the job in greasing this triangular trade. This trade, as well as rum sales to the southern and mid-Atlantic colonies, had been booming since 1740, fueled by cheap sugar products from the highly efficient slave plantations of French islands such as Saint Domingue (Haiti). Indeed, British West Indian molasses's share of the BNA market had fallen to around twenty percent by 1760. But with the new rigorous enforcement of the 1764 act, everything would change. So even with duties being cut in half, if they were actually paid the base price of molasses would rise by half, destroying the foundation of the whole West Indies-Africa trade controlled by New England.[33]

Massachusetts and Rhode Island merchants were naturally the ones most upset by the new rules under the Revenue Act. But when the Stamp Act was announced in the spring of 1765, almost all the thirteen colonies began to protest. As noted, being forced to put stamps on items of daily commerce (such things as newspapers and legal documents) was not new, but only an extension of the half-century-old postal stamp program. So, the outrage over "internal taxation" had less to do with the tax itself (although its extent did seem egregious) but the fact that the Stamp Act, if put into effect, would mean an even greater outflow of hard coin at a time the Revenue Act was already restricting triangular trade and the new Currency Act outlawed the printing of colony-issued paper money.

Colonial leaders quickly understood the long-term impact of all three new measures in their combined effect. They thus mobilized public opinion in the most effective way possible, arguing that these measures were violations of traditional British liberties—most importantly, not to be taxed without consent. But behind this principled argument was the material impact of the new British measures on trade, and what those measures signaled about British strategic thinking. As the leader of the Stamp Act revolts in Massachusetts in 1765, Sam Adams, told the colony's agent in December that year, the people of the province believed that Parliament was seeking to "greatly obstruct" BNA trade and that unless a remedy could be found, they feared that they would soon be ruined. The Revenue Act (which he slyly labeled "the Sugar Act") would force American merchants to trade mainly with British West Indies islands, which were too small to supply molasses for the whole system. "To confine us then to those islands must diminish [our] trade" and this, Adams warned, would have deleterious downstream effects. New England fishermen who sell fish to the sugar plantations of the French and British West Indies would not be able to find alternative markets in Europe, since more than a third of this fish was fit only for slaves on sugar plantations. This would reduce the acquisitions of specie, reducing trade even further. Four months later, Adams explained to his colleagues what was really behind London's new behavior: the British feared the "rising greatness" and "growing strength" of Massachusetts and its sister colonies.[34]

The Americans' often violent behavior in 1765, combined with the nonimportation program established by the "Stamp Act Congress" of October, convinced Parliament to withdraw the Stamp Act in May 1766. It was William Pitt's arguments in Parliament, along with Ben Franklin's eloquent speech in February on the economic costs to both sides, that made the difference. Yet the staples-oriented elite had not caved in completely. Not only did the terms of the Revenue and Currency Acts remain on the books, but by the Declaratory Act of 1766, the British signaled that Parliament had ultimate control of the imperial economic system "in all cases whatsoever." The tone of the Declaratory Act made it clear to Sam Adams that the fight was not over. There were still those within the British government, he wrote in mid-1766, "who have to this day sought our ruin."[35] Adams's words seemed to be confirmed in the spring of 1767 when Parliament passed the notorious Townshend duties. These duties, pushed through by Chancellor of the Exchequer Charles Townshend over the objections of sickly Prime Minister William Pitt, imposed small export duties on goods shipped from England, including paints, glass, and most infamously, tea. As in 1764–65, London made it clear that these new taxes would be used to not only pay for the new larger standing army in BNA, but also for administrative expenses of British officials, even governors.

These taxes did signal that there was a strong faction in London that was determined to control BNA both politically and economically in order to prevent its rise. As Sam Adams wrote to Massachusetts' agent on behalf of its

House of Representatives in January 1768, the British had moved from a system that emphasized mutual benefits through trade and the advancing of imperial power through population growth to one where London was forcing
colonists to pay taxes on goods British producers and companies like the East
India Company controlled. The system was becoming what we would now call
a zero-sum game. In Adams's words, "the loss . . . to the colonists" from the
new policy "is equal to the gain which is made in Britain."

For Adams, this was adding insult to injury. American colonists were already
paying upwards of £400,000 in hard cash through duties on enumerated staples
such as tobacco. Now they were being asked to pay duties on British-shipped
goods such as tea that, in theory, they could not get elsewhere. This placed a
"great weight" on struggling colonies such as Massachusetts. The fact that these
taxes were used to pay for the administration of justice and civil government
only reinforced that Americans must fear that London intends "[to] introduce
an absolute government in America," perhaps on the Quebec model.[36]

Sam Adams's greatest fears seemed to be coming true in the latter half of
1768, when the British moved their army into the city of Boston to quell protests and to help the governor suppress molasses and tea smuggling. The leading men of the colony, including Adams, organized a second round of BNA-
wide nonimportation to get London to retract at least some of the new and
old duties. Adams used the opportunity to spread the argument that essentially all British mercantile restrictions—and not merely those after 1763—
were part of a larger effort to keep the Americans down politically and economically. In an editorial in the *Boston Gazette* in August 1768, he argued that
by seizing vessels of even the most respected of Boston merchants (specifically
John Hancock) and by threatening British subjects with military force, the
British were making them "the slaves . . . of arbitrary power." He referred to a
British writer's calculation that all these various forms of taxation, including
enumeration, constituted close to fifty percent of the value of the goods being
taxed, or about £2,000,000 a year, and he appealed to Shelburne's well-known
sympathies for freer markets to reduce this burden on the beleaguered Americans. In a follow-up *Gazette* article a year later, after it was clear that the power
of the Pitt and Shelburne faction had been gutted, Adams argued that the
"great men" now running Britain were not only not always wise, they were also
"not always good." Intoxicated by power and greed, they were undertaking
policies that would lead to the "ruin" of the empire.[37]

The years 1770 to 1772 were not terribly good ones for the radical cause.
London made important accommodations that undermined arguments that
the British were determined to restrict the Americans' ability to grow. By early
1770 Lord North was prime minister. He and his faction were followers of
staples mercantilists Lords Bedford and Grenville, but they smartly

understood that recent policies were damaging overall trade with the BNA colonies. To restore a sense of normalcy, they did away with all aspects of the hated Townshend duties—all, that is, except for the three-pence tax on tea.

The British retreat from most of the 1767 duties, along with a further reduction in the duty on French West Indian molasses, seemed to do the trick. From mid-1770 until early 1773, relations between BNA and Britain seemed to be back on track (a puzzle of course for domestic and ideological paradigms). The Americans ended their nonimportation of British manufactures, and the pent-up demand led to a boom in Atlantic trade. Even John Hancock, one of the supporters of the anti-British colonial movement in 1768–69, seemed assuaged. Rejecting Sam Adams's pleas, he was pleased to go back to a full-time focus on his import/export business, as were most other East Coast merchants after the lean years of 1768–69. John Adams, after successfully defending British soldiers charged in the Boston Massacre, decided he would give up politics altogether.

Within the American political elite, Sam Adams was left largely alone to keep the flames of resistance going and to remind New England and the wider reading public that the faction running Britain's government had not changed its spots, and that it still planned to keep BNA from rising in its own right. In a series of articles from 1770 to the end of 1772, issued under a series of pen names such as "Candidus" and "Vindex," Adams hammered home a single point: the British had a master plan, and were using the remaining taxes and restrictions to fund their campaign to control crown governors, judges, and officials across BNA. He also restarted a series of correspondences with both influential towns in Massachusetts and with sympathetic popular leaders across BNA. The theme was the existential threat posed by the British to the colonists' way of life. Personal security, personal liberties, and the rights of property were all threatened if the colonists did not fight back. The balanced "mixed" government of the kind the provinces had enjoyed would be replaced by executive-dominated colonies guided by London. Restrictions on BNA trade and iron manufacturing, tied to duties that made the Americans pay for their own repression, were critical elements of Britain's overall strategy to keep the colonies in their place.[38]

Adams's ongoing problem during these years is that London would not oblige him with ill-chosen policies that would support his claims. Britain's problems with Spain over the trade in South America and concerns about the loss of tax revenue due to a terrible famine in India had put BNA on the back burner, at least in the short term. Increased duty revenue resulting from renewed trade with BNA had also made the situation seem more acceptable from London's perspective.

All this came to an end in mid–1772/early 1773 when the Indian situation became critical. In 1766–67, a deal struck between the East Indian Company

(EIC) and the government promised the latter a £400,000 share of the company's revenue in return for naval protection against the continued threat to the Asia trade from French bases in Mauritius and Pondicherry. Yet the drought-induced famine in British-controlled India, greatly exacerbated by the high taxation imposed on Indian peasants by the British, made the EIC unable to pay its promised sum. Moreover, a financial crisis in Britain starting in 1772 had caused a contraction in overall demand, including for the goods from Asia imported by the EIC. As millions of pounds of tea had piled up in London warehouses, the company went even further into debt.

To be sure, this affected holders of EIC stock, including many of the government elite, giving them a personal incentive to act. But all top officials, as well as the king, recognized that if the EIC were to go under, the *geostrategic* effects on the empire would be catastrophic. Britain would have to retreat from its hard-earned position in northeast India, would have to forgo not just the promised stipend but the regular duties on imported Asian products (including tea and Indian textiles), and would probably have to cede the Asian trade to the French and Dutch. The existing American sugar and tea duties could not come close to making up this shortfall in government revenue.[39]

The result was the infamous Tea Act pushed through Parliament by Lord North's government in May 1773. By the act, the EIC was to be given a monopoly on the transport and sale of British-shipped tea to BNA. The three-pence duty on tea from the 1767 legislation would remain. Yet by allowing the EIC to ship tea to America without having to pay the twenty percent duty, the price of tea to American consumers would be *reduced* significantly. The main goal of the Tea Act was not to raise revenue from the Americans (although if EIC sales increased, as was anticipated, this would be the effect); rather, the core objective was simply to get the EIC through its crisis period and back on the road to profitability so that Britain could maintain its dominant position in India and the Asian trade.[40]

The story of what happened in North America is well known and can be related briefly. In the fall of 1773, Americans in the main merchant cities— Boston, Newport, New York, Philadelphia, and Charlestown—collectively resisted the importation of the EIC tea, blocking its unloading and thus the collection of duties. The ships were told to return to Britain with the tea in their holds. In all the cities except Boston, British merchants complied. In Boston, however, Governor Thomas Hutchinson, on point of principle, would not let three EIC ships leave the harbor unless the tea was unloaded and duties paid. In December, Sam Adams and his associates proceeded to dump the tea into the harbor, leading Parliament to pass the Coercive Acts in spring 1774 that shut down Boston Harbor and imposed military rule on the colony. Many moderates wanted to pay the EIC for the cost of the lost tea and end the crisis, but patriots in Boston resisted this solution. They gained support from the other colonies as the full extent of British military rule in Massachusetts became clear. In September–October of 1774, the colonists held the first Continental Congress, agreeing to an immediate nonimportation policy to be overseen by BNA-wide committees of enforcement. This was a replication of the moves taken in 1765 and 1768–69 to convince British merchants to pressure the government to change its policies. But given the severity of the crisis this time—in the previous crises, the British had never thought to end a colony's charter or impose military rule—the Congress also agreed to implement a *nonexportation regime* starting in September 1775 if London had not reversed its policy by that point. This double whammy on British commerce, as we shall see, would lead Britain to impose a blockade on American trade that led to the final decision to break from Britain for good.

How could a relatively minor legislative act in 1773—one that actually reduced the price of tea to American consumers—be the action that broke three years of détente and create a spiral of hostility that led to the Declaration of Independence, an act that no one could have anticipated in 1771–72? Part of the answer of course is wrapped up in the economic impact on individual American smugglers of Dutch tea as well as on shopkeepers of non-EIC tea who would find their offerings underpriced or made illegal. British North Americans were some of the biggest tea drinkers in the world, consuming around six million pounds of tea a year. Only 300,000 pounds of that amount came from the EIC company prior to 1773.[41] If an EIC monopoly was enforced and American consumers forced to switch to the now-cheaper EIC tea, there would clearly be an immediate impact on this sector of the North American economy. Yet this does not explain why the vast majority of Americans in 1773, at least along the East Coast, were so concerned about the Tea Act's implications for their way of life that they would physically block the implementation of the act and risk total war.

The key to explaining the above puzzle is the broader impact of this piece of British legislation on the Americans' long-term trade expectations. The act not only signaled once again that Parliament would impose acts affecting BNA commerce without the consent of those affected but even more importantly, it suggested that the British long-term plan was to take over the BNA economy and run it for Britain's ends, not for the ends of Americans. London's move seemed to confirm all of Sam Adams's warnings through the years of calm from 1770 to 1772—namely, that the elite controlling British foreign policy did indeed intend to keep the American colonies so weak and compliant that they would be unable to pose a long-term threat to British dominance.

For the Americans, the Tea Act was not seen simply as a way to prop up the East India Company during its time of crisis. It was seen as a foot-in-the-door strategy to get the EIC into the American economic system where, once entrenched, it would be able to spread its tentacles beyond tea to other sectors of the economy. The Americans, the most literate population in the world, were active followers of British political debates. They had seen, following the takeover of northeast India in 1763, a dramatic shift in British thinking about that area of the world. The 1766–67 deal to bring £400,000 of revenue into British coffers on the backs of Indian peasants and the subsequent famine and deaths of perhaps one million Indians from 1769 to 1771 was certainly distressing to supporters of Pittite imperialists such as Burke and Shelburne. It suggested a shift to a formal colonization strategy over the informal approach focused on trade up to that point. But saving this vicious imperialist company—the one that had launched wars against not only the French but against local Indian rulers—seemed to signal that the staples-driven mercantilists were now overwhelmingly dominant within the British political system. As Arthur Schlesinger summarizes in his exhaustive analysis of American pamphlets published in October and November 1773 (prior to the Boston Tea Party):

> The writers sought to show that the present project of the East India Company was the entering wedge for larger and more ambitious undertakings calculated to undermine the colonial mercantile world. Their opinion was based on the fact that, in addition to the article of tea, the East India Company imported into [Britain] vast quantities of silks, calicoes and other fabrics, spices, drugs and chinaware, all commodities of staple demand; and on their fear that the success of the present venture would result in an extension of the same principle to the sale of the other articles.

Schlesinger goes on to note that "perhaps no other argument had greater weight than this; nor, indeed, was such a development [given previous British moves] beyond the range of possibility."[42]

A short sampling of some of these pamphlets shows Schlesinger's point. A writer in Philadelphia opined in the *Philadelphia Gazette* on December 8, 1773, a week before the Tea Party, that if the EIC succeeded in their present experiment, "they will send their own factors and creatures to establish [EIC trading] houses among US, ship US all other East-India goods . . . and undersell our merchants till they monopolize the whole trade." A *New York Journal* article of October 28 stated that if the EIC tea was accepted, "you will in [the] future have an India warehouse here; and the trade of all commodities of [India] will be lost to [American] merchants and be carried on by [the EIC], which will be an immense loss to the colony." This was not just American paranoia. A British customs commissioner stationed in Boston wrote home to his government around this time that the Americans were rightly concerned that "once the East India Company has established warehouses for the sale of tea, all other articles commonly imported from the East Indies and saleable in America, will be sent there by the Company."

Another *New York Journal* article argued that this was not a question of taxation without consent. Even if the minor tea duty was taken off, the East India Company "scheme" was "too big with mischievous consequences and dangers to America." It may "introduce a monster," one "too powerful for us to control." It would "devour every branch of our commerce, drain us of all our property and substance, and wantonly leave us [as in India] to perish by the thousands." After all, the company had already showed its brutality and avarice in the late 1760s with its plan to reduce Indians to mere suppliers of staples and tax money, a plan that would strengthen Britain and the company alone.

Indeed, it was not farfetched to believe that the British might try to use the EIC's latest exploits as a model for a much larger plan of repression. As another New Yorker wrote to a friend in Philadelphia in early December 1773,

> would not the opening of an East India House in American encourage all the great companies in Great Britain to do the same? If so, have we a single chance of being anything but *hewers of wood and drawers of waters* to [the British]? The East Indians are a proof of this.[43]

The fear of the EIC, with the active support of the British government, repeating its "rapacious" strategy from India in North America was real. A writer in the *Pennsylvania Gazette* in early December 1773 wrote that once the company got a footing it would "leave no stone unturned to become your masters," the company being "well versed in tyranny, plunder, oppression and bloodshed." A town meeting in Connecticut in June 1774 went as far as to compare the company's "recent cruelties" in India and its overall "history of . . . rapine" to the "Spanish brutalities" when Cortez conquered Mexico.[44]

From Sam Adams's point of view, all of this was just another brick in the British effort to construct a ceiling to BNA's expansion. By its recent actions, Parliament had shown its deep fear of BNA's rise and had thereby killed any lingering confidence regarding its motivations and intentions. That did not mean he wanted war. He wrote a colleague in London on April 4, 1774 (before word of the Coercive Acts had reached Boston) to say that if the British would return to a policy of moderation and equity, he could certainly accept a permanent union with the mother country. But he was pessimistic. Since the British could see that providence was erecting "a mighty empire" in North America, one that was growing rich and powerful through emigration and trade as the British sank into obscurity, their policies were laying "a foundation of distrust, animosity, and hatred" that would be hard to reverse.[45]

When the elite of British North America met in Philadelphia in September–October 1774 for the first Continental Congress, not one of the participants, not even Sam Adams, wanted to break away from Britain and its empire. But they did want a major rehauling of the economic and political terms of that arrangement. Unlike in 1765 and 1768–69, the objective was not simply to end the most objectionable aspects of recent legislation (the Stamp Act and the Townshend Acts, respectively), but to force Parliament to rescind essentially all its legislation since 1762.

This included British moves such as the Quebec Act. This act of Parliament in June 1774, coming three months after the Coercive Acts, did not seem to involve commerce directly. But over the long term, from the American point of view, it was seen as part and parcel of the British plan to restrict the Americans' ability to build their economic power base. For one thing, it reorganized Quebec's government to give the hated French Canadians—a people that had spilled American blood for more than a century, often in alliance with Native American tribes—a share in provincial decision-making. Yet the Quebec Act also made sure that the province would have a governor appointed by London. Colonists in the American colonies saw this as yet another sign of the move away from representative government in North America.

Of greatest concern, however, was the unexpected provision to quadruple the size of Quebec itself and to extend Quebec's boundaries to include the area north of the Ohio River (present day Ohio, Indiana, Illinois, Michigan, and Wisconsin). This area was precisely the region that the Americans had fought and died for during the French and Indian War. Combined with the continued restrictions on settlement past the line of the 1768 Fort Stanwix treaty, the Americans saw this action as just one more effort to contain BNA's overall territorial and manufacturing growth and to keep its population producers of staple products for the Atlantic system. As Boston's shadow government noted in its Suffolk Resolves sent to the sitting Continental Congress in September 1774, the Quebec Act was "dangerous in an extreme degree" both to the Protestant religion and to the civil liberties of all Americans, and thus the people were obliged "to take all proper measures for our security."[46]

Documentary evidence shows that the Americans were right to be suspicious. The reorganization of Quebec's government had been in the works for some time. But the quadrupling of the province's size and the assigning of the territory north of the Ohio River to Quebec's political jurisdiction was inserted just before the bill on Quebec was presented to Parliament in 1774. During the debates on the bill in May, the new minister in charge of North America, Lord Dartmouth, wrote to the man he had replaced, Lord Hillsborough, to explain the rationale for this late addition. Extending French law to the Old Northwest, Dartmouth noted, would serve as a deterrent to settlement by the English-speaking colonists. When the bill came up before the House of Lords in mid-June, William Pitt warned that this legislation would be seen as a "cruel, oppressive, and odious measure" that would "finally lose the hearts of all his Majesty's American subjects." Lord Lyttelton responded that with the subjects of British America already resisting London, "he saw no reason why the loyal inhabitants of Canada should not cooperate with the rest of the Empire in subduing them and bring them to a right sense of their duty."[47]

To pressure the British into repealing the Tea Act, the Coercive Acts, and the Quebec Act, the colonial elites at the October 1774 Continental Congress agreed on a punishing commercial strategy. Imports of all British goods (except certain necessities) would be suspended immediately and backed by a continent-wide enforcement regime to expose and punish violators. As noted, the colonists also agreed that by September 1775, should their demands not have been met, the colonies would not *export* to the British Isles. This was a new and highly threatening gesture. The British not only relied on duties from the import of enumerated staples to help pay for the navy and empire, but without key naval stores such as white pines for masts and tar for the bottoms of ships, the United Kingdom's naval power would be significantly reduced over the long term as its ships deteriorated and were not repaired or replaced.

The British governing class, upon the news of the Congress's demands and the economic restrictions they had agreed upon, fell into an acrimonious debate over whether concessions should be extended to avoid a war. In February, the indomitable supporter of the Americans, William Pitt, put forward a compromise plan that would reduce some taxes and increase the Americans' political autonomy for promises of loyalty to the British empire. But his suggestions failed to gain support in either house of Parliament. With the new commercial threat of the united Congress as well as the training and arming of militias in Massachusetts, the majority of British elites felt they had to show resolve or lose the one thing that made BNA a useful addition to the empire: its compliance with the British mercantile system. From February to April 1775, the houses of Parliament debated and then passed new legislation that would extend the commercial blockade of Boston to all of New England. The goal was not only to demonstrate a willingness to play the economic coercion game and force the most rebellious areas to see the costs of their position, but to prevent New England from trading with France and other European powers.[48] Parliament also hoped that by not blockading trade with the mid-Atlantic and southern colonies in the short term, but by threatening to extend the embargo to all of BNA should the nonexport provision be implemented, the other colonies would be convinced to end their support for the Massachusetts rebels.

The clash of arms at Lexington and Concord on April 19, 1775 and the summer of conflict over the control of Boston did of course greatly reinforce the arguments of Massachusetts leaders such as Sam Adams and John Hancock that the British would stop at nothing to keep the colonists in their place. Yet even with the second Continental Congress's sending of George Washington to Boston in July 1775, the vast majority of colonial elites still held out hope for a diplomatic solution to the crisis. An Olive Branch petition was sent to King George in the early summer in the hope that the king would, as he had done in the past, override the corrupt and vicious men of Parliament and restore a peace both sides could live with. In October, the king publicly rejected the Olive Branch petition. But word was not received in BNA until early January, and many colonists were still under the impression that a deal could be struck to avoid a declaration of independence and war. To avoid the possibility of a last-minute agreement, Thomas Paine published the incendiary pamphlet *Common Sense* on January 14, 1776, arguing that the time for reconciliation had passed, and that a war was necessary even if the British offered concessions.

Paine's pamphlet was a phenomenal success, with one in five American white males possessing a copy by the spring of 1776, and most of the rest hearing of its contents through public readings of it in taverns and political meetings. But this did not mean independence was inevitable. By most estimates, only about four in ten American adult males wanted actual war in mid-1776; about two in ten strongly supported Britain (enough to fight as "Tories" during what would become the first American civil war) and the remaining number sat on the fence.[49] What finally pushed the Americans to a formal declaration of war were the British economic actions of February and March of 1776. The Americans had been suffering from shortages of all products, as well as of military supplies through the fall of 1775. But in late February 1776, word was received in the colonies that Parliament had enacted new legislation stating that after the first of March *all American vessels sailing in and out of American ports would be seized and confiscated*, and that after June 1st all foreign vessels trading with the Americans were also to be seized. In short, as Schlesinger summarizes, "the colonies were to be isolated from the world, save such districts that would make submission."[50]

Arguments that a declaration of independence and a final severing of all political and economic relations with Britain were needed in order to get European trade and financial assistance to sustain the BNA economy now came to the fore. The American colonies had to declare that they had truly rejected the British mercantile system and were now completely open to commerce with the rest of the world. Otherwise, the European powers would have no incentive to break the British blockade or to support the American military buildup and plans for overseas trade. Yet the Americans knew in early 1776 that to announce their break with Britain's economic system would bring down the full force of Britain upon them. As John Adams later stated in his autobiography: "This measure of opening the ports [to non-British vessels]" through a formal rejection of the last vestige of the British mercantile system "labored exceedingly [in the halls of Congress] because it was considered a bold step to independence." In those heated debates, Adams himself argued that it was nonetheless necessary to state formally that BNA was no longer a part of the British economic system. But those against him, understanding the risks, "had an art and influence as yet to evade, retard, and delay every motion that [Adams's faction] made."[51] Word of Britain's complete BNA-wide embargo, not just for American shipping but all foreign ships, changed this debate. By April–May, the majority was now in favor of formal independence.[52] From their perspective, the colonists had been given no choice. Without a declaration, they would economically decline into poverty and "slavery." But with a declaration, they stood a good chance of securing European commercial and financial backing for their stand against British oppression.

This of course does not mean that the ideology of liberty and the personal interests of key leaders did not help nudge them toward a final break with Britain, while facilitating the mobilization of individuals from across all classes and regions. But without the increasingly harsh commercial measures on both sides, and specifically London's drive for a complete blockade as of June 1776, majority support across all thirteen colonies would likely have been lacking. As it was, even in late June/early July 1776, states such as New York, South Carolina, and Delaware had strong factions opposed to full independence. The severity of the British trade measures and the clear signs that these measures would continue unless the Americans caved into British demands meant that the Americans were, by the late spring of 1776, left with only one remaining option: an all-out war organized by Congress and supported economically through trade with France and other European states.

## Conclusion

This chapter has suggested an alternative explanation for the War for Colonial Independence that reveals the true tragedy of the conflict. Had the British not been worried about the rise of British North America, and had they been able to trust assurances from individuals such as Ben Franklin that the Americans were loyal to Britain and would remain a part of the British empire even if their population, land mass, and economic wealth far outstripped that of the British Isles, then war would probably not have occurred.[53] To be sure, the crisis of the 1760s had clarified the ideological orientation of many Americans and reinforced their sense that political and economic liberties constituted core foundational values. But the vast majority of colonial elites, from

Massachusetts to Georgia, were strong royalists who until late 1775 had believed, or at least hoped, that the king would see the need to rein in his overly aggressive Parliament to avoid war. Parliament, apparently at the king's urging, had made a number of concessions in 1766 and 1770, and they hoped it would do so again.[54]

The ideology of liberty was certainly a necessary condition for what was to come. Without it, American elites would have had a very hard time mobilizing the people of such diverse colonies for a war with the world's most formidable imperial and naval power. But this was a war initiated to *defend* traditional liberties, and the writings that inspired the rebels were almost all written by English and Scottish Enlightenment thinkers or by individuals such as Montesquieu who admired the British system. Thomas Paine's more radical anti-monarchy tract *Common Sense* was a huge hit, but it was not published until January 1776, and with the goal of undermining any last-minute efforts to reach a peace deal that he knew the majority would accept.

It is thus hard to see ideological fervor as the main propelling force pushing colonial elites to accept the necessity of war. Rather, they felt pushed into a lesser-of-two-evils choice by the economic and political restrictions that the British government had embarked upon since the Tea Act and the subsequent Coercion Acts of 1773–74. Without British concessions, the incredible economic growth that the colonies had made since 1730—a growth driven by commerce with neighboring colonies (realm one) and with the European world (realms two and three)—would have been negated. The colonies' future power would likely hit a glass ceiling, meaning that colonial life would be increasingly dominated by decisions out of London. Given this untenable situation, American elites who had formerly been proud "Englishmen" bearing the standard of liberty had to act. But without the Tea Act and the spiral of trade restrictions and signals of resolve to back them up, the compromise peace of 1770–72 would almost certainly have continued into the future.

Overall, it was problems inherent in the rise and decline of states that led to this break between London and its American colonies. Some British politicians such as Pitt and Shelburne felt London should trust the Americans. But the majority were trapped by the age-old issues of whether rising states will be as nice later as they are now once they have more power, and whether the very fact of their rise will make them demand even more from the declining power even if they still want cooperation to continue. As I will discuss in chapter 10, these same problems are with us today when it comes to the relative rise of China and the concomitant decline of the United States in economic and commercial power. The American-British war of 1776 to 1783 was undesired by both sides. Both knew that the costs would be high, and that third parties might take advantage of any conflict to pick apart what remained of the belligerents after the war. Likewise, today leaders in Washington and Beijing have no desire for a major war of any kind, with or without nuclear weapons. Yet the anticipation of China's rise might lead both parties in Washington to push for a true "cold war" economic containment of China that would slow its growth substantially and sustain America's preponderant position in the system. Fortunately, as we will see, there are ways to reassure American and Chinese leaders today that were not viable two and a half centuries ago. A repeat of the past is not inevitable.

# 4

# The United States and the World, 1790–1848

THIS CHAPTER examines the commercial factors behind U.S. foreign policy between the late eighteenth century and the first half of the nineteenth century. The overall goal is to evaluate the extent to which these factors were critical to explaining the outbreak of crises and wars during this period in comparison to the many noncommercial factors that scholars of American foreign policy have identified. As with all the empirical chapters, my intent is not to prove other theories wrong, but to show that by neglecting the commercial security-based drivers of U.S. behavior, their historical accounts are incomplete or have only revealed the facilitating factors that allowed American leaders to act, leaving the true propelling reasons for their actions unexplored. The bulk of the chapter will center on the lead-ups to the two large-scale wars that the United States initiated and fought during this period: the War of 1812 and the Mexican-American War of 1846–48. The next chapter will consider U.S. foreign policy from 1850 to the end of the nineteenth century, with a focus on the origins of the Spanish-American War of 1898.

In unpacking the causal forces leading to these three important conflicts, I show that commercial forces not only played dominant propelling roles in pushing political elites from peace to war, but that the logic for the initiation of crisis and war followed closely the dynamic realist logic detailed in the first two chapters. American leaders of all stripes were driven by the need to safeguard the nation's access to resources and markets, whether abroad or between the individual American states themselves. Building a strong economic power sphere (realm one) within North America through western expansion was an ongoing goal. Recognizing the tension between expansion and interstate mistrust, U.S. leaders continually sought to extend the republic while minimizing the risk of a spiral to war with Britain or any other European power. Yet whenever commercial access was threatened by these powers—that is, whenever American expectations for future trade with western territories (realm one) or with Pacific and Far East states (realm two) were reduced because of the current or anticipated actions of others—U.S. leaders quickly became more hard-line, implementing harsher policies commensurate with American military power.[1] When, however, expectations were improved through agreements or because the European powers were distracted by their own issues, U.S. foreign policies became more moderate. The entrenched sense of "cultural distance" of America from Britain and the rest of Europe—especially in the ideological divide between the aristocratic hierarchical order and more liberal republican ways of life—provided the backdrop for American interpretations of European actions as potential threats to the young republic. Yet it was the implications of these actions for the U.S. commercial and territorial sphere that almost always were at the forefront of the American definitions of "threat." And while at times more purely domestic political factors did play important causal roles in leading the United States from peace to conflict, these factors were rarely the primary propelling drivers of conflict. Rather, they served to facilitate the mobilization of the population for dangerous crises and wars that were being chosen for more dynamic realist reasons.

This chapter thus seeks to push the understanding of this period of American history in a new direction. There is little question that American expansionism westward did have much to do with the individual drives of settlers and the desire of Southern economic elites to maintain slavery's viability in the face of depleted soil and growing population. These factors, however, proved less important when it came to dealing with significant powers with important interests in North America, such as Britain and Spain. Here, strategic calculations of commerce and territory predominated. Sometimes a more purely opportunistic dynamic realist logic prevailed. In particular, the U.S. efforts from 1810 to 1819 to grab West Florida and East Florida from Spain were less about new threats and more about opportunities to extend the American economic power sphere as a hedge against potential future competitors. In both these two situations, the risks of spiraling were low and the potential gains high, making an opportunistic territorial grab that would build long-term economic power a rational response to the situation. More generally, however, U.S. leaders were only willing to take on the risks and costs of actual war when one of the main European great powers actually threatened to restrict the nation's future access to resources and markets, either in the west or with states in the neutral zone such as China.

The variations in the intensity of American expansionism and hard-line diplomacy toward outside powers from 1790 to 1850 were therefore primarily a function of changes in the level of external economic threats and only secondarily a function of changing levels of opportunity. U.S. leaders certainly had an entrenched understanding of the need to expand the American economic power sphere to increase future control and commercial access, as per the offensive realist economic baseline of dynamic realism.[2] But they also understood trade-offs. They knew that the drive to expand the U.S. economic sphere went hand in hand with the risk of sparking costly wars on the borders of the United States. Almost invariably, therefore, it was only when expectations for future trade turned negative did American presidents turn to more extreme hard-line options.[3]

It was thus with great reluctance that John Adams entered into a "Quasi-War" with France from 1797 to 1800 after the French began to impose commercial restrictions and seemed unwilling to negotiate a deal. His successor Thomas Jefferson entered office in 1801 with a very different ideological outlook, initially seeing foreign policy as part of a general strategy of promoting the well-being of the average individual, especially those making a living by farming. In fulfillment of his "Revolution of 1800," he spent his two years in office trying to reduce military spending to pay down the debt and return any surplus to the people.[4] Yet by 1803, after failing to stop some of the Barbary states of North Africa from threatening U.S. commerce in the Mediterranean, he decided to fight a full-scale naval war with Tripoli, the main Barbary offender.[5] More importantly, he was willing to risk a war with France in 1803 after Napoleon made clear he would reoccupy the Louisiana territory previously held by a weaker and more compliant Spain. After 1805 he increasingly contemplated initiating war with the British in the face of vicious depredations to U.S. trade. Jefferson's secretary of state James Madison, once president, completed the task by initiating war against Britain in 1812 as a last-resort option when Britain refused to end its attacks on U.S. trade.

The period from 1815 to 1848 was ostensibly a period of relative peace for the United States and the European great powers. Yet pretty well every major dispute except for the 1839–42 struggle with Britain over the Maine-Canada boundary was driven by fears of European encroachments that might constrain American commerce and reduce U.S. economic growth and thus long-term security. After much reflection, President James Monroe announced his famous doctrine in late 1823 to deter not only monarchical states such as France, Austria, and Russia from intervening in the rebellions of Spanish America, but also to minimize Britain's role in the trade and defense of the newly emerging Latin American states. By the 1830s and especially into the 1840s, American officials' anxiety over who would control the territories of Texas, Oregon, and California became palpable. Perhaps surprisingly, this anxiety had, in the end, little to do with the slavery question then dividing the country. National leaders from the South were initially worried that the incorporation of Texas would only exacerbate the North-South divide, and they understood that it was highly unlikely that the Oregon and Californian

territories would accept the extension of slavery. The dominant pressure leading to active U.S. incorporation of these areas came from outside—namely,
the fear that the economic juggernaut Britain would dominate these areas and
the trade relations in the Caribbean and the Pacific unless the United States
acted forcefully.

This chapter and the next reveal that American foreign policy from 1790 to
1900 had a common but important thread running through it. Almost every
time the United States was threatened with an immediate or looming cut-off
or restriction in its access to resources and markets, U.S. leaders, regardless of
their stripes, reacted swiftly and harshly. Domestic pressures and ideological
pathologies did have important causal roles to play in the "mix" of forces that
provide recipes for conflict across time and space.[6] Yet these unit-level factors
acted more to reinforce the more basic strategic logic for action, to rationalize
acts of aggression, or to facilitate the mobilization of domestic support for
strong action. As we will see, James Madison in mid-1811 had already decided
on war to counter British trade restrictions before he stirred up nationalist
sentiment with his addresses to Congress later that year. And out of the fear of
a British move against Californian ports, President Polk deliberately pushed
Mexico to fire the first shot so he could start a war of "manifest destiny" that
would secure America's claim to the Pacific trade into the future.[7] In the vast
majority of cases, it was declining trade expectations that propelled U.S. leaders into conflict. Domestic-level factors were supportive of this dynamic realist
reasoning, but not determinative.

## The Early Republic and the Origins of the War of 1812

This section's primary focus is the lead-up to the War of 1812 over the years 1805
to 1812. I will also briefly explore the crises from 1794 to 1804 as background
to this significant conflict. The United States was clearly the initiator of the
War of 1812, insofar as it was the first to launch military attacks and did so while
the British government was still hoping to avoid a direct conflict. The key
question on the table is: why? The prime competitors to my dynamic realist
argument here are a variety of domestic-level explanations compatible with
liberalism's overall views, including the arguments that as U.S.-British trade
plummeted, President Madison and his supporters in Congress used war to
consolidate their party's hold on power and to satisfy the greed of sectional
interests.

I will show that such factors were not the primary propelling reasons that
pushed the key American officials to choose war over peace. President James
Madison and his secretary of state James Monroe were at all times driven only
by their sense of what was best for the national interest—namely, the survival

of the United States as a strong, cohesive country. They only stirred up support in Congress once they had decided (in mid-1811) that war with Britain was the only means to break the harsh economic restrictions on the United States that Britain, the stronger power, had been imposing since 1805. The tragedy of this war is that while Madison was reluctant to go to war, the British felt they could not back away from the costly economic restrictions on America if they were going to defeat their primary enemy, Napoleonic France. In short, this is a classic case where third-party pressures on state X (Britain) from state Z (France) cause it to restrict trade with state Y (the United States), despite X's understanding that the restrictions pose a high risk that Y will ultimately initiate war.[8] In our case, Britain's cabinet understood, especially near the end, that its policy had completely undermined American expectations of future trade and was thus driving Madison into war. Yet given the exogenous threat of Napoleon, London could not moderate its demands or restrictions. War was then chosen by U.S. leaders as the lesser of two evils, the greater evil being the long-term economic and political decline of the United States.

For the first three decades after independence, the main foreign policy challenge to the new nation was the building of a vibrant economic foundation for national security in the midst of the ongoing mercantilist and war-economy policies of Britain and France. Almost all leaders across the Federalist-Republican ideological divide that soon split the nation agreed on one thing: that the young republic needed seaborne commerce to develop and unify the various sections of the country. Jefferson, Madison, and their Republican followers may have disagreed with the Hamiltonian Federalist emphasis on the renewing of the deep prerevolutionary trade ties with Great Britain, yet their goal was not to stop or reduce seaborne commerce but to diversify it away from the high dependence on Britain that emerged after 1783.[9]

Unfortunately for the Americans, both Britain and France were determined to maintain mercantilist spheres that built their productive and shipping capacities at the expense of their main rivals, meaning especially at the expense of each other. In 1783, the British cabinet issued its first postwar Order in Council to prevent all American ships from doing business with the British West Indies. The logic behind this policy was stated nicely by Lord Sheffield later that year when he argued that unless Britain sustained its dominant position in shipping and manufacturing, it would lose out to a rising American state that had already begun to show its abilities in both areas. U.S-British trade had constituted two-thirds of all external trade by the American states before the Revolutionary War, and the new nation was keen to restore it. The British postwar exclusionary measures were therefore quite devastating. The young nation, having just come out of an eight-year war and needing to rebuild, was of course in no position to risk war to force Britain to rescind the measures.

The British mercantilist dictates of the 1780s were thus allowed to go essentially unchallenged.[10]

Things with France initially seemed more promising. In particular, the French freed up trade with their West Indian colonies after 1784, a move that was quickly exploited by northeastern shipping interests. Yet overall, U.S.-French trade failed to take off as the decade of the 1780s came to a close. The fact that the decrees that had initially opened French West Indies trade to foreign shippers were gradually rescinded did not help. But the deeper reasons were more structural and entrenched: British-manufactured products were simply far more sought after in the United States than the equivalent French products; and British firms were much more able than the French to extend the credit necessary to fund cross-Atlantic ventures, ventures that often took months to complete. This reality meant that by the early 1790s, the United States was still highly dependent on trade with Britain, despite the desire of the federal government to reduce this dependency.[11]

The situation with France and Britain became progressively more problematic after the two states fell into war in 1793 after the beheading of King Louis XVI in January. On the one hand, American shipping to Europe had taken off as soon as France began to fight the continental powers in the spring of 1792. Total war in Europe (as in 1914 to 1916) was in fact a godsend for the Americans. With European seamen and merchant ships requisitioned by the navies or vulnerable to attack, neutral U.S. ships were needed to supply the demand for vast quantities of raw materials and food that the Europeans needed for their armies and populations. The overall value of U.S. trade grew threefold from 1790 to 1794, and most of this was still with Britain.[12] Yet British leaders were not pleased. Not only was America supplying goods to the French that directly or indirectly aided the French war effort, but transatlantic British shipping itself was being hurt by the fast growth of the U.S. competitor. The British government argued that by its self-declared "Rule of 1756," any trade that was illegal during peacetime must also remain illegal during wartime. And most of the new American trade growth was precisely of this kind: shipping of goods that the British and French merchant fleets could no longer handle. The British navy was thus given license to seize American ships to Europe that contained goods suspected of originating in the French West Indies. The British went further, however, seizing American ships that simply brought U.S. goods directly to France, labeling such goods contraband (military goods) regardless of their nature.[13]

These actions led to the first war scare of the postrevolutionary period. In early March 1794, as Congress was in the process of passing a bill that would establish a modern navy, word was received of a new British Order in Council that greatly increased the sweep of actions directed against U.S. shipping. For the rest of 1794, in the midst of America's first naval buildup, the country debated the wisdom of economic retaliation against Britain. Intuitively aware of the trade-security dilemma, President Washington knew that such retaliation might well lead to a spiral of hostility and the British initiation of war against the United States. Despite pressure from Madison and the Republicans in Congress, he thus resisted the call for sanctions, understanding well the short-term weakness of the U.S. navy. He instead sent John Jay to London to negotiate a peace. Jay came home in early 1795 with a treaty that secured this objective while getting British assurances that they would quit their remaining military posts on U.S. territory. But the Jay Treaty solved essentially none of the outstanding American commercial complaints against Britain—most importantly, the broad British definition of contraband, London's unwillingness to revoke the Rule of 1756, and the British impressment of U.S. sailors. The only major British trade concession of the treaty was London's agreement to allow trade between America and the British West Indies on ships under seventy tons, a size that northeastern shippers saw as greatly limiting the size of the trade itself. To avoid a devastating war, however, a slim two-thirds majority in the Senate approved the unpopular treaty.[14]

The logic of dynamic realist theory was clearly at play here, and if not for the strong constraining force of U.S. military weakness, an actual shooting war would likely have occurred. This is made evident by what transpired with France in the late 1790s. The French government was outraged by the Jay Treaty, seeing it as a betrayal of the still existing U.S.-French treaties of commerce and alliance from the late 1770s when France helped the American states win their independence. For the French, the simple fact of the Jay Treaty demonstrated that the United States had realigned with Britain against France. Paris thus began to issue a series of increasingly harsh decrees that led to brazen seizures of American ships and their cargo off the coast of northern Europe and in the Caribbean.

By the time John Adams assumed the presidency in March 1797, the French decrees had plunged the United States into its second full-scale militarized crisis in three years. Fortunately, this time the United States was more or less a match for the adversary, at least at sea. Three more of the six modern frigates authorized by Congress in 1794 were slated to be on line by the end of the year. Moreover, Adams was only up against the French navy, not the British, and he could rely on Britain to constrain the French in the Caribbean out of its own self-interest. Adams was therefore much better positioned in power terms to stand up to the French and their economic restrictions. His inclination, however, was still to avoid drawing his young but growing nation into war. Despite strong pressure from the War Hawks within the Federalist party and his own cabinet, he sent a delegation to

Paris to seek a peace deal. The delegation was more than rudely rebuffed. Foreign Minister Talleyrand would not even open negotiations until the United States agreed to offer cash-strapped France a substantial "loan" and to provide him and his primary officials with a substantial bribe. When word was received in the U.S. capital in March 1798, outrage over the "XYZ Affair" quickly turned into war fever.[15]

Adams managed to resist the hard-line Federalists' demand for a formal declaration of war from Congress. But the naval conflict that began in the Caribbean Sea in late 1798/early 1799, lasting for almost two years, was a war nonetheless. Historians later labeled it the "Quasi-War" because the military engagements occurred only at sea and the war itself was undeclared.[16] But the more accurate term is the one Adams himself later used: namely, a "half-war."[17] It is a war that fits nicely with dynamic realist logic and its focus on expectations of future trade and the risks of a trade-security spiral. The French, given the exogenous pressures of European war, felt compelled to counter the rebounding of trade between the United States and Britain that would naturally follow the Jay Treaty. The Americans, given their deteriorating trade situation and the fact that diplomacy had failed to restore U.S.-French commerce, felt compelled to wage at least a naval war to protect their trade with the Caribbean and with Europe. The difference between the resolution of the war crisis with the British in 1794–95 and the beginning of an actual naval war with France in 1798–99 reflects the difference between U.S. relative naval power in the two situations.[18] In the first, the naval buildup was still in its infancy and America was facing the world's naval superpower at a point of total military inferiority. In the second, the United States now had three frigates ready to go and three in production against a naval power which, at least in the Caribbean, it was more or less a match for.[19] In short, declining trade expectations and high dependence were propelling forces for war in both cases, but differences in the constraining factor of relative military power explain Washington's and Adams's differing foreign policy responses.

In the fall of 1800, Napoleon resolved the dispute with America at the exact time that, unbeknownst to the Americans, he convinced the Spanish to give Louisiana back to France. This was part of his grand plan to reestablish a colonial empire in Saint Domingue (Haiti) and North America to compete with his main rising threat, the industrializing British empire.[20] When Napoleon's secret deal with Spain became known in the spring of 1801, it caused consternation across the United States. The primary concern was the status of the port of New Orleans. All traffic down the Mississippi River had to go through the city. If the French decided to close New Orleans or to greatly restrict American trade through the port, it would have devastating consequences for the whole U.S. economy. Jefferson, the Republicans, and even most Federalists

understood the importance of the developing West to the continued economic health of the original thirteen states. Because it was much cheaper and
faster to ship western food and raw materials down the Mississippi than over the
Appalachian Mountains, the territories and states west of the mountains—
and thus the unity of the nation—would be greatly affected by the closure of
New Orleans. But given the growing integration of the U.S. economy, the eastern states would be greatly hurt as well: two-thirds of all produce traded in the
country now came down the Mississippi, and the more developed Northeast
and mid-Atlantic states saw the West as a key market for their manufactured
goods. Since the 1795 treaty with Spain, trade through New Orleans had flowed
quite freely. The impending reacquisition of the city by Napoleon thus created
an atmosphere of dread and foreboding across the nation and in its halls of
power. Considering Napoleon's personal history, it seemed highly likely that
he would either use the port as leverage against the United States or to hurt
American economic growth directly in order to fuel the development of
France's now larger imperial realm.

In the face of declining expectations of future trade, Jefferson and Secretary of State Madison acted in ways consistent with dynamic realism but
contrary to both their ideological predispositions and their historically
warm feelings toward France. They played a carefully calibrated game of
brinksmanship, signaling that they might not be able to hold back growing
American war fever, while strongly hinting that they would align with Britain
to take New Orleans by force in any ensuing war. By late 1802 as the war crisis
heated up, Jefferson and Madison embarked on a strategy that would become a cornerstone of U.S. diplomacy throughout the nineteenth century.
They offered to purchase the disputed territory—namely, the city of New
Orleans and its immediate surroundings—but made it clear they would go
to war if the offer to buy was refused. By combining carrots with sticks, Jefferson and Madison were, in the best mafioso fashion, making Napoleon "an
offer that he couldn't refuse."

By March of 1803, Napoleon understood that he was indeed in no position
to refuse. With his attempt to retake Haiti a complete failure, his dreams of
building an overseas empire to compete with Britain faded. In the face of continued British industrial growth, he knew he had to provoke Britain into another war in order to destroy it before it was too late. He thus surprised the
Americans by offering to sell the *whole* of the Louisiana territory, and not just
New Orleans and its environs. Unfortunately, he asked for a sum of money
that was much more than U.S. negotiators Livingston and Monroe had been
authorized to offer, given that Jefferson and Madison had been focusing just
on the city of New Orleans. Livingston and Monroe decided to take the plunge
and agreed without awaiting Jefferson's approval on a price of $15 million.

When Jefferson received word of the deal, he was delighted, and quickly asked Congress for its approval, which it gave. The two sides got what they wanted. The United States had just acquired territory that effectively doubled its size with a stroke of a pen. But of more immediate importance, Jefferson and Madison had resolved the primary issue behind the war crisis itself—the free passage of American goods through New Orleans. Napoleon not only avoided war, but he pocketed money essential to funding the invasion force he was building up to attack Britain. Moreover, he knowingly built up the United States as an Atlantic power that could divert British attention and power westward.[21]

For our purposes, the most significant thing to note is that declining American trade expectations were not just the dominant force driving Jefferson and Madison's behavior in 1802–3—they were pretty much the only thing. All other possible explanations for their actions fall flat. It is clear that the two men were not propelled by some dream of an "empire of liberty" stretching across the continent, or by land greed or the hope of saving slavery by acquiring new untapped territory for slavery's expansion. The crisis itself was sparked by news that the Spanish were returning the Louisiana territory to France, and by nothing else. And Jefferson and Madison's goals were very limited: if they could not get a return to the status quo (Spanish control of Louisiana and New Orleans), then they sought to purchase only the city of New Orleans and surrounding territory. It was Napoleon who surprised all Americans, including the president and secretary of state, by offering the whole of the territory for purchase.[22]

Also significant is the fact that the vast majority of Federalists and Republicans were united from the start in their determination to prevent a French takeover of New Orleans. This rare unity on foreign policy came about for the same economic reasons driving Jefferson and Madison. Dreams of a larger empire across the continent had floated through the heads of American leaders for some time. But most, including Jefferson, believed that with American demographic growth and migration, the vast Louisiana territory would eventually fall to the United States like a ripe fruit. Spain was seen as simply not having enough manpower to control such a vast swath of land over the long term.[23] Prior to word of the secret transfer to France and the sudden threat of cut-off, therefore, there was no call for government action to acquire the Louisiana Territory. Hence the key point: Jefferson did not enter into or initiate the war crisis in 1802–3 in order to force the immediate transfer of this land to American hands. He was only concerned about the threat to Mississippi trade through the bottleneck of New Orleans. To explain why the United States came close to war with France in 1802–3, therefore, it seems that only dynamic realism can do the job.[24]

## The Onset of the War of 1812

The resolution of the war crisis with France in 1803, partly aided by the U.S. threat of alignment with Britain, was not the end of troubles with European powers but only the beginning of a whole new set of commercial problems, problems that would lead ultimately to the initiation of war against Britain in 1812 and the simultaneous decision not to start a war with France. The renewal of all-out war between France and Britain in 1803 would lead these two powers to impose increasingly harsh economic blockades on each other. Once again, as in the 1790s, the United States found itself caught in the middle. Both Jefferson's and later Madison's presidencies would seek to supply both sides with the food and resources they needed to sustain their war machines. But as France and Britain set out to destroy the adversary's economy, they understood that it was essential to control America's "neutral" trade, use it for their own purposes, and above all deny the other any U.S. goods that would prevent a total victory. The combined effect was the devastation of the American economy by 1811. Because of America's greater dependence on the British economy and the impossibility of fighting both parties at once, President Madison decided to overlook French depredations. The American initiation of war began in the summer of 1812 with a full-scale attack on Canada. By this action, Madison hoped he could force Britain to remove its economic restrictions as the price for the return of Canadian territory. But for Madison this was the last resort, the only thing that might reinstate open trade after eight years of failed U.S. efforts to convince the British to lift their restrictions. As I will show, he was operating under a tragic least-of-many-evils logic forced on him by British economic policy. Domestic and ideological factors for war played only facilitating roles in Madison's actions—they helped him mobilize the public support for the war he needed to get it going but did not push him into it.

With the return of war in Europe in 1803, Britain had sought to reimpose its "Rule of 1756" which was designed to stop the United States from shipping French West Indies goods to France. American ships found to be violating this rule were seized and the goods confiscated. The Americans sought to get around this by sending French West Indies goods to the United States first, taking them off the ships as imports, and then reloading them as exports to France from America. In 1805, with the Essex decision, British courts ruled that such "broken voyages" were illegal. The rate of seizures of American ships increased dramatically. But the true beginning of the end of free-flowing U.S.-British trade began in 1807. In December 1806, after victories over Austria and Prussia, Napoleon announced his infamous Berlin Decrees, the start of his efforts to set up a "Continental System" that would prevent Britain from selling its goods in Europe. Britain responded to Napoleon's decree with new Orders in Council (OIC) in January and November 1807. The British navy proceeded to blockade the European coastline and demanded that all neutral ships seeking to sell to Europe pass through British ports first. The British strategy was not to stop all trade with Europe, but rather to ensure that Britain completely controlled that trade every step of the way. If Britain were able to confiscate any goods deemed contraband (ones that helped Napoleon's war effort), collect exorbitant duties on any U.S. goods that London did allow to go through, and force most of these goods to be shipped on British ships, Britain would win the game of relative economic power and force France to its knees. From the British point of view, such a strategy was a simple matter of life and death in the context of total war. It was this attitude that would drive British economic policy right up to the summer of 1812.

When Napoleon issued the Milan Decree in December 1807, the United States found itself for the next four years stuck between a rock and a hard place. The new decree stated that any neutral ship that obeyed the British OICs and stopped in Britain first would be subject to seizure and confiscation by French ships implementing his Continental System. The American dilemma was straightforward: if U.S. ships tried to meet the British requirements, they risked capture by the French; if they tried to obey Napoleon's decrees and sail directly to the Continent, they risked capture by the British. Because the British and French were fighting a total war of survival in which American "neutral" shipping might make the difference between victory and defeat, neither could afford to relax these restrictions without endangering their respective war efforts.

Jefferson and Madison had been advocates of economic coercion as a tool of statecraft going back to the early 1790s. As president and secretary of state, respectively, they finally had a chance to use this tool in 1807. In December 1807, Jefferson got a Republican-dominated Congress to approve a complete embargo on all American trade with both Britain and France. Going beyond an earlier nonimportation of select British goods, the U.S. government now forbade all imports from and all exports to Britain and France and their colonies. This was solely a tactical move to compel a reversal of European policies: Jefferson believed that Britain in particular would wake up to its great dependence on American food and raw materials and rescind its OICs. Unfortunately, with Britain's control of the Atlantic and with new trade opening up with Latin America, London was able to stand tough. The OICs remained in place, and in all diplomatic discussions, the British proved unwilling to budge on any core issues.[25]

The embargo, a complete failure that only ended up further devastating the U.S. economy, was allowed to lapse in early 1809. A replacement bill that outlawed only British and French imports was itself replaced in May 1810 by

Macon Bill #2. Macon #2 constituted an interesting reversal of policy. It ended all U.S. sanctions against Britain and France but stated that should either Britain or France unilaterally end its sanctions against America, Washington would immediately reimpose a full embargo against the other great power. Napoleon, the consummate calculator, pretended to take the bait by having his foreign minister Jean-Baptiste Cadore issue a letter to the Americans in August 1810, implying that his Berlin and Milan decrees would no longer apply to the United States after November 1810. The Cadore letter was vague enough in its specifics to allow France to relax or tighten restrictions on the Americans as suited French purposes in 1810–11. Napoleon was playing a tricky game. He could not truly end his restrictions without allowing the British to sell their goods to the Continent through U.S. shipping. And yet by occasionally appearing to make concessions, he could compel the Americans through the provisions of their own legislation to reimpose an embargo against Britain. This would force Britain and the United States into total economic warfare and possibly into war itself—fulfilling the strategic objective that had animated his sale of Louisiana seven years before.[26]

Madison was not fooled. Through 1810 and into 1811, he understood that France's ending of its trade sanctions was partial at best and cynically manipulative at worst. Britain continued to argue that Cadore's initiative was a sham and refused to change its policies. Strategically choosing to ignore France's depredations, Madison argued to Congress that it should abide by Macon #2 and reimpose nonimportation on Britain now that France had relaxed its restrictions. Congress agreed. But despite the passage of a new nonimportation bill against Britain in March 1811, Madison knew he was running out of options. He certainly hoped that Britain, given its own economic depression, might see both the absolute loss caused by nonimportation and the relative loss caused by increased U.S. trade with France as a reason to end its OICs against America. Yet if this measure failed, war was the only option left, and both he and former president Jefferson knew it.[27]

Once again, however, the British refused to concede to U.S. demands. London's fear of helping France grow economically was just too strong. In fact, when new British ambassador Augustus Foster arrived in July 1811, he adopted an even more intransigent stance than the British had previously. He told Madison and the new secretary of state James Monroe that Britain would only agree to relax its OICs if the United States could get Napoleon to open up the European continent to British products. This demand went beyond the simple argument that Britain would end its OICs once France proved that it truly had ended *its* restrictions against the United States, as per Cadore's promises. As both Madison and Monroe immediately understood, London was now asking the Americans to perform an impossible task: that they act as intermediary to convince Napoleon to end the Continental System, the linchpin of his overall strategy to force Britain to surrender.[28]

Madison made the decision for war with Britain in late July 1811, confirming that decision by discussions with Monroe over the next month. The next year was then used by Madison and Monroe to prepare a reluctant nation for war should last-ditch diplomatic coercion fail to convince the British to end their economic sanctions. There has always been some controversy over the question of when Madison made up his mind to start a war. There are a number of pieces of evidence, however, that together show that the decision was set in place by the end of July 1811, long before there was any domestic pressure for a war with Britain.

The first is Madison's behavior toward Congress during the summer and fall of 1811. In July, Madison took the unusual step, prior to leaving Washington for a vacation, of telling Congress it would have to reconvene a month early— that is, in early November 1811 rather than December. On November 5, as the new legislative session began, Madison immediately presented his annual message to Congress. It was a diatribe against British violations of American commerce and a call to prepare the nation for war. Madison began by arguing that with "confirmations" of the end of the French decrees (something he knew had not really occurred), he had hoped that the British would have been induced to repeal their Orders in Councils and thus remove "existing obstructions to [their] commerce with the United States." Instead of taking this "reasonable step," Britain went in the opposite direction, putting its OICs into "more rigorous execution" and then communicating through its envoy (Foster) that commerce would be restored only when France allowed British goods into the continent. In the meantime, London had told Washington that a continuation of the U.S. nonimportation policy "would lead to measures of retaliation." This coercive British threat had already been carried out, Madison noted. He spent the next three paragraphs reiterating British violations of American neutral commerce, noting that Britain showed no intention of providing compensation for the "great amount of American property, seized and condemned, under the [OIC] Edicts." In short, Britain was not only increasing its level of commercial hostility, but even more importantly, there was no evidence that it would vary its policy except under a condition (the end of France's Continental System) that the United States could not possibly hope to meet. In the face of this "hostile inflexibility," Madison argued, Congress should "feel its duty of putting the United States into armor." He spent the remaining part of his address stressing the actions needed to prepare the nation for war.[29]

The second piece of evidence is Madison's cagey and secretive behavior from July to October 1811 during the period when he would have been thinking about and preparing his national address. He made no public statements on his feelings about the new hard-line British position revealed by Ambassador Foster in mid-July, nor did he share the content of his exchanges with Foster with any member of Congress. Private letters, however, indicate that he now understood that there was little hope of a peaceful solution. On July 23, 1811, he wrote to friend Richard Cutts that Britain was using continued French violations as a "pretext for the refusal of [Great Britain] to revoke her orders in Council." Foster himself "stroaks [*sic*] with one paw and scratches with another." The same day, in a letter devoted to the crisis with Britain, he told Jefferson's former secretary of war, Henry Dearborn, that Foster's arrival "has yielded nothing that promises an amendment of things with [Britain]." London's condition for a repeal of the OICs was the French decrees "be repealed not only as they relate to the U.S. but as they relate G.B. [Great Britain]," such that "the ports of her Enemy [i.e., France] shall be opened to her trade." "Our present conclusion," Madison continued, was that Congress should be convened on the first day of November, a day that was "as early as will be convenient" and would give enough time to lay before Congress any new information received from Europe.[30]

When Madison arrived home at Montpelier in August, he sought to keep in contact with his two main confidants, his secretary of state James Monroe and former president Thomas Jefferson. Jefferson himself had argued a number of times during his own presidency that should economic coercion fail, war would ultimately have to be chosen—at a time when America was capable of waging it, of course.[31] On August 23, Madison wrote Monroe that he looked forward to a visit from the secretary, and that Foster's recent condemnatory letters to Monroe had such a hostile spirit that they must be reflecting directly the sentiments of the British government.[32] Monroe wrote back a few days later, explaining that his delay was due to an injured leg, mentioning that he would bring the Foster papers with him when he visited. In late August, the two conferred at Montpelier. Although we have no documentary record of their discussions,[33] we do know that soon after Monroe's return to Charlottesville, he received word from Madison that the president wished to come to Charlottesville to confer with Jefferson at Monticello. On September 13, Monroe wrote a letter to Madison on a "subject of peculiar delicacy." He advised Madison to cancel his impending visit to Jefferson, for fear that the newspapers and congressmen would conclude that Madison was taking marching orders from his mentor and former president, Thomas Jefferson.[34]

Madison wrote back immediately that he understood Monroe's concerns, but that prudence dictated that he come to Monticello regardless.[35] But this sense of prudence soon pushed him in the other direction, and he cancelled his trip as per Monroe's advice. A pessimism about the future haunted him throughout his stay at his home in Montpelier. On September 30, he wrote

Richard Cutts that "nothing has occurred latterly to vary the complexion of our foreign relations." The only ray of hope was that the British king, whom Madison characterized as "insane," was expected to die soon and his successor might push for a more pro-American cabinet.[36]

That Madison had decided on war soon after the failure of talks with Foster in July is affirmed by postwar accounts given by two individuals close to the president during this time: Edward Coles, his private secretary, and Joseph Gales, the editor of the *Intelligencer*. Some forty years after the start of the war, Coles wrote to a friend that the president during the summer of 1811 had not entirely despaired of peace—not until Britain "contended that France must not only repeal her decrees against us, but against all the world" before Britain would repeal its OICs. From that moment on, Coles continued, Madison's mind was "irrevocably fixed on war as the only course left us." It was only in July 1811 that Madison first learned of this new British position after discussions with Foster.[37] As for Gales, using his contemporaneous diary to aid his memory, Gales recounted a similar picture: Madison and Monroe "within some two months prior to the [November] session of Congress" decided that the United States must fight. Both men had "appear[ed] to have made up their minds that no option remained to the Government but open War" with Britain, given that "for several years [Britain] had been making covert war by her hostile edicts and her maritime supremacy upon the United States."[38]

The final piece of evidence confirming that Madison had decided on war prior to the reconvening of Congress—and that he therefore was not pushed into war by so-called War Hawks in the Congress—is Madison and Monroe's actions in late 1811 and early 1812 after the presentation of the war message on November 5 (see chap. 4, n. 42 in this volume, on Monroe). On November 15, Madison wrote a private letter to his ambassador in Russia, none other than John Quincy Adams, son of John Adams and an individual with whom he had consulted in the past. Adams was widely recognized as the most experienced diplomat in the country, and had been keeping Madison abreast of commercial and political developments in Europe for some time.[39] Madison was no doubt aware of Britain's increasingly successful effort to subvert Napoleon's Continental System by the smuggling of British goods through Russia.[40] In his dispatch to Adams, which included a copy of the war message to Congress, Madison argued that Britain showed "a predetermination to make her orders in Council [remain in place until the end of] the war," given that London knew that "nothing but a termination of the war, if even that, will fulfill the condition" that it had laid down for the repeal of its OICs. Madison's pessimism regarding future trade could not have gotten much worse: Britain was set on continuing its sanctions as long as war with France continued—and might even keep them on afterwards. So, for Madison the only question to be decided by Congress was whether "all trade to which the Orders are, and shall be applied, is to be abandoned" or whether the Orders are to be "hostilely resisted." Congress was unlikely to accept the first option, he believed, but it might still delay the preparation for the second option until the end of its current session. Regardless, the mere arming of U.S. merchant ships would likely "bring on war in its full extent," unless perhaps the British finally came to understand U.S. determination and backed down.[41] This logic was reiterated in a letter Madison wrote to the Tennessee legislature in late December or early January, asserting that war was a "necessity" when the only alternative was "a surrender of [a people's] sacred rights and vital interests."[42]

The story after December 1811 can be told quickly. A tight-fisted Congress approved of the general idea of war preparation but refused to raise the money needed to fund the kind of buildup Madison required for war. Madison's disappointment in the pace of effort and fear that the push toward war might be derailed led him and Monroe to do an unusual thing: they spent $50,000 on letters in the possession of John Henry indicating that James Craig, the British Governor-General of Canada, had conspired with New England Federalists to bring about the dismemberment of the United States. In early March, Madison presented the letters to Congress, and they had the desired effect of inflaming public opinion and increasing the leverage of congressional War Hawks within the legislative branch.[43] Madison and his War Hawk supporters in Congress were able to get a 90-day embargo imposed on Britain in April 1812 as a final attempt to coerce Britain into reversing its policies and to reduce the number of vulnerable U.S. merchant ships at sea. In June 1812, after much debate, both houses of Congress voted for a declaration of war on Britain.

In what may seem like a tragic irony, a new British cabinet voted that same month to revoke a number of the OICs, mainly as a stimulus to the British economy but also partly to placate the Americans. But the idea that somehow word of this policy switch, had it been received in time, would have averted war is a false one. As Madison made clear after he heard of the new British policy in early August, the British move was too little, too late. There was no reason to believe that London was doing anything other than temporarily trying to divert the Americans from war. In short, the British move did not do enough to convince the American leadership that London was serious about normalized trade relations. U.S. expectations of future trade could not be improved by this last-minute ploy, and the Americans knew that absent a concerted British effort to commit to future trade, London could easily revert to strict OICs as soon as the Americans put their guns back in their cupboards.[44]

There are two main historical explanations for the War of 1812 that compete with dynamic realism and the trade expectations approach. The first is the ideological argument, consistent with the liberal paradigm, that this was a war driven by Republican War Hawks in the Congress, specifically Henry Clay and Felix Grundy, and that Madison—still guided by pacifist Jeffersonian sentiments—was reluctantly pressured into war by the new breed of "nationalist" Republicans. The second, also consistent with liberalism, is the related idea that the war reflected the greed and ambition of certain key sections of the nation, in particular the South and West, who saw the war as an opportunity to gain land from the British in Canada and from the Spanish in Florida.[45]

These two arguments are "bottom-up" explanations that posit domestic pressures (either from specific regions or from legislators with regional or personal interests) as the propelling factors driving the nation into war. Without question, domestic variables were important in helping Madison mobilize popular support for such a risky and potentially costly war. But in light of the above evidence, we can see that they did not push him into war. Madison's decision for war came well before the rabble-rousing efforts of the War Hawks in the late fall of 1811. Moreover, the War Hawks in the Twelfth Congress of 1811–12 were a minority, and Madison had a difficult time getting congressional support for the buildup and the war itself. It was only with Madison's persistent push for war after November 1811 that a reluctant Congress finally approved a war declaration in June 1812. War Hawks such as Clay certainly aided the process once Madison had made his intentions clear. But they were not determinative of the decision for war itself.

Perhaps even more importantly, it is not at all clear that the legislative supporters of war were driven by either sectional or personal interests in agreeing with Madison's decision. Congressmen and senators from the South and West voted overwhelmingly in favor of war, but there was no clear pattern in the northern states. The New England states went both ways: a majority of representatives from New Hampshire and Vermont voted in favor of war, with the senators from the former split and the single voting Vermont senator voting in favor. All of the representatives and senators from Rhode Island and Connecticut voted against war, as did the majority of New York representatives (New York's senators were split). But sixteen of Pennsylvania's eighteen representatives voted in favor, as did both its senators. Even Massachusetts, a state which, like New York, Rhode Island, and Connecticut, was highly dependent on trans-Atlantic shipping, was split. Six of Massachusetts' fourteen representatives voted for war, and one of its two senators.[46]

These results make it hard to argue that a sectional alliance between the South and the West drove the country into war. Those in Congress favoring war could understand the basic economic logic that Madison laid out in his annual message. Most were not driven by a drive for land, but by a fear of economic decline should the restrictions not be lifted. It is noteworthy that the small handful of western congressmen that sought a guarantee that Canada would be annexed by the United States after a successful war failed to get any such guarantee included in a legislative resolution or bill. Madison and the majority of legislators looked at Canada primarily as a bargaining chip: Washington would give it back to the British once they agreed, in the peace talks, to reinstate open trade relations.[47] East Florida was also taken off the table prior to the war declaration. Most of West Florida was already in U.S. hands by 1811 and thus could not have been an objective of war.[48]

The only domestic-level explanation that has some plausibility is one that I have not yet discussed. This is Roger Brown's argument that Madison and Monroe recognized that in the face of British economic restrictions, war was needed to maintain a uniquely "Republican" vision of the future of the country. Continued confidence in U.S. commercial and political liberties and thus the American way of life was at stake; to not act would endanger those liberties and perhaps undermine the unity of the nation. Brown's thesis is supported by the fact that while there was no consistent sectional pattern to congressional voting, all Federalists voted against the war. The main limitation of Brown's argument is simply that the line between acting for national security and acting to maintain a certain way of life is a very thin one. All his evidence overwhelmingly confirms that Madison and Monroe not only drove the process, but they did so because they believed in the overall importance of renewed commerce for the health of the whole nation and its long-term development. Is this a uniquely "Republican Party" outlook? Not really. Madison's presidency had moved by 1811 quite far away from many of the original Jeffersonian ideals of the 1790s (as in fact had Jefferson's after the purchase of Louisiana). Notwithstanding the traditional Republican emphasis on small government, low military spending, and the promotion of yeoman agriculture still promoted by many old-time Republicans such as Virginian John Randolph, Madison and especially Monroe understood the need for balanced economic growth through seaborne commerce and industrial development. As Madison wrote to the House of Representatives of South Carolina in early January 1812, the effect of allowing the British to continue their trade restrictions would be to "recolonize our commerce by subjecting it to a foreign Authority." Should the United States allow Britain to prevent U.S. exports from being sold to Britain and Europe even as Britain smuggled its goods into America, London would "drain from us precious metals; endanger our moneyed Institutions; arrest our internal improvements; and would strangle in the cradle the manufactures which promise so vigorous a growth."[49] Alexander Hamilton could not have put it better.

The key point here is a simple one. Brown may be right that Madison and Monroe feared the decline of this unique experiment in republicanism called the United States of America. But that decline was being caused by British trade restrictions, as Brown's book confirms. And given British unwillingness to repeal its OICs, the American leaders saw no other way to sustain the economic and thus political security of the nation over the long term. Thus, war was reluctantly chosen as the lesser of two evils, the only way to keep this unique republic going. This is the trade expectations argument to a tee. National leaders act for the whole, understanding that without moderately free access to resources and markets, the nation's power will decline over time and its way of life will be threatened. If nothing can be done short of war to reinstate this vital commerce—if the negative trade expectations are exogenously determined, as they were in this case by the nature of the conflict Britain and France were fighting—then war is the logical option and a "necessity." Madison and Monroe operated according to this logic every step of the way.

To sum up this section, we have seen that the period from 1790 to 1812 fits well with the predictions of dynamic realism and the trade expectations logic. U.S. leaders certainly were keen to expand the scope of U.S. trade, but they were reluctant to get involved in militarized disputes or war with European great powers when commerce was growing, and trade expectations were positive (1790–93 with Britain and France and in 1800–4 with Britain). Yet whenever there was a fall in trade expectations due to a new threat to long-term commerce, American leaders reacted quickly and with hard-line policies whenever they had the power to do so. Given America's position of extreme naval inferiority in 1793–94, the war crisis with Britain caused by British depredations on U.S. trade was resolved without a fight. But against a weaker France and at a time of new naval strength, the United States challenged similar French depredations in 1797–1800, fighting an undeclared naval war to protect American shipping and neutral rights.

The Louisiana crisis of 1802–3 also came close to war as the result of the emerging French threat to Mississippi trade. This case illustrates well the value of taking a dynamic future-oriented approach to the question of economic interdependence. The French threat was a purely future one, since the French had not yet taken over New Orleans. But Jefferson nonetheless put the French on notice that war might occur if Napoleon refused to sell the city to the United States. Jefferson was acting for security, not for domestic reasons. It was the expectation of a major decline in trade, one that would be hard to reverse once France entrenched itself in New Orleans, that drove the process.

The War of 1812 also supports dynamic realism over liberal domestic-level arguments. Madison and Monroe did not choose war because low trade levels unleashed domestic drives for war, as commercial liberals would argue. Rather, Madison and Monroe understood that given high dependence on overseas commerce, the U.S. economy as a whole would be hamstrung by the continued existence of harsh British Orders in Council. War against Canada was needed to give American officials the bargaining chip necessary to get these OICs removed. While it is certainly true that Madison needed a country committed to war in order to get the war going, strong nationalist sentiment and popular support for the war were the *products* of his and Monroe's efforts to bring on a war after October 1811, not the cause of those efforts. To be sure, many individual members of Congress and U.S. soldiers may have had parochial motives for wanting a big war with Britain. But Madison and Monroe understood just how risky such a war would be. They only decided to initiate war after their repeated efforts to cajole or coerce London into relaxing its restrictions had failed. Once it became clear in mid-1811 that there was nothing Washington could do to restore relatively open access to European markets, war became the only option left to uphold U.S. security.

## U.S.-British Relations 1816–46 and the Origins of the War with Mexico

The period from the end of the war with Britain in early 1815 to the onset of war with Mexico in May 1846 was a pivotal one in U.S. history. It marked the completion of an expansion across the North American continent that secured a dominant territorial and resource base that would lead America to preeminence in the following century. By the Adams-Onis Transcontinental Treaty of 1819, the United States acquired Florida and a claim to territory from the edge of Colorado to the Pacific Ocean (above Northern California). Relations with Britain, except for a short interlude from 1816 to 1822, remained tense as the two nations competed over control of Latin America, the Oregon territory, Texas, and California. Through the unilateral declaration of the Monroe Doctrine in late 1823, the United States established a claim to a sphere of influence from North America to the tip of South America. Even if the claim could not be initially implemented because of U.S. military weakness, it provided the impetus for aggressive moves to absorb Texas, the Southwest, California, and ultimately half of the Oregon territory into the U.S. nation by the 1840s. For many European observers, U.S. demographic and economic growth seemed unstoppable. But American leaders were anything but relaxed about their future within the larger geopolitical system. Tangible fear of the British regional encroachments in North America remained right up to the end of the 1840s. It was only with the successful Mexican-American War that we see an end to an intense trade-security competition that on more than one occasion brought the two powers close to war.

In this section, I argue that U.S. policy throughout this period had a common objective—namely, to protect the nation from European, particularly British, encroachments that would threaten the long-term commercial and economic trajectory of the nation. This policy culminated in Polk's decision to launch a war against Mexico, a decision driven above and beyond all else by a need to prevent Britain from securing control of the key harbors of California. These harbors, along with Puget Sound (in the future state of Washington), were seen as critical to an American ability to compete with Britain for the vast emerging trade of East Asia. American leaders after 1815 understood that only Britain could stop the long-term rise of an American economic and political juggernaut. Thus, while relations with other European powers occasionally occupied the time of U.S. statesmen, particularly in 1818–19 and 1823, it was the British-American political and commercial competition that shaped the overarching concerns of U.S. foreign policy during these three decades.

War weariness and a desire to renew a strong commercial relationship led to several years of détente between Britain and the United States after war ended in 1815. The two states tentatively renewed trade ties on a most-favored nation basis, reduced their navies in the Great Lakes, and agreed that citizens of both states could "jointly occupy" the disputed Oregon territory until a more permanent solution was found.[50] This breathing space in the U.S.-British relationship allowed President Monroe and Secretary of State John Quincy Adams to advance the territorial interests of the nation against the tottering Spanish empire. In 1818, General Andrew Jackson made an unauthorized move into Spanish East Florida to punish the Creek Indian tribe for interfering in the settling of lands in Georgia and Mississippi. Adams convinced Monroe to let him use Jackson's action as leverage in his stalled discussions with Spanish minister Luis de Onis. Following Jefferson's lead, Adams made the Spanish an offer they couldn't refuse. He offered to buy Spanish Florida as part of a larger continental settlement, but warned Onis that should the Spanish be unable to control the Indian population in Florida, the United States would feel obliged to repeat a Jackson-style invasion, this time with government approval. Adams knew of course that with rebellions occurring across the Spanish Latin American empire, Madrid was in no position to meet his condition. Onis and Adams thus concluded the Transcontinental Treaty in early 1819, in which Spain sold Florida and relinquished all claims to Oregon territory in return for U.S. recognition of Texas as part of Spanish Mexico.[51]

This move by Monroe and Adams illustrates nicely a point made in chapter 2: namely, that under certain circumstances we can use the offensive realist aspect of dynamic realism as a special case of the larger paradigm. Dynamic realism argues that great powers are always looking for opportunities to expand their economic power spheres at a reasonable cost (the offensive-realist baseline), but they simultaneously worry that overly hard-line behavior might provoke a spiral of mistrust and hostility that leads to costly security competitions and potentially devastating wars (the defensive-realist baseline). Under most circumstances, both dimensions are at play, and thus great powers can be expected to be cautious in their imperialist policies. But when there is almost no chance of great power spiraling—as in the 1819 case—then the "pure" offensive realist economic logic can take over. Grabbing Florida through coercion was a near-perfect opportunity to expand the U.S. realm: not only was Spain distracted by Latin American revolutions, but more importantly Britain and France were preoccupied with national rebuilding after the Napoleonic Wars. Narrowly speaking, since there was no threat to existing or future trade coming from Spain, the trade expectations logic loses out to offensive realist thinking as an explanation for the case. Yet as chapter 1 makes clear, the *reason* why offensive realist theory seems to work best here is that the constraining aspect of fear of great power spiraling was absent, making the opportunistic aspect of dynamic realism predominate. In short, dynamic realism as a framework is still upheld, even as one gives credit to offensive realist theory for its insights into this case.

In 1822–23, a new threat to U.S. economic growth did emerge in the form of possible European intervention in Latin America to squelch the rebellions against Spanish rule that were sweeping the area. Monarchical France, with the permission of the Holy Alliance, had invaded Spain in April 1823 to put down a republican revolution against the Spanish king. For both the British and Americans, there was the fear that this might lead members of this alliance—France in particular, but also Russia—to bring forces to the New World to restore Spanish imperial control or to take over the Spanish colonies for themselves. In the spring of 1823, British Foreign Minister Canning proposed to the Americans that they make a joint statement to the Holy Alliance powers that any interference in Latin America would not be tolerated. Initially, President Monroe, backed by favorable reactions from former presidents Jefferson and Madison, was ready to take the British up on the offer. With the British navy doing what the smaller U.S. navy could not, together they could deter France and Russia from moving into the region. But Adams offered a larger strategic vision that ultimately convinced Monroe and the rest of the cabinet. The United States would make a unilateral declaration that it would not tolerate the new colonization of any territory in the western hemisphere or the interference by any European power with its independent governments. At the same time, Washington would promise not to intervene in European conflicts, such as the one underway in Greece.[52]

Such a declaration, which Monroe insisted be made public as part of his annual message to Congress in December 1823, would have two main effects. First, it would draw a clear line between Old World monarchies and New World republics, signaling that the western hemisphere was not to become a joint British-American sphere of influence, but solely an American one.

Second and relatedly, by acting alone and implicitly including Britain in the gaggle of European monarchical powers, Monroe and Adams were signaling to Britain that it must not think about increasing its own colonial control in the region. Monroe's cabinet had been concerned since the fall of 1822 that Britain might do more than simply oppose European intervention; it might grab territories itself.[53]

The primary concern was Cuba. Cuba was still firmly in Spanish hands, but revolution could spread to there as well. Monroe and his cabinet actively considered acquiring Cuba for the United States. Yet they realized that this would likely lead to war with Britain, a war that Britain would likely win. By the spring of 1823, the fear was more tangible: should Cuba also fall into revolution, Britain might preemptively grab the island to prevent it from falling into French hands. Adams's overall vision was one of a western hemisphere of free republics engaged in active trade with each other and led by the United States, and Cuba was critical to this vision. As Adams wrote to his minister in Madrid in 1823, Cuba "from a multitude of consideration, has become an object of transcendent importance to the commercial and political interests of our Union." Cuba's safe harbor of Havana, its profitable commerce, and its "commanding position" in the Caribbean all give it "an importance in the sum of our national interests with which that of no other foreign territory can be compared."[54] Any control by Britain of this central linchpin in any commercial system in the Americas would destroy Adams's long-term vision and lead to British, not American, commercial ascendancy into the distant future.[55]

Overall, then, as James Lewis summarizes, American unilateral action "would not only meet the threat from the Holy Alliance, but also prevent new ties between Spanish America and Great Britain."[56] In the short term, of course, given British naval superiority, the United States had to rely on London's own interest in preventing France from moving in on Spanish territories. But by sending a signal of U.S. determination now, Monroe and Adams raised the costs and risks to the British as well as the French for any active attempt to colonize or control any Latin American territory. Over time, as U.S. economic development allowed the growth of the American navy, Washington would be able to put muscle behind its words.

In briefly summarizing a complex picture, I do not mean to imply that the strong stance of the Monroe Doctrine was driven solely by falling expectations of future trade should the Europeans, particularly the British, gain a colonial foothold in Latin America. Monroe and Adams were also fearful of the direct military presence of Britain in the region and what that might mean for a narrower definition of U.S. territorial security. But for Monroe and Adams, as for almost all American leaders since the beginning, commercial access and U.S. trade had always gone hand in hand with long-term territorial security. If the

United States found itself unable to grow into its "natural" potential, European powers could take advantage of it down the road. Monroe and Adams thus knew that they had to act forcefully to keep European influence on Latin American development to a bare minimum. Otherwise, the great U.S.-dominated commercial sphere envisioned for the western hemisphere would never come to pass, and U.S. security would suffer accordingly.

By the end of 1823, with Russia agreeing not to challenge Spanish possessions and with France promising Britain that it would not intervene in the New World, only Britain remained a significant rival for commercial and political dominance in the western hemisphere.[57] Not surprisingly, the period after 1823 saw an end to the British-American détente of 1816–22 and a return to a great power competition punctuated by serious war crises and an ongoing security-dilemma spiral of suspicion and hostility.[58] If not for London's even more problematic relations with France and Russia—and the severe logistical problems involved in crossing the Atlantic Ocean to fight the American upstart—war between Britain and America would have almost certainly occurred sometime during the three decades after the Monroe Doctrine was announced.[59]

Fluctuating trade expectations in an environment of global commercial growth were central to the ongoing conflict. By 1825, under the push from "Nationalist Republicans" such as President John Quincy Adams and his secretary of state Henry Clay, the United States was increasing tariffs on manufactured goods as it sought to use government-subsidized canals and roadways to bring America into the industrial era. The British rightly saw Monroe's declaration in December 1823 as part of an American effort to keep Britain from exploiting the vast trade potential of the newly independent Latin American states. These states, freed from the confines of the closed Spanish mercantile system, would be seeking new trade and shipping partners. Should the Americans, under the guise of the Monroe Doctrine, gobble up this trade, British global economic dominance would be threatened. As British prime minister Lord Liverpool wrote his cabinet at the end of 1824, "if we allow these new states to consolidate their system and their policy with the United States of America, it will in a very few years prove fatal to our greatness, if not endanger our safety." In a series of memoranda, he and foreign minister George Canning noted that in terms of industry, the Americans were becoming "more formidable rivals to us than any other nation which has ever yet existed." In shipping, the Americans were seeking to supplant the British "in every quarter of the globe," and as the U.S. commercial fleet was augmented, "their military marine must proportionally increase."[60]

In 1826 the British retaliated against high American tariffs by closing the valuable West Indies to American trade. The British also increased their naval presence in the western Atlantic and Caribbean, and they began a program of improving the fortifications along the Canadian border with the United States. Fearing bombardment of major East Coast cities—the War of 1812 was still fresh in everyone's memories—U.S. administrations countered by throwing money at a massive system of fortifications on the Atlantic seaboard and the Gulf coast. During the first half of the 1830s, the two states managed to moderate somewhat the tension of their growing cold-war competition: President Jackson was preoccupied with domestic reforms and the South Carolina nullification crisis, while the British were caught up in a crisis with France and Russia over control of the Levant.[61]

From 1837 to 1846, however, Britain and America entered into a series of war crises of increasing severity. In 1837, as isolated Canadian rebellions against British rule broke out in Ontario, sympathetic Americans began to run guns and supplies across the border to aid the rebels. In December of that year, British forces launched a punitive raid into the United States, capturing and burning the American ship *Caroline* and killing one American in the process. American public opinion was outraged by this violation of U.S. territory, and war fever spread. President Van Buren called up the militia and asked Congress to appropriate funds for a military buildup. The British did not help the situation by initially painting the *Caroline* as a ship of a "piratical character" whose destruction was justified.[62] The key issue was whether the attack was the act of the British government or simply the unauthorized move of a local British commander. Taking the latter position would have helped the British smooth ruffled feathers by making amends, but British Foreign Minister Palmerston dug in his heels, calling the attack an act of "necessity" driven by the need to maintain control of the border. The crisis was not fully resolved for five years, but the danger of war dissipated by early 1839 by the failure of the Canadian rebellion and the willingness of London to offer reforms that satisfied many of the rebels' demands.

It is tempting to link the war scare over the *Caroline* to increasing trade restrictions between Britain and the United States after 1824. But in this case, aside from the fact that trade had been growing in the 1830s under the more pro–free trade policies of U.S. presidents Jackson and Van Buren and British liberal leaders, there is simply little direct evidence that trade and commerce had any causal connection to the crisis on the Canadian border. The crisis appears to be driven more by local initiatives sparked by domestic upheavals in Canada and the need to project national resolve as mistrust within a security dilemma spiral increased. The same is true of a similar dispute over the Maine boundary. British and American subjects fought a small, month-long war—the "Aroostook War"—in 1839 over control of timber lands in the disputed territory of northern Maine, which both countries claimed as their own. Despite the timber interests involved, neither London nor Washington felt that the economic stakes were high enough to turn a local skirmish into a full-scale war. But both sides realized that national passions might cause an unwanted escalation. Ongoing low-level disputes over the Maine boundary led Secretary of State Daniel Webster and British Minister Lord Ashburton to conclude a treaty in August 1842 that essentially split the disputed territory in half.[63]

Commercial variables were not directly implicated in the *Caroline* and Maine disputes; other factors had primary causal salience. One might argue that the liberal argument that trade can constrain domestic-level drives for war does have some validity here. Even archnationalist Lord Palmerston in 1839 understood that a large-scale war over Maine would hurt U.S.-British trade. He thus refrained from fanning the flames of nationalist passion over the Orostrook skirmish, even if trade apparently did not push him to moderation over the *Caroline* incident.[64] And to the extent that trade expectations had improved in London and Washington, dynamic realism does get the correlation right. Nevertheless, it seems clear that domestic-level forces were the primary propelling factors in both the *Caroline* and the Maine cases. Higher trade levels and positive trade expectations played more of a constraining role here, keeping both sides from escalating either crisis to the point of war. Expressed differently, one might say that because trade expectations were not negative, there was little reason for either side to turn the Canadian disputes into something much more serious. Still, the 1837–41 period is a case where local political interests were responsible for the crisis, not commercial forces. And as Trubowitz shows, the deep depression of the 1837–40 period imposed a major domestic constraint on just how far any U.S. executive would have wanted to take the crisis.[65]

## The Texas, California, and Oregon Crises of the 1840s

A much better comparative test of competing international relations theories comes with the struggle over control of Texas, California, and Oregon that arose in the 1843–46 period. I will argue that these disputes, particularly the latter two, were primarily driven by growing American concerns about British encroachment and British containment on the U.S. periphery. With the rapid growth of railways and steamships, Americans could envision for the first time a truly continental state, economically and politically unified by the new transportation technologies.[66] The British had good reason to fear the growth of an American leviathan and actively worked to restrict U.S. expansion beyond the core territorial base resulting from the Louisiana Purchase of 1803 and the Transcontinental Treaty of 1819. Moreover, the late 1830s and early 1840s was a time of new economic penetration of the potential riches of China and East Asia more generally. American leaders of all stripes were thus worried that should the British succeed in taking the key ports of the Oregon and California coastlines, U.S. long-term economic development would be trapped within the confines of the 1819 boundaries. The fear of successful British containment even extended by 1842 to the question of an independent Texas. Should the United States continue to reject Texan bids for annexation out of a concern for exacerbating sectional tensions—as it had on numerous occasions since Texas independence in 1836—the British might succeed in controlling the economy of the Texan republic on U.S. southern shores. Combined with British efforts to exert influence over the economic policies of Mexico and some Caribbean states, the "loss" of Texas to the British sphere posed a threat that even most Northerners understood. Southerners had coveted Texas as a new slave state for some time, of course. But it was the arising British assertiveness in the region that led formerly reluctant Southerners and Northerners to put aside fears of a sectional fight over slavery to bring Texas into the union.

The main competing arguments to dynamic realism for the 1844 to 1848 period are ideological (that Americans, especially in the western territories, were driven by a sense of "manifest destiny"), domestic-political (that Southern elites needed to expand slavery), and greed-based (that Northerners wanted land and profits in the west). Such arguments do help explain the motivations of certain political elites in Congress and some of the main constraints on the decisions of President John Tyler and his successor, James K. Polk.[67] But they do not necessarily capture the drives of the leaders and officials in the executive—the ones with the ultimate say over policy and the level of aggressive expansionism. And while American trade with Britain was rising at the time, the documents show that dependence on its own was not enough to push U.S. leaders into conflict. The United States had been steadily becoming more dependent on Britain since Jackson's move to freer trade policies and the British reopening of the West Indies in 1830, yet the severe war crises with Britain did not begin until the early 1840s. It is thus primarily the British turn to containment after 1840 that led America, in a defensive response, to move quickly into these areas to secure long-term U.S. dominance.

Overall, liberal arguments have trouble understanding how Britain and the United States could reach the brink of war by 1845–46 in the midst of growing British-U.S. trade. One might try to save an aspect of liberalism here by falling back on the argument that domestic pressures from below were pushing U.S. leaders into adopting a harder-line expansionist posture. According to this view, it was this aggressive posture of manifest destiny, rather than the effort of British containment, that led to the war crises of the period.[68] As I will discuss, there is something to this unit-level argument:

Southern drives to extend slavery, an ideological belief in a U.S. continental destiny, and simple greed for land did put pressure on presidents Tyler and Polk to extend the U.S. nation beyond its 1819 borders. But as with the run-up to the War of 1812, these variables acted more as facilitating factors that the executive branch manipulated when necessary to get its policies enacted. Throughout their tenures in office, Tyler and Polk and their primary advisors were "their own men." Whenever they decided to push hard for expansion, it was in response to a British threat to national interests. In these moments, they knew that holding the nation back from hard-line policies would damage long-term national interests.

In short, there is not much evidence that the Tyler or Polk administrations were either parochial in their objectives or felt pressured into expansion by sectional or ideological forces. That these forces existed there is no doubt. That Tyler and Polk as Southerners saw certain forms of expansion as being potentially useful in the protection of Southern interests is also beyond doubt. But these factors on their own were simply not powerful enough to justify the great risks of war with Britain that the two men knew they were running. What pushed them away from their initial cautiousness to policies that risked a great-power war was the larger national interest—the need to prevent British restrictions on future U.S. growth. Sectional interests helped build a consensus behind their policies but did not determine the policies themselves.[69]

The case of Texas after its independence from Mexico in 1836 poses a key puzzle for all theories: Why did U.S. presidents from both parties, as well as the U.S. Congress, reject calls for annexation from 1836 until 1841, and then slowly but surely move to absorb the state by 1845? One answer is that personalities and domestic pressures changed to breathe new life into the annexation issue by the early 1840s: President Tyler and President-Elect James K. Polk were both Southerners with a big interest in extending slavery into Texas, and Southerners themselves saw Texas as a place that would maintain cotton's supremacy while increasing the South's strength within the Senate. The problem with this argument is twofold. First, Southerners could only absorb Texas if Northerners also got on board, and from 1836 until the early 1840s, Northerners used Congress to block any attempts to annex the independent republic. Second, Southern leaders themselves recognized that absorbing Texas would greatly exacerbate the North-South divide and probably bring on a war with Mexico, which still refused to recognize the independence of Texas. For both these reasons, there was little progress toward annexation until 1843.

Something changed between 1836 and 1843, therefore, to make fence-sitting Southerners argue that the risks of a sectional divide and a war with Mexico were now worth it and to convince a sufficient number of Northerners that Texan annexation was now necessary. That change was the perception of growing British intervention in both Mexico and Texas. The fear after 1843 among Southerners and Northerners alike was a simple but tangible one: namely, that Britain would convince Mexico to recognize Texas so that Texans would choose to maintain Texas as an independent state. This would set Texas up as a British-influenced buffer republic between the United States and a Southwest (New Mexico, California) that was still under the control of a Mexico shaped by its growing dependence on London finance. Underlying this fear were layers of specific motives that brought enough Northerners and Southerners together by March 1845 to get an annexation bill through both houses of Congress on a majority basis. For Southerners, British involvement in an independent Texas would mean Britain's control of an alternative source of cotton for their mills. The concomitant reduction in British dependence on southern U.S. cotton would mean a fall in the long-term price of the South's key export—the export that was the linchpin of the whole Southern economy ("King Cotton"). Southerners also worried that the British, having outlawed slavery in their own colonies, would push Texan lawmakers to ban slavery in Texas as the price of British economic and political support. This was forecast to have a dramatic effect in the slave South. If plantation owners could not move into Texas as cotton depleted the soil in the existing Southern states, then costs of production would rise, and yields would fall. Moreover, by not having a safety valve for the export of surplus slaves, Southerners feared increasing internal unrest within their states.[70]

Politically, the main problem was convincing enough Northerners to come on board to get a Texan annexation bill through Congress. After another Senate rejection of an annexation treaty in the summer of 1844, outgoing president Tyler used the momentum of Polk's election in late 1844 to secure majorities in both houses of Congress in March 1845, just days before he stepped down. Importantly, the vote was not on sectional lines but party lines. Of the twenty-seven senators voting for the bill, thirteen came from the North and fourteen from the South. All thirteen Northern senators were Democrats. The same result obtained in the House. What brought these Northerners into the annexation camp?

The answer is a combination of economic self-interest and racial anxiety, driven by the implications of British involvement in an independent Texan republic. Many Northerners began to see by late 1844 that an independent Texas that had outlawed slavery would, given the above reasoning, hurt the Northern manufacturers and shippers that depended on the booming trade in cotton from the South. Britain's manufactures would gain as Northerners lost out. Moreover, the racial arguments of Mississippi Senator Robert Walker began to gain traction by the latter half of 1844. Walker argued that the decline in the South caused by an independent and British-influenced Texas would mean that surplus slaves, freed by their masters on economic grounds, would go north rather than west into Texas. In short, without Texas as a safety valve, the Northern economy and way of life would be radically undermined. Walker's argument worked its magic by early 1845 to create the slim majority needed for annexation.

The above shows how Tyler was ultimately able to get legislative support for his goal of Texas annexation. But in causal terms, Congress served only as a roadblock (a constraining factor) to Tyler's ambitious agenda. There is no evidence that he kept pushing for annexation over his last two years in office because of domestic pressure. Moreover, since he knew by 1843 that he did not want to run for reelection, he had little reason to respond to those within the South who favored absorbing Texas despite the risks. To understand the propelling causes of the case, therefore, we must explore his own reasons for his unceasing efforts for Texan annexation. Most importantly, was he driven by a national vision or by parochial concerns? While the fact that he was a Virginian slaveholder no doubt made him lean in the direction of annexation, the evidence shows clearly that his actions were driven by his larger view of what was needed for national growth and security.

In the autumn of 1841, he sent his friend Duff Green to Britain to find out information on Britain's grand strategy in the hemisphere. Green's reports over the next two years painted one consistently unnerving picture. Britain, Green argued, was frightened by America's commercial and economic growth, and was determined to keep the United States down. The British now realized they had made a mistake in freeing the slaves in their colonies, fearing that the U.S. cost advantage would only reinforce U.S. growth at Britain's expense. In early 1842, Green wrote that Britain sought to control Texas to make the world "dependent on [Britain rather than America] for the supply of *the* raw material [cotton] for the manufacturing of [textiles]." Britain's "war on slavery," regardless of its original motives, was now simply a "war on our commerce and manufactures." In conjunction with its colonies in the East Indies, Britain sought to dominate world trade in raw materials and to simultaneously "control the manufactures of other nationals and thus compel all nations to pay her tribute."[71] Controlling Texas was simply part of this larger British strategy to keep the United States in an inferior and subservient relationship over the long term.

Green's arguments had a big impact on Tyler, his secretary of state Abel Upshur, and John Calhoun, who became secretary of state in 1844 after Upshur's accidental death. In the summer of 1843, Upshur had received additional reports of British scheming in Texas. In mid-August he wrote Calhoun that Britain sought abolition throughout North America to revive the competitiveness of its colonies and would use Texas to flood the United States with its goods.[72] In September, Upshur informed U.S. ambassador to Britain Edward Everett that Britain's main objective was to find new markets for her surplus manufactured goods and "to destroy, as far as possible, the rivalry and competition of the manufactures of the United States."[73] It was right around this time that Upshur used Everett to find out more information on British efforts in Texas.[74]

President Tyler, clearly drawing from Green's warnings, told Congress in his annual message in December 1844 that if Mexico recognized Texas and it stayed independent and then Texas abolished slavery, this "would operate most injuriously upon the United States and might most seriously threaten the existence of this happy Union."[75] By the fall of 1844, it was clear that the rumors of British intrigues were correct. The British cabinet had sent envoy Charles Elliot to Texas and Mexico to convince the latter to recognize Texas and the former to accept this recognition and to remain an independent republic. Elliot had one advantage over the Americans in his negotiations with outgoing Texan President Sam Houston and incoming President Anson Jones: both these two political players, especially the latter, had a personal incentive to remain a dominant player in an independent nation rather than become a small fish in a much bigger pond. The late fall and early winter of 1844–45 thus saw a scramble of American and British suitors for the Texan hand, and it appeared to Tyler and his advisors that Britain might win out in the end.[76]

Tyler had sent Andrew Donelson, nephew of Andrew Jackson and friend of Sam Houston, to Texas in November 1844 to secure a deal. Donelson found both Houston and President-Elect Jones wavering between independence with British support and annexation by the United States. Donelson wrote Washington in December 1844 that the U.S. government must go all out to win Texas, and that America should try to get annexation "on any terms we can."[77] Tyler's rushed annexation treaty, approved by Congress in March 1845, shows that he followed this advice. In the *Richmond Enquirer* two years later, the now ex-president Tyler argued, in response to Houston's admission that in 1844–45 he had played London and Washington off against one another, that he indeed did fear that Texas would fall into the British sphere. Tyler had been "startled" by intelligence reports showing British efforts to move on Texas, and he was determined to "scatter [this] web of intrigues" before it was too late. Without prompt action, he believed at the time, the Texan "coquette" would "very soon fall into the arms of another [i.e., Britain] and thus be lost forever to the United States." He ends his argument by noting that he well understood at the time "the value of the virtual monopoly of the cotton plant, secured to the United States by the acquisition of Texas," and how this monopoly gave the nation more potential power in the affairs of states "than millions of armed men."[78]

We thus see that the push to acquire Texas only became intense once it became clear in the early 1840s that Britain was seeking to use Texas to contain U.S. economic growth, and indeed (in American eyes) to hurt the United States by undermining its dominance in cotton production through the promotion of the abolition of slavery. We can say in retrospect that the American fear of an end to slavery through British action was no doubt greatly overblown. But the concern that London was actively seeking to contain U.S. growth was not. Britain had been trying to restrict U.S. territorial and thus economic expansion since 1839–40, and its efforts heated up in 1844. The British envoy Charles Elliot in late 1844 had in fact successfully secured Mexican agreement to recognize Texas in return for a British promise to help Texas stay independent. He rushed to Texas in early 1845 to convince the Texans to reject annexation, armed with the argument that such a move was no longer necessary now that the fear of war with Mexico had dissipated.

With the passing of the annexation bill in March, however, the momentum toward annexation among the majority of Texans was now too great. Notwithstanding President Jones' preference for independence, the Texan legislature approved the annexation treaty on July 4, 1845. Elliot had failed, but just barely. And Tyler was correct to believe that without his hasty push, the result might have gone the other way. In sum, it was the British threat that energized the executive branch to work so hard for annexation. President Tyler, far from being pressured into annexation, had to overcome congressional hurdles to it at every step of the way. It was only the British threat that helped secure majorities in both houses of Congress. Without this threat to the long-term commercial future of the nation, Tyler would not have pressed so hard and congressional opposition would have continued to squelch any deals, leaving Texas as an independent republic on the U.S. southern border.

The Oregon Crisis with Britain and the U.S. war with Mexico, from the perspective of this book, must be seen as part and parcel of the same geopolitical problem: namely, the problem of Britain. In both cases, the Americans worried that the British would try to restrict U.S. long-term growth by grabbing the key ports of the West Coast, thereby ensuring continued British dominance over Pacific and specifically East Asian trade. The timing of the two events is not coincidental: the two countries came close to war over Oregon in early 1846 and did not resolve the situation until June of that year, just after the United States declared war on Mexico in May. President Polk and his advisors deliberately provoked a war with Mexico in order to grab California and its ports, and he wisely pulled his country back from the brink over Oregon to avoid two simultaneous wars. But Polk's diplomatic style would have made Godfather Vito Corleone proud. He made it clear to both Britain and Mexico that the United States would go to war if they did not concede to his demands. In the end, Britain understood that it could not fight a costly war over a far-off territory when its relations with France were deteriorating around the globe. It thus accepted a U.S. demand to split the Oregon territory in a way that gave America the valuable harbors of Puget Sound. In the now hallowed tradition of Jefferson regarding New Orleans and Monroe/Adams regarding Florida, Polk gave Mexico an offer he thought it couldn't refuse— namely, sell California and New Mexico or face war with the United States. But in this case, refuse it Mexico did. The ensuing war and U.S. victory allowed Polk to grab the very territory he had sought to buy and thus secure the ports that would ensure a strong American position in Pacific commerce for the foreseeable future.

The Oregon situation had been on a low boil since 1818 when London and Washington agreed to postpone a final settlement and allow "joint occupation" of the disputed territory stretching from Spanish California to Russia's Alaskan panhandle. Things started to change in the early 1840s when "Oregon fever" swept the midwestern states and migration along the Oregon trail significantly shifted the demographic balance in the Americans' favor. Midwest congress- men began to agitate for formal U.S. control over Oregon right up to the Alas- kan panhandle. Southerners were generally less keen, not only because the new territories would turn into free-soil states that would shift the balance of power in the Senate, but because any war with Britain would harm the lucra- tive cotton trade with that manufacturing giant. Individuals with the North- eastern and mid-Atlantic states were more divided, seeing both the commer- cial potential of Asian trade through control of northwest ports and the potential costs of a war with Britain. The internal debates over California in the early 1840s largely mirrored the ones over Oregon: midwestern and some northern commercial interests were keen to assert U.S. claims to the territory, while most Southerners and much of the mid-Atlantic region initially saw little reason to press for annexation.[79]

As with the question of Texas, therefore, the initial sectional divisions of the early 1840s do not tell us why the country would eventually come together by 1844–46—notwithstanding the substantial risks of both sectional conflict and costly foreign war—to support a hard-line push by the executive to grab new, far-off territory. For the answer, we must look again at presidential decision-making and why, under both Tyler and Polk, they would see the West Coast as so important that it justified such risks and costs.

Both presidents, despite their Southern agrarian roots, fully understood that a growing and industrializing America would need new markets in Asia if it were to compete with the British economic colossus. The recession that had followed the bank panic of 1837 had reinforced the widespread opinion that overseas markets were essential to U.S. growth.[80] As historian Thomas Hietala notes, both John Tyler and Abel Upshur were strict states' rights Jeffersonians, but they often put aside their principles to push for active federal involvement in the exploitation of new commercial opportunities in the Pacific. When Upshur was secretary of the navy in 1841, he argued for a doubling of the Pacific fleet, noting that commerce "may be regarded as our principal interest because, to a great extent, it included within it every other interest." Commerce, he wrote a year later, anticipating Alfred Thayer Mahan by a half-century, "*demands* the protection of an adequate naval force."[81] Tyler shared these sentiments. In June 1842, as Britain was imposing trading terms on China following its victory in the first Opium War, Tyler stated that he "had his eye fixed on China and would avail himself of any favorable opportunity to commence a negotiation with the Chinese empire."

Tyler and Upshur had strong support from Caleb Cushing, the renegade Whig congressman from Massachusetts, who as chairman of the House Foreign Affairs Committee in 1842 had authored a report condemning Britain's "immense and still increasing injury" to U.S. trade and its attempt keep America in a subservient position. Cushing recommended increased naval spending to "[safeguard] commerce of all parts of the country in peace and in war." His unflagging support of Tyler led to a friendship. In late 1842, Cushing urged Tyler to make a deal with China akin to China's agreement with Britain after the Opium War, which had opened five ports to trade. The Chinese government should be keen, given that it was only the United States "by the extent of our commerce [that could] act in counterpoise . . . of England." Cushing also warned Tyler of British efforts to dominate Japan, Hawaii, and the Columbia River. If it succeeded, Britain would possess "a complete belt of fortresses environing the globe, to the imminent future peril, not only of our territorial possessions, but of all our vast commerce on the Pacific."[82]

Tyler's thinking was directly in line with his friend's. Using an argument more often associated with the 1890s than the 1840s, Tyler asserted in his annual message to Congress in December 1842 that the "greatest evil which we have to encounter is a surplus of production beyond the home demand, which seeks, and with difficulty finds, a partial market in other regions." Congress must pay particular attention to trade with Asia, he contended. Trade with China had already doubled, and now was the time to go further. He recommended that the United States send an envoy to China to sign a treaty opening China to U.S. products. In May of 1843, Cushing himself would assume this post, and a year later he would sign the Treaty of Wanghiya, which opened five ports to U.S. ships. In the 1842 address to Congress, Tyler also extended the Monroe Doctrine to cover Hawaii. He warned that any attempt by another power to colonize or control Hawaii would create "dissatisfaction" on the part of the U.S. government.[83] When a British commander launched an unauthorized takeover of the islands in the spring of 1843, Tyler sent a sharply worded protest to Britain. The British disavowed the commander's action, but as Hietala notes, "the damage was done." Along with British interference in Texas, "Tyler and his advisors viewed this seizure as yet another indication of Britain's campaign to hem in the United States."[84]

The Oregon and California questions during Tyler's term revolved around the need to ensure U.S. control of the main West Coast ports. The San Francisco harbor, seen as the best potential port facility on the whole coast, was his ongoing obsession. During the 1842 talks on Oregon, Tyler's secretary of state Daniel Webster even offered to give Britain the area north of the Columbia River if Britain would use its influence to get Mexico to cede San Francisco and the surrounding areas of Mexican California to the United States. British envoy Lord Ashburton replied that he had no authority to secure such a deal. That same year Webster, almost certainly in consultation with Tyler, sought a more direct route to this goal: he asked the U.S. minister to Mexico to investigate whether Mexico might be open to selling the desired area to the United States.[85]

Fears that Britain would preemptively grab California had been growing for some time, as David Pletcher and others have shown. The British Hudson's Bay Company had begun to explore the fur-trading potential of California more actively after 1838. In 1842–43 it sent an expedition into the interior and opened a post in Yerba Buena. In addition, in October 1843 Robert Wyllie, a prominent Anglo-Mexican merchant with a significant stake in Mexican bonds, made a formal proposal to Mexico City for British colonization of California. The Mexican government postponed a decision on this until additional bondholders would sign on to an agreement.[86] While British governmental support for these ventures and for subsequent English and Irish migrants to the territory turned out to be quite minimal, American officials did not know this. They saw British encroachments as a prelude to formal occupation, using London's leverage over the Mexican economy to facilitate this end. Thus in 1844, the last year of Tyler's administration, the new secretary of state John Calhoun instructed Duff Green, who was now in Mexico City, to again put forward an offer to purchase California from Mexico. Should he succeed, Calhoun wrote, "our commerce in the Pacific will, in a few years, be greatly more valuable than that in the Atlantic."[87]

By the time of Polk's inauguration in March 1845, Oregon and California had become the primary foreign policy questions of the day. Polk was determined from day one to ensure that the United States beat out Britain for the best West Coast ports. Just after his inauguration, Polk told his navy secretary George Bancroft that along with the settlement of the Oregon question, one of the four key objectives of his administration would be "the acquisition of California."[88]

Newspapers in the spring of 1845 were full of reports of British designs on California. The common thrust of the articles was that now that Britain had failed to control Texas, it would work even harder to absorb California. The *New York Herald* stated bluntly that Britain would simply purchase California to make up for the Texas loss. Such sentiments fit with rumors circulating at the time that Mexico might sell California to Britain to offset debts to British bondholders. The British had been lending a great deal of money to Mexico through the 1820s and 1830s to build influence over the newly independent state, a common British tactic throughout the nineteenth century.

By the early 1840s, in fact, the Mexicans owed the British $50 million, an enormous sum for the time, especially considering the size of the Mexican economy.[89] Given past British practices of using another state's debt to extract territorial and other concessions, it was therefore not surprising that Americans were concerned about British encroachments. The fact that a British consul in Mexico City and an Irish missionary were circulating a plan to develop California as a check on American expansion via the migration of ten thousand Irish colonists did not help matters. Indeed, the rumors that Britain was preparing to buy California were so pervasive that Prime Minister Peel felt obliged to deny them in a public session of Parliament. As it later turned out, the British government was in fact reducing, not increasing, involvement in California. But this was not at all clear to American leaders at the time.[90]

The documentary evidence paints one overwhelming picture of Polk's logic and calculations leading up to the war with Mexico. His first preference was to purchase California without a war. This would secure the ports with minimal disruption and risk. But he preferred war with Mexico and a forced annexation of California and New Mexico to any status quo that might allow Britain to act first to grab the California ports.

To achieve his ends, Polk had to play a very careful game through 1845 and into 1846. He needed to coerce Britain into giving him at least half of the Oregon territory to ensure U.S. possession of Puget Sound and its wonderful harbors. Yet he also needed to finalize the seizure of California one way or another before Britain intervened or preempted the United States. If he were successful, he would grab the whole of the West Coast up to Vancouver Island without war or with only a short war with Mexico. But the risks were high: if he failed, he might find himself in war with not just Mexico, but with the world's greatest naval power. By the early fall of 1845, California had become the top priority. Reports were coming in from the U.S. consul in California, Thomas Larkin, that both British and French governments had suspiciously set up consular posts in California, despite the lack of any immediate commercial reason for their presence. As Norman Graebner relates, Larkin's reports created much excitement in the administration. Secretary of State James

Buchanan wrote Larkin back in October that the appearance of the two con-
suls at the time of "this present crisis" leaves the impression that "their respective governments entertained designs on [California]." Buchanan also wrote
the U.S. minister in London about the administration's suspicions that Britain
and France were "intriguing in both Mexico and California with ambitions of
acquiring the latter."[91]

Through the summer of 1845, Polk was still hoping for a negotiated solution
but preparing for the possibility of a fight in order to achieve his objectives. In
June, he sent instructions to John Sloat, the commander of the Pacific squadron, that he should be ready to seize San Francisco and occupy any other port
his capabilities permitted if he "ascertained with certainty" that Mexico and
the United States were at war.[92] Notwithstanding the agrarian roots of his own
Democratic party, Polk's focus was commercial. In July 1945 he acknowledged
that his obsession was controlling the ports of Oregon territory to further
future U.S. trade.[93] Late that month, the British minister in Washington rejected the U.S. offer to split the Oregon territory at the forty-ninth parallel, a
split that would have put Puget Sound firmly in U.S. hands. By late August,
Polk was telling his cabinet that in reply, Washington would revert to its demand for the whole of Oregon up to the 54-degree 40-minute line of latitude.
Secretary of State Buchanan felt that this would lead to war with Britain. Polk
stated firmly that he was willing to take that chance.[94] As was to become clear
over the next four months, Polk had no real interest in territory above the
forty-ninth parallel, notwithstanding his party's public stand that it wanted to
extend the United States up to Russia's Alaskan panhandle (the "Fifty-four
forty or fight" line from the 1844 election). But he did want perception of his
resolve to meet the party's demands to help him coerce the British to back
down and accept the forty-ninth parallel as the final settlement.[95]

On September 16 the cabinet met to discuss the recent internal instability
in Mexico. Polk agreed that the United States should reopen diplomatic relations with Mexico and send John Slidell to Mexico City to negotiate the purchase of California and New Mexico. Importantly, the mission was to be kept
secret from the British and French to prevent their thwarting of U.S. objectives.[96] Polk's anxieties about California were rising. On October 11 the administration received an alarming report from Larkin written some three months
earlier. An expedition had left Acapulco, led by a European and financed by
the Hudson's Bay Company, whose apparent purpose was to reimpose Mexican rule over California with the support of British financing. "There is no
doubt," Larkin wrote, that the force being sent to California was being sent "by
the instigation of the English Government, under the plea that the American
settlers in California want to revolutionize the Country."[97] Larkin's report
overlapped with a report from William Parrott, Polk's main secret agent in

Mexico City, that "everything coming from California excites great interest here in English circles," and that on such occasions, the British legation is "all alive" with activity.[98]

By October, Polk and Buchanan were working confidentially with a key player in the Senate—Thomas Hart Benton of Missouri, a man keen on expansion in both Oregon and California. On October 24, Polk met with Benton and assured him that he would fight hard for Oregon, employing the Monroe Doctrine principle that there should be no additional foreign colonization in the area. The conversation then turned to California. Polk's diary account that day is revealing:

> I remarked [to Benton] that Great Britain had her eye on that country and intended to possess it if she could, but that the people of the United States would not willingly permit California to pass into the possession of any new colony planted by Great Britain or any foreign monarchy, and that in reasserting Mr. Monroe's doctrine I had California and the fine bay of San Francisco as much in view as Oregon.

Benton replied that he agreed with this, and that the same logic applied to Cuba.[99]

This was certainly not the first time Polk had expressed a belief that the United States had to act forcefully should Britain show signs of moving against a key territory in North America. In 1844 he had publicly argued that should the United States not annex Texas, "there is [an] imminent danger that she will become a dependency if not a colony of Great Britain," an event that no American "anxious for the safety and prosperity of this country could permit to occur without the most strenuous resistance."[100] By October–November 1845, mobilized by the mid-October reports, Polk and Buchanan prepared to face any British move against California with the equivalent level of resistance. Their strategy was a simple one: to try to buy California and New Mexico if they could, but failing that, to seize them by force before Britain could act.

On October 16–17, Polk made two important moves as part of this overall strategy. He completed a reply to be sent to Larkin, instructing him to avoid direct involvement in the struggle between native Californians (mostly American immigrants) and the Mexican government but letting Larkin know that if the Californians won independence and wanted to join the Union, Washington would move quickly to accommodate them. Buchanan wrote a companion letter to Larkin, telling him more boldly to "exert the greatest possible vigilance in discovering and defeating any attempt, which may be made by foreign governments to acquire a control over [California]."[101] Polk that day also instructed that Commodore Robert Stockton, a known expansionist, be sent to join Commodore John Sloat off the west coast of Mexico with updated instructions. Recall that in June 1845, Polk had notified Sloat that his fleet should seize California in the event that war was declared against Mexico. Polk's new instructions reinforced the spirit of his previous ones. But they also now indicated that Sloat need not wait for an official declaration of war before acting.[102] By sending Stockton, Polk was not only making sure that Sloat understood the full significance of his orders, but that he would act quickly, even if Sloat had only received preliminary reports of U.S.-Mexican border clashes.[103] Polk clearly understood the importance of his new moves. To make sure that both Larkin and Sloat received their instructions, he dispatched a young marine, Lieutenant Archibald Gillespie, to carry a second copy of the instructions to both Larkin and Sloat, just in case. In a wonderful bit of geopolitical cloak-and-dagger, Gillespie was to cross Mexico posing as an ailing Bostonian merchant, give the Stockton message to Sloat at Acapulco, and then turn north to meet with Larkin.[104]

It is important to note that Polk did all of this prior to dispatching Slidell to Mexico in November to negotiate the purchase of California and New Mexico from the Mexican government. Clearly, Polk saw that Mexico might be unwilling to sell California, and he had to be prepared to move quickly to his second option, acquiring the territory by force. In a revealing private communication to Slidell in November, Polk told Slidell that should he fail to achieve a satisfactory solution, hopefully before Congress adjourned in March 1846, "we must take redress for the wrongs and injuries we have suffered into our own hands, and I will call on Congress to provide the proper remedies."[105] California and its ports were the focus, not New Mexico. Polk told Slidell that he was "exceedingly desirous to acquire California." And while Slidell was to offer up to $25 million for California and only $5 million for New Mexico, "[I] am ready to take the whole responsibility, if it cannot be had for less, of paying the whole amount" of $30 million just for California.

Buchanan's instructions to Slidell reinforced this prioritization. Buchanan noted that "both Britain and France have designs upon California," and that Washington had to act to prevent California "from becoming either a British or a French colony." Securing San Francisco Bay and its harbor was "all important to the United States," and "money would be no object when compared with the value of the acquisition."[106] Thus it is clear that even if the South's drive for the extension of slavery was at least a reinforcing motive for the annexation of Texas, the same cannot be said for Polk's policy in 1845–46. Polk was thinking about the long-term commercial competitiveness of the United States vis-à-vis Britain, not about sectional interests. Indeed, the fact that California would almost certainly become a free-soil state, hurting the South's relative power in the Senate, reinforces that the slavery question was a constraining, not a propelling, force in this case—because it held Polk back, his fear of

America's commercial future in the Pacific had to be that much stronger before he could contemplate acting.

Having set the stage for either the purchase of California or for a war to grab it, Polk spent most of November and December on the still-simmering problem of Oregon. Buchanan was still very much concerned that the dispute would lead to war with Britain, a view reinforced by Polk's meeting with an agent of the British company Baring Brothers in late October. At this meeting, which Polk saw as an effort by the British to ascertain his intentions regarding Oregon, the agent had intimated that war was likely if the United States continued to seek the whole of the Oregon territory.[107] In a cabinet meeting on November 29, Buchanan suggested that many in Congress would accept a deal splitting Oregon at the forty-ninth parallel; otherwise, war was a danger. Polk, however, maintained that there was a danger in compromising at this stage in the negotiations.[108]

This divide on strategy between Polk and Buchanan would continue for the next two months. Polk would use his first annual address to Congress in December to chastise "European governments" for their "vain diplomatic arts and intrigues" in North America against "that system of self-government which seems natural to our soil, and which will ever resist foreign interference." American growth had triggered a European effort at a "balance of power" against the United States, Polk argued, but his administration would resist any attempt to colonize new territories in pursuit of that policy.[109] Buchanan himself was forced by Polk to maintain a hard-line stance in negotiations. Yet by early 1846, the British were starting to bite back. London had already been increasing naval allotments through 1845 in response to Polk's belligerent attitude. Now Prime Minister Robert Peel and his ministers decided to show that Britain could not be pushed around by the American upstart. In January, Peel argued in Parliament for a continuation of the naval buildup. On February 3, Foreign Minister Lord Aberdeen had a harshly worded exchange with U.S. minister Louis McLane, and McLane communicated this new British tone to Washington. When McLane's report and other news from London arrived on February 20–21, it was a mixed bag. On the positive side, the Crown had made a conciliatory speech in Parliament in late January. Peel was also pushing hard for the repeal of the Corn Laws, which from the U.S. perspective meant the British government was temporarily constrained by domestic politics. On the negative side was McLane's report of Aberdeen's new threatening tone in his discussions of February 3.

On February 24, Polk called a cabinet meeting to discuss the news from London. Buchanan took the opportunity to push for an idea that he had been promoting since December—namely, that the British government be immediately informed that if it were to resubmit its old suggestion to divide Oregon at the forty-ninth parallel, the President would send it directly to the Senate for its "advice". Polk had warmed to this idea over the previous month, and the cabinet meeting ended with agreement to pursue it.[110] If the British were seen as offering a compromise to avoid war and the Senate recommended its acceptance, Polk would have political cover from the remaining hard-line congressmen that still demanded the whole of the Oregon territory.

Polk was clearly now worried about the risk of a military clash with Britain that might occur just as he was bringing the United States into war with Mexico. But with the whole of the West Coast up for grabs, he felt compelled to continue with his risky policy. The British envoy Richard Pakenham had harshly rejected the idea of splitting Oregon back in the summer of 1845. With Polk only suggesting to London that he would accept the Senate's "advice" should the British reintroduce the forty-ninth parallel option, the British might smell a rat and decide to reject such a deal once again. But Polk was willing to stay on the slippery slope to war—and indeed pull both parties closer to the abyss—in order to force Britain to back down on its original demands for continued access to the Columbia River. He had been pushing since his December annual message for a congressional abrogation of the joint occupation treaty. In late February, the House finally passed such a bill. After a heated two-month debate, the Senate followed suit in late April and word was sent to London.

The abrogation of the treaty meant that in a year the Americans could lay sole claim to the area now inhabited by the thousands of American settlers coming across the Oregon Trail. This policy tactic was self-consciously provocative, and the months from February to May were filled with tension and a widespread fear of a slide into another disastrous war with the superior British state. (The calamities of the War of 1812, including the invasion of New York and Maryland in 1814 and the burning of Washington, were still fresh in most Americans' minds.) It was only in early June 1846—after war with Mexico had been declared—that word was received that the British had finally agreed to propose the division of Oregon at the forty-ninth parallel and to accept time-limited access to the Columbia River. Polk immediately forwarded the British offer to the Senate and the Senate quickly advised that it be signed as a formal treaty. On June 15, 1846, with the Senate ratification of the treaty, the Oregon crisis was finally over. The resolution of the crisis gave Polk what he most wanted: access to the harbors of Puget Sound. But it is significant that to get it, he was willing to run a very real risk of war with Britain. The commercial significance of Puget Sound for trade with Asia and the need to keep Britain from controlling its valuable harbors drove Polk's risk-taking behavior.

What is perhaps most remarkable is that Polk kept the pressure on Britain even when he knew in February–March that war with Mexico was inevitable—and that the United States had to be the one to provoke it. Slidell had arrived in Mexico City in December thinking he could begin negotiations on the purchase of California and New Mexico. The shaky Mexican government under President José Herrera refused to treat Slidell as an official envoy of the U.S. government until Washington resolved the main outstanding issue between the two states: namely, the annexation of Texas. Slidell wrote Polk and Buchanan of his problems and of the corruption and instability of the Mexican regime. Indeed, in late December the Herrera government fell to a coup by General Mariano Paredes, and Paredes quickly made clear that the United States had to give Texas back to Mexico before any other negotiations could proceed.[111]

In the midst of these pessimistic developments, Polk took a momentous step. On January 13, he reiterated instructions to General Zachary Taylor that Taylor should march his troops stationed at Corpus Christi to the northern bank of the Rio Grande. He also ordered the U.S. Gulf Squadron to position itself off Vera Cruz. There is no diplomatic paper trail to help us understand his reasoning for these directives. But given everything else that came before and given what followed in late April, only one conclusion seems plausible: Polk believed that if this move did not coerce Mexico into quickly selling California and New Mexico, he could provoke the Mexicans into firing the first shot and thus would be poised to implement his second choice, a war to grab what he could not buy. Even if Mexico were to accept the loss of Texas, both sides knew that the area between the Rio Grande and the Nueces rivers was in dispute.

To have asked Taylor's forces to occupy Corpus Christi on the southern bank of the Nueces was provocative enough, since the city was already in territory Mexico claimed as its own. But to then have instructed Taylor to advance deliberately down to the Rio Grande—that is, to move further into Mexican territory knowing that Mexico had not yet even accepted the loss of Texas—was only asking for trouble. As one of Taylor's lieutenants, Ulysses S. Grant, later recorded, Taylor's troops were being asked to serve as bait in order "to provoke hostilities." Mexico had shown "no willingness to come up to the Nueces to drive the invaders from her soil, [so] it became necessary for the 'invaders' to approach to within a convenient distance to be struck." Another of Taylor's lieutenants noted that the U.S. move served as a "pretext for taking California" and as much of Mexican territory as America might choose.[112]

What transpired in late April and early May is perhaps even more instructive of Polk's Machiavellian strategy. Taylor received his instructions in February and by mid-April he had crossed the disputed territory and positioned his small army at Laredo, directly across the Rio Grande from the Mexican forces. Given the time lag in communications, Polk in late April still had no idea what was transpiring in this standoff. Earlier that month, on April 9, Polk had sat down with Senator Benton to privately inform him that the Slidell mission was a failure. Both agreed on the "steps proper to be taken . . . especially if the principal powers of Europe should attempt to force a Foreign Prince on a throne in Mexico".[113] On April 18, Polk met with Calhoun, and told him that relations with Mexico had "reached a point where we could not stand still but must assert our rights firmly." Thus, he saw "no alternative but strong measures towards Mexico."[114]

Three days later he informed the cabinet that the situation could not stay the way it was, and that he should send a message to Congress "decidedly recommending that strong measures be adopted to take the redress of our complaints against [the Mexican government] into our own hands." He argued his case "at some length" and achieved what he saw as an initial concurrence from the cabinet. A week later, on April 28, he secured unanimous cabinet support.[115] This set the stage for Polk and Buchanan's preparation of a message to Congress detailing Mexican "wrongs" against the United States and arguing for the necessity of war. On May 3, still with no word from Taylor, Polk again met privately with Benton to sound him out on the Mexican question. Benton was worried about war with Britain over Oregon, and he advised Polk to wait on Mexico until the Oregon question was resolved. Polk dismissed Benton's concerns, telling him that he had "ample cause of war" and promising only to wait until Slidell, who was expected momentarily, arrived back in Washington. After Slidell's return a few days later, the envoy met with Polk on May 8 and told him that there was "but one course . . . left": namely, war with Mexico. Polk agreed, stating that it was only a matter of time before he would make his case to Congress on the subject.[116]

The next day, Saturday, May 9, is perhaps the single most revealing day of the crisis. Polk met with his cabinet during the day, and after a full discussion of the Mexican question, cabinet members unanimously agreed that should word be received that Mexican forces had fired on Taylor's army, the president should immediately send his message to Congress. Polk argued against any delay, stating that no word had yet been received of open aggression by the Mexican army, but that "the danger was imminent that such acts would be committed." The United States thus "had ample cause of war" and "it was impossible that we could stand in *statu quo*, or that I could remain silent much longer." Indeed, it was his "duty" to send a message to Congress immediately— namely, by the coming Tuesday, three days away. Discussion ensued, with debate focusing on the question of whether the message should include an explicit declaration of war. Everyone except Secretary of the Navy George Bancroft agreed with Polk's position that it should. Bancroft was not against war; he simply wanted to wait for word of Mexican attacks to help justify the

U.S. invasion. The formerly cautious Buchanan sided with Polk, noting that while he would prefer a declaration of war after such word was received, "as matters stood we had ample cause of war against Mexico."[117]

As things turned out, later that day at 6:00 P.M., after the cabinet had adjourned, word was received that Mexico had indeed crossed the Rio Grande in late April and attacked Taylor's forces, killing a number of men. The news spread like wildfire through Washington the next day. Polk now had the perfect pretext to present his message to Congress containing the call for a declaration of war, and he did so on Monday, May 11, a day earlier than planned. The message argued quite disingenuously that "after repeated menaces, Mexico has passed the boundary of the United States, has invaded our territory, and shed American blood upon the American soil." That night, the House of Representatives passed the war measure by an overwhelming margin, 173 to 14, and the next day the Senate followed suit 42 to 2.[118]

We thus see just how strong Polk's drive to acquire California was. Following the failure of the Slidell mission, he was willing to initiate war against Mexico even without the pretext of Mexico having fired the first shot. It is instructive that most of his cabinet officials felt this pretext was worth waiting for. It was Polk who convinced them to proceed without it. It was only by sheer luck that word of the Mexican attack on Taylor's forces arrived three days before Polk was to present his war measure to Congress. Had this news arrived after that Tuesday, there is little question that Polk would have sent his war measure up to Capitol Hill without it.

In the face of this evidence, three conclusions are warranted. First, Polk ordered Taylor's forces to move down to the Rio Grande in order to provoke Mexico into a war should they fail to coerce Mexico into the sale of some forty percent of its territory. Second, by May Polk was so keen to proceed—and so fearful of a move in the West by Britain—that he was willing to forgo the pretext and move straight to war if he had to. Third, Polk's primary objective in all this was to acquire California, and he would risk a costly war not only with Mexico, but potentially with Britain, to get it.

This last point is reinforced by what happened in a heated cabinet discussion the day after the Senate passed the declaration of war measure. With the Oregon crisis still bubbling along—notice of the Congress's ending of joint occupation had only gone out in late April, and word of British reaction would not be expected for weeks—Secretary of State Buchanan strongly reiterated his worries about a war with Britain. In his view, if the United States did not deny that California was a territorial aim in the Mexican war when questioned by British leaders, war with Britain was "almost certain." Indeed, France would probably join Britain, since neither power could sit back and allow California to be absorbed by the United States. Polk responded that California's acquisition must be included in any peace terms as part of Mexico's payment for past wrongs, and that as president he would not "permit or tolerate any intermeddling of any European Power on this continent." Indeed, before making any pledge not to take California, he would "let the war . . . with England come and would take the whole responsibility."[119] This exchange nicely summarizes key aspects of Polk's orientation over the past year. Following in Monroe's footsteps, he would not let any European power, especially Britain, involve itself in North American territorial questions. If he had to risk war with Britain and France to keep these powers out and ensure that the United States controlled the key ports of California, so be it.

In sum, then, we have seen that the Oregon crisis and the war with Mexico were, like the Texas question, driven primarily by American leaders' fears of the future. Without forceful action, the United States might lose control of these areas to Britain or other European great powers, to the detriment of long-term U.S. economic growth and security. Alternative explanations fall flat or can only explain parts of the overall story. There is no way to explain, using sectional or personal interest arguments, why two Southern presidents with agrarian roots would be so obsessed with Oregon and California from 1841 to 1846. Neither Tyler nor Polk believed that Oregon and California would be conducive to the expansion of slavery or useful as places to grow traditional Southern crops such as cotton, tobacco, or rice. And when these free-soil territories became free-soil states, they would shift the balance of power in the Senate against the South. We are left with only one good causal explanation for the executive's behavior: the ports of the West Coast had to be kept out of British hands if the United States were to continue to develop its future economic power and its trade with Asia. The fact that the economic benefits from such expanded trade would accrue to Northern industrial and shipping interests more than Southern plantation owners only reinforces the argument.

We also cannot argue that Tyler and Polk were simply responding to public pressure from Westerners and Northerners who saw the future potential of the region. When Tyler took over after President Harrison's death in 1841, he quickly alienated Northerners and many Westerners such as Henry Clay by distancing himself from the platforms of his own Whig party. As for Polk, he was clearly his own man in office. Like Tyler, he had no interest in running for a second term, and thus little reason to kowtow to Northern and Western public opinion. Moreover, as with the debates over the annexation of Texas, it was not at all clear, given the risks of war with Britain, that the majority of Southerners and Northerners supported the acquisitions of Oregon and California. Both presidents knew that securing majorities in both houses would be difficult, as Polk discovered when he tried to get the Congress to repeal the joint occupation treaty in early 1846. Midwesterners and their new enthusiasm for "manifest destiny" would not be enough. Thus, Polk had to adopt a carefully calculated strategy of pressuring both Britain and Mexico to meet his demands, knowing he had to be ready for war should peaceful negotiation fail. In the end, Polk's strategy succeeded wonderfully. He was able to make it appear that Mexico was the aggressor so that he could move to absorb California before any European power did. And he was able to coerce and cajole Britain into splitting the Oregon territory such that the valuable Puget Sound would fall into the American lap. Few U.S. presidents have played the geopolitical game of brinksmanship and coercion with such aplomb. But this should not blind us to the incredible risks they sometimes take to secure a strong commercial future for the country.

## Conclusion

This chapter has demonstrated that shifting trade expectations, combined with the anticipation of growing dependence and rising American military power, drove many of the key decisions of American foreign policy in its first sixty years. In the 1790s, presidents Washington and Adams calibrated their approaches to Britain and France based on the U.S. need for continued trade with Britain and the West Indies (even as the country expanded its realm-one strength through westward expansion). In the process, they used diplomacy to avoid a war with London (the Jay Treaty), even though the move led to the French economic retaliation that produced the Quasi-War of 1798–1800. Jefferson's worry that a French reoccupation of the Louisiana Territory would restrict trade down the Mississippi pushed this cautious geopolitician to threaten Napoleon with war should the French dictator prove unwilling to sell New Orleans and its environs to the Americans. Madison reluctantly took his country into war in 1812 as a response to continued British Orders in Council that were destroying the economic viability of the American state. In the 1840s, a series of crises over Texas, Oregon, and California—each one of them driven by fears of British encroachments into areas American officials understood to be essential for long-term trade and economic growth—led presidents Tyler and Polk to turn to hard-line policies to ensure U.S. access to these vital areas.

Dynamic realism did not work perfectly across the board. The grabbing of West and East Florida from Spain from 1810 to 1819 was probably less a function of immediate commercial threat than of a territorial need to secure the American southern flank (although the 1819 treaty did also help secure the U.S. claim to Oregon territory to help extend commerce to the Far East). Commercial forces were secondary during the disputes with British Canada from 1839 to 1842. The temporary postponement of the Oregon question did serve American commercial interests in the Pacific, since the United States had a much easier time placing its own settlers and traders on the ground there. But the larger dispute over the border with Canada had more to do with domestic and personal drives than external trade factors.

Yet the dynamic realist approach showed strong explanatory power relative to liberal unit-level arguments across the broad sweep of time from 1790 to 1846. Considering that the Jeffersonian vision dominated American domestic politics after the collapse of the Federalist party's popularity following the election of 1800, this result is particularly noteworthy. It suggests that a realist-based logic focusing on the changing expectations of the future trade environment and their impact of perceptions of long-term power and security can explain the conditions under which systemic pressures will drive actors to aggressive, expansionist policies, even when their ideological predilections might otherwise incline them to peace. Against a base-line drive to expand the American economic power sphere in North America to build a foundation for long-term economic growth, U.S. officials proved highly aware of the threats to the commercial basis for this growth. When those threats were minimal, they cooperated with European powers such as Britain and with the Mexican governments. The fact that the British nation was still America's main antagonist into the 1840s, despite the diminishing level of cultural differences, demonstrates that uncertainty about the future can drive aggressive behavior even when other states are relatively similar in character type, as Britain increasingly was after the political reforms of 1832 and the orientation toward freer trade by the mid-1840s. Fears of slowing growth due to the other's commercial and imperial policies, most obviously in 1812 and 1846, can lead to war even when nations see themselves as similar in religion, ethnic background, and even liberal ideology.

# 5

# American Foreign Policy from 1850 to the Spanish-American War of 1898

THE PERIOD after the Mexican-American War until 1890 is generally seen by historians as a quiet period of retrenchment in U.S. foreign policy, when Washington turned away from vigorous territorial expansion to focus on issues at home. America's true insertion into global politics, from this perspective, only occurred in the late 1890s with the outbreak of the Spanish-American War and the acquisition of an overseas colonial empire in the Philippines and Guam. To a large degree, this picture is accurate. But as Fareed Zakaria has emphasized, this does not mean that leaders and officials in the U.S. executive were not keen to continue expansion after 1848; for the most part, they were, and in ways consistent with the idea that the larger the U.S. commercial sphere beyond the continental states and territories, the greater the American long-term economic and military power. The problem was rather that the U.S. executive after the turmoil of the Civil War was greatly constrained by domestic politics from pursuing an activist agenda on the foreign front. Only after the executive branch had gained a semblance of domestic power was it able to embark on the imperialism of the 1890s.[1]

This chapter will use Zakaria's work as a springboard for the exploration of the relative importance of trade and economic dependence in the shaping of U.S. foreign policy in the second half of the nineteenth century. His book is one of the few that uses international relations theory to explain this broad time period, and it is certainly the most prominent.[2] Zakaria argues that the domestic constraints were a function of the U.S. constitution, which allowed the legislature to check executive power. Drawing from both offensive realism and neoclassical realism, he contends that as the United States grew in overall economic power, it should have expanded territorially regardless of external threats, but could not do so until the legislature's power was reduced by the late 1880s. Insofar as my logic asserts that great powers are driven by anarchy to seek to expand their economic power spheres but may be constrained from doing so by domestic politics, it would agree with Zakaria's overall explanation for why the United States did not fight any external wars from 1850 until the 1890s. In particular, the need to resolve the North-South dispute over slavery, the reconstruction period after the Civil War, and the desire to consolidate gains in the West make it clear that expansion had to be off the table in the short term, even without considering the increased power of the legislature after 1865. For similar reasons, trade with the outside world also remained largely flat, and even as the industrial North grew after 1875, the expansion of the railways system meant that north-south and east-west trade *within* the United States was much more important than finding markets and cheap raw materials abroad.

To the extent that the period up to 1890 largely revolved around the preservation and consolidation of internal strength rather than the expansion of U.S. trade with the outside world, arguments revolving around commerce and the development of a state's economic power sphere, such as those discussed in chapters 1 and 2, are unlikely to have as much causal force as they do when the domestic situation is stable. Consequently, this chapter will move quickly through this period in order to focus on the bigger question hanging over the historiography of the late nineteenth century: namely, why the United States shifted from a relatively uninvolved position on the world stage up to 1890 to plunging into the global imperialist struggle, marked in particular by the initiation of war against Spain in 1898. This war led to the acquisition of America's first overseas colonies (in the Philippines, Guam, and Puerto Rico) and the greatly enhanced presence of U.S. forces in the Caribbean/Central American region. For a country that was born in a fight against colonial oppression, this move to imperialism was both morally surprising and politically controversial, and it foreshadowed the emergence of the United States as a true "global" power, something that would be solidified by U.S. entry into World War I (chapter 6). What explains this dramatic change in American foreign policy?

Because of the relative nonactivity of U.S. foreign policy until the 1890s, this chapter will proceed in a different manner from the other chapters of this book. Instead of focusing on how falling expectations of future trade interacted with the need to expand the nation's economic power sphere to drive leaders to adopt hard-line *behaviors*, including the initiation of war, I will show how these commercial factors gave leaders *the incentive* for such behaviors, even if they could not fully act upon them for domestic reasons. I will agree with Zakaria that the simple need to hedge against future problems pushed the executives to desire expansion, even in the absence of immediate threats. In this sense, the 1850 to 1890 period nicely illustrates the value of positing an offensive realist taproot within the larger dynamic realist paradigm: Even when threats are low, leaders are *propelled by uncertainty regarding the ability to maintain access and long-term economic growth* to seek opportunities to expand their state's economic power spheres as a hedge against future threats. But the practical execution of these desires will be *constrained* by both anticipated re-action of other great powers and resistance from domestic factions at home. When those constraints were low, as with U.S. expansion against divided Na-tive American groups, that expansion proceeded with alacrity. When those constraints were significant, as with attempted expansion in the Caribbean during the tumultuous 1850s, expansionist desires were put on hold. Dynamic realism can therefore explain the propelling forces behind U.S. strategic think-ing, even if liberal domestic-level factors explain why a more expansionist policy was not undertaken.

This chapter will show that changes in executive interest in expansion across the latter part of the century were primarily a function of changing ex-ternal threats to commerce, not simply growing dependence levels tied to growing state power. The initiation of war against Spain in 1898—part of a general shift in policy that included pressing forward with the absorption of Hawaii the same year—is the clearest example of this. The administration of President William McKinley initiated war against a fellow liberal democratic state not simply because it saw an opportunity for expansion, but because the European powers represented growing threats to U.S. commerce in both the Caribbean/Latin American region (realm one) and in the Far East (realm two). War with Spain would consolidate the U.S. ability to protect and develop its trade with these areas in the face of these new and unnerving threats.

This does not mean that the expanding and safeguarding of America's com-mercial sphere was the only thing shaping McKinley's decision-making. McKinley was a master politician, and he well understood that his domestic popularity would be enhanced by a quick war that both protected business interests in Cuba and ended a humanitarian crisis that had been played up by newspapers (the "yellow press") across the country. Yet in assessing the rela-tive causal salience of these differing and reinforcing motives for hard-line behavior, the timing of his move against Spain must be seen as significant. The crisis in Cuba had been going on since 1895. Yet McKinley only acted in early 1898 to mobilize his country for war. As the chapter shows, this shift corre-sponds directly to the increased efforts of European powers, particularly Brit-ain, Russia, and Germany, to increase their commercial control over trade in the Far East and with China in particular. Protecting and enhancing U.S. com-mercial penetration of this area, as well as establishing the dominance of the Caribbean and of any isthmus canal needed to grow America's Pacific trade was fundamental to McKinley's decision to act—indeed, to *create* for the first time a true overseas commercial empire on the British model (the model that Alfred Thayer Mahan had described so well in his highly influential book from 1890, *The Influence of Sea Power Upon History, 1660–1783*).

American concerns about the Far East and the Caribbean were for the most part about the character types of the adversaries in question. Liberal English-speaking Britain in the 1890s was often viewed as just as much a threat as Germany and Japan, and this reality continued into the early twentieth century, as the next chapter will show. Nonetheless, in 1898 Germany's more authoritarian regime type and its status-driven Kaiser did add to fears that Berlin was serious about grabbing the Philippines as a colony for its trade expansion in the region. This helped convince McKinley that he could not just grab Manila as a jump-off point for the China trade but would have to take the whole island. Domestic motives, including reelection, certainly played some role in the president's decision-making that year. But his careful manipulation of the crisis from January to April 1898 and his ongoing ties to Mahanian expansionists such as Teddy Roosevelt and Henry Cabot Lodge indicate that the exigencies of U.S. global trade were, in the end, the most critical part of his decision for actual war, and to why he rejected Spanish compromises that would have satisfied most of his domestic objectives.

## The Dynamics of American Foreign Policy from 1850 to 1890

With the consolidation of control over Texas, Oregon, and California complete by 1848, U.S. executives turning their attention to more far-off threats in Asia, the Pacific, Latin America, and the Caribbean. The constant concern of U.S. executives from 1848 to 1890 and beyond was to prevent, when possible, any European power from controlling the trade and naval routes to and through these areas. This concern transcended party affiliation and leader personal disposition across these four decades. From 1847 to 1860, for example, U.S. leaders worried about British efforts to control trade access through the Caribbean and to build an isthmus canal through either Nicaragua or the Columbian province of Panama. In 1845, the British government provoked U.S. fears by declaring a protectorate over the Mosquito Coast, an ill-defined 800-mile coastal region extending from what is today northern Honduras to Nicaragua. In 1847–48, as the Yucatan Peninsula in western Mexico underwent a revolution, American leaders considered occupying the region to forestall a British move against the peninsula (the end of the revolt in 1848 rendered the question moot).[3] And from 1847 on, it appeared once again that Britain, as Frederick Merk summarizes, had "designs on Cuba," an island seen since the days of Jefferson as critical to U.S. trade access to the Caribbean.[4]

At issue was the larger U.S.-British battle to control world trade. At the center of it all was the question of an isthmus canal linking the Pacific and the Atlantic. Because both Britain and America were contemplating such a canal, the British protectorate over the Mosquito Coast was seen as a direct challenge. President Polk before he left office negotiated an alliance with Nicaragua to counter Britain. Out of fear of war with the British, his successors Zachary Taylor and, upon Taylor's death, Millard Fillmore pulled back from this commitment. By 1850, Washington and London had negotiated the Clayton-Bulwer Treaty in which both sides agreed that they would not seek exclusive control over any isthmus canal nor colonize any part of Central America. This treaty, however, was only a stopgap measure to keep London at bay until the United States could secure the canal region for itself. As Taylor and Fillmore's agent to Nicaragua, Ephraim Squier, wrote publicly in 1852, the control of Nicaragua and any canal was key to the "rule of the East," that "vast and incalculable trade upon which is mainly based the maritime power of England." Britain wanted to snatch Nicaragua, but if Washington moved first and kept it free from foreign threats, the United States could "gird the world as with a hoop," thereby dominating both Atlantic and Pacific trade.[5] This foundational logic would dominate U.S. thinking on the canal issue for the next fifty years, until Washington finally convinced the British to give America exclusive control over any future canal.[6]

Cuba and which power would dominate it was also a critical geopolitical question for the second half of the nineteenth century. Even prior to 1850, American presidents had understood the island's importance. President John Quincy Adams, aware of its strategic and commercial value and worried about British intentions, had sought to buy it in the 1820s. For very similar reasons, President Polk made a similar effort in 1848.[7] In both cases, Spain had refused to sell this last significant remnant of its once mighty American empire. In the 1850s, the Cuban question became embroiled in the vicious debates over slavery that were tearing the country apart. It was now no longer simply a matter of Cuba's economic and geopolitical importance. The 1850s were a time when control of the U.S. Senate was up for grabs and both sections were eager to add new states, either slave or "free-soil," to their side.[8] Southern politicians saw the absorption of Cuba as a way to add to their total and avoid a loss of internal power. Filibuster efforts out of the South in the early 1850s to grab Cuba by force were abject failures. An attempt under the Democratic president Franklin Pierce to purchase Cuba for up to $130,000,000 was also thwarted. Northerners reacted sharply to leaked details of the government's apparent plan to take Cuba by force should Spain turn down the offer to buy.[9] In the end, Spain refused the offer and Cuba's status was once again left in limbo. Republican president James Buchanan (1857–61) again sought to purchase Cuba for strategic reasons, but the intensifying sectional division and Northerners' fear of Cuba becoming a slave state made such a move domestically impossible. Cuba in the 1850s was not like California in 1846 or even Texas in 1845, in which security fears could overcome sectional quarrels to create a united front to forestall Britain. Cuba seemed more important to the internal balance of power in the Senate than to the economic balance of power in the hemisphere. In the face of such a constraining force, nothing was done.

Things were different in the Pacific since there was no possibility of changing the slave/non-slave balance in the Senate. Both Whig and Democratic presidents during the 1850s sought to increase U.S. penetration of the untapped markets of Asia. Fearful of a British head-start, President Tyler had secured the opening of five trading ports in China in 1844, mirroring a similar treaty signed between London and Beijing in 1842. The so-called Chinese treaty system that emerged was reinforced by the British and French treaties imposed on China by force in 1857–58 but extended to America through Washington's most favored nation status. As we shall see, it was the breakdown of treaty system guarantees by the 1890s that helped push the United States into a new round of forceful self-assertion and war by 1898. But the key point to remember is that by the end of the 1850s, in the words of John King Fairbank, the "spirit of the Open Door" in China was already in place, with Washington piggybacking on the coercive diplomacy of European powers.[10]

Of more immediate anxiety for U.S. leaders in the early 1850s was the case of Japan, which had been closed to all but some limited Dutch trade for two and half centuries. The potential for trade was thus enticing to American and British eyes. Yet for the Americans arriving from the east, Japan was also strategic. It not only was reputed to possess large deposits of coal essential for refueling, but the Americans also believed that if another country controlled its waters, it could restrict U.S. access to the huge China market and to Southeast Asia. Whig President Millard Fillmore and his secretary of state Daniel Webster sent Commodore Matthew Perry to Japan in 1852 in order to secure coaling stations and to seek a limited opening to trade. To ensure he could act in the national interest, Perry was allowed to rewrite his instructions to suit the situation.[11] Perry understood that Britain had already helped the United States by opening up China. But he worried that with secure ports at Hong Kong and Singapore, Britain already possessed "the most important points in the East India and China Seas," and thus had the power "of shutting us up at will, and controlling, the enormous trade of those seas."[12]

With his black ships, Perry was able through two visits to Edo (Tokyo) Bay in 1853 and 1854 to secure an agreement that gave the Americans most favored nation status and would allow American ships to resupply in two ports. A full commercial treaty would await the arrival of America's first envoy to Japan,

Townsend Harris, in 1856 (the treaty would be signed in July 1858). While Britain, Russia, and other powers would soon follow suit to establish trade relations with Japan, Perry and his ships had been the first in two centuries to successfully pry open the isolated nation. And Perry did so with the full support of both Whig and Democratic administrations. American executives, as in the pre-1850 period, thus proved more than willing to use coercive diplomacy to advance U.S. economic interests when they saw new threats to long-term trade and were not constrained by domestic factors.

There is little need to try to explain the lack of U.S. expansion from 1861–65. For Lincoln and his secretary of state William Seward, the Civil War made all foreign policy questions secondary to winning the internal conflict.[13] After the devastating war was finally over, Seward, serving now under Andrew Johnson, moved quickly to renew the executive branch's ongoing efforts to acquire more territory both to extend America's commercial reach and to frustrate British plans to contain U.S. economic growth.[14] The number of places that Seward sought to acquire or at least investigate for possible acquisition between 1866 and 1868 boggles the mind. The list includes Alaska, Iceland, Mexico, the Darien Islands, Hawaii, the Danish West Indies, Santo Domingo, Haiti, French Guiana, Cuba, and Puerto Rico. Reflecting the embedded attitudes of Americans since the revolution, Seward was highly suspicious of Britain's intentions, believing that even a few of these territories would improve U.S. commercial power projection capabilities while keeping Britain at bay. He saw Alaska and Hawaii as particularly important in this regard, given how far they might extend the U.S. presence in the Pacific westward.[15] That his expansionistic efforts were a failure except for the purchase of Alaska and the occupation of the uninhabited Midway Islands does reflect the constraining influence of domestic politics. But contrary to Zakaria's argument, this has less to do with the constitutional "power" of the legislature per se than with the fallout from the Civil War. The enormous costs of the war not only made most American legislators turn inward to focus on the rebuilding of the country but Lincoln's centralization of control during the war naturally led many legislators to desire to reassert some influence over foreign and domestic policy. Seward was not responding to immediate threats when he sought this huge expansion in the number of U.S. possessions. Instead, he was trying to build a larger economic and strategic realm that would ensure U.S. trade dominance into the future.[16]

The 1870s were a period of relative calm in American foreign policy. President Ulysses S. Grant (1869–77) and his successor Rutherford Hayes (1877–81) both pushed hard for a U.S.-controlled isthmus canal—in violation of the 1850 agreement with Britain—and for acquisitions in the Caribbean to ensure American domination of access routes. In 1869 Grant, to supplement his plans for a canal, took up Seward's effort to establish naval bases on Santo Domingo. His envoy to the island returned home with more than Grant had imagined—a treaty for the annexation of Santo Domingo, approved by the island nation's president. Grant pushed hard for ratification of the treaty. But the Senate, led by Charles Sumner, rejected it in 1870. As Zakaria himself notes, the rejection reflected the "economy and retrenchment" that pervaded Washington as a result of the phenomenal costs of war and the ongoing process of reconstruction.[17]

Grant's failure to annex Santo Domingo despite his strenuous efforts did chasten future executives. For the next quarter century, presidents would generally refrain from presenting large-scale and expensive annexation proposals to the Senate. But Zakaria's argument that the period from the 1870s to 1890 was one of "passivity and inactivity" on the part of the executive due to the strength of the legislature cannot stand.[18] New threats to U.S. commercial growth arose from a resurgence of European imperialism and shipping tied to the rise of a unified Germany as a global competitor and Europe's concomitant industrialization (see chapter 7). And when these threats became salient, U.S. presidents responded accordingly.

The Hawaiian Islands, strategically located at the center of Pacific trading routes, were one particular source of concern. The islands gained renewed emphasis in the early 1870s as Grant's secretary of state Hamilton Fish noted the waning of U.S. influence on the islands. Britain and France had been projecting power into the Pacific since the 1830s, and by the late 1840s Britain controlled New Zealand and the Fiji Islands and France had acquired Tahiti, among others. President Tyler had extended the Monroe Doctrine to Hawaii in 1842–43, and this had helped convince Britain and France to pull back from their evident efforts to control the islands. By the 1850s, however, there was growing perception in Washington that the Hawaiian kingdom was starting to tilt toward Britain. In their summary of the 1850–90 period, Rawi Abdelal and Jonathan Kirshner note that presidents after 1850 sought to bind Hawaii through trade agreements that would give preference to Hawaiian sugar to reduce the influence of other powers. Until the early 1870s, domestic sugar interests within the United States kept blocking any reciprocity treaties that were put forward.[19]

After the Senate's rejection of another reciprocity treaty in 1867, however, Hawaii started to explore connections with the British empire that would compensate for restricted access to America. By the early 1870s, even the Senate was starting to wake up to the potential threat. In 1875, by a vote of 51 to 12, the Senate ratified a reciprocity treaty that everyone understood was designed primarily to prevent Hawaii's shift toward the British sphere. Indeed, it was only through the inclusion of Senate amendments requiring Hawaii to deny other powers special access to its ports and territory that the treaty went through. In the 1880s, as the costs to domestic sugar producers (in lost sales) and to the U.S. government (in lost tariff revenue) became clear, pressures arose to deny the renewal of the reciprocity treaty. A foreign threat appeared on the horizon, however. Canada had just completed its transcontinental railways, and the *London Times* was reporting that Britain would push for a reciprocity treaty between Hawaii and Canada should America fail to renew theirs. The fear of Britain having economic sway in Hawaii caused senators to fall in line, and in January 1887 the Senate extended the treaty for another seven years.[20]

It is worth noting that this extension occurred under the administration of Grover Cleveland, the one president in the 1865–1900 period who was personally predisposed to resist U.S. expansionism. But as Cleveland told the country in his annual address in December 1886, he was unhesitatingly supporting the renewal of the treaty with Hawaii, since "those islands, on the highway of Oriental and Australasian traffic, are virtually an outpost of American commerce and a stepping stone to the growing trade of the Pacific." No one else could be allowed to control such a valuable outpost smack in the middle of the Pacific Ocean.[21] The Hawaiian case in 1887 is also significant since it again shows that when an external threat is clear and tangible, internal support for U.S. expansion can be garnered. As Abdelal and Kirshner note, the Senate added an amendment to the treaty giving the United States control of Pearl Harbor, something that would "end once and for all the question of political influence in Hawaii: keeping the Americans in and the Europeans out."[22]

A similar economic and strategic logic guided the United States into its involvement with the Samoan Islands in the 1870s. The Grant administration had sent out special agent Albert Steinberger in 1873 to investigate Samoa's value as a possible coaling station on the way to New Zealand and Australia. Steinberger reported that Samoan ports would greatly aid the development of U.S. trade in the area. Through the 1870s, however, both Germany and Britain were trying to establish their own port facilities on the islands. When Rutherford Hayes became president in 1877, he continued to project America's interest in Samoa's ports. By January 1878, he had secured a treaty granting the United States the right to build a coaling and naval station in Pago Pago in Western Samoa. In an executive session two weeks later, the Senate ratified the treaty.[23] We have almost no documentary evidence indicating why the Senate would so quickly approve a treaty that was very similar to one it had rejected only six years before. But the best explanation is probably the simplest one: the Senate was worried about German and British moves in the region and felt the urgency of countering them before it was too late.[24] Fear of foreign encroachment had pushed the Senate to overcome internal disputes in 1875 and approve the reciprocity treaty for Hawaii. It is hard to think of any other factor of sufficient force to have caused such an equivalent shift in the Senate's think-ing on the Samoan Islands in so short a time.

In the late 1870s and 1880s, the issue of an isthmus canal joining the Pacific and the Atlantic Oceans was suddenly thrust into the political limelight. Amer-ican financiers had completed a profitable 48-mile railway across Panama in 1855 to exploit the California goldrush. This railway, though clearly not as ef-ficient as a canal, facilitated the free flow of goods and individuals while giving the United States, in the words of Walter LaFeber, a "hammerlock on the isth-mus."[25] But in 1875 Ferdinand de Lesseps, the builder of the Suez Canal (which had opened in November 1869), announced his intention to build an isthmus canal. Over the next three years he gathered French financiers behind him to fund the project, and by 1878 appeared ready to begin building. President Hayes now faced the possibility of a foreign-controlled canal in America's backyard. The fact that the British government consolidated majority control of the shares of the Suez Canal in 1877–78 certainly did not help matters. De Lesseps sought to reassure President Hayes in a visit to the United States in early 1880 but Hayes refused to be placated. Extending the Monroe Doctrine to include privately financed construction projects, Hayes told Congress in March 1880 that any canal built on the isthmus, whether across Panama or Nicaragua, had to be "under American control." Indeed, such a canal would be "virtually a part of the coastline of the United States." It was thus an Ameri-can "right and duty" to "to assert and maintain such supervision and authority over any interoceanic canal . . . as will protect our national interests."[26]

When James Garfield took over from Hayes in 1881, he and Secretary of State James Blaine informed the British of their dissatisfaction with the 1850 Clayton-Bulwer treaty. In Blaine's view, the existing treaty would leave Britain with de facto control of any canal, given its naval superiority. Thus, the U.S. government "will not consent to perpetuate any treaty that impeaches our right and long-established claim to priority on the American continent."[27] The British government refused to renegotiate the treaty and continued to do so until 1901.

De Lesseps's slow progress over the next decade and its final failure by the late 1880s helped moderate immediate U.S. worries. Two things are worth noting, however. First, the fact that the Garfield administration would direct its concerns to the British government, even though De Lesseps's project was largely backed by French money, indicates the extent to which the executive feared the British might attempt another Suez-type coup, this time with much more negative implications for the United States. Second, it was becoming increasingly clear to the majority of U.S. politicians that without greater naval strength, America would always be the weaker cousin in any and all impor-tant negotiations with European great powers.

The problem with the U.S. navy had become clear immediately after the outbreak of the War of the Pacific in 1879 between Chile and Peru. In the conflict, both sides employed British-built destroyers that were more powerful than anything the United States possessed.[28] With a treasury now yielding strong surpluses, the parsimony of the reconstruction era was replaced by a new congressional willingness to support a navy commensurate with the huge increases in U.S. economic wealth. In 1881, Garfield and his navy secretary William Hunt held a series of policy meetings between influential legislators and naval officials. These meetings quickly concluded that the U.S. navy was in terrible shape, and that a modern steel and steam navy had to be built. After Republican president Garfield's death in late 1881, Chester Arthur gained congressional approval for the construction of a modern fleet that could hold its own against the European great powers, at least in terms of defending U.S. hemispheric interests. When Democrat Grover Cleveland took over in 1885, he continued Chester's buildup and, for the most part, received backing from a Democratic Congress. By the end of his first term in 1889, thirty ships totaling 100,000 tons were laid down. This was a big improvement, but the navy was still significantly inferior to the likes of the French navy, let alone the British navy. So when Benjamin Harrison took over in 1889 he and his navy secretary Benjamin Tracy embarked on an even larger program to bring the United States on par with some of the strongest navies in the world.[29] It was this naval buildup that would allow McKinley to quickly defeat the Spanish in the Philippines and Caribbean in 1898, and then to project power in the Far East in support of U.S. open door policies.

In this section, we have seen that events of the 1850 to 1890 period fit the larger dynamic realist logic of trade expectations theory quite well, but with some caveats. Because the major territorial issues in North America were resolved by the Mexican War and the Oregon treaty, the threats to U.S. commerce that emerged after 1848 were not as viscerally salient as the ones in the first half of the century. Accordingly, internal divisions, particularly the North-South divide on the slavery question in the 1850s and the Civil War and its reconstruction aftermath, made it much harder for presidents to extend national power to counter emerging but less manifest threats in the Pacific and Caribbean. Yet as these threats arose, a succession of presidents from both parties acted to deter European encroachments that would damage U.S. commercial and strategic interests and to project American political control out beyond the continental base. American presidents were able to prevent the British from dominating the potential canal routes across the isthmus. They agreed on the importance of penetrating East Asian markets, and thus supported the use of subtle coercive power to open ports in China, Japan, and, in the early 1880s, Korea. Presidents from both parties also saw the importance of Hawaii as a jump-off point to trade dominance in Asia. Fearing that the French and especially the British would try to control Hawaii for their own commercial ends, U.S. administrations sought and ultimately secured Senate-approved reciprocity treaties that kept the Europeans out and the Americans in.

Liberal arguments that focus on the peace-inducing effects of increased trade do quite poorly for this period. Dependence on trade tied to growing industrialization was increasing, but this only heightened U.S. executives' desires to project power and to fight for the country's interests. The very buildup in the navy in the 1880s shows that the United States was not going to rest on the hope that higher trade meant greater security cooperation between the great powers. In this regard, dynamic realism, through its stress upon a state's need to expand its economic power sphere as a foundation for future geopolitical power, does quite well across most of the 1850–90 period: the increase in U.S. global trade is nicely correlated with an overall push, at least by the executives, for greater control over ports and markets. This offensive realist aspect of dynamic realism helps explain two cases particularly well: Seward's efforts to acquire a vast number of new possessions from 1865 to 1867, and Grant's move to absorb Santo Domingo to help the United States manage trade in the Caribbean. The fact that these moves came at a time when Bismarck was fighting wars in Europe to consolidate the modern German state is not coincidental. Seward and Grant could see that Britain and France would be too occupied with European issues to resist any American efforts to expand the U.S. economic sphere. Dynamic realism can also explain the fluctuations in the *intensity* of executive interest in expansion and hard-line posturing over the four decades. Shifting trade expectations tied to changes in European involvement in the Pacific and the western hemisphere explain the on-again/off-again U.S. involvement on questions such as the isthmus canal, the Hawaiian and Samoan islands, and trade ties with China and Japan.

What is remarkable about this period is that despite domestic upheavals and an inadequate navy, the United States suffered no major geopolitical losses across the four decades, and in fact made a couple of very notable gains, including the acquisition of Alaska and the domination of Hawaii and its key naval port, Pearl Harbor. Effectively using Monroe Doctrine logic to project a resolve beyond actual American power, U.S. presidents had managed to deter any nascent British plans to build an isthmus canal or take control of a French-built one and dissuaded new European takeover bids in the Caribbean or against the Hawaiian Islands. Needless to say, the multipolarity of the larger global system helped: the British and French had their hands full during this period dealing with the rise of Prussia and, after 1870, a unified German state. The British in particular had long-standing commercial interests in these areas, and yet in the end decided to concede the advantage to the Americans. For the most part, the executive branch's intermittent assertions of American power to counter the intrusions of the Europeans had paid high dividends. Hence by the 1890s the United States was poised to jump into the great power imperialist game feet first in order to claim its commercial rights in the Far East and Latin America.

## The Origins of the Spanish-American War and Formal Imperialism in the 1890s

The year 1898 marked what was, for most historians, a distinct break in the trajectory of U.S. foreign policy. By the year's end, the United States had acquired formal imperial colonies in Philippines, Puerto Rico, and Guam, and had annexed the Hawaiian Islands. These moves turned the United States into an imperialist power in the European mold. America now controlled "overseas" territories far from its shores, thus becoming responsible for managing the affairs of a large number of non-American peoples, often through the application of brutal force.[30] In this section, I will show that the push to formal imperialism was not as much of a dramatic break with the past as it is often portrayed. There is no doubt that 1898 marked America's arrival as a great power with truly global reach. But the actions in 1898 that led to the new acquisitions were for the most part simply extensions of the strategic logic—the great power imperative to expand one's economic power sphere and protect it against all comers—that had been driving the United States since 1800. The main difference between 1860 or 1880 and the late 1890s is that the threats to U.S. commercial access to Asia and Latin America were now more salient and the naval power needed to execute an expansionistic program that much stronger. At the heart of the "new" American imperialism after 1895, therefore, was the same propelling force behind U.S. territorial expansion since Jefferson and the Louisiana Purchase—namely, the fear that if Washington did not act swiftly and forcefully, the future commercial base for long-term U.S. economic growth would be harmed, and so accordingly would overall national security.

The campaign for formal overseas imperialism gained steam throughout the 1890s and was spearheaded by key political entrepreneurs such as Theodore Roosevelt and Henry Cabot Lodge. Yet as I will discuss, even supposedly reluctant imperialists such as President William McKinley understood the need to counter threats to America's control of its trading sphere, and to do so before those threats got worse.[31] To emphasize the economic pressures on U.S. decision makers is itself not new.[32] But in this section, by building on previous work on the role of U.S. trade in the Caribbean and East Asia, I seek to show exactly how these pressures—strategic and not just corporate and electoral— manifest themselves in McKinley's careful manipulation of the U.S.

relationship with Spain to get a war going when he wanted it, and for larger national security purposes. In the end, the Spanish-American War was a war where a U.S. president saw that he could kill many birds with one stone. He could certainly assuage domestic critics who saw him as weak on the humanitarian issues that the horrific civil conflict in Cuba brought up. And he could, by winning a quick and successful war, make himself more popular going into his reelection campaign in 1900. But he could also use the war to establish America's dominant geostrategic position in the Caribbean against the threats of German and British commercial intrusion and he could build the U.S. position in the Far East at a time when Germany and Britain were threatening existing and future U.S. trade interests.

In what follows, I will focus on the strategic commercial side of the mix of motives that drove McKinley into war in 1898 and pushed him to ensure Congress's support not just for the fruits of victory, but for the inclusion of Hawaii in the new American economic power sphere. Since it has been covered well elsewhere, I will not spend much time discussing the more domestic-level forces that convinced McKinley that war by the spring of 1898 would be in his personal and his party's interest.[33] My goal is to demonstrate that the geostrategic reasons, rooted in fears of America's commercial future, were as important if not more important.

As in the past, there were a great number of congressmen who, for personal or ideological reasons, opposed U.S. expansionism and were particularly concerned about acquiring overseas colonies. Yet also as in the past, the existence of concrete threats to U.S. commercial strength allowed the executive to overcome the doubters and proceed with territorial expansion. Zakaria is correct to note that by the 1890s, the United States now had the naval strength to proceed with formal imperialism. Yet it was not just the ability to expand that was important. The *need* to expand had jumped considerably by this period. European great powers had already gobbled up Africa in the 1880s.[34] By 1895–97 they were actively engaged in a similar effort to carve up China. They had also significantly increased their efforts to tap the economic potential of Latin America and were projecting their military power accordingly. The new player in all of this was Germany. German growth since 1870 had been nothing short of phenomenal.[35] Its rapid industrialization had greatly increased its need for raw materials and overseas markets, and this in turn had led global imperial powers such as Britain and France to worry about Germany's ability to supplant them in established open-trade areas such as the Far East and Latin America. The United States found itself caught in the middle of what looked like a new race for economic dominance in a globalizing world economy. For a large and growing number of influential Americans after 1890, it appeared certain that if the United States did not assert its right to be a major player in this race, it would be denied access to the growing benefits of late nineteenth-century globalization. The strength of its own economic power sphere would suffer accordingly.[36]

We have seen that U.S. executives, recognizing the importance of protecting overseas and regional interests, were already beginning to rebuild the navy in the early 1880s. Benjamin Harrison's administration would push this buildup strongly after he assumed office in March 1889. Harrison's Secretary of the Navy Benjamin Tracy understood the reasons. If the United States allowed any European power to achieve "commercial supremacy" in the western hemisphere, this would threaten the "independent existence" of the country. With great maritime powers—with obvious reference to Britain—"it is only a step from commercial control to territorial control."[37] The case for the buildup got a huge boost in 1890 with the publication of Alfred Mahan's *The Influence of Sea Power upon History, 1660–1783*. Using the British empire as his model, Mahan argued that the key to its historical success was its ability to project naval power around the globe in support of trade. Britain concentrated its sea-based firepower to force open markets for its goods, gain access to valuable commodities, and deter other great powers from in any way restricting British commerce.[38]

For American leaders, the implications of this argument for the rising U.S. nation were self-evident: America also needed a series of coaling stations and safe harbors around the world to increase its naval power projection capability in critical regions and to ensure ongoing trade access. By 1899–1900, after the absorption of the new imperial possessions, Mahan's logic would become formally enshrined as U.S. policy as part of U.S. Secretary of State John Hay's famous "Open Door" diplomatic notes.[39] But as we have seen, the United States had had been formally pressing for open-door treaties in the Far East and the Pacific since the 1840s, not to mention Latin America. Its policies toward Japan, Hawaii, and Samoa from the 1850s on had been consistent with this logic. Mahan's influence therefore came less from his originality than from his ability to support traditional U.S. strategic thinking with clear historical evidence from the most famous of global economic powers and America's main commercial competitor for more than a century: Britain.

Cuba played a key role in this emerging globalist vision. It had been seen as essential to protecting a future isthmus canal since 1848. But by the 1890s, U.S. trade and investment with Cuba had grown substantially. It was thus even more important to prevent Cuba from falling into complete internal chaos than it had been during President Grant's tenure (chaos that had provoked his attempt to purchase the island). Domestic strife would not only endanger immediate U.S. commercial interests, but might entice other European powers—most importantly after 1885, Britain and Germany—to intervene in a way that pulled Cuba out of the U.S. sphere. This long-standing fear was renewed in intensity in the 1890s by the renewal in 1895 of Cuba's civil war.

American political elites also had growing concerns about another key area of the world: China and the Far East. By the mid-1890s, it was clear that the European great powers as well as Japan were keen to increase their economic penetration of the region. France and Britain had gone from simply consolidating their hold on French Indochina and British Burma to using their military and economic power to directly control parts of southern China. For both Paris and London, there was a great deal at stake. As the famous French traveler in Asia, Prince Henry of Orleans, wrote in a book released in 1894: "It is in Asia . . . that will be decided the destinies of the world," and whoever dominates Asia will dominate Europe.[40] Japan had been growing in industrial power since 1870 and was now poised to establish a colonial empire of its own. In 1894–95, Japan used a victorious war with China to annex Taiwan (Formosa), grab China's Liaotung peninsula and its valuable harbor at Port Arthur in northern China, and exert a predominant influence in Korea.[41] Through the combined pressure of Germany, France, and Russia, Japan was convinced after the war not to accept the Chinese concession of the Liaotung peninsula.

The East Asian problem began in earnest two years later. In late 1897, St. Petersburg betrayed the spirit of the 1895 peace and began to strong-arm the Chinese government into leasing to Russia the exact same area the Japanese had been forced to give up: Port Arthur and its neighboring area on the Liaotung peninsula, including the valuable commercial port of Taleinwan. By that time Russia had already commenced construction of a trans-Manchurian railway system, which would ensure Russian economic penetration of northern China. Britain and France meanwhile were competing to build railways and gain exclusive access to key rivers in southern China. The German government, feeling left out, also got into the game of carving up China into spheres of commercial influence. Germany was second only to Britain in its level of trade with China, but it had no territorial concessions and it remained completely dependent on British Hong Kong for coaling and supplies. In November 1897, anticipating the imminent Russian takeover of Port Arthur, Germany occupied the harbor of Tsingtao in the north and then forced the Chinese to relinquish large pieces of the surrounding peninsula.[42] The next month, under intense Russian pressure, China finally agreed to a twenty-five-year lease of Port Arthur.[43]

By late 1897/early 1898, therefore, it was perfectly clear to U.S. leaders that the treaty system that had been sustaining relatively open trade access to China since the 1840s was disintegrating and doing so with rapid speed. The vision of penetrating the vast "China market," a vision that had entranced Americans since the first New England merchant ships of the 1790s, was now in the process of fading forever—and just at a point when American goods could compete on quality and price with those of any European power.[44] A number of individuals in 1897–98, in particular Assistant Secretary of the Navy Theodore Roosevelt and Senator Henry Cabot Lodge of Massachusetts, understood the connection between the Cuban and Far Eastern problems. The problem of disorder in Cuba had to be resolved and resolved soon, or else U.S. economic and strategic interests in the Caribbean and the future isthmus canal would be threatened. But a war with Spain over Cuba would also allow the United States to take a major step to mitigating the Far East problem. By defeating the Spanish Pacific fleet and capturing Manila harbor, America would be able to project power directly against the great powers scrambling over China. From a Mahanian perspective, the full exploitation of Far Eastern and Pacific trade required an isthmus canal controlled by the United States. And to protect access to such a canal, the giant fortress of Cuba had to be in neutral or American hands. To complete the logic, the United States needed to project effective naval power in East Asia, and ports in the Philippines and Guam would give it that.

The evidence remains ambiguous as to whether President McKinley was more focused on the Cuban question or the Far East question when he initiated war against Spain in April 1898. The president was a notoriously secretive individual, and he left no diary or letters that might illuminate his inner thinking during his presidency. All analyses of the causes of the war with Spain are therefore necessarily interpretive exercises based on circumstantial evidence, behavior, and logic. In what follows, I seek to show that there is a good case to be made that the strategic and security-driven motives for war, shaped largely by commercial fears, were as important if not more important than domestic-level reasons for war within the "mix" of motives that led McKinley into war with Spain. In geoeconomic and geostrategic terms, McKinley saw a successful war against Spain as a nice way to solve the Cuban and Far Eastern questions simultaneously. While McKinley started off in mid-1897 with a primary concern for Cuba, discussions with Teddy Roosevelt in the fall of 1897 and the European scramble for China in late 1897/early 1898 seem to have convinced him by early March 1898 that the Far East was an equal if not more important problem. By mid-March he was apparently so convinced that the issue at hand was much bigger than Cuba that he made sure that his ambassador in Spain, Stewart Woodford, would be unable to solve the Cuban question diplomatically. Hence in the latter half of March we see an odd spectacle emerge, with Woodford desperately trying to find any way to keep the peace and Spain agreeing to almost every American demand, and yet McKinley constantly adding new extreme demands every time a diplomatic solution seemed possible. Even when Madrid seemed willing to hand over the island to the Americans without a war, McKinley upped his demands to make sure no peace could be found.

This behavior, as I will discuss, strongly indicates that by the middle of March 1898—weeks before McKinley used the sinking of the USS *Maine* in Havana harbor to mobilize Congress and the nation for war—the president had decided he needed a large-scale war with Spain. The key to my interpretation is this: the Spanish willingness to give the United States almost everything it wanted regarding Cuba without a war, combined with the fact that congressional pressures during the key period of negotiations were quite muted. Since it was McKinley himself who made it impossible to reach a diplomatic solution with Madrid, it is likely that he had geopolitical objectives that went beyond Cuba, even if solving the Cuban situation was still important. He realized that only a war with Spain would solve both the Cuban problem and the larger problem of naval bases in the Pacific and the Far East at the same time. Hence, when Madrid in March began to cave into his earlier demands made in February and before, including the possible sale or transfer of Cuba to the United States, McKinley knew he had to make sure that no deal was struck. In a classic diplomatic tactic to squelch a peace, he simply kept raising his demands until the other side was incapable of agreeing without completely undermining support at home. When war was finally declared in late April, he moved quickly to secure the valuable port of Manila. Knowing that he needed Manila for his whole Pacific strategy, he refused to give it up after the end of the war. Yet when he learned that Manila could only be properly protected by having the whole of the Philippines in U.S. hands, he reluctantly proceeded by the end of the year to take over the islands as America's first large-scale colonial possession.

There are two main interpretations of the Spanish-American War that compete with the above argument, both of which contribute to full understanding of McKinley's motives. The first argues that McKinley felt domestic pressure to enter into war with Spain—in particular, the pressure coming from nationalist and humanitarian concerns sparked by the reports of the "yellow press."[45] The second position is the well-known neo-Marxist argument of LaFeber, McCormick, and others of the so-called Wisconsin school, which contends that American leaders were pressured into war by business interests that saw war and expansion as the best way to overcome the problem of massive industrial overproduction. The phenomenal post-Civil War growth of the U.S. economic base, tied to a deep depression from 1893 to 1896, led many to believe that overseas imperial expansion was the only way to sop up the vast new production capacity of the manufacturing and agricultural sectors. War and territorial acquisitions solved this problem by providing the markets and raw materials for future business growth.[46]

There are limitations to both arguments that make it unlikely that either is the whole story. Against the first is the evidence that key geostrategic thinkers such as Roosevelt and Lodge not only wanted war but helped to convince the president to bring it on under the most optimal possible conditions.[47] And while the second argument does correctly argue that U.S. industrial growth after 1865 combined with periodic depressions and labor unrest had pushed some Americans in the mid-1890s to contend that only colonial expansion would avert future economic downturns, there is not a great deal of substantive evidence that by late 1897 and early 1898, as McKinley prepared for conflict with Spain, the business classes were demanding a war. Most large firms and business elites were in fact against a war, fearing that its disruptions would hurt the economy and overseas trade.[48] The argument has a problem with timing. The economy had largely turned around by 1896–97 following the depression that started in 1893. Needless to say, McKinley knew that a successful war that increased U.S. commercial control in the Caribbean and the Far East would, in addition to securing the American geopolitical position, *also* help U.S. firms over the long term. But in the absence of short-term pressure from these firms for a war, we must conclude that the attitudes of American business were less salient to his decision-making than the clear national strategic interests on the table.

For the rest of this chapter, I will present the evidence for the alternative perspective of this book. Given the complex nature of the evidence and the lack of a single "smoking gun" document, we will have to explore the documentary record in some detail. But the stakes involved in this case are high. The scholars of the school that sees the Spanish-American war as a war driven by humanitarian outrage tend to believe that McKinley did not want war but fell into it by an inability to find a diplomatic solution to the tragic civil conflict in Cuba.[49] This view that the United States tends to stumble into wars rather than willfully initiating them allows many Americans to sustain a feeling that their nation is still an exceptional one, one that responds to bad situations rather than brings them on. Interpretations of America's role in the start of the Pacific War in 1941 parallel this, as I show elsewhere.[50] On the other hand, the left-wing revisionists of the "Open Door" school see the 1898 war as one of their best example of how capitalist pressures push the United States into wars that are against the broader interests of the nation.[51] If both arguments are incomplete or wrong in terms of the forces propelling McKinley into war, then their arguments about the foundational roles of domestic politics and social pressure will be less useful in understanding the factors that might lead Washington in the twenty-first century into a truly "unwanted war."[52]

To understand McKinley's actions in March and April of 1898, we need to go back in time to understand what role key individuals such as Roosevelt and Lodge played in his decisions. The neo-Marxist view is correct to note that with steep increases in U.S. productivity, American elites across the board recognized that the United States had to be able to penetrate foreign export markets if U.S. economic growth was to be maintained. Yet for these individuals, noncolonial access to markets, raw materials, and places for investment in Asia and Latin America was generally preferred to formal imperialism. This was for one simple reason: large-scale occupation was costly, and U.S. products could now compete on quality and price with the best German and British products. Thus, while securing coaling stations and safe strategic harbors had been an ongoing presidential objective for three decades—and the open door to China for three decades before that—formal colonialization was largely avoided and was contemplated only when stability in the surrounding area was needed to safeguard the ports and when there was a direct threat of European encroachment. The problem after 1895, as we have seen, is that the days of open access in the Far East were ending, while European great powers such as Britain and Germany were pushing their goods on Latin American states like never before. Moreover, if the United States were to control a future isthmus canal, it had to keep order in the Caribbean and keep Europeans from dominating key choke points, such as the waters around Cuba.[53]

Large-scale colonial expansion was thus a fallback position for almost all American elites, including McKinley as we will see. For a new industrial power such as the United States, it was the second-best option to open-door trading backed by key overseas ports. But it was certainly better than being shut out of markets in Asia or losing secure access to an isthmus canal and trade in Latin America. It was this lesser-of-two-evils thinking that came to dominate U.S. decision-making. It is quite evident that McKinley understood the strategic logic behind such difficult choices. Despite the dearth of documents on his inner thinking, a strong pattern emerges from the evidence we do have. As a Republican, McKinley was a clear nationalist. Since his early days in Congress he had supported high tariffs to promote U.S. industrial development, but he also sought increased U.S. exports, an expanded merchant marine, and a large navy. He also strongly supported Cleveland's willingness to challenge the British over Venezuela in December 1895.[54] When arch-expansionist Henry Cabot Lodge visited him in December 1896, just after he had won the election, the conversation turned to the question of Hawaii, Cuba, and other foreign policy matters. Lodge later told Roosevelt that the president-elect's "whole attitude of mind struck me as serious, broad in view, and just what we all ought to desire."[55]

The Republican platform during the 1896 presidential campaign, reflective of McKinley's thinking, called for the annexation of the independent nation of Hawaii. This hard line reflected the widespread view that Japan was now a direct threat to the islands. By carving out a colonial sphere in China through war in 1894–95, Japan for the first time posed a larger threat to the northern Pacific region than either Britain or France. Hence when Japanese immigration to the Hawaiian Islands greatly increased during the 1890s, McKinley and key

Republican leaders began to fear that Japan might emulate the American model applied earlier with Texas and Oregon and use nationals on the ground to pull the islands into its sphere. By the time McKinley assumed office in March 1897, the U.S.-Japanese relationship had already heated up. That month, the Hawaiian government had rejected 1,200 Japanese immigrants on technicalities and Japan had reacted fiercely. In early May the Japanese warship *Naniwa* sailed into Honolulu to put teeth behind Japan's demands for a return to open immigration. As Charles Campbell notes, McKinley was "not the man to permit Japan to seize the strategic archipelago."[56]

As the crisis intensified, McKinley asked his subordinates to renegotiate the annexation treaty abandoned in 1893 because of President Cleveland's resistance. Roosevelt, Lodge, and Assistant Secretary of State William Day were instrumental in convincing McKinley to pursue such a treaty, notwithstanding Secretary of State John Sherman's concerns about escalating an already tense situation.[57] The treaty was quickly finalized on terms similar to those of the failed attempt in 1893, and then presented to the Senate in late June 1897. The traditional domestic objections from Southern sugar interests, however, once again held up passage. During the summer of 1897, Japan lodged protests against U.S. annexation and sought, unsuccessfully, to bring Britain into the equation to avert what the Japanese saw as a deteriorating balance of power in the central Pacific. Secretary Sherman told the U.S. minister to Hawaii to remain vigilant and to be ready to declare a U.S. protectorate over Hawaii if Japan went too far. The minister was authorized to request American naval support and to land troops if necessary.

Parallel instructions were given to the American fleet, and four warships were moved into the area, leading Admiral Mahan to tell his good friend Roosevelt that there was a "very real present danger of war."[58] Fortunately, the Japanese backed down, withdrew the *Naniwa* in September, and tensions abated. Mistrust between Washington and Tokyo was now high, however. In March 1898, just as McKinley was preparing to initiate war against Spain, a report of the Senate Foreign Relations Committee on Hawaii was released. Summing up the main reasons to proceed with annexation, it noted that the critical problem remained the Japanese threat: "The policy of Japan toward Hawaii will become aggressive," and hence the United States "must act NOW to preserve the results of its past policy, and to prevent the dominancy in Hawaii of a foreign people."[59] Four months later, in July 1898 in the midst of the Spanish-American War, the security argument finally overcame the domestic objections and McKinley got his Hawaiian annexation bill through the Congress.[60]

Also significant in demonstrating McKinley's strategic thinking prior to the war with Spain are his views on an isthmus canal. The 1896 Republican platform had called for a Nicaraguan canal and for the purchase of the Danish West Indies, the latter serving to protect access to such a canal. McKinley had also spoken in favor of a Nicaraguan canal route in his inaugural address. Both President Harrison and President Cleveland had pushed for a U.S.-controlled isthmus canal after the French-led project fizzled out in 1888, but the financial resources of private American canal companies had come up short. Moreover, there was still fierce debate as to whether a Nicaraguan or Panamanian route was preferable. McKinley appointed a Nicaraguan Canal Commission in the spring of 1897 to confirm the viability of the Nicaraguan route, but the project got sidetracked over the next year because of the Cuban crisis. After the 1898 war, however, McKinley spoke of the necessity of an isthmus canal. In his December address to Congress, he argued that a canal was "now more than ever indispensable to that intimate and ready intercommunication between our eastern and western seaboards demanded by the annexation of the Hawaiian Islands and the prospective expansion of our influence and commerce in the Pacific."[61]

The Hawaiian and canal questions were relatively easy ones for McKinley, since the costs and risks were low. The same was not true of the Cuban question. Full-scale rebellion against Spanish rule had broken out on the island in 1895 and was increasing in ferocity by 1897. McKinley, as we have seen, had strong expansionist inclinations of his own. But on the Cuban question, he initially preferred a peaceful resolution that would restore order under Spanish auspices, an outcome that was seen as better than a potentially costly war with Spain, now a fellow liberal democracy and thus a state with which, all things being equal, the United States should be able to negotiate.[62] In the spring and summer of 1897, he thus resisted calls from more extreme expansionists such as Assistant Secretary of the Navy Teddy Roosevelt who from the beginning saw a chance to use the Cuban crisis to secure America's strategic and economic position in both the Caribbean and the Far East. During the fall of 1897, however, while McKinley remained reluctant to give up his first option—a return to the pre-1895 status quo—evidence indicates that he gradually came to see Roosevelt's plan as better than continued chaos in Cuba, and something that might also help the United States in the Far East.

Through the summer of 1897 and into the fall, influenced strongly by their correspondence with Mahan, life-long friends Roosevelt and Lodge worked out what Lodge would later call the "large policy"—namely, a policy of war with Spain that would yield not only U.S. control over Cuba and Puerto Rico, but would allow the capture of the valuable harbor of Manila. McKinley had known of Roosevelt's strong imperialist ideas ever since, at the invitation of Lodge, he had sat down with Roosevelt as president-elect in December 1896. Roosevelt's plan for the immediate occupation of Manila in any war with Spain was not his own. It derived from the writings of Lieutenant William Kimball of the Office of Naval Intelligence. Kimball had formulated the idea in 1896, and by early 1897 he and Roosevelt were in close contact, discussing "our hopes as to the Spanish business."[63] By the start of summer, Roosevelt had become concerned with Russian penetrations into Manchuria and northern China (as of course had Britain, Japan, and Germany). In June 1897, he began to spread his ideas on the larger global question, telling the Naval War College that "The enemies we may have to face will come from Asia . . . Our interests are as great in the Pacific as in the Atlantic."[64]

By all accounts, McKinley and Roosevelt began to establish a friendship in the early fall of 1897. During long horseback rides and dinners, the assistant secretary would brief McKinley on his larger strategic plans. During this time, McKinley also examined a Navy Department memorandum written by Roosevelt that argued that in the event of war with Spain, the U.S. Pacific fleet "should blockade, and if possible take Manila."[65] Even if McKinley was still hoping to avoid war at this point, as he apparently was, Roosevelt's briefings could not have failed to inform him that a war with Spain over Cuba could also have important side benefits in the Pacific. And his behavior shows that he did understand the possibilities before him: in December 1897, long before there was any immediate crisis with Spain, he agreed to a Navy Department plan that called for an attack on the Spanish fleet in the Philippines in the event of war.[66]

Actions that McKinley either undertook or allowed to occur after this important decision in December reinforce the idea that in late 1897 or early 1898 McKinley was starting to see war as a way out of his larger strategic concerns, both in the Caribbean and the Far East. In early January, he approved the sending of the battleship *Maine* into Havana harbor, an obviously provocative step that could easily lead to escalation (and of course did). Then on February 25, when Secretary of the Navy John Long was out of the office and Roosevelt was serving as Acting Secretary, Roosevelt was permitted to put the United States one step closer to the taking of Manila. Amidst a flurry of activity that afternoon, Roosevelt, with his friend Lodge hanging over his shoulder, wrote to Admiral George Dewey in Hong Kong. He told him to be ready at a moment's notice to launch offensive actions against Manila should war be declared with Spain. He also put the fleet in Asia and most of the U.S. naval ships around the world onto an immediate war footing.

When Secretary Long returned to his office the next day and discovered Roosevelt's unauthorized actions, he was understandably furious. After Long's discussions with McKinley regarding the action, Long rescinded around two-thirds of the instructions Roosevelt sent out that day. Significantly, however, *he did not cancel the instruction to Dewey*. Hence, when war was declared in late April, Dewey immediately received a telegram telling him to proceed to Manila Bay to carry out his assigned mission. Responding with alacrity, Dewey arrived five days later and on May 1 quickly engaged and defeated the Spanish fleet. This is prima facie evidence that even if Long was not happy about Roosevelt's telegram to Dewey in February, his superior at the White House believed it was a necessary step.[67]

Moreover, what transpired immediately after Dewey's attack in April shows the depth to which McKinley understood and agreed with Roosevelt and Lodge's "large policy." On May 2, with only preliminary newspaper reports of Dewey's victory in front of him, McKinley made a decision to send an army of occupation from the West Coast to secure the city of Manila. On May 4 he issued a call for volunteers to reach his objective of sending 20,000 men to the Philippines, four times what Dewey himself had said was necessary to control Manila. As Thomas McCormick notes, this was three days before an anxious Long received confirmation that the Pacific Squadron was safe and not immobilized by heavy damages.[68] A week later, on May 11, McKinley approved a memorandum from the State Department that called for Spain's cession of a suitable "coaling station" in the Philippines, which in the context undoubtedly meant Manila and its nearby bays. Significantly, Spain was to retain possession of the islands themselves.[69] On June 3, as it became clear that the long distance between Honolulu and Manila required an intermediate coaling station, McKinley went further and ordered the occupation of an island in the Spanish Marianas. Soon after, the U.S. seized control of Guam.[70]

Given these facts, it stretches credulity to believe that McKinley during the winter of 1897–98 did not understand the huge advantages to grabbing Manila as a point for power projection against East Asia and that he only fell reluctantly into involvement in the Philippines (as the inadvertent war thesis asserts). He had been told in the fall of 1897 by none other than Orville Platt, the Connecticut senator who later proved so critical to postwar U.S. control of Cuba, that "Manila had become one of the most important ports of the Orient and that the importance of that station demanded most careful attention."[71] It is worth noting that his order in early May 1898 to send 20,000 men to secure Manila was taken *some six weeks before the United States engaged the Spanish off the coast of Cuba.* In fact, because of the size of the Manila venture, critical ships and resources from the West Coast that could have been used against Cuba were diverted across the Pacific, greatly reducing U.S. firepower in the Caribbean and perhaps delaying U.S. victory there by a number of weeks. Since McKinley knew by early May that the U.S. fleet had already won a devastating victory in Manila Bay and he never rescinded this order, it is impossible to argue that McKinley saw the navy's plan for war against the Philippines as merely a tool to reduce Spain's overall strength in preparation for victory in the Caribbean. If he had, then all West Coast forces should have gone immediately to the Caribbean theater. It is thus clear that McKinley had a strong need to take Manila Bay for its commercial and strategic value and was prepared to sacrifice the war effort in the Atlantic to get it.

Historical accounts have led us into confusion by rightly pointing out that McKinley had no prewar desire to colonize the Philippine archipelago and only reluctantly came to the conclusion that the whole of the island chain had to be seized from Spain. But wanting a single port to project power into Far East waters and wanting the responsibility of managing a large and dispersed colony are two very separate things, and McKinley knew this. His agreement with the State Department memorandum of early May to demand a coaling station in the islands but to leave the sprawling archipelago itself in Spanish hands makes this very clear.[72] Indeed, his initial desire to take *only* Manila soundly defeats any neo-Marxist logic that McKinley believed that the islands would be useful in absorbing U.S. surplus production and investment capital. He knew they would serve no such purpose.

Yet once control of Manila and its surrounding bays was assured by July 1898, McKinley was forced to make a separate decision as to whether to take the whole chain and make it a U.S. colony. A secure port was an important addition, but a U.S. imperial possession was something much more problematic and much more potentially costly. In the summer of 1898, domestic opponents of American expansion were already having a field day arguing against the immorality and economic foolishness of taking the whole island chain.[73] And McKinley largely agreed with their reasoning. But with Germany projecting naval power into the area and demanding a slice of the Philippine pie, and with Spain too weak to crush a growing insurgency, he came to realize that unless the whole chain was appropriated, he could not secure the thing he most wanted—the port of Manila. Thus in October 1898, after much soul-searching, he announced the plan to absorb the Philippines as a U.S. colony.[74] It was McKinley's pessimistic assessment of his ability to hold onto Manila and thus to protect U.S. commercial interests in the Far East that led him to go much further than he would otherwise have wanted.

## Last Days of the Crisis and the Plunge into War

Turning to the specific events and diplomatic actions that led to the war with Spain in April 1898, we see a logical progression in McKinley's strategic thinking. From mid-1897 when he started to rachet up the pressure on Spain until late 1897, his focus was on restoring order in Cuba to protect U.S. economic investments and trade. He wanted Spain to make concessions to the rebels in terms of promises of autonomy and human rights that would end the rebellion and reestablish peace. His preference at this time, as mentioned, was to avoid a costly and risky war and to achieve his ends through both sticks (threats of

U.S. intervention) and carrots (offers to buy Cuba, discussions of freer trade, etc.). Yet by early 1898, we see a distinct and puzzling shift in McKinley's behavior. Despite the fact that Spain began to make larger and larger concessions to satisfy U.S. demands, McKinley became less and less willing to strike a deal. By late March and early April, with Spain having given in to almost all of McKinley's demands, the president adopted an intransigent stance that made it impossible for his minister in Madrid to find a solution that would avoid war.

It is this shift from a cooperative attitude to an intransigent posture that any historical account must explain. The inadvertent war thesis contends that McKinley was pressured into war by events such as the sinking of the *Maine* in February and the growing humanitarian outrage in America over human rights abuses in Cuba. The neo-Marxist position argues that business classes put pressure on the president in February–March to safeguard their economic interests in Cuba and around the world. As discussed, the second argument collapses once we see that the vast majority of firms were against a war until April, and only came on board because they saw the war crisis itself as being bad for business.[75] The first argument is a tougher one to defeat given the lack of documents on McKinley's inner thought processes. The very fact that humanitarian and hard-line pundits in the United States had been pushing for intervention since the outbreak of civil war in 1895, yet little was done until 1898, should make us suspicious of the inadvertent war thesis. Why did things get "out of hand" in March–April 1898 but not before? Indeed, how could a consummate political animal such as McKinley let himself be pushed into a war he didn't want?

Once we see the Machiavellian nature of McKinley's diplomacy in the last two weeks of March, the explanatory value of the inadvertent war argument starts to crumble. McKinley not only actively prevented the finding of any diplomatic solution, but he strategically introduced inflammatory evidence into public fora when he needed to move public opinion to the side of war and to obstruct further diplomacy.[76] As with Madison in 1812 and Polk in 1846, McKinley knew that he had to appear to have no other options and thus forced into war by the circumstances and the intransigence of the other side. Otherwise, majority support in Congress for war would not have been forthcoming—and Congress, as always, held the purse strings. As with Madison and Polk, McKinley manipulated public opinion to achieve the war he wanted when he wanted it. It is important to reiterate that this does not mean he started his presidency preferring war to peace. Rather, it means that as the external situations he faced with regard to Cuba and especially the Far East got progressively worse through 1897 and into 1898, he came to see that trying to maintain the pre-1895 status quo of a stable Cuba and an open-door China was no longer realistic. Like any good decision-maker, he thus chose war as the lesser of two evils, once his preferred choice was off the table. It is in this sense, and this sense only, that McKinley was a "reluctant imperialist."[77] But as we have already seen with his actions regarding Manila in late April and early May 1898, once his choice set was constrained, he chose expansion through force as the best option to achieve the long-term economic and strategic ends of his country.

I will now turn to the diplomatic evidence supporting the above argument. When McKinley began his sustained effort in mid-1897 to push Spain to solve the Cuban rebellion, his thinking followed the trade expectations logic but was confined to Cuba's economic importance to the United States. The Russian, German, and British scramble for port cities in China would not begin in a big way until November 1897, so the Far Eastern situation had not yet become acute. From 1890 to 1894, trade with Cuba had grown significantly, but the rebellion that had begun in 1895 had caused huge damage: the $96 million in trade in 1894 had fallen to $26 million by 1897. By the late 1890s, Americans also had $50 million in investments on the island, mostly in sugar plantations, mines, and railways, and these investments were devastated by the civil war.[78]

The instructions given to new U.S. minister to Spain Stewart Woodford on July 16, 1897 upon his departure—as well as all the correspondence Woodford received from Washington for the next six months—reveal that the declining economic situation was the primary U.S. concern, with humanitarian concerns being distinctly secondary. Woodford was told that the two-year civil war had caused significant damage to American property and commercial ventures on the island, and the Spanish government could not expect the United States to sit back and allow its "vast interests to suffer."[79] U.S. economic concerns became Woodford's primary refrain in his discussion with both the Spanish and with other European ambassadors. To the British ambassador to Madrid in September Woodford emphasized the fact that America was very dependent on supplies of Cuban sugar and Cuba as a market for U.S. goods, and that U.S. investments in Cuba had been made "practically unproductive and in great danger of being finally and completely lost." Trade and commerce must resume "promptly." The problem, Woodford noted, was that Spain did not seem able to crush the rebellion, forcing Washington to seek an end to the conflict.[80]

In discussions with Spanish ministers over the next four months, Woodford pressed his interlocutors to end the war by making concessions to the rebels, warning that U.S. economic losses would otherwise force the United States to intervene.[81] The Liberal party in Spain had taken over the government in October and quickly implemented a partial autonomy plan for Cuba to meet U.S. demands. Unfortunately, Cuban elites and Spanish soldiers in Cuba launched protests against this plan, serving only to heighten the instability on the island. By January 1898, it was clear that there was little Spain could do to restore order to the island. It was in that month that McKinley decided to send the warship *Maine* to Havana harbor, ostensibly to protect Americans on the island. Since this move came less than a year after Japan had caused a crisis over Hawaii by moving a warship to Honolulu, McKinley undoubtedly knew that he was taking a step that might escalate the crisis.

The deployment of the *Maine*, combined with the failure to rescind Roosevelt's message to Dewey, indicates that by the start of 1898 McKinley was gearing up for something big. This shift is made clear by his new approach to diplomacy with Spain. For one thing, he takes the highly unusual step of corresponding directly with Woodford in Madrid or using Assistant Secretary of State Day as his intermediary, rather than having all his messages go through Secretary of State Sherman. The reasons seem clear. Day was an old friend while Sherman had been appointed for political reasons. Sherman was also known for his cautious personality and reluctance to get out on the slippery slope to war.[82] Thus McKinley and Day's turn to a more direct control over diplomacy with Spain indicates the president's desire to ensure nothing happened contrary to his wishes in those critical three months from February to April.

The reports coming into the president's office from Woodford were not encouraging. On March 2, Woodford wrote McKinley that the Spanish were trying to delay any further concessions until late April when the new Cortes (Spanish parliament) was to meet. Knowing that McKinley had given him a deadline of April 15 to secure a deal, Woodford suggested that the Spanish be told more directly of the president's deadline so they might still be able to make the necessary concessions prior to that date. Otherwise, it might be hard to justify a U.S. military move against Cuba that would meet "the sober judgment of our people and the final judgment of history."[83] Woodford and McKinley had been friends prior to the former's appointment. So, such direct language from Woodford about McKinley's artificially imposed internal deadline—given at a time when the U.S. Congress had little inkling that military action might be imminent—suggests that McKinley was already preparing his nation for war by early March and was doing so for reasons removed from domestic pressure.

Through the months of March and April, McKinley would consider no conciliatory measures offered by Spain, notwithstanding the strenuous efforts made by Madrid to meet U.S. demands. On March 1, Woodford had written McKinley indicating that the Spanish government was very upset by reports of American filibusters landing ships on Cuban shores in support of the rebels.[84] Assistant Secretary Day replied to Woodford on March 3. Instead of investigating the charges, he simply denied the reports of American filibusters.[85] And in yet another provocative move, the U.S. navy deployed two of its ships to the coast of Cuba for the ostensible purpose of providing supplies to hungry Cubans. The Spanish government told Woodford that this move could be seen as official U.S. support for the Cuban insurgents, and it requested that any supplies be delivered only by merchant ships, not "ships of war."[86] Once again, McKinley refused to budge.

By early March it was becoming clear that the Spanish were at a loss as to what they could do to satisfy the Americans. On March 7, Woodford had met with an unnamed influential merchant who had direct connections to the Spanish minister of colonies, Prendergast Moret. The merchant, clearly acting as Moret's go-between, listed for Woodford all the concessions Spain had made since the Liberal party came to power in October, including granting Cuba autonomy, getting rid of a hated Spanish commander, closing the concentration camps, and offering a full pardon to all rebels. The only two things Spain could not do was to grant Cuba complete sovereignty or sell the island to the United States.[87] On March 17, however, Woodford wrote McKinley to tell him that his impressions of the situation had changed, and that he had reluctantly come to believe that the purchase of Cuba was the only viable way to ensure a peace between Spain and the United States. The current government in Madrid could not end the Cuban civil war until the late fall, and it believed it had made all the concessions it could make in the short term without endangering its own power and that of the Spanish monarchy. Perhaps the offer of a substantial sum for Cuba, given that the United States would likely take the island anyway should war occur, might make a transfer palatable to the majority of the Spanish elite. As things stood, however, "[the Spanish] will fight, if what they have done does not secure our continued neutrality."[88]

This is where things get especially intriguing. Over the next few weeks, Woodford worked tirelessly to try to convince the Spanish to sell the islands to the United States, believing that since McKinley had favored this option since the fall, he would still favor it over an actual war. Yet McKinley not only refused to help Woodford in this task, he also made it increasingly hard for the Spanish to find a deal that would satisfy the president and avoid war. We thus have the strange situation of a U.S. ambassador struggling to find a way to avoid war, and a U.S. president and his friend Assistant Secretary of State Day doing almost everything possible to impede any conceivable solutions.

In a long telegram on March 18 summarizing the day's events, Woodford informed McKinley that he had learned at midday of a heated meeting of the Spanish council of ministers. The ministers of war and navy had pushed for immediate military preparation for war. But Minister of Colonies Moret had "argued for peace" and Prime Minister Mateo Sagasta had "positively declared for peace on any terms at all consistent with Spanish honor." Three hours later, Woodford met with a pale and anxious Moret, who stated bluntly: "We must

have peace with honor to Spain. Tell me what can be done." Seeing his opening, Woodford told Moret that while he was speaking only for himself "since
I have no authority from my Government or my President for what I am going
to say," Spain could get out of its dilemma by selling Cuba to the United States.
Surprisingly, Moret did not dismiss the suggestion. Instead, after some reflection, he asked Woodford if he thought the American people would approve of
the idea and assume Cuba's debts in the process. Woodford said he thought
they would, given that they "would prefer to buy rather than suffer the pains
of war." Woodford proceeded to press the case for selling, listing no fewer than
ten good reasons for Spain to cede Cuba now. With time running out, Woodford was clearly pulling out all the stops, and finally he seemed to see a light at
the end of the tunnel—the minister of colonies and his president were grasping at any straw, and now were at least considering the option of selling.[89]

The next day, March 19, Woodford wrote the president a follow-up memorandum (telegram no. 45) to recommend holding off on immediate action,
unless the imminent release of the report on the *Maine* explosion required it.
Woodford told McKinley that the Spanish government might offer a settlement that would be "satisfactory to both nations." Given the context of his
telegram to McKinley the previous day, such a settlement would undoubtedly
entail the sale of Cuba to America.

Assistant Secretary Day, acting for McKinley, responded the next day. The
content of his telegram makes clear that he and McKinley were determined to
keep Woodford from pressing ahead with the sale option. Day said upfront
that the president was confused as to whether the telegram on the nineteenth
(telegram no. 45) involved just reparations for the loss of the *Maine* or covered
"the whole situation." To pretend that Woodford had been talking about the
*Maine* question when it was clear his dispatches concerned the sale of Cuba
was clearly disingenuous. The words "the whole situation" show that McKinley and Day did understand that Woodford was talking about something much
bigger. But the rest of the three-paragraph telegram focused solely on the issue
of *Maine* reparations and said nothing about the key issue at hand: namely,
whether McKinley would approve of the sale of Cuba if Woodford could get
the Spanish to offer it.[90] Day made clear that the confidential report on the
*Maine* concluded that it had been blown up by a submarine mine—that is, that
Spain was responsible for its destruction—and that the president could not
hold off on the report, but would be sending it to Congress "soon." He went
on to indicate that even if Spain sought to make amends for the *Maine*, the
"general conditions" in Cuba "demand action on our part." Unless Spain restored an "honorable peace" to Cuba by the April 15 deadline—something
Woodford had already told McKinley and Day was impossible—things would
move forward on America's end. Day ended the telegram by telling Woodford

that "it was only proper that you should know that, unless events otherwise indicate, the President, having exhausted diplomatic agencies to secure peace in Cuba, will lay the whole question before Congress." In short, McKinley would seek a war declaration from the legislature. Hence, Woodford should keep the president fully advised, "as [the] action of the next few days may control [the] situation."[91]

For a president who was supposedly reluctant to go to war and seeking every opportunity to keep the peace, this is a very odd telegram to send to the one person in the world—Stewart Woodford—who could break the deadlock. If Woodford was positioned to convince the Spanish to sell, and restoring order in Cuba was the president's only objective, then why not jump on Woodford's suggestions and do everything possible to arrange a last-minute deal? Why not at least try to offer a modest sum to entice the Spanish into a sale, as Jefferson had done with France in 1803 over Louisiana and John Quincy Adams had done with Spain in 1819 over Florida? The Spanish in their desperate state might just take it, as Woodford had been implying. Yet instead of considering Woodford's suggestions, McKinley and Day ignored them completely, focused on the spurious question of *Maine* reparations, and then stated emphatically that even these reparations would not delay McKinley's "laying of the question" before Congress.

Something profound had evidently shifted McKinley's strategic preferences by March 1898. The idea of purchasing Cuba had been on the table since 1897. And Woodford's logic was impeccable: if the regional problem was restoring order in Cuba to allow commerce to flow again, and Spain had proved incapable of doing this, then the United States had to occupy the island anyway to do the job. So why not use a small outlay of cash now to effect this outcome rather than fight a potentially costly war that might bring in other great powers? As we have seen, solving the Cuban problem peacefully had been McKinley's first preference since the midsummer of 1897. Even in late February he was still playing around with the idea of purchasing Cuba.[92] So why in March did he not encourage Woodford to pursue the idea when it was the last hope for peace?

One possibility is that he knew he couldn't get a purchase through Congress. When McKinley approached some senators in late February about buying Cuba for $300 million, he received a lukewarm response. Believing that Spain was about to lose Cuba anyway, they wondered why the United States should pay for it.[93] Yet this leaves more questions than answers. For a man of McKinley's consummate negotiating skills, had he believed a Cuba purchase was truly better than war, he could have found a way to convince legislators of this. Most obviously, given that the Spanish were getting increasingly desperate and fearful, he could have offered a much smaller sum—say, for starters, the $100–$130 million figure tossed around in the 1850s—and at least hoped that the Spanish would bite. Or he could have simply agreed to assume Cuba's debt, which Woodford had told him was an albatross around the Spanish neck. Yet he did not even attempt either negotiating option—something any actor with peace as a first preference would almost certainly have done.

The other possibility is that McKinley knew that Spain would not sell and thus it was a waste of precious time to try. This argument also falls short in terms of plausibility. Woodford had been telling McKinley directly that two very important individuals—Minister of Colonies Moret and Prime Minister Sagasta—were desperate for peace and might in the end accept a sale to avoid war. He was also telling McKinley bluntly that the sale option was essentially the only way to avert a war, since the Spanish were incapable of establishing order on the island—especially before the start of rainy season in early May. Given McKinley's own self-imposed deadline for a deal of April 15, he should have pushed Woodford hard to secure this one remaining option for peace.

But all this assumes that he still wanted a peaceful resolution to war. And by mid-March it is evident that he did not. Through his intermediary Assistant Secretary Day, therefore, McKinley made sure that Woodford understood that he was to focus solely on the *Maine* reparations issue. He also made sure that Woodford knew that even a solution to this problem would not stop him from taking the Cuban question to Congress. Woodford could not have been pleased by this lack of interest in his diplomatic pursuit of a sale. He had broached the sale option with Moret on March 17, knowing that he had no authority to do so, and in his March 18 telegram to McKinley, had reminded the president of this fact, presumably to nudge him to provide such authority. Yet on March 20, Day not only told Woodford that the *Maine* was the key issue but stayed silent on both the question of whether Spain would sell Cuba and Woodford's authority to negotiate such a purchase.

For a seasoned individual such as Woodford, this was the equivalent of a presidential censure of the sale option. And Woodford's short telegram to the president on March 21 indicates that he got the message but had personally decided not to drop the idea altogether. Since Woodford was writing to McKinley and not to Day, he used the first part of his telegram to repeat Day's March 19 telegram word for word, presumably to make sure that McKinley was fully in agreement with his assistant secretary of state's terse language or perhaps simply to confirm that these limiting instructions were the only guidelines he was to follow. Recognizing that he had perhaps already overstepped his ambassadorial authority in showing enthusiasm for a "final settlement" in his March 19 dispatch (telegram no. 45), he told McKinley somewhat sheepishly that he had "no intimation of the character of report on the *Maine* when

I telegraphed my No. 45, but reserved your full liberty of action if such [a] report should require it."

Turning to the main subject of Day's telegram, he unapologetically informed the president he had not broached the subject of the *Maine* with the Spanish government. This was Woodford's not-so-subtle way of telling McKinley that, given the level of crisis and the short time frame, the *Maine* question was really beside the point and should be dropped. Indeed, by not engaging the Spanish in a new discussion regarding *Maine* reparations, he was explicitly defying the instructions and spirit of Assistant Secretary of State Day's March 20 telegram. Knowing that it was a diplomatic dead end and would only enflame the situation, he was apparently hoping that McKinley himself would accept this insubordination as necessary to the task at hand—namely, getting a peace deal. Woodford goes on to say that "all other suggestions in my No. 45 [telegram] should be [kept] absolutely secret." This was a direct reference to the "settlement satisfactory to both sides" he had broached in that March 19 telegram. Woodford was clearly still holding out hope that Moret and Sagasta, the two individuals still seeking a peaceful solution, would state explicitly their willingness to sell Cuba. Woodford ended his telegram to McKinley by noting that the situation was "so delicate and yet so pressing" that he would offer no more suggestions that day. He would think on the situation that night, meet with Moret the next morning, and "say and do what shall then, after reflection, seem wisest." He promised to keep McKinley fully advised. In essence, Woodford was telling McKinley that despite not receiving authorization to negotiate Cuba's sale, he might still try to sound out Moret as to its viability.[94]

By the next day (March 22), Woodford, having heard nothing back from the president and evidently chastened by McKinley's continued lack of support, decided to play it safe and not broach the sale option in either an official or unofficial manner. He met with Moret in the morning and asked him whether he should talk officially or personally. Moret said personally. Despite this opening, Woodford proceeded to read from a prepared text. He reminded Moret that he (Moret) had been allowed to read the March 19 dispatch to McKinley (telegram no. 45), and that Woodford had now received a reply (Day's March 20 telegram). Still reading to ensure he got his words exactly right, Woodford told Moret the following:

> I ought to now say to you that the report on the *Maine* is in the hands of the President. I am not today authorized to disclose its character or conclusions, but I am authorized to say to you that . . . unless some satisfactory agreement is reached within a very few days, which will assure immediate and honorable peace in Cuba, the President must at once submit the whole question of the relations between the United States and Spain, including

the matter of the *Maine*, to the decision of Congress. I will telegraph immediately to the President any suggestion that Spain may make, and I hope to receive within a very few days some definite proposition that will mean immediate peace.[95]

The amazing nature of this text may not be apparent at first glance. Moret was the one Spanish official (other than Prime Minister Sagasta) who knew of Woodford's unauthorized initiative to secure the sale of Cuba and had expressed some interest in it. Indeed, Woodford had taken the radical step of reading him the exact wording of his March 19 telegram to McKinley. So, for Woodford to now not be able to tell Moret anything about the possibility of a sale, even in an informal capacity, could only communicate to Moret that the U.S. president had rejected the idea and would be satisfied only with some unnamed action that created "immediate peace and stability in Cuba"—an impossible condition, given the circumstances. In Spanish eyes, being told that McKinley would present "the whole question" of Spanish-American relations to Congress and not just the *Maine* report, and that the resolution of the *Maine* question would not be enough anyway, could only mean that the president had decided either to push Spain to the wall or to go ahead with war anyway. And yet Woodford, despite having to follow these elements of Day's unpalatable March 20 telegram, ended by stating that he would immediately telegraph to McKinley any suggestion that Spain might have, and that he himself still hoped to receive a proposal that would mean immediate peace. Since Woodford had personally given up on all options except the sale, and Moret knew the full background of his efforts to convince McKinley of this, Woodford was subtly telling Moret that there was still some hope of a deal. But Moret had to initiate the sale offer, since Woodford could not.

Moret quickly understood this implication, and he asked Woodford if he was authorized to state officially to the Spanish Foreign Minister Pio Gullón what he had just said unofficially to Moret, since this would be "in the interest of [an] early peace." Woodford said he was, and a meeting was set up for the next day, with Moret attending.[96] Given that Moret with Sagasta had been leading the peace wing of the cabinet, and given that Woodford's prepared statement, except for the final sentence, was disheartening to say the least, the fact that Moret would believe that the foreign minister needed to hear the statement "in the interest of peace" can only mean that he—like Woodford—still believed a sale was possible. At this meeting of March 23, which Woodford related in a separate telegram to McKinley, the ambassador repeated "in exact terms" the statement he had read to Moret the previous day. The foreign minister was largely noncommittal: he asked for a delay until the beginning of the rainy season, by which time a "secure arrangement with insurgents" would have been worked out. This was clearly not what Woodford wanted to hear. The foreign minister was not doing what Woodford and Moret had hoped he would: namely, broach a sale of Cuba as the "suggestion" he could take to McKinley to get an "immediate peace." He was only buying time. Woodford told him that time was of the essence, and that "unless a satisfactory agreement is [reached] within a very few days, [McKinley] must submit the whole question to Congress"—that is, almost certain war. The meeting ended without any resolution, but with the hope that a cabinet meeting that afternoon would discuss Woodford's statement further.[97]

The next day, Thursday, March 24, Moret met with Woodford in a "purely personal" capacity. The news was not good. Instead of coming back with the news Woodford had wished for—a Spanish offer to sell—Moret could only offer a much weaker proposition. The Spanish government would declare an "armistice or truce" enforced by its own army—that is, an end to all fighting— as part of a peace plan to be submitted to the now autonomous Cuban congress in early May. There was one main condition: Washington would have to agree to secure the insurgents' acceptance of the truce.[98] For Woodford, the Spanish position could only have come as a big disappointment. The sale option was now apparently off the table—unless McKinley himself introduced it, which of course he never did.

For the next three weeks, the idea of a mutual armistice for warring Cuban factions was the only major option for peace discussed. The armistice idea went nowhere, precisely because McKinley had already artificially set a deadline of April 15 to "solve" the Cuban question, and all armistice options required approval of both the Cuban parliament and the insurgents. Moreover, and quite to the frustration of the Spanish government, McKinley adamantly refused to pressure the insurgents to accept an armistice. Once again it must be asked: if McKinley truly sought peace above all else, then why not give the armistice idea a chance? Woodford himself, having had to abandon the sale option, did signal to McKinley that a stable armistice might still be secured.[99] This did not motivate McKinley to do anything that would have helped this option be realized.

On the afternoon of Friday, March 25, Woodford met again with Foreign Minister Gullón to find out more on the armistice plan broached by Moret the day before. Speaking of the need to secure a peace in Cuba at once, Woodford asked Gullón if Spain could agree to an "immediate and effective armistice" if the insurgents would also agree to it. Gullón replied that he could give no final answer until he had consulted with his cabinet colleagues, but that he personally believed such an armistice could not be reached. The foreign minister was also adamant that the *Maine* report not be sent to Congress but should instead be the subject of "diplomatic adjustment." The Spanish obviously understood that once the report reached the U.S. legislature, heightened emotions would make it almost impossible to find a peaceful solution.[100]

That Friday night at 9:00 P.M., Woodford received a memorandum from Gullón detailing Spanish views on Woodford's prepared statement given to Moret on Tuesday and then Gullón on Wednesday (March 22–23). Recall that Woodford's statement had followed Day's hard-line instructions carefully, but ended with an enigmatic sentence that he would "telegraph immediately to the president any suggestion that Spain may make" and that he hoped to receive "within a very few days [from Spain] some definite proposition that shall mean immediate peace."[101] Moret had most certainly informed Gullón of the sentence's hidden meaning—namely, that this was Woodford's way of saying to Spain that it should offer to sell or give Cuba to the United States or simply declare an immediate armistice to avoid a war. Gullón's terse one-paragraph note to Woodford and McKinley went right to the question of the "suggestion or proposal that might be made by Spain in order to secure an immediate and honorable peace." Gullón argued that if Washington was now inquiring about conditions related to Cuba's future "political system," then the Spanish government felt obliged to remind Washington that "nothing could be done in this direction without the natural participation of the [Cuban] parliament" which was set to meet on May 4.[102] Behind his convoluted language, Gullón was communicating a simple point: Spain might indeed allow the transfer of Cuba to some form of U.S. control should the Cuban parliament allow it, even if the island was not formally "sold." This was a small ray of hope in an otherwise deteriorating situation.

But Gullón also warned in a second memo the next morning that if McKinley placed the report on the *Maine* before the U.S. Congress "without correction, explanation, or counterproof of any kind," it would only stir up emotion, hurting the possibility of future discussion. Yet to keep hope alive, Gullón ended the memo by repeating word for word the paragraph on "the suggestion or proposal" that he sent Woodford the night before.[103]

In essence, Gullón's memoranda to Woodford were signaling that while the Spanish government would not be pushed around, a transfer of Cuba to the United States might still be possible. Foreign Minister Gullón was known as an individual who in the past had opposed giving concessions to Washington at the point of a gun. His memoranda thus indicated that the sale/transfer option had now been discussed with some of the more hard-line cabinet members, and that they agreed that it might be a solution to help avoid war. Yet because Cuba now had an autonomous legislature—ironically, because of 1897 reforms made to placate U.S. demands—the decision was not solely up to Madrid. The Cuban parliament had to agree to the move.

On Saturday, March 26, Woodford received a further bit of encouraging news. Moret visited him and told him that Prime Minister Sagasta would like to meet with Woodford and talk to him informally about an immediate armistice in Cuba. The next day, Woodford wrote Assistant Secretary Day to clarify instructions from a telegram that Woodford had received from Day late Saturday night. The FRUS documents, released just three years after the 1898 war, do not include this important telegram. But from Woodford's reply it is clear that McKinley and Day had suddenly—and without consulting Woodford—upped the ante one more time. The telegram instructed Woodford that the United States would only accept a peace in Cuba that gave Cuba "full self-government" with a "reasonable indemnity." Out of the blue, and at a time of intensely delicate negotiations, McKinley and Day seemed to be demanding that Spain could only have peace if it guaranteed Cuba's complete independence *and* gave the Cuban people a large sum of cash to compensate for years of oppression. And Spain was supposed to agree to all this within just a few days.[104]

In short, just as the Spanish seemed to be actively considering either the armistice or transfer/sale options (or both, since the first could facilitate the second), McKinley was adding new and impossible conditions to the mix. Note, moreover, that these new conditions were being added just three days prior to McKinley's (voluntary!) release of the *Maine* report to Congress— that is, just prior to the massive outpouring of congressional and national outrage that would facilitate the securing of the final congressional resolutions for armed intervention on April 19. The only logical explanation for this telegram is that McKinley and Day suddenly realized that the Spanish government, given its reasonable fear of war with the more powerful United States, might cave in and accept either the armistice or transfer options. And the last thing McKinley wanted at this point was peace.

Woodford was evidently taken aback by this significant and deal-killing increase in U.S. demands. On Sunday, March 27, he wrote Day a telegram that related his positive news about Sagasta's interest in an immediate armistice, but then noted his confusion as to his new instructions. He asked Day pointedly: "Do the words 'full self-government' mean actual recognition of independence, or is nominal Spanish sovereignty over Cuba still permissible?" He also wanted full instructions "as to what the words 'with reasonable indemnity' mean and imply." Woodford went on to tell Day that under the Spanish constitution, the ministry could not recognize the independence of Cuba. Only the Spanish parliament could do so, and it would not meet until April 25—that is, not until after McKinley's self-imposed deadline of April 15. Grasping at straws, Woodford went on to ask whether, if he could secure an immediate armistice between Spanish troops and insurgents "to take effect on or before April 15 . . . this [will] be satisfactory." Such an armistice, he believed, would mean a "present and permanent peace."[105]

Day's response to Woodford on Monday, March 28 is highly instructive. Now fully aware that there was no possible way for the Spanish prime minister and his cabinet to approve a deal that gave Cuba its full independence before April 25, Day told Woodford in a short four-sentence telegram that "Full self-government with indemnity would mean Cuban independence." To add to Woodford's difficulties, Day referred him to a telegram from the day before in which Day had added yet another new demand—namely, the "immediate revocation of [the] reconcentrado order" to allow people to return to their farms and be supplied with provisions from the United States. That this was a bogus demand designed only to impede negotiations and give a humanitarian reason for war is clear. The ruling Liberal government, under U.S. pressure, had made significant progress since October 1897 in closing the reconcentration camps established under the previous regime. Indeed, McKinley had already acknowledged this progress in early 1898. To introduce it now, the day after sending a rambling and self-righteous telegram to Woodford on how the president could no longer sit back and watch the horrors in Cuba that had "shocked and inflamed the American mind, as it [had] the civilized world," could only mean that McKinley was gearing up to make his "humanitarian" case for armed intervention.

Woodford was in a bind. He was preparing himself for what he knew were the final few days in which he might be able to hammer out some sort of deal to avert war, perhaps on the basis of Sagasta's signaling of his willingness to consider an immediate armistice. And yet his superiors in Washington were now requiring him to demand, even as part of an armistice settlement, full independence for Cuba, an indemnity, and an immediate end to reconcentration camps that had already been largely dismantled—three things that would be impossible to achieve in the short time frame he was given. Over the next five days, as Woodford informed Day of his critical meeting with Sagasta, Gullón, and Moret on Tuesday and of a follow-up meeting on Thursday, Day kept sending him one- or two-sentence telegrams that offered no sense of any flexibility on Washington's part. Rather, they simply stated the vital importance of finishing his negotiations as soon as possible—by Thursday, March 31 at the latest—and that feelings in Washington were "intense."[106] These were not the words of an administration seeking to cobble together a peace now that war was imminent.

But the final nail in the coffin for the argument that McKinley was seeking peace but was forced by domestic politics into war is provided by a telegram sent by McKinley directly to Woodford over the weekend of March 26–27. This telegram was conveniently not included in the FRUS documents, but we know of its existence and contents by Woodford's dispatches over the next week. In his telegram, McKinley gave Woodford detailed instructions for how he must conduct himself in his forthcoming meetings with Spanish officials, including the importance of saying that the United States wanted immediate peace in Cuba and an end to the reconcentration camps. This of course is the kind of language a leader uses so that he can later show his public, when selected documents are released, that he wanted peace and was driven by good humanitarian motives. But out of the blue, McKinley also added something new. Woodford was told to include in his prepared statement that he would read to the Spanish that "The President instructs me to say that we do not want Cuba," that is, that the United States would not accept authority over Cuba under any circumstances, presumably either by sale or by a simple transfer.[107]

In his meeting with the Spanish President on Tuesday, Woodford dutifully carried out these instructions.[108] But why would McKinley suddenly introduce the issue of a transfer of Cuban sovereignty to America at this late point in the negotiations? This issue had only been mentioned explicitly in a Woodford memo more than a week before (March 18) and only hinted at in veiled language by the Spanish since then (the "suggestion or proposal" memos). It had never formally been taken up by either party and certainly not by McKinley. Yet here was McKinley suddenly saying that the United States did not seek the possession of Cuba.

Once again, only one interpretation seems to make sense of this. As with McKinley's fear that an armistice might be negotiated before the April 15 deadline—necessitating Day's deal-killing note that Cuba must be given its full independence and provided with an indemnity—now the only remaining fear was that Spain would suddenly fall back on the ultimate logical solution: namely, the peaceful transfer of Cuba to short-term U.S. control. (And of course, both sides knew a U.S. victory in war would lead to exactly this outcome.) Hence, right in the midst of Woodford's final set of negotiations, McKinley forced Woodford to read a prepared line from McKinley saying that he did not want Cuba.[109] By this simple act, McKinley could ensure that the Spanish government did not even offer Cuba as a "suggestion."

On Wednesday, March 30, the day after Woodford read the above instructions from McKinley to Sagasta, Day wrote Woodford yet another deal-killing telegram. Woodford on the previous day had sent a quick four-sentence summary (telegram no. 60) to McKinley right after the meeting with Sagasta, offering a surprisingly optimistic assessment but noting that another meeting was necessary and would be held Thursday afternoon. He told McKinley:

> I have [a] sincere belief that [an] arrangement will then be reached, honorable to Spain and satisfactory to the United States, and not just to Cuba. I beg you to withhold all action until you receive my report of such a conference, which I will send Thursday night, March 31 [i.e., right after his meeting].[110]

If McKinley had been seeking peace, he should have jumped at this, sent encouraging support, and generally reinforced Woodford's efforts. Instead, he had Day send back a two-sentence telegram the next morning which speaks volumes as to the president's intentions: "Your No. 60 is encouraging, but vague as to details. The United States cannot assist in enforcement of any system of autonomy."[111]

Why would McKinley have Day say such a strange thing right before the most important and decisive meeting of the whole crisis? Both men knew—because they had told Woodford that he had to finish his negotiations by Thursday, March 31—that Woodford's meeting would either offer up a peace deal or mean McKinley would proceed to Congress to ask for war. Once again McKinley, just as he had with the line that America "did not want Cuba," was providing a new obstacle to avert any last-minute deal—in this case, a deal on a possible armistice. Day and McKinley were saying to Woodford that they would not help in any plan that involved continued "autonomy" for Cuba, as opposed to something greater—namely, complete independence. But given the short-term restrictions imposed by Spain's constitution—the need to get parliament's approval—continued autonomy was exactly what any armistice would necessarily involve should any deal be made over the next two weeks. McKinley and Day were thus reinforcing to Woodford that he could only discuss solutions that guaranteed Cuba's complete independence, something the ambassador knew was impossible to realize.

Woodford certainly could see that he was being boxed in, and that McKinley was using the constraints imposed on Spain's government by its own democratic constitution to make peace highly unlikely. But he did not give up. Later in the day on Wednesday, he wrote McKinley to provide more details on his Tuesday meeting with Prime Minister Sagasta and to try one more time to convince the president that only some form of a transfer of Cuba to U.S. control would solve the diplomatic stand-off. Woodford reiterated that Sagasta believed that given Spanish domestic politics, it would be almost impossible for the government in Madrid to offer an armistice. But the prime minister had introduced the idea *that if the insurgents were to make the offer*, it would be instantly accepted by his government. He did need six more weeks so that the nominally independent Cuban parliament could meet and agree to such an armistice. But Sagasta hoped that since the United States had waited so long, it could now wait just a bit longer.

Woodford ended his telegram with his personal assessment of the situation. He told McKinley that he had accepted Day's deadline to get a deal by Thursday after the follow-up meeting with Sagasta, Gullón, and Moret. But what Woodford said next constituted a highly unusual move for an ambassador, one justified only by his long friendship with McKinley, the seriousness of the moment, and his suspicions that the president was perhaps being misled by his enthusiastic assistant secretary of state, William Day. He stepped back from his summaries to tell McKinley his personal frustrations regarding the situation. He wrote:

> I have obeyed your instructions literally in stating to [Prime Minister] Sagasta and his colleagues that you do not want Cuba. But I ought, with all respect and in the entire frankness with which you have permitted me to write you, to say that my judgment grows more strong each day that we shall probably have to accept the ownership and the responsible management for Cuba in order to establish permanent peace in the island.

Woodford concluded by asking McKinley to give "due consideration to what I have written so frankly and so fully" while reassuring the president of his loyalty in trying to carry out his wishes.[112]

This telegram was clearly Woodford's last-ditch effort to get McKinley to see the reasonableness of the idea of gaining control of Cuba peacefully rather than fighting a war to achieve the same result. Not surprisingly, since it is clear that the president wanted no such last-minute peaceful solutions, neither he nor Day responded to the substance of Woodford's telegram. The assistant secretary's last dispatch before Woodford's momentous March 31 meeting was apparently written late into the night of March 30 and sent very early Thursday, since Woodford only received it that morning (Madrid being six hours ahead of Washington). It simply stated that there was a "profound feeling in Congress, and the gravest apprehension on the part of most conservative members that a resolution for intervention may pass both branches in spite of any effort which can be made." Day told Woodford that Congress was holding off from immediate action only because of McKinley's assurance that he would submit all the facts of the case "at a very early date" should negotiations fail. Woodford was then informed that "The President assumes that whatever may be reached in your negotiations tomorrow [i.e., that Thursday, March 31] will be tentative only, to be submitted as the proposal of Spain."[113]

Once again, we have a telegram whose hidden meaning defies belief. It was only on Tuesday, March 29 that McKinley had decided, by his choice and free will, to send the *Maine* report to Congress, despite pleas from both Spain and his own ambassador not to do so. He could have easily postponed such a decision for a few days until after he knew of the results of the Thursday meeting. So, for McKinley to argue that radical members of Congress were pushing the nation to war "in spite of any effort that can be made" was disingenuous to say the least. McKinley was making absolutely no effort to achieve peace, and instead putting up roadblocks to Woodford's efforts at every turn. But to add insult to injury, Woodford was being told just before his big meeting that the president was expecting that even if a deal could be reached, it should be considered only "tentative" and "submitted as a proposal of Spain." In short, anything Woodford could come up with as Spain desperately grappled to meet America's impossible demands would not be considered an "agreement" between the United States and the Spanish government, but only a tentative proposal from Spain that McKinley could then consider or reject.

This is devious and cynical Machiavellian politics in the extreme. And yet because of McKinley's finely finessed language, to an outside observer—most importantly, the American public who were given a select number of the telegrams to read when the *Foreign Relations of the United States (FRUS)* book was released in 1901—the telegrams seem to paint a picture of McKinley and Day at least trying to reach an agreement, and then failing because of time pressures and congressional demands. Indeed, McKinley did such a good job in his deception that even today the inadvertent war thesis is the one most Americans and historians accept. But had McKinley truly wanted peace, he simply had to take one of the following actions: ask for an impartial review of the *Maine* case; simply hold off sending the incendiary report of the Naval review board by a few days; help Woodford achieve the transfer/sale option; or facilitate one of the armistice options on the table. Given how desperate the Spanish were to concede to almost any U.S. demand to avoid war, any one of these would have been sufficient to secure a peace. That he did none of them, that he used the Congress's April 19 joint resolution supporting "armed intervention" to declare on April 25 that a "state of war" existed with Spain, that he would immediately send a message that day to the Asian fleet to attack Manila, and that he ordered the occupation of Manila by 20,000 troops only two days after learning of Dewey's victory—all of these actions point to a clear desire for an expansive war on McKinley's part. McKinley could not accept any peace deal because he *needed* a war with Spain to grab overseas territory in the Pacific and the Caribbean (Puerto Rico) to facilitate his Mahanian vision. Any deal would only give the United States short-term control of Cuba in the midst of a civil war—not exactly a great reward for all of McKinley's hard diplomatic work.

The predictable end of the story can be told in short order. Needless to say, Woodford's meeting on March 31 was not successful. On Friday, April 1 he wrote McKinley that the Spanish leaders believed they had "[gone] as far as they could possibly go." They would still accept an armistice, but domestic politics required that the proposal come from the insurgents; otherwise, there would be a revolution within Spain.[114] On Sunday, Woodford told McKinley that the Pope, with the support of a few European powers, was willing to provide his mediation services to achieve the armistice, and that Spain had agreed to this. Woodford still held to his belief that once an armistice was proclaimed, "permanent peace will be secured." Day quickly wrote back, dismissing the idea that the Vatican might play any mediating role, given that he and McKinley understood that Madrid had "already rejected" the possibility of an armistice.[115] For Day to state that the Spanish had rejected the armistice when he and the president *had just been informed that Spain would immediately agree to one* means either that both men had lost their basic faculties, or that they had other plans.

Yet just to make sure that Woodford had not forgotten the president's final condition for peace—the true deal-breaker—Day ended the telegram by stating: "Would the peace you are so confident of securing mean the independence of Cuba? The President cannot hold his message longer than Tuesday [April 5]."[116] This message was of course McKinley's prepared war message to Congress asking Congress to authorize armed intervention against Cuba. The long war message had already been written and was ready to go, but on April 4 and 5 the American consul in Havana, General Lee, wrote McKinley that he needed a delay to ensure he could get Americans off the island before the war started. Belying the supposed power of events and his inability to control them, on the morning of April 6 McKinley announced publicly that he would delay delivering his message until April 11. He explained that he wanted to allow Americans time to evacuate the island. But he said nothing about the collective efforts of the Pope and the European powers a few days before to mediate an armistice, despite the fact that he would have heard of any results in hours.[117] This was a man controlling events down to the last detail—pushing forward or holding back depending on what suited his agenda.

On April 11, as promised, the president presented his war message to Congress. He did so despite the fact that on April 9 a desperate Spanish government had retracted its one and only demand—that the insurgents ask for the armistice first—and then had unilaterally proclaimed an armistice under the auspices of the Pope. The Spanish had now agreed to every one of McKinley's demands, at least as Woodford had presented them: they had declared an armistice, ended the reconcentration camps, and not challenged the *Maine* report. (Woodford had wisely never mentioned McKinley's demand for Cuban independence, and so the Spanish did not offer it.). Yet McKinley still went to Congress with his war message.

In the message, McKinley argued that both material U.S. interests (lost trade and investments) and humanitarian concerns had forced the United States to intervene in Cuba to restore order. He also told Congress that granting Cuba independence after a U.S. victory was not practicable since it would mean recognizing the belligerents and would do nothing to achieve the key U.S. end, the restoration of order.[118] This must have come as a shock to Woodford, given that McKinley had made Cuban independence a key condition for a negotiated peace just three weeks earlier. Clearly, McKinley never had any intention of giving Cuba its immediate independence, regardless of how the United States ended up gaining control of the island. He knew that handing authority over to either the Cuban parliament or the insurgents would only mean continued chaos, and he needed to build order on the island from the ground up. He would thus not allow himself to be restricted by anyone or any legal body from establishing peace on the island as he saw fit.

After a week of debate, a joint resolution in support of armed intervention (the word "war" was never used) was passed in both houses of Congress. Conservative senators were able to insert language, borrowing from the Declaration of Independence, that the people of Cuba were and of right ought to be free and independent. But they dropped their demand that Cuba be recognized as a sovereign republic.[119] McKinley thus had his way. He could agree that in principle the Cuban *people* were free and independent—for Americans, a "self-evident" fact of any colonized people going back to 1775–76 (and soon forgotten when it came to the Philippines). But he could use the lack of recognition of any Cuban government on the ground, whether existing or insurgent, to give him free reign to implement his occupation plans for the island.

Through brilliant manipulation of both U.S.-Spanish diplomacy and American public and congressional opinion, McKinley had the war that he wanted, largely on his own terms. In a parallel to events of 2002–3 regarding Iraq, the U.S. president would be able to conduct war operations against Cuba and Spain in any way he chose, and with the freedom to define war aims in any way he saw fit (aside from annexing Cuba itself). McKinley proceeded to do exactly that. When the congressional intervention resolutions reached his desk on April 21, he waived a ten-day waiting period and immediately signed them into law. The next day, he ordered that a naval blockade be set up around Cuba, which in diplomatic parlance was a direct act of war. Then on April 25, he declared that a "state of war" now existed between the United States and Spain and ordered the Asian fleet to attack Manila.[120]

This declaration of a state of war is the final piece of evidence needed to close the door on the inadvertent war argument. McKinley had every constitutional right to wait ten days to sign the resolutions—time that might have been used to see the insurgents' reaction to Spain's declaration of an armistice, or even to push them to accept it. And the resolutions themselves did not authorize war per se, but only supported the president in demanding that Spain "relinquish its authority . . . [in Cuba] and withdraw its land and naval force from Cuba and Cuban waters."[121] McKinley therefore had no constitutional or domestic need to rush a declaration of a state of war between the countries, especially since he would not be able to actually fight the Spanish in the Atlantic for some two months. But he did have to attack the Spanish in the Philippines in a matter of days. And he did want to ensure that no more diplomatic initiatives—from Spain, the Pope, the European great powers, or his own ambassador—were put forward to divert him from his task. The war was on. And for the United States, it would mean the plunge into the difficult ethical waters of great power imperialism. In the end, however, McKinley would be able to protect U.S. commercial interests in both the Caribbean and the Far East against the threats that had arisen by 1897–98, while providing a chain of strategic positions that would be completed with the building of an isthmus canal. For these important ends, a short war over Cuba seemed well worth the costs and risks.

## Conclusion

This chapter has shown the value of taking a dynamic approach to trade and security in explaining cases that seem to be about liberal ideology and the domestic pressures on U.S. executives. There is certainly no doubt, as Za-karia has shown, that domestic politics acted as a *constraining* force on U.S. presidents and their advisors for two and half decades after the Civil War. But for the most part, the *propelling* forces of policy lay at the systemic level. American leaders and officials clearly wanted to expand the scope of the American economic power sphere after 1865, both because of opportunities to acquire European holdings (the baseline drive of all great powers to ex-pand their realm-one economic power spheres) and because of the percep-tion of increasing threats to current and future U.S. commercial interests for the neutral states of realm two. After 1890, as the United States played the great power game and built up its navy, rising threats in the Pacific and Far East, as Japan and the European powers acted to carve up imperial realms and keep others from enjoying the economic benefits, became more and more self-evident. Thus in 1897–98, President McKinley moved to acquire Hawaii and then stepping-stones to an economic empire in the western Pa-cific. Such an empire would protect U.S. trade interests with China while increasing American leverage over access to Japanese and European holdings and to Japan itself. A war with Spain over Cuba was seen as a useful means to secure ports at Guam and in the Philippines. Formal colonial control of the Philippines was not initially desired, but with internal chaos in the is-lands and the clear intent of Berlin to make a deal with Spain if Washington did not, McKinley reluctantly agreed to incorporate the whole island chain into the growing set of "overseas" territories useful for power projection and the protection of trade routes (Alaska, Hawaii, American Samoa, Guam, and the Philippines in the Pacific; Puerto Rico and Cuba's Guantanamo Bay in the Caribbean).

The Spanish-American War is a critical case for both liberal and neo-Marxist theories. Commercial liberals would hold to the logic that as trade benefits with Cuba fell, domestic pressures to use force—in this case to solve the humanitarian crisis according to Western liberal values—took over and pushed McKinley to act.[122] This we have seen is an incomplete view of the pressures McKinley felt by late 1897 and early 1898. Yes, the pressures of the yellow press and the general outrage in the country over Spanish actions in Cuba raised the domestic costs for McKinley of *not* acting. Most obviously, he might have a harder time getting reelected if popular opinion turned against him over his response to Cuba. But the liberal argument has a hard time understanding why McKinley waited a year to start acting on these pressures, and why he did not jump at Spanish concessions if the war was truly "unwanted." Something in addition to domestic public opinion must have been driving him. Neo-Marxist revisionists, on the other hand, use the 1898 war as one of their best cases for the role of capitalist firms in the conduct of foreign policy. To be sure, during the depression of 1892–96 the heads of firms did talk about their surpluses of production capacity and their need for foreign markets. Yet as the economy turned around after 1896, these demands lessened, and by 1897–98 when the Cuba crisis was heating up again, far fewer firms had an interest in a war to "free" Cuba to make it safe for American investment and trade. And there is little evidence that McKinley listened to the few firms suffering big losses in Cuba when he made his decisions for war. War, if it had to be initiated, was going to be about something much bigger and more important than simply the profits of a few angry capitalists. This is where the commerce of great power politics comes in. States such as Germany and Britain were expressing the age-old need of great powers to expand their trading realms to increase access to resources and markets. But in seeking to increase their penetration of two areas of historical importance to the United States—the Caribbean and the Far East—they directly threatened the long-standing drive to increase America's commercial presence in these regions. Moreover, in Mahanian terms, the thing that would link the regions—the proposed isthmus canal through either Panama or Nicaragua—was at stake. With the trading realms essential to American long-term security at risk, McKinley had to act, and act quickly.

As a final note, it is worth emphasizing the implications of the 1898 war for established democratic peace theory. The case suggests not only that two liberal and democratic states—as both the United States and Spain increasingly were by 1898—can indeed fall into war. More importantly, it shows that if one of the democratic states truly wants war, it can use *the liberal democratic institutions of the other states to prevent a diplomatic solution from being found*. It is a truism of the democratic peace literature that liberal institutions, particularly legislatures, act to extend negotiations and check any "illiberal" aggressive tendencies of executives.[123] Yet in this case, U.S. policy makers effectively used the existence of Spanish legislative institutions—and a new parliament in Cuba established by a liberal government in Madrid to placate previous U.S. demands—to give Spain's executive the impression that it had time to negotiate a solution that would avoid war, and then to hamstring that executive when it learned McKinley was on a very short timeline of his own choosing. In short, the vaunted "added negotiation time" said by democratic peace theorists to help democracies find a deal they prefer to war can also be manipulated by war-desiring leaders such as McKinley to put the other off the scent until it is too late.

In the case of U.S. worries about Germany, of course, it seems clear that the German government's more authoritarian nature did indeed heighten McKinley's belief that Berlin might be seeking its place in the sun in the Pacific and the Caribbean at the Americans' expense. McKinley thus made sure he averted a diplomatic solution that would have put off the U.S. seizure of critical strategic ports in the Pacific (in the Philippines and Guam) and the Caribbean (in Cuba and Puerto Rico). But the fact that he also worried about British moves with regard to China and the Caribbean islands, and that he chose war over peace with a democracy (Spain) indicates that the fear of the future can drive democracies to plunge into conflict or war even against states like themselves. Future research on democratic peace needs to explore other cases where leaders manipulate the constraining or propelling effects of the other democracy's legislature to bring on wars that only those leaders want.

# 6

# The U.S. Entry into the First World War

THE AMERICAN entry into the First World War in April 1917 is one of the great puzzles in the study of American foreign policy. After all, the United States had done very well for itself by *staying out* of the Great War for the two and half years from August 1914 until March 1917. Its economy by late 1916 was booming, having pulled itself out of the recession of 1913–14 through a quadrupling of exports to Europe. And by sitting on the sidelines while others bled themselves dry, it was not only growing rapidly in relative economic and military power, but it had shifted from a debtor nation to the world's primary lending state—with New York overtaking London as the center of global finance.

Why not let this favorable situation continue, and then bring America in only at the very end to secure the peace? With U.S. relative power transcendent, Washington would have both the clout and the moral influence to perhaps solve the problem of great power war once and for all. This scenario was indeed President Woodrow Wilson's fervent hope through 1916. The fact that Wilson *chose* to move his nation to war against Germany in late March 1917, even though Berlin hoped he would not, only adds to the mystery. Yes, Germany had returned to unrestricted submarine warfare in late January 1917, and this greatly increased the threat to U.S.-European commerce. Yet German subs had been sinking American merchant ships throughout the war, and on two occasions in 1915 and 1916, after Germany sunk passenger ships with Americans on board, the two countries had been close to war. Yet Wilson had always found diplomatic ways to avoid a war he both feared and found morally distasteful. So why switch to a war footing in March 1917 when diplomacy had succeeded in the past?

Historians over the past half-century have offered a number of explanations for the puzzle. Most in one way or another revolve around the notion that Wilson reluctantly moved to war because Germany's shift to unrestricted sub warfare signaled that his preferred option, a mediated peace, was now off the table. Entry into the war was thus the only way left for Wilson to achieve his ideological agenda—namely, to rebuild international relations on the basis of the liberal principles of self-determination, democratization, freer trade, and collective security institutions. The old European notions of balance of power politics had to give way to a new way of thinking—to the building of trust through "communities of power" rather than the building of arms and alliances to facilitate imperialist expansionism.[1] For almost all historians, Wilson's actions in March–April 1917 constitute the preeminent case of deeply rooted American ideology overriding calculations of advantage and selfish national interest. Wilson had a liberal vision, paraphrasing Thomas Paine, to remake the world anew; and nothing, not even the likely deaths of hundreds of thousands of American boys in history's most bloody war, was going to stop him.[2]

If this established historical view is correct, the American entry into World War I constitutes a decisive case against the realist-based theory put forward in this book. And Wilson does seem to be the preeminent example in U.S. history of a leader driven from an early age by a vision of reshaping the world according to the best elements of American republicanism. Yet this historical perspective faces two big problems. First, it tends to ignore or greatly underplay the geopolitical dimension of Wilson's mindset, his ability to understand traditional notions of power positioning and the use of force to realize a nation's ends.[3] Second, by portraying Wilson as a starry-eyed idealist or as a brilliant visionary who was ahead of his time, historians on both sides of the ideological spectrum miss one crucial aspect of his pre-1919 mindset: namely, his fundamental pragmatism, in particular his ability to make trade-offs between goals and to put in place policies that promised slow and steady "progress" as opposed to instantaneous changes for the better. (Such progress was more in line with the thinking of his intellectual hero, British Whig Edmund Burke, than with the social democratic radicals of the late nineteenth century with whom Wilson is often associated.) It is true that by the time of the Versailles peace conference in 1919, Wilson had become more an idealist than a realist.[4] And we can certainly fault him for trying in 1919–20 to impose his singular vision on a reluctant world and a divided U.S. Senate. Yet if we examine Wilson prior to April 1917 without filtering our observations through the lens of the postwar disaster of Versailles, a quite different picture of the man emerges.

The goal of this chapter is a simple one. I seek to show that existing side by side with Wilson's ideals and his constantly developing vision for a new international system was a deeply geopolitical outlook on global politics and the role economic power and trade play in the security of the United States. Wilson and his closest advisors, in particular Colonel Edward House and Robert

Lansing, understood a basic fact of all great power politics: that if the state does not defend its economic power sphere, the long-term security of the state and its way of life may be called into question. In the U.S. case, the key to a large and growing economic sphere over the previous nine decades had been the upholding of the Monroe Doctrine and its various corollaries. Wilson's predecessors, Teddy Roosevelt and William Howard Taft, had placed great emphasis on keeping the European powers out of the Caribbean and Central America and in reducing their financial influence both there and in South America. Woodrow Wilson, notwithstanding his efforts to project a new and more cooperative U.S. policy toward Latin American and Caribbean states, was in the end very similar in his obsession with U.S. protection of these states from European political and economic influence.

There is no question that he cultivated a public persona that was more "liberal" regarding the western hemisphere—including the promotion of freer trade, the seeking of a Pan-American pact of collective security, and the recognition of rights to national self-determination.[5] But in practice, in the face of the violent rise of revolutionary and counterrevolutionary movements in the western hemisphere, he chose the promotion of order over democratic change and the encouragement of the independence of regional states from European great power agendas over the economic growth of those states. In short, prior to 1918 and much like his predecessors James Madison and James Monroe, Wilson was a liberal pragmatist: while he certainly *hoped* that the world and the U.S. neighborhood would become more democratic over time, he was more than willing to sacrifice this long-term objective for the immediate goal of ensuring the dominance of U.S. economic and commercial power in the western hemisphere and beyond. And by 1915–16, he was prepared to back this up with a level of American naval strength that he believed had to be superior by the war's end even to Britain's.

This chapter shows that Wilson's obsession with protecting America's economic power sphere must be placed side by side with his idealism in any comprehensive explanation for his entry into World War I. And once we do so, we can then have the true scholarly debate this fascinating case demands— namely, about the relative causal salience of systemic commercial and power-political pressures versus the bottom-up forces of Wilson's ideology and his need for domestic political support, including from his own advisors. My deeper position in this chapter is a controversial one: that despite his ideological goals and concern for internal support, he made his decision for war in March 1917 based on the impact a German victory would have on America's ability to uphold its commercial and geopolitical position in the western hemisphere and around the world. This was primarily a realist calculation, and only secondarily a liberal or idealistic one. It was a decision that fit well with his foreign policy behavior from March 1913, when he entered office, until April 1917.

As I will show, even before the war began in 1914, Wilson had been gravely concerned that Germany was seeking to use upheaval in Mexico and certain Caribbean states to increase its financial and political penetration of the region and to reduce America's economic role.[6] Once the war in Europe got underway, this concern gradually morphed into a fear that Germany might use Mexico and the Caribbean to set up military bases, encourage conflict with the United States, and to establish a beachhead for further political and military control of the region. Any German success here might not only hurt direct regional trade with the United States; it might also endanger the Panama Canal and thus the established policy of expanding U.S. economic and strategic control over the Pacific region, from the west coast of South America to the Philippines and East Asia.

As the European powers settled into the military stalemate that characterized the years from 1914 to 1916, Wilson could remain confident not only that no European power could directly threaten America's sphere, but that the United States could gradually replace Britain and Germany as primary suppliers of loans and manufactured goods in the region. Wilson thus placed great emphasis on increasing U.S. trade ties within the hemisphere, and with the building of a merchant fleet and an inter-hemisphere banking system that would displace the Europeans. Yet all through the first years of the European war, he worried that one side or the other would win a decisive victory. This would fundamentally shift the distribution of power away from the multipolar standoff that had served the United States so well for so many decades. If Britain and its allies were to win, London might use its predominant naval position to dominate global trade and commerce, not just in Latin America but around the world. Yet even more frightening than British "navalism," as he called it, was the prospect of a German victory over the Allied Powers that would leave Germany hegemonic on the Continent and perhaps in control of a certain percentage of British colonies and naval ships. Given Germany's ongoing desire to cause trouble for the United States in Mexico and the Caribbean, German hegemony in Europe could only mean a significant increase in the threat to America's economic sphere in its own backyard (especially if Germany were to align with Japan to split U.S. power between two oceans).

What made the situation of February–March 1917 different from previous tensions in 1915 and 1916 was the now very real risk that Germany might actually win by knocking Britain, the linchpin of the whole Allied cause, out of the war and by forcing France and Russia to sue for peace. This would very likely mean an unequal peace that would lead to Germany's absorption of British and French colonies, trade routes, and perhaps even naval ships. Up until late

January 1917, Wilson had believed that he might still forge a "peace without victory"—that is, a peace between relatively equal great powers bound within a collective security system and able to deter future aggression by the combined strengths of many great powers. Yet if Germany won the Continent and beat Britain, such a stabilizing peace could not be realized, and the United States would then have to try to deter Germany's economic and political expansionism on its own.[7]

Berlin's announcement of its return to unrestricted submarine warfare in late January 1917 thus constituted a direct threat to America's economic power, not only by reducing ongoing trade to Britain and France, but more importantly, by credibly threatening a German victory that would quickly change Germany's ability to penetrate the western hemisphere. Yet in February Wilson still hesitated. He cut off diplomatic relations with Germany and sent its ambassador home. But he did not push for an immediate plunge into war. The reason was simple: given the German willingness in 1915–16 to back away from sub attacks on neutral shipping when Washington expressed outrage, he still held out hope that Berlin might use the threat of sub warfare to deter American shippers but hold off from actual attacks in the face of Wilson's strong stance and the arming of U.S. merchant ships.

Two things changed his assessment of German intentions. The first was the revelation of the so-called Zimmermann telegram in late February, showing that Germany was seeking an alliance with Mexico and possibly Japan should it fall into war with the United States. This reinforced that Germany was serious about gaining a strategic foothold in the New World, possibly in the most strategically important state of all—namely, Mexico. It also suggested that German leaders were driven by more than a mere fear of neighbors. The second shock came on March 16 to 18 when the Germans, after giving the American merchant ships a grace period in February and early March, sunk three ships without warning over as many days. With many more subs in the waters surrounding Britain than they had in campaigns of 1915–16, this signal of German seriousness meant that neutral shipping to Britain would be devastated, and Britain's economic survival gravely threatened. Moreover, it made clear that Germany was going all-out with one final effort at total victory.

The "peace of equals" that Wilson had called for in January was now clearly off the table, and with Russia temporarily weakened by revolution, the risk of a decisive German victory was very much heightened. The day after a crucial cabinet meeting on March 20, Wilson made up his mind. He informed Congress that he would speak to a special joint session in less than two weeks. On April 2, he stood before Congress and asked it for a declaration that a state of war existed between the United States and Germany. The long-standing policy of Americans staying out of European wars—a policy going back to George

Washington—was now officially over. The perilous systemic situation had made this necessary.

In what follows, I will show that Wilson's thinking about international relations from March 1913 onward was both calculating and highly geopolitical. While he did have lofty goals for long-term global progress—goals that grew exponentially *after* America's first year in the European war—he knew from 1915 on that trade-offs regarding his objectives had to be made, and that he could never sacrifice regional order and U.S. economic control of its sphere for any idealistic visions that he or others (such as his first secretary of state William Jennings Bryan) may have been entertaining. In particular, he resisted any efforts by any other great powers—whether Germany, Japan, or Britain—to increase their economic and political influence in Central America and the Caribbean region. An updated version of the Monroe Doctrine was the key to his whole international outlook because it provided the basis for U.S. economic dominance in both the western hemisphere and in global affairs. And when this doctrine was threatened in late 1916 and early 1917, he reluctantly accepted the necessity of war as the only means left to protect America's long-term security.

## Chaos in Mexico and the German Connection, 1913–14

In 1910–11 Mexico fell into revolution, the first major social revolution of the twentieth century. The dictator Porfirio Diaz, who had ruled Mexico since the 1870s, was overthrown. By the fall of 1911, the liberal Francisco Madero had assumed the office of president and began a program of limited social reform to improve the conditions of Mexico's lower and middle classes. When Madero himself was overthrown and killed in a coup by military leader Victoriano Huerta in February 1913, European leaders, concerned about Madero's efforts to reduce the influence of foreign capital, were quite pleased. Incoming U.S. president Woodrow Wilson was not. Upon assuming office in early March, Wilson made it clear he would not recognize Huerta's new government and signaled that he expected the European great powers to do the same. Wilson saw Mexico as a test case for his new approach to American foreign policy. Part of this approach was ideological: he did not want the United States to be seen as just another imperialist power, acting against smaller states to promote the interests of private corporate interests. He thus explicitly rejected Taft's "dollar diplomacy"—the encouragement of private lending and investment in Latin America and East Asia to shape these regions' development, and the use of U.S. forces to protect company holdings and to ensure repayment of outstanding loans. Wilson understood that past U.S. support for dictators and local business interests had helped increase the level of left-wing revolutionary activity across Central America, and in Mexico in particular. Yet he also wanted to signal that Washington would not tolerate leftist revolutions that sought to overthrow established governments. His logic was clear: the path to development was the "slow and steady" middle course of orderly government and the gradual modernization of a country's economy. Either extreme—right or left—would only lead to revolution and chaos, allowing European powers and Japan to intervene to improve their economic prospects at the expense of the U.S. sphere.

One week after inauguration, on Tuesday, March 11, Wilson held a cabinet meeting to discuss Mexico. Washington, he stressed, must demonstrate to states in the region that it favored "stable government." In particular, the United States must stop selfish leaders from fomenting troubles for personal aggrandizement or hoping that America would "wink" at revolution and do nothing.[8] The next day, Wilson stated this publicly, adding that he would accept only constitutionally authorized changes in government within Central and South America. In addition, he would act not for any special interest groups but only for the "development of personal and trade relationships" that would redound to the advantage of both sides.[9] Within a week of taking office, therefore, Wilson had established a middle-ground position toward smaller states in the western hemisphere that he would largely follow for the rest of his time in office. He would help them create order and good government (as defined by his administration) while protecting themselves from either greedy dictators on the right or violent revolutions on the left.[10]

Over the next eight months, Wilson worked to push Huerta to step down and allow a constitutional government to form. Huerta agreed to call elections for October. But when October came, he refused to relinquish the presidency, manipulating the legislative elections to ensure the dominance of his factions against the "constitutionalists" that opposed him. During 1913, Britain not Germany was the main thorn in Wilson's side. British private investments in Mexico were second only to the United States, and Britain was particularly dependent on Mexican oil exports out of the east coast port of Tampico to run its navy. The British government ignored Wilson's pleas and recognized Huerta's government in April 1913. It then sent to Mexico City as its new minister Lionel Carden, a diplomat with years of experience in Central American affairs, but with a known hatred for America's efforts to displace Britain as the preeminent economic power in Latin America. In October 1913, Carden signaled that Britain accepted Huerta's decision not to step down, and that it would work with Huerta and his legislature.

For Wilson, this constituted a clear threat to America's position in the region. At a speech in Mobile, Alabama on October 27 to the Southern Commercial Congress, he outlined how he saw the tie between global commerce and regions such as Central America. American industrialization had made the United States the number one manufacturing nation in the world, and to sustain that growth, it needed foreign markets and places for investment. He told the Mobile audience that "The future . . . is going to be very different for this hemisphere from the past." The states to the south had to be drawn closer to America by a common understanding of both their commercial interests and shared history. He wondered if the audience realized "the significance of the tides of commerce" that would be created by the opening of the Panama Canal, planned for the summer of 1914. The canal would link the manufacturing and banking heartland of the eastern United States with the west coast of Latin America, opening up a commerce that the world had not known before. The importance of this shift could not be overstated; indeed, "we are closing one chapter in the history of the world and are opening another of great, unimaginable significance."[11]

Yet there was a looming problem. Latin American states were being forced to grant concessions to "foreign interests," which allowed these interests to "dominate their domestic affairs, a condition of affairs always dangerous and apt to become intolerable." The United States, therefore, must prove to these states that it was a different sort of great power, that it showed itself as a friend that comprehends their needs and was there to help them develop not simply their economies but their "constitutional liberty" and "national integrity." Wilson was using the occasion to signal in the clearest way possible that while America would act strongly in the western hemisphere, it would do so to promote a middle way that created a balance between economic growth, political order, constitutional rule of law, and independence from the European great powers.[12]

His discussion the next day (October 28) with his main advisor and confidante, Colonel Edward House, reveals just how much Central America and fears of foreign influence were driving U.S. policy in a harder-line direction. The "Mexican question" was "absorbing his attention," House wrote in his diary. Both men recognized that the Monroe Doctrine had been driven by the need to keep Europe from securing political control of states in the western hemisphere. But for Wilson, "it is just as reprehensible to permit foreign states to secure financial control of these weak and unfortunate republics," and he would make this the key point of his December speech before Congress. Wilson wanted to let the British public learn of what London was up to in Mexico—namely, the propping up of Huerta's regime and the effort to maintain and extend concessions to British oil companies.

Relations with London would likely deteriorate, House noted. Yet the president accepted this, and setting a precedent for the future, he was prepared even to risk war to uphold America's position in the region. In their conversation, House reminded the president that when House had been speaking in

London with British foreign secretary Edward Grey, he had emphasized that Wilson was a much tougher individual than Secretary of State Bryan, and that "he [Wilson] did not look upon war in the same spirit as [Bryan], and he was not a man to be trifled with." The president noted that he might need to declare war on Mexico even if the United States did not immediately attack the country. Wilson's purpose here "[was] to keep the powers from interfering and entirely out of the situation" as he reduced Huerta's resistance by blockading ports and reducing his customs revenue.[13]

The riskiness of what was being contemplated was clear to both men. Utilizing an ancient Roman metaphor, House's diary continues:

> The President seems alert and unafraid. He realizes that his course may possibly bring about a coalition of the European Powers against this Government, but he seems ready to throw our gauntlet into the arena and declare all hands must be kept off [Mexico] excepting our own.[14]

By this point, the British were getting a sense of U.S. anger over London's support for Madero. Once again, Europe's multipolar situation played to the Americans' advantage. Unwilling to alienate the Americans when they had the Germans to worry about, the British acquiesced to Wilson in mid-November, such that Bryan could tell the press that "the foreign powers [would] not offer any objection" to the United States carrying out its preferred policies in Mexico. Yet the Germans were not at all happy about this turn of events. Berlin had been letting London take the lead in opposing Wilson over Huerta and had been signaling that it would support the British had they been willing to resist. Britain's back-down forced Germany to also acquiesce, at least for the near term.[15]

The crisis that he had believed might risk war with Britain and Germany was over. Germany resigned itself to merely trying to clarify Washington's intentions in Mexico. When Wilson proved unwilling to do so, German suspicions of American intentions grew. By February–March 1914, Berlin knew only that Wilson wanted a "free hand" to pursue a policy suited to American interests.[16] By that point, London had given Wilson this free hand in return for a promise to reverse a U.S. policy that would have imposed discriminatory tolls on non-American ships moving through the soon-to-be-opened Panama Canal.[17] Wilson had decided in February–March to begin supplying the Constitutionalists with weapons to help overthrow Huerta. But when he increased the U.S. naval presence in the Gulf and began to escalate the conflict with Huerta through a minor diplomatic incident in early April, the Germans had had enough. They decided to act.

On April 9, 1914, the Mexican authority at Tampico arrested two Americans from Admiral Henry Mayo's flagship the U.S.S. *Dolphin*. The Americans were soon released, and the incident seemed over. But Mayo, clearly aware of Wilson's desires, demanded a formal apology and the firing of a 21-gun salute to the American flag. Huerta's government resisted, and Wilson used this resistance to escalate the crisis. On April 20 he addressed Congress and asked for a resolution authorizing the use of armed force. He stated he would take action against Huerta, not the Mexican people, but was vague as to the actual steps he was contemplating. As the crisis escalated, the German steamship *Ypiranga* was loaded with arms for Huerta's army and moved into the Gulf of Mexico. In the very early morning of April 21, Bryan was informed that the *Ypiranga* was scheduled to unload its arms at Veracruz later that day. Wilson was awakened and updated by Bryan over the telephone. Wilson told the normally cautious Bryan: "you understand what drastic action [this] . . . might mean." Bryan said he had fully considered this before phoning. The equally cautious secretary of the navy, Josephus Daniels, was now brought into the discussion, and said he agreed that immediate action should be taken to prevent the Germans from unloading the arms. According to bystander Joseph Tumulty, Wilson's personal secretary, Wilson said to Daniels, without a moment's delay, "Daniels, send this message to Admiral Mayo: Take Vera Cruz at once." Wilson confided to Tumulty just afterward that "we are now on the brink of war and there is no alternative."[18]

U.S. forces attacked Veracruz at dawn the same day, and by 11:00 A.M. had control of the city. The *Ypiranga* arrived two hours later, and was detained, an illegal act since the United States and Germany were not at war. To avoid further escalation, Bryan apologized to the German ambassador, and the ship was allowed to depart without further incident. But the feeling among U.S. officials that war with Mexico was already underway and that the Veracruz incursion would soon escalate was palpable. As House wrote in his diary, "Of course we are all distressed over the beginning of war with Mexico . . . It will be difficult to restrict the sphere of war to Vera Cruz. The war feeling will grow on both sides of the Rio Grande, and there is no telling where it will end."[19] Fortunately, both sides decided to accept the diplomatic intervention of Argentina, Brazil, and Chile, and the crisis did not lead to any further military clashes over the next few weeks. The Germans continued to support Huerta privately through May, seeking to gain concessions in the oil-rich area surrounding Tampico in return.[20] Once it was clear to Huerta, however, that he could not maintain his hold on power, he agreed to have the German navy transport him to safety outside the country. On July 17, 1914, Huerta boarded the ship *Dresden* for a short trip to Jamaica.

The first phase of the ongoing 1912–17 crisis with Mexico was over. The United States had managed to avoid a clash with both Britain (October 1913) and Germany (April 1914). It had also kept the Mexican incursion to the barest minimum needed to pressure Huerta to leave the country. But the fact that Wilson had been willing to take a stand that could have spiraled to all-out war with Mexico or even another great power is a clear sign that protecting the U.S. political and economic sphere of influence from European intrusion was one of his top foreign policy priorities. As we have seen, Wilson and House's new view of the Monroe Doctrine—that the United States must resist the efforts of European powers to shape the behavior of regional powers through foreign direct investments and not just increased trade and bank lending—was now a critical aspect of Wilson's strategy for the western hemisphere.[21] This view would set the stage for how Wilson and House understood World War I and its significance for U.S. interests.

## The Early Stages of the European War, 1914–15

In the late spring of 1914, Wilson and House were becoming increasingly aware that the growing hostility between the European great powers could lead to actual war. In June, Wilson sent House over to Europe to see if American "New World" insights into the causes of conflict and war might help the Europeans avoid a horrific war. A core premise of Wilson and House's perspective at the time was one that Wilson would hold onto for the next two and a half years— namely, that major wars were less the result of calculated aggression than a function of misunderstanding and poor means-end thinking. Wrong-headed views of others' motives and of the best way to realize security led leaders to believe that their security was best satisfied by massive military buildups, re-strictions on others' economic growth, and hard-line posturing in negotia-tions. Such behaviors would create spirals of hostility and the desire to attack first for fear of the other's attack. When in Europe in June, House thus sought to convince the Germans to slow their arms and naval buildups to reassure their neighbors of their moderate intentions, and to convince the British to grant Germany greater access to colonies and trade around the globe.[22] The effort of course failed, and by early August, all the major powers except Italy were locked into a devastating war that would drag on for more than four years.

In historical writing about Wilson for the 1914–16 period, it is almost always assumed that his perspective on the war was shaped primarily by ideational factors—his outrage at the personal costs of the war; his concern for the viola-tions of neutral rights; his desire to end the war on terms that would make the repetition of such a horrific war impossible; and so forth.[23] Yet as this section will make clear, Wilson's high ideals and "idealism" went hand in hand and indeed operated in tension with his savvy understanding of geopolitics. For Wilson, great power politics had to be seen in terms of threats to America's economic sphere, and he thus shaped his policy choices to maximize their impact on America's long-term economic and military power position. After all, none of Wilson's ideals could be realized over the long term if the United States could not sustain its now clearly dominant global economic position.

In mid-August 1914, Wilson made his first major public statement on the war. He cautioned Americans that despite the troubling news from abroad, citizens needed to put America "first in our thoughts" and maintain a posture of neutrality and "undisturbed judgment."[24] In straightforward geopolitical terms, this self-centered America-first attitude made perfect sense. With three thousand miles of ocean between Europe and the United States, there was no immediate threat to America's position in the western hemisphere. The war itself, like the Napoleonic Wars, the last general European conflict, would likely lead to massive increases in U.S. exports and growth in American shipping—at least as long as the United States could skirt the blockades without being drawn into war, as in the War of 1812 (a conflict Wilson knew well as a historian).[25] This would help the United States get out of its current recession and replace the European powers as suppliers of manufactured goods to Latin America. Moreover, as a sideline-sitting state, America could be expected to grow immensely in relative economic and military power as the European states whittled themselves down through costly warfare.[26] His ambassador in London, Walter Page, had already told him on August 9 that no matter who won the war, all the European powers would be bankrupt, and that "relatively" speaking, "we shall be immensely stronger financially and politically." Thanking heaven for the Atlantic Ocean, Page warned his old friend to "be ready; for you will be called on to [resolve] this huge quarrel."[27] For the next two and a half years, Wilson would follow this advice, using diplomacy to position the United States to dominate world affairs and establish what he would later call a properly crafted "scientific peace."

In the first three weeks of the war, as the German army pushed on toward Paris, Wilson and House began to discuss the long-term geopolitical implications of different possible outcomes. Japan had come into the war in mid-August on the side of the Allies (it had been allied with Britain since 1902), and quickly began to move against German possessions in China and the South Pacific. Edward House, having learned that Britain was worried that Japan might try to grab German Samoa (next to American Samoa), wrote Wilson on August 22 that he was worried that Japan's behavior might force the United States into the war. House then pressed a theme that would become crucial to his and especially Wilson's thinking for the next two years: that if *either* side won a decisive victory, this would constitute a threat to American security and way of life. The "saddest feature of the [current] situation" was that there "was no good outcome to look forward to." Should the Allies win, "it means largely the domination of Russia on the Continent of Europe," while

if Germany wins, "it means the unspeakable tyranny of militarism for genera-
tions to come."[28]

When House and Wilson met on August 30, they engaged in their first
detailed discussion of the geopolitical implications of the war and its causes.
Looking into the long-term future, Wilson presciently noted that it was "quite
possible that eventually there might be but two great nations in the world,
Russia . . . and [the United States]." As for the immediate war, Wilson agreed
that if Germany won "it would change the course of our civilization and make
the United States a military nation." As for the war's causes, Wilson reiterated
his view that the prewar arms race had created a "powder magazine" of mistrust that had led the nations to stumble into an unnecessary war.[29] Wilson
would hold to this view until March 1917, and it would undergird his and
House's peace efforts for the next two and a half years. Both men strongly
believed that if European leaders could be made to see that efforts to build up
naval and land-based power did not enhance security but undermined it, they
would reject Old World realpolitik thinking and replace it with a new and
more "scientific" version of power politics. At its core, this was not inherently
naïve. From the perspective of international relations theory, we can say that
both Wilson and House were "spiral modelers" who recognized that states
worried about their security may build up their military power and yet end up
creating spirals of hostility that lead them to plunge into wars that they might
have otherwise avoided—with the First World War being the preeminent
example.[30]

House and Wilson through the fall of 1914 sought to convince both sides
that their enemies were not pathologically aggressive but rather acting from
distorted views of the best means to security. In an effort to get the British to
consider negotiations with Germany, House met with British ambassador
Cecil Spring-Rice on September 20, 1914. House suggested that London seek
a disarmament agreement with Germany in return for German concessions
on Belgium. Spring-Rice liked the idea but believed the Germans could not
be trusted. House replied by warning of the risks of *not* making a deal and then
grappling with "the stupendous consequences of [Allied] defeat"—that is,
German hegemony in Europe. House also added an acute geopolitical point:
Spring-Rice should see that "if the Allies won and Germany was thoroughly
crushed, there would be no holding back Russia, and the past situation [i.e.,
pre-1914 Europe] would hardly be less promising than the future."[31] Russia, in
sum, was a long-term threat to the system and Britain should recognize it
now—a view similar to the way the Germans thought prior to the war.[32]

The president was wholly in agreement with House's thinking. On September 28, House and Wilson met to discuss a possible mediation role for the
United States. Neither could see any possibility for such a role immediately,

or at least not until the war became a draw. House related his conversation with Spring-Rice on the geopolitical dangers of postponing negotiation. He also mentioned German ambassador Johann von Bernstoff's signaling of Berlin's willingness to discuss peace and his suggestion that House go to London to "see what could be done." Wilson was against moving too quickly, telling House that he would be sent when the time was right. (House would in fact make such a trip four months later). Wilson was not avoiding the issues but rather preparing the ground for a later mediating role. He told House that he should write Grey directly "and tell him of the dangers of postponing peace negotiations. If Germany and Austria are entirely crushed, neither of us [Wilson or House] could see any way by which Russia could be restrained." This, Wilson thought, should be brought "strongly to Sir Edward's attention."[33]

We can see that by September 1914, Wilson and House, concerned that either Germany or Russia would win the war, were seeking to convince Britain, the linchpin to the Allied cause, to consider a negotiated peace before either outcome became a reality. Yet as Wilson waited for the right moment to offer his services, he was also seeking to increase U.S. trade both with Europe and Latin America. In mid-September, he and House started discussing the idea of pushing Congress to pass a shipping bill that would build the American merchant marine, with government support. He also protested to London about British orders in council that allowed the interception and seizure of neutral shipping to Europe. Wilson was well aware that British behavior could lead to a U.S. response that might even end up in a British-American war. In a September 29 meeting with House, Wilson read a passage on the War of 1812 from his five-volume *History of the American People*. He told House that "The circumstances of the war of 1812 and [the current situation] run parallel. I sincerely hope they will not go further."[34]

British restrictions on U.S. shipping to the Continent were, in the short term, hurting the U.S. economy. Of particular concern were bales of cotton that were sitting in Southern warehouses awaiting shipment to Germany. From October to the end of November, relations with London were tense to say the least. State department counsellor (and future secretary of state) Robert Lansing was pushing for a hard-line stance against the British, even at the risk of war. Ambassador Page in London wrote to Wilson and Bryan on October 15 to urge caution, arguing that the British were in a life-or-death struggle with Germany, and that America would be doing the same if in Britain's place.[35]

It seems clear that it was the fear that Germany might win in Europe and then pose a threat to the western hemisphere, rather than any moral inhibitions, that helped Wilson decide not to press London to end its restrictions on U.S. shipping, despite the short-term economic costs. Aside from fearing a repeat of the War of 1812, Wilson was receiving advice from both Page and

House indicating the implications of a German victory. In the above memo to the president and Bryan, Page had reiterated a point he had made to Wilson in early September that if Germany were to win, "we shall see the Monroe Doctrine shot through" and the United States would be forced to build both "a great army and a great navy."[36] Page had also been writing directly to House, warning him that Lansing's hard-line stance would not cause the British to buckle and would only antagonize them.[37] When House met with Wilson in late November, he emphasized that Germany, should it win, would move forcefully into the U.S. sphere of influence.

> I told him that I had it on fairly good authority that the Kaiser had it in mind to suggest to us that the Monroe Doctrine should extend only to the Equator, which would *leave Germany free to exploit Brazil and the other South America countries* [should Britain be defeated]. Brazil seems to be the main object of Germany's desires.

Wilson's response is instructive. Instead of dismissing House's view as paranoid or extreme, the president replied "that the war [in Europe] was perhaps a Godsend to us, for if it had not come we might have been embroiled in war ourselves."[38] Here is Wilson voicing out loud his concern that given Germany's commercial and political ambitions in Latin America, had the Allies not been fighting to contain Germany in Europe, the Americans might have had to fight it in their own hemisphere.

Not surprisingly, it was in the same late November meeting with Wilson that House also broached the idea that the United States needed to rethink its relationship with the states of the western hemisphere. We have seen that with the Mobile address of October 1913, Wilson had signaled what House lauded as "a new interpretation of the Monroe Doctrine," one designed to keep Europe from securing political control of the hemisphere's smaller states through financial means.[39] But with war raging in Europe, it was now clear that the relationship with the hemisphere had to change. At the November meeting, while praising Wilson's 1913 domestic reforms, House advised him that it was time to "pay less attention to domestic policy and greater attention to the welding together of the two Western Continents." This required a new constructive policy that would "show the world that friendship, justice, and kindliness were more potent that the mailed fist." The old U.S. approach of "wielding the 'big stick' and dominating the two Continents"—one that Wilson himself tried to follow since March 1913—was ultimately self-defeating, since by doing so "we [had] lost the friendship and commerce of South and Central American and the European countries had profited by it."[40]

Initially, House had no clear plan for making this happen. By mid-December, however, he had developed a bold outline for a hemispheric security system; one that, as he told Wilson on December 16, would not only bring the western hemisphere together, but would "serve as a model for the European Nations when peace is at last brought about." Wilson was so excited by House's ideas that he took up a pencil and wrote down the agreed points for a potential Pan-American pact—points that included "mutual guarantees of political independence under republican forms of government" as well as government control over "the manufacture and sale of munitions of war."[41] As Marc Gilderhaus notes, these ideas were not wholly new to Wilson; a Columbian diplomat had suggested a treaty outlawing "the conquest of territory" in early 1914. Yet prior to the European war, Wilson's reaction had been largely dismissive.[42] Clearly, dangers and opportunities created by the war had changed Wilson's risk calculus. He now needed something that would not only solidify the U.S. position in the Americans' own backyard, but an institutionalized structure that, if it worked, could be used to convince the Europeans to make peace on terms that would prevent the emergence of any hegemon in Eurasia.

As we will see, it would take until 1916 for Wilson to publicly embrace the idea of a full-blown *great power* collective security system, and here he would draw inspiration not just from idealists but from realists such as former presidents Taft and Roosevelt.[43] But until then, Wilson had an idea that would, at the very least, solidify America's own sphere and keep the Europeans at bay. To his great disappointment, the Pan-American Pact would never be consolidated prior to America's entry into the war. Yet in December 1914, Wilson and House felt they now had a foundation for solving the problem of trust between nations—even if it was designed only for a hemisphere that the United States already dominated.

## A Time of Uncertainty, 1915–16

Through the year 1915, Wilson struggled hard both to keep the United States out of the war in Europe and to help the belligerents find a way back to some form of the multipolar status quo ante—what he would later call, in January 1917, a "peace without victory." The initial ideas for a great power collective security system were first broached by the liberal group the Women's Peace Party in January 1915 and the conservative group the League to Enforce Peace in May 1915. It would take more than a year—until May 1916—for Wilson to solidify and publicly announce his own ideas on what British foreign secretary Edward Grey had labeled back in April 1915 a "League of Nations."[44] This is a significant fact, given that we often assume it was Wilson himself that drove the campaign for a global collective security system. In this, he was a follower not a leader. He would of course be its greatest champion by late 1916/early 1917. But until May 1916, his focus was on protecting the U.S. backyard and achieving a peace in Europe that would *maintain* the checks and balances standoff created by having many great powers in Eurasia. Such a stand-off would of course help the United States to grow to dominate world politics after the war. Part and parcel of his thinking here, as we will see, was the development of a U.S. navy that would be second to none and could support Wilson's efforts to create a dominant U.S. economic position in Latin America and East Asia as the "waterbirds fought."[45] This was smart geopolitics, and it used the ideological similarity of states in the U.S. sphere—based on republicanism, not liberal democracy—to facilitate its cohesion and strength.

In late December 1914 and January–February 1915, the building of a Pan-American Pact was, at Wilson's direction, pushed strongly by both House and Bryan's state department. Chile proved to be the main constraint, given its leaders' concern that committing to such a pact would call into question the legitimacy of its territorial gains in its 1880s war with Peru and Bolivia over a nitrate-rich coastal area belonging to Bolivia. Chile would remain the main stumbling block to a treaty over the next two years. Mexico, meanwhile, had fallen back into civil war in late 1914 as the Constitutionalists that had helped overthrow Huerta in July had split over who would control the government, with Venustiano Carranza's forces controlling the area around Veracruz and Pancho Villa's forces controlling the north. Domestic chaos on the island of Haiti had intensified and was threatening to lead to either French or German intervention. As we will see, increasing direct U.S. involvement in Mexico and Haiti would reinforce Latin American cautiousness regarding the value and purpose of a regional security pact.

Wilson's thinking had shifted in February 1915 as the Germans significantly upped their level of submarine warfare against shipping to Britain. Given the large increase in American exports to Britain—backed by private loans from U.S. banks that were now permitted to finance British purchases of both supplies and munitions—such a German campaign posed a direct threat to American commerce. Prior to the new German policy, Wilson had decided to send House to Europe to investigate the possibility of a mediated peace. In meetings with Grey, it quickly became clear that no peace could be arranged in the short term with Germany occupying much of Northern France and Belgium and still showing itself the strongest military power in Europe. As House wrote to Wilson on February 23, "Germany may be successful [in its 1915 campaigns]. If France or Russia gives way, she will soon dominate the Continent." But if the Allies held and the war continued, House felt that the British government would be "ready to make great concessions [in a peace treaty] in regard to the future of shipping, commerce, etc. during periods of war."[46]

This latter comment is revealing of the underlying motives behind Wilson and House's diplomatic initiative, considering U.S. anger over the naval policies of both Britain and Germany. Two weeks before, on February 10, the State Department had issued strongly worded statements to both London and Berlin warning them to stop restricting neutral trade and, in the case of the British, to stop using neutral flags on British ships, since this might lead Germany to attack truly neutral ships by mistake.[47] Bryan had followed this up with a memo to both capitals on February 20 providing details of a suggested British-German agreement to "relieve neutral ships engaged in peaceful commerce from the great dangers" which they were incurring in trying to trade with Europe.[48] In short, while House's mission did hope to help the warring parties find a way back to peace, its primary goal was a selfish one—to keep American trade flowing to both sides, and to reduce the threats to that trade. The ghost of 1807–12 was again hanging over the peace-loving American nation, a nation seeking only to secure its commercial interests in its own hemisphere. Wilson was anxious to usher this ghost out the door without having to repeat the disaster from a century before.

On May 7, 1915, the British luxury liner *Lusitania* was sunk off the coast of Ireland, leading to the deaths of over a hundred Americans. This incident led to the first major U.S.-German crisis that might have led to American entry into the European conflict. Neither side, however, wanted war. Wilson knew that America was not prepared either mentally or militarily for war and that increased trade to Europe was building the U.S. power position over time. The Germans had no desire to add another adversary to the Allied cause. Even as Wilson was composing his diplomatic note to Berlin in late May, he continued to push House and Bryan to reach out to the Germans regarding the neutral trade agreement that House had just spent four months in Europe seeking to secure. His eventual "Lusitania note" to Berlin in early June was sufficiently harsh in its language that it caused Bryan, ever the pacifist, to resign in protest. (Robert Lansing quickly assumed the role of secretary of state.) The crisis chugged along through the summer of 1915, but with Wilson opposed to the kind of strong signals he would later use in 1917—most obviously, the severing of diplomatic relations—it is not surprising that the Germans found a way of satisfying the Americans without conflict. In early September, the German ambassador pledged that liners would no longer be sunk without warning and without the safety of its passengers taken into account.[49] This moderate concession greatly pleased Wilson and was enough to deescalate crisis tensions.

It is significant that during the months of crisis from May to September 1915, Wilson's main concern was not about a possible war with Germany (which he knew was unlikely to happen without his decision for it) but with America's overall economic and naval position in the western hemisphere and the world. With negotiations for a Pan-American pact bogged down, he decided to give a major public address to the delegates of the first Pan-American Financial

Conference meeting in Washington in late May. His purpose was to lay out his new vision for the hemisphere, one where the United States would be a true partner in the hemisphere's economic growth and security. On May 24, he rose before the delegates to say that mutual understanding and "successful commercial intercourse" were the bonds holding "the American republics" together. Yet Wilson made clear that any union of the hemisphere's states should be more than merely commerce for commerce's sake. "I cannot [help] harboring the hope, the very high hope, that by this commerce . . . we may show the world . . . the way to peace, to permanent peace."[50] Two of the three pillars for Wilson's eventual plan for global peace—greater trade and cooperation through large-scale institutions—were beginning to emerge (albeit without any other great powers participating). The promotion of "democracy" would not come until quite late—April 1917 and his request for a congressional declaration of war. But for now, it was enough that these states were republics, even if the vast majority were authoritarian-leaning republics, if not brutal dictatorships.[51]

American actions in the hemisphere in 1915–16 spoke volumes about Wilson's overall prioritization of commerce and regional cooperation over the promotion of liberal democracy. In the summer of 1915, the long-simmering unrest within Haiti came to a head. Wilson had been worried since the beginning of his administration that foreign governments, particularly Germany, would exploit Haiti's ongoing domestic turmoil to increase their economic and political presence on the island and in the region.[52] To ensure U.S. dominance, Washington had sent Assistant Secretary of State John Osbourne to Haiti in June 1913 to negotiate the purchase of Môle St. Nicholas, an area on Haiti's northwest coast with a deep harbor ideal for a future American naval base (the talks failed). In January–February 1914, pitched battles between two Haitian factions had led to the massing of a thousand U.S. troops along the coast and the landing of a hundred and fifty U.S. marines on Haitian soil to help establish order. When the faction led by Orestes Zamor triumphed in February, Bryan quickly ordered the recognition of his government and for the next year, American troops helped stabilize Haiti's fragile situation.[53]

In September 1914, worried about German desires to participate in the financial restructuring of Haiti's customs collections, Wilson himself had composed a memorandum sent to Berlin stating that the United States had long taken the position that "neither foreign mercantile influences and interests, nor any other foreign influence or interest proceeding from out the American hemisphere," could be allowed "to constitute a control, either wholly or in part, of the government or administration of any independent American state." Any participation by Germany in Haiti's customs administration would constitute a serious departure from that principle.[54]

By November 1914, Haiti's other major faction, led by Davilmar Théodore, had assumed control of Haiti's governmental apparatus. Bryan made it clear to Théodore that Washington would recognize his government as long as he agreed to let the United States run Haiti's finances and to ensure that Môle St. Nicholas was not given to any other power. Negotiations stalled, and in February 1915, Théodore was overthrown by his former comrade in arms Vilbrun Guillaume Sam.[55] Sam in turn was overthrown in late July and the outbreak of mob violence led to the initial landing of four hundred marines on July 28 and the assumption of control of Haiti by the United States upon reinforcements from Guantanamo naval base. A treaty turning Haiti into a semi-protectorate of the United States was approved by the Haitian legislature in November.[56]

As things were winding up in Haiti, Secretary of State Lansing sent a long memorandum to Wilson reiterating the relation between America's recent policy and its overall strategy in the region. Lansing noted upfront that he was considering only America's national security and making no arguments "on the ground of benefit" to the peoples of the states affected by U.S. policy. Support from European capitals for revolutions in Central America and the Caribbean had created the danger of foreign "political control," which "may be as great a menace to the national safety of this country as occupation or cession." To counter this threat, Washington had to reestablish stable government in states undergoing domestic upheaval and prevent their revenues "from becoming the prize of revolution and of the foreigners who finance it." He went on:

> The possession of the [recently opened] Panama Canal and its defense have in a measure given to the territories in and about the Caribbean Sea a new importance from the standpoint of our national safety. It is vital to the interests of this country that European political domination should in no way be extended over these regions.

The logic for military intervention in places such as Haiti, Lansing reminded Wilson, was consistent with what the United States had already been doing for years in Cuba, Panama, Nicaragua, and the Dominican Republic, and it should guide "what may have to be done" in other neighboring republics. He also advised Wilson not to forget about the Danish West Indies and other European colonial possessions that might become a "serious menace" to U.S. interests should they change hands.[57] (The islands would be purchased in early 1917 to keep them out of German hands.)

The years 1914–15 were also the years that Wilson made a concerted effort to expand U.S. trade beyond the immediate Caribbean region. Britain and Germany had traditionally been South America's top trading partners and investors. But with the war raging in Europe, neither side could afford to spend precious capital abroad or develop new trade ties. Moreover, with U.S. manufacturing booming and the economy coming out of recession, Wilson saw with even greater acuity that America would need foreign markets to utilize U.S. excess manufacturing capacity. Right from the beginning of the war, Wilson had encouraged American shippers to buy German ships stranded in U.S. ports and had pushed for a shipping bill that would significantly expand the U.S. merchant marine. In mid-August 1914, Treasury Secretary William McAdoo told him of a plan for the government purchase of merchant ships, operated by a federally controlled corporation. Consistent with dynamic realism's view that states will expand their economic power sphere when they can do so at low cost, McAdoo noted that the war had given America "an unusual opportunity for South American trade." Without more ships the opportunity would be squandered, but with them "we can quickly establish business and political relations that will be of inestimable value to the country for all times." By November Wilson had convinced key officials in the administration to support McAdoo's larger strategy.[58]

The calling of the May 1915 Pan-American financial conference was one aspect of this strategy (discussed above). Also important was the relaxation on restrictions on U.S. banks setting up branch offices in key South American capitals. Commerce secretary William Redfield discussed with McAdoo plans to encourage larger U.S. banks to invest in the southern continent and to free up U.S. dollars to allow easier Latin American access to credit. As Redfield wrote to McAdoo on November 19, comparing South America's trade with the United States versus Germany and Britain:

> You will see from the above that some of this trade is necessarily cut off by the war. In the frankest way South America says "United States can secure it." It is a tempting opportunity of permanent worth to us and to them. The problem it presents is a financial one. We have the goods; they want to buy them. We must provide the method of financing the sales; they cannot now do so. It is for our bankers, therefore, to furnish the necessary credits.[59]

Soon afterwards, National City Bank of New York (NCBNY) opened its first foreign branch in Buenos Aires, Argentina. As Burton Kaufman relates, "By this action, American businessmen for the first time challenged Europe's financial hegemony in South America."[60]

While it would take until September 1916 to get Congress to pass the shipping bill allowing a government-led coordination of the U.S. merchant marine, Wilson and his officials took other steps through 1915–16 to build trade and financial ties with the states to the south. In addition to the two hundred delegates from Latin America and the Caribbean that attended the May 1915

Pan-American conference, the U.S. government invited 145 of the most prominent American business leaders to attend. After the conference, the foreign
delegates were taken on a two-week tour of major commercial centers in the
United States, including New York and Chicago. McAdoo then appointed
prominent business leaders to represent America in discussion with Latin
American nations.[61] The Federal Reserve Act of 1913 had permitted American
banks to open branch outlets outside of the United States, but until the war
American officials had done little to promote this practice. In 1915, NCBNY
led the way with additional branches opened across South America and the
Caribbean.[62] Treasury Secretary McAdoo even recommended to Wilson in
September that the Federal Reserve banks open foreign branches to further
facilitate the free flow of credit in Latin America.[63]

By the above actions, Wilson consolidated America's hold on business in
Latin America and the Caribbean, while reducing the influence of Britain and
Germany. While many of his actions could be seen as consistent with neo-
Marxism and not just dynamic realism, the push for these actions was coming
from the top down, not from the bottom up. There is little evidence that Wilson and key officials felt pressure from business groups to push for greater U.S.
control of the western hemisphere. Indeed, they would incur pushback against
Wilson's initiative from a number of business groups and their congressional
representatives in 1916.[64] It was the larger great power context that drove Wilson. And as we shall see later, in the latter half of 1916, the American position
and the Monroe Doctrine would be increasingly under threat, not just from
Germany but also Britain.[65]

## Getting Ready for Globalism, 1915–16

Colonel House had felt from the start of the European war that the United
States had to build up its military power, both to ensure the Europeans did not
push America around and to prepare for possible entry into the war. Wilson
had initially resisted any major new arms spending measures. But by mid-1915,
in the face of British naval blockades and German submarine attacks, greater
military preparation seemed necessary. Also significant, although greatly underplayed in most accounts of Wilson's wartime decision-making, was the
sense of Japan as an emerging threat to America's trade interests in Asia and to
the North American west coast. Japan's occupation of parts of China's Shan-
tung peninsula in August 1914 and its subsequent efforts to impose "Twenty-
One Demands" on China were bad enough. But in November 1914, rumors
stirred that the Japanese were seeking to control Magdalena Bay on Mexico's
Baja peninsula, an action reminiscent of a similar scare in the spring of 1913.
Tokyo acted to squelch the rumors. But in December, the Japanese cruiser

*Asama* ran aground in Turtle Bay on the peninsula, and the Japanese navy refused American help to re-right the ship. The *Los Angeles Times* reported in April 1915 that five other Japanese cruisers had visited the bay, and that the guns from the *Asama* were to be brought ashore to protect a future Japanese naval base there. When the *Asama* was finally refloated in August and able to sail home to Japan, the U.S. navy found no evidence of Japanese plans to build a naval base. Yet Japanese ships, the admiral in charge of the investigation concluded, had indeed used the bay in the early stages of the European war as a "temporary coaling station," itself a violation of Monroe Doctrine principles.[66]

The *Lusitania* crisis of the summer of 1915 and the *Asama* incident combined to lead American officials to contemplate a possible Japan-Germany alignment against the United States, an alignment that might include Russia, the power that Wilson had initially feared the most. Lansing in early July 1915 composed a memorandum noting that Germany, Russia, and Japan were seeking to divide the world between them. His views aligned with a report from U.S. ambassador to Germany Gerard from February that there was much talk in Berlin "of Japan's making [a] separate peace and attacking America." A former naval attaché just returned from Japan gave a speech at the Naval War College in February noting that "Japanese admiration and like for Germany" had "visibly increased" and that Germany was "losing no opportunity to complicate matters to her own advantage." As historian William Braisted notes, given these widespread concerns about a Japanese-German rapprochement it is not surprising that the Navy's General Board in 1915–16 prepared plans for war in both oceans against a combined Japanese-German coalition.[67]

In the face of these growing military threats, President Wilson was not just sitting back and waiting. On July 21, 1915, he asked Navy Secretary Josephus Daniels to prepare estimates from his experts on what the U.S. navy would need "to stand upon an equality" with the world's largest navies. Rather than a crash program, he wanted a plan for "consistent and progressive [naval] development," one that Congress would get behind. Soon afterward, the General Board voted seven to one to build a navy "equal to the most powerful [nation] . . . by not later than 1925." From the Board's perspective, drawing from Mahan, the United States had to defend its growing commercial interests from states such as Japan and Germany, which had large populations but little unsettled land. And while the Panama Canal facilitated the movement of U.S. ships from one ocean to the other, the new potential for air power meant that the United States had to start planning for a two-ocean war that would divide the U.S. fleet between two theaters.[68]

Interestingly, over the last five months of 1915, while the planning continued to focus on both the Japanese and German naval threats, the navy was more concerned about Japan while Wilson was more worried about Germany. Navy officials were under the impression that Russia and Japan had already reached an understanding over China that would free Japan to fight the United States without fear of its traditional East Asian enemy entering the fray.[69] Wilson, perhaps influenced by House's pessimism regarding Germany's power and ambitions, appeared to be more concerned about a future German takeover of Europe. In his diary notes of September 22, 1915, House records his surprise when Wilson, in discussing U.S. relations with Germany, remarked that "he [Wilson] had never been sure that we ought not to take part in the conflict and if it seemed evident that Germany . . . [might] win, the obligation upon us was greater than ever."[70] But strength at sea, not on land, was Wilson's focus. When the two men met on September 24, they discussed the navy more than the army "because we both think . . . it is the more important." House stressed that if the United States fell into war with either Japan or Germany, it must directly confront their fleets to deter to them from "prey[ing] on our commerce."[71]

By December 1915, Wilson was preparing for his biggest policy step yet: the announcement to the American people that the United States must build up its power in order to play a more active role in both its own hemisphere and the world. The venue for this seminal announcement would be his December 7 annual address to Congress. In the address, he argued that the foundation for this new globalist posture—active engagement across both oceans backed by military power—would be the construction of a strong political and economic sphere in the western hemisphere. Yet when peace returned to Europe, large-scale "economic readjustments" would have to be made in that region, and America must be prepared to play a leading role. Specifically, he called on the American people to "fix your attention . . . [on] the full significance of [this task]" and to see clearly what was required to achieve it: "I mean national defense." This was Wilson's first major public call for the United States to become a global leader in not only the economic and commercial realm, but in the military realm as well.

Knowing his policy shift would meet resistance, Wilson spent much of the rest of his speech justifying his plans for a U.S. naval and armed forces buildup. It would not only keep the hemisphere "free from all outside domination," but would also support the necessary expansion of America's merchant shipping fleet. The United States could not just rest on its vast reserves of capital (accumulated, in large part, by wartime trade with Europe). "Something must be done at once . . . to open routes and develop opportunities where they are as yet undeveloped," and a government-supported merchant marine backed by a strong navy was needed to help private capital open the door to further trade. If other nations used the war to hurt each other's commerce, he warned, U.S. merchants would be at their mercy. But with a larger merchant marine and navy, the United States could have its cake and eat it too. Growing commercial cooperation in the "American hemisphere" tied to U.S. naval power would allow this hemisphere to enjoy "independence and self-sufficiency," but it would also help it avoid being "drawn into the tangle of European affairs." Wilson ended with a call to make sure the country lacked no instrument needed to play its new role and protect its "national efficiency and security." And this was no ordinary role: "In this we are not partisans but heralds and prophets of a new age."[72]

This was Wilson's first big speech setting forth his plan for a new global role for the United States, and he clearly designed it to mobilize a reluctant nation to play this role. Combined with the speech's occasional one-liners about democracies not seeking war but only individual liberty,[73] we might believe that he was preparing his nation for a liberal internationalist crusade we have come to associate with the man: the promotion of free trade, democracy, and security institutions around the world. But this speech is not that at all. It is a clear and forceful statement of the power-political notion that one is only safe if one has a strong and vibrant economic power sphere, controlled from on high, but with (in this case) the veneer of republican liberty for both citizens and member states. There is no mobilizing of Americans to spread democracy, even in the U.S. backyard. The "new age" he is calling for is really one where the United States makes sure no other great powers intrude in its sphere while it reshapes the world economy in its own image.

## The Preparedness Campaign and the Naval Buildup, January to August 1916

Having now declared that the United States would move to active engagement backed by force, Wilson began his so-called preparedness campaign to gain popular and legislative support for increased military spending, particularly for the navy. His many public speeches from December 1915 to February 1916 had a common theme, one building on his December address: the world was changing economically, and without more military power to back U.S. diplomacy, the country would be left behind after the war ended and the great powers returned to their previous efforts to improve their commercial positions and control. In his "Address on Preparedness" in New York on January 27, for example, he stressed that America was being forced by global changes to be the world's "chief economic [guide]" in the decades ahead. Yet "money brings with it power which may be well or ill employed." The United States had been thrust from its "provincial" status onto a world stage to do "the business of the world." While Americans would still only use their new power to render "service . . . to the rest of the world," its first obligation was to liberty and free institutions at home and "to stand as the strong brother of all those in this hemisphere who will maintain the same principles."

Wilson went on to address critics who were demanding U.S. intervention in Mexico. In a highly ironic remark, given that in less than three months he would send troops into Mexico, he argued that the United States had "slowly, very slowly" begun to win back the confidence of the other states in the hemisphere. Yet if the United States went into Mexico, the sympathies of the hemisphere would "look across the water [to Europe]" and "[not] to the great republic which we profess to represent." He then revealed a critical facet of his geopolitical thinking. Have those in favor of intervention in Mexico truly reflected on global politics?

> No one seriously supposes that the United States needs to fear a direct invasion of its homeland. What America had to fear, rather, are indirect, roundabout, flank movements upon her [predominant] position in the western hemisphere.

Without mentioning democratic norms such as free elections and the separation of powers, Wilson stressed that America must therefore "win the spirits" of southern nations if it was going to be a true leader of republicanism against Old World values in the hemisphere. He then returned to his larger theme, stressing that the world was undergoing "an economic revolution," one with great uncertainties that were hard to understand. Yet a militarily prepared America, while avoiding actions that would disturb the global peace, would be ready to defend the things that Americans stood for "against every contingency that may affect or impair them."[74]

In eight separate speeches over the next two weeks, Wilson reiterated these themes, stressing the importance of building U.S. commercial dominance backed by naval power to deal with such uncertain times, while saying next to nothing about ideological goals. On January 29 he noted that the European war was a struggle that would determine the history of world. In this struggle, Washington's goal was to "[maintain] the processes of peaceful commerce." Yet because of its neglect of its merchant marine, America had not provided itself with the means by which it could carry on its commerce without the "interference" of other nations. America may have a high-quality navy, but in numbers it was still only fourth in the world. And since the navy was the country's "first arm of defense," everything possible should be done to bring it up to full strength.[75]

On February 2, Wilson told his audience that Americans had looked to him to do more than keep America out of the European war. They had also counted on him "to see that your energies should be released along the channels of trade." Yet the U.S. navy was still not strong enough to deter other nations.

Shaped by the Navy Board's warnings about Japan and Germany, Wilson noted that the world war had "engaged all the rest of the world outside of [the western hemisphere]" and "this flame [may begin] to creep in upon us . . . towards both coasts." Given this threat, the navy must be "as rapidly as possible brought to . . . a numerical strength which will make it, practically, impregnable to the navies of the world."[76]

Reluctance within the Congress held up passage of any new naval bill until the summer. In May 1916, Colonel House encouraged Wilson to lean harder on his fragile Democratic coalition in Congress to get a bill passed, reminding him that a strong navy would not only enhance U.S. influence in any European settlement and in ongoing Pan-American negotiations, but would reduce the threat of Japan.[77] On June 1, House received word from French ambassador Jean Jules Jusserand that the Russians and Japanese had created an initial alliance, and that Germany might join it. He wrote in his diary that it was of critical importance to build America's navy to match its economic and political position in the world. In early July, a Russo-Japanese agreement to confer should their territorial rights in the Far East be threatened was made public. This reinforced the navy's continued public arguments that both Japan and Germany were the primary adversaries, alone or in combination. The pressure worked: in mid-August 1916 both houses finally passed a new naval bill.[78]

Wilson clearly understood the geopolitical implications of this developing naval strength. In a conversation in late September about worsening relations with Britain, House told the president that London was not happy about the U.S. naval buildup and that American commerce was "expanding beyond belief." In fact, the United States was "rapidly taking the position Germany occupied before the war." Wilson casually dismissed British concerns with the remark: "Let us build a bigger navy than her's [sic] and do what we please." This was not a man simply waiting for Europe to wake up to its disaster. Wilson was actively preparing to position the United States for global economic and political dominance over the next decades, even at the expense of potential allies such as Great Britain.

## The Growing American Distrust of Both Germany and Britain, March–December 1916

In late March 1916, a new crisis between Germany and the United States emerged after a German sub attacked the steamer *Sussex* as it crossed the English Channel with 325 passengers abroad. The steamer did not sink and was towed to safety, but eighty people died in the incident and four Americans were injured (but none killed). By this act Germany had broken its pledge after the *Lusitania* sinking not to go after passenger ships. This left Wilson having to decide whether to break relations and accept a possible spiral to war. Yet with its Verdun campaign stalled, Germany feared bringing America into the war. In early May, when Wilson accepted Berlin's expression of "sincere regret" and its pledge to observe the rules of cruiser warfare, including no attack on passenger ships and provisions for crews of unresisting merchant ships, the crisis ended. But the incident once again left American officials, especially Robert Lansing, highly suspicious of Germany's intentions and character. These suspicions were heightened over the summer by a series of explosions at East Coast munitions factories that the Americans had good reason to believe were carried out by German agents.[79]

Yet the biggest problem remained Germany's clear desire to get the United States mixed up in a war with Mexico. In mid-October 1915, Washington had given de facto recognition to Carranza in Mexico City and had lifted the U.S. arms embargo on his government, while abandoning its previous support for Villa in the north. Secretary of State Lansing summarized the logic behind this decision in his diary: "Germany desires to keep up the turmoil in Mexico until the United States is forced to intervene; therefore, we must not intervene. Germany does not wish to have any one faction dominant in Mexico; therefore, we must recognize one faction as dominant in Mexico." In short, "it comes down to this: Our possible relations with Germany must be our first consideration; and all our intercourse with Mexico must be regulated accordingly."[80]

By early 1916, the hope of sustaining good relations with Mexico would fade. On March 9, with Germany replacing America as his main supplier of arms, Villa attacked the border town of Columbus, New Mexico, killing eight civilians and seven American soldiers while ransacking the town. Wilson quickly made the decision to launch what was called a "punitive expedition," led by General John Pershing, to capture Villa and bring him to justice. On March 15, four thousand U.S. troops crossed the Mexican border. In Wilson's mind, this was not an intervention or invasion, since he had no desire to change Mexico's government or regime type, just a temporary incursion to punish a bandit and thus deter future attacks. In a meeting with House on March 29, Wilson reiterated that he was "determined not to intervene in Mexico," and would tell Congress that "under no circumstances" would he do so, given "the foreign situation, and because the enemies of the United States so ardently desire it." It was clear which enemy he meant: twelve days earlier House had written in his diary that Wilson's "determination not to allow Germany to force him into intervention" was accounting for his relatively mild response to Villa's actions.[81]

The Mexican incursion went awry, however, and by May some seven thousand American forces were 350 miles into Mexico, unable to find Villa and surrounded on three sides by Carranza's army. The two sides came very close to war when, on June 21, Mexican troops fired on American forces seeking to move without permission through the town of Carrizal. Wilson wisely decided not to retaliate, and Carranza chose to release the American prisoners and not press his military advantage. The two nations stepped back from the brink, and the crisis soon petered out (although U.S. forces would remain in Mexico until early February 1917). Wilson confided his reasons for his caution to his personal secretary Tumulty. German "propagandists" were in Mexico, "fomenting strife and trouble" between Mexico and the United States. "Germany is anxious to have us at war with Mexico, so that our minds and our energies will be taken off the great war across the sea." America must harbor its resources in case war with Germany were to transpire, Wilson argued, despite his hope that it would not.[82]

Turning to the second half of 1916, a review of the documents reveals a surprising fact: Wilson and many of his advisors became almost as anxious and suspicious of the British as they previously had been of the Germans. Since September 1914, American officials had been frustrated with Britain's increasingly tight blockade of neutral shipping to Germany and to states that might supply Germany with goods (especially Holland and the Scandinavian countries). By 1916, things got much worse. It was becoming increasingly clear that London was worried that a continuation of the war would lead to Britain forgoing its predominant commercial and financial position to the Americans. British officials were thus preparing to shift from their traditional free trade policy to a neo-mercantilist policy that would create a relatively closed economic sphere to protect Britain's overseas markets and investments. Washington did not know about the secret Sykes-Picot agreement of May 1915 dividing up the Turkish empire in the Middle East into postwar British and French spheres of influence and control. But with the precipitous decline in British commercial power since the start of the war, by January 1916 American businessmen were already hearing talk that London wanted to build a "preferential trade" bloc with its allies.[83]

Then came the true shock. In mid-April American officials learned of plans to hold an Allied economic conference in Paris in May or June 1916, with discussions centered on a proposed "economic alliance between Entente powers to regulate trade after [the] war." The scheme was leaked to the Americans by the Japanese envoy to the conference prior to his departure for Paris. He feared that the alliance would "divide [the] commercial world into three hostile camps: the Entente nations, the Germanic allies, and the neutrals, unless the last two [America and Japan] unite."[84] Lansing immediately told the U.S. ambassador in Japan that the State Department also opposed the proposed economic alliance, and that he could say to Japanese officials that it "would regret any combination that might restrict commerce between Japan and the United States."[85]

The secret conference began in Paris on June 14 and lasted three days. In May, Lansing had told the U.S. ambassador to France William Sharp to find out as much he could, but to use his discretion in obtaining the information.[86] By June 22, Sharp had obtained a complete copy of the resolutions adopted by the conference and he transmitted the document to Lansing. Its preamble claimed that the Central Powers (read: Germany) were engaging in a "struggle in the economic domain" that "will not only survive the reestablishment of peace but, at that very moment, will assume all its amplitude and its intensity." The Central Powers sought to establish "their domination over the production and the markets of the whole world and to impose upon the other countries an [un]acceptable hegemony."[87] In the face of this grave danger, and in their own defense, Allied governments would have to work together to "secure for themselves . . . full economic independence . . . on a permanent basis." During reconstruction after the war, the Allies would deny Most Favored Nation status to all enemy powers. They would conserve for the Allied countries, before all others, their natural resources during the period of reconstruction and establish "special arrangements" to facilitate the exchange of these resources. The Allies' overall objective was to increase production within their imperial realms in order to "maintain and develop their economic position and independence in relation to enemy countries."[88]

Robert Lansing was astounded by this news, and immediately wrote the president, attaching the ambassador's report and the resolutions of the conference. In his cover note, Lansing warned that the results of these measures "may be very far reaching on the commerce and trade of the whole world" after the war ended. Since the measures envisioned continued economic warfare on the Central Powers after the war, the agreement would make peace negotiations very difficult. But neutral nations such as the United States also had to be concerned, Lansing argued. They would face "a commercial combination which has as its avowed purpose preferential treatment for its members." Given Britain's and France's vast colonial possessions and their strong merchant marines, the restrictions on trade would cause "a serious, if not critical, situation for the nations outside the union by creating unusual and artificial economic conditions." Lansing recommended immediate counteraction. A "Congress of Neutrals" should be held to coordinate a response; acting independently would leave them impotent against the Allied commercial combination. Lansing concluded this memo by reminding the president that he (Lansing) had traditionally been against America becoming involved in multilateral economic organizations. But the proposed British-French economic condominium would "materially affect our industrial and commercial life." It therefore had to be countered in some way, "and the best way to fight combination is by combination."[89]

It is not clear that Colonel House was immediately made aware of the Allied signing of an economic alliance. But Britain and France's concomitant rejection of his and Wilson's proposals for a peace conference, accepted in theory by Grey in February 1916 but now put on hold until the Allied position on the ground improved, had soured him and raised his suspicions. In his diary of June 23, the day after the details of the Paris conference were received, House wrote that he believed the French and English were prolonging the war unnecessarily. The "permanent peace" which the American plan promised would have meant the "end of militarism"—that is, the end of arms racing and aggressive land-based expansionism. But such a peace also required an end to navalism, and "that is perhaps where the shoe pinches." Britain desired to destroy militarism "and at the same time perpetuate navalism." And the war had shown that of the two, "navalism might be the more oppressive of the two branches of the military service." The problem here was uncertainty about Britain's future type. Under a liberal government, House noted, neither navalism nor militarism would be a menace. But "under a reactionary government such as Great Britain might have, it could be made a serious menace to the happiness and freedom of mankind."[90]

Washington did not have to wait long for Britain's new neo-mercantilist strategy to rear its ugly head. In July 1916, a month after the British-French conference, London released a "blacklist" of companies that would not be permitted to do business with the United Kingdom or its colonies, under the premise that these firms were trading with the enemy. American officials instantly understood what this was really about: the effort to reduce U.S. firms' penetration of the traditional British markets in the western hemisphere and East Asia and their acquisition of cheap raw materials for America's booming domestic industry. London's action, along with the continued blockade on trade with continental Europe, led to a very intense six-month crisis between the two nations that by November–December even threatened a possible war. Since this crisis arose just as U.S.-German relations had been improving, the very fact that relations with Britain continued to deteriorate through the fall of 1916 says much about Woodrow Wilson's larger orientation to the threats to postwar U.S. trade and economic dominance. War would eventually be declared on Germany not Britain, but this had little to do with Britain being seen as a democracy.[91] The long-term German threat to American commerce simply proved to be greater, since only Germany had the chance of achieving hegemony in Europe and then using that base to go after the western hemisphere.

In late August of 1916 when old friend Walter Page, the highly pro-British U.S. ambassador in London, returned to the United States for consultations,

Wilson initially refused to talk to him about U.S.-British relations and what could be done to relieve tensions. In early September, Congress pushed through a Wilson-sponsored retaliatory act giving the president authority to embargo exports to America from countries discriminating against American firms or refusing to accept American ships.[92] Finally, on September 23, Wilson and Page spent a morning together to discuss the key issues at hand. The president sternly lectured Page that the Allies had sacrificed American sympathy by their arrogant and high-handed attitude. The war, Wilson said, while it had many causes, was perhaps primarily the result of "England's having the earth, [and] of Germany's wanting it." Wilson, according to Page's post-meeting account, "showed a great deal of toleration of Germany" while complaining of British behavior "the whole morning." Page got him to promise not to invoke the retaliatory legislation until after the election. But Wilson indicated that if Britain were to be continuing with its provocations at that point, he would.[93]

It was in a discussion the next day that Wilson responded to House's point that London was worried about U.S. naval and commercial growth with his statement that the United States should build a navy bigger than Britain's and then "do what we please." House, who had for some time believed it essential to come in on the Allied side should a mediated peace prove impossible, reminded the president that it was Germany's naval rise that had pushed the British into the war. Hence "it was unlikely the British would be willing to permit us to build a navy equal to theirs if they could prevent it." But he also noted that London's alignment with France, Russia, Italy, and Japan—now not simply military but also commercial—made the British "a formidable antagonist" should the Allies win the war. Wilson and House came to no conclusions on policy, and then broke for lunch.[94]

For the next three months, and despite his pro-British leanings, House worried excessively about a possible British preventive attack on the United States sparked by the growing commercial rivalry and America's naval buildup. On September 25 he asked Page whether he thought that Britain's outlook toward the United States was driven by the new U.S. naval program, "and whether we were not getting in the same position, from the British point of view, as [prewar] Germany." Britain and Germany, after all, had been friends until Germany had begun "to cut into British trade and to plan a navy large enough to become formidable." Perhaps, House speculated, the British saw the United States "as a similar menace both as to their trade and supremacy of the seas."[95] Notwithstanding his concerns, House through October and November would work diligently to avoid a war with Britain. But by December, as we shall see, his optimism started to fade.

After winning reelection in early November, Wilson made it clear to House that he was ready for one final effort to convince the Allies and the Germans to make peace before either side achieved a decisive victory. Wilson was well aware that Germany was threatening to resume full-scale submarine warfare if Britain would not let up on its efforts to starve Germany into submission, and this would likely lead the United States into war against Germany.[96] Over the next two weeks, House continually advised against a peace initiative, knowing that British officials felt they needed to improve their battlefield situation first and that London might see Washington's efforts as implying an alignment with Berlin's desires over the Allies' interests.[97] House was worried that Wilson might exacerbate the already growing spiral of hostility and lead Britain to strike out militarily at America. On November 15, House told Wilson that if Germany accepted his peace foray and the Allies did not, the United States might find itself at war with the Allies, either because of American public opinion or because the United States, if Berlin did not resume all-out sub warfare, would inevitably drift into a "sympathetic alliance" with Germany. And if this eventuality arose, England and France "might, under provocation, declare war against us." Wilson believed they would not. House disagreed, arguing that Britain might try to destroy the U.S. fleet and, with its ally Japan, land troops in sufficient numbers "to hold certain parts of the United States." Wilson's response is shocking, at least for those who have come to think he believed democracies could never possibly fight each other. He told House, almost nonchalantly, that the British and Japanese "might get a good distance [into U.S. territory] but would have to stop somewhere," to which House agreed. Wilson was ready for any eventuality. House records that he even "went so far [as] to say that if the Allies wanted war with us he would not shrink from it."[98]

These were not merely idle fears. On December 12 the Germans seized the initiative by making their own public proposal for peace talks. This left Wilson in a bind: if he were to now offer his own proposals to London and Berlin, he might be seen to be aligning even more toward Germany than under a scenario where Washington had been the first to act. This could trigger the very spiral to war with Britain that House and Wilson had discussed a few weeks earlier. House tried to comfort Wilson, whom he saw as "depressed" by these developments. Despite his own reservations that London would react negatively, he suggested that Wilson go forward with the peace plan. He then met with Navy Secretary Daniels to ask him how prepared the United States was for war "if it should come tomorrow." In a remarkable exchange revealing the level of internal turmoil and uncertainty within the administration, Daniels replied "war with whom?" House replied: "with Great Britain." House noted that "there was no need to await a reply since his face told the story." Yet Daniels, rather than dismissing House's comment, simply said it would take a year to set up mines to protect the U.S. coast from British ships. House then turned to his envisioned war scenario. Britain and Japan could "put us out of business" by assembling troops in Canada for an attack from the north. Given the state of American unpreparedness, "we should be as helpless to resist" as Belgium was to Germany in 1914. Following the meeting, House met again with Wilson and informed the president of the conversation with Daniels. He urged Wilson "not to place our country in the position where we should either have to back down or fight the Allies." He did not record Wilson's response.[99]

Since we know that the United States would end up fighting Germany, not the Allies, when it entered the war in 1917, we may dismiss the internal fears of House and Wilson in the waning months of 1916 as simply the paranoid worries of uncertain individuals. Yet they reveal something quite deep. American officials were concerned primarily with the threat to the western hemisphere and to America's increasingly dominant economic position there and around the world. They understood that the very effort to take advantage of the war to build a second-to-none navy, and to create new markets and investment ties in the region—and by extension, East Asia over the long term—would threaten Britain and Japan and encourage these states (who were, after all, allies) to fight back. Yet should Berlin feel forced to turn to unrestricted warfare to relieve hungry German citizens and to seek to knock Britain out of the war, it would threaten German hegemony in Europe and a German threat to the Monroe Doctrine. Wilson and House were caught between two terrifying scenarios, neither of which they could fully control. How this would all play out would be seen over the first three months of 1917.

## The Final Decisions for War, January to March 1917

In early January, Wilson was still hoping to avoid entry into the world war. He strongly believed that if the two European camps knew that the United States would join a collective security system designed to build trust, a concert of essentially equal great powers would be created that would solidify a "permanent peace." Given Wilson's belief that the war was caused by a spiral of fear and mistrust, a shared faith in a future collective security system would allow them to make peace now.[100] Yet his dilemma was clear: with the new prime minister of Britain, Lloyd George, having rejected any notion of early peace talks, Wilson knew that a German plunge into unrestricted sub warfare would likely require U.S. entry into the war, on one side or the other (House and Lansing of course preferring the Allied side). The president had to hope against hope that he could make a rational appeal to the powers to talk peace, and that they would agree to do so prior to any German decision on submarines.

Wilson's strategy was to offer a new public peace plan while simultaneously scaring the British into submission. Since Britain's financial and trade situation had been tenuous for months, he thought this might just work. On January 2, House warned British ambassador Spring-Rice that unless Britain accepted the necessity of talks, Germany would institute "unbridled submarine warfare," and that even if the United States jumped in to help, it might not be able to save the Allies from disaster. He could see from Spring-Rice's reaction that he had "hit the mark."[101] Through mid-January, German ambassador Johann Heinrich von Bernstorff continued to indicate his government's willingness to negotiate an arbitrated peace, reduce armaments, and to join a collective security league.[102] This gave Wilson the confidence to continue to refine, with House's help, his "Peace without Victory" speech for his January 22 address to the Senate. He clearly believed, as he wrote in an early draft, that the war "was brought on by distrust of one another"—the exact thing a league could help reduce. But House convinced him to remove such language for fear of upsetting the British (who believed the war was due to a German drive for world hegemony).[103]

Wilson also felt he needed peace to make sure that Japan did not take advantage of any European war that America entered into to expand further its influence over China, and perhaps even threaten the U.S. position in Central America (especially the Panama Canal). In an argument he would soon reveal to his cabinet, he told House in early January that the United States should try to stay out of the war, since "We are the only one of the great White nations that is free from war today, and it would be a crime against [Western] civilization for us to go in."[104] Back in December, Washington had protested Japanese efforts to exclude the United States from foreign lending arrangements with Beijing's government. On January 17, Lansing informed Wilson of the U.S. ambassador to China's report that Japan was trying to step into the banking vacuum created by the British, French, and Russian focus on Europe, and to lend to Beijing as long as it agreed to break off loan negotiations with American banks. Japan hoped to keep China weak and divided, he argued, and "to take advantage of the preoccupation of her allies to obtain control of China."[105] Such information could only have reinforced Wilson's long-standing concerns about the expansion of Japan's economic sphere in the Far East.

Then there was the continued problem of Mexico. U.S. forces had been kept in the country in the second half of 1916 as leverage over Carranza's government. In addition to wanting greater assurance over border security, Wilson sought assurances that Mexico would not nationalize major resources industries owned by Americans or restrict their ability to explore and export. Carranza had successfully resisted these demands, arguing that the latter could be discussed only after American withdrawal from his country.[106] In October–November, to increase his leverage and to deter an American attack, Carranza approached the German government to ask Berlin to declare that it would not view a U.S. intervention with favor, and to supply arms and sign a commercial and maritime treaty with Mexico. In return, Mexico would offer "extensive support" for German subs in the area.[107] The Americans had found out in June of German efforts to obtain a grant of land on a peninsula south of Veracruz, with an ideal harbor for a submarine base.[108] Given that Carranza had allowed or encouraged Japanese naval intrusions into the Baja region from 1913 to 1915, Washington had good reason to be worried about any new Mexican connections with either Germany or Japan. In January 1917, with Carranza still balking on concessions, Wilson wisely reduced his risks of a U.S.-Mexican war and ordered the unilateral retreat of Pershing's forces back to Texas. They would be out in early February.[109]

It was in the midst of this deep uncertainty—east, south, and west (and even north, if one includes the possibility of a British-Japanese attack from Canada)— that the president delivered his address on January 22. In light of the commonly held view that Wilson was driven by a desire to spread democracy, either through a peace deal or by entering the war,[110] it is significant that the speech focuses solely on the importance of a new league to establish peace, on the need for freedom of commerce on the high seas, and on reduction of armaments. Given that, even at this late date, Wilson believed the war was caused by mistrust and arms racing rather than by aggressive autocracies, this true "Wilsonian triad" (collective security, more open commerce, and low military spending) made perfect sense.[111] But even there he ended his speech with a provocative call on all nations to "adopt the doctrine of President Monroe as the doctrine of the world." This, of course, was Wilson's updated version of the doctrine which he had been trying (unsuccessfully) to codify as a Pan-American collective security treaty, now described as the idea that "no nation should seek to extend its polity over any other nation or people, but that every people should be left free to determine its own polity, its own way of development." The triad plus the revised Monroe Doctrine, Wilson concluded, were "American principles" but also "the principles of mankind," and they "must prevail."[112]

Just over a week after his address, Wilson received news that destroyed his plans for a peace deal: Germany had begun an unrestricted sub campaign that would include all neutral ships heading toward England. It was clear that Berlin had decided on one final roll of the dice—to starve Britain into submission and, because of London's key role in propping up the Allies, to end the war on terms acceptable to Germany. German leaders obviously hoped that neutral ships would simply be deterred from crossing the Atlantic. This would achieve the effect desired—Britain cut off from all food and raw material imports— without having to sink U.S. ships and risk drawing the United States into the war. But from the American perspective, the dilemma was straightforward and existential: if the Americans did *not* keep exporting to Britain and the Allies, it would not simply destroy the trade that had pulled America out of recession and made it the world's leading creditor and exporting nation. Even more importantly, it would risk Germany's victory on the Continent, and its potential takeover of British colonies and even portions of the British fleet, depending on the final terms of the "peace."

When House talked to Wilson on Thursday, February 1, the president was "sad and depressed." The discussion shows how their bubble of optimism had burst: "We had every reason to believe that within a month the belligerents would be talking peace." Now, Wilson felt the world "had suddenly reversed itself." They agreed that Bernstorff should be handed his passport and relations with Berlin severed. Yet Wilson was still determined that "he would not allow it to lead to war if it could possibly be avoided."[113] Over the next month, as Germany gave the Americans a grace period where no neutral shipping was attacked without warning and accommodation to the crew, Wilson continued to hope that perhaps the Germans were just bluffing and would regain their senses in time before disaster struck. After all, on two previous occasions, Germany had backed away from the brink once it was clear its sub campaign might lead to war with America. Wilson continued to believe until mid-March that Germany wasn't truly serious in its new and much more severe threats. He also hoped that U.S. negotiations with the Austrians—negotiations that accepted the continuation of the Austria-Hungary multiethnic empire— might convince them to leave the war, forcing Berlin to see that only a negotiated solution would realize their aims.[114]

On February 2, Wilson held a cabinet meeting to get feedback from its members. Many felt that the issue was now settled, and conflict with Germany inevitable. Wilson disagreed. Asked at one point which side he hoped would win, he replied that he did not "wish to see either side win." Here he was, faced with imminent German attacks on U.S. shipping, seemingly still clinging to the peace without victory logic. Yet his view was not merely a function of wishful thinking and cognitive closure. When Secretary of the Interior Franklin Lane suggested that a German-Japanese-Russian alliance was likely after the war, Wilson remarked prophetically that perhaps the Russian peasant, through revolution, "might save the world this misfortune." Russian dominance of Eurasia had been his and House's first fear way back in the early months of the war. Yet by this point he was evidently more worried about Japan using the total war of the "white" nations to expand its sphere at America's expense. He told the group with emphasis that if "in order to keep the white race or part of it strong to meet the yellow race . . . it was wise to do nothing" and he would do exactly that.[115] In sum, we can say that while his hope for peace was perhaps delusional, his logic remained quintessentially geopolitical (if also shaped by Wilson's racial views of politics).

Through February, Wilson came around to the idea that American merchant ships should be armed, with U.S. government help, not only to protect themselves but more importantly to signal U.S. resolve and force the Germans to back away from their stated plans. On Friday the twenty-third, Wilson held a heated cabinet meeting and was pressed to consider not just the arming of U.S. merchant ships but convoying them via the U.S. navy as he prepared public opinion for war. Wilson accused those supporting such ideas of being bent on pushing the country into war.[116]

Yet by Monday the twenty-sixth, Wilson was willing to formally ask Congress to requisition funds for arming merchant ships. At a cabinet meeting the next day, when members pressed Wilson to acknowledge just how involved Germany was in Mexico and the Caribbean, Wilson needed no convincing. He and the cabinet decided that day to send a division of soldiers to Cuba to help its government fight a new threat from "revolutionists." Wilson told the group that "so many things are happening [that] we cannot afford to let Cuba be involved by G[erman] plots." He went on to relate a note from U.S. ambassador James Gerard in Berlin stating that former foreign secretary Gottlieb von Jagow had warned Gerard that should war break out between the United States and Germany, there would be "500,000 German reservists [within the U.S.] ready to take up arms for [the] mother country and you will have a civil war." Lane and McAdoo piled on, stating that there were rumors that there were now five hundred German reservists in Mexico, and that two hundred Japanese citizens had arrived to make munitions for Mexico. Secretary of Labor W. B. Wilson was puzzled: "Strange that G[ermans] and Jap[anese] both going to Mex[ico] seeing they are at war."[117]

Woodrow Wilson, however, was not puzzled. Although he chose not to reveal this to his cabinet, on the previous day, Sunday, February 25, he had received word that Germany was actively seeking, should war come with America, to form an alliance with Mexico and Japan, and in fact was encouraging Mexico to attack the United States to recover territory lost in the 1846–48 war. In mid-January the new German foreign secretary Arthur Zimmermann had sent a coded telegram to Mexico City proposing such an alliance. The British had decoded the infamous "Zimmermann telegram" in early February but had not allowed the American leadership to learn of it until the twenty-fifth.[118] It was Wilson's learning of this telegram on that fateful Sunday that provoked his new hard-line policies on Monday and Tuesday.

The Zimmermann telegram was not the complete "shock" it is often portrayed to be. As we have seen, the Americans were well aware of active German efforts to cause turmoil in Mexico and draw Mexico and America into war with one another from 1914 on. Yet the telegram did have a fundamental impact on Wilson himself by seeming to confirm all the warnings from Lansing, and increasingly House, that the German leaders were not just security-seekers wrongly viewing other powers as threats, but rather militaristic aggressors bent on world domination. They thus had to be stopped now, before they went further. This mental shift from seeing the other as a security-seeker to seeing it as having a pathological drive for glory and dominance is critical to explaining Wilson's willingness to risk and then choose war with Germany in March 1917. A Germany that had gotten involved in the war because of fear and mistrust was one thing—it might be willing, as Berlin had so often implied in 1915–16, to accept a peace of "equals" that protected German security through a collective security league. But a Germany bent on total victory in Europe and an expanded presence in the western hemisphere posed an existential threat to America's economic and political sphere, and perhaps even to the U.S. homeland itself.

On Wednesday, February 28, Wilson decided to give the Zimmermann telegram to the Associated Press. This move itself represented a significant shift, since it would stir up public opinion in a way that just five days before he had dismissed as "propaganda of hatred" against Germany.[119] When Congress ended its session on March 3 without passing legislation to support the arming of merchant ships, Wilson on the eighth used executive privilege to proceed anyway. During the next week, Wilson approved the purchase of the Danish West Indies to make sure that Germany did not grab the islands and their ports first, either through purchase or the coercion of Denmark.

The final coup de grâce came on Sunday, March 18, when Wilson learned that three U.S. merchant ships had been sunk without warning over the previous three days by German submarines off the British coast. After giving the Americans a grace period to see if deterrence would work, the Germans were now signaling that they indeed meant to choke Britain off from all neutral shipping, regardless of the risks of an expanded war. This news came at the same time as word of revolution in Russia and the overthrow of the czar. Russia's "democratic" revolution would certainly help facilitate a U.S. entry into war by making it seem to the American public that this was indeed a war of democracy against autocracy.[120] But there was also an important geopolitical implication. As House noted after a dinner with notable friends, there was "general agreement that [a] democratic Russia would not join Japan in the future in the exploitation of China, and that Japan would probably moderate her policy in that direction."[121] In short, the Americans had to worry less about any U.S. entry in the European war leading to Japan's further penetration of China. This would help moderate Wilson's fear of "the yellow race" controlling the Far East as the western great powers fought each other. Moreover, as House had told Wilson two days before, helping democracy in Russia survive "will end the peril which a possible alliance between Germany, Russia, and Japan might hold for us."[122]

March had been a month of waiting for Wilson. But with final confirmation on March 18 that the Germans were indeed determined to pursue unrestricted sub warfare until Britain sued for terms, Wilson could no longer avoid the inevitable. House and Lansing, his two closest advisors, both wrote separate letters to Wilson on March 19, urging him to see that there was now no other choice but war. Lansing argued that there was no point in waiting any longer. Germany would never declare war on America, for it served no purpose, but it would not relent until the autocratic Central Powers had defeated the democratic Allies. For Lansing, this was an ideological war, and for the welfare of mankind and the establishment of peace, "Democracy should succeed."[123]

House, more attentive to Wilson's geopolitical core, said nothing about ideological goals. For him, the problem was simple: France was badly in need of bullets, coal, and raw materials; and the "strain upon the English" to furnish materials for Russia, France, and Italy had been so great that Britain couldn't even recruit more men for its army. (British finance and supplies had been keeping the other Allies going for more than two years.) In short, the United States could not wait any longer. As House told Wilson: "the English and the French tell me that if we intend to help defeat Germany that it will be necessary for us to begin immediately to furnish the things the Allies were lacking."[124] He did not have to mention the obvious alternative outcome: that if the United States stayed out now, and did not use its navy to protect the shippers as they crossed the ocean, Britain itself would soon starve or be defeated, or at the very least be unable to resupply the Allied armies fighting on the Continent.[125] This would mean German victory in Europe.

On Tuesday, March 20, 1917, an internally torn Wilson held the most important cabinet meeting of his four-year-old presidency. Wilson began by stating that he had told Congress that he did not believe Germany would do what it had threatened, and now it had. He mentioned how much he opposed German militarism on land—but also British militarism at sea. "Both were abhorrent," and hence he was still "disinclined to [make] the final break."[126] He then went around the room and asked each of his cabinet members for their opinions. Each one to a man, even the former doves such as Daniels, argued that Wilson had no choice but to take the United States into the war.[127] The meeting ended with Wilson offering no sense of what decision he would make, saying only to Lansing after the meeting he would sleep on it.[128] The next morning, however, he came to the conclusion that the cabinet was right, and he sent a note to Congress to set aside time on Monday, April 2 for a special address. That Monday night, Wilson rose to the podium to ask Congress to declare that a state of war existed between the United States and Germany. America was now in the Great War. Wilson's great reluctance, driven both by moral and geopolitical concerns, had been overwhelmed by what Polybius had famously called the "pressure of circumstances." He knew there was no other way to prevent Germany from dominating Europe and, potentially, important aspects of trade and political alignments across the globe and, of course, in the western hemisphere.[129]

## Conclusion

This chapter has offered a highly revisionist account of the reasons Woodrow Wilson took his nation into the bloodiest war in human history up to that point. But this is not revisionism in the neo-Marxist reading that by the 1930s would be promoted as the main explanation for intervention: namely, that American "death merchants"—the producers of weapons and the suppliers of war materiel—pressured Wilson to act to protect their profits. Undoubtedly there were many firms by 1917 that were worried that if Germany succeeded in blocking U.S. shipping to Europe, their huge annual sales of goods to Britain and France would suddenly dry up. But there is simply no evidence that these were the kinds of economic concerns driving Wilson in early 1917. Nor is there any evidence that he felt pressured by regions of the United States dependent on continued sales to Europe to act before these regions suffered economic downturns, as Benjamin Fordham claims,[130] although Wilson was no doubt aware of the direct implications for the U.S. economy of not acting. He was, after all, a keen student of the reasons for Madison's plunge into war with Britain in 1812 as Napoleon sought hegemony in Europe.

Even if neo-Marxism is wrong, this still leaves the traditional historical account that Wilson finally accepted the necessity of war because he saw no other way to achieve his ambitious liberal goals of remaking the world system in the American image. As we have seen, there are a number of problems with this view considered on its own. First, if Wilson was driven by his ideological vision, then why did he wait so long to get into the war, and why did he seem to be so unsure by the end of 1916 as to which great power in Europe was the greatest threat to the system and to long-term U.S. interests, Britain or Germany? Second, if he saw the spreading of liberal democracy as the key to a peace that would end all war, why did he propose as late as January 1917 a "peace without victory" that would have preserved each belligerent's political system intact and not have forced Germany or Russia to change its stripes? Moreover, if he wanted to use the war to break up oppressive multiethnic empires, why would he work *until the end of 1917* to pull Austria-Hungary out of its alliance with Germany, promising that it would be able to keep its empire in the Balkans?[131] Third, if collective security was such an integral part of Wilson's liberal understanding of world politics, why was he so slow to accept it as part of the solution to balance of power politics? Why indeed was collective security initially pushed by realist-leaning leaders such as Howard Taft and Teddy Roosevelt in 1915, with Wilson only jumping on board in 1916? And why, as late as January 1917, did Wilson believe Germany would be a necessary part of a successful collective security system, especially as a tool to keep Russia contained and to offset a likely commercial condominium between postwar Britain and France?

The liberal view that Wilson's idealism or his drive to uphold international law propelled him into war is largely driven by post hoc analysis. Since we know that Wilson by 1919 did indeed have a starry-eyed liberal vision for the world that he tried to force down the throats of *realpolitik* leaders in Britain and France as well as in the U.S. Senate, we tend to assume that he must have been thinking in such ideological terms all along. But as we have seen, Wilson was the consummate pragmatist when it came to both domestic and international politics. To be sure, he had a strong faith in the American way of life and what he perceived to be its superior values and progressive culture. But he was more than willing to set aside his ideals when push came to shove and American interests were at stake. Most significantly, he understood that without U.S. commercial dominance in the western hemisphere (realm one) and a strong trade position in East Asia (realm two), other great powers would slowly be able to reduce America's relative economic power and even assume control in its own neighborhood. The Zimmerman telegram was thus the most important piece of information that pushed Wilson into war. It was bad enough that Germany through unrestricted submarine warfare might hurt short-term U.S. economic power. But the Zimmerman telegram confirmed what more than five years of intelligence on German activities in Mexico and the Caribbean had already suggested—namely, that Germany was actively seeking to penetrate the western hemisphere, secure its raw materials and markets, and then use its global economic power to coerce the United States into submission. The main threat posed by unrestricted submarine warfare, therefore, was that Britain might be forced to sue for peace, offer up some of its navy and its trade connections in Latin America to avoid invasion, and then retreat stage-left as Germany realized its plans for economic hegemony, both in Europe and around the world.

Once we understand what was really going on in this crucial case, we can see the true power of dynamic realism and its focus on commercial expectations as a driving force in great power politics. Even highly moral and ideologically inclined individuals such as Woodrow Wilson and Edward House, once they get into power, find themselves pressured by the exigencies of the system and by the need to expand their nation's economic power sphere to ensure its long-term security. Their liberal predispositions certainly shaped the *way* they ultimately implemented their policies, including their use of liberal values to mobilize the American people to join a terrible war in Europe. But Wilson's continual delaying of action, and the reasons for his reluctance, reveal that geoeconomic and strategic objectives overrode his more idealistic goals when trade-offs had to be made. And as any good systemic realist would have to suggest, putting such goals on hold whenever they conflict with geopolitics is simply the prudent thing that any responsible statesman must do—even a Woodrow Wilson.

# 7

# The Second World War and the
# Origins of the Cold War

THIS CHAPTER focuses on two questions. First, to what extent did commerce play a role in drawing the United States into the Second World War in Europe and the Pacific? Second, to what extent did the reasoning that drove the United States into the Second World War also help lead to the Cold War that broke out with the Soviet Union soon after the defeat of Nazi Germany and Japan?

For most scholars of international relations and diplomatic history, the answer to the first question is easy: commerce had almost no role to play in Franklin D. Roosevelt's decision-making from 1939 to 1941 that pulled the United States into the war. If there was a connection, it was only an indirect one: U.S. economic sanctions against Japan pushed Tokyo to attack Pearl Harbor, which led Hitler to declare war on the Americans. But even if one wanted to argue that FDR needed this attack to get the American public to support a war against Germany—an argument for which there is little direct evidence—commerce would only be at most a facilitating factor, not a propelling one.[1] The standard view, repeated across thousands of books and articles, is that Roosevelt's desire for war came from his visceral opposition to Hitler's ideology and his need, as an acolyte of Woodrow Wilson, to protect liberal democracy from totalitarian regimes seeking dominance in Eurasia.[2] There is little question this view has something to it. There had never been a threat to American values quite like that of German Nazism. Yet for a complete picture, other layers of explanation need to be added.

Neo-Marxist revisionist scholars suggest that while the ideological fight against fascism may have been important, Roosevelt and his officials were equally or even more intensely driven by the need to protect the capitalist order. They needed a military-territorial victory over Germany and Japan that would stimulate growth and firm profits to avert a postwar slide back into a depression and social unrest. Securing foreign markets and cheap raw materials were critical to this plan. Yet the idea that Roosevelt from 1939 to 1941 saw broad commercial objectives as critical to *the long-term national security* of the United States is ignored by revisionists, given their focus on elite wealth and the avoidance of domestic revolution as the supposed ultimate ends of American statecraft. Yet as this chapter shows, Roosevelt and his officials from September 1939 onward were convinced that without U.S. involvement in the war, American security would be directly threatened. Nazi Germany would establish a dominant geopolitical position that would hurt American access to raw materials, investments, and markets on the Eurasian periphery and Africa, and likely challenge U.S. access to South America. Even if the Nazis could not ultimately be beaten and the world was to become a bipolar stand-off between Germany and the United States, the Americans would need a superior commercial position across the Atlantic to keep Germany bottled up and unable to undermine long-term U.S. economic and military strength. The combination of growing German power and the perception of Hitler's irrational, glory-driven character made the Nazi state the biggest threat the United States had ever faced in its existence.

The second question is also an easy one for most scholars, at least those subscribing to the traditionalist interpretation of the Cold War. If the Second World War was about stopping totalitarian fascism, then the Cold War came about because of Harry Truman's desire to stop totalitarian communism. One aggressive enemy, Nazi Germany, fell by the wayside and was replaced by another, Soviet Russia. Despite the cooperation displayed in the alliance against Hitler, traditionalists argue, Stalin after May 1945 quickly showed his intentions to expand his sphere beyond Eastern Europe. This new threat to liberal democracy had to be stopped, this time not by total war but by an expansive containment policy that kept the Soviet bloc within the confines of its present territorial realm.[3] In this chapter, I accept one big part of the traditionalist argument: namely, that the nature of Russian communism played an important role in exacerbating the American perception of the postwar threat the Soviet Union posed. But the full story of the origins of the Cold War is much more complex and power-political than what the traditionalists put forward.

Neo-Marxist revisionists would draw parallels between needing to beat Nazi Germany to restore prosperity and domestic order within the capitalist West and the imperative of stopping communist Russia in its effort to undermine capitalism around the world. But once again their perspective is limited by their focus on the wealth and position of U.S. elites as the primary ends of statecraft.[4] The notion that this chapter supports—that American officials really did care about the security of the whole nation when they sought to restrict Soviet growth and build up U.S. economic power—is fundamentally at odds with the revisionists' neo-Marxist starting point; namely, that elites are ultimately driven by selfish class-based material interests. Yet as I show, from June 1940 onward, U.S. officials worked tirelessly to secure a position of commercial and political dominance in Eurasia that would counter the profound threats to the liberal way of life of all classes of American citizens that the totalitarian powers posed, whether Nazi Germany or Soviet Russia.[5] The policies of FDR from 1943 until his death in April 1945 and of Truman from that April until 1947 were direct offshoots of the politico-economic reasoning put in place from June 1940 to the end of 1942. The Americans would build a new international order that was founded on absolute U.S. dominance of the global commercial system. If the Soviets accepted their lesser sphere of influence in Eastern Europe and worked with the Americans on a stable peace, great. But if not, then they would be restricted in their ability to grow economically and kept within the territorial confines of what the United States had allowed them.

We can see by the brief sketch above that this chapter is highly revisionist, but in a dynamic realist way, not a neo-Marxist way. It shows the critical importance of the American drive to extend the U.S. economic power sphere significantly beyond the original "Monroe Doctrine" sphere of the western hemisphere. U.S. leaders and officials from June 1940 on realized that without a dominant economic position after the war ended, the United States might face either a German or Russian superpower that, through its control of Eurasia, would slowly but surely whittle away at America's commercial connections and thus its long-term power base. Without this power base, the security of the United States from attack or from great power efforts to undermine America's social order would fall dramatically. And the threat to commerce was real—indeed, even worse than the one faced by Wilson in 1917.

President Wilson, as we have seen, had to act to protect the established economic sphere the United States had in the western hemisphere. But Roosevelt and Truman both realized that the multipolar world of many great powers in Eurasia was falling apart. That world had allowed European states to fight as the United States dominated North and South America. Yet after June 1940, it became very clear that Nazi Germany had destroyed that multipolar "balance of power" once and for all. With U.S. help, the Soviet Union was able to win critical battles in 1942 that made it clear that Germany would lose the war. But this only meant that, with the death of multipolarity, the Soviet Union would be the main new threat to American commercial connections to Europe, the Middle East, Southeast Asia, and Africa. FDR thus went beyond Wilson's regional concerns and reoriented American grand strategy to the geopolitics of Eurasia. He took the recommendations of his advisors and made sure that the United States would establish an economic-political position that would encircle the Soviet empire and keep it subordinate to the American. His strategy worked so successfully that to this day, Chinese and Russian leaders decry the "hegemonic sphere" of alliances and economic connections that surround their countries and restrict their "natural" developments, from Russia's connection to Eastern Europe to China's extension of its Belt and Road Initiative.

The chapter proceeds in two parts. In the first, I provide a summary of the evidence for the importance of commerce to FDR's efforts to get the United States into the war in Europe. Because Roosevelt was responding to German aggression rather than being the initiator or cause of conflict, I will keep this section short, and focus on the way the Nazi threat to Europe translated into a perceived threat to the American economic power sphere and long-term U.S. security. The bulk of the chapter will focus on the much more complicated issue of the American role in the onset of the Cold War. Most scholars still argue that U.S. officials were only responding to postwar Soviet expansionism and that the Cold War conflict only arose in 1946–47 as a necessary defensive move to contain the Russian threat.

Against this position, I argue that the Americans helped provoke the spiral of hostility and mistrust we call the Cold War, and they did so by actions as early as 1943–44 that were designed to secure for the United States a position of economic, political, and military dominance in the Eurasian periphery and beyond. While the Americans were hoping that the Soviets would peacefully accept their inferior sphere and even create commercial ties with it, they were well aware that the building of a truly globalist posture—for the first time in U.S. history—might be upsetting to Moscow. Yet the establishment of a strong economic power sphere was a critical foundation for postwar U.S. security, given both the potential growth of the Soviet Union and the strong perceived differences in character type between the two great powers. The Soviets were not only communists, but they believed that they needed to build an autarkic economic sphere to survive. States that fell into its sphere would thus be largely cut off from trade with the West. Hence, after it became clear by the spring and summer of 1945 that communism might spread to the U.S.-led realm—even if only because of its appeal in a poverty-stricken Europe and Asia—the willingness to accept a trade-off between avoiding a spiral of hostility and protecting the long-term American power sphere changed, and American actions grew progressively more hard-line and antagonistic. By the second half of 1945, the United States had already embarked on an active containment of the growth of its former World War II ally, even if the actual word "containment" would not be used for another two years.

## The Commercial Foundations for the U.S. Entry into the Second World War

The period after World War I was a time of rebuilding for the United States and the other great powers. The Versailles Treaty and its offshoot the League of Nations were, much to Woodrow Wilson's chagrin, rejected by the U.S. Senate. But this result did not mean, contrary to popular mythology, that the country retreated into "isolationism" in the 1920s. American commercial expansion into South America and the Far East, facilitated by the government-sponsored growth of the U.S. merchant marine during the war, continued unabated. Britain and France did seek to use their colonies and their League of Nations "mandates" in the Middle East and Africa to rebuild their trade ties and counter U.S. economic growth, but they were never able to consolidate the plan for a commercial condominium that had so worried Washington in the summer of 1916. In fact, because of the huge costs associated with both rebuilding in Europe and paying off war debts to the United States, London and Paris found themselves seeking American financial support to help jump-start the European economy again—without Germany if they could do it (1919–24) and eventually *with* Germany given its importance to global trade and commerce (1925–29). Through the Dawes Plan of 1925 and the Young Plan of 1929, American financial clout was employed to reduce Germany's reparation burden while at the same time providing relief for the struggling British and French economies. Until the crash of October 1929 and the subsequent Great Depression, the "roaring twenties" appeared to foreshadow a new era in increased global trade and technological development, fueled by the mass production of automobiles, refrigerators, transistor radios, and lower costs for transportation and tourism.[6]

With the shock of the global depression, the great powers resorted to ill-advised economic policies such as the imposition of high tariff barriers (starting with the American 1930 Smoot-Hawley Act) and the retreat into closed economic spheres (e.g., the British-inspired "imperial preference" schemes of 1931–32 on), which led to a massive drop in global trade. States with small or nonexistent imperial spheres such as Japan and Germany were particularly hard hit. Japan, for example, saw its total trade fall by two-thirds from 1929 to 1931.[7] The exacerbation of hard economic times led to dramatic domestic changes on the ground: Japanese "Taisho democracy" of the 1920s was destroyed by a right-wing authoritarian reaction in 1931–33, and Germany of course found itself led by Adolf Hitler by January 1933 after his party received the plurality of votes in the December 1932 election and President Hindenburg appointed Hitler chancellor. By March 1933, Franklin Roosevelt was president of the United States, and was caught between trying to restore economic confidence and prosperity to a country with over 20 percent unemployment and deal with the simultaneous growth of both German and Japanese authoritarianism Soviet communism. For the next three years, FDR would place his primary emphasis on solving the first concern. By 1936, however, with Hitler's reoccupation of the Rhineland and clear evidence of his massive military buildup, it was clear that the German threat would have to be countered sooner rather than later.[8]

The specific dimensions of the Nazi threat were up for debate. The German use of aerial bombing in the Spanish Civil War from 1936 to 1939 made it clear that cities could now be on the "front lines" of any future war. But the fear of long-range bombers being able to hit the United States was not yet in the consciousness of U.S. officials, let alone most American citizens. The initial fear, as with Woodrow Wilson from 1913 to 1916, was that the Germans would use government agencies to help German firms penetrate the economies of Latin America at the expense of American political and commercial dominance. In 1934–35, the German government began a concentrated effort to increase both exports to and imports from South America. The impact was immediate. German exports to Latin America doubled in a year, and by 1936 Germany had surpassed the United States as Brazil's largest trading partner. Over the next three years, Germany continued to use special "Aski" marks that could be used only to buy German products to divert even more Latin America raw materials to Germany in return for German manufactured goods. Berlin employed a similar strategy for trade with Eastern Europe.[9] By early 1939, Roosevelt was worried about Germany's neo-mercantilist efforts to create a closed bloc harming U.S. interests. He told a group of visiting senators in late January that the "whole threat" emanating from Germany was wrapped up in effort to dominate world trade by putting an economic fence around the United States akin to what the British did to Napoleonic France in 1807.[10]

Roosevelt and his advisors insightfully understood that part of Hitler's economic strategy and his preparation for war had been driven by a feeling that Germany had been excluded from the global economic system by the other great powers. From 1937 to 1938, therefore, Washington had made moves to coordinate an "economic appeasement" plan with London that would involve giving back to Germany some of its pre-war colonies in Africa now controlled by the British. Neville Chamberlain, however, refused to work with Roosevelt on such a plan, focusing instead on appeasement within Europe itself.[11] But once war began in September 1939, preceded by Germany's pact with Soviet Russia to divide up Poland and avoid war with each other, Roosevelt knew that Hitler could not be appeased, and that Germany now constituted a direct threat to American access to Eurasian and African resources and markets, and not just U.S. commerce with the western hemisphere. He told a friend in a private letter in December that if Germany and Russia had contracted to divide up Britain and France and their empires, then American civilization was in peril. "Our world trade would be at the mercy of the combine," and despite recent gains, South American countries would start to reorient their relations back to Europe "unless we were willing to go to war on their behalf against a German-Russian dominated Europe."[12]

Through 1940 the "nightmare of a closed world," as historian Patrick Hearden calls it, became increasingly intense, and not just due to Germany's behavior directly. By January–February, American officials Cordell Hull (secretary of state), Norman David (Council on Foreign Relations), and Ambassador Jay Pierrepont Moffat believed that Britain, in response to Berlin's policies, would have to extend its wartime economic restrictions into any postwar peace, and as in 1916 would have to create, in Moffat's words, "a pound-franc area designed to exclude us."[13] German military expansionism combined with its mercantilist policies, however, remained the near-term threat. But the real shock came in April–June 1940 when Germany quickly defeated and occupied Norway, Denmark, Belgium, the Netherlands, and then beat France in a six-week war that led to the British near-disaster of Dunkirk. Britain was on the ropes, and might fall, while the German-Soviet alliance remained intact, providing the buffer for Germany to begin to move across North Africa toward British-held Egypt, the gateway to the Middle East and its vast oil reserves.

Stephen Wertheim's recent book, backed by earlier work by Laurence Shoup and William Minter, shows beyond any doubt that June of 1940 was a turning point in American thinking about the threats emanating from Europe and Eurasia and what must be done about them. A good two years before Nicholas Spykman began writing his famous series of analyses on the geopolitical importance of maintaining control of the "rimland" from Britain through the Middle East, Southeast Asia, and China, and keeping it out of the hands of any continental great power (whether Germany or Russia or a combination of the two), U.S. policy-makers, aided by insightful reports from the quasi-official Council on Foreign Relations (CFR), understood that America now had to step up and play a decisive global role far beyond the western hemisphere.[14]

Prior to the spring of 1940, as Wertheim shows, State Department officials and their compatriots in the CFR had expected a long defensive war in Western Europe akin to 1914–17, not a quick German takeover. Roosevelt even hoped the United States could play the role of intermediary to achieve the equivalent of Wilson's plan of January 1917, a "peace without victory." The shock of France's defeat in June changed everything. Suddenly the United States faced the very real prospect of the end of a multipolar Europe and the emergence of a single state that could use its domination of the region to control global trade and political/colonial affairs around the world. From June until December 1940, as Wertheim summarizes, American officials and their CFR advisors feared the "specter of a Nazi-led world order," with "the first problem [being that] such a world might be closed to U.S. trade and other liberal forms of intercourse."[15] Five study groups within the CFR, in coordination with the Department of State (DOS), had already been set up to study such things as the economic-financial and territorial questions coming out of the war in Europe and the nature of U.S. aims for the postwar peace. Over the next four years, CFR members would attend over 350 meetings and write almost 700 separate reports for the DOS.[16]

Immediately after the defeat of France, the key issue on the table was whether the western hemisphere was a sufficiently large trading zone to ensure the United States could resist a Nazi hegemon across the water. In a key shift from Woodrow Wilson's hemispheric focus of 1914–16, top CFR and DOS officials realized the world had changed. Not only could the United States no longer rely on the checks and balances of multipolarity in Europe to ensure commercial access to Eurasian and African resources and markets, but the increased complexity of the commodities required for a modern economy made such access absolutely essential. A CFR report from September 1940 analyzing more than 90 percent of world trade across all commodities concluded that the American economic bloc of North and South America would be significantly less self-sufficient than a German-dominated continental bloc. Since many key raw materials such as rubber and tin would have to be drawn from British colonies in Southeast Asia, a larger bloc that included Britain's commercial sphere would have to be created. But of course, this strategy depended on Britain surviving as a great power, and from June 1940 until the first half of 1941, this could not be assumed. The CFR recommendation for the United States to trade fifty old American destroyers for leases on British bases in the Caribbean was accepted by Roosevelt in September, and the president soon explored the importance of securing Greenland and Iceland in order to protect the Atlantic sea lanes for both U.S. and British ships.[17]

It is important to realize that in the fall of 1940, CFR-DOS planners had no idea that the Soviet Union would eventually become the true "other pole" of a postwar bipolar world order. At the time, they were expecting that any such order might very well result from a military stand-off between the United States *and Nazi Germany*. The Soviets were expected to continue to play the role of raw material supplier and peaceful junior partner to a Berlin-controlled Eurasian-African economic power sphere. Only with Germany's surprise attack on the Soviet Union on June 22, 1941, did the possibility of a U.S.-Soviet postwar order emerge, and that was only after the Soviets proved by early 1942 that they might well be able to stop the German juggernaut. So, in the planning from the fall of 1940 to December 1941, the focus of CFR-DOS strategic thinking was on how to prevent Germany from dominating the world system, assuming that Germany might not be defeatable in war. From July 1940 through 1941, the CFR offered DOS officials a series of reports, complete with Mercator-projection maps of the world, arguing that the United States (always shown in light gray) had to create a "Grand Area" that would counter and contain the Nazi menace (always shown in black).

The maps of the fall of 1940 showed Germany controlling all of Western and Eastern Europe, North Africa, and the Middle East up to Persia (Iran). Britain remained outside the German sphere but a part of the U.S.-led Grand Area that included all of South America, China, British India, Southeast Asia, Australia, and (by October's map) Sub-Saharan Africa. The language used is important here. On every one of the maps, the gray-shaded areas were labeled the "U.S.-led postwar area" and the black areas "the Axis-led postwar area." Dotted lines were used to show "shipping lanes" connecting the American eastern and western ports with Britain, Africa, and Asia all the way to Japan, which was assumed to be a part of the U.S.-led Grand Area, not the Axis. The Axis-led area was shown to have no shipping lanes beyond its core area, implying the complete economic encirclement of Germany's economic power sphere by the American one.[18]

The above should not lead us to conclude that commercial factors were the only things leading Roosevelt and his officials after June 1940 to seek to join the war against Germany as quickly as they could, and to support Britain and then (after June 22, 1941) the Soviet Union as much as they could. But they were absolutely central to American thinking. By 1940, U.S. officials were envisioning a loss of about two-thirds of American trade should the United States fail to protect, with the help of the British navy, global shipping beyond the western hemisphere. But even with control of North and South America, they worried that the United States would become isolated from world history if the Nazis won, left alone to protect liberal democracy while the rest of the world fell to one form or another of totalitarianism. Already in June 1940, shocked by France's fall, Roosevelt warned the nation that if it continued to avoid getting into the war, it would find itself "a lone island in a world dominated by the philosophy of force."[19]

So began a strenuous campaign through all levels of government to paint those who continued to resist U.S. entry into the war as ignorant "isolationists" who were endangering the universal cause of liberal republicanism that American leaders in history had worked so hard to protect and promote.[20] Roosevelt's meeting with Winston Churchill in August 1941 and the joint declaration of the Four Freedoms may have been primarily driven by a desire to commit the British to dismantling the closed imperial sphere of their empire in return for American aid.[21] But it is also clear that he truly believed that the war was not just a fight against fascism but a struggle to extend the benefits of the American way of life to as many countries as possible, without also provoking spirals of mistrust.[22] The majority of the world, in short, had to be globalized according to American principles of at least liberal trade, if not necessarily liberal democracy. And to achieve this, the United States had to have a global military presence and rework consciousness at home in support of this new strategy. As early as October 1940, CFR reports to the DOS indicated that the country needed an "integrated policy to achieve military and economic supremacy for the United States within the non-German world." Given that Nazi Germany would still exist, this policy would not achieve perpetual peace, but rather give Washington "the greatest measure of economic bargain[ing]-power to maintain economic superiority which, in turn, [would] lead to decisive military superiority." This would one day allow America to defeat Germany and make the world whole again.[23]

With the strategy of the Grand Area already set by the end of 1940, the year of 1941 was spent on tactical questions such as how to prop up Britain beyond the deal on destroyers. With Roosevelt having ended most of the restrictions of the Neutrality Acts by November 1939, he was able to get Congress to approve a Lend Lease Act in the spring of 1941 that funneled military equipment and supplies into Britain at no immediate cost to London. The original planning for the postwar world, since it assumed Nazi Germany's continued dominance of continental Europe, did not envision a reliance on collective security institutions. The term "United Nations" would only be coined in December 1941 once the United States was in the war, and it initially was only a term to describe the anti-Axis grand alliance. And since this grand alliance was made up of many nondemocracies, including the Soviet Union and Latin America dictatorships, all Wilsonian allusions to a coalition of liberal states were avoided. The logic was power-political, and economic power was at its heart.

The economic and financial group within the CFR was particularly influential, not just in shaping the notion of a Grand Area linked by shipping lanes, but in stressing the importance of raw materials from Southeast Asia and Africa to the long-term viability of the "U.S.-led area." This kind of thinking was closer to Wilson circa 1916 rather than Wilson 1919, and of course much more globalist in orientation.[24] By May 1941, CFR planners were actively discussing the need for a policy that was "essentially offensive in character," one that required that the United States establish "advanced bases" overseas that had no geographic limits. These planners realized that some of these bases would require the use of British territories and colonies and would project not just American naval power but air power as well. Working with the British, the United States would need air and naval bases "which will enable [the two states], acting jointly or in close cooperation, to contain any possible hostile force."[25] These words were penned in mid-June 1941, just before the German invasion of the Soviet Union. While they clearly are directed against the Nazi threat, by 1943 they would apply as well against the Soviet Union.

The German invasion of Russia on June 22, 1941, suddenly brought Stalin's Russia into the war against Hitler. As I have shown in detail elsewhere, this led

Roosevelt to immediately pledge full support to Moscow and to make sure that Japan did not create a peace with China and the United States that would allow it to go north against Russia. Such an attack would force Stalin to fight a two-front war when his war against Germany required not just everything he had, but the crack Soviet forces of the east that had been battle-hardened by two wars with Japan over Manchuria in 1938 and 1939. Although this is a little-known story for why Pearl Harbor occurred when it did, the evidence is over-whelming that Roosevelt and his secretary of state Cordell Hull used severe economic sanctions against Japan to draw it south and prevent it from going north against Russia. They were willing to engage in negotiations on three occasions (spring 1941, late August, and November 1941) if Tokyo was willing to agree not to attack anywhere in the Pacific in return for renewed trade. Since the Japanese leaders were willing to commit to peace everywhere *except* in the north, Roosevelt and Hull on November 26 decided to "kick over" negotiations and accept a Japanese attack in the south in order to save the Russians from a two-front war. Given its declining economic situation, Japan had no choice but to switch from a Go-North strategy to a Go-South one. On December 7, 1941, it attacked the United States at Pearl Harbor. With Hitler declaring war on America four days later, the United States was now in the war until its bitter end. Protecting America's access to the Grand Area that would ensure long-term economic security and growth was critical to the decision to support the ideological adversary Soviet Russia to destroy the even greater long-term threat, Nazi Germany.[26]

## The Commercial Origins of the Cold War, 1943 to 1945

The goal of the rest of this chapter is to show just how important commercial flows were to the origins of the dangerous U.S.-Soviet conflict we came to call the Cold War. As with what we have just seen, the need to prevent any great power, whether Germany or (after 1942) the Soviet Union, from dominating Eurasia pushed the United States to create a dominant economic power sphere extending from Britain through the Middle East to China. Maintaining America's "preponderance of power" helped to create mistrust in Moscow and was critical to the onset of an intensifying spiral of hostility by the second half of 1945.[27] But Washington's strategy from 1943 to 1945 was more than just a matter of stopping a great power from using a Eurasian power base to expand further, as it had been for dealing with Germany in 1939 to 1942. Nazi Germany did not possess a universal philosophy. The Soviet Union did. The Americans now also had to worry that the citizens of Western Europe, China, and other places on the Eurasian periphery would be drawn to communism in the face of the poverty and inequality left by the war. By securing a strong economic and political position on the periphery, the United States would be able to direct the post-war recovery of most of the globe and keep the Soviets from drawing large parts of it to its side. If the Soviets decided to work with Washington and keep order within their own smaller sphere, great. But if not, then the United States would have the power base needed to deal with anything that arose in the future, and with the problems on the ground in the present.

I will be talking about the causes of the Cold War and the way it played out over forty-five years for the next three chapters. Before I proceed, therefore, I need to briefly address what might seem to be a self-evident truth: that economic interdependence could have had little to do with either the Cold War's origins or with the crises and tensions that pockmarked its history until the late 1980s. After all, U.S.-Soviet trade from late 1945 onward remained at very low levels given what seemed to be strong geopolitical reasons for not trading, particularly American fears that trade would promote Soviet relative economic growth within the new more zero-sum, bipolar world Washington now faced. It would thus seem that economic interdependence drops out as a causal variable that might explain both the start of the Cold War and its dynamics over some four decades. Indeed, both realists and liberals usually completely ignore the economic aspects of the U.S.-Soviet relationship from 1945 to the 1980s, presuming that low or almost nonexistent trade could not possibly have had much of a role in the Cold War struggle. The two camps thus tend to fight over the relative salience of other variables: realists stress the importance of power and nuclear technology in shaping arms-racing dynamics, fears of surprise attack, and the competition for territorial position, while liberals argue for the importance of ideological and domestic motivations and the role of international institutions and arms control regimes.[28] When it comes to the specific causes of the Cold War itself, liberals typically align with the traditionalist argument that Moscow's drive to spread communism led to the spiral of hostility between the two wartime allies. Systemic realists generally adopt the post-revisionist view that both sides brought on the Cold War spiral out of fear of the other side's present and future territorial intentions. The economic dimensions of great power politics have typically played little or no role in either camp's analyses.[29]

To garner any insight into the role of economics in the Cold War, one has had to fall back on revisionist scholars who argue that the United States started the Cold War to protect the profits of American firms and to ensure sufficient prosperity to avoid revolution within. As we will see, revisionists have uncovered important historical documents on the role of commerce to force us to rethink the nature of the U.S.-Soviet conflict.[30] But their efforts to show commerce was only about the wealth and survival of the capitalist class ignores the profound national security implications of economic interdependence that arose for America as World War II wound down and a new era began. Moreover, their focus on Western capitalism leads them to miss a key fact: that Russia also had strong economic needs that made its leaders quite concerned about Soviet ties with both new spheres of influence in Eastern Europe and northern China and with the United States itself.

This chapter and the next two chapters seek to rectify the lacuna in the international relations and historical fields by showing the truly powerful impact of economic factors on the dynamics of U.S.-Soviet relations after 1942. The problems with realist and liberal thinking about economic interdependence are starkly revealed by the Cold War case. The theoretical logics for both camps are based on the actual present trade between great power spheres. But in situations where current trade and commerce is low or nonexistent, leaders' expectations of *future* trade and commerce can still be critical to their decision-making processes. So even when there is little present trade, if a state needs what the external system has to offer, the other's commitment or lack of commitment to the provision of future economic benefits may be critical to a leader's assessment of the state's future security.

This was the Soviet situation from 1943 to 1945. From late 1941 onwards, the Americans had been shipping millions of tons of lend-lease aid to Russia, asking nothing in return. After it became clear by 1943 that the allies would win the war, Moscow began to probe Washington's willingness to create a permanent trading relationship, one that would be sustained in the short term by U.S. trade credits and loans. Russia had been completely devastated by the war and needed American goods to rebuild. America's unwillingness by 1945 to keep lend-lease aid flowing and to extend the credit needed to jumpstart the trade relationship severely undermined Soviet confidence in cooperation. With Soviet suspicions already rising as a result of Truman's efforts, beginning in mid-1945, to constrain Russian economic and political growth, Stalin was forced to turn to hard-line measures to stabilize the Soviet economic position. He thus began to use coercion to further Soviet interests, starting with Iran in the late winter/early spring of 1946 (see chapter 8). Moscow's actions against Iran were resisted by the United States, sparking an action-reaction spiral, including further reductions in East-West trade, that led to an all-out Cold War struggle by 1947–48.

Yet it was not just the Soviets that were anticipating and worrying about the future of global trade and commerce. Both presidents Roosevelt and Truman and most of the Washington foreign policy elite believed strongly that without a global "open door" for U.S. trade, America could not sustain a vibrant and growing economy after the end of the war.[31] While some individuals such as Cordell Hull held to a broad Wilsonian belief that open trade was needed for a general postwar peace between nations, the vast majority of political elites had a much more U.S.-centric and realpolitik-driven focus. They believed that a failure to maintain American access to markets, raw materials, and overseas investments would lead to a decline in U.S. economic power, leaving the country vulnerable to rising powers such as the Soviet Union. To maintain power preponderance and security into the future, therefore, it was critical to ensure continued access to the peripheral states in Europe and Asia that held the bulk of global production and resources outside of Russia and America per se.[32]

As this chapter will show, during the period from 1943 to 1945 both superpowers sought to solidify their economic power spheres as a hedge against the other's potentially malevolent character going into the future, an uncertainty exacerbated by the clear cultural differences between the two states—not just due to the political ideological differences (communist totalitarianism versus liberal democracy) but different orientations to economic nationalism versus relatively open trade.

Despite both states wanting control over their own spheres, they found themselves economically dependent on developments within the other's sphere. But their expectations for the future arose from different sources. Soviet expectations for the postwar trade environment were essentially a function of the explicit policy of the U.S. government. Like Japan in the late 1930s, Russia was dependent upon decisions originating in Washington that would either lead to trade between the U.S. and Soviet spheres or restrictions on it. And by the middle and latter parts of 1945, Truman and his officials had firmly decided in favor of economic restrictions. Washington not only ended lend-lease aid and denied crucial loans, but it also limited Russia's ability to extract reparation payments from the country that had just destroyed its infrastructure, Germany. This policy shift was driven both by a fear of the rise of Soviet power in the postwar era and by the intervening impact of third parties—specifically, the need to redirect U.S. money and goods to the devastated Western European states that would serve as the first line of defense against communism. Given these exogenous constraints, Truman felt compelled to restrict Soviet economic growth while he built up the power of the western sphere and ensured U.S. access to all its parts. But the result was a fundamental undermining of any basis for long-term superpower cooperation.

American "dependence" was about the great arc of influence, from Britain to the Middle East to China, that Roosevelt's brilliant post-1940 policy had left the United States. By 1943–44, the Americans had used this arc to establish military bases around the periphery of the Soviet Union and to consolidate a preponderant economic power sphere constituting more than three-quarters of the earth's landmass. This sphere was secure in the short term. Primary U.S. fears now revolved around one thing above and beyond all else—namely, the strong possibility that in the future peripheral states in America's realm two might fall to communism, even without Moscow's active encouragement. The fundamental problem was rooted in the nature of communism and in the overall logic of Soviet foreign economic policy. What the Americans knew is that any small state that "went communist" would automatically want to realign its commercial policy toward the Soviet sphere and away from the American realm. Such a desire would reflect more than a mere hatred for capitalism. The Soviet Union represented the new model of political economy. Under communism, Russia had not only quickly built up its economic power, but it appeared to have dramatically improved the conditions of the lower classes. In the face of the devastation of World War II, the material goods that Soviet-style communism seemed to be able to deliver to the masses made it very attractive to millions of workers and peasants having trouble even finding food to feed their families.

The threat of fragile peripheral states in western Europe and Asia going communist was very real. During the war, communists had played dominant roles in almost every resistance movement against German and Japanese aggression. They were now poised to exploit their newfound power and popularity and the devastated conditions at home to seize power—by either the rifle barrel or the ballot box. If key states such as France, Italy, Greece, and China fell to communism and were pulled into the Soviet economic sphere, America's economy and thus its long-term power position would be severely undermined. Through 1945, American leaders looked to the Eastern European states as precedents, and they did not like what they saw. The Americans had hoped in 1944 that the commercial policies of states such as Bulgaria and Romania would remain open. But by mid-1945 it was clear that these states would orient themselves economically toward Russia, either by choice or through Soviet coercion. If positive feedback loops kicked in—started, say, by the fact that Western European states could not get access to critical Eastern European food and raw materials—then other peripheral states might fall into the Soviet sphere. This would further reduce prosperity in the West, which would in turn shrink the American economic surplus needed to support the faltering economies of the still remaining allies. As more peripheral actors fell, the process would accelerate, and the United States would find itself trying to use a steadily deteriorating economic base to face down a superpower that now controlled most of Eurasia. Over the long term, the Soviet Union might find itself the dominant global superpower without having to fire a shot.

In the face of these threats, there was only one thing any responsible American statesman could have done: contain Russia's growth by restricting its access to western trade while redirecting U.S. goods to the faltering economies of the western sphere, notwithstanding the evident risks of provoking an intense trade-security spiral. This chapter will show that U.S. leaders began to take such measures as early as May–July 1945, a good two years before the Marshall Plan and the Truman Doctrine were announced. The United States also built up a strong position in the Middle East and China/the Far East, a position that would help reduce both Russia and Britain's economic and political roles in these regions after the war. The moves to assert regional hegemony were already well underway by the time of Franklin Delano Roosevelt's death in April 1945. Always the shrewd geopolitician, Roosevelt was well aware of the importance of establishing a strong American sphere around Russia as a hedge against future problems, even as he tried to maintain cooperative relations with the emerging Russian superpower. But U.S. policy from April to August 1945 took a decided turn to the hard-line end of the spectrum, and for one major reason: by the late spring of 1945, it was clear to every key official, including the newly installed president Harry S. Truman, that if the United States did not act forcefully to build up Western Europe and China and to restrict the economic growth of the Soviet Union, states in the western sphere might very soon start falling to communism. If this occurred, the snowball would quickly become too large to stop.

The emerging threat to America's access to the resources and markets of the periphery was thus a fundamental cause of its switch to harder-line policies by mid-1945, and thus of the subsequent spiral into Cold War hostility. This was not the only cause, however. Also important, as I have discussed elsewhere, was the simple need to maintain America's ongoing power preponderance given Russia's vast potential for future growth. There is overwhelming evidence that through the summer and fall of 1945, Truman liked Stalin and believed he could do business with him. Yet he also worried that if the United States did not act to constrain Russia, it would grow significantly, and future Soviet leaders might not be as restrained in their behavior.[33] Because I have detailed this evidence elsewhere, I will not repeat it here (although I will summarize some of its key elements at the end of this chapter). Rather, this chapter's goal is to extend this work by showing that Truman and his advisors were equally worried in 1945 about the economic implications of the immediate loss of peripheral states to the beguiling appeal of Soviet communism. I also push the analysis back to 1943 to show that Roosevelt recognized the critical importance of protecting America's economic access to the periphery and took active steps to further U.S. military and political penetration of key strategic areas.

In making the above argument, this chapter directly challenges the argument, rooted in traditional liberalism, that the Cold War was caused by Soviet aggression, aggression which forced the Americans by 1947 into a containment posture they would otherwise have avoided.[34] I show that the move to a strong proto-containment position had already begun in mid-1945. But while it is clear that the Americans were the first to shift to a grand strategy designed to restrict and reduce the strength of the other's sphere, I am not out to put moral "blame" on Truman for starting the Cold War. In purely causal and chronological terms, it was indeed American actions that brought on the Cold War spiral of mistrust and hostility. The Soviets, after all, were desperate to buy time to rebuild their devastated society, and they had strong self-interested reasons to appear moderate and reasonable. Yet from a normative standpoint, Truman did exactly what was required of him given the uncertain circumstances that he faced. Moreover, the nature of the Soviet state—its mercantilist economic practices and its authoritarian leadership structure—played a significant role in his calculation. It is important to stress, however, that from a theoretical perspective Russia's communist regime type had an indirect rather than direct causal impact. It was not Soviet "aggression" in 1945 that sparked the Cold War, as traditionalists would argue. Rather, it was U.S. worry that communist revolutions would lead to the loss of smaller states to the closed Soviet economic sphere, combined with the concern that Moscow's intentions might not stay moderate into the future, that led to the hardening of U.S. behavior.

In sum, both states can be held "responsible" for the Cold War, but for different reasons: the United States because it was the first to turn to hardline policies known to be provocative; the Soviet Union because its regime type and internal economic policies undermined American confidence in the future.

## Roosevelt and the Geopolitics of Hedging, 1943–44

In the first decade after World War II, a popular notion emerged that Franklin Delano Roosevelt, because of his beliefs in the value of centralized government to help overcome inequalities in society, had not seen the Soviet Union to be a true threat to the system, as he clearly had with Hitler's Germany. He had thus naively allowed Stalin to expand his empire at little cost. With the work of Warren Kimball, Robert Dallek, and Stephen Wertheim, among others, we can now see that Roosevelt was far more "realist" in his geopolitical strategies than he was "Wilsonian," and indeed saw himself that way. His approach to foreign affairs involved avoiding hard and fast principles to give himself the flexibility needed to adjust to new situations and circumstances as they arose. By issuing no "doctrines" and by allowing vague public statements (such as the 1941 Atlantic Charter) to be violated when necessary, Roosevelt was able to push his larger agenda for the postwar world without hindering either side's ability to adjust its policy along the way.[35] He was the master of subtle deception that came in the form of a jovial cajoling and an affable willingness to bargain even at the expense of his stated principles. As he described himself in mid-1942: "I am a juggler, and I never let my right hand know what my left hand does . . . I may be entirely inconsistent, and furthermore I am perfectly willing to mislead and tell untruths if it will help win the war."[36]

Because of this penchant for flexibility and deception, and because he left few substantive diary notes or personal reflections when he died suddenly in April 1945, it has been frustratingly difficult for scholars to determine Roosevelt's ultimate strategic objectives from 1943 to 1945 as the United States began preparing for the postwar world. I will therefore follow the standard historical practice of trying to build the most plausible interpretation of his deeper aims and plans through an examination of his actual behavior and practices. Drawing from recent scholarship, I argue that Roosevelt had a subtle, intelligent plan to allow the building of a postwar order that recognized the legitimate spheres of both the Soviet Union and the United States, even as he reduced the influence and significance of the British Empire. His goal was to reassure the Soviets that Eastern Europe would be completely within their sphere of influence and thus would no longer be a conduit for an invasion of Russia. But from 1943 on, Roosevelt also prudently sought to hedge his bets. He acted to maintain a strong U.S. presence on the periphery of the Soviet Union, both through overseas bases and by a series of U.S. "trusteeships" in occupied territories. And like most Americans of the time, he was a strong believer in the importance of the open door as a means to sustain and increase American economic growth after the war. As we will see, sustaining this open door was becoming increasingly important as the United States, due to the rebounding of the economy and allied resource needs, found itself running out of oil and key raw materials. Roosevelt thus made sure that America could project its power along the whole of the Eurasian periphery and that, in particular, it achieved a dominant position in the oil-rich Middle East.

His actions in 1943 and much of 1944 fit nicely with the offensive realist baseline logic of dynamic realism discussed in chapter 1. In a period when the risk of communist revolution in Western Europe was not yet evident, Roosevelt seized opportunities to build up the American position to reduce U.S. vulnerability to future trade cut-offs. To the extent that Roosevelt was simultaneously using Lend Lease to buy Soviet cooperation on postwar issues, liberal arguments also have some value. But by late 1944/early 1945, shifting trade expectations start to play a predominant role as threats to the stability of the periphery were becoming clear. These threats led Roosevelt (and then Truman) to shift to a strategy of redirecting credit and goods to the propping up of Western Europe, even at the expense of souring relations with the Russians.

The year 1942 proved to be the worst of the war, as Japan established an empire in Southeast Asia while Germany pushed toward the oil-rich Caspian

Sea. But in November–December 1942, the Soviets finally stopped the Germans at Stalingrad. They launched a counteroffensive that encircled the German army and caused its first major defeat. Stalingrad, as all the Allies quickly understood, was the turning point in the war. Despite the hard battles to follow, it was increasing clear after December 1942 that Hitler would be defeated. The Americans now had to confront the question of the postwar order and how the Allies might divide Europe. The first internal report on this question came from William Bullitt, FDR's first ambassador to the Soviet Union. In January 1943, Bullitt, now the undersecretary of the navy and an informal confidant of the president, wrote Roosevelt a blunt analysis of U.S.-Russian relations. Roosevelt had asked Bullitt to prepare such an analysis two months earlier, but the tone and directness of Bullitt's arguments must have taken Roosevelt by surprise.

Bullitt's objective was to dispel the myth propagated by such Roosevelt aides as Special Assistant Harry Hopkins and Vice President Henry Wallace that the United States could only overcome Soviet distrust by continuing massive lend-lease aid to Russia and by helping to rebuild devastated areas of the country after the war. Instead of resting on the faith of so-called liberals, Bullitt argued, America should approach the issue of Soviet intentions "with the same admirable realism with which Stalin approaches all questions affecting the Soviet Union." Stalin puts Soviet national interests first and lets no ideological objectives influence his actions, meaning that he is cautious in his efforts to extend communism to other countries. He "moves where opposition is weak" and stops when opposed. "He puts out pseudopodia like an amoeba rather than leaping like a tiger. If the pseudopodia meet no obstacle, the Soviet Union flows on." And what we know, Bullitt argued, is that "the areas annexed by the Soviet Union will be withdrawn, as heretofore, from the area of normal trade between nations, which it is our policy to extend."[37]

Given this, U.S. policy must be geared up to "prevent the flow" of this amoeba into Europe. The small states of Western Europe on their own could not hold back this flow, Bullitt stressed. The United States, acting with Britain, therefore had to play an active role in creating an integrated democratic Europe, "pacific but armed" that would not only form a balance of power against direct Soviet expansion, but would be stable enough internally to "keep the Bolsheviks from replacing the Nazis" as masters of Europe. In addition, Washington had to take a strong position on future aid to the Soviets, at least to compel the opening of discussions on U.S. terms.

Bullitt was not calling for actions that would directly harm Soviet power and control within its realm. He agreed with the president's overall policy of allowing the Soviets a sphere of influence, just as America and Britain had theirs.[38] His argument, rather, aligned with ideas later pushed by American ambassador to Russia Averell Harriman and his aide George Kennan after July 1944. By firmly resisting Stalin's demands, Bullitt believed, Washington could convince the Soviets of the costs of extending their tentacles further. And yet by providing benefits, Stalin could also be convinced to be cooperative. In short, by using "the old technique of the donkey, the carrot and the club [,] you might be able to make Stalin move in the direction in which we want him to move." And Roosevelt did have a substantial carrot—namely, "post-war aid for rebuilding the Soviet Union," as well as the promise of genuine security for the Soviet Union in Europe by way of agreements. The club included opposition to Soviet predatory policies, the possible diminution or cessation of war aid, and the quiet signaling to Stalin that it might be difficult domestically to secure postwar aid for the rebuilding of the Soviet Union if he did not play ball. Now was the time to act, Bullitt stressed, since U.S. relative power was at its height.[39]

Roosevelt took seriously Bullitt's remarkably prescient analysis. In February 1943 he established a working committee to study options for the postwar period on a weekly basis. In March he met with visiting British foreign minister Anthony Eden and asked him his opinions of Bullitt's analysis. Eden replied that Bullitt's view, if fully implemented, would undermine Soviet trust in the West, thus endangering the postwar peace. Roosevelt told Eden that he was more in his camp than Bullitt's.[40] But the president's subsequent behavior indicates that he took Bullitt's warnings to heart. Given that the Soviet army was not expected to move into Eastern Europe proper until early 1944—and given that there was little the Americans could do to stop its progress even if they wanted to—there was no immediate need to start blocking the movement of the "Red amoeba." Moreover, Roosevelt was well aware that the Red Army would remain the primary fighting force against Nazism until the oft-delayed British-American invasion of France. He thus rejected the idea of withholding lend-lease aid to the Soviets. Yet in a number of important ways, Roosevelt would hedge his bets about the postwar world and the potential threat that the rising Soviet state posed.

The first was a critical decision made in mid-1943 to not divulge any information about U.S.-British work on the atomic bomb—not even the fact that the two countries were working on such a weapon. Roosevelt continued this policy even after it became clear after 1943 that Soviet spies had learned of the Manhattan Project.[41] The second important dimension of Roosevelt's hedging strategy was his determination to establish a ring of U.S. bases around the perimeter of the postwar Soviet sphere. In December 1942 he had asked the Joint Chiefs of Staff to investigate America's postwar basing needs. In March 1943 he was provided with a report from the Joint Strategic Survey Committee arguing that overseas bases were essential to U.S. security, given that international institutions could not be counted on to keep the peace. Thus "their acquisition . . . must be considered as among our primary war aims."[42] In November, Roosevelt approved the policy document JCS 570, which stressed the importance of projecting power against future enemies while keeping *their* bombers as far away from U.S. shores as possible. To this end, the document noted that America needed bases in the western Pacific, west Africa, Iceland, Japan, and the East Asian mainland. Clearly this constituted a massive extension of U.S. global reach. And as the documents make clear, it was done in the expectation of having to counter a rising and future threat.[43]

For Roosevelt, however, the question of bases went beyond just the projection of air power into the Soviet Union to keep Russia cooperative. In February 1944 he told Secretary of State Hull to push the state, war, and navy departments as well as the Joint Chiefs to examine how overseas bases could be used for naval and ground forces as well.[44] Since his time as secretary of the navy under Wilson, Roosevelt had firmly believed in Mahan's vision of global power projection as a means both to protect one's security and to build one's trade and economic power.[45] His fateful policy decision in 1943–44 to build a vast web of overseas bases on the Eurasian and African periphery was thus driven both by the immediate fears of strategic attack and the more general need to protect American commercial ties around the world.[46]

Roosevelt's efforts to leave the United States in a preponderant position after the war also led him to take major steps to enter the great power struggle over who would control access to Middle East oil. As I discuss elsewhere, by 1941–42 his administration was well aware that the United States was running out of oil. Domestic production was peaking, and demand was skyrocketing as a result of the United States' industrial recovery and the needs of its now-huge overseas military machine. If trends continued, the United States, the world's largest oil producer, would soon move from a position of net exporter to net importer. To compensate for this future vulnerability, Roosevelt encouraged U.S. multinational oil firms to increase their presence in the Middle East, and even explored the establishment of a U.S. government-owned oil company on the British model to ensure future access.[47] Most importantly, in 1943–44 he plunged the United States into a political struggle over the postwar fate of oil-rich Iran. Roosevelt convinced the Shah to work with U.S. advisors at the highest level—including the appointment of an American as finance minister—and to convince the Soviets, who had occupied northern Iran during the war by agreement with Britain and America, to leave his country. The president saw Iran as what he called his "test case" for his postwar vision of stable peripheral states connected to an open global economy. The Soviets, for obvious reasons, pushed back against U.S. penetration of what had been historically a British and Russian sphere of influence. But with their need for continued American economic and military assistance to win the war against Germany, by late 1944 they conceded the Americans predominant influence over the Iranian government and over affairs in the southern two-thirds of the country. Moscow kept forces in northern Iran until mid-1946 but was ultimately convinced to pull them out to prevent a further spiral of hostilities as the Cold War heated up.[48]

## Europe and the Ending of the War, January–May 1945

By January–February of 1945, Roosevelt's policies had left the United States in a highly favorable position, one that would allow his successor to begin shifting to a containment stance by late June/early July. The United States now had a string of bases around the Eurasian perimeter. It had a secure foothold in Saudi Arabia, and it had helped stabilize the Iranian state so that it could block further Soviet penetration. By reversing himself and rejecting the extreme version of Morgenthau's plan to break up Germany into a number of agricultural provinces, Roosevelt had laid the basis for the integration of the coal and industry of western Germany into the larger Western European economy. It was this integration that proved essential to preventing Western Europe's fall to communism. At Yalta in February, Roosevelt would have to acknowledge what he could not prevent—namely, the future Soviet hold over Eastern Europe. But Yalta also allowed him to get Stalin's assurance that he would not insist on a Soviet role in Italy's recovery. Moreover, secret agreements at Yalta had assured Roosevelt that Stalin would come into the war against Japan three months after the war in Europe ended. This, as his military had been insisting, would help avoid a costly prolongation of the Pacific War that would only hurt America's relative power should the Soviets sit on the sidelines. For his part, Stalin's terms had been relatively moderate. In return for agreeing to recognize the Kuomintang as the legitimate government of China and to hand control in Manchuria over to Chiang Kai-shek after the Soviet troops withdrew, he sought only a warmwater port on the Liaotung peninsula and some role in the running of the trans-Manchuria railway system.[49] Finally, Roosevelt's continued pressure on the Manhattan Project organizers meant that the atomic bomb would be ready to test by midsummer and that the United States would retain monopoly control over its use.[50]

Three main economic issues, however, hovered over U.S. policy discussions from January to September 1945. The first was the question of a Soviet request for a $6 billion postwar loan to facilitate Russia's rebuilding process. The second was Western Europe's devastated economy and the fear that simple hunger and cold might cause the states of this region to fall to communism, either through elections or revolution. The third was the matter of the open door to

China, given Stalin's agreement to invade Manchuria and Mao's obvious strengths in northern China. Two other economic issues were also tied to these primary concerns: the reparations policy toward Germany and the question of U.S. access to Eastern European trade and investments. This section will cover events up to May 1945. Subsequent sections will take us through the Potsdam conference to the breakdown of cooperation in the fall of 1945.[51]

The Soviet loan request was made in an odd yet revealing way. Soviet foreign minister Molotov met with American ambassador Harriman on January 3 and handed him the following statement:

> Having in mind the repeated statements of American public figures concerning the desirability of receiving extensive large Soviet orders for the postwar and transition period, the Soviet Government considers it possible to place orders on the basis of long-term credits to the amount of 6 billion dollars.

The memorandum also noted the type of goods Russia would buy (mostly manufactured goods and industrial equipment) and suggested the interest rate terms it could accept (an initial rate of 2-1/2 percent). Finally, it requested that the U.S. government grant a 20 percent discount in price for all goods purchased prior to the end of the war via the loaned funds.[52]

The Americans had been expecting a formal request for postwar credits for some time. When Harriman had first arrived in Moscow in October 1943 to take up his ambassador's post, he had publicly announced the United States' willingness to fund Russia's postwar recovery. Throughout 1944, tentative ideas were floated regarding a postwar loan that would facilitate the securing of American goods after lend-lease aid, which was legally required to operate only during wartime, was ended. But the size of the Soviet request and the manner in which it was sought took U.S. officials by surprise. The Soviets were presenting their request as though they were responding to America's plea for trade orders that would help the United States get through the difficult postwar "transition period."

The Americans interpreted the tone of the request as simply an opening gambit in an extended bargaining process. They believed that the Soviets, in an obviously weak position, needed to reduce the perception that they were supplicants to an American economic giant. This interpretation captures part of the truth. But Molotov's memorandum also reflects Soviet perceptions of the American need for trade. Through the years 1943 and 1944, hundreds of newspaper articles had reported that without extensive trade after the war, the United States might easily fall back into a severe depression. Indeed, Roosevelt and the State Department had regularly promoted the idea that without opendoor access to the world's resources and markets, the U.S. economy could not grow to its full potential. Underpinning this logic was Roosevelt and Hull's recognition that the United States needed world trade even more than it did when the open-door policy was first articulated in the late nineteenth century. Such thinking fit perfectly with Soviet communist ideology, which empha-sized that without the global extension of their trade tentacles, capitalist econ-omies would suffer from economic downturn and domestic unrest. The United States thus needed Russia as much as Russia needed the United States, meaning that the Soviets could secure reasonable terms in the final loan agreement.

Predominant American opinion by this point, however, viewed the poten-tial loan in a very different light. From the spring of 1944 onward, Harriman had been pushing Roosevelt and Hull to use any postwar loan to Russia as a tool to compel Moscow into concessions over Eastern Europe and the Far East. In Harriman's oft-repeated language, the Americans had to take a "firm but friendly" stance toward the Soviets, exacting political concessions as a "quid pro quo" for U.S. loan guarantees. Indeed, from Harriman's point of view, the prospect of loans was the only major lever the United States possessed to truly influence the way the Soviets managed their expanding territorial spheres in Europe and Asia.[53]

Roosevelt agreed with Harriman's overall point, and on several occasions he conveyed his opinion to subordinates that American economic power should be used to shape negotiations with the Soviets. On January 10 he told the new secretary of state Edward Stettinius that it was "very important that we hold back on [the loan] and don't give them any promises of finance until we get what we want." Roosevelt agreed with Stettinius's point that the issue should not be raised at Yalta, and at the conference a month later, Roosevelt studiously maintained his policy of silence. Roosevelt believed that by keeping Moscow uncertain about the loan, he could shape its behavior in desired ways.[54] In March when the president was advised by Leo Crowley, the head of the Foreign Economic Administration, that Washington should continue to hold off on the loan until Russian peacetime objectives were made clear, Roosevelt said he "concurred very definitely."[55]

Until his death in April, Roosevelt gave the Soviets no hint as to which way he was leaning on the loan question. Treasury Secretary Henry Morgenthau had made it clear to both the president and the State Department in January that such a policy of delay and obfuscation would only raise serious suspicions in Moscow as to American postwar intentions.[56] But he was overruled by Roo-sevelt and Stettinius, who were prudently waiting to see if Stalin would hold to his promises from Yalta. March proved to be a month of increasing suspi-cions on both sides. Stalin was upset by reports that the Americans were se-cretly negotiating with German generals for the separate surrender of German troops in the west. Roosevelt and his advisors were becoming increasingly convinced that Stalin had no intention of allowing free elections to proceed in Poland, despite Soviet assurances at Yalta. The president thus continued his policy of wait and see on the loan question, while keeping U.S. power strong. While FDR was again acting according to a prudent realism, his policy would only serve to hurt Soviet expectations about America's commitment to post-war trade.

Soviet trade expectations would be further affected by the American reaction to an important exogenous development. By the time of Roosevelt's death on April 11, it was becoming clear to all that Western Europe was in the midst of an economic crisis of unprecedented and overwhelming proportions—one that might well lead to communist takeovers across the board. In mid-April, Assistant Secretary of War John McCloy returned from a trip to Europe to tell his colleagues that the conditions were far more dreadful than he expected. Germany was in particularly bad shape. Secretary of War Henry Stimson noted in his diary of April 19 that McCloy "gave me a powerful picture of the tough situation that exists in Germany." It "is worse than anything probably that ever happened in the world. I had anticipated the chaos, but the details of it were appalling."[57]

Fears of economic crisis in Europe had been building since the late summer of 1944. In August of 1944, the State Department's Mission for Economic Affairs (MEA) issued a report on "The European Coal Problem in the Immediate Postwar Years." It argued that in 1945 and 1946 continental Europe would need between twenty and thirty million tons of coal just to meet basic needs. If Britain could return to its prewar level of coal exports, this would provide about ten million tons. But the rest would have to come from the Continent itself, where Germany's Ruhr region, Czechoslovakia, and southwestern Poland possessed by far the biggest coal reserves. The report recommended the creation of a European coal organization to coordinate the shipment of coal from areas with large reserves to areas with minimal or no reserves. If this were not done, desperate European states might "scramble for available suppliers," causing economic chaos and unrest, especially in poorer areas unable to afford the scarce coal supplies.[58]

Roosevelt and the State Department approved the recommendation. By January 1945, formal talks had begun in London to explore the formation of a European Coal Organization (ECO). Britain and the United States were the dominant players, but the Soviet Union, France, and other European states also participated. The State Department instructed its delegates to emphasize the importance of coordination across "all continental Europe," meaning that coal supplies from Eastern Europe and Western Europe should be integrated. In short, there should be no "economic regionalism." From the American perspective, this made a great deal of sense: Polish and Czech coal could supplement German coal in staving off collapse in the rest of Western Europe. France was a particular concern. French coal production was only at 40 percent of prewar levels, and British coal exports to the Continent were down to less than 15 percent of the 1938 figure.[59] The French communists had made great inroads between 1943 and 1945 through their leadership of the French Resistance, and the French Communist Party was the only serious challenge to De Gaulle's Free French organization. There was thus a strong possibility by early 1945 that De Gaulle would not be able to prevent a shift of public opinion toward the communists, despite his promises of massive nationalization and welfare programs.[60] From the Soviet perspective, however, the shipping of precious coal from Poland and Czechoslovakia to Western Europe made little sense when Soviet cities and villages were in dire need. America had come through the war unscathed, and thus could afford to export some 200,000 tons of coal per month. The Soviet Union had been devastated, and desperately needed both the oil and coal from Eastern Europe to meet immediate needs and to rebuild. For Moscow, these were realities that could not be simply ignored.

By March 1945 it was increasingly evident that the Soviets would not cooperate in the ECO scheme. On March 21, Ambassador Harriman told Washington that the Americans should make one last effort to reach agreement, and if this failed, "proceed with whatever measures we find it in our interest to take . . . independent of the Russians." Two weeks later, on April 4, Harriman sent the president and his officials his most dire warning yet. The situation in Western Europe was providing an ideal vehicle by which to trumpet the superiority of the Soviet system and to steer Western Europe toward communism without Stalin having to lift a finger.

> They have publicized to their own political advantage the difficult food situation in areas liberated by our troops, such as in France, Belgium and Italy, comparing it with the allegedly satisfactory conditions in areas which the Red Army has liberated . . . The Communist Party or its associates everywhere are using economic difficulties in areas under our responsibilities to promote Soviet concepts and policies and to undermine the influence of Western Allies.

If the United States did not act independently to help the areas under its control, Harriman continued, "the chances of Soviet domination in Europe will be enhanced." In short, U.S. policy now had to be one of taking care of allies and areas of U.S. responsibility first, and only after that responding to Russian needs. More than two years before the Marshall Plan, Harriman saw what had to be done. Economic aid to Western Europe was needed "to reestablish a reasonable life for the people of the countries who [share our] general outlook." The Soviets would extend their totalitarian system into their new Eastern European sphere. But the United States could not use such methods. Thus, the only hope of stopping Soviet penetration was "the development of sound economic conditions." Washington had to confront the new realities and orient its foreign economic policies accordingly.[61]

In saying this, Harriman was not giving in to pessimism. He ended his telegram by stressing the importance of building a friendship with Russia. This friendship, he reminded Roosevelt in now-familiar language, always had to be "on a quid pro quo basis."[62] Yet there was a key change in Harriman's overall emphasis. Previously he had recommended hard bargaining to secure a U.S.-Soviet peace deal. Now, in addition to a deal, he was stressing the buildup of the Western sphere, even if that should lead to greater Soviet mistrust.

It was this backdrop of growing concern that allowed McCloy's mid-April report on Germany to have the impact it did. Until his report, U.S. officials had a full sense of the economic chaos only in France, Holland, and Belgium. But McCloy now showed that Germany's condition was not only terrible, but much worse than expected. And without a viable Germany, the whole U.S. operation in Europe would be compromised, since Germany would be needed to supply coal to Western European homes and factories, especially if Russia restricted coal exports from Eastern Europe. Stimson and McCloy used their regular meetings with President Truman in the last two weeks of April to keep him informed of European developments and to bluntly warn him of the implications of inaction. One report to Truman was particularly direct, noting that "There is complete economic, social, and political collapse going on in Central Europe, the extent of which is unparalleled" since the collapse of the Roman empire. Without the reestablishment of a semblance of economic life, countries such as France and Belgium would be "torn apart."[63]

It is clear that the new president was absorbing the gist of the warnings and adjusting his behavior accordingly. On April 20, Harriman had told Truman that a workable basis for U.S.-Soviet relations could still be achieved, but the United States had to stand firm on key issues. Washington could afford to adopt a strong posture, since the Soviets "needed our help in order to reduce the burden of reconstruction." Truman agreed, noting that he intended to be "firm but fair" in order to get 85 percent of what he wanted.[64] Two days later, Truman began two days of talks with Soviet foreign minister Vyacheslav Molotov. While pleasant on day one, on the second day Truman forcefully argued that Stalin must uphold his Yalta promises on Poland, and that without this, Congress was unlikely to approve of any legislation providing economic aid to Russia. Through straightforward linkage politics, he was now making it clear that to receive valuable postwar aid, the Soviets would have to start playing ball in Eastern Europe.[65]

Despite his new rhetoric, Truman at this stage still sought U.S.-Soviet post-war cooperation. His objective with regard to Poland was quite moderate. Truman knew as well as anyone that he could not prevent the Soviets from dominating the country. Given this, his goal over the next two months was to get Stalin to make enough cosmetic concessions on Poland's domestic makeup to keep domestic public opinion on Truman's side. He hoped that Stalin, after hearing Molotov's report, would now see the importance of this public opinion to the ultimate securing of postwar loans. In late May he sent Harry Hopkins to Moscow to obtain these concessions. He told Hopkins before he left that he wanted a "fair understanding" with Stalin, and that Hopkins should make Stalin aware that what transpired in Eastern Europe "made no difference to U.S. interests" except in terms of the larger peace structure. Hopkins should try to get Stalin to make some gesture, "whether [the Soviet leader] means it or not," to "keep it before our public that he intends to keep his word."[66]

Contrary to many accounts, therefore, Poland was not the dealbreaker that led to the spiral of Cold War hostility. Indeed, the very agreement that Hopkins reached with Stalin in June 1945 demonstrates that Truman's primary concern was getting his fig leaf for domestic consumption. Stalin agreed to include London Poles in the interim Polish government until elections were held, but only as a minority part of the government. In early July, Truman publicly announced with "great satisfaction" Washington's recognition of the new Polish government. He did this even before he received any guarantee that elections would be held (they never were) and before recognizing other Eastern European governments under Soviet control. More telling still, Truman made no objections in July when Stalin proceeded to try sixteen leaders of the Polish opposition.[67]

The true point of contention that would divide the two superpowers and lead to the Cold War was something broader and more geostrategic. This was the question of Western European stability and the link between the way Stalin dealt with Eastern Europe and its economy and this stability. As with so many cases in the history of great power politics, it was the political realities of third parties that would lead to the decline in bilateral relations between the great power protagonists.[68]

Already by the end of April, U.S. policy was becoming more at odds with Soviet interests as Washington scrambled to address Western Europe's economic crisis. On April 30, the White House issued a long press release detailing a new internal report on Europe. Designed to prepare the American people for a new commitment of resources to stabilize Western Europe, the press release noted that the "immediate and long-range economic situations of [the] liberated countries are extremely serious." Seven million people had no food and no coal, and stable and democratic governments in Europe could not be fostered in such a situation. The "future permanent peace of Europe" thus depended upon restoration of the European economy.[69] Truman's central message was clear: without active U.S. assistance, Western Europe might very soon be lost to communism.

As an immediate step to implementing this wide-ranging policy, precious lend-lease aid would have to be redirected from supplying the most important U.S. ally of the war—the Soviet Union—to the countries of Western Europe most in need. This new direction was made concrete by the announcement on May 12 of the immediate ending of all lend-lease aid to Russia. Traditionalists would argue that this act could not have been perceived as a terribly unfriendly one, given that the blanket denial of all lend-lease aid was reversed the following day and U.S. goods for Russia's anticipated war against Japan were reinstated. Yet as we will see, the Soviets did view the May 12 cut-off as a further signal of American unwillingness to help Russia in its postwar recovery. Moreover, the U.S. documents show that Moscow did have good reason to worry. A new harder-line American policy was indeed emerging, driven by the choice to support Western European recovery over Soviet recovery and to use any U.S. economic goodies as leverage both to deter Moscow and improve its behavior. Declining Soviet trade expectations were therefore well justified.

On May 9, Secretary of State Stettinius had written his undersecretary Joseph Grew to argue that programs to assist what were already being called "western allies" should have priority over assistance to Russia, and that America should immediately curtail lend-lease shipments to Russia. U.S. policy on this "and similar matters"—presumably meaning reparation payments from western zones to the Soviet Union—should be one of "firm[ness] while avoiding any implication of a threat."[70] On the morning of May 11, Stimson met with Truman to convince him of the need for "a more realistic policy" regarding Lend Lease—namely, that this aid should end. Truman was enthusiastic, telling Stimson to write up a memorandum on the subject. After talking with Stimson, Grew later that day presented Truman with a report underscoring that the United States was formally committed to keeping some aid flowing until at least June 30—that is, the supplies to support a possible Soviet entry into the Pacific war. Yet all other lend-lease goods for Russia should end immediately and the goods "diverted to the approved supply programs for Western Europe." Truman immediately approved the memorandum.[71] The next day, however, after heated internal debate within the committee managing lend-lease shipments, it was decided to interpret the Grew memo aggressively and instantly stop all shipments to Russia. Later that day, not only were shipments at ports unloaded and those at sea turned around, but even goods slated for the Pacific War were blocked as well.[72]

The Russian embassy immediately expressed its outrage. When Harriman and Assistant Secretary of State William Clayton got word, they secured Truman's permission to countermand the order and put the supplies that had already been loaded or were at sea back on their way to Russia. Clayton explained to the Russian ambassador that the total cut-off had been a bureaucratic mistake that was now corrected.[73] But the Russian sense that U.S. policy had shifted was reinforced by a memorandum that hard-liner Grew sent to the Soviet embassy the same day, May 12. It stressed that future lend-lease deliveries would have to be "justified" on the basis of Soviet military needs and "in the light of competing demands for such supplies in the changed military situation." (The actors making competing demands on such goods were obviously the Western Europeans.) The Russians were then told bluntly that the future aid—including goods to facilitate Soviet entry into the Pacific war—would not be covered by a formal contract but would simply be set up to meet new military situations "as they arise."[74] The message was clear: the Soviets would get no more aid to facilitate reconstruction in western Russia, and lend-lease assistance for war against Japan would be dispensed to Russia on an ad hoc basis—that is, at Washington's discretion.

As the above shows, the May 12 incident was not simply some administrative snafu, as it is so often portrayed in simplistic historical accounts. While the officials that day certainly went too far, there is little question that Truman and the State Department hard-liners were shifting policy in a new and significant direction. The lend-lease flow to Russia would be dramatically reduced so that goods could be freed up for the struggling Western European states, most of which had played little or no role in the defeat of Hitler. The damage to Soviet perceptions of America as a state willing to help Russia recover from a devastating war was significant. As historian George Herring summarizes, the "sudden, drastic, even rude, stoppage of shipments on May 12—without warning and without consultation—needlessly antagonized the Russians at a critical juncture in Soviet-American relations."[75]

There is little doubt that Soviet perceptions of U.S. economic policies were hurt by the May 12 incident. This became clear during the course of Harry Hopkins's week-long meeting with Stalin in late May. Hopkins used his first meeting with Stalin on May 26 to lay out U.S. concerns regarding Poland. As per Truman's instructions, he noted that public support for Russia had been greatly diminished by its treatment of Poland. But Hopkins also stressed that Truman wanted to continue Roosevelt's policy of working with Moscow. He assured Stalin that Washington rejected a British-style policy of creating a cordon sanitaire around Russia via Poland and Eastern Europe, at which point Stalin said that the Polish question could be easily solved (as it was over the next week of discussions through the cosmetic concessions Truman sought).[76] A separate issue, however, was Stalin's new views on the likelihood of receiving U.S. support for the rebuilding of his country. In the second meeting with Stalin on May 27, Hopkins asked if Stalin had any concerns. Stalin began by stating that recent U.S. moves had created a "certain alarm" regarding Washington's attitude now that the European war was over. One of the most obvious examples, Stalin continued, was the curtailment of lend-lease aid. If the United States was no longer able to supply such aid, that was one thing. But "the manner in which it had been done had been unfortunate and even brutal." If the refusal to continue Lend Lease "was designed as pressure on the Russians in order to soften them up" then the Americans had made a fundamental mistake. Hopkins obfuscated, arguing that the May 12 cut-off was only a "technical mistake" and not a policy decision, and there was "no attempt to use [it] as a pressure weapon." Stalin interrupted, saying it was the action's form that he objected to most. If only proper warning had been given, there would be no ill feeling. In a rare admission of the Soviet need for what America had to offer, he noted that such warnings "[were] important to [the Soviet government] since [its] economy was based on plans," not market forces.[77]

One might dismiss Stalin's words as simply an effort to guilt the United States into restoring the flow of what were, after all, essentially free goods. But Stalin's admission that lend-lease goods were critical to Soviet planning and thus to his larger recovery objectives suggests that the Soviets were genuinely shocked as well as angered by the American cut-off on May 12, along with what it signified for the future. Through late May and June, the Soviets continually complained to Ambassador Harriman about their inability to secure critical lend-lease goods and about the diversion of aid to Western Europe.[78]

The State Department had no intention of moderating its policy, however. On June 26, Acting Secretary of State Grew told the Russians that lend-lease supplies not only had to be justified by military requirements but also could now only be secured by "cash payment." If the Soviets could not purchase the goods, Washington would take steps "to protect the interests of the United States by diverting machinery and equipment to other requirements"—meaning, most obviously, the requirements of Western Europe.[79] Hence by late June, Moscow understood that even lend-lease goods destined for the Pacific would be diverted to states in the U.S. sphere playing little or no role in the war against Japan. Grew did not mention whether these states were more able to pay cash for such goods, for the simple reason that he knew they would be receiving them under the old lend-lease terms—free of charge. The new policy of building up the western sphere at the expense of the Soviet recovery was clearly well under way. And the Soviets knew it.

# The Larger Questions of Germany and Eastern Europe,
## May–July 1945

I now turn to the role played by Germany in the hardening of Truman's foreign policy between April and July 1945. The redirecting of lend-lease aid and the delaying of loans to Moscow were only two steps in the larger strategy to prevent Western Europe from slipping into the Soviet sphere. Equally important was the need to reestablish trade between Germany/Eastern Europe and the Western European states. On May 16, Stimson held a critical meeting with the president on the issue of Germany—a meeting that Truman himself later recognized as a turning point in U.S. policy.[80] Truman was already getting pressure from Churchill not to implement any plan that would divide up Germany and prevent its reintegration into Europe. Stimson told Truman that

> all agree as to the probability of pestilence and famine in central Europe next winter. This is likely to be followed by political revolution and Communistic infiltration. Our defenses against this situation are the western governments of France, Luxembourg, Belgium, Holland, Denmark, Norway, and Italy. It is vital to keep these countries from being driven to revolution or Communism by famine.

The immediate problem, Stimson went on, was that a food shortage would likely begin by summer 1945 and get much worse by the coming winter. It was therefore critical to make sure Germany was allowed to rebuild its industry and play its necessary role in the European economy. The fate of eighty million Germans along with their ability to form a wealthy and democratic society, Stimson stressed, would "necessarily swing the balance on [the European] continent." Given what Germany had just done to Europe, reintegrating it into Europe was a touchy issue, requiring Russia's cooperation. A revitalized German industry would need Eastern European food, and the Soviet army, after all, was sitting on the best agricultural lands of Central Europe. Washington "must find some way of persuading Russia to play ball."[81]

After that meeting, a new and radical policy shift was implemented. The nation that had just plunged Europe into the bloodiest war in world history was now to be quickly reintegrated into the European economy and allowed to restore its industrial base. For a Soviet government that had been promised at Yalta a weak and subdivided Germany as a necessary foundation for Russia's long-term security, this was a highly problematic turn in U.S. policy. But with Truman now on board, there was no going back. On May 22, Truman sent a letter to the war agencies in Europe noting that the future peace of Europe depended on restoring the economies of liberated countries.[82] On June 24, he wrote a detailed letter to Churchill arguing that the "coal famine" that threatened Europe meant that every effort had to be exerted to increase German coal exports. "I believe that without immediate concentration on the production of German coal we will have turmoil and unrest in the very areas of Western Europe on which the whole stability of the continent depends."[83] In a meeting on July 3, when Stimson reiterated the importance of rehabilitating Germany, Truman said that was exactly the way he thought it should be.[84]

Part and parcel of the new policy was a decision to deny the Soviets reparations from the western half of Germany. At Yalta, Stalin, Churchill, and Roosevelt had agreed that Germany would be forced to pay $20 billion in reparations—$10 billion of which was to come from the western zones—to help the Soviets rebuild. These figures reflected Roosevelt's desire to placate Stalin's fear of a resurgent Germany and to recognize the great price the Soviets had paid in blood and treasure to stop Nazism. But by June, with the urgent need to restore Germany's economic health to save the rest of Western Europe, reparations made less and less sense. In late June there was much discussion between the state and war departments about how to finance Germany's imports of food and basic goods. Lend-lease aid was already being diverted from Russia to France, Holland, and other "western allies." But Germany in June 1945 was no ally; it was a defeated enemy. It was therefore imperative that most of the goods coming into Germany to avoid starvation and unrest be paid for in some way by the Germans themselves. Much of this German finance, as it would be called, would have to come from German "exports"—that is, allied-controlled transfers of coal from the Ruhr and other coal-rich areas of Germany.

But here was the problem: if the Russians had first dibs on any "exports" out of the western zones in the form of reparation payments, then Germany simply would not be able to pay for its imports. The whole plan for saving Western Europe—dependent on transfers of German coal to France and other countries in exchange for food and supplies (much of the latter in the form of American and Canadian aid)—would break down if Germany had to pay off the Russians first. Assistant Secretary of State Clayton had already told the War Department on June 18 that he was concerned about War Department statements that it would not be able to finance the procurement of imports into Germany needed to increase German production for export. This would undermine the achievement of "certain basic objectives of United States policy. These include the provision of relief for the benefit of countries devastated by Nazi aggression." The president had ordered, Clayton continued, "the taking of all feasible measures" to facilitate the production of German coal and other necessary goods to achieve this purpose. Since only the military authorities were in a position to implement this directive, he argued, it was up to the War Department to find a way to pay for German imports.[85]

After further state-war discussions failed to resolve the issue, Clayton wrote the War Department again on June 30 to press the department to take responsibility for procuring the necessary imports into Germany. He attached a document based on those discussions entitled "German Finance." In a key statement that would come to guide the discussions over reparations at Potsdam, the document noted that "The sum necessary to pay for imports into Germany should be a first charge on all German exports from current production or stocks on hand." That is, any other claims on goods coming out of the western part of Germany, such as those arising from Russian reparation demands, would have to come second, and would be only paid out *after* the imports were procured.[86] The line "or stocks on hand" was no doubt studiously added to make sure that the Russians could not insist that they had a claim to western Germany's current capital stock of railways, factories, machinery, and the like. The western half was, after all, the industrial heartland, and the Russians coveted such capital stock as the most direct means of restoring their devastated industries.

Clayton may not have understood just how significant his phraseology would become in the coming month. But he surely knew that his department had arrived at a formula by which the western Germany economy could be saved from a repeat of the reparations disaster that had destroyed Germany after World War I. On July 5, new secretary of state, James Byrnes sent a memorandum to Truman stating that there was now "full agreement" among all the key departments regarding how to approach the Soviets, British, and French regarding the question of the procurement and financing of essential German imports. Utilizing Clayton's logic, Byrnes noted that any discussions with the other occupying powers "would, of course, state that the sum necessary to pay for imports into Germany should be a first charge on all German exports from current German production or stocks on hand." Byrnes drew Truman's attention to an attached memorandum, which was only a slightly modified version of Clayton's June 30 report—this time entitled "German Financing," perhaps to make clear the active role the United States had to play in keeping western Germany solvent.[87]

This policy shift immediately found its way into the ongoing discussions with Moscow on reparations. Back in the spring, Truman had appointed Edwin Pauley to head the U.S. negotiating team. In the early stages of the discussions in June, the Soviets kept reminding Pauley of the Yalta commitment of $20 billion, half of which was to go to Russia from the industrialized western half of Germany. Pauley told Secretary of State Byrnes on June 19 that he was continuing to use the Yalta figure as a basis of discussion. Yet like other top U.S. officials, he was worried about Germany's ability to pay and what that meant for postwar Europe as a whole.[88] Until the internal debates were resolved, however, Pauley and the State Department had no formula that he could effectively use to counter the Soviet claims, especially in light of Russia's huge postwar needs and Moscow's visceral fear of a resurgent Germany.

By July 6, however, Pauley was able to inform Byrnes that he had tentative agreement among the British, Soviet, and American delegates of the Allied Commission on Reparations to a set of principles, the eighth and last of which read:

> 8. After payments of reparations enough resources must be left to enable the German people to subsist without external assistance. In working out the economic balance of Germany the necessary means must be [found for the] payment of imports approved by the [governments] concerned before reparation deliveries are made from current production or from stocks of goods.[89]

Clayton's formula, in an altered and probably deliberately vague form, had slipped its way into the reparation discussions. The Soviet delegate Ivan Maisky had obviously not understood principle 8's full significance when he agreed to it. The delegates on the commission took a brief recess to take the eight principles back to their respective governments. In the interim, the Soviets spotted the dangerous knife hiding within principle number 8. A week later, on July 14, just three days before the start of the Potsdam conference, Maisky met with Pauley. Maisky asked for one and only one change to the document: the Soviet government could not accept the second sentence of principle 8. This sentence of course was the foundation of Washington's new policy on reparations—namely, that Russia would be paid only after Germany paid for its imports. The Soviets had smelled a rat. If they accepted this principle, instead of getting the promised $10 billion from the western zone, they might get nothing. The Americans could simply claim that Germany had not yet paid for its necessary imports. But by this point Pauley not only had the language to resist the Russian claims; more importantly, he also now had the authority to do so. He told Maisky "that my own Government stands firmly on the principle that approved imports shall be a prior charge against approved exports of current production and stocks of goods," and it "would not recede from this position." To reinforce the point, Pauley then added that he felt so strongly about this issue that he would not even recommend, as the commission's U.S. representative, the deletion of this clause from the statement of principles.[90]

It is clear that Pauley would not have become so hard-line in his rhetoric unless he had been authorized to do so from above. Clayton's June 30 memorandum, built into Byrnes' July 5 memorandum to Truman, had done the trick. From the beginning of the Potsdam conference on July 16, the Soviets would be told that they would receive no fixed sum of reparations from western

Germany. Indeed, the figure of $20 billion itself was now discarded. In its place, Russia was offered only a certain percentage of what the western zones could afford to pay, after paying for imports. As the Soviets well understood, this meant Russia would receive few if any goods from the western zones, since the Americans could always claim that there was little surplus above and beyond what western Germany needed for necessary import payments.

At Potsdam, after much discussion, the Russians were forced to concede to the new U.S. position. Despite Molotov's willingness to reduce the figure of $10 billion down to $2 billion—but as a guaranteed amount—the final agreement specified only a figure of 10 to 15 percent of western Germany's surplus industrial production. The agreement thus ensured that there would be little coordination between western and eastern zones. The Soviets could take what they wanted from eastern Germany—a policy that of course would only hurt their sphere's overall strength. But they would receive little from the west. Since the west held most of Germany's industrial strength, this was a major blow to Soviet efforts to rebuild Russia's industrial infrastructure, a quarter of which had been destroyed in the war.

As historian Carolyn Woods Eisenberg notes, the American stand on reparations constituted a clear breach of the Yalta commitment regarding reparations, which was designed to recognize the great sacrifice made by Russia in defeating Nazi Germany. Now, just three months after Hitler's defeat, Washington was helping build up the western part of Germany as well as what were now called America's Western European allies. To be sure, the financing that was supplied to Germany and the other Western European states was not ultimately as substantial as the billions of Marshall Plan dollars that flowed to Europe after the spring of 1948. Still, because it bypassed Congress and was not held up by legislative wrangling, it was immediate and decisive in reversing the economic chaos that threatened to undermine the western sphere. The West would be saved from the specter of communism. If the Soviets found as a result that their economic development was constrained, they would just have to learn to live with it.

## Eastern Europe and the Lead-up to the Potsdam Conference

The causal role of Eastern Europe in effecting the shift to the constraining and containing American policies of mid-1945 is a fascinating and underappreciated one. From the traditionalist standpoint, Eastern Europe mattered because of Poland: by breaking his agreement at Yalta to allow London Poles into the government and to permit free elections, Stalin showed that he was an evil expansionist that had to be stopped. The problem with this argument has always been a simple one. Stalin made what Truman perceived to be significant concessions during Hopkins's mission to Moscow in late May/early June 1945, and the president thus recognized the Polish government in early July. The question of Poland's regime makeup was largely off the table during the Potsdam conference; when the country came up for discussion, it was almost exclusively in terms of the final delineations of Poland's new borders in the east and west.[91] In fact, by the end of the conference, the agreement on Poland was one of the few concrete successes from the three weeks of intense negotiations.

Truman and his officials had major concerns with Soviet policy not in Poland per se, but in the rest of Eastern Europe, particularly Romania and Bulgaria.[92] For this reason, Washington refused to recognize the Romanian and Bulgarian governments through the summer and fall of 1945, despite recognizing Poland's government in July. Clearly it was hoped that this might create some leverage to bring about desired changes. The complaint that the Americans had was less with Moscow's political policy than with its economic policy (although the two ended up going hand in hand). Here was the crux of it: in each of the Eastern European states that Russia occupied in 1944–45, the Soviets had imposed "trade agreements" on these states that amounted to little more than the forced reorientation of their trade policies away from their traditional trade partners in the west and toward Russia. As the chief of the Division of Eastern European Affairs told the director of European Affairs on May 30, 1945, while the United States was seeking to reduce tariffs by 50 percent, the Soviets were going in the opposite direction. The texts of recent trade agreements between Russia and Bulgaria in March and Russian and Romania in May were disconcerting:

> The general tenor of these agreements is very restrictive and are [sic] apparently aimed at excluding free trade in these areas by other powers. The agreements are in effect barter agreements and the prices for the goods delivered by the smaller countries are apparently very low.

In addition to the creation of artificial terms of trade that benefited only the Soviets, the treaty with Romania in particular created a jointly owned Russian and Romanian oil company and bank to exploit the country's oil resources and control its financial structure. The memorandum concludes by noting that

> it is fair to assume that the Soviet Government will make similar agreements with all other countries in the areas under its control and that by this method they will create an almost airtight economic blackout in the entire area east of the Stettin-Trieste line [dividing Eastern and Western Europe]. This blackout . . . presents a very serious problem [to] which we must give immediate consideration.[93]

Romania and Bulgaria remained of particular concern to the Americans for the rest of 1945, notwithstanding the fact that prewar trade with the whole of the Balkans region amounted to no more than 3 percent of overall U.S. trade. There were two main reasons for this concern, both of which were more about what the two countries signaled about the future of the postwar system than about any narrow material gains. First, ever since reports began to filter in from Harriman in January and February 1945 concerning the Soviet expropriation of Romanian oil equipment and its shipment back to Russia, U.S. officials had seen Romania as a test case for Soviet respect for global property rights law. American and British oil companies had a modest stake in the prewar Romanian oil industry, an industry that ended up being a major supplier of oil to Germany during the war. The Russians argued through the spring of 1945 that western companies no longer "owned" the equipment of these companies because the Romanians had served Axis oil needs and had acquired equipment from Germany during the war.[94] For obvious reasons, the American government found this argument specious and fought to have the equipment, at a minimum, returned to its rightful owners. The conflict would not be resolved at Potsdam, although a joint Soviet-American committee was established to investigate the issue.[95]

The second reason for the inordinate attention given to Romania and Bulgaria has to do with a grand commercial scheme that Truman had apparently conceived from discussions with Utah senator Elbert Thomas while Truman was still in the Senate. The plan was to link up the food-producing regions of the Balkans with the industrial area of western Germany, France, and Belgium through the use of a vast network of canals that would join the Danube and Rhine river systems. This would provide a large trading zone from the North Sea to the Black Sea that would facilitate economic recovery in Western Europe through the mutual complementarity of trade. It was critical to the success of his plan that the Danube become one of what Truman called his "free waterways for trade."[96] But if Bulgaria and Romania resisted this plan due to Soviet pressure, Western Europe would not receive the critical food supplies needed to stabilize the region.

As implausible as this scheme may sound in retrospect, it became an important part of the discussions at Potsdam, as Truman sought Stalin's support for the idea. As we will see, Stalin made little effort to accommodate the Americans, evidently viewing the plan as a way for the Americans to insert themselves into the heart of his sphere. Given Stalin's opposition, Truman left the Potsdam conference more pessimistic than ever about the possibilities for mutually beneficial trade between Eastern and Western Europe. Along with the failure in March–April to draw Czechoslovakia, Poland, and Russia into the European Coal Organization, it now seemed clear that Eastern Europe would not be allowed to play any real role in the stabilization of the Western European economies.

As I will show, the American effort to keep an open door between Eastern and Western Europe constituted a huge part of the Potsdam discussions both in document flow and time spent. This effort was directly stimulated by the profound fears U.S. decision-makers had regarding the future of Western Europe. With the growing concerns about Soviet trade deals with Eastern Europe in mind, Acting Secretary of State Grew sent Truman a memorandum on June 19 to update him on the key economic issues to be discussed at Potsdam. Grew stressed that the goods of Eastern Europe had to be used to relieve the needs of the rest of Europe. It was also important for Washington to obtain equality of opportunity for U.S. business interests in the region. Overall, the conference could be used as a venue for discussing key Soviet commercial policy questions, particularly such matters as export dumping, restrictive bilateral agreements, and Moscow's use of a trade monopoly to obtain political objectives.[97]

At the end of June, Grew sent Truman an additional series of detailed analyses on the situation in Europe and on the importance of Eastern Europe to American strategy. One of the longest reports, sent on June 27, considered the resurgence of European communist parties. In Eastern Europe, communist parties were exploiting the Soviet occupation to purge their countries of all democratic elements under the guise of destroying fascism. In Western Europe, largely because of circumstances, communist parties had been more moderate. But they were still advocating radical solutions to the political and economic problems facing their countries. Yet these local parties could be expected to increase their efforts to push Europe to the left. The communists would not be satisfied with simply nationalizing industries. Rather, as they saw it, the true "achievement of socialism" was "impossible to imagine without [the] preliminary conquest of power."

Grew did not charge Moscow with directly pushing local communists in Western Europe to overthrow their governments. He knew that Stalin had been refraining from supporting communists in western states, if only because he needed U.S. goodwill to rebuild his country. But local communists would not be restrained, regardless of Moscow's need for peace. "To a Communist, Europe today politically and economically represents a perfect situation for the propagation of their doctrines." Europe was emerging from probably the most devastating war in its history, while at the same time the Red Army's successes "have been so well advertised that the majority of Europeans regard them as their liberators." Europe thus now affords "a perfect background for spontaneous class hatred to be channeled by a skillful agitator."[98]

Three days later, Grew sent Truman an even longer analysis on subjects for discussion at Potsdam. He recommended the postponing of diplomatic recognition for Romania and Bulgaria, and if necessary, Hungary, until Washington and Moscow agreed to a satisfactory reorganization of their current government. While Hungary still had a "fairly representative" coalitional government, in Romania and Bulgaria Soviet authorities and local communists were actively engaged in establishing one-party regimes. Stalin's correspondence with Truman in late May had shown that the Soviet leader was keen to have U.S. recognition of all three states. Grew argued that providing this recognition at this time might help ease U.S.-Soviet relations in the short term (as it had regarding Poland). But "it might encourage the repetition of the same process in countries farther to the west"—namely, the spread of one-party systems to Western Europe. Grew thus recommended the deferral of recognition until the Soviets agreed to reorganize Romania and Bulgaria on a more representative basis.

Ironically, considering the way traditionalists blame Soviet behavior in Poland for starting the Cold War, the standard the United States was pushing for was the degree of domestic openness the Americans saw in other countries of the Soviet zone, such as Poland and Czechoslovakia. It was only in such countries where there were "elements not completely subservient to Moscow."[99] In short, by late June even the most consistent hard-liner at the State Department, Undersecretary Grew, did not see Poland's internal political makeup as the main problem. The problem—and thus the real litmus test for the rest of Eastern and Western Europe—was the nature of the Romanian and Bulgarian governments.[100] Moscow's policy in these two countries spoke volumes about the cultural divide that existed between the United States and the Soviet Union, especially on ideology and the desired degree of mercantilism in each one's political economy (see chapter 2). Combined with the strong possibility of postwar growth in Communist bloc power, the Americans had every reason to worry about the future.

We see how American officials were using Soviet behavior in Romania and Bulgaria to update their estimates of threat in three follow-up reports sent to Truman by the State Department on July 5, 1945. Each report covered specific background information on the three Balkans countries in question. The report on Bulgaria stressed that the Soviet-Bulgarian trade pact, signed while 200,000 Soviet troops were occupying the country, was contributing to the deterioration of a Bulgarian economy "already strained by Soviet demands for provisions for [their] military establishment and for export to Russia."[101] But in the short term, the Romanian situation was the most problematic—and most emblematic of the way Moscow used its satellites economically. The

Soviets had proceeded in Romania without reference to the views of the American and British representatives on the Allied Control Commission set up for the country. Excessive reparations payments and Romania's new obligations under its trade treaty with Russia

> probably will have the effect of breaking down Romania's economy, tying Romania economically to the Soviet Union to the exclusion of trade and financial relations with other countries [in the West] and making it impossible for American business interests to operate in [the country].

The effect of the treaty therefore would be to leave Romania "economically dependent on the U.S.S.R., without economic contact with other countries outside eastern Europe."

The section on America's long-term interest with regard to Romania is the most revealing of the document. It shows that U.S. policy makers were keenly aware that Romania's significance went well beyond any immediate American trade ties to the country. What happened between Russia and Romania signified something about Moscow's overall economic intentions in Eastern Europe, and how those intentions would affect Washington's concerns for Europe as a whole. The paragraph is worth quoting in full:

> The long-range interest of the United States in the maintenance of peace and stability in eastern Europe may be involved in the issues now arising in connection with the control of Romania during the armistice period and with the [Potsdam] peace settlement. The fundamental problem is the degree to which the United States will acquiesce in the exercise by the Soviet Union of a dominant or exclusive political and economic influence in Romania. It poses the need for reconciling, in this region, our policy of cooperation with the U.S.S.R. for the preservation of peace with our principles and commitments embodied in the Atlantic Charter, in the Yalta agreements, and in many general statements of policy.[102]

Romania thus had become the test case for Moscow's economic and political policy toward Eastern Europe and thus its overall policy toward the West. U.S. decision-makers wanted, as we have seen, Eastern Europe's full economic participation in the recovery of Western Europe. Yet if the Soviets proceeded to violate the Atlantic principles of sovereignty, open trade, and the protection of property rights in the other Eastern European states as they had been doing already in Romania, then expectations for the future of Western Europe's economy could not be positive.

In short, if Eastern Europe failed to play ball, Western Europe would have to go it alone, supported in the short term by massive infusions of American aid. This would not only slow Western Europe's recovery and the rebounding of U.S.-European trade, but more significantly, it also would have the effect of increasing poverty and despair within the western states, greatly increasing the chances of widespread and irreversible communist takeovers of nations critical to the U.S. sphere's economic and political strength. Given the existential significance of this, one of Truman's primary goals going into Potsdam was clear: Moscow would have to relax its economic grip on Romania and Bulgaria and allow greater openness to industrial goods, investment, and raw materials and food. As a State Department briefing paper noted in early July, Soviet trade agreements with Romania and Bulgaria had given Russia "predominant, if not exclusive" control of industry and trade. This kind of exclusive economic penetration was at odds "with the general commercial policy of [the U.S.] government, which looks to the expansion of trade and investment on a multilateral, non-discriminatory basis." Accordingly, Moscow should understand that while it may have special security interests in Eastern Europe, the United States was "vigorously opposed" to preferential economic arrangements, Soviet monopolies, and to "interference with American property or trade in these sovereign countries."[103]

## The Potsdam Conference

The conference at Potsdam represented the best and last opportunity for the Americans and Soviets to avoid a Cold War spiral. Yet aside from a secret deal on China (see chap. 7, n. 51 in this volume), little of substance was accomplished. Indeed, as the conference progressed, the U.S. position became increasingly hard-line. So, what prevented a grand bargain for peace from being realized? The answer cannot be found in disagreements regarding Poland, as traditionalists assert, since those were largely resolved prior to the conference. The fundamental problem that derailed the Potsdam conference, perhaps surprisingly, was not a territorial or military one but an economic one. The Soviets proved unwilling to meet U.S. demands that they commit to allowing Eastern Europe to trade freely with Western Europe and the broader world. From the American perspective, this meant that Western Europe would become increasingly vulnerable to economic decline and to the possibility of Western European states falling into the Soviet sphere. In what follows, I will summarize the key events of the Potsdam conference to show the critical importance of Eastern European economic questions to the deadlock that undermined any chances for an agreement that might have averted the Cold War.

Arriving at Potsdam on July 16, Truman wasted little time in broaching the question of the Balkans. In the very first plenary session with Churchill and Stalin on July 17, after some preliminary discussion on coordinating policies in Germany, Truman read from a prepared statement on the "Implementation of the Yalta Declaration on Liberated Europe." It was important for the show of unity between the allies, Truman argued, that obligations agreed to at Yalta be implemented. At present they had not yet been carried out. Truman went immediately to his main point: namely, that the three allied governments "should agree on the necessity of the immediate reorganization of the present governments in Romania and Bulgaria."[104] He mentioned nothing about Poland or any other Eastern European state. This is not surprising, given that the issue of the Polish government had been resolved while other Eastern European governments were politically more balanced and had not yet signed bilateral trade treaties with Moscow. The same could not be said for Romania and Bulgaria.

The big issue on the table on July 18, at the first meeting of the foreign ministers and the second plenary meeting of the three leaders, was the running of Germany. Poland was discussed only in terms of how to dissolve the London-based government in exile now that the London Poles had been brought into the existing Polish government. The atmosphere was cordial and cooperative. Indeed, the individual who for the previous five months had been the most concerned about Poland's fate in the new Europe, Winston Churchill, said that he "wished to take this occasion to rejoice in the improvement which had developed in the Polish situation and to express the wish for the success of the new Polish Provisional Government." Truman offered his hope for future elections, and the discussion quickly returned to Germany.[105] For the rest of the conference, talks on Poland focused on the question of its borders with eastern Germany and on the question of Poland's economic relations with the West.

At the third plenary session on July 19, the British introduced and guided discussion on four questions—namely, fighting along the Bulgarian-Greek border, the foreign ministers' deliberations on Germany and Poland, the disposition of the German fleet, and the question of fascist Spain. When it came time for Truman to lead the discussion, he immediately brought up the issue of the document on liberated Europe that he had introduced at the first meeting. To prevent a renewed debate, Stalin intervened to suggest that the discussion of Romania and Bulgaria be postponed because the Soviets were working on a document that they wished to submit. The three sides agreed to delay consideration of Truman's statement until that time.

Discussion then turned to the question of Spain. Stalin pressed hard for the Big Three to do something about Franco, the only remaining fascist leader in Europe. Churchill then made a diplomatic faux pas that would have important implications by the next morning. He argued that Britain had "an old and well-established trade" with Spain that it did not want to compromise, and that from his perspective the wartime allies "should not interfere in [other states'] domestic affairs." This was a question of principle, Churchill continued.

Undoubtedly to Truman's chagrin, Churchill went further. "There were many things in regard to Yugoslavia and Romania that he did not like," but one had to recognize that "a great danger" arose if outsiders interfered in the internal affairs of others. He might be willing to consider a general statement on which European states had not met certain democratic principles, "but . . . many governments in Europe now do not fulfil these principles." At this point, clearly not liking the direction of the conversation, Truman intervened to suggest that the three sides defer discussion on Spain to a later meeting, and Churchill and Stalin agreed.[106]

By the time of an 11:30 A.M. meeting of the foreign ministers the next day, it was clear that the Soviets were going to align themselves with Churchill's arguments and put them to good use. Molotov introduced the topic of "Liberated Europe" and then distributed the promised written Soviet response to Truman's statement. It offered no compromises. The Soviet government, it declared, "cannot agree to [Truman's] statement regarding Romania and Bulgaria." These states had restored order and legal power and had helped the United Nations defeat Germany. Borrowing Churchill's rhetoric, and with little sense of irony, Molotov's document continued: "Under these circumstances the Soviet Government sees no reasons for interfering in [their] domestic affairs." The document went on to encourage London and Washington to recognize the two countries' governments "in the nearest days."[107] Secretary of State Byrnes replied he had hoped that the spirit of Yalta would be honored in Romania and Bulgaria. It was the burden of all three governments to see that these two countries not discriminate economically against other states. Employing his one bargaining chip, Byrnes noted that in view of the attitude of the Romanian and Bulgarian governments, "we could not recognize them at this time." But if free and fair elections were held, this recognition would be forthcoming.[108]

Molotov countered with his ace in the hole: the British-American double standard. Any "excesses" in Romania and Bulgaria, he argued, were not comparable to those taking place in British-occupied Greece.[109] And he reminded Byrnes and Eden that no elections had yet been held in Italy. The discussion devolved to a set of angry exchanges between the three foreign ministers, certainly the most heated debate yet in the four-day-old conference. The meeting ended without a resolution. But the three sides agreed to prepare concrete proposals on what should be done regarding Romania and Bulgaria, with Greece, Hungary, and Italy now pointedly added to the list.[110]

At the fourth plenary session later that day, Molotov summarized the morning's meeting, noting that Byrnes had asked for an agreement regarding "the supervision of elections" in Romania, Bulgaria, Hungary, and Greece. After a tense discussion between Truman/Byrnes and Molotov over whether the

Russians had already agreed to the drafting of this agreement, Churchill intervened. Once again, he did so in a way that seemed deliberately designed to undermine the primary U.S. objective of the first five days of talks—namely, to get the Soviets to commit to opening Romania and Bulgaria up to outside political and economic influences. Churchill argued that the proposals should be written up but that the word "supervision" should be avoided "as the British had not contemplated control of the elections." Truman and Byrnes tried to moderate the effect of this by saying that they also did not want to supervise elections; rather, "observe" was a better word. But Churchill undercut even this. Evidently concerned that any agreement concerning Romania and Bulgaria would also be applied to British-occupied Greece, he replied that Britain did not mind knowing what went on but had no wish to assume the responsibility for elections. His implication was clear: the Allies should inform each other of what was happening in their respective spheres, but not push each other to have early elections.[111]

The next morning, July 21, Byrnes submitted a proposal at the foreign ministers' meeting that stressed the "immediate urgency" of holding elections and allowing freedom of movement and of the press in five countries: Italy, Greece, Bulgaria, Romania, and Hungary (in that order). By including the two western-sphere countries, and listing them first, he evidently sought to counter the Soviet charge of hypocrisy as he proceeded to push the Soviets to open up their Balkans possessions. Molotov claimed that the Soviets needed time to translate the document into Russian, and the three sides agreed to postpone discussion.[112]

When the fifth plenary session of the Big Three leaders began at 5 P.M., Truman sat down with a new air of self-assurance. Earlier that day, he had been briefed on the just-arrived report of General Leslie Groves, the official overseeing the Manhattan Project. On the first day of the Potsdam conference, Truman had received information regarding the bomb's successful test, but that information had been sketchy and preliminary. The Groves report, however, described in great detail how truly destructive the atomic bomb was, and how its power had far exceeded even the most optimistic expectations of the scientists.[113] When Secretary of War Stimson read the report to Truman, the president "was tremendously pepped up by it . . . He said it gave him an entirely new feeling of confidence."[114] This new confidence was on full display. The next day, after Stimson told Churchill of the Groves report, Churchill remarked that he now understood why Truman the day before was a "changed man." He told the Russians "just where they got on and off and generally bossed the whole meeting."[115]

The minutes showed that Truman and Byrnes did indeed dominate the July 21 meeting, with the president's agenda on Eastern Europe and Germany occupying the whole session. The two Americans introduced, for the first time, a new and subtle wrinkle on the Polish question. Truman presented a revision of a draft joint statement on Poland. In it, the United States took for granted that the Polish government in exile based in London no longer existed and had been replaced by an agreed provisional government. But a new second paragraph was added. It argued for the protection of property belonging to the Polish state against "alienation to third parties." Truman and Byrnes's remarks in the meeting clarified their reasons for adjusting the draft statement. They were worried that the Soviets would make heavy demands on the Poles to transfer assets from Polish territory. The Poles might then end up having to finance these transfers by way of loans from America and Britain. As Truman noted, according to U.S. business practices, one could not transfer assets "without taking liabilities [i.e. Poland's debts to other countries] into account." Churchill jumped in to agree that new loans to Poland required the assumption of liability for past and future debts. In short, Poland had to be kept economically sound enough to pay the West back. Byrnes went further, stating that the "settlement of property rights" was a matter that lay between Washington and the Polish government and no one else.[116]

It seems almost certain that Truman and Byrnes were not bringing up this issue just to protect a few small loans the West might make to Poland. In separate meetings on reparations, Pauley had been pushing the now-fixed U.S. line that the western German zones would not be able to pay reparations to Russia until they had covered their payments for imports first. This, as we have seen, was a way to ensure that western Germany could recover while preventing the massive transfer of capital goods to Russia. The Americans had been trying for months to get the Soviets to stop taking U.S. and British oil equipment from Romania. With the new confidence the bomb had given him, Truman was upping the ante in an effort to avert Moscow's wholesale reorientation of the Polish economy away from the West and toward the Soviet Union. At the very least, he and Byrnes were looking for some sign, any sign, that might indicate Moscow's willingness to keep Eastern Europe partially open to western commerce.

Probably to Truman and Byrnes's surprise, the Soviet leader quickly agreed to the addition of the new second paragraph. Poland had already redeemed its debt to the Soviet Union for previous "large credits," Stalin said, and he considered the account as closed. Needless to say, given that Russia over the past year had not been providing loans to Poland but rather feeding its own troops on Poland's surplus, Stalin was basically stating that he had decided against further exploitation of Poland's economy on the Romanian/Bulgarian model. Truman thanked Stalin for his cooperation. Byrnes then turned to the ongoing debate on the U.S. memorandum on liberated Europe—the one Molotov had countered earlier that day with his own alternative memorandum. Stalin once again surprised the two Americans by saying that he had no objections to the American document. He simply wanted an amendment to one of the paragraphs that "provided for [the] recognition of the [Bulgarian and Romanian] governments." Truman replied that he could not agree with Stalin's amendment. Only when these countries "were established on a proper basis" would Washington recognize them "and not before."[117]

This exchange reveals much about the two sides' agendas. By playing the good cop to Molotov's bad cop, Stalin could reinforce his established image as a reasonable actor. And if he could use his concessions to secure American recognition of the Bulgarian and Romanian governments, Moscow could then lock in the status quo in the Balkans, forcing the Americans to relax their pressure. Knowing that recognition was one of the few things Stalin seemed to care about with regard to Eastern Europe, Truman obviously feared losing his main bargaining chip. Until he had achieved his own objectives, he would therefore continue to dangle the carrot of recognition, with the hope that the Soviets would moderate their ways.

At the foreign ministers' meeting on the morning of July 22, Britain's Eden broached the issue of the American statement on liberated Europe. Molotov, again playing his bad cop role, rejected many of the specifics, including the supervision of elections. The discussion went nowhere.[118] At the plenary session that afternoon, Stalin made the startling announcement that Soviet troops would be pulling out of Austria, garnering the appreciation of both Truman and Churchill. Most of the meeting was taken up by Soviet requests for allied help in revising the Turkish straits treaty and with the possibility of a Soviet trusteeship for the former Italian territory of Libya. Stalin was obviously maneuvering for a deal: concessions on Austria in return for a Soviet position in the Mediterranean.[119]

At the plenary session of the next afternoon, the Turkish straits issue arose again. At Teheran in November 1943, Roosevelt and Churchill had tentatively pledged to help the Russians gain better access through the straits. This gave Stalin the opening to now argue that the 1935 Montreux Convention had to be substantially revised. That convention had allowed Turkey to block the straits to Russian commercial shipping not only if Turkey were at war but also if Istanbul simply believed that there was a threat of war. Stalin asked Churchill and Truman to imagine the commotion their countries would make if the Suez or Panama canals had to operate under such conditions. And just as the British and American navies had a presence in those waterways, Stalin contended, the Soviets should have a navy base within the Turkish straits to defend their shipping interests. (This of course had been a Russian economic and strategic objective since the early nineteenth century.) Churchill and Truman expressed sympathy for the Soviet position but argued that all three powers should act to defend the straits as a "free waterway" open to the world.

The president used this opportunity to launch into what one of his advisors would later call "Truman's favorite project at that time"—namely, the scheme for open inland waterways.[120] History suggested, Truman told Stalin and Churchill, that wars of the future could be avoided through free intercourse through the Turkish straits and Europe's main river systems—namely, the Rhine and Danube. He read from a prepared proposal that recommended equal treatment and uniform regulations for all nations using these waterways. America's ambition was to have a Europe that was "sound economically and which could support itself." This would be a situation in which Russia, Britain, France, and all other European countries would work together, and through which the United States could trade and become prosperous. Truman concluded his soliloquy by turning back to the Turkish straits question, which he said was really up to Russia and Turkey to solve themselves. Yet the question of the Turkish straits, Truman added ominously, "concerned the United States and the whole world."[121]

At the plenary session the next afternoon (July 24), after a heated discussion about Italy,[122] Truman asked if the others had considered the paper he had circulated on inland waterways. Stalin's immediate reply was blunt: this paper talked only about the Rhine and Danube, and he wanted a response to his proposal on the Turkish straits issue first. Truman then came to his main point, the one he had alluded to the day before: namely, that he "wished the two questions to be considered together." Any such linkage would of course be a major problem for the Soviets, since it might require them to open up the Danube to free commerce, thereby exposing Romania, Bulgaria, and Hungary to western penetration. Stalin quickly tried to postpone debate. But Churchill came to Truman's rescue. The prime minister stated that he had understood that the Big Three had agreed to work together to guarantee access through the Turkish straits, "and that the United States would come into that kind of an organization." Needless to say, this was a highly distorted summary of the inconclusive debate from the day before. There seems to be little doubt that the British and Americans had consulted prior to the meeting, for Truman immediately jumped in to say that Churchill "had clearly stated the position of the United States." The prime minister added that this proposed solution would be more than a substitute for the Soviet proposal of a fortified straits—that is, one protected by a Soviet naval base.[123]

This was a remarkable exchange. Here were the American and British leaders cooperating fully on a proposal that they must have known, given Russian history, that Moscow could not accept. They were essentially asking the Russian leadership to agree to having the U.S. and British navies patrol the

Turkish straits to keep the Black Sea open to merchant and naval ships of all countries, including of course those of America and Britain. For 150 years, there had been one constant in Russian strategic thinking: that Russian merchant ships should have free access *into* the Mediterranean Sea to promote Russia's economic development, and foreign navies should be kept *out* of the Black Sea to protect against attack via the Ukraine. And, of course, there had been one constant objective in British naval strategy: to keep the Russian navy bottled up within the Black Sea and to allow maximum access for British shipping. Churchill, as a keen student of history and a former naval secretary, undoubtedly jumped at this opportunity to work with the Americans to achieve British ends. Truman, perhaps more concerned about maintaining open access to the Danube but certainly also wishing to minimize the Soviet penetration of the Mediterranean, was obviously pleased to have the British on board for the task. And if Stalin agreed to the proposal, perhaps to achieve concessions on other issues, so much the better. Truman's inland waterway plan could go through, Romania and Bulgaria could be opened up to western commercial and political influence, and Western Europe would get the raw materials and food it needed to ward off communism.

The Soviets, of course, were not going to fall into such an obvious trap. Molotov entered the conversation to ask sarcastically if the Suez Canal might be allowed to operate under the same principle being proposed—namely, a three-way protection of its openness. Churchill responded that this question had not been asked. Molotov replied that he was asking it. After all, he said, "[if] it is such a good rule why not apply it to the Suez?" Churchill lamely countered that the British had established an arrangement that had worked for seventy years, and that they were satisfied with it. Molotov caustically suggested that Churchill should consult the Egyptians as to their satisfaction with the arrangement. The point was made: if the openness of waterways was the goal, it should be applied broadly, and not just in areas that would allow western interests to flourish. In the midst of the Molotov-Churchill exchange, Truman reminded the three sides of what he was envisioning by an "international guarantee" of the freedom of the straits: "it meant that any nation had free ingress [i.e., entry] for any purpose whatever."[124] From the Russian standpoint, this was exactly the problem. The Americans and British would be able to move freely into the Soviet realm, spreading their commercial tentacles as they undermined communist political control. And of course this was precisely what the Americans had in mind as they sought to save Western Europe from collapse.

The remaining week of meetings at Potsdam can be covered in short order. There were no major breakthroughs on any of the most contentious issues. Although Truman brought up the inland waterways question on two more occasions (with new British prime minister Clement Attlee now occupying Churchill's chair), Stalin refused to budge without American concessions on Russian control of the Turkish straits.[125] The waterways issue was left to be considered at future foreign ministers' meetings, while the three sides agreed to consult Turkey on revisions to the Montreux Convention.[126] In the sub-committee meetings on reparations and in discussions on reparations in the foreign ministers' sessions, the United States stuck to the formula that western Germany would only offer up reparations after it had paid for necessary imports. After much haggling over the details, the final agreement specified that Russia would receive 10 to 15 percent of western Germany's surplus production over and above what the latter needed to sustain its peacetime economy.[127] As noted, because Germany would have little or no surplus production after paying for imports, this meant in practice that the Russians would end up receiving essentially nothing from the western zones.

The three sides did agree to treat Germany as a single economic zone and coordinate some east-west shipments. But this also proved a dead end over the following months. There was little trade across the east-west divide, as the Soviets sent eastern German goods to Russia as reparation payments while the British, Americans, and French worked together to use their zones to help Western Europe. Accomplishments at Potsdam regarding Europe were few and far between. There was agreement on the final borders of Poland. And all three powers reiterated that they recognized the "Polish Government of National Unity." But despite American wishes, there was no final statement on "Liberated Europe," one that was supposed to have reflected Soviet concessions on Romania, Bulgaria, and Hungary. Instead, the Big Three agreed simply to work on revising the procedures for the Allied Control Commissions in the three Eastern European states. Since the real problem for Washington was not Hungary but the economic and political openness of Romania and Bulgaria, it was evident that the Soviets would make no adjustments to their controlling positions in these two countries. This intransigence would continue in subsequent foreign minister discussions through the fall.[128]

In sum, the Potsdam conference nicely demonstrates the explanatory power of dynamic realism. The Americans went to the conference deeply worried about the growing risk of Western Europe's complete economic collapse and its fall into the Soviet camp. They thus sought Soviet assurances that Eastern Europeans would be allowed to send raw materials and foodstuffs westward to help key states such as western Germany and France regain a measure of economic and social stability. Stalin's policy regarding Romania and Bulgaria thus became a litmus test for Moscow's overall foreign economic orientation in the postwar period. Once it became clear that the Soviets, in order to rebuild their war-shattered economy, would force the Eastern Europeans to trade almost exclusively with Russia, the Americans knew they had to do more to prop up Western Europe, even if this meant acting in ways that hurt Russia's economic recovery. Truman and Byrnes thus denied the Soviets reparations from western Germany and continued to redirect aid away from the Soviet Union and toward Western Europe. In a very direct and straightforward sense, then, negative trade expectations combined with the American desire to consolidate a realm-two economic sphere in Western Europe led to U.S. behavior that in turn caused Soviet trade expectations to plummet. The result was a rise in mutual animosity that made a postwar peace impossible.

## Conclusion

This chapter has had two goals. The first was to show that FDR's reasons for getting into the Second World War were fundamentally driven by his concerns for the commercial and economic position of the United States after the war. Like Wilson, he could not allow Germany to dominate Europe and then use that as a springboard for going after the commerce of the western hemisphere. But Roosevelt's dilemma by June 1940 was far more acute than even Wilson's by March of 1917. Nazi Germany had eliminated France, had control of Holland, Belgium, Norway, and Poland, and had a strong ally in Italy that would allow penetration of the oil-rich Middle East. Britain stood alone, and if Britain were to be forced to sue for peace, there was a strong likelihood that it would also lose part of its navy and its control of Egypt and give Germany a gateway to the Middle East and the Indian Ocean. If Germany could not be beaten, then it had to be contained where it was in Europe, with the United States controlling the commerce of the periphery. Once the Soviet Union was attacked in June 1941, there was suddenly the prospect of Germany controlling the vast bulk of Eurasia and then using that as a base for spreading south into the rest of Africa and even across the water to South America. Roosevelt worried that Japan might go north from Manchuria and split Stalin's forces into two. To avoid a Soviet defeat, he used severe economic sanctions to force Japan to go south to secure the oil of the Dutch East Indies. But his focus the whole time was defeating Hitler and avoiding a bipolar global standoff against Nazi Germany. By helping to save the Soviet Union, he ended up creating the context for a different sort of bipolar standoff, now with a communist Russia, not a fascist Germany.

The impending victory over Germany and Japan led FDR by 1943 to prepare for a different world order than the one envisioned by his advisors in late 1940. But the geopolitical and geoeconomic logic underpinning it was not terribly different. By building an economic power sphere that went beyond the western hemisphere to include essentially everything *but* the Soviet Union and Eastern Europe, FDR hoped to bottle up Stalin and make him a junior partner in the new international order he envisioned. The United Nations organization could be used as a collective security structure that now would allow the United States and the Soviet Union to potentially work together, in FDR's vision, as policemen for their respective spheres. A peace based on spheres of influence—without ever calling it that—would be possible if Stalin played ball. But if he didn't, FDR was ready: his dominant commercial sphere that spanned the globe would give the West such overall economic dominance and forward power projection capability that the Soviets would rationally be deterred by the sheer force of the U.S. position.

The second major section of this chapter demonstrated the critical role economic dependence and trade expectations played in the growth of U.S.-Soviet mistrust after 1943 and the ultimate onset of the Cold War. Although the struggle for position began with Roosevelt's strenuous efforts in 1944 to create a strong U.S. presence in the oil-rich Middle East,[129] the deepest concerns of the emerging superpowers came to a head in Europe during the first half of 1945. The Americans simply could not allow Western Europe to slip into the communist economic sphere. Yet the Soviets would not permit their newly acquired Eastern European satellites to open to east-west trade in a way that would stabilize the West. Perhaps even more important in terms of shaping American expectations, Moscow's posture also made it clear that should Western European states gravitate to the Soviet bloc after left-leaning domestic changes, the United States would be cut off from Europe, its traditional regional partner for trade and investment. A nation's military power is always founded on a strong economy. It was thus self-evident to Truman and Byrnes that without vigorous and potentially provocative action, America's economic power and thus its security in the postwar era could be gravely endangered.

We should not take this to mean that dependence and trade expectations were the only factors driving the two superpowers into the Cold War after 1945. As I have shown elsewhere, the sheer size of Russia's population and resources meant that as it reignited its prewar industrialization programs, it might overtake the United States in GDP and possibly military power within a few decades. It was therefore only natural that Truman and Byrnes would turn to measures that would restrict Soviet territorial and economic growth to improve the likelihood that America would maintain a position of overall economic and military superiority.[130] The cultural differences between the two sides in ideological goals—with Moscow explicitly committed to helping communism spread around the world—understandably made the Americans concerned about the future intentions of the rising Soviet state.

Yet the evidence of this chapter allows us to see exactly how economic orientation and the competition over third parties can interact to shape each side's expectations about the future global trade environment, expectations that in this case greatly reinforced U.S. fears that the Soviet bloc would grow to overwhelming proportions—at least if Washington failed to act to stop this growth. Moscow's neo-mercantilist orientation to the states in its sphere and its desperate need to recover from the war meant that the Soviets could not conceive of allowing Eastern Europe to "go west" in order to help rebuild the Western European economy. Yet this in turn meant that Western Europe would likely fall to communism, a result that would only heighten Soviet economic growth at the expense of American economic power. In short, even without Stalin directly wanting to foster revolution in Western Europe to build global Soviet power—and there is good evidence, which the Americans saw at the time, that Stalin was constraining rather than encouraging communist parties in Western Europe and Greece[131]—Washington understood that the indirect result of his economic policies would likely amount to the same thing.

Given the "triple whammy" of declining U.S. trade expectations for Western Europe, the likely development of Russia's potential power, and the ideological divide between the two states, it is not surprising that Truman and Byrnes decided to move to more hard-line policies by the summer of 1945. As I have detailed elsewhere, as of July–August 1945 the Americans began a concerted program to constrain and contain long-term Soviet growth. They did this not simply by acting to rebuild Western Europe and western Germany, by denying the Soviets economic reparations, and by ending economic aid to Russia; they also acted to reduce Soviet influence in the Far East by excluding Moscow from any role in the occupation of Japan and by helping Kuomintang forces retake Manchuria and northern China. Finally, the Americans quickly entrenched themselves in overseas bases around the Eurasian perimeter, bases that Roosevelt had farsightedly secured over the 1941 to 1945 period. This meant that the Americans could project conventional and nuclear power against the Soviet heartland far more easily than the Soviets could project power against the continental United States. With Truman's decision in the fall of 1945 to deny Moscow access to American atomic secrets, the United States seemed poised to maintain its overall power dominance, even at the well-understood risk of sparking a dangerous Cold War spiral.[132]

The fact that such a Cold War spiral did ensue soon after these U.S. actions, beginning with the crisis over Iran in early 1946, should not lead us to conclude that the American side is morally to blame for the onset of the Cold War. Given the circumstances that they faced, Truman and Byrnes really had no other choice than to shift American policy in a way that would ultimately be seen as provocative by Soviet leaders. At the deepest level, had Stalin not had such a neo-mercantilist perspective regarding Eastern Europe, and had Soviet potential power not been so daunting, Truman and Byrnes would likely not have anticipated that the future decline of the United States would have been as steep, absent a more hard-line policy. This would have allowed them to pursue a more cooperative stance that could have maintained the modest degree of trust the two sides had built up as allies during the war. Truman's efforts in May and June 1945 to resolve the dispute over Poland and the fact that he arrived at Potsdam with hopes of working out a modus vivendi (albeit on American terms) indicates that he was not implacably hostile to Stalin and Soviet interests.[133] Yet in the face of Soviet intransigence on trade within Europe and the prospects for long-term Soviet economic growth, Truman had to act to avert a significant and irreversible loss in American relative power. The fact that this preventive policy, by including restrictions in U.S. aid and trade, would only increase the likelihood of a Soviet backlash, was simply a risk he had to accept in order to protect America's power position.

In the end, therefore, we should see the onset of the Cold War as the tragic result of circumstances that were ultimately beyond the control of either of the two emerging superpowers. The devastations wrought by the Second World War on all of Europe, and especially on the Soviet Union, meant that Stalin had to think first about Russian economic interests and not about what might be good for Western Europe. But this meant that the Americans would necessarily anticipate Western European states falling into the communist sphere unless the Soviet sphere could be quarantined, and the western sphere rebuilt at the expense of Russian growth. Potsdam was the last hope to avert an escalation driven by these exogenous factors. With both Eastern and Western Europe lying in ruins as a result of Nazi aggression, it was almost impossible to expect that the Americans and Soviets could work out a deal that would preserve positive trade expectations and still have allowed both sides to ensure the stability of their respective economic power spheres.

# 8

# The Crises and Conflicts of the
# Early Cold War, 1946–56

THE GOAL of this chapter and the next one is a broad and probably overly ambitious one. I will try to sweep across forty-five years of superpower politics to examine one simple question: What was the relative causal importance of economic interdependence and changes in economic expectations to the ups and downs of Cold War history? Chapter 7 showed the surprising significance of U.S. and Soviet dependence and expectations from 1943 to 1945 for the origins of the Cold War itself. Once strong levels of mistrust and fear were in place by the fall of 1945, there was little doubt on either side that the future would be one of ongoing arms racing punctuated by highly dangerous crises—crises that might lead not just to small regional wars, but to a nuclear war that could destroy the planet. Yet throughout the forty-five-year Cold War, there was active desire in both Moscow and Washington to moderate the intensity of superpower struggle so that a self-destructive total war could be avoided.

This chapter and the following chapter will examine the major crises that raised the risk of actual superpower confrontation and war from 1946 to 1991. In addition to considering the periods leading up to these crises, the two chapters will also examine the efforts to achieve a lessening of tensions that would avoid such crises altogether. I do this not simply to avoid "selecting on the dependent variable," the methodological problem of looking only at months of crisis and not months of relative calm. I do this because we need to understand the conditions that can lead to the ending of cold war struggles ("enduring rivalries"), but also the conditions that prevent states from escaping those struggles, even though they clearly desire such an outcome.[1] In the late 1950s and again in the early 1970s, for example, both sides sought a détente that would allow for peaceful coexistence into the foreseeable future. Neither had any desire for a thermonuclear war that would wipe out their respective societies. Yet certain key factors intervened to thwart their efforts for peace. The true winding down of the Cold War only came in the late 1980s. So, we need to ask not simply what caused the periodic crises of the Cold War era, but what ultimately allowed it to end in a whimper and not a bang.

It would take many books to cover these topics adequately. The two chapters are therefore designed more to provoke than to fully convince; subsequent analyses can help to strengthen or refute certain more controversial arguments. My goal is simply to show the underappreciated and often surprising significance of economic factors in the ups and downs of the Cold War. In perhaps no other period of history have the economic dimensions of great power politics been as ignored as the Cold War era. Almost every major analysis of the crises of the period, aside from some neo-Marxist revisionist works, places primary focus on the military, political, and ideological dimensions of the U.S.-Soviet struggle. As I noted in chapter 7, this academic lacuna likely reflects the fact that there was little actual U.S-Soviet trade for almost half a century. Scholars could therefore safely assume that changes in the levels of peace or conflict could not be a function of changes in trade levels. Yet once we shift our thinking over to a more dynamic approach, we see that state behavior can be shaped by the anticipation of large benefits that could arise in the future should the other begin to open up to greater commercial ties. Conversely, an expectation that the other will continue to apply tight restrictions on trade and commerce can squelch efforts to build better relations. Moreover, because great powers have an incentive to expand their economic power spheres, leaders can also anticipate what might happen to the level of trade with current allies should the other great power succeed in drawing some of them over to its sphere of influence. On all three grounds, expectations of the future economic environment can play a determining role in the actor's behavior, even though there is literally no trade at the time between the two great powers themselves.

I will argue that expectations of future economic cut-offs, frustration at current restrictions, and anticipated losses tied to the other's expansion of its primary and second trading realms were dominant causal factors in many of the key crises of the Cold War and were particularly important in efforts to achieve a lessening of U.S.-Soviet hostility during the 1950s, 1970s, and 1980s. Expectations of a decline or a peaking in future economic power, combined with the stark ideological differences, combined to make both Washington and Moscow see the other as a potential external threat. And yet, as the next chapter explores, efforts to improve the other's expectations of future trade proved to be an essential aspect of any negotiated effort to lessen tensions and avoid war.

Notwithstanding the explanatory value of the dynamic realist argument, this chapter will also show that in two important crises, economic interdependence and trade expectations had almost no direct role to play in the outbreak of superpower confrontation. These cases are the first Berlin crisis of 1948 and the Korean War of 1950. As I discuss, both crises pose problems for both commercial liberalism and my trade expectations logic since they arose in the midst of a severe drop in trade between the two superpower blocs. In such a situation, we would expect trade variables to have had some relevance to the outbreak of conflict. Yet while economic factors are important overall, both crises were caused by Soviet fears of a decline in relative bloc power, not because of economic interdependence or trade expectations per se. So, even if the fact that it was U.S. efforts to build the Western economic sphere that caused this decline is captured by my theory, the response of the Soviets that leads to crisis and war is not.

The Berlin 1948 and Korean War cases are particularly problematic for commercial liberal scholars. They constitute two of the "most likely" cases in the Cold War for the liberal position that as trade falls, domestic-level pathologies get unleashed and lead to conflict or war. With trade levels falling off dramatically after 1946–47, liberals would expect to see evidence that it was greed or the drive for ideological dominance that was propelling Stalin into hard-line provocative behavior.[2] Yet the evidence strongly indicates that Soviet actions in both 1948 and 1950 were largely defensive reactions to negative trends caused by U.S. policies. The overwhelming historical consensus on Berlin is that Stalin was seeking to counter a Western move to unite the three allied zones in western Germany and to hand over power to an independent West German government, policies that would cause the economic and political decline of East Germany. Given this consensus, and given that I have covered this case elsewhere, I will only briefly summarize the evidence here.[3] The Korean War case is more controversial, however, and thus requires more discussion. The traditional historical perspective is that Stalin was indeed operating in an opportunistic way, seeking to expand communism's reach after learning in mid-January 1950 that U.S. Secretary of State Dean Acheson had placed South Korea outside the American defense perimeter. If this were true, the case would nicely confirm liberalism's contention that when trade falls, unit-level drives for war get unleashed. I will show, however, that this traditional view is very likely wrong. The declassified Russian documents show that Stalin's policy with regard to East Asia had shifted *prior* to Acheson's speech and was driven by a new fear of increased American involvement in the region. Moreover, the Soviets interpreted the speech as confirmation of a renewed American hostility and a growing rather than diminishing U.S. commitment to South Korea. Contrary to the liberal thesis, therefore, Stalin gave the go-ahead to North Korea largely because of fears of decline, not because domestic and psychological pathologies were unleashed after U.S.-Soviet trade levels plummeted.

Notwithstanding the fact that security motives were driving Soviet behavior in both 1948 and 1950, the trade expectations component of dynamic realism must be seen as weak in explanatory power for these two cases. The sharp downward trend in trade between the blocs during the 1940s should have given Stalin trade-related reasons for expansion. But it seems clear that his logic for upping the ante over Berlin and Korea, while fundamentally about the decline in the economic and strategic position of the communist sphere, had little to do with trade per se. These two cases thus show that the trade expectations logic can be lacking in causal explanatory power in situations where other causes of decline are existentially overwhelming.[4] Yet despite the logic's weakness here, I will also briefly consider an aspect of one case where it does surprisingly fit: the initial U.S. financial and military commitment to Vietnam in 1950 and through to 1960. As I will discuss, the fears of communist gains in 1949 that led the United States to increase its aid to South Korea *also* led to support for South Vietnam. Here the aid was driven by a deep concern that if Vietnam fell and much of Southeast Asia then lost, a key country— *Japan*—would lose the access to raw materials and markets it needed for postwar growth and a place in the American alliance system. Declining trade expectations regarding the overall Western economic sphere, in other words, drove early U.S. policy over Vietnam. So, while it is clear that the more purely political and geostrategic implications of dominoes falling took over after 1960 and led to the escalation of 1963–65, the original reasons for involvement were very much bound up with commerce and the American global position.

This chapter will take the story up to the end of 1956 and the following chapter will continue the analysis until 1991. In this chapter, special attention will be given to a comparison of the Iranian Crisis of 1951–53 and the Suez Crisis of 1956. Both crises arose in an area of the world, the Middle East, where American economic dependence was both high and growing. Aside from their contemporary relevance, therefore, the crises provide fertile ground for a direct comparison of the power of the main competing economic theories of this book. I will show that dynamic realism not only does a good job explaining both cases, but it can explain why President Eisenhower acted forcefully in one crisis (Iran 1953) and quite moderately in the other (Suez 1956). Neither liberalism nor a more purely military-focused realist argument can explain the two crises.

Overall, the focus of this chapter and the next will be on the lead-ups to actions that directly affected the chance of actual superpower conflict—both the ones that raised the risk of direct confrontation due to their nature (Suez Crisis) or location (Iran 1951–53) and the ones that lowered that risk via unilateral or bilateral efforts to reduce tension (efforts at détente in the late 1950s and early 1970s and the end of the Cold War itself).[5] By examining the events where there was distinct variation on the dependent variable, we can expose to the light of day the true explanatory power of economic variables versus noneconomic variables. The trade expectations logic of dynamic realism does not prove itself powerful in every case, to be sure. Yet it is not only much more powerful than one might expect, given low superpower trade levels, but in general it does better than either liberalism or a more military-driven realist logic. Variations in anticipated trade levels, combined with anticipated future needs for raw materials, markets, and investments, can indeed be powerful forces for shifts in great power behavior.

## Truman and the Early Cold War, 1946–49

The United States, as was discussed in chapter 7, was the first superpower to switch to hard-line policies designed to reduce the other's sphere and to contain its growth. In this sense, it must be seen as the superpower most causally responsible for the onset of Cold War tension, even if one can applaud (as I would) Truman's actions as the prudent response to a deteriorating situation. Stalin in 1945 was primarily interested in rebuilding his state after a devastating war. But by the fall of 1945, he was already beginning to react to the shift in U.S. policy that had occurred by June/July. We first see Stalin's change of policy with regard to Far Eastern questions. After Hiroshima, Truman had moved to exclude Russia from the occupation of Japan's four main islands, despite the fact that Moscow's entry into the war gave it a claim to share occupational duties. Japan had attacked Russia in 1904, in 1918, and again in the late 1930s, and Stalin had good reason to fear a renewal of Japanese militarism. He had Molotov push hard to secure a small role for Russia in Japan's occupation at the foreign ministers' meeting in September, but Secretary of State Byrnes blocked his efforts. In October, Stalin told ambassador Harriman that if Moscow was denied its rightful role regarding Japan, it would have to pursue a "unilateral course" in Asia. Harriman, by this time worried that U.S. policy had become too hard-line, warned Washington that U.S. resistance would only heighten Soviet fears that America was using Japan to contain the Soviet Union.[6]

It was soon after this that Stalin began to take a more assertive stance with regard to the long-simmering question of Iran. As I show elsewhere, in the fall of 1944, after Moscow had reacted to British and American efforts to secure new oil concessions, Teheran had postponed any discussion of such concessions until after the end of World War II.[7] Britain, Russia, and the United States had earlier agreed to remove all troops from Iran six months after the end of war, and the Iranians continued to refuse all discussions on oil until after the troops were removed. The U.S. troops were largely gone by

December 1945. The Soviet forces, however, were still in the north by the end of the year and seemed to have no intention of leaving by the first of March deadline. For Moscow, the reality of the situation was clear: while the Americans and British could promise large infusions of capital, advanced technology, and connections to world markets, the Soviets had no economic bargaining tools working in their favor. Their only point of leverage was the threat to continue military occupation until Teheran agreed to an oil concession. Thus, from late November 1945 onward they blocked all efforts by Teheran to quell unrest in the Soviet-occupied provinces of Azerbaijan and Kurdistan, and refused to remove Soviet troops until an oil concession was agreed to.[8]

The maneuvering turned into a low-level crisis in March 1946 when the Iranians, with American support, presented their case to the U.N. Security Council. The Soviet delegates walked out of the proceedings. A few weeks later, on April 4 Moscow and Teheran signed an oil agreement that promised an oil concession in the north in return for troop evacuation. By May 9, the Soviet forces had completed their withdrawal from Iran. American officials basked in what they saw as the first effective use of hard-line pressure to coerce a Soviet withdrawal from a key strategic area on the periphery. Yet in reality, as Natalia Yegorava's seminal work shows, the results the Soviets obtained were close to what they had been pushing for almost two years. Moscow was still importing oil in 1945–46 from Eastern Europe and was certainly far from achieving the strong export position in oil and natural gas it would enjoy by the late 1950s. Moreover, as Kennan had noted in the fall of 1944, the Soviets were worried about a growing British and American presence in a country on Russia's vulnerable southern border. The agreement of April 1946 was by no means a clearcut victory for Moscow. But it did ensure that the northern provinces would have a Soviet rather than British-American presence into the future.[9]

This first clear crisis of the Cold War era was fundamentally the result of great power maneuvering for economic and strategic position in the emerging postwar world. The U.S. side wanted to block Soviet penetration of Iran as Washington increased its own presence in this critical oil-rich region. The State Department emphasized to Truman through the summer and fall of 1945 what it had told Roosevelt for two years: namely, that Saudi Arabian oil—what one report to Truman called "a stupendous source of strategic power, and one of the greatest material prizes in world history"—had to be protected.[10] While Washington was ultimately prepared to allow the British primary control of Iranian oil, it would not allow the Soviet Union to have any role—military or economic—in such a pivotal state as Iran. Yet Soviet fears of being shut out of the oil wealth of Iran, combined with the simple geographic importance of the state, made it essential that the Soviets had at least some presence in the country. Trade expectations on both sides, therefore, as well as the need to increase their respective realm-two economic power spheres, were essential to the willingness of both sides to struggle over Iran's future. That the Iranians ultimately reneged on their promise to grant a concession in the north does not mean that the Soviets did not believe in April 1945 that they had secured their economic access to Iran and thus could reduce their military presence. Indeed, the crisis resolved itself precisely because Teheran had played upon Soviet expectations of *future* access to achieve an agreement that undercut the one Soviet lever in its bargaining—its military presence on Iranian soil. Once the Soviet troops had departed, Iran could break the agreement and seek better deals from the West, knowing that it would be much harder for the Soviets to reoccupy the north without sparking a larger war. Teheran won this round. But as we will see shortly, the Soviets were not through with Iran by any means.

The years of 1947–48 saw another jump in overall Cold War hostility with the announcement of the Truman Doctrine and the onset of the first Berlin crisis. In February 1947, the British government informed Washington that it would no longer be able to support Turkey or Greece in the face of a severe financial deficit at home. The Truman Doctrine of March and the subsequent announcement of the Marshall Plan in June came directly out of a strategic logic that had been in place since late 1944/early 1945: namely, that if the Soviets were able to draw peripheral states such as Turkey and Greece—or worse, Western European states—into their sphere, the United States would lose access to the benefits of trade that were needed to sustain its long-term power position. As a consequence, the Soviet Union would grow while the United States declined. Kennan's arguments in 1947 about the importance of maintaining U.S. dominance over the "military-economic potential" of Eurasia, made now from his position as the head of the Policy Planning Staff, reinforced these fears.[11] As Melvyn Leffler summarizes, despite Truman's need for domestic reasons to couch the Truman Doctrine in Manichean ideological terms, the intensified crusade to protect the periphery was underpinned by "deeply rooted geopolitical convictions that defined national self-interest in terms of correlations of power based on the control of critical resources, bases, and industrial infrastructure."[12] In April 1947, for example, the joint State-War-Navy Coordinating Committee (the forerunner to the National Security Council) recommended that long-term economic and military assistance for the periphery was critical. "It is important to maintain in friendly hands," the SWNCC report argued, "areas which contain or protect sources of metals, oil, and other national resources" and that represent "substantial industrial potential."[13] Such areas would determine the long-term economic future of the American superpower and thus could not be lost to Russia, a state which had been practicing neomercantilism for more than a century.

The United States, unlike the Soviet Union, was a democratic state that could not coerce allies into handing over its goods or accepting American products. These critical areas would only help sustain high U.S. economic growth through ongoing trade ties. But by 1947 it was clear that the Western European economies could no longer afford to trade: they simply did not have the U.S. dollars needed to buy American goods. In 1946 the Western Europeans imported approximately $4.4 billion in goods from the United States but exported only $900 million back. After lend-lease aid had been wound down in the fall of 1945, loans had sustained the Western Europeans in the short term. But American officials in early 1947 expected that the Europeans would have to reduce overall imports by 50 percent and imports from the United States by as much as 80 percent unless larger infusions of cash were provided. The Western European states would be forced to move even further in the direction of central planning and relative autarchy just to survive. And if they went communist as a result of their internal economic problems, the situation would be disastrous. As the State Department's committee on the European Recovery Program noted at the time, any communist state in Western Europe would be happy with a regimented economy and restrictive bilateral trade treaties with the Soviet Union. The Soviets would eagerly jump at the chance to use trade levers to control the critical resources of the area. Scandinavia, North Africa, and the Middle East would then have to follow suit, radically shifting the overall economic balance of power in the Russians' favor.[14]

The Marshall Plan and the Truman Doctrine were thus, as Truman famously noted, two halves of the same walnut; both were essential in the maintenance of U.S. economic and geopolitical strength over the long term.[15] The Berlin crisis of 1948 arose out of this general context of economic competition and the U.S. drive to consolidate an economic power sphere in Western Europe, although it was not directly a function of economic dependence per se. Because I have covered this case elsewhere, I will only briefly summarize its security-driven roots here.[16] By the winter of 1947–48, the importance of the German economy to the economic recovery of all of Western Europe loomed even larger than it had in 1945. At the London Conferences of January–March 1948, Britain, France, and the United States agreed to unite their three occupation zones in Germany and to hand political control over to an independent West German government.[17] This was a daunting prospect for a Russian state that had just lost twenty-seven million lives fighting Germany. The fear of a resurgent West Germany was only made worse by the flow of refugees from the Soviet zone that was weakening the East German economy and increasing the strain on the overall Eastern bloc. When Britain and the United States announced currency reforms in mid-June 1948 as a preparatory step to the creation of a unified West German state, the Soviets reacted. They blockaded all ground traffic to Berlin, hoping that this would pressure the West into reversing its recent decisions. The Americans understood that the Soviets' actions were a defensive reaction to Western moves. As U.S. ambassador to Moscow Walter Bedell Smith wrote to Washington in July, the Soviets desired "a return to [the] status quo," and would forgo a battle for Berlin if the London agreements were cancelled.[18]

In discussions over the next two months, the constant Soviet demand was for the reversal of the London agreements, but the Americans held firm. By June 1949, the Soviets ended their blockade and accepted the new status quo, ending the first Berlin crisis of the Cold War. Economic factors were a primary force in the Soviet initiation of the crisis. Moscow foresaw that the unification of western Germany would cause a relative loss of economic power for Russia. But it was not because of eastern German dependence on trade with the western zones that the Soviets feared the London agreements. They simply knew that these agreements would create a strong western Germany, further the rebound of Western Europe as a whole, and fuel the exodus of east German citizens to the West. In short, fears of economic decline drove the process, but these fears were not a function of interdependence and trading realms per se.

Berlin 1948 is a problematic case for liberalism. Levels of trade had been plummeting between the United States and the Soviet Union. American exports to Russia had dropped from $3.5 billion in 1944 during the height of Lend Lease to $149 million in 1947 and a mere $28 million in 1948.[19] For liberals, the ending of any economic restraint on Soviet behavior should mean that unit-level drives such as greed and ideological expansion should be operating as the primary propelling forces behind Soviet action. Yet it is quite clear that the Soviets were reacting out of security fears, and that they desired only a return to the status quo prior to the London agreements. Yet the case, at least in terms of Soviet behavior, also poses some problems for the trade expectations logic. My broader dynamic realist argument can certainly explain why U.S. leaders wanted to build a realm-two economic sphere in Western Europe, one that would have to include West Germany. But it was Soviet behavior in 1948 that created the crisis. And here Stalin was responding to the economic implications of the London agreements for eastern Germany and the Soviet bloc, independent of east-west trade per se.

## The Origins of the Korean War and American Involvement in Vietnam

This section will show that the Korean War of 1950 and the U.S. commitment to Vietnam that led to a tragic conflict in the 1960s have a common origin: they both reflect the hardening of American Cold War strategy by the late 1940s and the perceived need to protect America's larger economic and political sphere in Asia from the expansionist activities of communist Russia and China. Even before the Soviets exploded their own atomic weapon and China fell to Mao in the fall of 1949, Washington officials were already preparing to increase the U.S. commitment to East and Southeast Asia to stem the possibility of decline in this vital area. In particular, they believed that a revitalized Japan was the linchpin for the region, and without a strong economy Japan might very well fall to communism from within. In one of the great ironies of the postwar era, the very country that had acted from 1941 to 1945 to keep Japan from dominating the economy and trade of the region now acted to *defend* Japan's ability to get access to cheap raw materials and overseas markets for its industrial goods. In short, while the Americans did not act primarily to protect their own access to trade in Asia, they did act on the basis of a larger geoeconomic logic consistent with the trade expectations logic. They knew that by keeping noncommunist areas of Asia out of Soviet and Chinese hands they would enhance the overall economic strength of the "Western" sphere, while reducing the strength of the communist bloc.

It is important to stress upfront that in seeking to shore up the Western position in Asia, American officials were not seeking war per se. Both the start of the Korean War in June 1950 and the eventual escalation of the Vietnam conflict to war by 1963–65 were undesired events. And in both cases, a complete explanation for U.S. behavior requires that we bring in American beliefs in "domino theory"—the idea that if the United States failed to defend South Korea or South Vietnam from communist expansionism, other countries in Asia would also be more likely to fall and the whole area might be "lost" to communism as a global ideology.[20] This theory when applied to Asia, as Andrew Rotter and Michael Schaller show, was a simple extension of the lessons learned at Munich in 1938—namely, that if an evil force believed that smaller states would easily fall into its sphere, it would become even more inclined to spread its evil, through subversion or direct invasion.[21] In both Korea and Vietnam, such domino thinking is the most direct explanation for U.S. involvement in these "far-away places" (to borrow Chamberlain's line about Czechoslovakia from the Munich Crisis).

I do not contest this explanation, which is strongly supported by almost all the historical literature. Indeed, to the extent that domino logic dominated U.S. thinking with regard both to Korea in 1950 and Vietnam in the early 1960s, the explanatory value of my commercially driven argument is weakened. As I will show, however, part of the reason that American thinking after 1948 became obsessed with small states in East Asia had to do with perceptions of the long-term threats to the U.S. economic sphere and the need to keep the communist world economically contained within its present sphere of influence. Stalin's decision to support a North Korean attack on South Korea in June 1950 was not directly about trade. But it was shaped by important American decisions in late 1949 and early 1950 to increase U.S. economic and political support for states in Asia, including South Korea and French-occupied Vietnam. And these decisions were made as a response to U.S. fears in 1948–49 of a declining economic and military position in Asia. I will not cover the escalation into all-out war in Vietnam in 1963–65. It is covered exhaustively by other scholars, and there is little disagreement that John Kennedy and Lyndon Johnson both felt they had to stay the course in Vietnam because to pull out after having made a commitment to protect South Vietnam from communism would mean a dramatic loss in America's reputation for military resolve and the falling of dominoes across the region.[22] The argument of this book has trouble explaining this obsession with reputation and dominos.[23] My purpose is thus simply to show that without the initial fear in 1948–50 of a deteriorating economic sphere in Asia, the Americans would *likely have not become reputationally committed to Vietnam in the first place.* The decisions to up the ante in Asia taken in 1948 to 1950 thus set the course for U.S. military involvement in the region, and in the case of Korea, actually provoked a direct military attack that forced an immediate American response.

The shift in U.S. policy toward Asia began in early 1948. Up until that point, American officials had been concerned to keep Japan from reindustrializing, for fear that it would again become an aggressive power in Asia. But with continued Maoist victories in China despite America's best efforts to support Chiang Kai-shek, it became clear that Japan would have to be rebuilt as an economic power. The smaller states in the region needed Japan to buy their exports of food and raw materials, and Japan needed them for markets. George Kennan's Public Policy Staff (PPS) had issued an internal report on the global situation in November 1947, which noted that U.S. policy "must be directed to restoring a balance of power in Europe and Asia," but it had lacked specifics on Asia.[24] In March 1948, Kennan got more specific. He argued that it was now crucial to relax restrictions on the Japanese economy in order to speed Japanese industrial recovery. The initial goal was to reduce Japan's dependency on the United States by encouraging its exports to Asian states, and to turn Japan into the "workshop of the Far East." On October 9, Truman approved NSC 13/2, the document embodying this new policy direction, and in early December he appointed Joseph Dodge to oversee the revitalization of the Japanese economy.[25]

Within the overall grand strategic logic that Kennan and others had been developing, a revitalized Japan and Germany would help the smaller states of their regions develop over time and thereby help maintain America's dominant economic and political position. In December 1948, John Davies, the PPS's main expert on Asia, argued in a memorandum that to ensure successful containment in Asia, the United States should help create "economic stability and interdependence" among Japan and Southeast Asia while also encouraging the export of raw materials to Western Europe.[26] Early in 1949, Secretary of State Dean Acheson directed the PPS to rethink American policy toward Southeast Asia. The study that emerged in March, PPS 51, noted that Southeast Asia was now a principal target of Soviet expansionist aims, and its loss to communism would prevent it from making necessary "contributions to the [Marshall Plan] countries . . . or to the orientation of Japan's trade southward in search of survival." If the United States, by its policy, could stabilize Southeast Asia, it could then "vigorously develop" the region "as a supplier of raw materials and Japan, Western Europe, and India, as suppliers of finished goods." Japan's survival was thus intimately linked to the security of Southeast Asia. And once Japan's industrial power was stabilized, as Dodge argued in July, Japan could then play its role as a critical frontline state "in the world-wide clash between communism and democracy."[27] This was the first major internal statement of what would later become known as the domino theory for Southeast Asia (but which of course was part of the logic American leaders applied after the disaster of Munich 1938).

In July of 1949, Acheson hired three consultants to advise the State Department on Asia. In August, the group offered their recommendations to Acheson, arguing the United States needed to conclude an early peace with Japan and to increase economic and military aid to Southeast Asia. On November 17, the consultants presented these ideas to Truman, and included the suggestion that the United States should seek to detach China from Russia through a moderate policy toward Mao. Truman found the presentation "tremendously helpful."[28] During the fall, Acheson's State Department had been able to shape the emerging NSC policy on Asia toward its strategic ends, despite some resistance from the Pentagon. The key moment came at a December 29 NSC meeting when Truman approved as U.S. policy two documents, NSC 48/1 "The Position of the United States with Respect to Asia" and its accompanying summary statement, NSC 48/2.

NSC 48/1 begins by noting that "Asia is an area of significant potential power—political, economic, and military." Building up the states of this region while drawing them permanently into the U.S. sphere would enhance Asian security as it "strengthen[ed] the world position of the United States," while losing them to the Russian sphere "would threaten the security of both Asia and the United States." Keeping Japan within the American sphere was critical. If Japan, "the principal component of a Far Eastern war-making complex," were added to the communist bloc, there would be a "shifting [of] the balance of world power to the disadvantage of the United States." Japan's defeat in World War II had created an economic vacuum that had set back regional

development and made communism more attractive. It was therefore imperative that Washington facilitate the development of economic relations between Japan and its neighbors. This included Mao's China, which might be
drawn away from Russian influence by the economic benefits of Sino-Japanese
trade. The document also reinforced the importance of South Korea: Washington must continue to give it political, economic, and military assistance not
only to "contain the threat of expanding Communist influence" but to help
reunify north and south "on a democratic basis." Finally, NSC 48/1 made clear
that Southeast Asia and South Asia were key parts of the new policy, given
their economic ties to Western Europe and Japan. In particular, Japan's economy could be strengthened if it were able to secure more of its needed food
and raw material imports from Asia, its "natural markets," rather than the
United States.[29]

As we will see in the next section, Acheson's leaking of the essence of NSC
48/1 and 48/2 in early January fundamentally hardened Stalin's view of the
necessity of aligning with China and starting a war with South Korea. Stalin
could not allow the Americans to draw China away from the Soviet sphere as
they reinforced the economic and political power of U.S. client states, including South Korea and the much-feared Japanese. For now, what is critical to
realize is that the U.S. policy shift was made clear to the world by early 1950,
and that it not only pushed Russia into supporting China and North Korea,
but it led to a significant increase in American economic and military aid to
Southeast Asia—including, for the first time, the French colony of Vietnam.
As Andrew Rotter's seminal work shows in detail, the United States made
significant commitments in economic and military aid to Vietnam in 1950 as
a result of the new thinking about Japan and Asia's strategic importance to the
overall competition of power spheres within the Cold War. With the loss of
China, Vietnam as well as Malaysia and Thailand were now on the front lines
of the struggle to contain communism. Over the next four years, Washington
supported the French against Ho Chi Minh's Vietminh forces to the tune of
some $4 billion, until the French finally agreed to withdraw at the Geneva
Conference in May 1954.[30] The United States would remain committed even
after the French left, and by the early 1960s, as the situation within South Vietnam deteriorated, presidents Kennedy and then Johnson would find that the
risks of U.S. withdrawal were too great.

It might be easy to think that a president such as Eisenhower, had he continued on into the 1960s, would not have made the mistake of taking the
United States into a devastating war over a tiny country such as Vietnam. But
it was Eisenhower, in a press conference in April 1954, a month before the
Geneva Conference, who first gave a name to the idea that without a clear U.S.
commitment, small states in Asia might fall to communism. When asked to

define "the strategic importance of Indochina to the free world," he noted two things. First, there was the obvious significance of its "production of [raw] materials that the world needs." Then

> you have the broader considerations that might follow what you would call the "falling dominos" principle. You have a row of dominoes set up, you knock over the first one, and what will happen to the last one is the certainty that it will go over very quickly. So you could have the beginning of a disintegration what would have the most profound influences.

Interestingly, Eisenhower did not argue that falling dominos in Southeast Asia would somehow directly threaten the U.S. homeland. Rather, the losses of the Southeast states to the communist sphere would, he continued, "take away, in its economic aspects, that region that Japan must have as a trading area." Should Japan not be able to get raw materials from the area, or export its products, it would have "only one place in the world to go—that is, toward the Communist areas in order to live."[31] Eisenhower, in short, had fully absorbed the thinking that had driven Truman to increase the U.S. commitment to Vietnam and Southeast Asia in 1950 and to keep it going despite terrible French losses.

The domino thinking that got the United States into a full-scale war by 1964–65 may have been an extreme and ultimately irrational extension of the Truman-Eisenhower logic. In that sense, the "Vietnam War" can be seen as a problematic case for my dynamic realist argument, at least if we consider it only as a conflict from 1961 to 1975. From Kennedy onward, domino fears overrode rational calculation of commercial and economic self-interest. But the initial reasons for involvement from 1948 to 1954 did come out of the vicious geopolitical struggle for economic power spheres of the first years of the Cold War. Supporting Japan's recovery made sense, and because Japan could only do well through trade and finance ties with Southeast Asia, U.S. involvement in Vietnam was necessary given the trends at the time.[32] In sum, dynamic realism, while it cannot explain the gradual American slide into total war in Vietnam by 1964, does a good job explaining why U.S. leaders felt the need to be there in the first place.

Turning to the Korean War, it is clear that no commercially driven theory of international politics can explain Stalin's decision to support North Korea's attack on the south. Liberalism and my theory might seem to have a case here, since trade between the United States and the Soviet Union had fallen to very low levels by 1950.[33] The recently declassified documents, however, do not support either theory. Commercial factors in 1950, either current or anticipated ones, were simply not important in the Soviet calculus. Moreover, the liberal argument that domestic pathologies were allowed free reign once trade levels fell is also not supported by the new evidence. As I will show, Stalin and his officials were driven mostly by fear of North Korea's declining economic position relative to South Korea, a situation created by America's growing support for South Korea. In short, the Soviets acted out of fear for the future, but this fear was not induced by interstate commercial factors. The trade expectations logic may not explain Soviet decision-making, but it does explain why the Americans acted to increase their economic support for South Korea, thereby provoking Soviet fears of decline and the crisis itself. As we have seen, by the fall of 1949 Washington was prepared to greatly increase the amount of aid flowing to Japan and Southeast Asia. The new strategic logic of NSC 48/1 and 48/2 spilled over into U.S. policy for South Korea. While the United States was not yet ready to align *militarily* with South Korea (as it was now preparing to do with Japan), U.S. leaders would signal over the first half of 1950 a clear commitment to the south's *economic* growth. This commitment, combined with Acheson's leaks on the thrust of the new Asian strategy, led Stalin to worry about communism's long-term position in Asia. He thus made amends with Mao in January, and in March approved Kim Il Sung's desired invasion of South Korea.

The traditional argument for the Korean War is one of deterrence failure—namely, the inability of Washington to communicate its resolve to defend the status quo on the Korean peninsula. This argument focuses in particular on Secretary of State Acheson's foreign policy speech on East Asia to the Washington Press Club on January 12, 1950, as the trigger for war. The primary purpose of the speech was to lay out Acheson's argument for an intensified program of containment against the spread of communism in east Asia. He mentioned that a "defense perimeter" existed from Japan through the Philippines, with the United States committed to the defense of the states within it. According to the traditional accounts, by leaving South Korea outside of the perimeter, Acheson was giving the Soviets and North Koreans a green light to invasion. Extended deterrence cannot operate, after all, if the United States refuses to commit itself to a small state's defense.[34]

The Soviet documents indicate, however, that the Soviets were already switching to a more hard-line policy in Asia ten days before the Acheson speech and indeed saw the speech, when they received information on it in mid-January, as a statement that the United States was becoming *more* involved in the affairs of all of East Asia, not less. Mao Zedong had arrived in Moscow in mid-December 1949 with the hope of negotiating a Soviet-Chinese alliance, only to be told bluntly that he should expect no such thing. He was then summarily ignored by all senior officials in Moscow until a Soviet *volte face* on January 2. That day, completely out of the blue, the Soviets reversed their stance and agreed to work toward the immediate conclusion of an alliance.

It is hard to explain this dramatic change in Soviet policy as a bargaining tactic. For one thing, the Soviets that arrived at Mao's door that day (Molotov and an associate) did not ask for anything in return, but simply caved into Mao's primary demand. And they did so despite the obvious risks of inflaming the U.S.-Soviet relationship, the concern that had previously been holding them back. The best explanation for the policy shift seems to be the startling revelations in the *New York Times* on January 1 that the United States was embarking on a new hard-line policy in East Asia. During the early Cold War, the *New York Times* was clearly the best American newspaper for foreign news, and it served as a critical source of information for the Soviet leadership. Its most well-known investigative reporter was James "Scotty" Reston, an individual known to have direct personal connections with key players such as Dean Acheson and Harry Truman. The front-page article by Reston on January 1 provided key leaked details from a December 29, 1949 meeting of the NSC, in which Truman approved of a more aggressive containment policy for East Asia. As we have seen, the Americans had been secretly debating the need for a new East Asian policy for months. But this was the first revelation of the direction of the new policy.

Reston's article outlined the new U.S. strategy as one that was trying to "widen the breach" between Stalin and Mao, and it noted that Washington would now have to distance itself from Taiwan. This indicated that Washington hoped that Mao might go the way of Tito, the Yugoslav leader who had defected from the Soviet bloc in 1948. Reston also noted that U.S. leaders were considering ways to stop communism in Southeast Asia and would likely sign a treaty with Japan that would give the United States military bases on Japanese soil.[35] Perhaps even more disturbingly, it appeared that the United States would allow Japan to remilitarize as part of the deal. Next to Reston's piece was another front-page article on General MacArthur's New Years' Day address to the Japanese people. MacArthur indicated that with Soviet communism on the rampage, the Japanese people could not be expected to accept complete disarmament.[36] Overall, the trend was not reassuring. As yet another *Times* article that day opined, it seemed clear that the United States was embarking on "a more vigorous Oriental policy," with Japan as a critical link in the new chain.[37]

Such news, given past Japanese aggression against both China and Russia, would have been enough to push the Soviets to quickly change direction and agree to a Soviet-Chinese alliance. Such an alliance would keep China in the Soviet fold and help to deter any American attacks launched from future bases in Japan.[38] Supporting this interpretation is the fact that there were no other changes in U.S. or Chinese behavior between late December and January 2 that could explain such a dramatic and risky shift in Soviet behavior. By the process of elimination, therefore, we can say with fair confidence that it was Stalin's fearful reaction to the *New York Times*' revelations that provoked the policy change.

Yet if Stalin was only reacting defensively, then the Acheson speech on January 12 still seems like a puzzle for any theory emphasizing Soviet security concerns: if South Korea was placed outside of the U.S. defense perimeter on January 12, then why would the Soviets worry about this tiny nation? It now seems clear, however, that the Soviets did not even know that Korea was outside the perimeter when they were making their key policy decisions in mid-January. Since the text of the Acheson speech was not released for eleven days, Moscow had to rely on American press reporting, with the *New York Times* once again being the best source. The *Times* article on January 13 covering the speech mainly focused on Acheson's charges of Russian imperialism in East Asia, specifically against China. Russia, Acheson argued, was trying to annex four northern areas of China, an act that must bring upon the Russians "the hatred and righteous anger of the Chinese people." Such provocative statements supported the *Times*' January 1 report that Acheson and Truman were seeking to divide China from Russia.

The article later briefly covered Acheson's discussion of a "defense perimeter" running through Japan and the Philippines. Acheson noted that with regard to other parts of Asia, "no person can guarantee these areas against military attack." After North Korea's attack on June 25, such lines were used by critics and later historians to argue that Acheson had given Moscow a green light for invasion.[39] Yet Acheson in his speech went on to emphasize that should any area outside the perimeter be attacked, reliance would be on the people attacked to resist and upon "the commitments of the entire civilized world under the Charter of the United Nations." In short, even if the Soviets had believed that the Korean peninsula was placed outside the perimeter, this statement would have raised a red flag: at this time the Americans dominated the U.N., often using it to promote U.S. interests in Korea.[40] To say the U.N. would resist any aggression was close to saying, from Moscow's point of view, that the United States was committed to Korea.[41]

But here is the real shocker: the *Times* mistakenly reported Acheson as saying that "in the southern part of Asia, unlike Japan or Korea," America was just one of many nations who would provide assistance through the above U.N. mechanism. Thus, according to the *Times*, South Korea was actually *inside* the defense perimeter![42] *Times* reporters continued to hold to this position through the winter and spring of 1950, even after the complete text of the speech was released.[43]

A detailed record of the conversation between Molotov, Foreign Minister Vysinsky, and Mao on January 17 shows that the Soviets did indeed have a very different impression of the Acheson speech than is commonly supposed. Not only did Molotov and Vysinsky make no mention of the defense perimeter or Korea, they were totally preoccupied with Acheson's hostile remarks on Russian imperialism. Mao said he was puzzled by the speech: was it a "smoke-screen" to allow the United States to occupy Taiwan? Molotov replied that "the Americans [were] trying, with the help of slander and deception, to create misunderstandings" between Russia and China. He asked Mao to denounce the speech as an "insult" to China. Mao agreed to do so.[44] The Russian fear that Washington might detach China from the Soviet bloc, as it had with Yugoslavia in 1948, is tangible. It is thus not surprising that Stalin on January 22 made another concession, telling the Chinese that he would jettison the 1945 agreements that were so distasteful to the Chinese leadership (the ones giving Russia joint control of the northern railways and a port on the Liaotung peninsula).

Acheson's strategy had thus backfired: instead of drawing China away from Moscow, the secretary's comments had led to a Russian-Chinese alliance and increased suspicions of U.S. intentions. The Korean peninsula now had more direct salience for all involved. Back in April 1949, Kim Il Sung had made his first appeal to Stalin to support a North Korean attack on the south. Stalin had rejected the idea, telling the North Koreans "that they need [to exercise] caution."[45] The Soviets did agree to provide economic and military aid, but they pushed the North Koreans to achieve a victory through subversion, not direct attack. In September 1949, Kim again asked for the go-ahead, admitting that success through a southern insurgency was now unlikely. He was again told to exercise caution, given the risks of drawing the Americans into a war, and to keep trying to make subversion work.[46]

Through the winter of 1949–50, the South Koreans completed their annihilation of the insurgency in the south. Then on February 9, after strong appeals from the White House, the U.S. Congress approved another $60 million in U.S. economic aid for South Korea in addition to the $60 million already earmarked for the country.[47] On March 7, President Truman asked Congress for another $100 million for South Korea for fiscal year 1951, starting July 1, 1950. Translated into current dollars, these were clearly significant injections of aid: the equivalent of approximately $1.5 billion in contemporary dollars by July 1, 1950, and another $1.2 billion thereafter. Acheson told the Senate Foreign Relations Committee in early March that this aid was a "symbol of what we can do" for nations seeking democracy. He added that it would also have "a very great effect" on Southeast Asia. Moreover, Acheson continued, "it was generally recognized . . . that [America] had 'special responsibilities' in South Korea" due to the 1943 Cairo conference "just as it had [with] Japan."[48]

The U.S. public commitment to South Korea was thus not only strong—it was growing. For a Stalin that doubted North Korea's ability to survive,[49] this could only have suggested one thing: if he continued to deny Kim the right to attack, the south would grow to a point of dominance on the peninsula. It had twice the north's population, and with U.S. economic help it would surely overtake the north in the long term. Yet in the short term, according to Kim's assurances and embassy reports, the north had significant military superiority. As historian Charles Armstrong relates, in Kim's view South Korea "was vulnerable at the moment but might be more formidable in the future" and thus needed to be defeated now.[50]

By mid-March, Stalin made up his mind. On March 18 he wrote Kim directly to tell him he could now fully satisfy Kim's request for the arms and technical equipment needed for an attack on the south. A few days later, Stalin agreed to meet Kim in Moscow to finalize the details. By mid-April, Kim had his go-ahead from Moscow for the war, pending Mao's approval. A month later he had secured Mao's support, and on June 25 the attack on South Korea began.[51]

The origins of the Korean War thus appear to be quite similar to those of the Berlin crisis of 1948. The Soviets were reacting to the new moves by the Americans to consolidate the U.S. sphere and build up its combined economic and military power. Moscow was acting more out of fear than of a desire for gain or to exploit what they perceived to be a Western weakness. Stalin had been cautious about a North Korean attack from April 1949 onward. But with new evidence that the Americans were poised to increase their military presence in the Far East and were building their sphere's strength through economic aid to such front-line countries as South Korea, the Soviets had to act. In sum, the American fear of a decline in their economic and political sphere should the United States fail to increase its overall commitment to Asia had inadvertently triggered a *Soviet* fear of decline in the key strategic area of the Korean peninsula.

## The Iran and Suez Crises, 1951–56

The Iranian Crisis of 1951–53 and the Suez Crisis of 1955–56 should be considered together. Both superpowers, given the importance of oil, saw the Middle East region as a critical part of the larger postwar geostrategic struggle over the neutral "periphery" (realm two in the language of chapter 1). And unlike the 1947–50 period where both superpowers were focused on consolidating their post-1944 economic power spheres in anticipation of future threats, here specific changes in both dependence levels and trade expectations did play important causal roles in the shaping of U.S. behavior.

There are many commonalities across the two cases. Both crises were fundamentally about the flow of Middle Eastern oil. And as in so many cases, it was the independent actions of small third parties that shaped the calculations of the key great powers. Both Iran and Egypt were led by nationalistic leaders bent on gaining control over something of significant value to an American ally: in the Iranian case, the British-owned Anglo-Iranian Oil Company; and in the Egyptian case, the British-dominated Suez Canal Company. Moreover, in both cases there were worries that Soviet ties to the key leaders in power might permit Moscow ultimately to deny the United States access to the region and to its most important producer, Saudi Arabia. Finally, when the crises reached their heights in 1953 and 1956, respectively, the United States was led by the same individual, Dwight D. Eisenhower, who was supported by almost the exact same set of advisors, including Secretary of State John Foster Dulles.

Yet despite these similarities, American responses to the two crises were radically different. In the Iranian case, Eisenhower authorized a coup against the government. In August 1953, a military general with active Central Intelligence Agency (CIA) support overthrew the Iranian leader Mohammed Mossadeq and an authoritarian regime was installed that would work with the mercurial Iranian monarch, Reza Mohammed Shah. This risky move could have easily sparked a larger superpower escalation. As I will show, however, it was taken because it seemed less dangerous than letting the situation decline further. In the Egyptian case, Eisenhower's behavior was much more moderate. He rejected any covert effort to overthrow Nasser and the Egyptian government, and he took a strong stance against any military intervention by Britain or France or Israel—the states most keen on using force. When these three states did in fact attack Egypt in late October–early November of 1956, Eisenhower applied economic sanctions so devastating that Britain and France soon ended their occupation of Egyptian territory.

What explains why the U.S. government would adopt such different stances to deal with two seemingly similar problems? To my knowledge, there is no political science work that compares the two cases on this question. And while historians of U.S. Middle East policy have covered these crises thoroughly, they typically treat them separately and thus fail to answer the posed question. I show that differing trade expectations for the future, filtered through the fear of Soviet encroachments in the region, explain the differing U.S. responses across the cases. In both instances, U.S. elites were wary of overreacting to the nationalizations undertaken by the particular governments of the time. They worried that a strong response in support of Britain would only fuel anti-Western hatred, hurting the U.S. position just as Moscow was posing as the champion of "anti-imperialist forces" around the world. In Iran, however, the domestic situation was in chaos by 1952 as British oil sanctions devastated the Iranian economy. By the end of the Truman administration and the beginning of Eisenhower's presidency, there was a tangible fear that if the United States did not act, the country would fall to Iranian communists already aligned with Moscow. With Iran and its oil under their control, the Soviets would be poised to go after other regional actors whose oil went largely to the United States and continental Europe. Given this threat, Eisenhower chose to implement a plan for Mossadeq's overthrow first discussed in the waning days of Truman's presidency.

In the Egyptian case, in contrast, there was never any serious risk that the communists would seize control of the government. Egypt's president, Gamal Abdel Nasser, was certainly viewed as an unpredictable leader who employed Arab nationalism to build his domestic and regional popularity. But there was no evidence that Egyptian communists were strong enough to overthrow him. Indeed, despite accepting military and economic aid from the Soviet bloc, he had successfully repressed the Communist Party at home. When Britain began pushing for military action to counter Nasser's announced nationalization of the Suez Company, therefore, Eisenhower saw the risks of such action as much greater than any benefits. A British-led attack or coup effort would greatly enflame Arab sentiments across the Middle East, and if the United States was seen to support such moves, its reputation would be greatly damaged. Moreover, Nasser was acting moderately: he offered to compensate the Europeans for the nationalization of the Suez Company; assured the world that the canal would be kept open; and in September proved that Egypt could pilot ships through the canal without European help. In short, from Eisenhower's point of view, Nasser did not pose a threat to European or American oil, even if the president and his secretary of state personally disliked the man and what he stood for.

The British strongly disagreed with Eisenhower's assessment and believed that the threat to trade was high. Yet Eisenhower saw more clearly than the British that Nasser had every interest in keeping trade flowing—especially since he needed the canal's revenue to fund his Aswan Dam project. The Egyptian situation in 1956 was therefore quite different from Iran in 1953, where the threat to the resources of the region was very real indeed. Different expectations of future trade across the two cases explain nicely the different postures assumed. As we will see, both standard realism and commercial liberalism fail to explain either case, let alone the variation between them. Contrary to realists who argue that dependence always provides an incentive to use war to reduce vulnerability,[52] the United States was dependent in both cases, yet it acted only in Iran, and only when things got bad. And U.S. behavior was propelled by security fears, not the unit-level factors liberals propose.

The U.S. postwar obsession with the Middle East can be traced to Roosevelt's concern in 1943–44 about growing energy dependence and the renewed Russian interest in the region.[53] Iran of course had been a problem in 1946 when the Soviets refused to withdraw their troops until they had secured an oil concession. After India's independence in 1947, the impending collapse of European imperial influence around the world foreshadowed an ominous new chapter in the superpower competition. In September 1948, the CIA distributed its first major analysis of this new situation. The opening paragraphs sketched the logic that would guide U.S. thinking across the so-called Third World for the next three decades. The breakup of the colonial system had "major implications for U.S. security, particularly in terms of possible world conflict with the U.S.S.R." If the United States did not play its cards right, it could easily be "[deprived of] assured access to vital bases and raw materials in these areas." The Soviet Union, as a noncolonial and newly industrializing power, was effectively positioned to "champion the [anti]colonial cause," meaning that emerging states might align with Moscow, "adversely affect[ing] the present [East-West] power balance."[54]

Given this new reality, Washington had to act carefully with regard to growing Middle East nationalism or else it would be seen as "just another imperialist power." In 1948–49, major Middle East oil producers, including Iran and Saudi Arabia, began to renegotiate agreements with foreign multinationals to increase their share of oil profits. In July 1949, Teheran and London's Anglo-Iranian Oil Company negotiated an initial deal seen by most Iranians as falling far short of Iranian demands. The Majlis (Parliament) refused to ratify the agreement. In June 1950, the issue was referred to a special committee chaired by Mossadeq, the leader of the National Front, a coalition of nationalist groups. In November, the committee repudiated the agreement, announcing that only nationalization would secure Iran's interests as a sovereign nation.[55]

The Truman administration was deeply concerned that a British refusal to accept even limited nationalization would cause unrest that Moscow could exploit via the communist Tudeh Party. A July 1950 memorandum to Truman from R. H. Hillenkoetter, the CIA director, stated the problem starkly. Soviet forces on the border with Iran were "in a position to overrun Iran without warning." Should things get worse and Tudeh assume power, the Soviets would gain access to Iran's great oil resources and be positioned to penetrate the rest of the Middle East and the Indian subcontinent.[56] And things did indeed begin to deteriorate. Prime Minister Ali Razmara, who had supported a go-slow approach, was assassinated on March 7, 1951. Eight days later, the Majlis voted to nationalize the Anglo-Iranian Oil Company. On April 28, Mossadeq was chosen as Iran's new prime minister and three days after that the new law went into effect with the shah's approval.[57] London rejected the nationalization, kicking the crisis into high gear.

Truman's position over his last two years in office remained consistent. Britain should accept nationalization to avert unrest that might bring the communists to power, but Iran should provide adequate compensation for British losses as well as assurances that British and U.S. oil companies could still sell Iranian oil around the world. A January 1951 National Intelligence Estimate noted that if Middle East oil were cut off, not only would the United States suffer "substantial rationing" but Western Europe would have its industrial expansion halted, leading to "profound changes" in its economic structure.[58] The latter implication was of particular concern, given that Washington's primary goal since 1944 had been to stabilize Western Europe to prevent it from going communist.

Through the summer of 1951, Truman attempted to broker a deal between Iran and Britain via envoy Averell Harriman, but London and Teheran remained intransigent. Churchill's return to power in October only made things worse. Exports of Iranian oil had already fallen off, but Churchill acted to ensure Iran could not sell oil to non-British oil companies. By year's end, a total blockade of Iranian oil was in place. This would have an absolutely devastating impact on the Iranian economy through 1952 and into 1953.

The Truman administration was now caught between a rock and a hard place. Through 1952, Truman would continue his efforts to broker a British-Iranian agreement. The diplomatic discussions went nowhere, however, and Iran continued its descent into domestic chaos. In August 1952, Secretary of Defense Lovett began a push for a dramatic change in policy. The British no longer had clout in the region, he argued, and the United States had to step in and accept additional political, economic, and military commitments if Iran was to be prevented from going communist.[59] By the fall of 1952 Acheson and Truman, fed up with British and Iranian intransigence, came around to Lovett's point of view. When the two met with president-elect Eisenhower on November 18, Iran was second on the agenda. Acheson told Eisenhower that both the British and the Iranians were being "wholly unreasonable," and their standoff had led to the "very grave disintegration" of Iran's political structure. The British were too caught up in their own selfish concerns to see the broader issues at stake. Acheson vaguely stated that he and Truman were therefore "going forward under the President's authority to consider what [Washington] alone might do to solve the problem."[60]

What Acheson did not tell Eisenhower is that the State Department was already gearing up to implement Lovett's radical shift in policy—one that would leave no options off the table, including military force. The day after meeting Eisenhower, Truman and his National Security Council sat down to discuss the Korean and Iranian situations. The Defense Department's deputy secretary, filling in for Lovett, told Truman that it was now necessary for the United States "to proceed unilaterally to get Iranian oil flowing again and to get Iran back on our side." While he hoped that nonmilitary measures would work, his department had already reached tentative conclusions on the feasibility of military options.[61] The next day, an NSC document on Iran, NSC 136/1, was issued for Truman's approval. The loss of Iran to the Soviet bloc, it contended, would allow Moscow to seriously threaten Middle Eastern oil. Thus, if communists tried to seize power, the United States should support the noncommunist side via actions that included "military support." Planning for a cover operation began that November through contacts with the British government, such that by the first month of Eisenhower's administration, London and Washington had agreed on the details of a coup plot and had selected Teddy Roosevelt's grandson, Kermit Roosevelt, to oversee its implementation.[62]

The deteriorating situation in Iran and the threat to oil had, by the end of the Truman administration, caused it to shift toward risky military and subversive options. While everyone still hoped that the problem could be solved without war, the final section of NSC 136/1 showed the true seriousness of the problem. Should the Soviets move forces into Iran, Washington would have to assume that "global war is probably imminent." It would then have to "[take] action against the aggressor . . . in the manner which would best contribute to the security of the United States."[63] With the oil resources of not just Iran but the whole of the Middle East at stake, the United States was ready to go to war should Moscow seek to muscle its way into the region.

The end of the story can be told in short order. Even before Eisenhower came into office on January 20, 1953, he was already actively working on a solution to the Iranian problem.[64] London and Washington had a coup plan in place by February. By early March, it was clear that even if Mossadeq managed to hold onto power, he could only do so with Tudeh support.[65] At an NSC meeting on March 4, Dulles told Eisenhower that if Iran succumbed to communism, "there was little doubt that in short order the other areas of the Middle East, with some 60% of the world's oil reserves, would fall into Communist control." The talk around the table was extremely pessimistic. The secretary of the treasury asked Dulles if he already believed that Iran would go communist. Dulles replied affirmatively, prompting Eisenhower to argue that U.S. forces could be moved into neighboring states. The risks were obvious. If the United States was compelled to move forces into Iran itself, Eisenhower noted, Moscow would invoke its 1921 treaty of alliance and friendship, and "then we would find ourselves at war with Russia." Yet if the United States failed to act, he "feared that the United States would descend to the status of a second-rate power."[66]

In April, a million dollars was sent to CIA operatives in Teheran to bring about Mossadeq's fall. In mid-July Kermit Roosevelt entered Iran from Iraq to finalize the organization of "Operation Ajax." Street demonstrations in mid-August were going in Mossadeq's favor, and the shah fled the country. But on August 18–19, with CIA help, General Fazlollah Zahedi was able to arrest

Mossadeq and assume control of the state. The shah returned triumphantly to Iran, and the Soviets wisely chose not to contest the outcome. Within two years a consortium made up of U.S., British, and Dutch multinational oil companies agreed to share profits with Iran's nationalized oil company, thereby paralleling similar recent deals with other key oil producing states, including Saudi Arabia.[67]

The Iranian crisis was resolved without an escalation to regional war, or worse. Yet both the Truman and Eisenhower administrations were willing to risk such an escalation to prevent Moscow from gaining a foothold in the Middle East. Third-party instability had created a situation where a negotiated solution had become highly unlikely. Declining expectations of future trade, tied to the West's now high dependence on Middle East oil, drove the increasingly severe policies of both presidents. With dependence levels constant, traditional realism cannot explain the variation in U.S. behavior. Liberalism cannot explain U.S. leaders' risk-taking behavior during a period of high dependence, or the fact that security objectives were predominant. That the world avoided a war has more to do with Soviet caution, perhaps facilitated by Stalin's death in March 1953, than with U.S. restraint. Truman and Eisenhower were preparing themselves for a big fight, and economic fears for the future were determinative.

The Suez Crisis of 1955–56 mirrors the above, with the United States again finding itself in a crisis because of Britain's unwillingness to accept the loss of a Middle Eastern asset. On June 26, 1956, President Nasser announced the nationalization of the Suez Canal Company, the organization that had run the canal for almost seventy years. The British government under Prime Minister Anthony Eden instantly began to organize a military response, drawing into its plan the governments of France and Israel. Some two-thirds of all the oil Britain and Western Europe consumed passed through the canal. The British were worried that if they allowed Nasser to grab the waterway, not only would Britain's economy suffer, but its regional position would deteriorate rapidly.[68] Eisenhower tried to restrain Eden from taking military action, but Eden was hellbent on safeguarding European control of the canal. When the Israelis launched a preventive attack on October 29, 1956, British and French forces invaded the canal zone soon after. With the Soviet bloc supplying arms to Nasser through Czechoslovakia, Premier Khrushchev felt obliged to hint that Britain and France might be hit by Russian nuclear strikes should they refuse to retreat. In late November, London and Paris did decide to end their occupation. But the deeper reason for their exit was not Russian nuclear coercion, but instead the economic devastation created by Eisenhower's refusal to send Latin American oil to Europe or to support their rapidly falling currencies. As with Iran in 1953, however, the situation was a highly dangerous one. A misstep by each side—say, a U.S. decision to support Britain's use of force, followed by a Soviet decision to deploy conventional forces in the area—could have easily spiraled into a full-scale superpower confrontation.

The question before us is why Eisenhower chose such a moderate stance in this crisis despite the apparent challenge to the economic health of the Western world. Eisenhower and his secretary of state were indeed concerned about developments in Egypt after a military coup in July 1952 overthrew King Farouk and put a regime of generals in his place. Colonel Nasser emerged as the sole leader by early 1954, and then proceeded over the next two years to establish an image as the head of pan-Arab nationalism and a driving force behind the so-called nonaligned movement. For Eisenhower and Dulles, nonalignment in a struggle of such importance as the Cold War was more than mere nuisance; it was seen as a betrayal of the U.S. cause. Nevertheless, the stakes were too high to simply write Nasser off. By February 1955, the new Soviet politburo (now known as the presidium) under the leadership of Khrushchev and Nikolai Bulgarin was determined to increase Soviet influence in the south. Moscow began an "economic offensive" (so named by Washington) to draw away key Third World states through the promise of aid and trade. Moscow's initial focus was on newly independent states in Asia, including India, Burma, and Indonesia. But in mid-1955, Khrushchev and Bulgarin turned their attention to Egypt as the one major Arab state that was not in the clutches of either Washington or London.

An Israeli attack on the Egyptian-controlled Gaza Strip in early 1955, combined with Britain's formation of the Central Treaty Organization, convinced Nasser of the need to increase Egypt's military strength. In September 1955, he shocked the Western world by announcing a major arms purchase from Czechoslovakia. The U.S. government was worried, but unlike the Israelis and British, still believed that Nasser was a rational leader who would keep his radical nationalism within bounds. Moreover, Eisenhower and Dulles thought they had much bigger fish to fry: as long as Nasser continued to repress communism within Egypt and did not directly threaten commercial access through the canal, he could be tolerated. Seeing that Nasser was setting Moscow against Washington to get the best deal, Eisenhower decided to play the game. When the Egyptian leader signaled that he wanted massive foreign funding for the building of the Aswan Dam in southern Egypt, Washington was supportive. In December, Dulles indicated that the U.S. government would provide a substantial loan to supplement what the U.S.-dominated World Bank had already offered.

By that point, the United States' Cold War strategy had undergone a visible shift in focus. Until late 1955, the series of Basic National Security Policy papers that oriented U.S. foreign policy had still placed primary emphasis on the strategic military struggle and competition over Europe. On October 3, though, the State Department distributed a memorandum arguing for a new policy direction. Because the Soviets saw general war as irrational, they were now concentrating on the "non-military competition" in the developing world, especially in the Middle East and Latin America. To counter this, Washington had to increase efforts to foster economic growth in these areas.[69] This new view of the Cold War competition would be incorporated into the revisions of the Basic National Security Policy document undertaken over the winter and approved on March 15, 1956.[70]

We can thus see why Eisenhower and Dulles became so keen to maintain relations with Nasser in late 1955 to early 1956, notwithstanding his pan-Arab nationalism and purchase of Soviet bloc arms. Unfortunately, Nasser played his hand too hard: he was unwilling to make peace with Israel, continued his buildup, and signaled that he would turn to Moscow for economic aid should Washington continue to hold up U.S. and World Bank assistance for the Aswan Dam project. His recognition of Communist China and announcement of a new arms deal with Poland in May 1956 were the final straws. NSC and State Department officials now agreed that the carrot of U.S. and World Bank money could not dissuade Egypt from aligning more closely with the Soviet bloc. On June 19, Dulles told the Egyptians that the United States could not supply aid for the dam, nor would it encourage the World Bank to do so. A week later, on June 26, Nasser announced the canal's nationalization in a highly charged speech in Alexandria, noting that the money raised through transit fees would be used to fund the dam.[71]

Nasser's move took Eisenhower by surprise. On the morning of Friday, July 27, Eisenhower held an emergency meeting with CIA Director Allen Dulles and Undersecretary of State Herbert Hoover Jr (Secretary of State Dulles being out of town). Hoover argued that Nasser's move violated international law and might result in interference with the canal through which two-thirds of Middle Eastern oil passed. Eisenhower agreed, stating that "we and many others have a concern over [the canal's] operations," and Washington should issue a statement that it viewed the matter "with grave concern."[72] Soon after the meeting, Eisenhower received a letter from Prime Minister Eden, emphasizing that Egypt was incapable of running the canal and Britain was developing a military plan to counter the threat to the European economy.[73]

Eisenhower called Hoover back to the White House late that afternoon to discuss the letter. Hoover declared that the United States must move strongly or face a decline in the "whole Western position." Eisenhower, still feeling his way toward his own position, stated that the situation was so troubling that Congress might need to be called back from summer recess. Its leaders should be told that "this development has the most serious implications for the

Western world. If the movement of oil were interfered with, or if the pipelines were cut, we would be faced with a critical situation."[74] That afternoon, Eisenhower sent a vague reply to Eden, telling him that he agreed with many of Eden's points, but that other steps should be considered first, including consultation with affected maritime nations.[75] Eisenhower's initial posture was to slow down British decision-making to give diplomacy a chance, even as he kept the military option on the table. Over the next two days, however, as the costs of military action rose and the risks of not acting began to appear slight, his view moderated substantially. Critical to Eisenhower's moderate stance by late July was his understanding that Nasser's action was not only legal but also that the Egyptians were signaling they would keep the canal open and operating efficiently.

On Friday, a State Department legal advisor had written a memorandum underscoring that Nasser's nationalization decree agreed to provide compensation at full market value prior to the decree to the canal's European investors.[76] At a meeting the next morning (July 28), Eisenhower was informed that Egypt had agreed to abide by the 1888 convention guaranteeing states free use of the canal. Undersecretary Hoover also noted that Admiral Arleigh Burke, the Joint Chiefs of Staff's chief of naval operations, had said that piloting ships through the canal was not as difficult an operation as had been previously reported. The president summarized the costs and risks of the two main options. It would not be difficult for Western states to retake the canal militarily. Yet there was no real basis for such action in terms of global public opinion. Accordingly, he agreed with the State Department that Egypt "was within its rights, and that until its operation of the Canal was proven incompetent, unjust, etc. there was nothing to do."[77]

Hoover quickly tried to back away from such an interpretation of State Department briefings, saying that he felt action was necessary or else the Western position would be gravely undercut. But the president had now arrived at a policy logic that he would hold onto for the remainder of the crisis. The impact on global and especially Middle East public opinion of any form of Western military action would be huge. Even if only the British acted, the United States would be excused of aiding and abetting old-style European imperialism against a developing nation that was acting within its legal rights to reclaim an important national asset. And if the Egyptians were not only willing to keep the canal open, but also proved themselves more than capable of piloting the ships, then what was the real concern? Nasser was certainly a firebrand nationalist, but he had good self-interested reasons in keeping the canal open to maximize revenue for his Aswan project. As Eisenhower summarized his thinking in late July, the weight of world opinion was that Nasser had a legal right to nationalize the canal, and this right "could scarcely be doubted" as long as just compensation were provided. "The main issue at stake, therefore, was whether or not Nasser would and could keep the waterway open for the traffic of all nations, in accordance with the [convention] of 1888," Eisenhower continued, and "This question could not be answered except through test."[78]

Everything that happened over the next two months only reinforced for Eisenhower that the British were foolish in pushing for war and that an American "do-nothing" policy was in fact the best of many distasteful options. A telegram from the U.S. ambassador in Cairo arrived on July 30, describing his conversation with Nasser. Nasser emphasized that he had only taken the action to finance the dam, and that he would have greatly preferred direct aid from the United States and World Bank. The ambassador replied that Washington's key concern was whether the canal would remain open for international use. Nasser reassured the ambassador that he was committed to the canal's openness and had affirmed this in his recent declarations.[79]

This information may have helped Eisenhower relax somewhat, but his own military was proving a problem. The Joint Chiefs of Staff had submitted a study on July 28 specifying three options, from diplomatic support for British military action to actual U.S. military participation.[80] At a long White House meeting on the morning of July 31, the president and his advisors were told that Eden had taken a firm decision to initiate hostilities to "break Nasser," probably after six weeks of preparation. Eisenhower opened the discussion by saying that this was an unwise decision that was out of touch with present circumstances in the developing world. He and CIA Director Dulles agreed that precipitous action would cause the whole Arab world to unite against the West, Middle East oil would "dry up," and the United States would have to divert oil to Europe, leading to rationing at home. Admiral Burke adopted the opposite view, arguing that it was the Joint Chiefs' opinion that Nasser must indeed be broken, and that if diplomacy failed and Britain used force, Washington should support its action. The president gave no ground. Convinced that the British were making a deep error, he asked Dulles to go to London to explain his view. Asked what would happen if this caused a split between London and Washington, Eisenhower agreed that this would be a serious development, although "not as serious as letting a war start and not trying to stop it."[81]

Later that day, a Special National Intelligence Estimate on the crisis was issued that supported Eisenhower's reasoning. While Nasser was committed to reducing Western influence in the Middle East, his decision to nationalize the canal was apparently taken on short notice in reaction to Washington's decision not to fund the Aswan Dam. But the action was legal, and should Egypt fulfill its promise to abide by current rules and practices, there would be "little basis for legal action by the using powers."[82] This seemed to seal it for Eisenhower. He immediately wrote Eden, telling him that despite the canal's importance, concerned nations could exert enough pressure on Egypt that assure "the efficient operation of the Canal . . . [into] the future." The canal's openness and efficiency were the key issues, not who controlled it, Eisenhower stressed. Then came his warning. If the British went ahead with military action, "the American reaction would be severe," and most of the world would share that reaction.[83]

The events of August to November can be covered in short order, given that Eisenhower never wavered from his fundamental position that a British-led attack on the canal zone would be disastrous for both Britain and the United States. He held to this in spite of the arguments of his advisors, including at times Secretary Dulles, that British action should be given at least implicit support.[84] In mid-August and again in mid-September, two separate multiparty conferences were held in London to try to coordinate the key maritime nations' response. The British were adamant that an international consortium of non-Egyptian states should assume control of the canal zone. During the August meeting, Eisenhower told Dulles, who was acting as U.S. envoy, that the group should not adopt a position that was impossible for Nasser to accept. Thus, instead of having an international board assume operational control of the canal, it should have merely a "supervisory" role.[85] This suggestion, similar to Moscow's proposal, was summarily rejected by the British negotiators. After an eighteen to four vote in favor of the British position, Australian prime minister Robert Menzies travelled to Cairo with what amounted to an ultimatum: Egypt had to accept international control of the canal or face attack. As Eisenhower had predicted, Nasser rejected the terms as incompatible with Egypt's sovereign rights. A follow-up conference of the Western states in mid-September proved equally fruitless. The conference focused on Dulles's new proposal for a Suez Canal Users Association, a loose organization that would coordinate the flow of traffic through the canal, collect tolls, and pay Egypt its fair share of the revenues. Despite majority agreement in favor of this plan, it too was dead in the water, given lukewarm British support and Egyptian resistance.[86]

Eisenhower himself saw little value in the Suez Canal Users Association by the end of the month. And yet he was still resolute in his opposition to the use of force. The events of September 14 proved to be decisive here. That day, London and Paris ordered their canal pilots to leave the canal zone, hoping that this would expose the inability of Egypt to operate the canal. Over the next seven days, Egyptian pilots stepped in to guide 254 vessels safely through the canal—a new one-week record. This achievement not only showed the hollowness of the British and French arguments for action but also verified that Egypt was more than capable of running the canal by itself.[87] Eisenhower in his memoirs states his reaction in no uncertain terms:

> As it [turned] out, not only were the Egyptian officials and workmen competent to operate the Canal, but they [demonstrated] that they could do so under conditions of increased traffic and with increased efficiency ... The assumption upon which the Users Association was largely based proved groundless. Furthermore, any thought of using force, under these circumstances, was almost ridiculous.[88]

Positive trade expectations were playing their anticipated causal role. Eisenhower had no reason to push for force if the Egyptians were perfectly willing and able to keep commerce flowing through the canal zone and had every rational reason, including the funding of the Aswan Dam, for wanting to keep the toll revenues flowing in. British fears of a cut-off might be driving them into war, but these worries were simply irrational from Eisenhower's perspective; they had no basis in fact, as the events of September 14–21 showed. Yet if London did go ahead, and if Washington was seen to be supporting such holdovers from a dying imperialist era, the U.S. position in the Middle East and around the world would suffer a dramatic decline.

Hence when Israel, Britain, and France ignored his warnings and entered the canal zone in late October–early November, Eisenhower knew that he had to stand symbolically against the "aggressors." The United States and the Soviet Union, for the first time since the founding of Israel, stood together in the United Nations and condemned the attacks. Washington's subsequent unwillingness to provide oil to Western Europe or to support the British and French currencies signaled to the world that European imperialism would no longer be tolerated and that the United States stood on the side of progress in the developing world.

The trade expectations logic does a solid job explaining U.S. moderation in the Suez Crisis. Unlike Iran in 1953, there was little fear of communism taking over in Egypt and little fear that the nationalist government in power would restrict the flow of oil. Traditional realists cannot explain this moderation in the face of America's high and growing dependence on Middle East oil. And they certainly cannot explain the variation in U.S. behavior across the Iran and Suez cases. Liberals and neo-Marxists could at best try to explain the moderation in 1956 through the fear of a widening war that might lead to even greater costs to U.S. multinational oil firms and to the American lifestyle back home. But the documents show Eisenhower carefully calculating the risks of Nasser severing oil traffic through the Suez Canal in terms of the larger issue of national security and the Cold War struggle. In addition, he was more than willing to assume large risks of superpower war in 1953 given the implications for the United States of losing access to oil. We can thus safely conclude that it was strategic dependence tied to trade expectations that drove his decision-making, not domestic-level concerns.

## Conclusion

This chapter has covered the main crises of the first decade of the Cold War era. By examining the periods prior to the crises themselves, we can identify the changes in causal variables that pushed leaders to shift to more hard-line policies that increased the risk of war through unintended escalation. We can also isolate the factors that caused superpower leaders to dampen down the risks of escalation for crises that were largely the result of third-party actions. The trade expectations aspect of dynamic realism proved particularly useful in explaining the differences between American actions in 1950–53 over Iran versus in 1955–56 over Egypt and the Suez Canal. Washington's behavior in reaction to the Iranian nationalization of the oil industry was ultimately far more hard-line than its behavior in reaction to Nasser's takeover of the Suez Canal, even though both potentially threatened the West's access to Middle East oil. Trade expectations had become quite pessimistic in the Iranian case, given the growing fear of a successful communist revolution in Iran. In the Suez case, however, U.S. trade expectations were more positive: Nasser's ability and willingness to allow trade to continue to flow through the canal convinced Eisenhower that there was little real threat to Western oil interests.

The trade expectations logic was not driving Stalin's decision-making regarding Berlin in 1948 and Korea in 1950. It was Washington's effort to strengthen Western Europe through currency reforms that would unify the West German economy that led Moscow to fear the rise of a strong western German state. And it was the United States' strategy of revitalizing the South Korean economy as it consolidated its position in the Far East that helped convince Stalin to support Kim's plan to unify the Korean peninsula by force. Stalin's perceptions of decline were key, but in neither case was East-West trade itself shaping those perceptions. Yet concerns about declining future trade can explain the Americans' decisions after 1947 to build up their spheres in Western Europe and East Asia in the first place—including the shift to military aid to Vietnam in 1950. In short, we see an action-reaction cycle occurring in the 1947 to 1950 period that was ultimately deeply rooted in trade and economics. Since the British pullback from global politics and the announcement of the Truman Doctrine, the Americans had felt an increasing need to strengthen their realm-two economic power spheres in Europe and Asia to protect them from ongoing communist subversion. But the anticipated success of these efforts caused the Soviets to believe that *their* bloc's relative position would decline over the long term unless something dramatic was done. And of course, communist bloc actions in 1948 and 1950 only solidified in the American mind that the ideological and political-economic differences between the two sides were so severe that the United States must do everything possible to prevent the rise of Russian and now Chinese communist power. Cold War mistrust and hostility would ratchet up to a new level of intensity after June 1950.[89] And this would make it even harder to use trade as a tool to foster peace.

Overall, the chapter has shown how concerns about developments outside of a great power's immediate realm can push leaders into more risky and provocative policies. Even if Soviet moves in 1948 and 1950 were not about commercial flows per se, they were very much tied to the larger competition for economic power spheres and the fear that the other great power was winning the competition for allies and trading partners. As we will see in the next chapter, efforts to improve the prospects of future trade and investment between spheres can, under certain conditions, help adversaries to dampen this baseline drive to expand their power spheres, and even bring about an end to a dangerous rivalry. And this can occur even when cultural differences between states, including ideological and religious worldviews, remain quite strong. The need for trade and technology to consolidate one's economic power can lead even a state like communist Russia to seek expanded commercial ties in exchange for a greater willingness to accept the status quo.

# 9

# Trade Expectations and the Struggles to End the Cold War, 1957–91

THE PERIOD from 1957 to 1962 is probably the most puzzling of the Cold War. On the one hand, it contained the two most frightening moments of the Cold War era, and perhaps of world history: the Berlin Crisis of 1961 and the Cuban Missile Crisis of 1962. In both crises, particularly the latter, the world teetered on the brink of thermonuclear war, a war that would have wiped out hundreds of millions of people and perhaps destroyed Western civilization. On the other hand, by the mid-1950s both sides understood the horrors of nuclear war and were actively seeking ways to reduce tensions, to increase trust, and to avoid further spirals of arms spending and hostility that might push the superpowers to the edge of the abyss. If the desire for cooperation was there, why did détente not "break out" in the late 1950s or early 1960s? Why did it take until the early 1970s for such a détente to be realized, and why did it prove so ephemeral? Finally, why was a lasting relaxation of superpower tension—a true "end" to the Cold War era—not achieved until the late 1980s?

This chapter will attempt to sketch an initial answer to these important and difficult questions. The answer I propose is a surprising one, at least for liberal and realist scholars who have ignored the role of trade in U.S.-Soviet relations. I argue that by the mid- to late 1950s, Soviet leaders were already beginning to understand that they could not maintain Russia's long-term position in the system unless they were able to gain access both to Western technology and to the raw materials of the so-called Third World. The Soviets needed what the West and the Global South *could* do for their state, even if actual trade was at quite low levels because of America's containment policy. And when dependence is there *in potential*—that is, when actors recognize the large future gains to be had from initiating trade as well as the large costs of continuing to be cut off from that trade—then the expectations of future trade variable of dynamic realism can play a significant role in the shaping of state policy.

This chapter differs from the other chapters in this book. Because liberals who see high trade as peace-inducing and realists who see it, if anything, as war-inducing both agree that when trade has been low for some time it falls out as an important causal variable, there is little point in trying to test my argument about trade expectations against their arguments. My goal is simply to demonstrate the surprising empirical impact of changing trade expectations on great power behavior *even in environments where trade is largely nonexistent*. I will not try to argue for the superiority of the trade expectations argument versus noneconomic approaches. I accept that there were many noneconomic factors that mattered during the 1957 to 1991 period, especially military power, technology, and differences in ideology. But I will show how expectations of changes in commercial variables at important moments significantly exacerbated the mistrust between Washington and Moscow, increasing the intensity of spiraling tension and the risk of superpower crisis. In ways that have not been explored in the literature, we will see that in the struggle to expand and sustain their economic power spheres, their military and trade concerns interacted with their differences in ideology and political economy to significantly undermine the chances for peace during the 1955 to 1962 period. I will also demonstrate how trade expectations were integral to the unwinding of Cold War hostility, both in the early 1970s and in the 1980s. Rather than trying to show the limits of the noncommercial explanations, as I have in previous chapters, I seek here to add my economic logic to the standard discussions of the Cold War era and to show how trade expectations and each side's need for a strong economic power sphere interacted with noneconomic factors to drive behavior and outcomes.

My argument for the late 1950s/early 1960s is straightforward. By the late 1950s, as in the early 1970s and late 1980s, Soviet leaders were acutely aware of how much they needed trade in technology with the West in order to reenergize economic growth and thus Russia's long-term superpower position. The Eisenhower and Kennedy administrations, however, proved unwilling to offer the Soviet leadership any real hope that U.S.-Soviet trade would increase from its very low level, mainly because of fears that the transfer of technology would only enhance Russia's ability to catch up in overall strategic power. The Soviet leaders were still enthralled with communist ideology and neomercantilist foreign economic policies, and thus Washington had trouble trusting Moscow's future intentions; Khrushchev, while a reformer, was no Gorbachev. Despite an American desire for lessening of tensions in 1957 to 1962, this potent mix of fear of Soviet power and character type also came at a time when neither side could be assured of its second-strike capability. This made it ultimately impossible for Eisenhower or Kennedy to provide the kind of relaxations in trade restrictions that would help Khrushchev in his hour of economic need.

This Soviet pessimism about their economic prospects combined with Soviet fears about growing *American* strategic superiority by early 1961 set the context for the Berlin and Cuban crises of 1961–62. I will not argue that offers of higher trade by Washington would have necessarily averted these two crises. As I have shown elsewhere, both crises were driven by superpower fears of economic and military decline that were not directly tied to trade per se.[1] But the heightened atmosphere of superpower hostility by 1960 to 1962—an atmosphere of deep mistrust that put both great powers on a hair trigger—was indeed strongly shaped by the decisions of Eisenhower and then Kennedy not to give the Soviets what they were asking for: namely, more trade in higher technology goods. These decisions not only led Khrushchev to believe that Washington was determined to undermine his economic reforms—reforms that the Soviet Union needed to sustain long-term growth and thus its position in the system. They also sent a strong signal that the Americans had no true interest in accepting a "peaceful coexistence" between "equal" great powers. From the Soviet perspective, if the Americans were determined to maintain their level of superiority or in fact to increase it, then Moscow had to do everything to prevent decline (as with the exodus of East Germans from East Berlin) and to close strategic gaps where they existed (thus the placing of missiles in Cuba). The counterfactual question is therefore this: had Eisenhower or Kennedy made concrete gestures to convince Moscow that trade would grow significantly in the future—as each of them seriously considered doing—would Khrushchev have been as risk-taking as he was in 1961 and 1962? (Answers to this question will be important to understanding in chapter 10 how U.S. leaders should rationally respond to the rise—or the possible peaking and decline—of modern China.)

The comparison with later periods is instructive. By the early 1970s, and then again in the late 1980s with assured second-strike capability in place, the Americans were prepared to open trade with the Soviet Union as long as Moscow could demonstrate that it had dampened its desire to spread its ideology and economic philosophies around the world, and thus that it would improve its foreign policy behavior.[2] These mutual commitments served to improve expectations on both sides and to reverse the trade-security spiral. As I will show, the détente created by Nixon and Kissinger through "linkage politics" was indeed helping to moderate superpower hostility in the early 1970s. But it was undermined by unanticipated domestic troubles (Watergate and legislative opposition), troubles that undermined Soviet trade expectations once again. This ushered in another decade of Cold War hostility until Mikhail Gorbachev assumed control in 1985. Through a series of costly signals of his moderate character, Gorbachev was able to reduce American fears of relative loss through renewed trade ties. As Ronald Reagan and then George Bush signaled their willingness to commit to higher trade, the Cold War quickly wound down. The trade-security dilemma had been turned from a vicious cycle into a virtuous one. To be sure, positive Soviet trade expectations were not the only thing responsible for the ending of the Cold War. But the evidence shows that without them, given the Soviet obsession with economic decline, little real progress in the reduction of superpower tension could have been made.

## A Lost Opportunity? The Missing Détente of 1957 to 1962

With the formation of Coordinating Committee or CoCom in 1949, the United States, with Western Europe at its side, went beyond mere economic sanctions to adopt a posture of all-out economic warfare against the Eastern bloc.[3] The logic behind this strategy is not hard to figure out: Washington feared that trade would give Russia a huge relative gain within the global power struggle. America had little desire for Russian goods, but the Soviets needed both high- and low-tech Western goods to sustain economic growth. In late 1953/early 1954, proclamations of "peaceful coexistence" emanating from the post-Stalin Soviet leadership started to soften the Western Europeans, who realized that a restoration of traditional East-West ties would provide a needed economic boost now that Marshall Plan aid was petering out. It was none other than Winston Churchill, prime minister of Britain from 1951 to 1955, who argued publicly in February 1954 that "the more trade there is between Great Britain and Soviet Russia and the satellites, the better still will be the chances of our living together in increasing comfort."[4]

By August 1954, Western European leaders convinced the Eisenhower administration to slash the number of products restricted by CoCom by 50 percent. Allied trade with Russia immediately began to recover. Washington, however, chose to continue its almost complete economic embargo on direct U.S.-Soviet trade. To keep the allies happy, Eisenhower again agreed to further relax the CoCom list in 1958. But tight U.S. restrictions on most American exports remained in place, implemented either through embargo legislation or through the unwillingness of the Commerce Department to grant "licenses" to Russian firms seeking to buy supposedly non-embargoed goods. Total U.S. exports to Russia by 1958 had fallen to an almost negligible $7 million by 1959 and would hover between $20 and $45 million until the late 1960s—at a time when British and West German exports to Russia together averaged between seven and eight times this amount.[5]

As we saw in chapter 8, by 1955 U.S. officials had become quite concerned with Moscow's new push for a presence in the Global South, especially in the oil-rich Middle East. Soviet policy was seen, as it was, as part and parcel of an effort to increase the Soviet economic and political sphere of influence even as it undermined the American power sphere. In March 1956 Eisenhower approved a new Basic National Security Policy document (NSC 5602/1) that placed new emphasis on ensuring that so-called Third World states were not lured into the Soviet sphere through offers of trade and aid.[6] In January 1957, following the disaster of the Suez Crisis and the subsequent loss of British prestige, Eisenhower went further and announced a new policy for the Middle East. Washington would now assist any country in the region that was seeking to fight international communism.[7] This so-called Eisenhower Doctrine sent a signal not just to the Middle East but to the whole developing world that the United States would no longer sit back and rely on waning European powers to contain communism's expansion. A full-scale battle for the hearts, minds, and territory of key Third World states was now on, and it would be waged with the tools of economic aid, increased trade, and occasional military interventions (such as the marine landing in Lebanon in the summer of 1958).

By 1957–58, Eisenhower's Council on Foreign Economic Policy (CFEP), chaired by Clarence Randall, was playing a dominant role in shaping not only general economic policy toward Russia but also the countering the Soviets' so-called economic offensive toward the southern hemisphere. The two issues were seen by U.S. officials to go hand in hand. If the United States allowed Khrushchev to implement economic reforms at home, facilitated by imports of high-tech U.S. goods, then the Soviets would not simply have more economic wealth to devote to military growth. They would also have the surplus needed to offer developing states aid and trade packages that would reorient them toward Russia. The vision of the future was not a happy one: an economically strong Soviet Union with a strong military base could neutralize U.S. power at the strategic level while giving the Soviets a leg up in what Khrushchev was calling the "peaceful competition" for the loyalty of the developing world. In short, the competition for dominance in realm-two commercial spheres was now on, exacerbated by the rapidly escalating process of European decolonization.

Soviet decision-making after 1956, however, was pulled by two contradictory forces. On the one side, Khrushchev and his key advisors knew that the high growth rates of the early 1950s could not be sustained without the creation of a stronger technological base, particularly in the chemical, electronic, and oil industries. To achieve his goal of catching up to and overtaking the United States, Khrushchev needed the West to relax its restrictions on trade and the issuing of trade credits. CoCom's move away from pure economic warfare by 1954 had helped to build some trust with Western Europe. Yet most of the constraints on high-tech goods from Western Europe remained. More importantly, the United States was still by far the world's most technologically advanced state, and it was operating with full restrictions on U.S.-Soviet trade.

A moderation of the U.S.-Soviet relationship was therefore needed to get Washington to allow high-tech exports from America itself.[8]

Pulling from the other side, however, was the sobering reality of Moscow's precarious existential situation. The United States had maintained overall strategic superiority since the beginning of the Cold War. The Soviets needed to close the gap and to deter Washington during the transition period. Yet any actions to create and maintain a strong nuclear deterrent would obviously work against the larger effort to relax tensions, increase trade, and improve economic growth. In the late 1950s, military technology was changing so fast that both sides constantly worried about their ability to maintain their second-strike capabilities, ones that would dissuade the other side from contemplating a first strike. To speed up his economic reform program while protecting Soviet security, Khrushchev had decided in 1955 to reduce spending on the conventional army and increase the funds devoted to his missile program. The strategy worked. By the end of 1957, the Soviets appeared to be ahead of the Americans on missile technology: they had successfully tested the first ICBM in August, and in October launched into space the world's first satellite, the beeping steel ball known as Sputnik. Knowing that he was ringed by B-52 bombers that could deliver an overwhelming strike against Russia at a time when Soviet bombers could only reach the United States on one-way missions, Khrushchev chose to encourage the perception that Russia was rapidly turning out missiles that could hit not just Western Europe but the American homeland. As a result, fears of a "missile gap" that could give the Soviets a first-strike opportunity dominated the public discussions of U.S. foreign policy from October 1957 to the end of 1961.

Eisenhower in late 1957 understood that the United States was ahead in overall deliverable nuclear weapons. But he did worry that a future missile gap might arise if Washington was too complacent in the present. Moreover, he was convinced that the Americans might fall behind in overall scientific and technological strength if more effort was not made. At a November 4, 1957 meeting at the White House, Eisenhower told his advisors that the true critical period was not now, but five years hence.[9] To prevent a future gap from opening up, Eisenhower accelerated U.S. missile programs and redirected substantial resources to the training of more engineers and scientists. Because of Eisenhower's efforts, U.S. superiority on deployed missiles was maintained, a fact that John F. Kennedy learned in 1961 only after assuming office.[10] But the net result of the new arms race was that Washington continued to be unwilling to provide the kind of trade and credits that might accelerate Soviet economic and technological growth. Ironically, this happened just as Moscow's need for U.S. technology was rising significantly and as Eisenhower's desire for a superpower détente was peaking—that is, just as the opportunity for a trade peace that could spill over into a military peace was presenting itself. By 1958–59, Khrushchev was well aware that his earlier agricultural and industrial reforms were losing momentum and that the Soviet economic technology (if not military technology) was falling even further behind the United States.[11] For his part Eisenhower, now in his final few years of office, wanted to leave a legacy of stable superpower relations, embodied in an end to nuclear testing and progress on disarmament. And he understood that the carrot of increased trade with Russia was one of the few levers Washington held that could be used to buy Soviet cooperation.

The period from January 1958 until the collapse of joint discussions in May 1960 thus constitutes a strange mixture of acute arms racing at the strategic level—including often reckless statements of missile capability by Khrushchev—and the genuine effort on both sides to find a way to a stable peace. Added to the mix was the strong fear on the U.S. side that if the Soviet Union kept growing, the Global South would indeed gravitate to the Soviet sphere, seeing socialist planning and economic nationalism as the way to fast-track economic development with a minimum of social disruption. Eisenhower tried to square the circle of his conflicting desires and fears by seeking détente even as he maintained America's dominant economic and military position around the world. But without a willingness to relax the U.S. restrictions that were impeding Soviet economic development, this strategy was bound to fail.

In mid-February 1958, in discussions on trade controls with the British, Undersecretary of State for Economic Affairs Douglas Dillon summarized the new significance of the global economic struggle. The relationship of trade controls such as CoCom to Russia's economic penetration of the underdeveloped areas was "the most serious aspect of our struggle with the Soviet Union at this time."[12] Freer trade was seen as a carrot that might moderate Soviet behavior (as I discuss below). In his state of the union speech of January 1958, Eisenhower had talked about the need to win "a different kind of war"—namely, the "massive [Soviet] economic offensive" against free nations.[13] On March 3, Undersecretary Dillon explained to the Senate Foreign Relations Committee that this economic offensive was gaining momentum, and that the key issue was this: "How much farther can the Soviet leaders use the economic power of the bloc to advance the political objectives of International Communism?" The Soviet Union was not only producing machinery and capital goods that less developed states required for development, but it also had structured its economy to absorb large amounts of raw materials and foodstuffs from the southern hemisphere. Given the complementary nature of Soviet–Third World trade, therefore, there was little doubt that the Soviet bloc had the potential to intensify its economic relations with the less developed world, Dillon argued. Yet the main Soviet goal was the spreading of communist ideology and the "disrupting [of] economic relations among the free world." The expanded Soviet aid program was simply a new instrument directed toward "the same old purpose" of drawing smaller nations into the closed-door Soviet sphere at the Americans' expense.[14]

The Soviets by this point, however, were keener than ever to improve U.S.-Russian relations to help moderate the arms race and secure exports of U.S. technological goods. On June 2, 1958, Khrushchev sent a long letter to Eisenhower. It was of great importance that the two sides improve relations, Khrushchev wrote in the opening paragraph, and there are some "great and so far unused opportunities" to achieve this end. For twenty-three of the next twenty-five paragraphs, the letter focused solely on the question of U.S.-Soviet trade relations. With the Soviet people wanting increased consumer goods, opening trade would "further the cause of world peace." Khrushchev provided a long list of desired purchases—everything from chemicals to the equipment necessary for the manufacture of refrigerators and televisions. While Russia could export raw materials to buy these goods, Khrushchev indicated that some long-term trade credits and loans would be needed. He ended the letter by noting that a "positive solution" to the trade question would constitute "an important step toward a rapprochement between our two countries."[15]

Eisenhower's reply to Khrushchev on July 15—a short one-page letter that he made public—did not help matters. While expressing Washington's ongoing interest in trade, he disingenuously argued that the Soviets were free to sell their goods to the United States with few restrictions.[16] This ignored the thrust of Soviet complaints: that they were not free to *buy* U.S. goods. A memorandum circulated at this time by Eisenhower's Council on Foreign Economic Policy—an organization with powerful influence over U.S.-Soviet and Third World trade policies—observed that many of the items listed in Khrushchev's letter were still under explicit "embargo" due to the 1951 Battle Act: such things as pumps and compressors, television equipment, and mining machinery. Sixteen of the eighteen other items, while not explicitly banned, required licenses from the U.S. Department of Commerce and were under the "presumption of denial," including items as seemingly innocuous as air conditioning equipment, parts for televisions, and pipes for city gas lines.[17]

Eisenhower had little choice but to continue restricting Soviet purchases of even relatively low-tech goods, though. Another Basic National Security Policy review had been completed in May 1958. This review had made it clear just how much the world was changing. Eisenhower's national security advisor Robert Cutler had told him on May 1 that as the Soviets moved toward strategic parity, there was not only increasing doubt among allies as to whether Washington would use its nuclear capability to defend them, but Moscow also was becoming bolder in its economic and political policies toward developing nations. The final policy document that circulated on May 5 argued that the United States had to counter Moscow's economic offensive against the developing world even as it maintained U.S. nuclear superiority. So, while Washington should remain open to negotiations, the United States should not make concessions "in advance of similar action by the Soviets" simply from a hope of inspiring Soviet compromises.[18]

For the next two years, Eisenhower took this advice to heart. He did indeed want a modus vivendi to reduce the risks of nuclear war. But he continually refused to make concessions, particularly on the trade issues that mattered so much to Khrushchev, until he had first seen large concessions or improved behavior from Moscow. This bargaining strategy differed substantially from the one adopted by Henry Kissinger in the early 1970s. Kissinger sought to directly link Soviet concessions on military and political matters to U.S. concessions on trade; that is, the two sets of concessions would occur *simultaneously* and would be enshrined in written agreements to bind both sides. Eisenhower, however, remained unwilling to adopt such a "linkage" strategy. He wanted to see clear evidence of better Soviet behavior *prior to* accepting more trade openness. As we shall see, the adoption of this posture effectively sank any hope for a détente before he left office.

It is hard to believe that a man of Eisenhower's intelligence and experience would not have seen the advantages of practicing such a tried-and-true negotiating tactic as linkage. Something was clearly holding him back. This something, in essence, was the strategic situation the United States faced in 1958–60—a problem that was much more acute than the one confronting Kissinger and Nixon in 1970–72. In the 1958–60 period, there was no certainty that both sides would achieve and maintain a secure second strike to ensure stable nuclear deterrence. There was also great uncertainty, in the larger struggle for economic power spheres, as to whether newly independent Third World states would lean toward Moscow and thus restrict U.S. access to critical raw materials. Finally, it was unclear whether Russia might indeed catch up to and even overtake the United States in total economic strength, given that it had been averaging a growth rate almost double America's through the 1950s.[19] By the time Nixon would assume office, these concerns had been largely ameliorated: mutual assured destruction (MAD) was a reality, Third World alignments were clear, and the Soviet economic system was stagnating.

The United States of Eisenhower's era, in contrast, could not simply start free trading without expecting the Soviets to grab technologies that might catapult them to predominance. This created a tragic feedback loop: Washington could not afford to relax its economic restrictions without first seeing major Soviet concessions. Yet continued restrictions only hurt Soviet expectations of future trade, increasing Moscow's own fears for the future. This in turn led to more hostile Soviet behavior, making it even harder for Washington to make substantial trade concessions.

Concern about Soviet economic catch-up permeated the key internal analyses in Eisenhower's last three years. On November 16, 1958, a report to Eisenhower from the CIA's deputy director underscored that Moscow's new thrust was the "creation of the material-technical basis" for Soviet power. Moscow was investing heavily in chemicals, but success depended on its ability to develop the petrochemical industry. This would be difficult, "unless substantial assistance [in] petrochemical technology and equipment is procured from the West."[20] This report came at a moment when Moscow was engaged in what Bruce Jentleson calls the "Soviet Oil Offensive" toward Western Europe. Russian oil production had doubled from 1953 to 1958, and the country had gone from being a net importer to a net exporter of oil.[21] Moscow was anxious to sell large quantities of oil to Western Europe in return for some of the higher-tech items still denied by the United States. U.S. officials worried that the Soviets were using cut-rate oil prices to increase Western Europe's dependency, obliging it to realign eastward.[22]

These concerns coincided with Khrushchev's announcement in November that he would make Berlin a "free city" within six months if the wartime allies could not figure out a new arrangement. Notwithstanding this development, the Soviets were still pressing Eisenhower to reduce direct U.S. constraints on Soviet purchases. In December 1958, Anatas Mikoyan, Russia's number-two man and the acknowledged head of all trade issues for the Soviet Union, asked if he could make an "informal" visit to Washington. This prompted Clarence Randall, the chairman of the CFEP, to write Gordon Gray, Eisenhower's new national security advisor, to explain his evolving position on East-West trade. While there were government officials who wanted even harsher economic restrictions on the Soviet Union, Randall noted, U.S.-Soviet relations were "already too delicate" to take this further risk. Hence, "the time has come to let peaceful trade develop as it will."[23]

Randall's memo exposed a developing split within the administration. As dynamic realism would predict, this split reflected different views on the trade-offs between projecting peaceful intentions and upholding overall U.S. superiority. By January 1959, officials in departments of State and Defense had come to believe that increased U.S.-Soviet trade might indeed help to moderate overall relations and provide a foundation for a future détente. The heads of the Commerce Department, however, were adamant that the restrictions were critical to preventing relative decline. The approaching Mikoyan visit exposed this interagency division. At the January 8, 1959 meeting of the CFEP, Undersecretary of State Dillon emphasized that Eisenhower himself was "very clearly in favor" of developing "peaceful trade" with Russia. Randall pointedly argued that "certain agencies" were dragging their feet here, even though increased trade "would help the cause of the peace." Secretary of Commerce Lewis Strauss countered that even simple items like carbon black, used in tire production, could increase Russia's strength by helping it transport troops.[24] A follow-up State Department memorandum on "Peaceful Trade" with Russia outlined the key arguments on both sides but leaned in favor of increased trade. Although increased trade might help the Soviets convince "uncommitted countries" that communism was the fastest route to industrialization, trade was also an "important way of avoiding war" and "relaxing tensions."[25]

When Dillon met with Mikoyan on January 19, he began by stating that his government understood that improved commercial relations might help reduce tensions, but that "political complications" made it difficult to expand trade. Mikoyan quickly saw this as a statement that if Moscow were to improve its behavior, more trade would be forthcoming. He replied that while poor relations may not lead to greater trade, "trade expansion does contribute to good political relations," and U.S.-Soviet trade was still very low. One part of this was U.S. discrimination against Soviet exports such as manganese and vodka, which made it difficult for Russia to buy U.S. goods except by draining its gold reserves. This was not "friendly competition," Mikoyan noted, parroting one of Dillon's favorite lines. He went after the licensing system that restricted what the Russians could buy. The meeting ended in deadlock, with Dillon contending that the Soviets needed to resolve outstanding issues such as lend-lease payments, and Mikoyan maintaining that the sacrifices made by the Soviet people during World War II were payment enough.[26]

Despite the failure of the Mikoyan talks, the next nine months of 1959 showed signs of promise. A new State Department memorandum sent to Eisenhower in early March stated that it was now an assumption of U.S. economic defense policy that East-West commerce should be encouraged because the "benefits from peaceful trade" outweighed any impact it might have on Soviet economic, technological, and industrial growth.[27] Officials favoring trade still wanted to see concessions on Berlin and other issues before allowing Moscow to buy more goods.[28] But there was now for the first time in the Cold War a distinct possibility of using commerce and changing trade expectations to moderate the superpower conflict.

Eisenhower's strategy over the next five months was to dangle the possibility of future credits and relaxed trade restrictions to leverage the Soviets into concessions on Berlin and disarmament. He knew Moscow needed what the United States had to offer, and he was prepared to withhold all commitments to trade until he got progress in the security realm. On the Berlin question, Eisenhower could see that the Soviets were already softening to some degree:

he had been informed through British prime minister Harold MacMillan that Khrushchev did not view his original May 27 deadline as an ultimatum. This deadline did indeed pass without incident, suggesting that the Soviets would not press the issue in the short term.

The two sides restarted foreign minister talks in Geneva in May. The president believed these talks might lead to a broad set of agreements on outstanding issues: not just Berlin and strategic disarmament, but also a test ban treaty, assurances against surprise attack, and perhaps even limitations on the deployment of intermediate range missiles.[29] With a new, more accommodative secretary of state at the helm—Christian Herter had taken over in May after John Foster Dulles's death—there seemed reason for optimism. Hopes were therefore high when, in late September, the Soviet leader arrived for a prearranged two-week tour of the United States with direct talks with Eisenhower at the front and back ends.

State Department briefing papers for Eisenhower emphasized that trade would be high on Moscow's wish list. A September 8 paper reported that trade was "a major Soviet preoccupation" and Moscow wanted not just reduced restrictions but loans to fund its purchases of U.S. goods. The paper was cautiously optimistic, suggesting that both sides might now be able to move toward a signed agreement on trade. But this would depend on the Soviets continuing to moderate their behavior enough to create the "confidence" for long-term commerce.[30] Three days later, Eisenhower was told that Khrushchev would push for peaceful coexistence, using the argument that "expanded trade is the best road to improved U.S.-Soviet relations." The president was advised to tell the Soviet leader that history would see him as a great statesperson if he helped reduce the burden of the arms race.

> The U.S. and U.S.S.R. would then be able to confine their competition to peaceful fields. Of course, the ground rules would have to be agreed—and the competition, in ideas as well as the economic and cultural fields, would have to take place within the Communist as well as in the non-Communist world. The prospects for expanded economic relations . . . would then be bright.[31]

The repeated use of the word "then" in the above quotation is instructive. It underscores the overall orientation of the U.S. bargaining strategy: trade could expand, but only *after* major shifts in Soviet behavior on arms and the "ground rules" of competition. Eisenhower, in short, should not enter summit negotiations with the intention of securing a quid pro quo deal. Moscow would have to move first to build the confidence and trust needed for improved relations and sustained trade.[32] In short, knowing that this was a key concern of the Soviets, Eisenhower was to wait for Khrushchev to broach the issue and then state his position. This would permit the president to push the Soviet leader in a direction he wanted, dangling the potential for expanded trade as a carrot. But in both the raising of the question and the offering of strategic concessions, Khrushchev would have to move first.

Khrushchev arrived in Washington on September 15, and three hours later the two leaders held their first meeting. With both sides aware that the true give-and-take would come only after Khrushchev's ten-day tour, the first meeting was taken up with generalities about their mutual desires to build trust.[33] Khrushchev did not broach the trade question, and following the State Department's advice, Eisenhower did not bring it up. When Khrushchev returned to Washington on September 25, he and Eisenhower left for Camp David for two days of talks. Once there, perhaps because he sensed Eisenhower's need for something concrete upfront, Khrushchev quickly made a key concession: he agreed to withdraw his ultimatum on Berlin and allow the status quo to continue, at least for the near term. Eisenhower in return acknowledged that the current Berlin arrangements were abnormal and could not be maintained indefinitely. They also agreed to meet again in four-power talks that included Britain and France.[34]

On the second day of conversation, Khrushchev pushed hard on the trade issue. In a meeting with Dillon, when Dillon tried to encourage Russia to buy U.S. machinery to make shoes and textiles, the Soviet leader angrily cut him off, saying he was not interested in discussing minor items. He wanted one thing and one thing only: an across-the-board end to discriminatory practices. If the United States refused to end these practices, "this would mean that it wants a continuation of the Cold War." Dillon replied that if the Soviets wanted actions on trade, they must realize that it depended on Congress along with "the general state of the relations between the U.S. and the U.S.S.R." The message was clear. There could be no progress on the trade question until there was a noticeable improvement in Soviet behavior.[35]

Other than the informal agreement on Berlin, the Camp David talks led to few concrete achievements. Yet for the next few months, a "spirit of Camp David"—the sense, at least, that the two superpowers could sit down as equals and work toward compromise—infused both sides with an optimism that an agreement on key issues might be possible by the time the four-power summit convened in May 1960. Khrushchev in particular came away from Camp David energized and optimistic, telling advisors that the two sides had turned the corner and that he was confident a peace could be reached.[36] Such a peace was critical to reducing the economic strain of the arms race. He knew from internal reports that the growth rate of the Soviet economy was slowing down. Moreover, his U.S. visit had convinced him that America was still far ahead in technology and industrial techniques. Much like Gorbachev in the 1980s,

Khrushchev understood that unless he got the arms race under control, his country's economic performance would always lag considerably behind the United States. As he told his son, "If we are forced into [running this arms race], we will lose our pants."[37]

Khrushchev's solution was a radical and bold one. He would dramatically cut the size of the Soviet conventional army, hold to a bare minimum the installation of first-generation ICBMs, and continue to seek to acquire technology from abroad. In January 1960, building on Camp David's afterglow, he publicly announced that the Soviet army would be cut by between 1.0 and 1.2 million men, or about a third of its active force. This would not only reduce costs within but send a positive signal of the new Soviet spirit of cooperation and trust-building—just the sort of thing the Americans had been saying they were looking for.[38]

The separate decision to forgo a massive ICBM buildup and wait for second-generation ICBMs to come online was a huge strategic gamble. Khrushchev knew better than anyone that Russia was not equal in strategic military power, despite his claims to the contrary. But he hoped that he could get through the interim period of inferiority without a war so that secure, second-generation missiles could establish a viable deterrent within three to four years. This move would save money and avoid redundancies. On the other hand, it entailed an enormous risk: it would leave the Soviet Union vulnerable to U.S. blackmail and even war should Washington discover Russia's temporary inferiority.

The Soviets would also keep pressing for a relaxation in U.S. economic restrictions. And to get it, they were now willing to change their negotiating tactics. Most important, for the first time Moscow stated its willingness to resolve the ongoing lend-lease debt accrued during the war. Formal talks on Lend Lease began in Washington on January 11, 1960. Even allowing such talks to take place was a hugely symbolic concession to the American position. The Soviets had always found it insulting that despite having paid the highest blood price in the war, Russia was the only power asked to pay back a large percentage of the lend-lease loans—and without any compensating assurances of nondiscriminatory trade. Dillon's argument that resolving the lend-lease question was critical to getting progress on trade had obviously bent Moscow to Washington's will. Yet the Soviets wanted something in return. In a February press release, they noted that any lend-lease agreement must be concluded "simultaneously" with a trade deal offering Russia most favored nation status and trade credits.[39] Moscow was countering Washington's bargaining strategy with good old-fashioned linkage politics.

For the first four months of 1960, Eisenhower remained hopeful that by the end of May, a peace deal could be secured at the Paris summit. Then he made a fatal error of judgment. Despite the known risks, he allowed one more U-2 spy plane flight over Russia to help determine the true extent of the Soviet ICBM buildup. The U-2 plane was shot down on May 1, with the pilot, Gary Powers, being captured alive. This put Khrushchev in his own quandary. He could not allow such flights to continue without exposing the strategic inferiority that he himself had allowed to arise. Yet if he pressed too hard to get the Americans to stop the flights, they might become less inclined to compromise on the larger strategic and economic issues on the table. In the end, he decided to announce publicly that a U.S. spy plane had been shot down and the pilot captured, apparently believing that Eisenhower wanted peace and would use the incident to chastise the hawks within his administration. Eisenhower, however, refused to distance himself from the spy missions or agree to curtail them. In the first two days of the Paris summit, Khrushchev kept pressing for a commitment to stop the flights, and when it was apparent that Eisenhower would not budge, the Soviet premier walked out of the meeting. The U-2 crisis was a classic example of an action-reaction spiral that produced a result that neither side had wanted or foreseen.[40]

Eisenhower quickly understood the implications. In late May, he told his main scientific advisor "with much feeling . . . how he had concentrated his efforts [over] the last few years on ending the Cold War, how he felt that he was making big progress, and how the stupid U2 mess had ruined all his efforts. He ended very sadly that he saw nothing worthwhile left for him to do now until the end of his presidency."[41] We will of course never know what might have occurred had the U-2 incident not destroyed the May talks. Yet the deeper dilemma hanging over Eisenhower's last two years in office was the problem of trying to engage in economic diplomacy during a period of strategic uncertainty. Because neither side had guaranteed second-strike capability, neither side could relax its guard in a way that might allow positive expectations of future trade to do their work. The U.S. government believed it could not offer trade until it had seen significant concessions. The Soviets, painfully aware of their strategic inferiority, believed that major concessions now— including allowing U-2 flights to continue—might increase the United States' perception of its advantage, leading to coercive diplomacy or worse. With MAD not yet in place, both sides feared that even minor shifts in the nuclear balance might give the other an incentive for a first strike.[42] Trade thus could not be expanded until Soviet behavior improved, yet Moscow had little incentive to improve its behavior if Washington was so mistrustful it would not sell even low-tech industrial goods. Both sides were trapped in a vicious conundrum that could not be resolved until MAD became a reality in the late 1960s.

The Berlin Crisis of 1961 and the Cuban Missile Crisis of 1962 arose out of the failure of the talks of 1959–60 to curb arms spending as well as to achieve a preliminary trade-based détente. In the last six months of his tenure, Eisenhower continued to push forward with the U.S. arms buildup and modernization program. By the end of 1960, his administration had planned for eleven hundred ICBMs—a total which had been jumping each year since 1957.[43] The Kennedy administration, despite discovering the extent of U.S. nuclear superiority in its first month, continued this buildup, given the worry that Moscow might still achieve temporary superiority before new U.S. ICBMs were deployed in quantity.[44] A February CIA study also showed that the Soviet GDP was still growing at twice the U.S. rate. This was traced to capital expenditures which were almost at U.S. levels, even though the Soviet GDP was still only half of America's.[45]

The same dilemma that plagued Eisenhower hung over the Kennedy administration. Kennedy wanted a reduction in the intensity of the Cold War. But given the possibility of a future strategic deficiency, Washington could not afford to offer economic concessions, or at least not without evidence of increasing moderation in Soviet foreign policy. In the short term, it was clear that the Soviets wanted a peace to help them continue to build their economy (not unlike the Chinese from 1992 to 2007). At a February 11 meeting, Kennedy and his top advisors agreed that Khrushchev's "deepest desire" was to gain time for economic growth, and for this he needed "a generally unexplosive period" to achieve certain diplomatic successes, including progress on disarmament.[46] Unfortunately, an exogenous third-party problem was putting Khrushchev under intense pressure. In June 1961, Khrushchev announced that a new six-month deadline existed to solve the Berlin question. As I show elsewhere, the Soviet leader's move was driven primarily by fears that the exodus of East German refugees into West Berlin was causing the rapid economic decline of his most important Eastern European ally, East Germany. If East Germany collapsed, the Soviet bloc's power and global image would be greatly undermined.[47]

Although the Berlin crisis was the immediate result of a fear of economic decline, the larger context was important. Had the Americans and Soviets been able to reach a deal in 1959–60 that would have promised increased technology exports to Russia, Khrushchev would have had a stake in the fostering of future good relations. He would have worried that a crisis over Berlin would have led to the hardening of Washington's position on trade restrictions (as his upfront concession on Berlin at Camp David suggests). Moreover, the promise of trade would have given him greater confidence in Moscow's ability to overcome East German economic decline through transfer payments to the ailing state. In a meeting with East German leader Ulbricht in November 1960, for example, Khrushchev had agreed to "take over almost completely the East German economy . . . in order to save it."[48] Khrushchev knew that this would cost the Soviet Union in the short term. But had the Soviet economy itself not been slowing down in its growth rates, or at least had Khrushchev believed that the influx of U.S. technology would have given it a badly needed boost, he would have been more cautious in dealing with the exodus problem.

Such a counterfactual argument is, like all such arguments, ultimately unprovable. But internal efforts to moderate U.S. trade policy undertaken by the State Department during 1961 and the first half of 1962 indicate that American officials were well aware that the continuation of harsh trade restrictions was exacerbating tensions and limiting the chances of détente. In late February 1961, for example, Secretary of State Dean Rusk told Kennedy that it was of "great importance" to reduce restrictions, especially on insignificant items, to provide "a tangible demonstration of our desire to improve [U.S.-Soviet] relations" during a time of high tension.[49] Rusk's assertion reinforced the findings of a task force appointed by Kennedy during his transition period and headed by George Ball, Kennedy's undersecretary of state. The so-called Ball Report, completed just before Kennedy took office, argued that a more relaxed approach to U.S.-Soviet trade would both satisfy allies and give Washington a critical bargaining chip in future negotiations with Russia.[50]

By June, the Kennedy administration seemed poised to push Congress to amend trade legislation to give the president the flexibility to make the desired changes. Unfortunately, the crisis over Berlin restarted in late June right after the frosty Vienna summit between Kennedy and Khrushchev. This served to undermine any possibility in the short term of Congress agreeing to ease restrictions on East-West trade. Indeed, by the fall of 1961, Rusk and his officials had to spend time trying to prevent congressional leaders from *increasing* the severity of current trade sanctions. Given the state of U.S.-Soviet relations by late 1961, clearly a short-term relaxation in restrictions was impossible.[51]

Notwithstanding these problems, the State Department continued to promote internally the idea that expanded East-West trade could have important peace benefits. Even in the summer of 1962, amidst worrisome reports of a Soviet ICBM buildup,[52] Secretary of State Rusk saw the dangling of trade carrots as a tool to moderate Soviet behavior. On July 10, he presented a memorandum to the National Security Council arguing that continuing to deny license applications worked at cross-purposes with efforts to improve relations. The Soviets attached great significance to trade, Rusk argued, and they tended to view U.S. policies on trade "as indicators of our over-all attitudes." At a time of tension over Berlin and other matters, Washington should therefore avoid "giving the Russians a misleading impression . . . about the kind of [economic relationship] we hope ultimately to have with them." So long as the Soviets seemed to be ready for rational conversation, the Americans should avoid trade policies that seem to belie "our expressed readiness to maintain normal contacts of all kinds" with them. And while it was still important to retard Soviet war-making potential, it was equally necessary to expand trade contacts to help the Russians and Eastern Europeans "become more responsible and peaceful members of the community of nations."[53] In a follow-up memorandum, Rusk acknowledged that the Soviets sought U.S. technology to develop their productive capacity. Yet trade-offs had to be made, and he was "completely in accord with the often-expressed premise" that trade was one of the few means to push Russia toward more peaceful behavior. The United States should therefore shift policy and endeavor "to expand trade with the Soviet Union and other bloc countries."[54]

When he wrote these words, Rusk was of course unaware that the Soviet Union was already starting to deploy medium and intermediate range missiles in Cuba. The Cuban Missile Crisis, as I show elsewhere, arose from one overriding two-way dynamic. When the Americans publicly exposed Soviet nuclear inferiority in late 1961 and then began to talk about a "no-cities" counterforce strategy in the first half of 1962, Khrushchev believed he needed a stopgap measure to provide basic deterrence until his second-generation missiles came online. He thus copied the U.S. technique of deploying intermediate range missiles near the Soviet Union by convincing the Cubans to accept Soviet missiles on the island. Yet the very act of deploying such missiles caused the Americans to worry not only about a loss of superiority but a potential short-term gap of inferiority—one which might tempt the Soviets to launch a first strike as the United States rebuilt its power. In short, the dynamics of adverse power oscillations were at the heart of the crisis. The Soviet need to close the gap and establish basic deterrence led to the deployment of missiles in Cuba. And the American concern that the Russians would more than close the gap and then have an incentive to attack the United States before their own advantage waned put both powers on the nuclear precipice.[55]

Economic interdependence was not directly driving this process of fear, action, and reaction. Yet as with the Berlin Crisis, we can pose the counterfactual: Would Khrushchev have been as concerned about a short-term Soviet position of inferiority had he been more confident that the Americans were not seeking to drive Russia and its sphere into the ground economically? I would contend that had Soviet trade expectations been substantially improved by a deal between Eisenhower and the Soviet leader in 1960, or by positive economic signals from Kennedy in early 1961, Khrushchev would likely have felt more confident about Washington's willingness to accept peaceful coexistence in the interim as Russia built up its long-term economic and military strength. And as Alexandr Fursenko and Timothy Naftali show, Soviet leaders saw Kennedy's trumpeting of U.S. nuclear preponderance in the fall of 1961 as a sign of the opposite intent: that Washington would not allow Soviet growth and might even choose a preventive war to take advantage of short-term U.S. superiority.[56]

As with Berlin, we can never know if a trade deal would have smoothed the waters enough to prevent the most dangerous crisis in world history. And I do not want to push the trade expectations logic too far: the fears of losing one's second-strike capability were so strong on both sides that even with a new U.S. commitment to trade, it is quite likely that the period of 1961 to 1962 would still have witnessed some form of existential crisis. But such a crisis would probably not have pulled the two actors so close to the edge of ultimate destruction. Had an initial détente been established in 1959–60 or in early 1961, both sides would have felt more confident that any short-term gap in strategic power in the other's favor would not be used for a first strike. Greater caution during the transition period to true mutually assured destruction would likely have prevailed. Supporting this conclusion are Rusk's statements to the NSC that show that U.S. officials were greatly aware of two key things: the Soviets needed trade to remain confident about long-term growth; and trade was one of the few tools that Washington possessed to influence the direction of Soviet behavior for one way or another.

What we can conclude from the above analysis is that the lack of progress on opening up U.S.-Soviet trade and concomitant effects of Russian trade expectations played a far bigger role in the dynamics of Cold War politics during the Eisenhower and Kennedy administrations than has been previously understood. Given Soviet need, trade was a powerful bargaining chip, and the United States was prepared to use it for good measure. But the fragility of the nuclear balance forced Washington to insist on Soviet concessions before trade restrictions could be relaxed. This strategic conundrum proved a constant roadblock to what Kissinger would later call a stable "structure of peace."

In the next section, I show that Nixon and Kissinger were willing to build such a structure through the negotiating strategy of linkage—mutual concessions that would move the superpower relationship forward across many issues simultaneously. The option of such a strategy was facilitated by the new reality of MAD and the sense on both sides that with the Soviet economy stagnating, Russia was unlikely to catch up in overall economic power. This realization allowed the Americans to feel more relaxed about providing the Soviets with limited relative gains through trade. And if Washington could get major concessions from Moscow in return—concessions that would help the United States to sustain its dominant position at a time when the Vietnam War was reducing the perception of U.S. vitality—then a linked deal was more than worth it.

## The Emergence and Breakdown of Détente, 1963–79

The theory put forward in this book has stressed that behavior of actors can be changed even when there is little real trade between them, as long as needy states have expectations that the future trade environment will improve and remain open for some time. This was clearly the case as the two superpowers maneuvered toward a true peaceful coexistence in the late 1960s. Variations in the Kremlin's trade expectations after 1965, combined with the increasing Soviet need for Western goods to overcome internal stagnation, directly shaped the peacefulness of Soviet behavior, even when actual trade levels did not change significantly. And the increasing caution Moscow was showing helped convince Washington that the Soviet character type was starting to mellow at least enough to consider tying trade and technology carrots to direct concessions on Soviet foreign policy.

As we have seen, by the mid-1950s the Soviets had already understood that trade with the West could have potentially large benefits, especially if it secured technology unavailable or superior to indigenous Soviet technology. After consolidating their power following Khrushchev's ouster in 1964, the new Soviet leaders Alexei Kosygin and Leonid Brezhnev began a new push for greater trade. The impetus was declining rates of economic growth. From average annual growth rates of 6 to 10 percent in the first decade and a half after the war, the economy was registering only 5 percent growth from 1961 to 1965.[57] At the root of the decline was what Soviet analysts were now labeling the "scientific-technological revolution." The world was moving away from the emphasis on heavy industry characteristic of the Industrial Revolution. Growth was now seen to depend increasingly on the integration of technology—computers, scientific management techniques, information systems, and so forth—into the production process.[58] In particular, the Soviets were coming to realize that increasing GDP through extensive production—simply increasing the inputs of labor and capital—would be more difficult now that the economy had recovered from the war. To keep up with the Western bloc, intensive development was necessary—that is, growth through the more efficient use of a given level of inputs (greater productivity).[59] To achieve this, changes were needed to match the West's level of technological sophistication.

The man leading the charge toward technological improvement was Premier Kosygin. By 1965–66, he was arguing that the scientific-technological revolution was now the critical dimension of the superpower competition and Russia's "essential inadequacies" were having serious effects on economic growth. For the future, it was critical therefore to pursue "the most rapid . . . introduction of the results of scientific research into production."[60] His assessment was supported by analyses by Soviet economists such as Abel Aganbegyan, which showed that the U.S. economy was growing rapidly, supported by its superiority in such critical areas as computers and automation.[61] For Kosygin, the easiest solution to the problem was greater trade with the West, since foreign technology would save millions of rubles that would otherwise go into scientific research.[62] Kosygin's efforts to encourage greater trade were initially resisted by the majority of Politburo members, given their concern that trade dependence would leave the state vulnerable to Western political pressures. By 1969–70, however, Party Secretary Brezhnev began to see the wisdom of Kosygin's approach. Internal economic reforms begun in 1965 were not having a significant effect, and something had to be done.[63] At the party congress of March 1971, the new orientation was formally codified in a "Peace Program" linking increased trade and the slowing of the arms race to Soviet long-term economic growth. Moscow was now willing to seek "mutually advantageous" cooperation with the West, Brezhnev announced. Further economic growth would be hampered by continued high defense expenditures.[64] Moreover, Russia must keep up with the West in technology. The scientific-technological revolution must go forward, Brezhnev argued, and in this greater trade was essential.[65]

The Soviet need for Western trade gave Nixon and his national security advisor Kissinger the opening they were looking for. To build their structure of peace, trade would be offered in return for a moderation of Soviet behavior (including an arms control agreement, help in resolving Vietnam, and reduced interference in the Third World). For Kissinger, this so-called linkage strategy involved both carrots and sticks. Economic interchange would give the Soviets "incentives for . . . restraint," while U.S. strategic power and resolve would reiterate to Moscow the costs of expansionism.[66] In short, the growing network of ties would give the Soviets a "stake" in peace, making it "more conscious of what it would lose by a return to confrontation."[67] Tactically, Nixon and Kissinger made a distinct shift from Eisenhower's policy in the late 1950s. While Eisenhower wanted to see improved Soviet conduct before he would allow increased trade, with MAD now a reality, Nixon and Kissinger were willing to commit themselves upfront to more open trade and even trade credits as long as the Soviets simultaneously committed themselves to more cooperative behavior.[68]

The new U.S. willingness to trade with Russia was signaled by a series of deals and agreements in 1971 and 1972. In November 1971, a grain deal worth $136 billion was worked out. Later that month, the secretary of commerce facilitated the signing of $125 million in contracts between U.S. firms and the Soviet Union. In February 1972, export licenses for truck manufacturing equipment worth almost $400 million were approved.[69] The Moscow summit in

May focused on the signing of the Strategic Arms Limitation Treaty, but the two sides also announced they would work actively to build economic ties.[70] In October 1972, a formal trade agreement was signed, promising the Soviets most favored nation status and the extension of extensive trade credits. Both elements were important to the Soviets: being short of hard currency, they could not afford to buy U.S. goods unless they could both sell Soviet products and secure the short-term credit needed to expedite their purchases.

The impact of the new commercial spirit was felt quickly. Between October 1972 and May 1973, restrictions were removed on 477 of the 550 categories of products that were under U.S. export controls.[71] The Export-Import Bank extended a $202 million loan, and a trade council of three hundred U.S. firms opened a Moscow office. U.S. companies, needed for their technology, became involved in joint plans to develop the vast Siberian oil and gas fields.[72] Overall, the trend was definitely upward: total Soviet trade with America grew from an annual average of $60–$100 million in the 1960–70 period to $649 million in 1972 and then $1,577 million in 1973.[73] Even more significant for our purposes is the impact of the new relationship on Soviet expectations for the future. In February 1973, Brezhnev wrote to Nixon expressing his confidence that their upcoming June summit in Washington would lead to even more commercial agreements.[74] An internal Central Committee report written upon Brezhnev's return stated that the summit had provided "new prospects for the development of [U.S.-Soviet] economic-trade relations . . . on a long-term large-scale basis."[75]

If anything, Brezhnev's expectations for future trade with the West during 1972–73 were, as both Peter Volten and Raymond Garthoff note, overly optimistic.[76] The Soviets were slow to wake up to the implications of Watergate for Nixon's ability to control domestic opposition to U.S.-Soviet trade.[77] When the trade deal was signed in October, both sides committed to a tripling of bilateral trade over the next three years. Given that trade in 1972 had already reached $650 million, this effectively meant an anticipated jump to approximately $2 billion a year by 1975.[78] But the Soviet expectation—never of course realized—was for even more. A senior Soviet official with direct knowledge of U.S.-Soviet trade relations during this period has revealed that Soviet leaders "expected that annual trade with the United States would reach $10 billion by the end of the decade."[79] Indeed, by 1973, Brezhnev was staking the very success of his revitalization program on the continuation of a stable U.S.-Soviet relationship. Détente had to be made "irreversible," he argued through that year; it was the key to solving outstanding Soviet domestic problems.[80]

As I discuss shortly, growing domestic opposition to détente within the United States would ultimately destroy the prospects for significant future trade by January 1975. This led, as the trade expectations logic would predict, to an abrupt shift toward a much more assertive Soviet foreign policy in the

Third World. But during the period when Soviet expectations were still positive (1972–73), there was clear moderation in Moscow's behavior. As Kissinger had intended, the Soviets proved willing to sacrifice their interests on the periphery to secure the long-term benefits from U.S.-Soviet trade. Two examples stand out. Moscow used diplomatic pressure and the termination of military supplies to push North Vietnam to make the concessions that led to the Paris Accords of January 1973.[81] Even more significantly, the Soviets proved accommodating during the 1973 Israeli-Egyptian conflict, thereby allowing Washington to control both the diplomatic process and final outcome.

The superpower crisis ignited by the Yom Kippur War in October 1973 might suggest that détente had not moderated Soviet behavior. Careful analysis leads to the opposite conclusion. The Soviets not only did not want a Middle East war and acted to prevent it; they also sought to end it quickly, before too much damage to détente was done. Indeed, Kissinger acknowledges that he acted to exploit Moscow's evident caution in order to increase U.S. influence in the region. In sum, the Middle East crisis was provoked by the independent decisions of Egypt and Syria, *despite* Soviet efforts to dissuade these states from war. Once underway, the economic incentives embedded in détente significantly moderated Soviet behavior—much to the delight of Kissinger and Nixon.

By the spring of 1973, Brezhnev could see that despite his entreaties, Egypt and Syria were gearing up for war against Israel. Brezhnev told Nixon of this fact at the June summit, and in highly emotional terms, warned Nixon that unless America and Russia worked together on a Middle East settlement, he "could not guarantee that war would not resume."[82] Over the next three months, notwithstanding repeated Russia pleas to deal with the situation, Nixon and Kissinger kept shrugging them off. While they may have seen war as unlikely given Israeli superiority, it is also apparent, as Kissinger admits, that they viewed war (if it occurred) as a perfect opportunity to reduce Soviet influence in the Middle East. The Soviets' desperate need for the material benefits of détente would aid him in his task. As he puts it, he and Nixon were hardly the duped victims of a Soviet plan to use détente to expand Russia's sway in the Middle East via Arab proxies. Rather, "the opposite was true; our policy to reduce and where possible to eliminate Soviet influence in the Middle East was in fact making progress under the cover of détente." Without détente, Kissinger states, the Soviets would have been far more willing to intervene forcefully in a crisis not of their making. As it was, détente operated as "a tranquilizer for Moscow as we sought to draw the Middle East into closer relations with us at the Soviets' expense."[83]

The Soviets did indeed find themselves trapped between their need for a trade-based détente and their obligations to Egypt and Syria. According to insider Victor Israelyan, Brezhnev and his Politburo colleagues were very unhappy that their efforts to restrain Egypt and Syria over the previous eight months had failed to prevent the war. A few hours after Syria and Egypt had launched their surprise attack on Israel, the Politburo held its first crisis session. Brezhnev told the group that "the Arab action would whip up international tensions and complicate the Soviet Union's relations with the West, especially with the United States." Gromyko told Israelyan after the meeting that "negotiations between Brezhnev and President Nixon . . . had created a good foundation for a political solution to the Middle East problem" and a war there would "ruin these chances."[84]

Brezhnev's behavior reflected these concerns. In a hurried note to Egyptian leader Anwar al-Sadat, the Soviet leader wrote that Arab leaders were "interfer[ing] in the process of the development of political cooperation between the USSR and the USA," and he asked for an immediate ceasefire.[85] Sadat rejected the idea. His forces were seeing initial success on the battlefield, and he saw little reason to stop so soon. The Soviet leadership found itself trapped between its desire to end the fighting—which would minimize the risks to détente while preserving a role for Moscow in the subsequent negotiations—and its fear of abandoning Sadat, which would hurt its reputation in the Middle East. Brezhnev decided to supply the Arab forces with arms during the war, and to support them publicly. Behind the scenes, however, the Soviets were actively pressing for a ceasefire and a negotiated settlement throughout the month of October.[86]

In essence, Kissinger's strategy during October was to "induce Soviet caution by threatening the end of détente," thereby enacting a regional solution that best suited U.S. interests. He knew that Moscow had not colluded with the Arab states to initiate war, and that in fact the Soviets were reluctant to support Arab forces with either arms or diplomacy.[87] Even Kissinger's dramatic move on October 25—placing U.S. forces on temporary nuclear alert (DEFCON 3)—had little to do with fear of a superpower clash and almost everything to do with reducing Moscow's role in the final crisis settlement. With Egypt's army on the ropes, Brezhnev had been warning that he might have to send Soviet forces to Egypt unilaterally should Washington reject his idea of a joint U.S.-Soviet peacekeeping force to enforce a ceasefire. Kissinger worried that if Washington accepted a joint operation, it would legitimize a role for Moscow in Middle Eastern affairs and thus he escalated the crisis to deter Soviet action.[88]

The above analysis shows the strong moderating effect of détente on Soviet behavior during the 1973 Middle East crisis.[89] Without the incentive of high expected U.S.-Soviet trade, essential to Russia's reforms and continued superpower position, Moscow would have been more likely to have intervened actively in the Arab-Israeli dispute, and the probability of a dangerous superpower clash would have been that much greater. In the end, it is the U.S. leadership that must bear most of the blame for the October crisis, since it was Nixon and Kissinger who, out of a desire for geopolitical gain, did so little to avert or moderate the conflict.

While positive expectations for future trade were moderating Soviet behavior during the 1972–73 period, trouble was brewing within the United States. Liberal and conservative critics of Nixon's presidency found a common ground on which to oppose his foreign policy: they would attack it as insensitive to human rights, particularly the Jewish emigration problem. In March–April 1973, Senator Henry Jackson formally introduced an amendment linking most favored nation status to significant increases in Jewish immigration as part of the Trade Reform Act of 1973 (a similar amendment was introduced in the House by Representatives by Charles Vanik). Through 1973, the Jackson-Vanik Amendment slowly gathered momentum as the Nixon administration sank into the swamp of Watergate. In December, a month after the resolution of the Middle East crisis, the House passed a bill containing the amendment, and in June 1974, Senator Adlai Stevenson III added a further amendment, limiting credits offered to Russia by the federal Export-Import Bank to $300 million over four years. The Stevenson Amendment was significant, since the Soviets were counting on generous credits for the billions of dollars of purchases of U.S. products they expected to make (in particular, equipment needed to develop the vast Siberian oil and gas reserves).[90]

The Soviets struggled hard to satisfy congressional critics at a price that would not damage Russia's global reputation. In April 1973, just as Jackson was introducing his amendment, Brezhnev rescinded the exit tax that was restricting Jewish emigration, and that had so upset Jackson and his supporters. Jewish emigration rose from four hundred in 1968 to almost thirty-five thousand by the end of 1973.[91] Yet for Jackson this was not sufficient. In September 1974, he publicly indicated that he sought seventy-five thousand per year and would press for at least sixty thousand. The Soviets made it known through the back channels that they would go as high as fifty-five to sixty thousand, as long as the deal was kept private.[92] Yet Jackson, as Kissinger laments, "wanted an issue, not a solution."[93] On October 18, 1974, just after Jackson and Vanik signed letters at the White House apparently resolving the dispute, Jackson used the occasion to trumpet his victory, arguing that the Soviets had completely caved to his demands.[94] The Soviets were outraged at this public humiliation. The trade bill with the Jackson-Vanik amendment was passed on December 13. On January 3, 1975, President Ford reluctantly signed the Trade Reform Act into law. Ten days later, the Soviets indicated that the 1972 trade treaty was now null and void.

Hence by early 1975, as Garthoff summarizes, "the heart of the official American-Soviet trade component of détente had collapsed."[95] This domestic interference in the Nixon-Kissinger plan represented a huge blow to Soviet trade expectations. Moscow now understood that there was little it could do, short of appearing to capitulate to ever-increasing U.S. demands, to save the 1972 trade treaty. And given the evident weakness of the U.S. executive in the wake of Watergate, by December 1974 it was clear that further negotiations would serve no purpose.[96]

What is significant is how quickly Soviet behavior on the periphery moved back toward the previous policy of "adventurism." Reversing its two-year policy of restraining North Vietnam, in December 1974 Moscow reinstated weapons shipments to Hanoi. Four months later, the North launched its decisive assault on the South, undoubtedly with at least the tacit approval of Moscow. In 1973–74, the Soviets had only provided the barest of aid to leftist forces in Angola, and only after U.S. aid to anti-leftist groups was stepped up. This restraint vanished in 1975, when Soviet support for Angolan leftists increased dramatically.[97] By the late 1970s, Moscow made significant inroads in Somalia, followed by Ethiopia and Nicaragua. Then in 1979, with the invasion of Afghanistan, Russian forces for the first time in the Cold War invaded a country not formally a part of the Soviet sphere.

Although the internal documents on Politburo decision-making for the 1975–79 period are still sketchy, it is surely no coincidence that Soviet behavior changed so suddenly after the failure of the trade treaty.[98] As Bruce Parrott observes, "Soviet willingness to accept implicit linkages between trade and Soviet political behavior depended on how the prospective economic benefits fitted into a larger balance of political opportunities and risks. . . . By 1975, however, the balance of benefits and costs had shifted."[99] In sum, the end of the trade treaty represents a major reason for the collapse of détente and a return to a more conflictual superpower relationship.[100] The trade expectations argument provides a simple but powerful explanation for this. Without the anticipation of a stream of increasing trade benefits accruing from U.S.-Soviet cooperation, the Soviets no longer had the incentive to moderate their actions in the Third World, as they had in 1972–73. While this explanation may also seem to align with commercial liberalism, note that it was not current trade that constrained Soviet policy but rather the expectation of high future trade. Moreover, Moscow's ends were clearly security-driven, focused on Russia's long-term position in the superpower competition. This again demonstrates the value of taking a dynamic approach to great power decision-making within enduring rivalries.

## Economic Relations and the End of the Cold War, 1981–91

For many, the end of the Cold War is rooted in one fundamental fact: the ascendancy of Mikhail Gorbachev and his new liberal vision for Soviet society and its place in the world. By this account, Gorbachev's belief that his country had to become an open and democratic society translated into a desire to integrate Russia into the Western liberal system, thereby ending nearly half a century of mistrust and tension. This section shows that to the extent that this interpretation emphasizes ideational epiphany over self-interested material calculation, it is inadequate as an explanation of the Soviet leader's reasoning.[101] Gorbachev's reforms, at least for the first two years, were not that new (nor were they seen as such by the American side). They were an extension of the reform plan set down during the brief tenure of his mentor Yuri Andropov from late 1982 to early 1984. This plan in turn was based on the same goal that drove the Kremlin toward reform and trade in the late 1960s—namely, the need to overcome economic and technological stagnation. Gorbachev's "new thinking" became progressively more radical only after 1986; that is, only after the failure of his initial reforms. But even here his actions were largely materially driven: only by democratization within and greater peace and economic interdependence without did he believe that his country could pull itself out of decline. Without radical change, the Soviet Union could not remain a superpower into the twenty-first century. Growing expectations that the United States—and after U.S. approval, Europe—would offer the kind of trade and credits needed to further his reforms was an integral part of Gorbachev's larger strategy for peace. Yet Gorbachev was indeed able to project to American leaders and officials that he was a different type of Soviet leader—one that was less ideologically driven, and more pragmatic. This would help reduce American fears that helping the Soviets reenergize their economy would leave the United States in a vulnerable future position.

While estimates vary, all accounts agree on one thing: by the late 1970s/ early 1980s, the Soviet economy was in deep trouble. Annual GDP growth rates, which had been around 7 to 10 percent in the 1950s and 5 percent in the 1960s, were now at best zero to 2 percent. Productivity was flat, the quality of Soviet products far below that of the West, and inefficient factories were using up Soviet energy resources at rates many times greater than comparable Western figures.[102] Soviet leaders were not unaware of the problem. Before he came to power, and when still head of the KGB, Andropov established a secret department within the KGB to study what was seen, according to one official, as "the coming economic catastrophe."[103] A report in the spring of 1983 by the Soviet Academy of Sciences indicated that the centralized system was "incredibly . . . outdated" and was the primary cause of Soviet decline. Overall, it had to be made less rigid and complex, and market mechanisms were needed.[104] Andropov quickly followed up on its implications. In a June speech, Andropov emphasized the importance of reforms to increase technology-based productivity.[105]

Given Andropov's poor health, his protégé Gorbachev was primarily responsible for implementing the reforms. Gorbachev was fully supportive of Andropov's efforts, which at this stage were modest, focused primarily on greater discipline in the workplace (including an end to alcoholism). Gorbachev was well aware of the problem of relative economic stagnation versus the rest of the world. By 1982–83, he understood that "time was running out." The world was experiencing a sweeping scientific transformation. Yet while Western states were rising to the challenge, the Soviet system "spurned innovation and moved against the general tide of progress." Not only was the West ahead, Gorbachev maintained, but the gap in advanced technology "[has begun] to widen, and not to our advantage."[106] That Gorbachev's primary obsession was the maintenance of the Soviet Union as a superpower is shown by his speech at a conference of party officials in December 1984. Outlining his strategy for economic reform, he argued that "we have to achieve a breakthrough. Only an intensive and highly developed economy can ensure the strengthening of the country's position on the world scene and enable it to enter the next millennium in a manner befitting a great and prosperous country. . . . There is no alternative."[107]

By 1985, the question of decline was assuming overwhelming significance. On assuming power in March, Gorbachev was handed a top-secret KGB report that alleged that unless the country began fundamental reform, "[it] could not continue as a superpower into the twenty-first century."[108] In late February 1986, Gorbachev told the Twenty-Seventh Party Congress that should scientific and technical trends continue, the capitalist world might achieve "social revenge"; namely, "the recovery of what had been lost before."[109] To ensure Soviet economic and territorial security, Gorbachev had three priorities. First, he had to end the arms race in order to free up resources for consumer goods. Economic reform could not succeed if the Soviet Union continued to devote 20 percent of its GDP to the military.[110] Second, he needed to stop the U.S. effort to build a space-based missile defense system. This system, even if not successful, would force Moscow to squander precious investment capital needed for economic growth. And if it did work, it could undermine deterrence and spark a new arms race.[111] Third, and increasingly important as his reforms progressed, Gorbachev had to convince the United States to relax restrictions on trade and economic credits. Like Brezhnev, Gorbachev understood that integral to overcoming economic decline was access to superior Western products and information.

These three elements were essential to furthering a domestic reform program that was Leninist in its foundations, not liberal, as Gorbachev freely acknowledged. He sought not a revolution but rather an improvement of the existing socialist system, which he saw as having distinct moral and organizational advantages. As with Lenin's effort in the early 1920s to use trade and technology for Russian power, Gorbachev saw the importance of reestablishing good relations with the West.[112] In May 1986, he spoke to six hundred foreign aid and trade officials from the Foreign Ministry. Soviet diplomacy "must contribute to the domestic development of the country," he argued. The primary goal of foreign policy was therefore to "create the best possible external conditions" for internal growth.[113] While Gorbachev's subsequent actions indicate that ending the arms race was the key initial step, securing trade was also critical. In his first meeting with Secretary of State Schultz and Vice President George H. W. Bush immediately after assuming power, Gorbachev lamented the low level of contacts between the two countries. "[U.S.] technology can be transferred only with the express approval of the president. Trade is not permitted."[114] Two months later, in May 1985, Gorbachev told Secretary of Commerce Malcolm Baldridge that it was "high time" to improve economic ties—a theme he reiterated when the two met again in December.[115]

The Soviets had reason to believe the Americans were open to greater commerce. President Reagan had sent a personal letter to Andropov in July 1983 expressing hope for greater discussion on arms control and expanded trade. Five months earlier, Reagan had signaled that he believed the Jackson-Vanik Amendment was wrong and should be revoked.[116] Beginning in late 1984, the Commerce Department had started to relax some intra-Western export controls—a crucial initial sign since much of the technology desired by the Soviets was being garnered through Western Europe.[117] But Gorbachev knew that much more was needed. In a statement of fundamental principles coming out of the Twenty-Seventh Party Congress, the first principle in the economic sphere was the ending of "all forms of [trade] discrimination."[118] In his book *Perestroika* released in mid-1987, Gorbachev offered a message to Western leaders: "don't be scared by perestroika [restructuring] . . . but rather promote it through the mechanism of economic ties." Such ties "[will help] build confidence between our countries."[119]

Unlike in the early 1970s, it was clear to the Soviets that this Republican administration was unwilling to sign a quid pro quo deal linking arms control and better Soviet behavior to increased U.S. trade commitments. Reagan and his associates were simply too mistrustful of Soviet intentions.[120] Consequently, the Soviets understood that they would have to make a number of dramatic gestures that would signal that the new leadership was indeed different.[121] Gorbachev received a report in April 1985 from advisor Georgi Arbatov arguing that the changing of the guard in Moscow opened up significant opportunities for better relations. Yet to avoid disappointment, "we [must] change our negotiating style and take unilateral measures," including the reduction of Soviet forces in Europe.[122]

Gorbachev took this advice to heart. In January 1986, Gorbachev publicly proposed a three-stage plan for the elimination of nuclear weapons by the turn of the century. At Reykjavik that fall, the Soviets were willing to agree to far-reaching reductions in strategic missiles in return for limitations on space-based weapons. While no agreement was reached, Schultz saw the meeting as a turning point in demonstrating Moscow's seriousness regarding fundamental change.[123] This view was reinforced in 1987 when Moscow agreed to an intermediate-range nuclear forces treaty that entailed significantly disproportional cuts in intermediate-range missiles from the Soviet side.[124]

These dramatic gestures led to some moderation of U.S. trade policy. In early 1987, the U.S. embargo on oil and gas drilling equipment was lifted. This was an important step, given that energy exports were the primary source of foreign currency; indeed, Gorbachev recognized early on that such exports were critical to the overall success of reform.[125] At a special CoCom meeting in January 1988, Washington accepted a liberalization of the list of controlled items, including computers and telecommunications. In addition, a U.S.-Soviet agreement on scientific cooperation was signed.[126] Overall, however, the Soviets remained frustrated. At the Moscow Summit in May 1988, when Reagan asked about perestroika's progress, Gorbachev quickly turned to how the United States "persisted in maintaining a discriminatory trade policy towards the Soviet Union." Reagan's refusal to budge whenever Gorbachev raised the issue only led Gorbachev to believe that even more dramatic steps were needed to break the logjam.[127] In December, in a speech to the United Nations, he took his most radical step yet. He stated that the Soviet Union would reduce its troop presence in Eastern Europe over the next two years by five hundred thousand men—unilaterally and without relation to conventional forces talks going on in Vienna. The connection between this move and his economic goals was indirect but hard to miss. The global economy was becoming one organism, he told his audience, "and no state, whatever its social system or economic status, can normally develop outside it."[128] As Gorbachev later described it, one of the primary themes of this speech was that "perestroika . . . required a change in the way we conducted our foreign trade, an organic integration with the world economy."[129]

This speech, combined with the Soviet agreement to withdraw from Afghanistan, led Schultz to discuss further relaxations of controls with the defense department in the waning days of the Reagan administration.[130] Once George H. W. Bush assumed power, however, he decided to undertake a full review of U.S. policy toward Russia. A number of his advisors were worried that Soviet concessions were simply a ploy to give Russia the breathing space needed to restore its power.[131] Thus for many months, aside from a few vague statements applauding Soviet reforms, there was little concrete progress in normalizing relations. The Soviets were concerned. In September, Foreign Minister Edvard Shevardnadze met with Secretary of State James Baker and stressed that Russia was going through an important stage and needed to overcome the incompatibility of its economic system with Western states. Moscow did not want aid, but rather "economic cooperation" to help perestroika succeed.[132] To further the discussions, Shevardnadze offered two more critical concessions: the Soviets would delink arms control talks (START) from discussions on space-based weapons; and dismantle a radar station that Washington saw as a violation of previous agreements.[133]

This additional evidence of Soviet cooperation in the foreign policy realm seemed to do the trick. By late 1989, the Bush administration made a definitive decision that Gorbachev's reforms must be supported.[134] Baker made a major speech in mid-October confirming that Washington was prepared to provide technical assistance for Soviet reforms.[135] When Bush and Gorbachev met in Malta in December 1989, the Berlin Wall was down and the Soviet position in Eastern Europe was quickly unraveling. These developments gave new urgency to the need to help perestroika succeed in order to keep Gorbachev in power. Bush made the promise that Gorbachev had been waiting more than four years to hear: the White House would seek to secure most favored nation status for the Soviet Union and to end legislative restrictions on economic credits. In essence, this was a promise to return to the spirit of the 1972 trade agreement. Bush also offered Moscow observer status at the General Agreement on Tariffs and Trade (GATT), as a means to further integrate the Soviet Union into the world economy. Finally, Bush suggested that the two sides begin discussions on a new trade agreement, to be signed at the next summit.[136] The atmosphere at Malta turned optimistic, almost jubilant, with Gorbachev announcing: "The world is leaving one epoch, the 'Cold War,' and entering a new one."[137] Positive Soviet trade expectations were reinforcing the wisdom of the new peace program. A month later, Gorbachev submitted his report to the Politburo. He welcomed both the U.S. "readiness to give us certain practical aid in the sphere of the economy" and the "mutual understanding of the necessity for Soviet-American cooperation as a stabilizing factor" during this crucial stage of world history.[138]

Despite the new atmosphere, when Bush and Gorbachev met for the Washington summit in late May 1990, no formal trade agreement had yet been signed. The United States was still seeking to use Gorbachev's desperate need for trade and technology as leverage in realizing U.S. ends, especially the unification of the two Germanys within the North Atlantic Treaty Organization (NATO) and a moderation of Russia's presence in Lithuania. Despite the great sensitivity for the Russians of the first issue, Gorbachev chose the summit to make the dramatic move of allowing a united Germany to make up its own mind on which alliance to join. But he had a price. The next day, June 1, at a televised meeting with top congressional leaders, the Soviet leader stressed that the present trade relationship was "very primitive" and appealed for a "favorable gesture . . . on trade" from the U.S. Congress. This gesture, he noted, was "very important . . . from a political standpoint."[139]

Both sides were up against the clock: they had committed to a signing ceremony late that day. When Bush met Gorbachev after the televised meeting, he told him that he was still unsure about the trade agreement. Gorbachev reiterated it critical importance.[140] In the mid-afternoon, Baker phoned Bush to tell him that they should proceed with the trade deal. Shevardnadze's additional appeals that day, plus a breakthrough on the reuniting of the two Germanys within NATO, had apparently convinced Baker that America must show its concrete support for perestroika. Bush agreed: "Let's go ahead and do it."[141]

The president kept Gorbachev hanging to the last minute. Just before entering the East Room for the signing ceremony at 6:00 P.M., Gorbachev asked "Are we going to sign the trade agreement?" Bush replied that they would. Beaming, Gorbachev told the president, "This really matters to me." Bush also agreed that he would not explicitly link the deal to Soviet behavior on Lithuania.[142] Gorbachev thus came away with the deal he wanted. The United States was now committed to the normalization of trade relations in return for the Soviets' quiet acquiescence to the U.S. position on Germany and private suggestions of moderation regarding Lithuania.

It is clear that the Washington summit of May–June 1990 was a significant moment in the unwinding of the Cold War. From Gorbachev's perspective, the trade agreement of June 1 represented a "turning-point" in U.S.-Soviet relations, in which the Americans went "from verbal support for our perestroika to real action."[143] On the day of the signing, he spoke of the body of agreements as a step toward a "new world." Bush's speech that day noted that while the two superpowers did not agree on everything, "we [do] believe in one great truth: the world has waited long enough; the Cold War must end."[144] Cooperation did indeed become the norm after this point. Most surprising and immediate was the way both sides worked together during the eight-month crisis to end Iraq's occupation of Kuwait, which began less than two months after the Washington summit. By October 1990, the two Germanys were united, with the understanding that the new larger Germany would remain a part of NATO. By spring 1991, East-West relations were hardly recognizable. Gorbachev received an invitation in June to the July G7 summit of industrialized nations. On July 11, Gorbachev sent a personal letter to the Western powers, stating that the Soviet people "feel that the time has come to take resolute steps . . . for a new type of economic interaction that would integrate the Soviet economy . . . into the world economy."[145]

In one of the most remarkable events of the post-1945 period, the leader of the Soviet Union—a man still dedicated to the principles of socialism—arrived in London on July 16, 1991, to hold talks on international trade and investment with the seven leaders of the capitalist world. At a special meeting designed to represent the "7 + 1" formula—and on the same day that Bush and Gorbachev came to a final agreement on a START treaty to reduce strategic arms (July 17)—Gorbachev spoke to the G-7 leaders. He told them that the Soviet leadership now believed that "positive processes in the world could be sustained if the political dialogue we had established were to become rooted in the new economic cooperation." Of course, integration could be achieved only by "the lifting of legislative and other restrictions on economic and technical ties with the Soviet Union."[146] Gorbachev was pleased by his reception at the meeting. Chancellor Helmut Kohl of Germany spoke of the "historic moment": "if this process we are initiating . . . goes successfully, it will have the utmost importance for Europe and the entire world." Prime Minister John Major of Britain, host of the summit, noted that the Western states were in a position to help Russia at the macroeconomic level. The G-7 countries agreed to build a "special association" between the Soviet Union and the International Monetary Fund/World Bank, while expressing their resolve to reestablish full access to trade and investment. From his perspective, Gorbachev came away from the G-7 meeting "with a significant gain." He had achieved "a fundamental political agreement about the integration of our country [into] the world economy," thus "fulfill[ing] the national and state interests of our country."[147]

The above analysis demonstrates the profound importance of improving Soviet trade expectations on the winding down of the Cold War. Gorbachev recognized the need for trade and investment early on and worked tirelessly to secure U.S. and Western European agreement to a relaxation on existing restrictions. He understood that the probability of future trade was partly a function of his own behavior: unless he offered dramatic concessions in arms control and geopolitics, the Soviet Union would still appear to have a malign character type, and Reagan and Bush would be unlikely to use their political capital to press for the changes in CoCom along with domestic legislation. But he also used the promise of better behavior—and the implicit threat of the loss of his domestic authority and a return to an intense Cold War—as a tool to secure Western commitments to future trade. As a result, a virtuous cycle of

political concessions, signals of future Western trade, and further political concessions could be set in motion. The trade-security spiral that had been first
set in motion in 1945 had finally been reversed, leading to the end of nearly a
half century of intense Cold War.

## Conclusion

This chapter has shown the value of reorienting our thinking about economic
interdependence away from the established but static models of traditional
liberalism and realism toward a dynamic logic based on actor expectations of
future trade and commerce. Because trade between the United States and the
Soviet Union was very low for most of the Cold War era, liberals and realists
alike assume that the shifting dynamics of competition and conflict could not
have had anything to do with economic interdependence. They thus fall back
on other tools in their toolboxes: ideological, institutional, and domestic differences for liberals; and changes in relative power and military technologies
for realists.[148] These of course were important factors that helped create and
sustain mutual mistrust and perceptions of threat over many decades. Yet once
we turn to the possibility that the Soviets were thinking in terms of the *potential* for economic gains through trade and the possibility that Washington
would indeed commit itself to *future* exports and trade credits, we see the true
importance of economic interdependence in driving many of the key events
of the Cold War. Eisenhower's unwillingness to strike a grand bargain that
would open up U.S. trade in return for Soviet commitments to more moderate
behavior served to increase Khrushchev's fears for the future, setting the stage
for the dangerous crises of 1961 and 1962. Nixon and Kissinger's willingness to
make such a bargain underpinned the first superpower détente, helping Washington to dominate the Middle East peace process at a critical time. This détente might have held had it not been for the effect of unexpected congressional opposition on Soviet trade expectations: without confidence that the
U.S. executive could uphold its economic promises, Moscow had little reason
to play nice in the Third World and on nuclear issues.[149] Finally, Reagan and
Bush's ability in the late 1980s to convince Gorbachev that the Americans were
now truly committed to the relaxing of trade restrictions played a critical and
largely unappreciated role in the winding down of the Cold War.

Many of the economic lessons of the Cold War have apparently been
learned by post–Cold War U.S. administrations. In dealing with China, American executive leaders, and for the most part congressional leaders as well, have
recognized that trade restrictions that would contain Chinese growth would
likely push Beijing into a hostile stance that would lead to a new Cold War. So,
while Washington has been increasingly tough on Beijing since 2010, it has

avoided a true economic decoupling, with the significant exception of trade in high-tech computer chips and the machines that make them. The potential for an increasingly intense trade-security dilemma between the United States and China is still real. Washington decision-makers have therefore been smart to maintain relatively positive Chinese trade expectations to help stabilize the geopolitical relationship, despite knowing that this could allow China to grow economically. The downside of an all-out economic containment strategy against China is likely much higher than accepting a degree of Chinese GDP growth, especially now that China's growth rates have tapered off. Perceptions in Beijing that Washington was trying to drive China's economy into the ground would likely push Chinese leaders into military conflicts and even war over areas of long-standing dispute, such as Taiwan and the South China Sea/Southeast Asia.

Geopolitical tensions between China and the United States have been intensifying for the last decade, and fears of Beijing's intentions and a potentially deeper alignment with Russia could very well lead to a greater U.S. desire to restrict Chinese trade to hurt the power projection capability of this emerging authoritarian bloc. In the final chapter, I will explore different scenarios that could arise, depending on China's growth trajectory and the nature of its character and intentions. There are indeed very real risks that an undesired spiral of declining commercial expectations and military build-up could lead the two powers into a new Cold War, or worse. Yet because both sides are aware of these risks and have reason to want to reduce the potential for escalation to conflict, Washington and Beijing may well be able to adjust their policies and realize a cold peace that avoids regional crises and direct superpower war. Lessons from the U.S.-Soviet conflict from 1945 to 1991 can thus help moderate the probability that another all-out Cold War occurs, let alone one that has crises of the intensity of Berlin 1961 or Cuba 1962.

# 10

# Economic Interdependence and the Future of U.S.-China Relations

THE MOST significant geopolitical trend of the last three decades has undoubtedly been the rise of China from a second-tier developing nation to the status of a superpower or a superpower-to-be. In 1991, as the Cold War ended with the collapse of the Soviet Union, China's economy, despite its huge population, was a mere 10 to 15 percent of the U.S. economy, and it ranked seventh in the world in total GDP and eighth in total trade. By 2012, it was the second largest economy in the world, overtaking Japan, and by the beginning of the 2020s it had a GDP close to 80 percent of the United States. It was the world's largest exporter, and the number one trade partner for over one hundred countries, including the European Union and (off and on) the United States. The only question on the minds of Western political leaders seemed to be when (not if) China would overtake the United States in total GDP and whether it would continue to grow to a point of economic dominance, if not military dominance, in the subsequent decades.[1] By contrast, the only other potential peer competitor to the United States in the post–Cold War era, Russia, experienced devastating upheaval and decline in the 1990s from which it never fully recovered. Vladimir Putin's stabilization programs of the early 2000s did stop the freefall, but his reliance on energy exporting and not manufacturing has left Russia, even before its disastrous invasion of Ukraine in February 2022, with an economy the size of Italy and a technological base that has improved little over the last thirty years.

The great geopolitical struggle of the twenty-first century is thus one between a seemingly declining United States wanting to maintain a semblance of preeminence and a rising China seeking to establish itself as a dominant, if not *the* dominant, state in its region and perhaps the world, a position it has not come close to holding for more than two hundred years. Almost all the debates in the literature on the rise of China revolve around two key dimensions: the inevitability of power trends and the nature of Chinese ends or "intentions," now and into the future. Some analysts—those who can be called Sino-American "pessimists"—believe that China is indeed on a path toward power predominance over the next decade or so, and that under Xi Jinping the state has already shown that it has highly expansionistic ambitions for both its region and the globe.[2] Often drawing from the experience of the early Cold War, they argue that only a dramatic shift by Washington toward economic and military containment can moderate China's growth and deter Beijing from extending China's control over its near-abroad and the key sources of raw materials and oil in the Middle East, Africa, and South America. The logic underpinning their conclusions tends to mirror what Robert Jervis called in 1976 the deterrence model of international politics.[3] The other is assumed to have motives that go beyond mere security, such as an ideological mission and the status and glory of being a superpower. In the current situation, China is assumed to want to spread its repressive brand of techno-authoritarianism and to cultivate the pride of a rejuvenated Chinese nation. From this starting point, it stands to reason that only by standing up to China now can the United States prevent a dangerous Chinese expansion of its economic sphere and its military power projection capability.

At the other end of the spectrum are those that can be called Sino-American "optimists": namely, those who believe there are good reasons to doubt whether China can overtake the United States in total economic and military power, and that even if it could, it would have good reasons to be relatively moderate in its policies.[4] Adopting assumptions that parallel Jervis's other model, the so-called spiral model, optimists tend to focus on how Chinese Communist Party leaders since at least 2011 and the U.S. "pivot" to Asia have had reason to worry about U.S. efforts to use partnerships with local states to restrict China's ability to break out of its region. They also point to Washington's increasing use of trade sanctions and restrictions on high-tech exports such as semiconductors to keep China down economically. Aware of the risks of creating a destabilizing spiral of hostility between the two great powers, they suggest that Washington and Beijing seek to find areas of common interest—including absolute GDP growth and domestic order, climate change, third-party instability, and antiterrorism—that will help them avoid a new and intense Cold War with all its attendant risks and costs.[5]

This chapter will seek to go beyond this division between pessimists and optimists, using the book's theory and case studies to provide a deeper understanding of the various forces and factors that will shape future U.S. decisions regarding China over the next two decades.[6] There are two fundamental problems underlying this pessimist-optimist divide and the other arguments that draw from either position. First, the two main camps do not acknowledge that all great powers have, as chapter 1 explained, a natural predisposition to expand the size of their economic power spheres and to protect their trade routes with naval power. China's Belt and Road Initiative and its massive military buildup over the last decade seem to pessimists to be clear signs of current president Xi Jinping's drive to "dominate the world"[7]—or for optimists as the reactions of an insecure actor feeling trapped. But they could well be the normal policies of a rising state that has reached a point of being *able* to do these things (through having enough economic power) and that *needs* to do these things to ensure access to key resources and to avoid the problem of diminishing marginal returns that so often causes rising states to start to peak and then decline in world history. Chapter 1 laid out the theoretical reasons for understanding why great powers in history have been compelled to expand their realm-one and realm-two commercial power spheres and to reduce their vulnerability to cut-offs from the spheres of adversaries (realm three). And the empirical chapters demonstrated that the United States, on *its* rise to a dominant position from 1790 to 1945, regularly acted to expand the scope of America's trade and investment realms. It first moved westward in North America and then across the Pacific Ocean, and finally achieved a globally dominant position with Franklin Roosevelt's economic and political "Grand Area" from Britain and Western Europe through the Middle East to Southeast Asia and Japan—a position still largely intact today (what I later call "FDR's legacy"). If U.S. leaders have felt compelled by uncertainties about the future to undertake such actions, then why should we expect Chinese leaders on their rise to be any different?[8]

It is of course likely that China's motive for "going abroad" after 1996—that is, for adopting a policy that extends the reach of Chinese firms and diplomats around the world[9]—is only partially a function of this baseline realist drive and that other causal factors—non-security drives (for pessimists) and insecurity given U.S. policy (for optimists)—are also important. But we can't assume that either the pessimists or the optimists are right about why Chinese foreign policy has taken a more "assertive" turn since 2007 before including the third explanation and what it might mean for the prospects for peace or Cold War escalation. Moreover, if there is indeed a *mix* of forces pushing leaders in Beijing to be more hard-line on the world stage, then understanding how those forces interact will be crucial for any rational security-driven U.S. leader seeking to create a balanced policy that both signals resolve and power and avoids creating unnecessary spirals of mistrust and hostility.

The second problem underlying the pessimist-optimist divide is the way the two sides go about describing the realities that drive their analyses. They invariably seek to convince us that their picture of what is happening now and what will happen in the future is the only one that fits the facts. Yet China is a notoriously secretive nation whose officials often release misleading statistics or present only facets of the reality they want the world to see. More significantly, however, is the age-old problem of uncertainty in international relations. It is the *inherent nature of all great power politics*, even between democracies, that it is very hard to know for sure the adversary's true current power and motives, let alone what it will be like ten or fifteen years from now. Probabilistic estimates of its power and its character type, now and into the future, can of course be made, and indeed are essential to any "net assessment" exercises undertaken to calculate the costs and risks of alternative policies and to leave room for later adjustments as new information is received. But what we need for both scholarly purposes and for good policy-making is an understanding of *the different scenarios that may emerge* going into the future, and how smart actors will prepare for specific scenarios as the updated estimates become available.

This is what the bulk of this chapter will seek to do. I will lay out four main scenarios for the future, depending on changes in China's economic power position and its character type. The theoretical and empirical work of the previous chapters will be used to elucidate exactly what the implications are for each of the scenarios as well as for dynamic transitions between these scenarios. This allows me to avoid having to choose any one scenario or pathway as the one that indeed will come about, given current realities. Instead, I can simply do what any rational state would do under the kind of conditions of high uncertainty that constitute the current situation with China: namely, figure out the various possibilities, and then determine the best U.S. strategy for the most likely situations that might arise given the trends. Smart leaders understand that international politics is a world of tensions and trade-offs. They will thus try to avoid unnecessarily provoking the other through overly nasty policies, given the specific conditions at hand, even as they avoid letting their guard down through overly nice policies.

To create a balanced policy that suits evolving conditions, U.S. leaders will need to analyze how things might evolve across two main variables: *whether China can catch up and overtake the United States in economic power, or not*; and *whether Chinese leaders will increasingly deviate from the "rational security-maximizing" ideal over time*, either by pushing for non-security objectives such as glory and the spread of ideology, or by being less able to rationally use the best means to achieve their ends (or both).[10] By conceptualizing both dimensions in a single space, we can use the theory of the book to predict how the United States will likely act into the future, at least if its leaders remain both rational and driven above all by security ends.

In short, this chapter will avoid the tendency of scholars and pundits to try to gaze into the crystal ball and predict what the geopolitical reality will be like in a year or ten years. The fact is no one knows for sure. But we can lay out the various scenarios that could emerge and predict what the United States is likely to do about each scenario should it appear to be arising. Subsequent analyses by U.S. government agencies of changing conditions can then be undertaken to make probabilistic predictions about the likelihood of each scenario and how intense it will be should it come about. In this way, we can use the book's argument and evidence to make theoretically informed (yet practical) judgments about the way the United States is likely to respond over time to developments in China and East Asia.

## The Three Stages and the Four Scenarios

In any situation of emerging bipolarity, where a second-ranked state is catching up to the dominant state in relative economic power, we can usefully talk about three stages of great power competition over time.[11] The first stage is simply the catching-up phase, whereby a state such as China grows from a point of clear inferiority to one where it is still inferior but could, if positive relative trends continue, overtake the declining state in the near term. The second stage, given the current U.S.-China competition, is the most interesting. This is where scholars and policy makers wonder if the rising state will be able to sustain its rise in relative economic power or whether it will "peak early" and then start to decline before being able to overtake the declining power. The third stage, because of the uncertainty in the second stage, can itself have two possibilities. The first is where the rising state from stage one does indeed keep its growth going and overtakes the decliner, but then reaches its own peak in power later, either because the formerly declining state is able to reenergize its economic growth, or because strong diminishing marginal returns cause the rising state to simply "peter out" once achieving dominance. The second possibility is where the declining state in stage two is not only able to reverse its decline during that stage before the riser overtakes it, but then in stage three opens the relative gap between it and the now-falling former riser.

These possibilities are shown in figure 10.1. The solid line captures the core presumption of the pessimistic school—namely, that the rising state "C" (in this case, China) can and will significantly overtake state "A" (the United States, or "America") and achieve a position of dominance some decades from now before it finally reaches some sort of peak in its relative economic power. The optimist position is represented by the dotted line that begins as the powers enter stage two, showing China peaking early while still inferior or about equal and then declining into greater inferiority in stage three. This dotted line thus reflects the optimist's assumption that China is unlikely to ever overtake the United States, given the across-the-board strengths of the American state and the demographic, environmental, and debt-related constraints on the Chinese state.

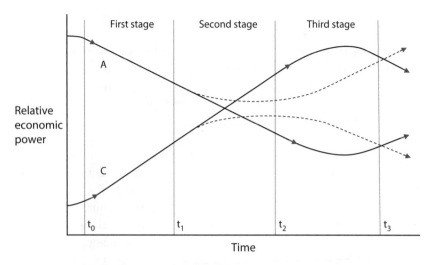

FIGURE 10.1. Stages in an emerging bipolar situation

The diagram, by focusing on the power dimension of the U.S.-China relationship, reveals what is missing in the debate between pessimists and optimists: namely, the causal impact of dynamic variations in character type over time. Each side in the debate starts with presumptions about "what China wants"—the relative weightings of glory and ideological expansion versus security—and thus fails to consider potential changes in the weightings and intensities of these ultimate ends over time. Moreover, the diagram captures a problematic assumption of both pessimists and optimists: namely, that the trends are exogenous to the behavior of the actors—in terms either of how easily they can *reenergize their own growth* in the face of economic slowdowns or how they can *hurt the other's ability to grow.*

Some scholars, most notably Hal Brands and Michael Beckley, have seen the weaknesses of the existing debate, and introduced the idea that China has indeed already started peaking, and that this peaking will cause China to act more aggressively in the near term. This is an important potential corrective to the optimist logic that says that Washington doesn't have to worry because China will never surpass the United States in overall economic and military power. Brands and Beckley, utilizing an earlier theoretical argument made by Copeland regarding the danger of states peaking and then declining in power, rightly show that uncertainty about the future can make such states—if indeed they have good reason to believe they *are* truly peaking—become more aggressive. Brands and Beckley, arguing that China has already hit its peak, thus believe that over the next decade China will invade Taiwan and likely move against Southeast Asian states such as the Philippines to shore up its declining position before it is too late.[12]

The problem with the Brands-Beckley argument is that it presumes, like the pessimists and optimists, that its assessment of China already having peaked is both a self-evident existing reality for leaders in Beijing and one that these leaders cannot do anything about short of war or policies that risk a spiral to war. This is wrong on both counts. Given that the vast majority of both pessimistic and optimistic scholars believe that China is still rising and that it is only a question of how far it will grow, it is premature to assume that China is already and unalterably past its peak and that it is all downhill from here. Certainly since 2008 CCP leaders have been aware that the double-digit growth of the early 2000s will be very hard to reestablish. And Xi himself acknowledged as early as 2014 that the "new normal" of Chinese GDP growth going into the future would be closer to 5 to 6 percent.[13] The period since the Covid-19 pandemic has been of course a rollercoaster for all economies. China itself achieved only 2 percent growth in 2020 before rebounding to around 9 percent in 2021. With the resurgence of Covid and an ill-advised Covid-zero policy, 2022 growth was only 2 to 3 percent. But China's exports in 2022 still grew at double-digit rates despite the disruptions created by the Ukraine war and a shortage of semiconductors. And if there is one thing we know from past downturns over the last three decades (1990–91, 1998–99, and 2008–9), China has an ability to bounce back and reorganize its society for a new round of economic vitality.[14]

The better approach is to suspend judgment on present realities and trends and instead to analyze different scenarios that *could* come about over the next decade or two, looking at both potential changes in power and in China's character type.[15] By looking at various future scenarios and how the United States is likely to react to each as it becomes a stronger and stronger possibility, we can examine the risks of conflict and great power war in each of them, and use theory and historical understanding to suggest ways to moderate these risks. The rest of this section will lay out the four main scenarios, with some predictions of how the United States will likely react to each scenario and variations in it.

I begin with an uncontroversial premise: namely, that the return to a more conflictual global system over the last fifteen years has been fundamentally driven by the worries of a formerly dominant state (the United States) that the rising state (China) will overtake it in economic and even military power and will then use its new position to force changes on the system that hurt U.S. interests and security. Were the Americans simply to accept the inevitability of China's eventual rise to preeminence and continue the relaxed, even encouraging, policies of economic engagement of the 1980 to 2010 period, then there would be little reason for scholars and officials to be concerned about the deterioration of the post–Cold War peace, let alone expect, as many do, that America and China are entering into a new Cold War. China would simply continue to use its increased trade connections with the United States, Europe, and the world to facilitate further technological growth, build the diversity of its economic base, and translate that into a global military position that would take over the American post-1945 role as the protector of sea lanes and regional order.

Since 2010–11, however, with President Obama's geopolitical pivot to Asia, it has been clear that the United States was now prepared to position itself to deter Chinese regional expansion and to increasingly constrain (if not "contain") China's growth relative to the United States.[16] While this move came before the rise to power of Xi Jinping, his assumption of the presidency of China in late 2012 and his desire to extend China's economic power sphere through the Belt and Road Initiative (2013) and its associated support mechanisms (e.g., the Asian Infrastructure and Investment Bank and the Export-Import Bank of China) has fueled American concerns that Beijing is more willing to whittle down America's traditionally dominant position than ever before. The fact that China, besides heightening the aggressiveness of its rhetoric, has rapidly built up both the size and technological sophistication of its navy and has militarized barren atolls in the South China Sea has only reinforced American beliefs that China is seeking a major revision of the post-1990 order, at the expense of the United States.[17]

The emerging consensus view of both Democrats and Republicans in Washington is that the U.S. officials of both parties naively assumed until the 2010s that economic engagement with China after 1990 would give China a stake in the continuation of the global rules-based system and might even help move the state toward the liberal democratic end of the spectrum, thus reinforcing the post–Cold War peace.[18] Xi's policies have burst this bubble, and now Democrats and Republicans alike want to prevent China from growing further in relative economic and military power. Both sides are now willing to project U.S. power into the Indo-Pacific region to make Beijing think twice about any further aggressive expansion of its influence and control.[19]

This leads us to the two core strategic issues that are now front and center for both U.S. parties: To what extent can China really catch up and overtake the United States? And to what extent will Chinese leaders become less concerned with the security of the nation and its domestic order and more concerned with non-security goals such as glory, status, and the spreading of ideology for their own sakes? The phrase "for their own sakes" is important here, since so often it is automatically assumed that any imagery and rhetoric projected by Xi Jinping to his people about the "great rejuvenation of the Chinese nation" and the reestablishment of its place in the system reflect goals that go beyond the security of the state. But this is not necessarily so. President Xi, for one, understands that liberal democratic states do represent a critical threat to the stability and cohesion of his state, for the simple reason that liberal ideals of individual rights and freedoms are appealing to many if not most of his citizens. The wake-up call here was the two-month-long Tiananmen Square crisis from April to early June 1989. Every Chinese leader since June 1989 has been obsessed with preventing a repeat of "Tiananmen," with its calls for individual rights, its hunger strikes for freedom, and its startlingly bold and revolutionary imagery—a Goddess of Liberty statue, modeled on New York's Statue of Liberty, sitting in the main square of the "People's Republic" of China for a week; and of course, a young man standing in front of a line of moving tanks in the square a few days after the massacre, grinding them to a halt with simple courage and a white flag.[20] The fact that Beijing would again bring out tanks to quell the bank-failure protests in Henan in July 2022 reinforces that the CCP leaders still believe that their country is fragile and that foreign ideas such as freedom of speech and association are fundamental threats to the cohesion of the Chinese nation.[21]

As I have stressed in chapter 1, any leader's concern for national security, at least since the French Revolution, has two dimensions: the fear of invasion of the homeland or critical allies by an adversary; and the fear that the adversary will seek to undermine the nation's domestic stability through the promotion of ideological subversion or ethnic division, often via economic tools. The threat that Moscow represented to the United States during the Cold War was largely the former (although the second seemed strong during the McCarthy era of the 1950s). But Russia's efforts to undermine the U.S. electoral process and to increase American polarization from 2016 to 2020 have reinforced the idea that national security can be undermined by tools that exist on a spectrum from direct military action to the use of rhetoric to undermine internal stability. Chinese officials have felt this dual aspect of security in an even deeper way than the Americans, precisely because authoritarian states do have inherent legitimacy problems, and Washington has for decades sought to encourage the liberalization of China through trade, Voice of America broadcasts, and the internet.

In the following discussion of the four main scenarios, I will start with the assumption that, at least at this stage, both the United States and China are largely rational security-maximizing states, meaning that the core leaders and officials of each state are primarily concerned with protecting their nation and its partners from either direct attack or from an adversary's efforts to subvert internal stability. The terms "largely" and "primarily" here simply mean that the leaders and officials of either state, when they have to choose, will not sacrifice national security for other non-security goals such as glory and the spread of ideology, and will rationally pursue the best means to the end of security. Some scholars might argue that Xi Jinping has already shown a willingness to trade off security for the glory of his nation and his own status as a "great leader." This may be so. But since it is hard at this stage to tell if Xi's touting of the "great rejuvenation of the Chinese state" (the China Dream) is simply his way of maximizing security by mobilizing his population for the "new challenges" China faces,[22] I will stay with the assumption that both the United States and China are largely RSMs worried about the future. This allows me to discuss *changes* from this baseline as the next two decades unfold.[23]

The first scenario for the future is that both America and China remain largely rational security-maximizers in a power situation where China stays below the United States in GDP—that is where it is unable to catch up and overtake the United States in economic power. In figure 10.2, I show this scenario number 1 in the bottom-left corner. The figure itself provides two main variables—China's level of future relative GDP and China's character type over time. Scenario number one is thus a situation where the current status quo as I have defined it continues, with the Chinese leadership continuing to primarily seek security in a rational way against an American leadership that is presumed to be rational and security-maximizing across time and all scenarios.

From the U.S. perspective, this can be considered the "best" scenario of the four I will outline, for the simple reason that China never achieves a position of economic dominance and has good reasons to stay moderate, given that security concerns are more important than glory, status, and the spread of China's socialist ideology. The one exception is where China is not able to hold its own in relative economic power and actually starts to plunge downward due to structural problems at home or overly restrictive U.S. commercial policies.[24] But let me first discuss the three other main scenarios before returning to the question of China's "peaking early" and feeling itself to be in deep decline, since all four of the scenarios and the pathways leading to or from them can involve this fundamental problem of "peaking and decline" that can greatly destabilize the system.

The second scenario is shown in the top left-hand side of figure 10.2—namely, where China remains a largely rational security-maximizing state in its character type but continues to achieve growth relative to the United States, to the point where it is quite superior in GDP relative to U.S. GDP. In the chapter's first figure, figure 10.1, this was the solid line of China growing through stage two to achieve a preponderant position in stage three, without changing its core character. We can predict that American leaders would have at least a "moderate to high" concern about this scenario coming to pass, since while Chinese leaders are still rational security-maximizers, they also have the kind of economic dominance needed to push for major changes in the principles

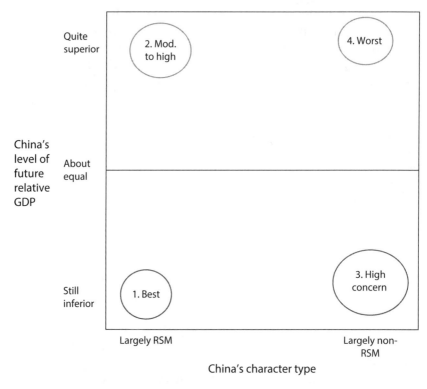

FIGURE 10.2. The four main scenarios and the U.S. level of geopolitical concern, from best or lowest of concern to worst or the highest.

of the "rules-based order" and to leverage better commercial deals with partners that are part of whatever form the Belt and Road Initiative takes over the next two decades. And since all great powers seek to expand their economic power spheres, a preponderant China would perhaps push even beyond the current plans for the BRI.

A different scenario is the third, in which China is not able to catch up and overtake the United States in relative economic power, but its internal makeup becomes decidedly "non-RSM" in character type; say, by an internal coup that puts Maoists in power in Beijing or by the deterioration of Xi Jinping's health and his ability to rationally calculate the best means to his determined ends, whether security or non-security in nature.[25] This scenario would probably be of equal or even greater concern to American policy makers as one were to see it coming about, simply because actors that are either driven by non-security objectives or are irrational in their means are, historically, typically quite aggressive, and China *already* has the economic and military power to do major damage if its leaders wanted to do so.

The final and fourth scenario, the top right corner of figure 10.2, is the one where China has not only overtaken the United States in relative GDP but *also* has clearly moved to the non-RSM end of the character spectrum. For obvious reasons, in a snapshot sense, this is likely the worst future scenario from the American point of view. It involves a China that is not only economically preponderant and thus has weight to throw around, but has strong glory, status, and ideological mission reasons for wanting to expand. Scenario number four, in a way, could look to Washington as the mid-1930s looked to Paris and London—as a situation where the rising state (in this case China) had reached a point where it could take on the system, and seemed to have pathological reasons for wanting to do so. The nuclear weapons of the modern era would moderate even such a state's desire to "go all out" in its expansionist ambitions. But this scenario would involve so many unknowns and potential regional flashpoints that we could expect increasing nervousness within an American polity that saw this top-right scenario coming about.

At this point, the picture of scenarios has been largely static in nature. I have dealt only with snapshots of different situations that could come about in the future. I have not shown the various pathways that would move the great power relationship from the current status quo—assumed to be the bottom-left situation of the United States facing an inferior but largely rational and security-maximizing China—toward one of the other three corners. Nor have I dealt with the implications of a China that is on its way toward another corner but then finds itself either peaking and declining in relative power or having internal changes that push the state back toward the rational security-seeking end of the character spectrum (as happened when Mikhail Gorbachev came to power in 1985).[26] As I have stressed throughout the book, it is generally the *anticipation* of future changes in power, trade, and character type that drive current changes in actor behavior.[27]

Figure 10.2 provides only a quick first cut at conceptualizing the future. A fuller, more dynamic picture of the future is shown in figure 10.3—with dynamic defined here both in terms of changes in power and character type over time and, as I'll discuss below, changes in trends in relative growth, including the phenomenon of peaking and then declining. Starting with the presumption that we are currently still in the bottom-left corner (China inferior in relative GDP and largely a rational security-seeking state), it shows five main pathways of change. The first, pathway A, is basically a situation where China cannot grow much further in relative GDP and stabilizes its relative position at where it is now, at about 80% of US economic power. This is a situation that could easily come about if the United States achieves, say, about 2-3% absolute growth over the next two decades on average and China's growth rate is about the same, making it hard for China to overtake America in relative power (and

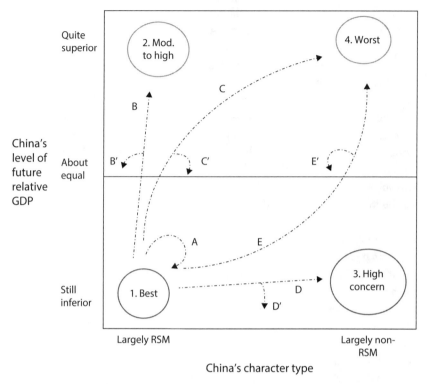

FIGURE 10.3. The five main pathways and their "peaking-and-decline" variants, with U.S. assessment of concern from best to worst.

of course still leaving it quite inferior in per capital GDP, given China's huge population). Provided that both states do indeed achieve similar and *positive* absolute growth figures, and neither side is worried about being overshadowed by the other, we can expect both sides will be relatively moderate in their foreign policies. Both will seek to assure the other that trade flows will continue, and both will be anxious not to hurt the absolute growth trends that not only provide enough popular support at home to deflect any efforts by the other to undermine the regime type, but enough economic growth to allow the projection of naval power necessary to protect trade routes.

Pathway A is likely to be the most stable and peaceful of the five pathways, with again the caveat that both can use diplomacy and foreign economic policy to achieve similar absolute growth trajectories and avoid creating negative expectations of future trade that make either state fear deep decline. China can help achieve this by forgoing overly militarized and exclusive connections to the countries in its Belt and Road Initiative. The United States can achieve this by reassuring China that it will continue to be able to get access to the oil, raw materials, and semiconductor-related inputs that it needs to achieve its goals of being a "prosperous" and "advanced" country by 2035 and a fully coequal great power by the hundredth anniversary of the founding of the PRC in 2049. This may be tough, given the baseline need of great powers to expand their economic power and to protect those spheres with naval power. Moreover, great powers anticipating decline have an incentive not only to coerce new trade partners into their existing spheres, but to try to reduce the economic growth of the adversary for fear of being made vulnerable down the road, as we saw with U.S. policy toward the Soviet Union from 1945 to 1985. And both of these pressures can lead to an intensification of the trade-security spiral, in which the decliner increases its economic restrictions, but the riser fears that it will thereby hit a glass ceiling if it does not act strongly to compensate for the restrictions. Such was the case with the origins of the colonial War for Independence: British fears of decline led to policies that convinced the Americans that London was trying to keep it down, and they came to believe that only an all-out war with the British empire would secure their established freedoms and ways of life. Chinese leaders could reach a point where they saw the United States as similarly determined to keep China in a second-ranked and more manageable position.[28]

Rational states, however, can also learn from history to respond subtly to complex changing conditions in ways that preserve security without risking war. The Berlin and Cuban crises of 1961 and 1962 and Japan's attack on Pearl Harbor have taught us that when states practice hard-line commercial and military policies that cause the other to believe it is potentially in deep decline, the latter will shift to expansionistic or risky coercive strategies to shore up its weakening position. If both Washington and Beijing prove able to internalize the lessons of the past, they can work to stabilize each other's expectations of both trade and future behavior, thereby creating the kind of trust that can allow for similar absolute growth levels that avoid significant relative decline.

The second pathway, pathway B, is more problematic. Here China achieves higher GDP growth rates than the United States, and thus moves over time toward the top left corner—namely, toward a position of clear economic superiority.[29] If this scenario were to be seen as unfolding, we can expect that U.S. policy would become progressively more inclined to hard-line policies across the board, notwithstanding the known risks of escalation. Washington would seek to use increasingly strong economic restrictions to try to slow Chinese relative gains in GDP, particularly if China was perceived to be intensifying, not decreasing, its use of neo-mercantilist strategies such as currency manipulation, generous subsidies, and the illegal appropriation of Western technology. It would also seek to use military buildups to ensure that a more powerful China did not think of using coercion to expand its footprint in Asia and elsewhere.

In a real way, we have already seen this pathway at work. Since 2011 and Obama's "pivot" to Asia, and especially since Trump's 2018–19 trade tariffs and Biden's intensification of Trump's restrictions on the transfer of high-tech inputs such as semiconductor software and hardware, U.S. administrations have been trying to maintain the American economic edge at the commanding heights of the global economy. The Biden administration's effort in 2022–23 to get the Dutch to stop exporting not only the machines that make the highest-tech semiconductors,[30] but also the ones making lower-level chips, demonstrates that the United States has already started pursuing a form of economic containment, albeit only at the high-tech level.[31]

It is worth reiterating that this pathway will be seen as worrisome in Washington even for those officials who expect China is and will remain a largely rational and security-driven actor. This is because, according to the logic of all systemic realist theories, even great powers that are rational security-maximizers (RSM) now *and know the other is also RSM* will be uncertain about whether the other might become a non-RSM character type in the future. It must also worry that even if the rising state *stays* rational and security-driven, as a future dominant RSM it will start to believe it must further expand its economic power sphere *as a hedge against others that might rise against it later* once it reaches a peak of its own power. A currently declining state will know that smart rising states will understand that they can't sustain relative growth forever. They thus will likely undertake actions—even as they are still rising—that will serve to stabilize their future power positions once they peak in relative power.[32] This was what FDR and Truman did from 1943 to 1945 to ensure that the United States after the war would indeed have full control of the so-called Grand Area stretching from Britain and Western Europe, through the Middle East and all the way to Japan.

The good news in terms of current American foreign policy is that the United States still inhabits this highly advantageous position, one that keeps China and Russia bottled up geographically and economically. The implications of this "FDR legacy" is that China has very few true aligned states in its sphere—North Korea, perhaps some Central Asian and African states, and Russia (for now). The American political sphere of aligned states constitutes almost all the wealthiest industrial nations or groupings in the world such as Canada, Japan, South Korea, Taiwan, and the European Union. It also has strong ties with most of the key states in particular regions, such as Saudi Arabia, Indonesia, South Africa, Mexico, Brazil, and Argentina. Unlike past great powers that have been economically on top but have feared long-term decline, such as Germany from 1905 to 1914, the United States has little reason to worry about its larger economic power base, since much of the globe is already aligned with it. Indeed, as the end of the Trump era quickly showed, most states in Asia *want* a strong American presence in their region, even if not necessarily with American boots on the ground (e.g., Vietnam and Malaysia).[33] Washington can use this base to shore up its economic position without having to resort to the kind of highly destabilizing policies that Germany and Japan had to engage in after their leaders began to anticipate respective peaks in power after 1905 and 1935.[34]

The next pathway, pathway C, is one where a China that is growing in relative GDP starts to become over time more and more demonstrably irrational or non-security-driven in its strategic thinking and behavior. Pathway B was problematic enough since a declining United States would be uncertain about whether rising China would be aggressive later at its peak (after time $t_3$ in figure 10.1) for either RSM or non-RSM reasons. But with pathway C, it is becoming increasingly obvious to Washington that China is not only growing in power but also turning into a non-RSM actor. All things being equal, we can predict that such developments, as they became increasingly self-evident, will convince U.S. leaders to expend even more effort to constrain China's ability to build its economic power and expand its commercial realms. They will accept heightened risks of escalation as the price for preserving a measure of deterrence capability.

Compared to pathway E (discussed below), by the nature of pathway C, China's changes in character type are delayed. This may mean that the United States may not react quickly enough to really stop China's relative growth trend. For offensive realists, the very chance of a rising China changing into a non-RSM actor over time should make the United States assume "worst case" and thus shift it to all-out containment now.[35] But as I have argued in chapters 1 and 2, because of the potential to set off a trade-security dilemma spiral that leads to unwanted war, smart actors will think probabilistically rather than in worst-case terms. After all, in the early stages of both pathway B and C, as figure 10.2 shows, it is very hard to tell whether China is headed toward the top-left corner (where it is RSM) or the top-right (where it is not), and indeed, one cannot know whether China's growth trends will taper off before they become preponderant. So, it is irrational to assume worst case until more data is in and a move toward the top-right becomes a given. Assuming worst case in the early stages, given the dynamics of spiraling, could create the very "bad apple" that one hopes to avoid—a rising state obsessed with the idea that only all-out expansion will save it or a situation where domestic hawks gain power and start promoting their status and ideologically driven agendas at the expense of pure security.

I will return below to the situations on pathways B and C where the rising state does indeed "peak early" before achieving preponderance and then starts to anticipate decline. These pathways B' ("B prime") and C' ("C prime") are potentially quite problematic, since as the riser starts to anticipate peaking and decline, it will have a greater incentive to increase the hardline-ness of its policies to shore up its trade networks and to secure the kind of naval and territorial positions around the world that either reenergize the state's economic growth or avoid further decline. But for now, let's look at the other two main pathways.

Pathway D is simply a situation where China remains inferior in GDP but is becoming more and more "non-RSM." If this pathway is looking increasingly probable, we should expect that U.S. officials, seeing the trend within China toward irrationality and non-security ends, will be increasingly willing to adopt a more purely "deterrence model" approach to policy. This may not necessarily involve increasing economic restrictions, since a China that had already been demonstrating an inability to grow through its own resources might be driven into decline and war by a U.S. economic containment strategy, as was Japan in 1941. In the early 1970s and late 1980s, Washington cooperated with Moscow partly out of a fear that driving the Russians into the ground economically might trigger *more* aggressive behavior from a Leninist state worried about long-term power trends. It worked, and the initial détente eventually turned into a trade-cooperation deal that ended the Cold War itself. With today's China, we cannot in the near term expect a Gorbachev to emerge. All things being equal, however, a movement by China toward the bottom-right corner would be a situation where Washington must deal with Beijing both firmly (to show power and resolve to dissuade regional plunges) and flexibly (to ensure trade access when Chinese leaders are moderating their behavior to help avoid making them feel desperate about the future, as happened to the Soviets from 1960 to 1962).

Pathway E is the most potentially dangerous of the five. It captures the situation where a rising China has been becoming increasingly driven by glory and a sense of ideological mission and is less rational in its pursuit of its ends, and yet is also increasing its relative GDP and thus feeling, at least initially, more and more confident that it can achieve preponderance and then impose its will not just on neighbors but on the United States itself. Extreme pessimists believe that this has already been happening, at least since Xi Jinping became president in 2012, and that China's increasing "assertiveness," if not aggressiveness, in its region and around the world is a direct reflection of both of its non-RSM regime type and its increased power in the system. Yet a more fully dynamic view of this pathway would emphasize how a still rising China has an interest in strong trade ties with both its neighbors and the larger U.S. sphere in order to keep its growth going. Hence, while Xi has certainly been more provocative in his rhetorical posturing and assertive in the promotion of the Belt and Road

Initiative, in terms of actual policy, including over Taiwan, he has talked a tough game but been reluctant to act on his hard-line rhetoric.[36]

It is certainly true that if Xi truly became an irrational non-security-driven actor, we might expect to see him taking great risks of war to achieve his status and ideological goals. But pathway E is typically, like the other pathways, a *gradual* movement away from the previous status quo. And because of its centralized domestic system, China will probably avoid a dramatic shift in character type, unlike Germany in early 1933 when Hitler came into power, partly through elections. American officials should therefore have enough time to ratchet up the *severity* of the deterrence strategy employed as a reaction to expectations about the severity of the shift in both power and character type going on within China. Xi is not Hitler, and not even Stalin—at least at this stage. He knows how to respond to U.S. and allied balancing, and he knows that an overly aggressive strategy could well lead to the kinds of restrictive trade policies imposed on Germany in the late 1930s and Russia after 1947.

Up until now, I have talked about the pathways as though they were movements across time that could not really be fundamentally reversed by either U.S. policy or through domestic changes within China. But of course, this is exactly one of the key questions that hangs over all of U.S.-China relations: To what extent can the United States *cause* China either to slow down in its relative economic growth—as Washington did successfully with the Soviet Union after 1946—or to experience a change in its domestic type? If we accept that Washington can indeed endogenously affect China's power or its type, we must face the separate issue of security dilemmas and spiraling from chapter 2: To what extent would trying to do either of these things tend to make the United States *less* secure because it would increase the mistrust Chinese leaders feel toward Washington, and would make their expectations for future trade and future domestic security plummet, forcing them to move against the U.S. sphere in ways that increased the risk of war?

Figure 10.3, through the "prime" variants of the pathways, captures the problem that U.S. policies combined with internal problems within China might lead not just to a stabilization of China's relative position at some point in the future, but to China's *peaking and decline* in relative power. The first two, B' and C', are where China has been growing toward equality in economic power and then finds itself peaking early and unable to hold its relative position in the system. Pathway D' ("D prime") is a situation where China remains inferior in GDP even as its type has become more glory- and ideologically driven, and then finds itself declining. Each of these first three variants are situations where one would expect China to become more aggressive the more it feels it can do little to reenergize its economic growth except through expansion and coercive policies abroad. The situation of D' might be less problematic than either B' or C', simply because China does not have the economic size to support a prolonged strategy of aggression and the absorption of new states into its political and economic spheres. But all three hold out the strong possibility of Beijing believing that preventive "now or never" measures are needed, and soon, to shore up its declining international and regional positions. To the extent CCP leaders view Washington as the cause of its peaking and decline, then they will be that much more aggressive in their pursuit of this policy.

Fortunately, to the extent that Washington is aware that it is pushing China into a decline, the more likely it is that U.S. officials will moderate the very policies that are creating this declining trend. This again was what Reagan and then Bush smartly did at the end of the 1980s, using the promise of trade and technology to reduce Russian fears that the Soviet Union would fall into the dustbin of history. In December 1991, it did of course end up splitting into separate republics. But no one foresaw this, except perhaps the generals that sought unsuccessfully to overthrow Mikhail Gorbachev in August 1991. If China ever reaches a point where its power trajectory resembles either B' or C', the best policy for Washington is to help give the Chinese state a soft landing in the hope that its fall will not be deep. As in the 1987 to 1991 period with Moscow, the commitment of the United States to open trade can help improve Beijing's trade expectations, and at least prove that any further Chinese decline is not being caused by vicious American policies.

Overall, the most destabilizing situation shown in figure 10.3 is pathway E when it morphs into the variant E'. Here, Chinese leaders, now fully non-RSM, feel they have reached a point of rough equality in power but expect the state to decline over time. They thus have an incentive to plunge into an expansionist mode that involves the use of military power and coercion, both to protect China's current position in the world and to make a bid for the larger China Dream of a coequal superpower that is respected around the world. The Brands and Beckley book's argument is essentially that China is already in this situation, and thus it will soon be going on the warpath, not just against Taiwan, but other states in the region and even beyond.

Yet their analysis is inherently flawed, as we have seen. In addition to the above critique, there are two additional points that can be made. First, they themselves show that China has been driven by security fears about the United States and the West for some time, and that CCP leaders expect Washington to try to undermine China's internal cohesion and make it more liberal and democratic. It thus follows that if these leaders perceived U.S. officials to be backing off from the promotion of liberalism, they would have reason to be less worried about the future disintegration of the Chinese state—in short, they would be less concerned that a repeat of the 1989 Tiananmen Square crisis would occur. Second, they provide little evidence that the *Chinese leaders themselves* believe that China is declining deeply and inevitably and that further reforms and government-directed investments cannot reenergize the state.[37] Indeed, the irony of the Brands/Beckley position is that it is the very centralized Leninist structure of the Chinese state—one of the things they believe makes China so aggressive—that gives Chinese leaders the confidence that their domestic system is superior to the U.S. system and will lead to China's eventual triumph over a polarized and self-centered American social order. With more than half of Republicans accepting Trump's Big Lie that the 2020 election was stolen and the January 6, 2021 insurrection a justified act of civil disobedience, we can perhaps see the reasons for their long-term confidence. But it does mean that in the short term, China's economic dependence will act as a major restraining force on any desires to revise the global status quo.[38] Why rock the boat if it might mean cut-offs from the trade that has fueled your growth for forty years?

The situation of E' is therefore quite a way off, if indeed we are even moving on that pathway currently. There are many unknowns, and any assertion that E is the true current pathway and that a domestically driven China is already at the peaking and decline point of E' is mere speculation. Indeed, were U.S. officials to follow the Brands and Beckley argument that a strong containment strategy is necessary now, they might adopt hard-line policies that *create* the very sense of peaking and decline that the authors think is already occurring (our E' scenario). And as Beijing's fears of the future increased and glory-driven hawks gained more power within the Party, the chance that China would go after Taiwan, the Philippines, or something bigger would grow. This would be a self-fulfilling prophecy of the worst kind.

In the next section, I move from simply outlining the implications of different pathways and how they might unfold in dangerous ways to focus on what I believe has been really going on within the Chinese state over the last three decades, and what this means for the various scenarios we have covered. This section may appear to be breaking my rule about not speculating on what the current situation is and where it is going, and to some degree that is true. But my goal is not to give, as most of the literature does, some sort of definitive assessment of "what Chinese leaders want" or whether China will overtake the United States. Like all scholars, I possess no crystal ball. I will therefore refrain from "picking a pathway." But by looking at some of the key points of Chinese history over the last three decades, we can arrive at an understanding of some of the key turning points and developments that almost all scholars of China agree upon. This will provide a foundation that allows policy makers to make probabilistic estimates regarding which pathway might come about and under what conditions. In this way, U.S. officials can decide for themselves what combination of military and trade policies seem best for the situation they seem to be facing, all the while knowing that overly hard-line policies can cause China to anticipate decline and become more hawkish while overly soft-line policies can lead to China's relative growth and to a weakening of Beijing's perception of U.S. power and resolve. Understanding the core trade-offs will allow policy makers to incorporate the insights of both deterrence- and spiral-model thinking as they move forward.

## How Chinese Leaders Think about Security

As the Cold War was winding down in the late 1980s, China was just starting to move toward a freer economic and political system at home after the repression of the Maoist era. It had tentatively opened four special economic zones to encourage foreign investment and joint ventures to bring technology and production techniques into China. It had for the first time allowed a measure of open discussion about the value of capitalism versus socialism and was tentatively experimenting with the distribution of American films and music. Then in 1989, out of the blue, but inspired by democratic reforms in South Korea, Taiwan, and the Soviet empire, a domestic crisis of monumental proportions hit. This was of course the two-month standoff from April to early June pitting students and then also workers against the CCP leadership at the very heart of China's cultural and political heritage, Tiananmen Square in Beijing. The students were moved by the death on April 15 of Hu Yaobang, the CCP leader who had been sacked two years earlier for pushing for even greater openness, to congregate in Tiananmen Square to seek a new round of reforms.

Student appeals for fundamental change struck a chord across the country, and in over two hundred Chinese cities, students and workers took up the protest, while hundreds of thousands took trains to Beijing, joining those already camping on the street. The CCP leadership was split, with moderate Zhao Ziyang seeking compromise and hard-liner Li Peng demanding a violent crackdown to restore order. As the Chinese government appeared impotent, the students ratcheted up their demands to include constitutional guarantees of basic rights and freedoms, symbolizing their efforts by constructing a large statue modeled on New York's Statue of Liberty and placing it in the center of the square, right in front of the Forbidden City. By late May, Deng Xiaoping, nominally retired from all his formal positions (except the head of the military) but still de facto leader of China, had had enough. He ordered the army to clear the square and restore order. On June 4, 1989, the tanks and soldiers entered Tiananmen Square and began firing. Thousands of students and workers lost their lives, and tens of thousands were subsequently arrested, many executed over the next few months. Order within the communist-controlled Chinese state, which had been tottering on the edge of collapse, was restored.[39]

Almost all China experts agree that this "incident" seared itself into the consciousness of all Chinese leaders and high officials alive today.[40] It demonstrated not only that the stability of this very populous state could be easily undermined by outside ideas of liberal democracy and freedom, but that the Western powers, the United States in particular, would seize opportunities to both spread these ideas and encourage dramatic liberal reform, even if it meant revolution and chaos. Deng himself set the foundation of this view when he spoke publicly a few months after Tiananmen and said that "The West really wants unrest in China." Later that year he was more direct, stating that "the United States was deeply involved" in the Tiananmen disturbances and the "counter-revolutionary rebellion," and that Western countries were waging "a Third World War without gun smoke."[41] As Rush Doshi and Sulmann Wasif Khan note, Chinese leaders since 1989 have been obsessed with preventing another Tiananmen Square.[42] The fact that Tiananmen was followed by the successful revolutions in Eastern Europe later that year and the subsequent downfall of the Soviet Union in 1991 only reinforced their fears of foreign ideas destroying the social order. The shock of seeing global communism quickly fall apart—with China almost one of its casualties—was so profound that for almost three years, Beijing pulled back from even economic reforms, believing that such reforms would automatically create increased pressure for political liberalization.[43] Only with Deng's "southern tour" in early 1992 to promote the idea that China's coastal areas could draw in foreign capital without undermining social order—and use economic growth to keep the population happy and help them ignore the new increase in political repression—did China get back on the reform track that led to its subsequent rise to superpower status.[44]

There is no question that when Xi Jinping came to power in 2012, he quickly moved to turn China into an increasingly centralized "surveillance state" that would ensure conformity through facial recognition technology, social credit systems to punish improper behavior, and the monitoring of each citizen's internet, economic, and social activities. Higher party members have been kept in line by Xi's ongoing crackdown on corruption and his intolerance for opposition. And both the many and the few have been subjected to a massive propaganda campaign, promoting the collectivist idea of the "great rejuvenation of the Chinese nation"—the great China Dream of the country taking its place as a coequal or even dominant state at the top of the great power hierarchy. This campaign, along with the teaching of "Xi Jinping Thought" in both schools and workplaces, seeks to solidify each individual's commitment to the larger whole even as they followed Deng's advice that "to get rich is glorious." Needless to say, the increasingly authoritarian trends within China that began after 1989 but which intensified significantly after 2012, have been highly distressing to those who had hoped China would become more Westernized as it became more modernized. And the fact that Beijing seems intent on sharing its surveillance techniques to help autocratic leaders around the world remain in power only seems to reinforce the point that China is indeed a "revisionist" power intent on overthrowing the current international rules-based order and replacing it with something more to Beijing's liking.

It is easy in the West to jump to the conclusion that the changes within China and in Beijing's behavior toward the outside world after 2008—the crisis with Japan in 2010–12 over the Senkaku Islands, the seizing and militarization of atolls in the South China Sea from 2009 to the present, China's "Wolf Warrior" diplomacy, the massive military buildup in East Asia, the extension of the Belt and Road Initiative to Latin America, and the ongoing coercive threats toward Taiwan—are clear confirmation that Chinese leaders seek to displace the United States as the dominant state in the world. And of course, pessimists use this evidence to support their position that China has goals that go beyond the rational security ends assumed by systemic realists.

But before we assume that China is already well along pathway E and that it must be countered by an all-out effort to match its military buildup and reduce its economic growth by trade restrictions, three issues must be raised. First, it is important to establish to what extent the Chinese understanding of security is shaped by an imperative that almost all great powers face, especially as they reached certain stages of development: namely, to expand their economic power spheres just to keep GDP growth going.[45] Second, we need to see how China's problem of domestic stability is quite different from any other great power in modern history. And third, we must determine to what extent Washington's own behavior, including the promotion of democratic liberalization around the world, can affect the way Chinese leaders see the level of external threats that surround them. Only after we have this foundational understanding of the Chinese view of security in place can we turn to the question of to what extent China's recent behavior goes beyond mere rational security maximization, and thus to what extent it will be difficult to reach an accommodation with Beijing that secures the future peace.

One key question that arises immediately is whether the current tensions in U.S.-China relations are simply a function of Xi's leadership and ambitions. The answer is no. As Andrew Chubb, Rush Doshi, and Susan Shirk have shown, China started to become much more assertive over such things as the Senkaku Islands near Taiwan and the atolls in the South China Sea just after 2007.[46] Moreover, while the push to extend China's economic footprint certainly got a lift with Xi's Belt and Road Initiative, this initiative, as Min Ye demonstrates, was really a new name for a series of policies that were started in 1997–98 and gained steam after 2007. They were part of a larger strategic decision to "go abroad"—to use investments in smaller trade partners to increase China's control over both export markets and sources of raw materials. Significantly, as Ye shows, the upticks in China's going-abroad policies came just after periods when China's growth rate had slowed dramatically and CCP leaders could see what might happen should China not be able to increase its production efficiency.[47] China had an annual growth rate of 14 percent in 1992 but this rate was falling every year thereafter and by 1998 growth was around 8 percent. A significant effort was made to integrate China even more into the global economy, including through the controversial decision to join the World Trade Organization.[48] China's growth rose again into the double digits, and again hit 14 percent by 2007. But the trend was again downward, and by 2009 China's growth rate fell below 10 percent and it has been steadily falling to the point that by the mid-2010s Xi was talking regularly about 5 to 6 percent growth as the future "new normal."[49]

The problem of diminishing marginal returns and declining rates of growth are of course classic great power concerns, as Robert Gilpin has stressed.[50] China's responses to the anticipation of slowing rates—the effort to extend China's trade into new areas, to energize Chinese firms to be more competitive, and to protect the new trade routes with naval power—are themselves traditional actions that great powers do to increase the scope and wealth of their economic power spheres. Bismarck cast aside his former concerns about colonialism to grab large parts of Africa in the 1880s, and officials in Berlin after 1895 made sure that the German navy could protect trade all the way to China and the Pacific. The United States began its naval buildup after 1888 and then secured its own empire in the Pacific through the war with Spain in 1898. Such behavior comes out of the fundamental great power drive to extend one's economic power sphere to sustain growth, and this drive only gets stronger over time as economic growth uses up raw materials at home and industrial firms need larger markets to cover high fixed costs. China is no different. We should therefore not be surprised that in an era of slowing growth Xi Jinping, like Chinese Communist Party leaders before him, has been seeking to extend China's economic reach, even if it means bumping into the vast American sphere that is the legacy of Franklin Roosevelt's wartime policies.

But China's problem with falling rates of growth goes beyond the traditional great power concern about sustaining one's power position relative to primary adversaries. China has domestic concerns unlike any other great power in history. Its population is huge—over 1.4 billion—and 90 percent of it is concentrated on around one-third of the land. Unlike the American West when the United States was expanding in the nineteenth century, the western half of China is too high or too dry for high-yield agriculture. Moreover, the

Xinjiang and Tibet provinces have non-Han-Chinese majorities, making it hard for Beijing to encourage western migration.[51] Over four decades of modernization, the cities in the eastern third of China have absorbed more than 300 million migrants from the rural areas, not only increasing the Chinese need to import food but creating an urban concentration of individuals per acre greater than any nation on earth, including India. As the widespread protests over access to bank accounts in July 2022 reminded every senior CCP official, even when the issues at stake are economic and not political, the potential for social disorder and chaos is great.

China's own history over the last two hundred years confirms that revolts and revolutions are not only common, but often devastating. Over twenty million died in the Taiping Rebellion of the 1850s and 1860s, started by a leader influenced by Christian ideas brought by missionaries. Millions more died in the chaos that began with the overthrow of the Qing dynasty in 1911 and led to almost four decades of regional fragmentation, warlordism, the clash of the Nationalists under Chiang Kai-shek and the Communists under Mao Zedong before the Japanese invasion of 1937, and the civil war that followed Japan's defeat. Chinese leaders today, for good reason, see these internal tragedies (the "century of humiliation") as directly linked to the invasion of foreign troops, ideas, and firms after China lost the Opium War of 1839 to 1842. Not only did foreign powers feel free to sell products that undermined traditional Chinese culture—the worst example of this being Indian and Turkish opium—but they used coercion and force to carve China into economic spheres over which they exercised a considerable degree of political and legal authority.[52] So bad was the situation that by the early twentieth century only foreigners were fully protected by the rule of law in the international settlements, and Chinese citizens were often denied access to their own city parks.[53]

Considering this history, it is not surprising that all CCP leaders since Tiananmen have worried first and foremost about maintaining the internal security of the state. They not only fear that Western powers such as the United States are seeking to undermine the communist nature of Chinese society, but that the mere presence of U.S.-aligned democratic states near its shores in the form of Taiwan, South Korea, and Japan increases the risks of another Tiananmen crisis. In their minds, they thus have reason to take actions both within and without to protect the security of the state from foreign influences. And we do need to remember that U.S. policy since the death of Mao has not been just sweetness and light. During the Tiananmen Square crisis, Western media and the U.S. government sided with the protestors, not only by promoting the heroic nature of their actions, but by severely condemning the June 1989 crackdown. While George H. W. Bush decided to repair the U.S. relationship with Deng, Bill Clinton ran a campaign in 1992 that, among other things, strongly criticized Bush for cozying up to the "butchers of Beijing." Once in power, Clinton spent most of his first year distancing his administration from China, even as he offered up his new vision of promoting economic openness and the spread of liberalism around the world. When in 1994 he finally agree to restore normal relations with Beijing, one of his key demands, which Chinese leaders accepted, was that the Voice of America be allowed to broadcast freely into China.[54] The very fact that this was an important issue only reaffirmed for CCP leaders that the Americans were seeking not only to consolidate liberal democracy within Boris Yeltsin's Russia, but hoping to see it spread into China, one of the last remaining self-proclaimed socialist states on earth.

Given all this, it is not surprising that Chinese leaders from Deng to Xi have stressed the importance of noninterference in the affairs of others as a foundational principle of the international system—indeed, as a core "rule" of any rules-based order. It is also not surprising that Xi and his cohorts believe that the more they can strengthen the sphere of autocratic states around the world, the more China itself will be protected against the pernicious influence of liberal democracy.[55] In this sense, Xi's effort to promote China's form of techno-authoritarianism has a very different end than Mao's efforts in the 1960s to spread peasant-based revolution in the Global South. Mao was trying to inspire the masses to rise up against the local elites that were, in his mind, running regimes supported by the West. Xi is trying to do the opposite: he wants to *prevent* the many from overthrowing the few who run oppressive regimes, to stop them from sparking revolutions from below that lead to another wave of liberal democracy akin to that which swept the world in the late 1980s. And as a nice side benefit, he sees this as stabilizing the trade relations China has created with these states and discouraging them from following Washington's lead on commercial policy.

Xi is learning that in order to do this he not only needs China and its fellow autocratic states to increase surveillance while providing the calming balm of economic growth. He needs a collectivist and nationalist ideology that unites the many around the idea of the glorious nation, supported by officials that have genuinely dedicated their lives to the task of national development and pride.[56] The example of the fall of the Soviet Union teaches China that it cannot neglect the role of ideas when it counters the power of the West. As he said to party members in January 2013, just after assuming the role of President:

> Why did the Soviet Union collapse? Why did the Soviet Communist Party lose its power? One of the main reasons is that . . . [under Gorbachev] the history of the USSR and of the CPSU had been completely denied [and] Lenin had been rejected . . . Ideological confusion was everywhere . . . The

Soviet Union, which had been a great socialist country, collapsed. This is the lesson we must learn from the errors of the past![57]

To make sure the lesson was indeed learned, a three-hour documentary was commissioned on the Soviet collapse and provided for private viewing by party members later that year. It demonized Gorbachev, accusing him of selling out his country to the Americans. The film ends by admonishing party members to never give in to the "hostile forces" that seek to "western-ize" China and "sow the seeds of separatism." Members should, above all, be attuned to Western efforts to use "financial and ideological manipulations . . . [to further their plans] to incite chaos by promoting governance from the streets."[58]

In sum, while it may seem clear to many Western observers and certainly to China pessimists that Xi Jinping is a glory-driven egomaniac bent on "domi-nating the world," we cannot ignore the powerful baseline level of security concerns that animate Xi as well as the CCP power structure more generally. Chinese officials must grapple with not only falling growth rates and the need for markets to absorb the great excess capacity of Chinese factories. They must also constantly worry about the ongoing appeal of liberal democracy and the possibility that economic downturns or social issues as simple as inadequate jobs for graduating students will lead to a repeat of May 1989. Security for Beijing, as it has for most great powers since the ideological turn of the French Revolution, means not just fear of attack but a concern that other great powers will use economic tools and propaganda to insidiously undermine domestic stability. And foreign ideas at odds with China's historically hierarchical soci-ety have been threatening Chinese regimes for seven centuries—from the Buddhist-inspired insurgencies of the fourteenth century through the Christian-inspired Taiping Rebellion of the nineteenth century to the Western-liberal-inspired revolt of Tiananmen Square in the late twentieth century.

Solidifying a uniquely Chinese ideological foundation for the state, com-bining Confucianism with a "socialism with Chinese characteristics," has been one of Xi's fundamental goals since 2012. Yet in today's environment, his efforts have widened the sense of cultural distance between the United States and China, a distance that includes all four of the elements of cultural difference mentioned in chapter 2: political ideology, foreign economic orientation, re-ligion, and ethnic identity. There is no question that China's collectivist cen-tralized approach to political organization is at odds with the more individual-ist and decentralized approach of the United States (even if both states remain highly nationalistic). And Chinese leaders since 2008 have reinforced a strong state-centered and mercantilist form of political economy, emphasizing the guidance of the state in all areas of economic activity. China is officially atheistic, and its crackdowns on religious groups from Tibetan and Falun Gong Buddhists to Christians and Muslims alienates Chinese leaders from the historically more tolerant, and generally more religious, Americans.[59]

Those three elements of cultural difference on their own exacerbate American fears of what China might be like in the future, depending on its power trajectory. But we should not discount the extent to which American officials, at least unconsciously, also find it disconcerting to deal with a nation that constantly touts its "5,000-year-old civilization," with its millennia-old philosophies, traditions, and language. In principle, America has a civic-based nationalism, based on universal ideas of individual rights, rule of law, and equality of opportunity for all citizens who accept its principles, regardless of original ethnicity, race, and religion. China's is largely an ethnic-based nationalism.[60] While the people and Party officials are immensely proud of the triumphs of socialism and see China's version of socialism as a model for others, at its heart Chinese nationalism revolves around a Han Chinese view of the state and nation. The Han Chinese as an ethnic group make up over 90 percent of China's population. It is thus not surprising that a Xi Jinping can so easily reintroduce Confucius and his 2,500-year-old principles of loyalty to the group as a set of foundational values to guide daily behavior, using Confucian social ideology to reinforce the Marxist-Leninist principle that one's ultimate commitment, even in the age of material accumulation, is to the collective whole. And while lip-service is given to the importance of minority groups in the "autonomous regions" of Tibet, Xinjiang, and Inner Mongolia, since the 1950s Beijing's long-term goal is to have citizens from the Han majority move into and dominate these regions for the good of "China proper"—the egg-shaped area from Beijing in the north to Guangzhou in the south and Chengdu in the east, where over 85 percent of Han Chinese live. So dominant has the Han basis for China's political and cultural identity been over the centuries that despite a major demographic shift that will leave China with only two to three workers for every retiree by 2050 (versus the seven-to-one ratio in 2000), few Chinese officials openly advocate using immigration as a solution to the problem.[61]

Yet despite the clear cultural distance between the American state and the Chinese state as shaped by CCP leaders over the last three decades, we should be careful not to assume that a rising China, regardless of which of the many possible pathways it eventually takes, will inevitably be as much of a threat as the two biggest rising threats the United States faced in the twentieth century: Nazi Germany in the late 1930s and Soviet Russia in the early Cold War. There has been much loose talk about Xi Jinping having global ambitions to dominate the world that imply parallels to the twentieth-century drives of Adolf Hitler and Joseph Stalin. Yet even if we think, as pessimists do, that China is already well along pathway E and will not only overtake the United States but be driven by drives for glory and the spreading of its ideology, we should not presume that a new all-out Cold War, let alone a hot regional war, is inevitable. Understanding what it means for Chinese leaders to seek non-security ends such as glory and the spreading of ideology, as well as what it means to improve national security, will help us see just how different the new Sino-American geopolitical competition is from previous periods that we have discussed in this book.

First off, as optimists note, there is simply no reason to believe China will "inevitably" overtake the United States in relative economic power, or that even if it does this is a huge problem for the Western world. The very scholarly debate over whether China's economy is already peaking or whether it will continue to grow significantly in absolute and relative power reinforces just how uncertain it is that China's GDP will ever significantly overtake America's GDP. But if it does, there are two key factors that will make this of much less practical salience than the similar fear of the Soviet Union overtaking the United States in the 1950s. First, China's huge population means that it will have for quite some time one-fourth to one-third the GDP per capita of the United States. This leaves the Chinese state with much less surplus, after fulfilling basic citizen needs of food, shelter, and health care, for power projection around the world. China is certainly now a regional power in East Asia. But to "dominate the world" it would have to be able, as the United States has for eight decades, to credibly position its army and navy forces around the globe and be ready to put boots on the ground when a crisis arises. Not only can China not do this now, but its small per capita GDP would make it hard to sustain such a global posture if it were to try.[62]

Second, China is highly constrained in its ability to build an "empire," even if its leaders wanted to, by the very fact of what I've been calling the FDR legacy. The core political grouping in the world right now, as it has been since the late 1940s, encompasses the geopolitical arc of nations from Britain, through Western Europe and the Middle East, to Southeast Asia and Japan/South Korea. And with the collapse of the Soviet realm, this arc now includes the states of Eastern Europe and Finland. Essentially all of these nations are either formally aligned with the United States or see America as their primary patron. China does not even have the equivalent of Comecon, the Soviet-era economic sphere in Eurasia, let alone the series of far-flung client states Moscow had during the Cold War such as Cuba, North Vietnam, and Nicaragua. Yes, China has done an effective job of using the Belt and Road Initiative to increase its economic penetration of some of the states that have historically been a part of the U.S. economic power sphere. But the accepting of Chinese money to build railways, ports, and infrastructure, as Malaysia, Indonesia, Kenya, or Greece have done, does not mean that when push comes to shove such countries will switch to trading exclusively or even primarily with China, let alone shift their political allegiance to Beijing.

For one thing, many countries within the BRI are already worried about becoming too dependent on Chinese loans and Beijing's "debt trap diplomacy." Sri Lanka having to give China a 99-year lease on its Hambantota port when it failed to pay its BRI loan was a wake-up call, and many countries, including Malaysia and Kenya, have sought to scale back the BRI projects and renegotiate the terms of the loans. Moreover, states that have used BRI to develop their abilities to extract and then export natural resources are not terribly interested in selling primarily to China. There is one simple reason for this: they need reserves of fully convertible currencies to pay for their own vital imports, including oil, food, and medical supplies, and China does not have *and is unlikely to ever have* a fully convertible global currency on par with the U.S. dollar, the Euro, or the Japanese Yen. Authoritarian states in history have always shied away from creating fully convertible currencies, since it would mean that wealthy citizens and their families that want to leave the country to flee political repression could simply take all their wealth with them. The capital flight that would occur when controls on capital flows are lifted could not only destroy the value of the currency but would also lead, perhaps even more importantly, to a massive transfer of "human capital" to more liberal and democratic great powers. The best and brightest citizens would leave for countries that not only protect their political rights, but also their property rights (their wealth).[63]

In short, China is stuck in a conundrum that has plagued all autocratic great powers in history: it must increase repression to keep the revolutionary ideas of liberal democracy from infecting a modernizing citizenry and causing rebellion (as they did in 1989). But this very repression increases the desire of the wealthiest and most innovative individuals to flee the country and take their financial and human capital with them. Hence, despite a decade of effort to create some form of a convertible Renminbi that China's trade partners will want to hold as a foreign currency, the Renminbi still constitutes less than 4 percent of global currency reserves, despite China's GDP being over 18 percent of the global economy.[64]

The final point is perhaps the most important of the three. Because the liberal democratic states in the U.S. economic sphere are also typically *politically* aligned with the United States—and unlike past imperial systems, are freely choosing to be so—Washington has significant leverage over their larger foreign economic policies and how those policies shape the U.S. relationship with China. We saw this in the 1950s, when the American government not only imposed almost a complete embargo on U.S. trade with China, but was able, through the CoCom agreements, to get most of its aligned states not to trade with China in anything more than basic goods. After CoCom was disbanded in the early 1990s, the United States allowed its high-tech European and East Asian allies to sell most goods freely to China, even ones that had a potential "dual use" in the military realm. Since the Obama pivot of the early 2010s, however, and especially under the Trump and Biden administrations, Washington has been much less willing to let either U.S. firms or firms from aligned countries trade freely with China in high-tech goods. And since U.S.-designed or manufactured components so often go into these goods, the Americans have an easy way to make their leverage felt: they can simply ban the sale of high-tech inputs to for-eign firms that use these inputs for manufacturing or assembling *their* products that are eventually sold to China. For example, the Chinese firm Huawei, not only one of the world's largest makers of 5G communication systems but also cellphones, was devastated by the 2020 ban on the selling of American-designed components, such as the Android operating system, for Huawei's popular smart-phone. Huawei's position in the global smartphone market went from number three to number twenty-four within a year and a half.[65]

The Biden administration has been in the process of greatly extending the number of firms on the "entity [black] list" that are banned from using com-ponents that have American technology, and as noted, it has convinced the Dutch to continue a Trump-era ban on the selling to China of the extremely complex machines that make the highest-tech chips in the world. Biden has also announced an Indo-Pacific Economic Framework of fourteen countries, not including China, to coordinate on supply chains in East Asia, as well as a narrower "Chip 4 Alliance" of South Korea, Taiwan, Japan, and the United States to organize the design, production, and sale of semiconductors. Note what this means from the Chinese perspective. Beijing sees itself faced with a united front of almost all the highest-tech countries in the world. And these countries, beholden to Washington for their security, are usually willing to go along with the larger geopolitical and geoeconomic strategies of the United States, designed to constrain China's ability to reach the levels of technological sophistication needed for the twenty-first-century superpower competition.

For these three reasons, the United States should not be as worried about China having a GDP that is larger or even significantly larger than its own. The collective economic size of America's "realm one"—the realm of commercial partners that it has strong political influence over—is so large, and its com-bined technological strengths so immense, that with a simple turn of policy, the United States and its allies can decide to make it hard for China to reach its dream of self-sufficiency in high-tech production. And by keeping China dependent on the U.S. sphere's design of semiconductors and software pro-grams and on the production of the high-tech chips themselves, Washington has the leverage needed to convince Beijing to act moderately in world and regional affairs.[66] China may not like it. But without its own high-tech sphere, there is little it can do short of invading neighbors, and this would lead, as we saw with Russia after February 24, 2022, to devastating sanctions that would defeat Beijing's goal of increasing its economic growth and concomitant internal stability. War in its region would end up killing the golden goose— international trade—that has laid so many golden eggs for so many years.

Yet by understanding the way Chinese leaders see their country's larger security problem, we can also see why a preponderant China in the future will be much more restrained than past authoritarian states that have achieved a certain level of dominance in either their regions or the system. As I have stressed, the CCP leaders' biggest security obsession is not with invasion— foreign troops are very unlikely to start landing on China's shores, as they did during the century of humiliation—but with liberal democratic countries undermining social stability from within, à la 1989.[67] And here the fear is not just the active efforts of the United States through Voice of America or the education of Chinese students to shape the mindsets of the Chinese upper and middle classes. There is also the ongoing "demonstration effects" of democratic neighbors such as Taiwan, South Korea, and Japan simply sitting there, providing the good life without the political repression that Chinese citizens face on a daily basis.[68]

What a Xi Jinping or any future Chinese leader knows, going forward, is that the ability of the Chinese state to resist the internal threat posed by liberal democracies will depend fundamentally on whether the economy keeps growing. And given the nature of China's post-Mao reforms, this growth will continue to depend on China's ability to bring in cheap raw materials and high-tech components and to sell its manufactured goods in foreign markets. CCP leaders thus face yet another conundrum: commerce exposes the people to foreign ideas, but trade is also the main way to create the wealth that sustains the Party's legitimacy. If one is inclined to doubt trade's importance, consider what happened from early 2021 to the middle of 2022. After essentially negative or no growth during the first year of Covid, 2020, China was able to achieve a remarkable 18 percent growth in the first quarter of 2021, relative to Q1 of 2020. Q2 saw a respectable 8 percent growth. Yet with the slowing of infrastructure and housing construction in the second half of 2021—spurred in large part by Beijing's decision to put "red lines" on lending to debt-heavy construction companies—China's GDP growth rates were only 5 percent for Q3 and 4 percent for Q4. So, while Xi could tout the 8 percent average growth for 2021 as a significant sign of China's rebound from the pandemic, the downward trend in growth across four quarters was a sign of problems. And if we unpack the components of GDP for the fourth quarter, we see something startling: growth in infrastructure and construction was basically flat. So how did China eke out a modest 4 percent growth in Q4 2021? Through a 30 percent increase in exports.

This strong growth in exports—itself fueled by Western countries coming out of *their* Covid downturns—continued into 2022, albeit at lower levels, enough to allow Chinese leaders to achieve around 3 percent growth for the year. Yet if such a growth figure—below Xi's desired "new normal" of 5 to 6 percent—is fundamentally still dependent on exports to the world, as it almost certainly is,[69] it means that the ten-year effort to shift China to a greater reliance on internal consumer demand has either failed or reached a major roadblock.

What this means for China's foreign policies going forward is significant. Chinese leaders, even if they do have desires to establish the glorious state and put China on the map as a true superpower, will be forced to confront major trade-offs in their ability to achieve these non-security ends.[70] Will Chinese leaders be so obsessed with glory and status, or their legacies in the history books, that like Putin they will undertake foolhardy military actions that jeopardize the long-term power and security of the state itself? Given that China's concentration of population is many times greater than Russia's, it seems clear that only the most irrational or poorly calculating of Chinese leaders would risk everything the Chinese state has achieved over four decades to indulge in actions that satisfy the status whims of certain individuals. And Xi at least has shown himself to be a highly cool and calculating Machiavellian on the world stage. In July–August 2022, for example, when he signaled with military displays his anger over House Speaker Nancy Pelosi's Taiwan visit, Xi avoided any actions that would hurt China's ability to import semiconductors and other high-tech goods from Taiwan or to trade with the United States and its allies. Five months later, he sought to improve relations with Washington by moderating his rhetoric while making changes at the top, including appointing a new and more accommodating foreign minister, which communicated his desire to avoid an action-reaction cycle that might lead to further restrictions on Chinese high-tech imports.

The above analysis suggests that in forecasting where U.S.-China relations will go from here, we cannot look simply at the different possible pathways shown in figures 10.2 and 10.3. We must also bring in the issue of *how American foreign economic policies will shape Chinese expectations of future trade* and thus Beijing's assessment of its likely future growth rates, both absolutely and relatively. We know from theory and history that actors that anticipate a deep and inevitable decline in their power positions tend to start big wars or engage in aggressive behaviors that increase the risk of such wars. And we also know that leaders that expect their states to soon peak in power will be inclined toward more assertive policies that can, through the creation of new trade linkages into the other great power's trade realm, reenergize the state's growth and perhaps put it on a new upward growth curve. They are not likely to simply *start* a war, as Germany did in the face of deep decline versus Russia and its alliance in 1914. Rather, they are likely to push their firms and navies into what the adversary sees as *its* trading realm to try to take advantage of economies of scale and to compensate for the high fixed costs of production that arise with large factories needed by such economies. And this can risk escalations of mistrust and hostility that increase the probability of an inadvertent spiral to regional war, or something worse.

Germany's more assertive policies after 1905 over Africa and the Middle East in the face of slowing German growth are, in this sense, parallels to the greater assertiveness of Hu Jintao in the South China Sea after 2008 and Xi Jinping with the development of the Belt and Road Initiative after 2013. The slow and steady drop in growth after 2007 was, as Min Ye has shown, a spur to an intensification of the "going out" strategy first adopted after 1993–97's slowing of growth.[71] But Ye downplays the necessity of supporting this larger grand strategy with the protective support of the Chinese navy. China's long-term thinking, at its core, is a pure Mahanian logic: commerce is key, but it cannot flourish if there are potential threats to that commerce from not just pirates and local insurgent groups, but from other great powers also seeking to protect their economic power spheres. And for China, given the FDR legacy, there is almost no ability to expand trade ties to Middle East, Africa, and Latin America *without* pushing into areas the Americans consider their own. Consequently, the number of Chinese "naval visits" to faraway places such as Jamaica, Senegal, and Ecuador have increased threefold in the last fifteen years. These visits are directly connected to new trade ties and loans, and thus have a clear signaling value to Washington: *we are here, in the area, to support our commercial expansion, so don't think you can leverage this trade for political ends.*[72]

So far, the Americans have not been nearly as upset as they were in the 1960s and 1970s about Soviet penetration of their backyard. But the U.S. restraint is itself, as the Chinese well know, a function of Beijing's willingness not to push political and ideological changes in the region as hard as Moscow did during the Cold War. Both sides, in short, seem to have learned that foreign policies, both political-military and commercial, need to avoid the in-your-face bombast of past great powers if positive expectations of the future are to be sustained.

## Final Thoughts: Using Theory and History to Reduce the Risks of War

The chapters of this book have laid out a dynamic realist theory of great power politics and shown the power of its deductive logic across a wide variety of different contexts in the history of American foreign policy. Americans may have a strong sense that theirs is an exceptional nation, one that is morally attuned to the importance of liberal values of individual rights and freedoms, and one that sees its values expressed in its foreign behavior through the visions of its leaders or the bottom-up pressures of social groups. Sometimes these internal forces do indeed shape important decisions, as we saw with ongoing efforts by Washington to spread liberal democracy during the Cold War and afterward, or by the constraining effect of public opinion on FDR's desire to get the United States into the Second World War. Yet across time the big decisions of U.S. foreign policy elites have been made (and continue to be made) primarily based on the intensity of external threats, not on the ups and downs of domestic politics. Indeed, Donald Trump's four years in power are seen by almost all scholars and pundits as an anomaly for a very good reason.[73] He was one of the few presidents in U.S. history willing on an ongoing basis to trade-off the foreign policy interests of the United States for his own personal status and position in power—including, most egregiously, his restricting aid for Ukraine's military and aligning with Vladimir Putin to help improve his chances of reelection.[74] Future American presidents will likely continue Joe Biden's resetting of U.S. foreign policy to its traditional focus on dealing rationally with external threats to national security.

This does not mean, of course, that American policy makers never make mistakes, or that they cannot improve their decision-making processes through a better understanding of both realist theory and U.S. history. The parallel to contemporary business school training is apt: business students are trained in the most up-to-date and well-supported theories of finance and marketing in order to *improve and hone* their abilities to make optimal decisions given various circumstances they may face in the future. Good political science theories have a similar role: they provide nuance and subtlety to the baseline rational calculations that political leaders are already making to maximize the state's ability to respond to threats of attack and efforts by others to subvert domestic stability.

The dynamic realist theory of this book offers three big pieces of advice to present and future U.S. officials. Given that, since 1991, the United States has had and still has a dominant position in the world, the first is both obvious and absolutely critical: Do not push adversaries that may be already experiencing slower growth to believe that they will in the future decline deeply and inevitably due to the policies being implemented by Washington. This point comes directly out of the study of the five pathways above, and the risks to the system when a rising state such as China starts to anticipate a long fall in power both because of domestic problems and perceived American efforts to restrict its growth. The lesson of 1941 and the Pacific War is clear: driving another state into the ground economically through sanctions—and giving it little way to find diplomatic solutions to get trade reinstated—will likely lead the now declining adversary to undertake very risky actions to preserve its position and security. China today needs trade to continue to grow, at least absolutely if not relatively. From the perspective of leaders in Beijing, a China that was expected to suffer from prolonged declining trends in GDP would be inclined, like Japan in 1941, to lash out at the United States and its partners if it were to see Washington as the main source of its problems.

Two sets of commodities come to mind here: energy and semiconductors. China was an exporter of oil until 1993. But its phenomenal economic growth over the past three decades has simultaneously reduced its internal reserves and increased its consumption, such that China now imports three-quarters of its oil from abroad, 80 percent of which comes through the narrow Malacca Strait between Indonesia and Malaysia. Currently, Chinese projections of military power from their atolls in the South China Sea help deter the U.S. and Indian navies from imposing any constraints on the flow of oil (or other natural resources) through the strait. Likewise, China's strong naval presence in both the South and East China Seas serves to dissuade Taipei or Washington from placing restrictions on the high-tech Taiwan-made chips that China needs to produce advanced electronics, robots, and electric and self-driving vehicles. It is critically important that the United States continue to use policy signals to assure China that it will *continue* to have open access to oil and semiconductors, at least as long as Beijing does not engage in aggressive military strikes against its neighbors. The situation over Taiwan, for example, can remain stable, even if tense, as long as the CCP leaders know that they will have access to chips if they maintain the status quo, but will be cut off from chips and other high-tech components should Beijing become expansionistic in the region.[75]

In short, Americans must remember that China's high level of economic dependence can act both as a constraining factor for peace (if positive expectations of future trade continue) and a propelling force for war (if these expectations turn negative). This means that the issue of peace or war in East Asia is very much in the hands of U.S. policy makers. The spirals of hostility associated with the trade-security dilemma are, in this sense, a choice, not a given reality. Knowing this can help the United States avoid decisions that lead to the second Pacific War in a century.

The second big piece of advice coming out of this study is that both American and Chinese leaders need to constantly remind themselves that all great powers have an incentive to expand their economic power spheres, and that this natural impulse arises because of uncertainty about the security of future trade and the desire to establish a position that can deal with any unforeseen threats to that trade. The Belt and Road Initiative, in this sense, is no more surprising than the American desire, after conquering the territories of western

North America, to keep expanding across the Pacific (1898 to 1935) and then establish an arc of aligned powers from Britain to Japan after 1945 (the "FDR legacy"). Had China not started to "go out" after 1997, it would have started to suffer diminishing marginal returns to growth, and it would have become more vulnerable to leveraging by the United States over its trade with Asia and Africa.

Understanding the great power drive to extend one's economic power sphere can help leaders in Washington be more relaxed about *why* China is spending so much time and effort on advancing its commercial presence in Southeast Asia, Central Asia, the Middle East, and beyond. The Belt and Road Initiative may not end up working as well as America's strategy after 1944 of expanding commercial connections around the world—after all, the war had left three-quarters of the globe under the oversight of the United States, and China is working against this legacy. But the fact that the BRI bumps up into the established American economic power sphere should not force the United States to adopt an all-out containment logic akin to what Washington did with CoCom against the Soviet Union from 1947 to 1971. Back then, U.S. leaders had reason to think that states that "went Communist" would automatically trade only within the Soviet economic sphere. But today the masses are not inspired by China's Confucian-Leninist authoritarian ideology, and even despots in the Global South know that they must sell their goods to the West to acquire the foreign currencies needed to buy the products that keep their populations happy (and themselves in power). China itself needs trade with the West for these reasons. Hence its two biggest trading partners remain the European Union and the United States (with total trade over ten times its trade with its political partner, Russia). Were Washington to really move on the talk of "decoupling" the U.S.-European-Japanese economic bloc from China—talk that could become a reality only if the Americans chose it—it would greatly increase China's suspicions of long-term U.S. goals and lead Beijing to employ military and not just political means to protect its own export and import markets. A return to the kind of intense trade-security spirals seen in the 1930s would not be unimaginable.[76]

Finally, U.S. officials must make sure they understand that the policies of the Chinese government that appear to be part of a larger drive for glory, status, and the spreading of techno-authoritarianism may be more the actions of leaders worried about threats to the cohesion and stability of their society. The United States has for decades sought to change China's centralized and authoritarian system, to push it either by external incentives or internal shifts in values toward the liberal democratic end of the spectrum. Throughout the 1990s, in the heady days of victory in the Cold War, Washington undertook a concerted effort to liberalize Yeltsin's Russia, just as it had previously sought to liberalize Gorbachev's Soviet Union. It also sought to create a more liberal if still nominally "Communist" China through increased trade ties, Voice of America broadcasts, and support for religious and non-Han ethnic groups within China. After the profound shock of Tiananmen Square in 1989, which CCP leaders saw as directly encouraged if not instigated by Washington, these actions in support of liberalization could only have been seen as reflecting a deep American aversion to Chinese efforts to build "socialism with Chinese characteristics." Threats to internal stability continue to obsess leaders in Beijing. And this is not surprising since the educated middle and upper classes *have* had access to foreign ideas through education and travel, and thus do know what life is like on the outside. Xi Jinping's clampdowns at home and his bombastic foreign policy rhetoric, as distasteful as they are, thus cannot automatically be seen as arising from a fundamentally non-security or irrational character type of the kinds the world saw in the 1930s and after. Indeed, they at least in part reflect the very success of the United States in using its soft power—the appeal of its culture—to reshape the values of a large segment of China's population.

This does not mean we shouldn't consider China's regime type as *potentially* pathological to some degree. But even if we accept some movement since Deng Xiaoping toward the non-RSM end of the spectrum, two issues remain: To what extent are Chinese leaders willing *to trade-off security from foreign attack and subversion to achieve their non-security objectives*? And to what extent *are U.S. policies themselves changing China's domestic make-up* such that more and more officials are becoming either non-security driven or irrational in their use of means to ends, or both? We must be careful not to become so disillusioned by the failure to moderate China's behavior through engagement that we jump to the equally incomplete view of many pessimists that Chinese leaders are akin to Hitler and Stalin and are bent on "world domination." The fragility of the Chinese domestic situation alone makes any CCP leader quite frightened about putting boots on the ground abroad, not only sacrificing valuable butter for uncertain guns, but taking soldiers away from their homeland where they may be needed for repression.[77]

If Chinese leaders are not like or Stalin, and China is not like Germany or the Soviet Union from the 1930s, then what kind of state *does* it resemble in history? While some scholars saw China of the early 2000s as akin to Bismarck's Germany from 1875 to 1890 (cautious, seeking to buy time for growth, and avoiding provocative policies),[78] Xi and his colleagues have clearly moved away from the earlier "hide and bide" strategies of the 1992 to 2008 period.[79] One could draw parallels to Germany after 1900. But China today has no Reichstag, and it is far more oppressive than Wilhelmine Germany ever was. I would suggest that the closest parallel to contemporary China is probably

Louis XIV's France from 1668 to 1688 (the middle decades of a seventy-year reign). Louis on the surface seemed to be obsessed with *gloire*, both for his state and himself, and his mercantilist policies after 1668 to build France's commercial empire mirror Xi Jinping's actions to combine statism with local markets. But as the recent scholarship shows, Louis saw his promotion of *gloire* as largely instrumental rather than being an end in and of itself. Like modern China, France had come out of a period of deep internal conflict—not just the intra-elite civil war of the Fronde in the 1648–53 period but the struggle to construct a centralized bureaucratic state with loyalty toward the larger state rather than to individual self-interest. Like Xi, Louis thus used the propaganda tools of his day to construct a shared vision of the unified corporatist state that gave each person a sense of his or her role in the furthering of the state's development and magnificence. Economic growth and domestic stability through trade, combined with the protection of the nation's frontiers, were the primary strategic objectives.[80]

I do not want to press the Louis XIV analogy too far, since clearly Louis operated in an age when religion was both a major source of legitimacy and a significant dividing force between nations. But what examples such as Louis XIV bring to the surface is that rising powers such as late seventeenth-century France and early twenty-first-century China may have good reasons to fashion centralized "absolutist" states as a way to deal with threats both within the state and beyond. In Louis's case, Protestant nations such as England and the Netherlands had been promoting a more individualist political order for decades, and their mere presence made Louis worried not just about France's Protestant Huguenots but those in the upper and middle classes subscribing to Catholic Jansenism and its promotion of the individual's relationship to God, independent of the king and clergy. Chinese leaders since Tiananmen have been obsessed with the presence of liberal democratic states near China and supported by the United States, and the impact they could have on a modernizing China whose best and brightest have absorbed "Western" ideals.

Going forward, U.S. leaders need to be aware of how cultural differences in ideology, economic thinking, religious belief, and ethnicity can impact not only the way Americans perceive the degree of threat a rising China poses to the United States and its partners, but the way Chinese leaders look at the threat the liberal world led by the United States poses to China. It is too easy to paint China as a totalitarian revisionist state ready to swallow the world—at least if not opposed by a containment policy that drives China into the dustbin of history, as the United States did to the Soviets many decades earlier. Such a view fails to understand how much more vulnerable China is to internal revolt compared to the Soviet Union during the height of the Cold War. CCP leaders are well aware that China's 5,000-year history shows that in a country with this level of population concentration—fifty cities of over two million people, and two (Shanghai and Beijing) over twenty million—protest can turn into rebellion and revolution at the drop of a hat.[81]

Being sympathetic to China's domestic fragility does not mean leaders in Washington should not project strong military power into the East Asian region, nor that they should shy away from assuring regional partners of America's resolve to protect them and to punish China commercially if Beijing attacks them. A strong military posture is essential, for the simple reason that all great powers, even security seekers, will seek to exploit opportunities to expand if they are not deterred by the high costs and risks of such expansion. But it does mean that in negotiations with Beijing, Washington must assure CCP leaders that the United States is not seeking to destroy China's economy, and that as long as China does not invade its neighbors, oil, raw materials, semiconductors, and other high-tech components will continue to flow into the country, while Chinese products will be accepted in markets around the world.

In a world where nuclear weapons make leaders disinclined to initiate any crisis that might unleash their missiles, diplomatic moves that shape the other state's expectations of future trade—positive or negative—can make all the difference between whether their policies end up fostering cooperation or lead to spirals of mistrust and hostility that heighten the risk of a slide into devastating war. If leaders in Washington and Beijing, knowledgeable about the past, can improve each other's expectations of both trade and future behavior, many more decades of peace in East Asia should be achievable.

# NOTES

## Chapter 1

1. Fukuyama 1989.

2. See Mearsheimer's updated edition of *The Tragedy of Great Power Politics* (2014, 451–52) for his mention of U.S. expansion in the western hemisphere. Note that his argument cannot explain, given the supposed "stopping power of water," why the United States went from regional hegemony to a global hegemonic position by the mid-twentieth century. He argues that regional hegemons such as the United States do have to prevent other great powers from establishing hegemony in their own regions, as America did in two world wars and during the Cold War. But when other great powers are not seeking regional hegemony, the United States should remain an "offshore balancer," avoiding commitments on other continents (2014, chap. 7). The fact that it has not acted in this way is a puzzle he later explains by arguing that Americans have a strong desire to spread their liberal democratic ideology (2018, chap. 1; see also 2014, 46–49 and 75–76). Christopher Layne (2002) nicely argues that a reformulated offensive realism that did away with the stopping-power-of-water assumption would indeed be able to explain why the United States has bases across Europe, Asia, and Africa. I will build on Layne's point below by stressing the economic foundations for an offensive realist starting point.

3. Because of their important archival work on the role of commerce in U.S. foreign policy, I often draw heavily on revisionist insights in later chapters. Their focus on capitalist elites' drives for profit and wealth, however, makes their larger theoretical position fundamentally different from this book's argument. Revisionists and I agree that American leaders seek large and secure economic power spheres. Yet my leaders do so because they know economic power is essential for territorial security and for resisting efforts by other states to subvert the nation's way of life and domestic order. The profits and wealth of capitalist firms are thus only means to the larger end of national security, rather than ends in themselves, as they are for revisionists.

4. This literature is huge, and I will refer to specific works in the empirical chapters. Works that capture the essence of the approach include Williams 1962; LaFeber 1965b; Gardner 1964, 1993; McCormick 1967; Kolko 1990; essays by Rosenberg and Fry in Martel 1994. See also Leffler 1994; Krasner 1978; Costigliola and Hogan 2016.

5. See in particular Pratt et al. 1979; LaFeber 1994; Herring 2008; Hixson 2016; Zoellick 2021.

6. Mead 2001; Nau 2013.

7. See, in particular, the recent books by three prominent realists John Mearsheimer (2018), Stephen Walt (2018), and Barry Posen (2014), which argue that liberal values and domestic factors have often dominated and distorted American policy making, especially after the Cold War (the triumph of "liberal hegemony"). For the parallel perspective in traditional realists, see

also Osgood 1953; Kennan 1951; Niebuhr 1953; Kissinger 1979. For references and an argument reinforcing realism's treatment of the Cold War as their best case, see Miller 2021. So-called neoclassical realists, who examine the way domestic-level variables filter the effects of systemic pressures, also suffer from the problem of using their theories for only narrow time periods, such as the late nineteenth century (Zakaria 1998) or the twentieth century (e.g., Layne 2006; Dueck 2006). See essays by Steven Lobell, Randall Schweller, Mark Brawley, and Jeffrey Talliferro in Lobell, Ripsman, and Talliferro 2009; and the argument and references in Ripsman, Talliferro, and Lobell 2016; Rose 1998. See chap. 1, n. 18 in this volume.

8. Peter Trubowitz's 2011 book is one of the few that applies liberal theory to U.S. cases from the eighteenth, nineteenth, and twentieth centuries. Unfortunately, his argument does not go directly up against the present book's logic. His theory focuses on explaining the *broad types of strategic postures* of U.S. administrations rather than changes in specific policy behaviors *within* or *between* these administrations in response to changes in causal variables (see Trubowitz 2011, chap. 1). Moreover, his cases are selected to illustrate these various postures rather than to explain the full scope of cases of conflict or peace from the eighteenth century forward. Michael Hunt (2009), Walter Hixson (2008), Anatol Lieven (2012) and Robert Kagan (2006, 2023) have written important books on ideology, national identity, and U.S. foreign policy since the founding. Their goals, however, are more to describe the often disturbing ideological and racial views that have animated policy elites' views of the world than to explain specific cases of conflict and war across time. For how some recent historians have incorporated religion into the study of American foreign policy, see Preston 2016.

9. For references and analysis of American exceptionalism, see Restad 2015; Lipset 1996; Jouet 2018; Lieven 2012.

10. This is equivalent to placing societal scope conditions on the applicability of one's theory, as Skocpol (1979), for example, does in looking only at modern social revolutions.

11. See Copeland 2015 for the application of a similar but earlier version of the argument to European and Asian great power cases from 1790 to 1991.

12. While I often employ the label "dynamic realism" to describe this book's theory, the term can be used to cover a family of different theories that share a common focus on how anticipation of changes into the future affect state decisions today. Such theories include power transition theory and preventive war logics. For references on power transition theory, see Cashman 2013; Levy and Thompson 2010 (for a critique, see Copeland 1996, 2000a). For the literature on preventive war, see Levy 1987; Kim and Morrow 1992; Van Evera 1999; Weisiger 2013; Debs and Montiero 2014; Copeland 2000a, 2015.

13. Kenneth Waltz's 1979 *Theory of International Politics* (chaps. 3–5) is the locus classicus of the external approach.

14. The German term *Aussenpolitik* is often used to capture this externalist orientation, while *Innenpolitik* is used to describe the internal approach summarized below. See Trubowitz 2011; Snyder 1991.

15. Waltz 1979; Mearsheimer 2001; Walt 1987, 1996; Tang 2010; Rosato 2021.

16. I will continue to use the labels realist and liberal to designate the externalist and internalist camps simply because these labels are so entrenched in the literature. The reader should understand, however, that it is the conceptual orientation of each camp that matters to what follows in this book, not the label per se. In short, this is not a book about "isms" but about types of causal arguments and when and under what conditions they apply.

17. For arguments and references within this vast literature, see in particular Moravcsik 1997; Lyon 2012; McCormick 2012; Peterson 1994; Restad 2015; Jouet 2017; Narizny 2007, 2017; Trubowitz 2011; Lake 1999; Rosecrance and Stein 1993; Solingen 1998; Hancy 2012; Ikenberry 2011; Fordham 1998, 2008; Frieden 1988; George 1980; Carter and Scott 2012; Foyle 2012; Owen 1994, 1997; Snyder 1991; Destler 2012; Schaffer 2012; Cashman 2013; Jones 2012; and essays by Jonathan Caverly, David McCourt, Risa Brooks, and Brian Rathbun in Balzacq and Krebs 2021. For a classical realist approach that accepts the importance of anarchy but centers its explanations on internal pathologies, see Kirshner 2022.

18. The development of neoclassical realism arose directly out of this belief in systemic realism's explanatory limitations. Neoclassical realists may start with the presumption that any state Y will face systemic pressures that shape its desired policies, but they derive most of their "value-added" from detailed explorations of the domestic-level variables *within Y* that serve to filter and constrain the choices of foreign policy elites (see Ripsman, Taliaferro, and Lobell 2016 for overview and references). Neoclassical realism can add nuances to the empirical understanding of specific cases. But for the purposes of this book, it has one major limitation. It assumes that we have exhausted the potential for developing purely systemic realist explanations of the behavior of any great power Y without referring to Y's unit-level characteristics. Yet because neoclassical realists *have not yet established a properly specified overarching systemic framework* for making first-cut predictions from external variables, they too quickly drop down to the unit level to explain behavior. Providing this overarching framework for neoclassical realists to use as they incorporate domestic and psychological factors is one objective of this book. For further references, see chap. 1, n. 7 in this volume.

19. Mearsheimer 2001. See also Labs 1997; Rosato 2021; Elman 2004.

20. Mearsheimer 2001. While Mearsheimer in 2021 stated that offensive realism can explain the emergence of a new strategic competition with China, he has no explanation for why U.S.-China relations were relatively peaceful for nearly three decades. He thus falls back on unit-level factors, blaming "liberal" policy elites who irrationally pursued engagement when they should have been containing the rise of the Chinese state (2021; see also Mearsheimer 2018; Walt 2018).

21. Jervis 1976, 1978, 1997; Glaser 1992, 1994–95, 1997, 2010; Tang 2010; Kydd 1997a, 1997b, 2005; Collins 1997; Booth and Wheeler 2008; Copeland 1999–2000, 2015; Montgomery 2007; Ralph 1999. Mearsheimer 2001 briefly discusses the security dilemma (35–36), using the first page from John Herz's seminal 1950 article to argue that security dilemma thinking forces leaders to maximize power. Yet Herz's larger argument in the piece, as with the above authors, is that leaders that know of the potential for spiraling will rationally seek to avoid assertive policies that provoke it. It is worth noting that Mearsheimer's theory, by asserting that states must assume "worst case" about other great powers, logically precludes the core insight of the security dilemma: that states "update" their probabilistic estimates of the other state being an aggressive type upon seeing that state build up its military and project its power. If the other is already seen as "the worst," then its behavior can have no effect on such estimates.

22. Copeland 2000b. This point is reinforced by the fact that intentions can change overnight, say due to a coup or revolution in the other (Jervis 1978), while it usually takes years to shift one's relative power, and the very effort to do so after falling behind can push the other into a preventive war (Copeland 2000a, chaps. 1–2). For summaries and references on preventive war, see esp. Levy 1987; Kim and Morrow 1992; Van Evera 1999; Weisiger 2013; Debs and Montiero 2014; Copeland 1996, 2000a, 2015.

23. The defensive realist focus on uncertainty about present intentions is made clear by their use of costly signaling models, which by their nature can only reveal current type, not future type. See Kydd 2005; Glaser 1994–95, 2010. Kydd 1997b is aware of the problem of changing future type that is particularly problematic when the other state is rising in power. But his response is simply to argue that empirically this is rarely a problem.

24. Offensive realists align with the Fearon 1995 point that states often have difficulty in trusting that the other will keep to its promises down the road, a phenomenon now generally known as the commitment problem. For arguments and references, see esp. Kydd 2005; Powell 2006. See my discussion in Copeland 2015, 12–13 and 43–45.

25. The most dramatic recent example of this would be the American push under three different administrations after 1992 to expand NATO into Eastern Europe. While this effort certainly was consistent with a desire to protect global democracy, it also clearly reflected fears of a future Russian state hoping to recreate its Cold War empire. Russia's invasion of Ukraine in February 2022 could either be seen as confirming these fears, making NATO expansion appear rational, or as provoking Russia into a reaction because of a lack of NATO restraint.

26. See Goddard 2018.

27. Grieco 1988; Mearsheimer 1992, 1994–95; Rosato 2021.

28. Haas 2005. See also Owen 2010.

29. Gilpin 1975, 1981; Knorr 1944, 1973, 1975; Ikenberry 2014.

30. See chapters 7–9.

31. Mahan 1890; FP: 6–9, 11; Mead 2007. See also Mead 2001, chaps. 2–3, on the differences between a sea-based approach such as Mahan's and the continental realism of a Bismarck or a Kissinger. Specter (2022) shows that Mahan and other American strategists helped shape the European view of realism as much as the Europeans shaped the American view. See also Findlay and O'Rourke 2007.

32. See chapter 10. Because of Trump's tariffs, Mexico and Canada narrowly beat out China as the top U.S. trade partners in 2020 and 2021.

33. Knorr 1973, 1975; Gilpin 1975, 1977, 1981; for further references, see Poast 2019. On mercantilism, see Knorr 1944; Hechscher 1933; Stern and Wennerlind 2013; Kirshner 2022, chap. 6.

34. Let me restate just how important it is that one does *not* assume that rational states must think "worst case" about adversaries, as Mearsheimer (2001) asserts. Aside from the fact that this prevents any updating of type, eliminating the security dilemma as a concept (see chap. 1, n. 21 in this volume), such an assumption presumes that states cannot make foreign threats more intense by their own behavior, and that they need not be aware of this fact. That modern leaders may be aware of spiraling risks and still push forward with strong policies to secure their economic power spheres is shown in Leffler 1992.

35. Copeland 1999–2000, 2015.

36. Hirschman 1980.

37. See Mastanduno 1992.

38. Mearsheimer 1992, 1994–95, 2001, 2018; Grieco 1988; Rosato 2021.

39. In 2022, U.S.-China trade set a new record of over $640 billion, despite ongoing fears that the two nations were "decoupling" from direct commercial relations with each other. *Financial Times*, 17 January 2023.

40. Waltz 1970; Copeland 2015, 8–9.

41. This paragraph and the next summarize a longer discussion found in Copeland 2015, 28–32, which draws from the so-called new trade theory of such scholars as Paul Krugman and Elhanan Helpman.

42. Gilpin 1981.

43. Aside from these three factors, the desire for trade with other great powers will also increase in multipolar environments, since state Y cannot afford to avoid trade with X and Z if these two states are trading with each other, since their absolute gains from trade mean a *relative loss* for Y. This simple imperative not to fall behind can explain periods of intense great power trade, such as between the pre-1914 European great powers. See Copeland 2015, 30; Gowa 1993, 1994; Keohane 1993.

44. In a previous book (Copeland 2000a) I referred to these core endowments and a state's baseline level of technology as dimensions of a state's "potential power."

45. Copeland 2015. In U.S. history the most direct parallel to the German and Japan situations would be American dependence on overseas oil after 1945, and the crises that arose in the Middle East with the Soviet Union in 1944, 1946, 1956, and 1973 over control of that region's oil reserves.

46. See Copeland 2015, chaps. 4–5.

## Chapter 2

1. More precisely, I assume for the sake of deepening the theory's deductive logic that state Y has a moderate but fixed baseline drive to expand its core economic power sphere (realm one) into the neutral zone of realm two. This allows me to focus on Y's changing levels of dependence and expectations of trade with realms two and three as these levels are tied to state X's behavior. In the empirical chapters and in the final chapter on U.S.-China relations I will relax this assumption. But it is worth noting upfront that *this assumption only pertains to Y's decision-making.* As a rational security-maximizing state, Y remains aware that *state X* may be intensely seeking to expand its realm-one power sphere, and that this will affect Y's expectations of future trade, especially regarding Y's realm two.

2. As I discuss below, the complex nature of uncertainty does not in any way justify a logical leap to worst-case thinking about the other, as Mearsheimer (2001, 2014) and Rosato (2021) claim. As David Kearn notes (2014), there is a third major form of uncertainty—uncertainty about the impact of future military technologies on the offense-defense balance—that can hurt the ability of great powers to cooperate in the present. For sake of isolating the causal impact of the above two forms of uncertainty, I will assume that the offense-defense balance is "neutral" in the short term—neither offensive nor defensive dominant—and that it will remain so into the future (this parallels the theoretical assumptions in Copeland 2000a, 2015). See Proposition 3b below for how these assumptions can be relaxed in the case studies.

3. Haas (2005) returns to Kenneth Waltz's second of his three ways to define systemic structure in international politics: the characters of the units. (The other two are the ordering principle of the system—whether anarchic or hierarchic—and the distribution of capabilities of the actors; Waltz 1979, chap. 4.) In Waltz's theory, this second element drops out because Waltz believes great powers are forced by anarchy to become "like units." Haas brings the character of units back in as a systemic variable by examining the differences in states' political ideology as they change across space and time. See also Owen 2010.

4. It is this set of assumptions—that we are only trying to explain state Y's behavior, not X's, and that Y is solely driven by forces outside of itself (relative power, trade, and the other's type)—that keeps the theory parsimonious and predictive. In practice, of course, Y may well be driven by non-security goals as well as domestic-level pressures. But for the purpose of creating a deductive and testable theory, those goals and pressures are assumed away (as in keeping with economic modeling since the late nineteenth century). When we come to case studies, as I do later, this set of assumptions can be relaxed to see how powerful the theory is versus its domestic level ("liberal") counterparts and to what extent one needs a combination of external and internal forces to explain Y's behavior in any particular case.

5. Copeland 1999–2000, 2015.

6. See Copeland 2019. This is an important extension of my argument about declining and rising states from my first book (Copeland 2000a), which puts most of the blame for conflict in world history on declining states, under the assumption that rising states always have an incentive to buy time for future growth. If leaders of rising states anticipate an imminent peaking in power and then subsequent decline, they also have incentives to act aggressively, especially on third-party issues, in order to either lock in a strong power position or reenergize their upward trajectory. This can help explain, for example, why Germany became more assertive over Morocco and other colonial issues after 1903 and over the question of Czechoslovakia after 1937.

7. On resolve, see Fearon 1995; Mercer 1996; Copeland 1997. On risk tolerance, see Schelling 1966; Fearon 1992; Ellsberg 1968.

8. Defensive realists will refer to Mikhail Gorbachev's dramatic gestures in 1987–89, including the willingness to pull Soviet soldiers and missiles out of Eastern Europe, as a clear sign that Moscow had no intention of attacking Western Europe and was more interested in peaceful trade than imperial expansion. Previous Soviet leaders, by this analysis, likely did have desires to spread communism or build a glorious empire, given their unwillingness to stop funding communist rebellions around the world. American hard-line policies prior to 1985 thus made sense as a counter to the likely drives of the Soviet leadership. See Kydd 2005.

9. Mearsheimer 1990, 1994–95.

10. Mearsheimer 2001; Rosato 2021.

11. Indeed, the great irony here is that by their current reasoning, offensive realists *accept that there is a democratic peace* of sorts; namely, that all things being equal, two democratic states Y and X who are not currently backsliding should be more moderate and limited in their revisionist tendencies than two authoritarian or totalitarian states Y and X. If this were not the case, there would simply be no reason to talk about the risk of backsliding in the theory, nor for bringing up the famous case of quasi-liberal Weimar Germany *becoming* a state led by a Hitler and his disturbing unlimited-aims ideology.

12. Jervis 1968, 1976; Lebow 1981.

13. See Yoder 2019b and Haynes and Yoder 2020.

14. The potential for an adversary to be irrational even if security-driven is nicely noted by Glaser, and my own conceptualization below has been strongly influenced by his argument (Glaser 1992). Unfortunately, in his later work to develop a more general theory of international politics (2010) he returns to the standard realist assumption that both actors are rational so as to focus on the differences in the other's motives for acting (greedy or security-seeking). I should also note that in my analysis, I treat the other's tolerance for the risks and costs of hard-line behavior as an implicit

part of both its motives for acting and its degree of rationality. An individual such as Hitler, for example, given that he had both strong non-security motives for acting and was often irrational in the pursuit of his ends, was in practice a highly risk- and cost-acceptant actor. Conceptually, one could treat risk- and cost-tolerance as third and fourth dimensions of character type. But since they are so obviously tied to the first two, this would unnecessarily complicate the analysis.

15. For Mearsheimer, the costs that deter expansion are not simply the battlefield costs, but the "stopping power of water" when one tries to project military power across oceans (2001, 2014). But as Layne has pointed out, the latter should not deter if a state already has a beachhead on another continent, as the United States has had in Europe and South Korea since 1945. The stopping power of water is thus a purely ad hoc variable that can play no consistent role in a theory of great power politics.

16. The metric of "expected probability of survival" as the thing security-seeking states are trying to maximize captures the idea that rational states will have to think probabilistically in uncertain environments. See Copeland 2000a, 38–40 and 265n13. As is commonly understood by security specialists, leaders of Y will be interested not just in protecting the state from direct attack (reducing the probability of war via deterrence or increasing the probability of victory if war does occur). They will also seek to counter actions that adversaries might take to subvert the political and social order within Y or its allies (for example, the fear of Russian and Chinese efforts to promote communist revolutions abroad during the Cold War or recent efforts to interfere in U.S. elections).

17. Note that if X is currently RSM but expected to change to another type in the future, then all bets are off. This allows us to explain why two RSMs might still find themselves in an intense rivalry, especially if one of them is currently in decline: the fear of the future overshadows the ability to trust the other's type in the short term.

18. In the language of economics, X no longer has a lexicographic preference for security, and thus is willing to reduce its expected probability of survival to some degree to improve the realization of other ends of statecraft. The RNM is equivalent to Charles Glaser's rational "greedy" state (Glaser 1994–95), since "greed" for Glaser is a catch-all concept that includes any ultimate end that is not national security.

19. In other work, I have shown that there were strong elements of rational security maximizing to the Nazi German state up until late 1941, especially within the German military high command (which saw a second major war in Europe, as in 1914, as necessary to prevent the rise of the Russian juggernaut). But Adolf Hitler himself had clearly irrational and non-security reasons for total war—most horrifically, the genocidal cleansing of Europe of Jews, gypsies, and other "non-Aryan" peoples. Copeland 2000a, 2015.

20. Defensive realists rely on costly signaling models to help states show their own security-driven motives. But like all game-theoretical set-ups, it must be assumed that *both sides are rational* (and indeed know that the other is rational and that the other knows as well) for costly signaling to work as intended.

21. This aligns with two of the four variables shaping threat in Walt's balance-of-threat theory (1987): relative power and the perceived intentions of the adversary. Walt's other two variables—geography and offensive-defense balance—I place to the side for now by assuming states are equidistant from one another and that neither offense nor defense has the advantage. (This aligns with the assumptions in Copeland 2000a, 2015.) By relaxing these assumptions in the empirical chapters, I turn them into additional parameters shaping perceived threat.

22. Copeland 2000a, 2000b, 2015.

23. I say "likely" to highlight that it is the *probability* of the state peaking and then declining later that will drive the intensity of its leaders' beliefs that something must be done now to keep the state rising and avoid this peaking of economic power. See Copeland 2019. See chap. 2, n. 6 in this volume.

24. Copeland 2019; Brands and Beckley 2021, 2022.

25. Copeland 2000a, chap. 2.

26. Copeland 2015.

27. Haas's focus (2005) is on the variable of ideological *distance*—how much two states differ in their ideologies—rather than on the *content or nature* of their specific political values and strategic thinking. This allows him to talk about two communist states or two absolutist monarchies as having the same ideological distance as two democracies, and thus predict similar levels of threat perception. My notion of "difference" includes both Y's sense of its distance from X and its sense of whether the content/nature of X's political ideology make X a potential threat to Y's territorial existence and domestic order. This holds also for X's foreign economic orientation, religion, and ethnicity. Such a theoretical move allows my theory to discuss how aspects of X's culture may be very unnerving to Y, even if X looks quite similar to Y in an overall sense. For example, in the nineteenth century Britain and the United States were the most liberal of great powers in the system. Yet the British saw the specific dimensions of American-style liberalism—republican not constitutionally monarchic; more neo-mercantilist than free trading; and devoted to individualism rather than hierarchical order—as a threat to the British definition of liberal democracy.

28. This list is drawn both from Haas's (2005) definition of political ideology (5–6) as well as from the aspects of ideology he explores in his case studies. The *breadth* of the leadership group's respect for citizen rights across a population can of course vary greatly across time: the United States itself had slavery until 1865, did not give voting rights to women until 1919, and needed civil and voting rights acts in 1964–65 to provide a measure of equality to nonwhites across all the states. Nevertheless, it is still possible to talk about the core political ideology of the United States from 1788 onward as fundamentally liberal and democratic using the definition Haas provides, even if the extent of the "liberal democratic-ness" of the polity waxes and wanes over time.

29. Haas (2005) explores only internal economic ideology as part of "political ideology."

30. For arguments and references, see in particular Owen 2010; Philpott 2001.

31. Tellingly, the ancient Greek word for foreign peoples—*barbarians*—derives from the way the Greeks heard the languages of non-Greek ethnic groups, which for the Greeks sounded like an incomprehensible noise ("bar-bar") rather than a "civilized" language such as Greek.

32. See Greenfeld 1992; Mearsheimer 2018; Gellner 2008.

33. Copeland 2000a, chaps. 3–4. This would of course change by the 1930s, when political ideology and foreign economic orientations constituted major differences between a waning German state and the ascendent Soviet state. See Haas 2005, chap. 4; Copeland 2000a, chap. 5.

34. Owen 1994, 1997.

35. Weeks 2014.

36. See Copeland 2000a, chap. 2.

37. This section is underpinned by recent work on inter-state signaling in dynamic environments where the relative power and future behavior of adversaries may change. See especially Yoder 2019b, 2019c; Yoder and Spaniel 2022; Haynes and Yoder 2020; Spaniel and Poznansky

2020; Trager 2011, 2017; Joseph 2021; Debs and Monteiro 2014; and Wolford, Reiter, and Carrubba 2011. This work identifies conditions under which foreign policy signals allow the rational updating of type as background variables change. It thus goes beyond both first-generation bargaining models of war (shaped by Fearon 1995) that treat incomplete information and shifting power separately, and the more static approaches to reassurance pioneered by Kydd (2000, 2005). For now, I simply assume that this new work is largely correct on the specifics so that I can focus on the more general picture of how states are driven by their perceptions of threat to shift the intensity of their policies on the hard-line/soft-line spectrum and how their behavior feeds back on those perceptions. In my next book, I develop a formal model that shows how changing perceptions of power, character type, and the level of a state's demands for changes in the status quo work together to drive the likelihood of escalation to crisis and war.

38. See Jervis 1976, 1978, 1997; Glaser 1994–95, 1997, 2010; Kydd 1997a, 1997b, 2005; Tang 2010; Booth and Wheeler 2008; Collins 1997; Brooks 1997.

39. See especially Jervis 1976; Glaser 1994–95; Kydd 1997a; and Tang 2010.

40. Defensive realists thus need to vary other factors, such as the offensive-defense balance and the technology of war and logistics, to explain why states that otherwise would be peaceful turn aggressive.

41. Copeland 2015, 36–44; Copeland 2011. See also Rosato 2021, chap. 1, which draws on Copeland 2015.

42. Defensive realism's focus on whether adversaries are or are not driven by security or non-security ends and its focus on parameters such as the current offense-defense balance make the theory one of "comparative statics." It is snapshots of current factors—power, perceptions of other's present intentions/motives, offensive or defensive technologies, and so forth—that matter. Offensive realism is more inherently dynamic since it does stress the importance of uncertainty regarding a state's future power and the other's type. Yet through its worst-case assumption (Mearsheimer 2001) and its assertion that leaders can rarely reduce their uncertainty about other's intentions (Rosato 2021), offensive realism, like Waltz's neorealism, ends up being a largely static theory of international politics. It ends up explaining the dismal recurrence of "security competitions" with little sense of why the intensity of these competitions varies so dramatically over time. As mentioned earlier, other dynamic realist theories include preventive war theories (see especially Levy 1987; Kim and Morrow 1992; Van Evera 1999; Weisiger 2013; Debs and Montiero 2014; further references are in Copeland 2000a, 2015). David Edelstein (2017), by varying states' time horizons, also brings in time, but with a focus on internal psychology rather than actor estimates about changing external variables.

43. These two senses of the term "dynamic" have analogues in economic theorizing: dynamic as theory that brings in expectations of the future as determinants of current behavior (e.g., rational expectations theory); and as theory that explains the pathways that phenomena take over time to get from one relatively stable equilibrium to another (as in supply and demand economics) or to unstable results due to positive feedback effects (as with "Cobweb" effects in agricultural markets).

44. Jervis 1997.

45. Note that offensive realists would claim that Y cannot make X believe it has limited aims when Y grabs small opportunities to "revise" the system, given that both Y and X think the worst of each other. But such a claim is only a mere stipulation of the theory. Empirically, we see great powers regularly accept that adversaries have limited aims. Theoretically, once we allow variance in type between RSM and non-RSM actors, it only makes sense that two RSMs would

"understand" that the other must occasionally act against smaller states in its neighborhood, given the offensive-realist baseline. But this would not mean the other's intentions are unlimited.

46. A background condition for figures 2.2 and 2.3 is Y's current military power, since while military power within the theory is not directly driving Y to adopt more hard-line policies except as it is affected by economic and commercial trends, it does act as a facilitating factor for such policies when Y is strong.

47. This is reinforced by relaxing the third assumption in figure 2.3, such that X is facing new exogenous constraints arising from such things as third parties and the depletion of raw materials, and thus is less *able* to trade freely with Y.

48. Note that while negotiations may be an important part of how Y and X assure each other of their willingness to cooperate economically, my model is quite different from the core premises of the Fearon "bargaining model of war" (1995). There is no uncertainty about present power or resolve (willingness to pay costs) in my logic, only uncertainty about the likelihood of the other state being willing to allow open RIM access into the future. There may be a "commitment problem" that makes it hard for rising states to commit to being open traders down the road, but in my argument state Y examines the other's *type*, not its public or private promises, to determine the likelihood of future trade. On the commitment problem, see esp. Fearon 1995, 1998; Powell 2006; Kydd 1997b.

49. Because defensive realists expect states to be moderate to avoid spiraling, they can only explain extreme conflict by either invoking initial misunderstanding of the other's type or by simply assuming the other is indeed aggressive and must be contained. The offensive realist focus on uncertainty about the future helps explain why even two rational security maximizers might still struggle for position as a hedge against problems down the road, but they can't explain why great powers cooperate economically and politically, nor can they understand why very extreme measures such as major war may be needed when a state anticipates severe decline in its commercial and economic position.

50. For further discussion, see Copeland 2000a, chap. 1; and Copeland 2015, 30, which draw from Gowa 1993, 1994; Keohane 1993. For example, the British after 1820 allowed the United States to grow without ultimately going to war with it, largely because London saw other rising states as more threatening to Britain's long-term security.

51. In short, the neoclassical realist approach of bringing in domestic-level factors as constraints may have validity in empirical cases, but dynamic realism predicts that leaders will not simply accept these constraints but find ways to mobilize public and elite opinion to achieve the desired policy. Roosevelt's maneuvering from 1935 to 1941 to overcome isolationist sentiment in the United States is one of the clearest examples of this.

52. My discussion draws from a more detailed exposition in Copeland 2015, chap. 2 and Copeland 2018a, 2018b.

53. This is the "effects of causes" logic that Goertz and Mahoney (2012) nicely summarize.

54. Mackie (1980) famously refers to a situation where multiple bundles of different factors can explain event E as INUS (which stands for a factor that is an "insufficient, but necessary part of an unnecessary but sufficient condition").

55. Historians who want to "really understand" specific cases often do what I am saying intuitively—they look at a whole host of factors that came together to create the "conditions" for the outbreak of the rare event they are studying.

56. This is the classic divide between preventive war theorists and diversionary war theorists in explaining why Germany in 1914 would risk a long and costly major war with the system. See Copeland 2000a.

57. For example, in the late nineteenth century the American state was able to expand westward against Native American nations in a "pure" offensive realist way, since the European powers were focused on themselves and there was no real risk of a defensive-realist spiral of hostility from doing so. In short, no trade-offs had to be made, and the offensive realist argument that states expand when costs are low could predominate. Such a logic, however, is perfectly consistent with dynamic realism's predictions, given the absence of spiraling risks.

58. For scholars taking the ideational approach, and for references, see Restad 2015; Nau 2002, 2013; Hunt 2009; Hixson 2008; Lieven 2012; Preston 2016; Owen 2010. Neoclassical realists such as Dueck 2006 and Layne 2006 fuse cultural ideas as driving forces with power as constraining and facilitating factors.

59. Russett 1993; Doyle 1997; Russett, Oneal, and Davis 1998.

60. Owen 1994, 1997.

61. Destler 2012. Zakaria (1998), as we will see in chapter 5, focuses on the legislative constraints on American expansionism in the post–Civil War era up until the 1890s.

62. Allison and Zelikow 1999; Jones 2012.

63. Posen 1984; Levy 1986; Allison and Zelikow 1999.

64. See essays by Vincent Auger, Jerel Rosati and Scott DeWitt, Peter Dombrowski, and Loch Johnson in Hook and Jones 2012.

65. Milner and Tingley 2015; Trubowitz 2011.

66. Troubowitz 1998; Fordham 1998, 2008.

67. For example, the "Israel Lobby," Mearsheimer and Walt 2007.

68. Jervis 1976; Lebow 1981; Mercer 1996; Yarhi-Milo 2014.

69. On prospect theory, see Levy 1997; McDermott 1998.

70. Jervis 1976; Mercer 1996.

71. Crawford 2000; Costigliola 2016. See also Yarhi-Milo (2018) on the importance of a leader's enbedded self-monitoring and hawkish tendencies.

72. Janis 1982; Mercer 1995.

73. Yarhi-Milo 2018.

## Chapter 3

1. The justification for this labeling is reinforced by the fact that it wasn't until 1777 that the Articles of Confederation were agreed upon, and not until 1781 that they were ratified: in 1776 and in the months leading up to the Declaration of Independence, the colonies were much more interested in the writing of their own constitutions than in creating a "national" constitution binding them all. And of course, the Articles of Confederation was an agreement of individual states, not of "the people" of the United States (as in 1787).

2. See chapter 10.

3. See in particular Holton 1999; Egnal 1988; Breen 2004; and Nash 1979 (further references in Gibson 2009).

4. I mentioned in the introductory chapter that there are two aspects to national security: the protection from invasion from outside, and an outsider's subversion of one's political and social culture from within. The second aspect is more important here, although when British troops did occupy Boston in 1768, many Americans understandably saw the first aspect as also under threat.

5. See especially Wood 1998, 1991, 2011; Bailyn 1965; Maier 1991 (further references in Gibson 2009).

6. Wood 1991, 3–7, 11–24. See also Eric Nelson's seminal work (2017) on the extent to which American elites loved their king and saw him as a critical check on the British Parliament within the ideal of mixed government established after 1688.

7. Advocates of the first two approaches might argue that protecting one's way of life is wrapped up in preserving one's ideological values and social structures, and therefore consistent with their arguments. While this is so, the third perspective is distinct. Recall from the first chapter that for all realist theories there are two possible types of threats posed by an outsider— either actual invasion of the homeland ("nation") or the other's subversion of its political and social order. The realist perspective assumes that leaders are willing to sacrifice personal and even class interests to protect their homelands from both types of threat. The focus is on the external threat as the propelling force causing leaders to choose actions that may risk much that they hold dear in the short term for the long-term security of the transcendent nation.

8. See in particular Draper 1996; Alvord 1917; Tucker and Hendrickson 1982; Edelson 2017; Knorr 1944. While Jack Greene's influential work over more than fifty years is highly eclectic, he clearly shows that fear of decline in the face of rising British North America as well as London's inability to find a "constitutional" solution that would not reinforce this problem were central to Britain's decisions to restrict American economic and political development after 1762. Of his many books, see in particular Greene 1990, 2010, 1995; Greene and Morgan 2008; Greene1970. Interestingly, the founder of the ideological school, Bernard Bailyn, wrote in the preface to the fiftieth anniversary of his seminal *The Ideological Origins of the American Revolution* that in relooking at his own work half a century later, the thing that struck him the most was "the Americans' obsession with power. It was not just one among many concerns; it was their central concern" (Bailyn 2017, viii). This suggests that while political ideas were indeed flowing freely during the period, their focus was less on the purely ethical or normative aspects of British policies—whether it was "right" or "legitimate" for London to do what it was doing—but on the relative power implications of those policies.

9. Authors detailing this divide in thinking include Pincus 2005; Alvord 1917; and Vaughn 2019. Needless to say, had there been no trade-offs in choosing between these two policy perspectives, all British mercantilists would have wanted *both* an increase in staples trade and in markets simultaneously. But they knew that in practice this was impossible. The question here thus comes down to the *relative* emphasis the two factions placed on the two main forms of trade.

10. As their economic and political expectations declined, American elites came to realize that their colonies would have to fight to preserve a way of life that, ironically, the war of the Glorious Revolution of 1688 had made possible. Not surprisingly, John Locke's writings justifying the actions of 1688 were seen as directly parallel to what the British North Americans were going through. On the truly revolutionary nature of the 1688–95 period in England, see the seminal work of Pincus 2005. For the impact of the Glorious Revolution on the colonists, see Lovejoy 1987.

11. See especially Dickerson 1975 for summary and references.

12. Schlesinger 1918, 97; Beer 1907, 31.

13. Andrews 1938, chap. 5; Schlesinger 1918, 95–99; Beer 1907, 31–36.

14. This summary is drawn from Warden 1970; Newell 1998; McCusker and Menard 1991; Andrews 1938.

15. McCusker and Menard 1991; McCusker 1989.

16. Exports from Britain to BNA had more than doubled from 1746–47 to 1766–67 and were larger than imports. British exports rose from £267,000 for the decade 1700–10 (versus £266,000 in imports) to £812,000 by 1740–50 (versus £708,000 in imports) to £1,760,000 by 1760–70 (versus £1,044,000 in imports). See Beer 1907, 139; Draper 1996, 128; McCusker and Menard 1991.

17. Quoted in Horne 2014, 4. The French in the 1730s were also well aware of the possibility that as BNA grew, it would be likely to seek independence from Britain. See Draper 1996, 79.

18. PTBF, 62–71. As early as 1747, Franklin believed that Americans represented the "spirit of a rising people"; Wright 1986, 78.

19. Quoted in Simms 2008, 387.

20. Draper 1996, 81–82.

21. Stourzh 1969, 54–55 sees Franklin's 1751 missive as at least partly a response to the British fears of BNA's rise as reflected in the Iron Act.

22. Draper 1996, 9.

23. Draper 1996, 13; Wright 1986, 176–77.

24. This was not surprising, since markets-based mercantilist William Pitt was still prime minister during the 1760–61 period of debate. The argument that the British West Indies' sugar interest pressured British politicians to give up Guadeloupe is weak. Many of the plantation owners, knowing the productivity of their own islands' soil was declining, were already investing in the captured French islands, and indeed Grenada and Dominique were retained and added to the British Caribbean empire.

25. Draper 1996, 17–19.

26. See Beer 1907, 142 on Pitt's views of the value of Canada and BNA overall in expanding markets for Britain. See also pages 154–55, that while taking Canada would not generate positive net income in the short term, it likely would in the longer term.

27. Beers 2007, 122–30; Andrews 1938, chap. 5.

28. See e.g., Tuchman 1985; Speck 1979; Christie and Labaree 1975.

29. This group usually included traditional landed elites who were not tied to the export trade and who saw a staples-based mercantilism as a way to reduce the high land taxes that came with imperial wars.

30. Galloway 2006.

31. See Knollenberg 2002, 92–101. This logic was certainly not forgotten over the next decade. In 1772, the Board of Trade wrote the Privy Council to remind it that immediately after the 1763 peace treaty with France, the "principle" was adopted of restricting western settlement in order to keep the Americans close to the seacoast. This would ensure that their settlements "should lie within the reach of the trade and commerce of this kingdom, upon which the strength and riches of [Britain] depend." Knollenberg 2002, 101.

32. Andrews 1938; Wallerstein 2014.

33. William 2005; McCusker and Menard 1991; McLoughlin 1986.

34. WSA I: 62–63, 72.

35. Massachusetts and its sister colonies have been "exerting our growing strength" in service of the mother country, and this worried British elites (WSA I: 72).

36. WSA I: 134–52. That month, Adams wrote directly to Lord Shelburne, now colonial secretary and an acolyte of Pitt who had been sympathetic to BNA desires for territorial and market expansion. He reminded Shelburne that it was the colonists who had been responsible, mostly at their own expense, for enlarging the British empire and who already paid a huge cost because of restrictions on their right to trade with the rest of the world. Forcing Americans to send enumerated and duties staples only to Britain was "in reality a tax, though an indirect one," one that was on top of the new Townshend duties. WSA I: 152–62. See also memos by Shelburne in LWES.

37. WSA I: 236–40, 386–91.

38. See the whole second volume of Adams's writings (WSA II), which cover January 1770 to February 1773, especially 350–69.

39. For summary and references, see Vaughn 2019.

40. Vaughn 2019.

41. Breen 2004, 304.

42. Schlesinger 1918, 268–69. See also Vaughn 2019; Andrews 1938.

43. Schlesinger 1918, 269–73 (emphasis in original). A New York commissioner wrote to the Boston Committee of Correspondence in February 1774 that giving in to the EIC on tea would mean "they will obtain liberty to export their spices, silks, etc."

44. Schlesinger 1918, 274–76.

45. WSA III: 101–2.

46. Quoted in Stoll 2008, 135–36. On the anti-Catholic fear created in New England by the Quebec Act, see Metzger 1936; Lawson 1989.

47. Quoted in Gipson 1967, 162–63 and Alvord 1917, II: 246. When debate in Parliament to repeal the act came up in 1775, two Pittites, Lords Camden and Shelburne, expressed their sense of the act's intent in no uncertain terms. Camden said bluntly that the act extended Quebec's boundaries to the west of the English colonies "so as to prevent their further progress." Shelburne noted that aside from restricting western settlements, the act effectively handed over the whole of the western fur trade from the Ohio River to Hudson's Bay to the French Canadians. English-speaking colonists would naturally see themselves excluded by this "total monopoly" (quoted in Alvord 1917, II: 243–44). Since parliamentary debates by this point in British history were widely reported in English newspapers, such discussions could not have improved American confidence in London's intentions.

48. As Lord North was said to have stated in March during the debates, if the Americans refused to trade with Britain, "we should not suffer them to trade with any other nation." Schlesinger 1918, 538.

49. These figures come from averaging statistics provided in a broad range of historical works.

50. Schlesinger 1918, 578–79.

51. Quoted in Schlesinger 1918, 578–79.

52. Schlesinger 1918, 578–79.

53. The inability of the colonies to commit politically to staying a part of the British empire—a form of Fearon's commitment problem (1995), but one that also involves concerns about the future commercial intentions of the rising powers—made it very difficult for the British to remain confident about the future, especially given what the Americans in New England were already signaling about their character and desires.

54. Nelson 2017.

# Chapter 4

1. In the language of chapter 2, they "leaned" more to the hard-line end of the spectrum as threats increased, accepting the risk of provoking higher inter-state mistrust in order to prevent a relative decline in economic growth.

2. And this was true of both Hamilton and Jefferson, despite their considerable differences. See Mead 2001, chaps. 4 and 6; Onuf 2000; Tucker and Hendrickson 1990.

3. I am of course referring only to relations with significant states such as Britain and Spain, as opposed to relations with Native American groups, in which opportunistic expansion from 1790 until the 1890s was the order of the day.

4. Mead 2001, chap. 6; Onuf 2000.

5. Because this First Barbary War from 1803 to 1805 had no risk of escalation to war with the great powers, I do not cover it here. Suffice it to say that it aligns well with the logic of the trade expectations approach. For overviews, see Wheelan 2003; Tucker and Hendrickson 1990; Pratt et al. 1979.

6. See Mead 2001, 2007; Pratt et al.1979; LaFeber 1994; Zoellick 2021; Herring 2008.

7. We often forget that John O'Sullivan's famous proclamation of August 1845 that the United States had a "manifest destiny to overspread the continent" was written in the context of the ongoing struggle with the British to control Texas and California. Just before this famous line, O'Sullivan stressed that "other nations" were seeking to "intrude themselves into [the Texan question] . . . for the avowed purpose of thwarting our policies and hampering our power." The article then took up the question of California, and its "immense utility to the commerce . . . with the whole [of] Eastern Asia," especially after a transcontinental railway was built. For the document, see *IAFP*, 56–58.

8. See Copeland 2015, chap. 1 on the theoretical impact of third parties on the Y-X interaction and the probability of crisis and war.

9. Herring 2008, chap. 1; Hamilton, *Federalist Papers*, FP, nos. 11–13; Jefferson in TJW, 834–1015. It is worth remembering that Jefferson's main function as ambassador to France in the late 1780s was to increase U.S.-French trade.

10. See Herring 2008; Marks 1986. As Marks shows, the calling of the Constitutional Constitution of 1787 was itself fundamentally driven by the trade restrictions from European powers such as Britain after 1782. Without a consolidation of federal power, the newly formed "United" States would lack the bargaining leverage to secure favorable trade deals, and would continue to impose tariffs on each other, both of which would hurt long-term U.S. growth and the ability to stop European efforts to draw vulnerable states into their own spheres. See also the first eleven Federalist Papers, esp. 6–9 and 11 by Hamilton.

11. See Elkins and McKitrick 1993.

12. Elkins and McKitrick 1993, 382–83.

13. See Elkins and McKitrick 1993, chap. 9; Flexner 1972, chaps. 14–15; Bemis 1962.

14. See in particular Bemis 1962; Flexner 1972, chaps. 14–15, 21; Herring 2008.

15. Summary drawn from Smith 1962, vol. 2; Herring 2008; Elkins and McKitrick 1993; Wood 2009; Pratt, DeSantis, and Siracusa 1979; Deconde 1966.

16. U.S. and French land forces never fought one another, notwithstanding Alexander Hamilton's desire to lead a reconstituted U.S. army into such a fight. But the very fact that this army was hastily cobbled together in late 1798 shows the extent of Adams's and the Federalists' fear that the French might indeed land their troops on the U.S. coast or use Spanish territory in the west or Florida for this purpose. DeConde 1966 remains the most complete account of the conflict with France from 1797 to 1800 and is the basis of my short summary here. See also Herring 2008; Elkins and McKitrick 1993; and Pratt et al. 1979.

17. Malone 1962, 383.

18. Again, this is consistent with figure 2.3 and current military power as a constraining factor that after improvement becomes a facilitating factor for action.

19. Toll 2008.

20. See my discussion in Copeland 2000a, chap. 8; and Copeland 2015, chap. 8.

21. My summary is drawn from Tucker and Hendrickson 1990; Cerami 2004; Onuf 2000; Herring 2008; Wood 2009; Cogliano 2014. See also Copeland 2000a, chap. 8.

22. See Tucker and Hendrikson 1990; Onuf 2000. Francis Cogliano shows that Jefferson's larger plans for the area west of the Appalachian Mountains were at least partly shaped by concerns about slavery's long-term viability. But Cogliano accepts that his policy toward Napoleon was a function of the immediate and unanticipated threat to commerce on the Mississippi. Cogliano 2014, chap. 6.

23. Onuf 2000.

24. The more purely offensive realist argument of Elman 2004—that Jefferson was grabbing an opportunity for more territory in the face of future military threats—fails for the same reasons the domestic-level explanations fail. Jefferson did not act because of opportunity but out of fear of economic cut-off, and his goals were limited not expansive.

25. Above summary based on Herring 2008; Perkins 1961; Pratt et al. 1979; Brant 1970; Stewart 2015; LaFeber 1994.

26. Hill 2005, chap. 11.

27. See Burstein and Isenberg 2010, chap. 13; Ketcham 1990, chaps. 18–19.

28. Ketcham 1990, chap. 19.

29. MP 4: 1–5. For Treasury Secretary Albert Gallatin's detailed critique of an earlier draft of Madison's message, a draft that was apparently more hard-line than even the one he presented to Congress, see MP 3: 535–40.

30. MP 3: 389–90.

31. See Malone 1972.

32. MP 3: 427.

33. A discussion of Foster's letters was a center point of the meeting, however, as seen in Monroe's letter of September 7, 1811, MP 3: 451. See Ammon 1994, 299.

34. Later in the letter, he wrote that "every step you take at this time is watched and criticized with severity . . . Some friends have been cooled, other made enemies." MP 3: 459.

35. September 13, 1811, MP 3: 459.

36. September 13, 1811, MP 3: 473 (Madison underlined the word "insane" in the text). Jefferson understood Madison's feelings and sought to dispel even this hope. As Jefferson wrote Madison on October 10, one might wish that the prince would improve relations with Washington, but that was "barely possible" given his character. MP 3: 483.

37. Quoted in Perkins 1961, 105.

38. Quoted in Brown 1971, 30.

39. See MP 4: 17, n. 4.

40. Indeed, this smuggling, implicitly supported by the czar, became the basis for Napoleon's attack on Russia seven months later, in June 1812. See Copeland 2000a, chap. 8.

41. November 15, 1811, MP 4: 16–17.

42. Secretary of State Monroe's thinking at the time mirrors the president's. On December 6, 1811, he wrote his brother that the U.S. government "is resolved, if G. Britain does not revoke her Order in Council . . . to act offensively towards her." In a mid-June 1812 letter to Virginia farmer John Taylor, Monroe admits that he and Madison had accepted the necessity of war following the failed talks with Foster. It was clear by late summer 1811 that "Nothing would satisfy [the British] short of unconditional surrender." Hence, the only remaining alternative "was to get ready for fighting, and to begin as soon as we were ready. This was the plan of the administration, when Congress met in November last . . . and every step taken by the administration since has led to it." Quoted in Brown 1971, 30–31.

43. See Horsman 1962, 242–43; Ketcham 1990, 517–18.

44. See discussion in Brown 1971, chap. 6.

45. For summaries and references, see Brown 1971 and Perkins 1961.

46. See Brown 1971; Horsman 1962.

47. Horsman 1962. It is worth remembering that Madison and Monroe were from Virginia. Neither they nor Southern legislators had any interest in seeing Canadian provinces become new non-slave states, a move that would have shifted the domestic balance of power against them.

48. Ketcham 1990; Silverstone 2004.

49. MP 4: 123–24.

50. See Bourne 1967.

51. Summary based on Weeks 1992; Pratt et al. 1979; 1950; Herring 2008; Bemis 1949; LaFeber 1965b.

52. Summary drawn from Crabb 1982, chap. 1; Weeks 1992; Bemis 1949; May 1975; Weinberg 1935.

53. Weinberg, 1935; May 1975.

54. Quoted in Bourne 1967, 63–64.

55. Lewis 1998, 172–80.

56. Lewis 1998, 180.

57. For almost the next four decades—until French intervention in Mexico in 1862–63—France played only a minor role in hindering or facilitating America's foreign policy objectives in the western hemisphere.

58. See esp. Bourne 1967.

59. The counterfactual here is this: had Britain not been constrained by having to worry about other great powers (European multipolarity), would it have been as cautious in the nineteenth century about engaging in war with a rising new threat, the United States?

60. Quoted in Bourne 1967, 64–65.

61. Bourne's evidence suggests that both sides were deterred by the potential costs of war: the British were still vulnerable in Canada despite the new fortifications, and the Americans feared what the British could still do to the coastal cities (Bourne 1967, 70).

62. Jones and Rakestraw 1997, 35–36. See also Bourne 1967; Herring 2008; LaFeber 1994.

63. Jones and Rakestraw 1997; Herring 2008; LaFeber 1994.

64. Jones and Rakestraw 1997, 19.

65. Trubowitz 2011, chap. 5.

66. These technologies had dropped the costs of transporting goods by more than ninety percent from 1820 to 1840, while reducing the time involved by four-fifths. For the phenomenal changes in the North American political economy, Howe 2009, chaps. 1–4 and 14–15.

67. Merk 1966; Weinberg 1963; Horsman 1981; Hietala 1985; Pletcher 1973. David Pletcher and Thomas Hietala in particular show how fear of a North-South split in the country acted as a restraint on Tyler and Polk's desires to absorb Texas and later California.

68. For summaries and references, see esp. Merk 1966, 1978, 1985; Hietala 1985.

69. Overall, the sectional argument for the push to expansion works far better for the 1850s than 1840s. By this point, because of the western territories added by 1848, there was an intense North-South struggle to control which of the new territories would allow the extension of slavery and which would be "free soil" (non-slave) territories. The Southern struggle to increase the number of slave states led to the filibustering exercises in Central America and the Caribbean and the effort to purchase Cuba as a future slave state (the Ostend Manifesto of 1854). In a real sense, therefore, the sectional drives to shape the nature of U.S. expansion did not cause the land grabs in the West from 1846 to 1848. Rather, they resulted from them. See Pratt et al. 1979.

70. Much of my summary below, unless otherwise noted, is drawn from the seminal book on the Texas case, Pletcher 1973.

71. Quoted in Hietala 1985, 18; and Merk 1966, 14.

72. Pletcher 1973, 126–27.

73. Quoted in Hietala 1985, 22.

74. Merk 1966, 18.

75. Quoted in Hietala 1985, 223–23.

76. Pletcher 1973.

77. Quoted in Pletcher 1973, 178.

78. Tyler's note, LTT, 428–31. He repeated this logic in a private letter to his former secretary of state Daniel Webster in April 1850; see Hietala 1985, 69.

79. Merk 1978.

80. Hietala 1985, 56–57.

81. Quoted in Hietala 1985, 57.

82. Quoted in Hietala 1985, 58–59.

83. Hietala 1985, 60–62.

84. Hietala 1985, 61.

85. Jones and Rakestraw 1997, 144–45; Pratt et al. 1980, 83; Graebner 1983, 71; Pletcher 1973, 99. Andrew Jackson had made a similar offer in 1835, but the debate over the Texan war for independence precluded any deal. Weeks 1992, 109.

86. Pletcher 1973, 96–97.

87. Quoted in Graebner 1983, 72–73. See also Pletcher 1973, 212, for another move by Calhoun to buy California.

88. Quoted in Leonard 2001, 136; see also Pletcher 1973, 230–31 and Hietala 1985, 84. Polk's keen interest led him to send William Parrott, a friend with knowledge of Mexican politics, to Mexico City in April to collect information on Mexico's willingness to sell California in return for forgiving Mexican debt. See Wheelan 2007, 67–68.

89. Chace and Carr 1988, 77.

90. See Pletcher 1973, 261–62; Graebner 1983, 86.

91. Quoted in Graebner 1983, 109–10.

92. Quoted in Graebner 1983, 116.

93. Graebner 1983, 116–18.

94. PD I: August 25, 1845.

95. In the August 26 meeting, Polk emphasized the importance of not giving the British any sense of "hesitancy and indecision on our part" by immediately communicating Polk's now harsher terms. PD I: August 26, 1845.

96. PD I: 16 September 1845.

97. Quoted in Pletcher 1973, 281.

98. Pletcher 1973, 283; Chaffin 2002, 273; Leonard 2001, 137.

99. PD I: October 24, 1845.

100. Quoted in Merk 1966, 136.

101. Pletcher 1973, 283.

102. Chaffin 2002, 273.

103. A third move on October 17 was also significant. Polk instructed Zachary Taylor, the commander of the U.S. army in Texas, to approach the Rio Grande River "as near . . . as circumstances will permit" to counter any Mexican or Indian attacks. Taylor's forces had been in position in Corpus Christi on the southern bank of the Nueces River since early fall. This note, along with an even more assertive one sent in mid-January 1846, would compel Taylor to move across the disputed land between the Nueces and the Rio Grande and place his troops directly across from Mexican forces (Pletcher 1973, 364–66).

104. Senator Benton convinced Polk to also instruct Gillespie to carry instructions to his son-in-law, the pathfinder John Frémont, who had left for California the summer before, apparently on another fact-finding adventure. The nature of the instructions to Frémont, both before he left for California and the ones he received from Gillespie when Gillespie arrived in May 1846, have been a matter of great historical debate. After all, Frémont played a critical role in May–June 1846 in organizing the rebellion of American immigrants that led to the Bear Flag republic and subsequent absorption of California into the Union. There is not the space to engage this debate here. Suffice it to say that even if the instructions to Frémont were not specific, as they apparently were not, Gillespie almost certainly informed Frémont of the general thrust of Polk and Buchanan's letters to Larkin, which had instructed Larkin to counter the designs of foreign governments and to bring California into the Union should its residents declare independence. Frémont later claimed to have understood at the time that he was being given implicit instructions as a U.S. army officer to "foil England by carrying the war now imminent with Mexico into the territory of California," a claim that seems quite plausible. After all, the strategy Polk and Buchanan had envisioned in October 1845 when the

letters were sent via Gillespie was clearly conveyed in the letters themselves. See Van Alstyne 1965, 140–41; Chaffin 2002, 303–6.

105. Quoted in Pletcher 1973, 289.

106. Quoted in Binder 1994, 101–2; Wheelan 2007, 71–72. See also PD I: March 28, 1846, where Polk reiterates the importance of acquiring San Francisco.

107. PD I: October 27, 1845.

108. PD I: November 29, 1845.

109. Quoted in Pletcher 1973, 305–8.

110. PD I: February 24, 1846.

111. Wheelan 2007, 75–78.

112. Quoted in Wheelan 2007, 85.

113. PD I: April 9, 1846.

114. PD I: April 18, 1846. Through April, Washington received reports from London and Mexico City on continued British machinations with the Mexican leadership. See Pletcher 1973, 370–71.

115. PD I; April 21 and 28, 1846.

116. PD I: May 3 and 8, 1846.

117. PD I: May 9, 1846.

118. NPD 87, n. 4.

119. PD I: May 13, 1846. At another point, he told Buchanan he would face either Britain or France or both and "stand and fight until the last man among us fell in the conflict."

## Chapter 5

1. Zakaria 1998.

2. Other IR theory books cover specific cases, such as the Venezuelan crisis of 1895 and the Spanish-American War but tend to ignore the previous four decades. See Owen 1997; Kirshner 2007.

3. Merk 1995.

4. Merk 1995, chap. 9; LaFeber 1989, 1994.

5. Quoted in Van Alystne 1965, 158–59.

6. See McCullough 1979; LaFeber 1989.

7. LaFeber 1994; McCullough 1979.

8. Ironically, it was the very territorial acquisitions made in the first half of the century, driven as we have seen largely by economic concerns, that intensified the internal struggle that made further expansion so difficult to implement.

9. This was the notorious "Ostend Manifesto," a secret report to the secretary of state stating the importance of Cuba to the United States and the need to take Cuba if Cuba's internal disorder endangered the internal peace and security of the United States. See Pratt et al. 1979, 132.

10. Quoted in Van Alystne 1965, 173. See also LaFeber 1994.

11. Hane 1972, 245–49.

12. Quoted in Van Alystne 1965, 173. One hears here echoes of contemporary Chinese concerns about U.S. control of the Indian and Pacific Ocean trade.

13. Because the U.S. Civil War is generally considered an internal war rather than a case of American foreign policy, I do not consider it here. I am currently working on a separate paper, however, that shows that in large part President Abraham Lincoln was unwilling to let the South go peacefully (as it certainly preferred to do) since as a separate nation it would have greatly harmed the rump United States economically over the long term. The North would no longer have had access to cheap raw materials, including cotton, or at least not on terms superior to competitors such as Britain. The U.S. government would also have had to forgo tariff revenue on European manufactured goods that the South, the country's major exporting region, had tended to pay disproportionately. Moreover, tariffs imposed by the Confederacy on U.S. manufactured goods would have ended the benefits of the customs union and given the advantage to British products, which were still relatively cheaper and of higher quality.

14. Seward successfully used coercive threats in 1865–67 to get the French out of Mexico and to deter Vienna from supporting Austrian Maximillian's shaky hold on power in Mexico City, leading to Maximillian's execution in 1867 and Mexico's return to the republican fold. Because these actions had little to do with economic questions, I do not cover them here.

15. See Zakaria 1998, 59.

16. See Zakaria 1998.

17. Zakaria 1998, 60–61.

18. Zakaria 1998, 75–76.

19. My summary below relies heavily on Abdelal and Kirshner 1999–2000. See also Maass 2019.

20. Abdelal and Kirshner 1999–2000, 126–28.

21. Quoted in Campbell 1976, 71.

22. See Abdelal and Kirshner 1999–2000, 131. Zakaria recognizes that Grant and Fish's actions over Hawaii and the Senate's approval of the deal were both driven "by fear of British encroachment" (1998, 74).

23. Campbell 1976, 72–76; Zakaria 1998, 76–77.

24. In early 1889, in the face of German intervention in a Samoan civil conflict, the Senate approved Cleveland's request for money to protect the U.S. base in Pago Pago. A year later, under the new administration of Benjamin Harrison, the Senate approved a three-way treaty between America, Britain, and Germany that kept Samoa independent under its original king but divided up responsibilities for maintaining civil order. Campbell 1976, 76–83.

25. LaFeber 1989, 12.

26. Quoted in Pratt et al. 1979, 148; see also Campbell 1976, 62–63.

27. Van Alystne 1965, 163.

28. Love 1992, 345.

29. See Love 1992, chap. 21.

30. For summaries and references, see esp. Hunt and Levine 2012; Immerman 2012; Zoellick 2021; Pratt et al. 1979; LaFeber 1994. More than 200,000 Filipinos died in the three-year insurgency. Over 125,000 Americans were deployed, and more than 4,200 died.

31. On McKinley's character, see Dobson 1988.

32. See, for example, LaFeber 1965b; Campbell 1976; McCormick 1967; Williams 1962; Pratt et al. 1979.

33. See Offner 1992; Musicant 1998; Perez 1998; Schoonover 2003; Karp 2010; Thomas 2010.

34. See Copeland 2015, chap. 8.

35. See the statistics in Copeland 2000a, appendix 1.

36. Pletcher 1998, 2001.

37. Quoted in Smith 2012, 28.

38. Mahan 1890; Mead 2007.

39. Campbell 1976; Layne 2006; Mead 2007.

40. Quoted in Langer 1951, 391–93.

41. For more on this period and the lead-up to Japan's war with Russia in 1904, see Copeland 2015, chap. 3.

42. Langer 1951, 167–90, 385–412, and 445–90.

43. Graebner 1985, 341; Schoonover 2005, 67–68.

44. Graebner 1985, 341.

45. See Offner 1992; Schoonover 2005; Perez 1998; Hunt and Levin 2012; Herring 2008; Kagan 2023.

46. See LaFeber 1965b; McCormick 1967.

47. See esp. Gould 1981; Dobson 1988.

48. See Campbell 1976; Pratt et al., 1979.

49. See esp. Offner 1982.

50. Copeland 2015, chaps. 4–5.

51. See Layne's (2006) summary of the Open Door school.

52. This phrase of Offner (1992) to describe the Spanish-American War may be wrong for 1898, but of course it is perfectly appropriate in an age of thermonuclear weapons.

53. LaFeber 1989.

54. I will not cover this crisis here since the case is straightforward and has been nicely covered elsewhere (see especially Owen 1997; Layne 1994; see summary in Copeland 2015, chap. 8). Suffice it to say that Cleveland took a strong stand and was willing to bring the nation to the edge of war to reduce the threat of British intrusion into what was seen as a U.S. sphere of influence.

55. Quoted in Gould 1981, 32.

56. Campbell 1976, 232.

57. Beale 1984, 57. Mahan and Roosevelt were in regular contact on this issue, with Mahan of course also supporting annexation. Sherman, unaware of treaty negotiations, assured the Japanese that no such negotiations were underway. This only exacerbated Japanese mistrust when they were told of a signed treaty in late June.

58. Love 1992, 386.

59. Quoted in Campbell 1976, 237.

60. Abdelal and Kirshner, 1999–2000.

61. Quoted in Gould 1981, 196. See also Campbell 1976, 222–30; Dobson 1988, 25. Full-scale development of a canal would await the formal British acceptance of U.S. future control over any isthmus canal in November 1901. Theodore Roosevelt's calculated move to separate Panama from Columbia in 1903 was designed to move the project forward. See McCollough 1978; LaFeber 1989.

62. See Owen 1994, 1997.

63. Quoted in Chace and Carr 1988, 131.

64. Quoted in LaFeber 1965b, 361.

65. See Pratt 1964, 221–22; Chace and Carr 1988, 130–31; LaFeber 1965b, 361. Quotation is from McCormick 1967, 107.

66. Love 1992, 390; also LaFeber 1965b, 361.

67. See Beale 1984, 60–62; McCormick 1967, 107–9; Zimmermann 2004, 242–44; Pratt 1964.

68. McCormick 1967, 108.

69. McCormick 1967, 108–9.

70. McCormick 1967, 109.

71. Quoted in McCormick 1967, 107.

72. McCormick 1967.

73. Mayers 2007.

74. See esp. Welch 1979, chap. 1.

75. Pratt et al., 1964; Campbell 1976.

76. To make this case for an "unwanted war," scholars such as John Offner must proceed by downplaying or ignoring all of McKinley's efforts to absorb Hawaii and his connections to expansionists such as Roosevelt and Lodge from late 1896 on, to focus largely on the 1897–98 events as seen by the public at large, rather than from the perspective of the key participants who could have halted the move to war. (Offner 1992; see also Musicant 1998 and Kagan 2023).

77. Offner 1992; Zimmermann 2004; Dobson 1988.

78. See Campbell 1976, 247.

79. FRUS 1898: July 16, 1897, 658–61.

80. Woodford to Sherman, September 13, 1897, FRUS 1898: 562–65.

81. He was following Washington's lead here. See Sherman's long note to Woodford, November 20, 1897, FRUS, 603–5 on the need to end the conflict given "the losses occasioned to our commerce, our industries, and the property of our citizens." See also FRUS, 647–48, for Woodford's use of this language in discussions with the Spanish.

82. Dobson 1988.

83. Woodford to the President, March 2, 1898, FRUS 1898: 673–75.

84. See Woodford's attached note to the March 2 correspondence, which is a translation of his confidential ciphered dispatch to McKinley sent on March 1. FRUS 1898: 675–66.

85. FRUS 1898: 676. Day's separate confidential report that day (FRUS 1898: 680–81) makes clear that Day and McKinley are in constant contact on the issue, and that Day is keeping the president "thoroughly advised of the situation."

86. See Woodford's letters to Sherman, March 3 and 4, FRUS 1898: 677–78.

87. FRUS 1898: 681–84.

88. FRUS 1898: 685–88.

89. FRUS 1898: 688–92.

90. The Spanish were understandably unwilling to take the blame for the *Maine* sinking. They rightly saw it as an accident that the Americans were using to push the Spanish into a corner while they mobilized public opinion around a hard-line option.

91. FRUS 1898: 692–93.

92. Offner 1992, 143–44.

93. Offner 1992, 143–44.

94. FRUS 1898: 695.

95. FRUS 1898: 696.

96. FRUS 1898: 696.

97. FRUS 1898: 697.

98. FRUS 1898: 697.

99. FRUS 1898: 697–702.

100. FRUS 1898: 698–702.

101. FRUS 1898: 696.

102. FRUS 1898: 702.

103. FRUS 1898: 701–3.

104. FRUS 1898: 710–11.

105. FRUS 1898: 712–13.

106. See two telegrams on March 28 and telegrams on March 29 and 30, in FRUS 1898: 713, 718.

107. FRUS 1898: 719, Woodford's dispatch on March 29 to McKinley.

108. See FRUS 1898: 719.

109. See FRUS 1898: 719.

110. FRUS 1898: 718.

111. FRUS 1898: 718.

112. FRUS 1898: 718–21.

113. FRUS 1898: 721.

114. FRUS 1898: 727–28.

115. FRUS 1898: 732–33.

116. FRUS 1898: 732–33.

117. Offner 1992, 168.

118. FRUS 1898: 750–60.

119. Offner 1992, chaps. 10–11; FRUS 1898: 769–72. Senator Henry Teller was also able to include a clause stating that America would disclaim any intention of exercising sovereignty over Cuba (the famous "Teller amendment").

120. Offner 1992, chap. 11.

121. FRUS 1898: 761–62.

122. See Copeland 2015, chap. 1 for review of the commercial liberal argument.

123. See in particular Owen 1994, 1997; and Russett 1993.


# Chapter 6

1. From Wilson's January 22, 1917 "Peace without Victory" speech, discussed below.

2. In this vast literature, for references and core arguments, see esp. Mead 2001, chap. 5; Smith 2017; Berg 2013; Cooper 2009; Knock 1992; Calhoun 1986; Gilderhus 1986; Heckscher 1991; Link 1960, 1964, 1965; Ikenberry 2020; Tucker 2007.

3. For historical accounts that do take into account realpolitik aspects of Wilson's thinking, see Kennedy 2009; Doenecke 2011.

4. Kyle Lascurettes (2020), however, shows that in 1919 Wilson also saw his plans as a way to use institutions to contain and reduce the growth of Soviet communism.

5. Mead 2001, chap. 5, 2007; Ikenberry 2020; Cooper 2009; Knock 1992.

6. He also had strong fears of British penetration into Mexico and the Caribbean, suggesting that his perception of the German threat was due more to the particular intensity of Berlin's efforts in the area than to its regime type per se. Ido Oren (1995) shows that prior to 1917, despite Germany's nonelected executive branch, Wilson saw its political system as having many liberal democratic elements.

7. In short, Wilson wanted to preserve a centuries-old multipolar structure that had European great powers so concerned with each other that they let the United States build its economic power sphere in the western hemisphere and eastern Pacific in relative freedom.

8. Cronon, ed., *Cabinet Diaries of Josephus Daniels* (hereafter CDJD): March 6–7, 11, 1913.

9. Link, ed., *Papers of Woodrow Wilson* (hereafter PWW), 27: 172, March 12, 1913.

10. His policy toward China in the aftermath of its 1911 revolution and the assumption of power of strongman Yuan Shih-kai was similar. See Cohen 1980.

11. Although Wilson's belief that the world economy was fundamentally changing was a long-standing one, the wording of his speech and his subsequent behavior was likely influenced by a wired memorandum from the U.S. ambassador to Britain, his old friend Walter Page. Two days earlier, Page had informed Wilson of his emerging view that the United States was destined to play a dominant role in world politics over the next decades. A man only needed "two economic eyes in his head," Page argued, to see that the "leadership of the world" was passing from Britain to the United States and that "the future belongs to us." In language similar to Wilson's, Page wrote that "The great economic tide of the century flows our way," and with big questions on the table, "we shall need world policies." LLWP, 1: 144–51, October 25, 1913.

12. For Wilson's Mobile speech, see MPWW, 1: 32–36.

13. HD, October 28, 1913.

14. HD, October 28, 1913.

15. Mitchell 1999, 189–92.

16. Mitchell 1999, 194.

17. See Grieb 1969, 136–39.

18. Tumulty 1921, 151–52.

19. HD, April 22, 1914.

20. Katz 1981, 240–42.

21. His policy would be codified by Robert Lansing, the State Department's primary counselor and future secretary of state, just before Huerta's exile. In a memorandum to Wilson on June 16, 1914, Lansing wrote that the Monroe Doctrine had always been about U.S. "primacy" in the western hemisphere. Traditionally, the doctrine had mostly reflected concerns over European acquisition of territory. But with their vast increases in wealth over the last quarter century, Britain and Germany were now stressing investments and increased penetration through steamship lines, mining, and agricultural exports. America was operating under the same pressures, and thus "[U.S.] commercial expansion and success are closely interwoven with political domination over the territory which is being exploited." Yet the threat to U.S. interests was clear: the Europeans would use Latin American debt obligations to control governments "as completely as if it had acquired sovereign rights over the territory through occupation, conquest or cession." See "Present Nature and Extent of the Monroe Doctrine and Its Need of Restatement," FRUS, Lansing Papers, 1914–20, 2: June 16, 1914, 460–65.

22. See Gilderhus 1977; Calvert 1968; Katz 1981.

23. See references, chap. 6, n. 2 in this volume.

24. PWW, 30: 393–94, August 18, 1914.

25. See below for Wilson's discussions in September 1914 on the parallels to the War of 1812.

26. On sideline sitting, see Copeland 2000a, chap. 1.

27. LLWP, 1: 310–11, August 9, 1914.

28. PWW, 30: 432–33, August 22, 1914; HD, August 22, 1914.

29. HD, August 30, 1914.

30. Jervis 1976, chap. 3; Glaser 2010; Van Evera 1999. I show elsewhere (2000) that this explanation is incomplete: while it captures the behavior of Russia, France, and Britain in July 1914, it does not cover the thinking of leaders in Berlin, which was driven by the fear of the long-term rise of Russia.

31. HD, September 20, 1914. House seems to have gotten through to the British ambassador. Spring-Rice told Grey afterwards that the "following considerations seem to force themselves on the attention of the world. If war continues, either G[ermany] becomes supreme or R[ussia]. Both alternatives would be fatal to the equilibrium of Europe." IPCH, 328–29 (no date given, but likely sent between September 20 and 22, 1914).

32. See Copeland 2000a, chaps. 3–4.

33. HD, September 28, 1914. House wrote to Page in London on October 3 that he felt Germany would soon be willing to discuss terms, since "It is manifestly against England's interest and the interest of Europe generally for Russia to become the dominating military force in Europe, just as Germany was." LLWP, 412–15, October 3, 1914.

34. HD, September 29, 1914.

35. PWW, 31: 160, October 15, 1914.

36. PWW, 31: 160, October 15, 1914.

37. LLWP, 380–84, October 22, 1914.

38. PWW, 31: 354–57, November 5, 1914 (italics added). See also the December 3 discussion where House told Wilson that the Kaiser's "whole economic scheme [for South America] seemed to me wrong and wholly material." PWW, 31: 387.

39. Gilderhaus 1986, 18.

40. PWW, 31: 354–55, November 25, 1914; Gilderhaus 1986, 49. See also House's memorandum to Wilson on November 30 stressing that the "opportunity to weld North and South America together in [a] closer union, is at your hand." PWW, 31: 363.

41. PWW, 31: 468–73, December 16, 1914.

42. Gilderhaus 1986, 51.

43. Knock 1992.

44. See Grey's note to House, April 24, 1915 in IPCH 1: 425, where Grey states that if "Germany would enter after the war some League of Nations where she would give and accept the same security that other nations gave and accepted against war breaking out between them, their expenditures on armaments might be reduced and new rules to secure 'freedom of the seas' made."

45. Blainey (1973) gives us the image of animals sitting on the sidelines taking advantage of the tendency of waterbirds to whittle down their strength by fighting amongst themselves. This is equivalent to the strategy of "sideline-sitting" discussed in Copeland 2000a, chap. 1.

46. IPCH, 1: 383–83, February 23, 1915.

47. MPWW, 1: 219–25, February 10, 1015.

48. MPWW, 1: 225–26, February 20, 1915.

49. Link 1960, 584–85.

50. MPWW, 1: 119–21, May 24, 1915.

51. Given this context, Wilson's request on April 2, 1917, that the United States help make the world "safe for democracy" can be interpreted more as a desire to *protect* existing democracies than to actively increase their number. In short, the "regime promotion" aspect of Wilson's later "liberal internationalism" was a secondary or insignificant part of his thinking during the years and months leading up to the entry into the war itself, and indeed until 1918. Cf. Smith 2017; Berg 2013; Ikenberry 2020.

52. Plummer 1988.

53. Plummer 1988, 194–99.

54. Quoted in Munro 1964, 339–40.

55. Link 1969, 525. In February the Germans were again asking to participate in Haiti's financial reorganization given the preponderant influence of German merchants on the island. As Bryan told Wilson, in explaining why such demands had been turned down, participation by the European powers "would be [a violation] of the spirit of the Monroe Doctrine and would open the door to all sorts of requests." It seems he and Wilson were unaware of the hypocritical nature of historical U.S. demands for "open doors" to Asia trade as they shut those doors back home! FRUS, Lansing Papers, 1914–20, 2: 465–66, February 25, 1915.

56. Link 1960, 532–38; FRUS 1915, Supplement, The World War: 473–96. American forces would not leave the island nation until 1924.

57. FRUS, Lansing Papers 2: 466–68.

58. Quoted in Kaufmann 1974, 99.

59. Quoted in Kaufmann 1974, 102.

60. Kaufmann 1974, 104. Kaufman's seminal work on this issue is unfortunately marred by his assumption, drawn from the Wisconsin school of diplomatic history founded by William Appleman Williams, that the U.S. executive branch was doing all this for the sake of firm profits and elite wealth. My discussion shows that Wilson is acting primarily for the long-term security of the nation as a whole—that is, for realist propelling reasons, not neo-Marxist ones. The support of business elites was a facilitating factor for Wilson since he could not expand the U.S. economic power sphere without them.

61. Kaufmann 1974, 113–16.

62. Congress adjusted the Federal Reserve Act in 1916 to allow national banks to create foreign banking corporations (as distinct from domestic banks with foreign branch offices). Kaufmann 1974, 118.

63. Kaufmann 1974, 119. As McAdoo told Charles Hamlin, the governor of the Fed, in August: "Our duty is to protect the commerce of the United States," and "Our foreign commerce is just as essential to our prosperity as our domestic commerce." Kaufmann 1974.

64. See Kaufman 1974.

65. My realist argument here parallels that of Krasner 1978, when he discusses Franklin Roosevelt's "statist" efforts during World War II to create a new government oil corporation to increase U.S. oil security in the Middle East, despite resistance from business and congress.

66. Braisted 1971, 163–65; Widenor 1980, 135–36.

67. Quotations and summary from Braisted 1971, 187–88.

68. Braisted 1971, 188–89.

69. Braisted 1971, 189.

70. HD, September 22, 1915.

71. HD, September 24, 1915.

72. MPWW, 1: 133–55, December 7, 1915.

73. MPWW, 1: 137.

74. PWW, 36: 11–12, January 27, 1916.

75. PWW, 36: 42–45, January 29, 1916.

76. PWW, 36: 101–3, February 2, 1916.

77. Quoted in Braisted 1971, 197 from House diary/papers, May 17 and 24, 1916.

78. Braisted 1971, 198–202.

79. Blum 2014.

80. Lansing's diary note from October 10 is quoted in Katz 1981, 302.

81. HD, March 29, 1916; PWW, 36: 335, March 17, 1916.

82. Quoted in Katz 1981, 311. As Ross Kennedy shows, by October 1915 Washington was aware that German agents were busy encouraging internal conflict within Mexico (Kennedy 2009, 28).

83. Perini 1969, 32.

84. FRUS 1916, Supplement, The World War: April 17, 1916.

85. FRUS 1916, Supplement, April 24, 1916.

86. FRUS 1916, Supplement, May 3, 1916.

87. Germany from the start of the war had clear plans for economic hegemony in Europe (see Copeland 2015, chap. 3). The Allies had apparently caught wind of these plans.

88. FRUS 1916, Supplement, The World War: June 22, 1916.

89. PWW 37: 287–88, June 23, 1916.

90. HD, June 23, 1916.

91. Recall that Wilson actually saw Germany as the more democratic state prior to the war (Oren 1995).

92. LLWP 2: 184.

93. LLWP 2: 185–86; Cooper 1977, 339–46.

94. HD, September 24, 1916.

95. HD, September 25, 1916. Page could see that House was hinting at the possibility of U.S.-British war. He rejected this line of argument, telling House that while the British would never allow the Americans to create an equal or superior navy, they would respond simply by building more ships.

96. HD, November 14, 1916.

97. See HD, 14, 15, 20, November 26, 1916.

98. House Diary in PWW, 38: 658, November 15, 1916.

99. HD, December 14, 1916.

100. See HD, January 2, 1916. His view aligns with how defensive realists such as Robert Jervis view the origins of World War I and the role collective security institutions can have in preventing such disasters. See Jervis 1976, 1982; and Kupchan and Kupchan 1991.

101. HD, January 2, 1916.

102. HD, January 15, 1917.

103. See HD, January 11, 1917.

104. HD, January 4, 1917. Wilson's use of language here clearly reflects his well-documented racism, which in the more neutral terms of chapter 2, can be seen as Wilson increasing his sense of the Japanese threat due to perceptions of strong differences in ethnicity.

105. PWW, 40: 512–13, January 17, 1917.

106. Katz 1981, 312–14.

107. Katz 1981, 348–49.

108. Tuchman 1958, 83.

109. Katz 1981.

110. For the most recent version of this long-standing argument, see Ikenberry 2020.

111. Cf. Ikenberry 2020. Far from wanting to promote "democratization" or even ethnic self-determination, Wilson would actively encourage negotiations with Austria-Hungary from February to December of 1917, promising to keep the nation intact and part of the new league as long as Vienna broke away from Berlin and made a separate peace (see Lansing's memoirs, 1935). I have found no evidence that Wilson spoke of war "for democracy" until his famous April 2, 1917 address to Congress asking for a declaration of a state of war with Germany. His most used phrase up until April, and one used on January 22—that governments should have the "consent of the governed"—was a wonderfully vague phrase that he had used since 1913 to justify U.S. interference in Latin America and the Caribbean when he wished to oppose revolutionary efforts by armed minorities.

112. PWW, 40: 533–39.

113. HD, February 1, 1917.

114. See chap. 6, n. 111 in this volume.

115. All quotations from WWLL, 6: 455–56.

116. See quotations from Lane's letters in CDJD, 106.

117. CDJD: 106–7, February 27, 1917.

118. Tuchman 1958.

119. From the cabinet meeting of February 23, CDJD: 106.

120. Englund 2017.

121. HD, March 19, 1917.

122. PWW, 41: 422–23, March 17, 1917. It is significant that he did not mention any other reason for aiding Russia—the importance of Russian democracy or the value of Russia as a future partner of an alliance of democracies against autocracies. Surely if Wilson had been truly driven by notions of making the world safe for democracy, House would have at least appealed to these ideals.

123. PWW, 41: 425–27, March 19, 1917.

124. PWW, 41: 428–29, March 19, 1917.

125. Moreover, without America in the war, the U.S. government could not offer loans to finance the goods that did manage to get across the Atlantic. Page had warned on March 5 that the Allies were in a "most alarming" financial situation. Should America enter the war, "the greatest help we could give the Allies would be . . . a direct grant of [government] credit." WWLL, 6: 495.

126. CDJD: 117–18, March 20, 1917.

127. Lane at one point noted that public indignation against Germany was now intense, and that the people would "force us to act even if we were unwilling to do so." Wilson strongly resisted this notion, replying that "I do not care for popular demand. I want to do right, whether popular or not." (From Lansing's and Daniel's accounts, in PWW, 41: 436–44 and CDJD: 117–18, respectively. See also HD, March 22, 1917.)

128. PWW, 41: 444.

129. Wilson in late March was taking no chances with regard to Germany in the Caribbean. In addition to sending troops to Cuba to counter German-assisted rebels and ordering the immediate purchase of the Danish West Indies to keep them out of German hands, Wilson on March 28 conferred with Lansing and Secretary of War Baker about protecting Panama and Cuba should their governments also declare war on Germany. See CDJD: 123, March 28, 1917.

130. Fordham (2007, 2008) bases his argument on the statistical correlation of the growing dependence of certain regions on burgeoning U.S. trade and American action by 1917. But correlation is not causation. Since he cannot point to any documentary evidence that Wilson took the concerns of regions into account when he shifted his policies in February–March 1917, we must put aside his argument as merely suggestive.

131. See chap. 6, n. 111.

## Chapter 7

1. See Trachtenberg 2006 for a restatement of the "backdoor to war" argument and references.

2. For overviews and references, see in particular Dallek 1979; Herring 2008; Kimball 1991, 1997; Smith 2007.

3. Traditionalists would include Arthur Scheslesinger, Herbert Feis, Adam Ulam, Philip Moseley, George Kennan, and Henry Kissinger. For references, see Jones and Woods 1993; Leffler 1994a; Costigliola and Hogan 2016.

4. The most well-known revisionists are Gabriel Kolko, William Appleman Williams, Thomas McCormick, and David Horowitz. For references, see Jones and Woods 1993; Leffler 1994a; Hogan and Paterson 1991.

5. As Stephen Krasner pointed out decades ago (1978), it is often hard to separate an action a leader takes to build a nation's economic power sphere from an action that helps corporate interests. Yet when documents reveal that these leaders are undertaking actions that they know either hurt those interests (e.g., FDR seeking to create a national oil company in 1943–44; Krasner 1978, 188–97) or shape the state's economic position and wealth without fundamentally altering the profits of influential firms, then we can infer that national security is taking precedence over the self-centered drives of capitalist elites.

6. See Leffler 1979, 2019, chaps. 1–3; Herring 2008.

7. Copeland 2015, chaps. 3–5. See also Copeland 2000a, chap.5 and Copeland 2012a, 2012b.

8. By recognizing the Soviet Union in 1933 and then encouraging commercial ties with the state, Roosevelt became part of the emerging effort to create a "common front" against Germany (France, for example, signed an alliance agreement with Moscow in 1935 that anticommunist elites in Britain did not oppose). See Dallek 1979; Kimball 1991.

9. Haglund 1984; Hirschman 1980; NDR, vol. 2.

10. Quoted in Friedman 2003, 86; see also Gardner 1964, 122.

11. See Haglund 1984, 64; Dallek 1979.

12. Quoted in Haglund 1984, 158.

13. Hearden 1987, 233.

14. See Spykman 1942, 1943.

15. Wertheim 2020, 49–50.

16. Wertheim 2020.

17. Shoup and Minter 2004, 126–30. Iceland would be occupied by the United States in July 1941 as part of this plan.

18. See Wertheim 2020, 64–69; Shoup and Minter 2004, 135–40.

19. Wertheim 2020, 56–58.

20. Wertheim 2020, 78–79 and chaps. 3–4.

21. Hearden 2002, 34–35; Dallek 1979, 281–86, Woods 1990, 51–54.

22. Engel 2015.

23. Wertheim 2020, 69–70.

24. Wertheim 2020, 120–26.

25. Wertheim 2020, 101–4.

26. Copeland 2015, chaps. 4–5.

27. Leffler 1992.

28. The literature here is too vast to cite, but for a general overview of the two sides' positions and references, see Buzan 1984.

29. For overview articles on the debates, see Gaddis 1983; Jones and Woods 1993; Leffler 1994a. Neoclassical realists, because of their emphasis on unit-level factors, have typically sided with liberals (Kydd 2005; MacDonald 1995–96). Trachtenberg 1999 provides a systemic realist account stressing the impact of the competition over the control of postwar Germany. The only realist scholar that focuses a great deal of attention on economic factors is historian Melvyn Leffler (1984, 1992, 1996, 2007), and my perspective has been strongly influenced by his writings.

30. See in particular Kolko 1990; Paterson 1973; Williams 1962: Hearden 2002; and Gardner 1993 and 2009. For summaries and additional references, see Gaddis 1983; Jones and Woods 1993; Leffler 1994a.

31. See Layne 2006. Layne sees this open-door outlook as the product of a unique American cultural history. Yet by looking only at the U.S. case after 1898, he ignores the almost universal great power obsession with open access to resources, markets, and places for investment, as chapters 1–2 of this book and Copeland 2015 demonstrate.

32. See esp. Leffler 1992; Wertheim 2020; Hearden 2002.

33. See Copeland 2000a, chap. 6, which draws from the seminal work of Leffler 1984, 1992, 1994b, and 1996.

34. For references, see chap. 7, n. 3 in this volume.

35. Kimball 1991, 1997; Dallek 1979; Wertheim 2020.

36. Quoted in Kimball 1991, 7.

37. See Gardner 1993, 156 for more on this.

38. As Kimball (1991) has nicely argued, Roosevelt's push for Russia, Britain, China, and the United States to assume "spheres of responsibility" within his notion of the "Four Policemen"

of the postwar order was a spheres of influence policy by another name—that is, a name that was less upsetting to an American public unused to thinking in straightforward geopolitical terms.

39. FTP: 576–90. See also Vice President Wallace's diary note, PV: 171–72.

40. Hearden 2002; O'Sullivan 2008.

41. Sherman 1987.

42. NA, JSSC 9/1, "Post-War Military Problems—with Particular Relations to Air Bases," RG 218, CCS 360 (12-9-42), Sec. 1, Box 269, p. 10.

43. Sherry 1977, 44–47. See also Copeland 2000a, 152–53.

44. NA, JCS 570/4 and "Supplemental Instructions to the State Department Concerning Post-War Military Bases," RG 218, CCS 360 (12-9-42), Sec. 2.

45. Ninkovich 1994, 101.

46. His interest in 1943–44 in the linking of countries in the western sphere by a system of fully functional international airports fits with this vision. The airports would not only serve the U.S. air force in an emergency, but they would facilitate the growth of commerce and the penetration of U.S. firms and trading companies in far-off places. See Kimball 1991.

47. See Krasner 1978; and Yergin 1991.

48. See Copeland 2015, 252–58.

49. See Plokhy 2010; Harbutt 2010; Leffler 1986.

50. Sherman 1987.

51. Given space limitations, I will not cover U.S. concerns over China from April to July 1945. Suffice it to say that prior to Potsdam, Truman and his officials were deeply worried that the Soviets might use Manchuria to block a return to U.S. economic access in northern China. On the first day of Potsdam, however, Stalin proved surprisingly accommodating. He agreed to recognize Chiang Kai-shek's Nationalist Party as the only legitimate government in China, to comanage Manchuria's railway system with Chiang, and to ensure that Dairen was maintained as a free port open to all nations. Truman was highly pleased, telling the secretary of war that he had clinched the open door in China (Stimson Diary, 17 July 1945, LC).

52. FRUS 1945, V: 942–43.

53. See Paterson 1973, 35–36; Herring 1973; Harriman and Abel 1975; Martel 1979.

54. Quoted in Herring 1973, 170; Paterson 1973, 39–40. See FRUS 1945, V: 967–68.

55. Quoted in Herring 1973, 40n27 from Crowley's postwar recollections.

56. See Paterson 1973, 39–40, and FRUS 1945, V: 963.

57. Quoted in Leffler 1996, 16.

58. Quoted in Kapstein 1990, 22–24.

59. Figures and quotations from Kapstein 1990, 25–27.

60. See Dallas 2005, 102–13, 318–21, 502–4, and 526–39; Lacouture 1992, chaps. 5–9.

61. Quoted from the documents in Forrestal's possession, in FD: 39–40; see also Kapstein 1990, 28.

62. FD: 40.

63. Quoted in Leffler 1996, 16–17.

64. HSTL, April 20, 1945, Memorandum of Conversation, Papers of HST, PSF: Subject File Foreign Affairs, Russia: Molotov.

65. HSTL, April 22 and 23, 1945, Memoranda of Conversation, Papers of HST, PSF: Subject File Foreign Affairs, Russia: Molotov. See also FRUS 1945, V: 256–58.

66. Quoted in Maddox 1988, 65. This aligns with Chief of Staff Leahy's advice to Truman that Washington should focus on simply giving Poland the "external appearance" of independence (Leahy Diary, LC, April 23, 1945).

67. See FRUS 1945 Potsdam I: 735; Davis 1974, 237–48; McJimsey 1987, 386; and Trachtenberg 1999, 12–14.

68. On the theoretical role played by third parties in the creation of declining trade expectations, see Copeland 2015, chap. 1.

69. HSTL, April 30, 1945, Papers of HST, Office File 426 (1945–46).

70. FRUS 1945, V: 998.

71. HSTL, May 11, 1945, Papers of HST, PSF: Subject File, 1945–53, Foreign Affairs, Lend Lease; see also FRUS 1945, V: 999–1000.

72. Herring 1973, 204–5.

73. Herring 1973, 205–6.

74. Quoted from Grew's summary of his May 12 memorandum in a note to Soviet chargé in Washington on June 26, 1945, in FRUS 1945, V: 1027–28.

75. Herring 1973, 20.

76. FRUS 1945, Potsdam I: 24–31.

77. FRUS 1945, Potsdam I: 31–41.

78. See Grew's "Memorandum for the President" from early June in Papers of HST, PSF: Subject File Foreign Affairs, Reports: Current Foreign Developments. Harriman himself wrote Hopkins on June 21 that he was "gravely concerned" over delays and hoped Hopkins could use his connections (i.e., to Truman) to rectify the problem immediately (FRUS [1945], 5: 1020).

79. FRUS 1945, V: 1027–28.

80. Truman 1955, 235–36; Stimson diary, LC, May 16, 1945.

81. Stimson Diary, LC, May 16, 1945.

82. Leffler 1996, 17.

83. FRUS 1945, Potsdam I: 612–14. It was thus not coincidental that around this time Grew sent his harsh note to the Russians regarding Lend Lease.

84. Stimson Diary, LC, July 3, 1945.

85. FRUS 1945, Potsdam I: 468–69.

86. FRUS 1945, Potsdam I: 477–79.

87. FRUS 1945, Potsdam I: 491–93.

88. See FRUS 1945, Potsdam I: 510–11.

89. FRUS 1945, Potsdam I: 528.

90. FRUS 1945, Potsdam I: 537.

91. See the briefing papers prepared for Potsdam from late June and early July in FRUS 1945, Potsdam I: 714–32; Truman and Churchill's correspondence in early July, FRUS 1945, Potsdam I: 733–34; and the detailed summaries of the Potsdam meetings in FRUS 1945, Potsdam II.

92. See in particular Leffler 1992.

93. FRUS 1945, V: 852–53.

94. See Paterson 1973, 102–3.

95. A few weeks after Potsdam, Byrnes told the Romanians that any "equitable settlement" would require either the equipment's return or monetary compensation (FRUS 1945, V: 657–58).

Moscow and Bucharest made little effort to meet these demands. The meetings of the joint commission ultimately went nowhere and were formally ended in July 1947 (Paterson 1973, 103).

96. Truman 1955, 236.

97. FRUS 1945, Potsdam I: 178–82.

98. FRUS 1945, Potsdam I: 267–80.

99. The full report containing the above quotations is found in FRUS 1945, Potsdam I: 198–205, 357–62, and in the other annexes referenced in the footnotes of 198–205.

100. My understanding here has been strongly shaped by the work of Leffler (1992).

101. FRUS 1945, Potsdam I: 362–66.

102. FRUS 1945, Potsdam I: 370–74.

103. FRUS 1945, Potsdam I: 420–23.

104. His second and third points filled in the details on what had to be done. FRUS 1945, Potsdam II: 53, 643–44.

105. FRUS 1945, Potsdam II: 92–94 for the minutes of the two meetings; see also 66–79, 88–98.

106. FRUS 1945, Potsdam II: 127.

107. FRUS 1945, Potsdam II: 698.

108. FRUS 1945, Potsdam II: 150–51.

109. Stalin had given Greece over to Churchill in their infamous October 1944 spheres of influence agreement, and the British had proceeded to occupy and brutally suppress the communist uprising in the country.

110. FRUS 1945, Potsdam, II: 143–57.

111. FRUS 1945, Potsdam II: 164–77. On British-Soviet collaboration on spheres during the 1944–45 period, see Harbutt 2010.

112. FRUS 1945, Potsdam II: 194.

113. FRUS 1945, Potsdam II: 1362–65.

114. Stimson Diary, LC, 21 July 1945.

115. Stimson Diary, LC, 22 July 1945.

116. FRUS 1945, Potsdam II: 204–5.

117. FRUS 1945, Potsdam II: 205–7.

118. FRUS 1945, Potsdam II: 210–13.

119. FRUS 1945, Potsdam II: 275–285.

120. Quoted in Paterson 1973: 110 from Robert Murphy's memoirs.

121. FRUS 1945, Potsdam, II: 299–317, specifically 303–4; see also 654.

122. Stalin challenged Washington and London's desires to admit Italy into the United Nations when they had not yet recognized Romania, Bulgaria, and Hungary. Truman and Churchill responded that they could not recognize these countries until they became more open to the West. Stalin countered that the Soviets had been given no representation on the control council for Italy, a state that could hardly claim to be democratic (a former fascist general under Mussolini having been allowed to become prime minister).

123. FRUS 1945, Potsdam, II: 365–66.

124. FRUS 1945, Potsdam II: [pages].

125. Truman's obsession with the inland waterways idea was so strong that he used the last day of discussions to push the three powers to insert the plan into their final declaration. See Mee 1975, 275.

126. FRUS 1945, Potsdam II: 1496–97.

127. FRUS 1945, Potsdam, II: 1485–86.

128. See Boll 1984, chap. 6.

129. Copeland 2015, 254–58.

130. See Copeland 2000a, chap. 6, drawing from the seminal work of Melvyn Leffler 1984, 1992, 1996.

131. See inter alia Pechatnov 1995, 1999; and my discussion in Copeland 2000a, chap. 6.

132. See Copeland 2000a (chap. 6) for the details of this multifaceted policy shift and for Truman's recognition of the risks of cold war escalation resulting from this shift.

133. Indeed, it is quite clear that Truman liked Stalin at the time and thought he could do business with him. For a summary of the documentary evidence, see Copeland 2000a, 165–67.

# Chapter 8

1. On the vast literature on enduring rivalries, see in particular Diehl 1998; Cox 2010; Maoz and Mor 2002; Colaresi Rasler, and Thompson 2008.

2. See Copeland 2015 (7, 18–21) on how the logic of commercial liberalism ties low trade to unit-level drives to expand.

3. See Copeland 2000a, chap. 7.

4. The case does support the overall logic of dynamic realism, of which trade expectations theory is a part, since it was Soviet fears of long-term decline in both cases that drove Moscow's behavior. It is simply that *commercial* factors were not critical to this anticipation of decline.

5. Because they posed little risk of superpower escalation, I will not discuss cases such as Guatemala 1954 and the Dominican Republic 1965 (but see Krasner 1978 for evidence on such cases that generally aligns well with the strategic logic of this book).

6. See Copeland 2000a, 169–70 for a fuller treatment.

7. Copeland 2015, chap. 6.

8. Yegorova 1996.

9. Yegorova 1996. For a fuller discussion of this crisis, see Copeland 2015, chap. 6.

10. FRUS 1945, VIII: 45–48; Leffler 1992, 80.

11. Leffler 1992, 143; Gaddis 1982.

12. Leffler 1992, 146.

13. Leffler 1992, 147–48.

14. Leffler 1992, 159–63.

15. Jones 1965.

16. Copeland 2000a, chap. 7.

17. On the London conferences, see FRUS 1948, II. The Americans were also active in Italy during 1948 to prevent the Communist Party from utilizing the electoral process to take over the government.

18. FRUS 1948, II: 984–85.

19. Figures are from the Department of Commerce (FCY).

20. For summary and references, see Jervis 1991.

21. Rotter 1987; Schaller 1985.

22. See analysis and references, see especially Herring 2002, 2008; Logevall 2001, 2012; LaFeber 1994; Martel 1994; Kaiser 2000; Selverstone 2022.

23. Although see Copeland 1997 on why reputation-driven arguments are typically valid.

24. DAPS, 90–97.

25. Schaller 1985, 127–34.

26. Quoted in Schaller 1985, 138–39.

27. Quoted in Schaller 1985, 148, 159–60. As Shoup and Minter (2004) note, however, the importance of the whole of Southeast Asia as a critical source of cheap raw materials in the postwar era was first noted in a series of commissioned Council of Foreign Relations studies from the fall of 1943. Shoup and Minter 2004, 225.

28. Schaller 1985, 200–205; Rotter 1987, 104–5.

29. See NSC 48/1 in DAPS, 252–68, as well as NSC 48/2 in DAPS, 269–76.

30. Rotter 1987. See also Borden 1984 on the importance of helping Japan increase its exports to overcome the "dollar gap" that was impeding its postwar recovery.

31. See document #2 in TRW.

32. I thus consider the "Vietnam case" to be a partial confirmation of dynamic realism, even if the theory works less well for the period of direct U.S. combat involvement.

33. From the already low level of $27 million in 1948, U.S. exports to the Soviet Union fell to $7 million in 1949 and to an almost negligible $700,000 by 1950 (see FCY). This reflected Washington's imposition in 1948–49 of formal barriers to U.S.-Soviet trade and the establishment with Western allies of the infamous CoCom restrictions on overall East-West trade. By denying the East almost every imaginable product, U.S. officials sought to keep Soviet economic growth as low as possible. See Mastanduno 1988, 1992.

34. For the seminal version of this argument and further references, see George and Smoke 1974.

35. *New York Times*, January 1, 1950, A1.

36. *New York Times*, January 1, 1950, A1.

37. *New York Times*, January 1, 1950, A20.

38. The final wording of the alliance document released on February 14 emphasized the two states' concern with preventing the revival of Japanese imperialism and aggression from any state that might collaborate with Japan. See Goncharov, Lewis, and Xue 1995, 260–61, doc #45.

39. I have not found a single statement by political analysts or historians prior to June 25 interpreting Acheson's speech in this way. That no one except the South Korean ambassador was concerned is discussed in McLellan 1976, 210–11.

40. Dobbs 1982, chaps. 5–7; Lee 1995, chap. 2; Cumings 1981 and 1990.

41. Indeed, given South Korea's ambiguous status—a creation of the U.N. but not yet a member—Acheson could hardly have said otherwise. The U.N. was thus the perfect cover to protect the fledgling state while maintaining the posture of impartiality, a posture that would help calm China and draw it away from Russia.

42. *New York Times*, January 1, 1950, A1.

43. DSB, Vol. 22, January 23, 1950; Cumings 1990, 424.

44. CWIHPB, Issues 8–9: 232–34, doc. #17.

45. CWIHPB, Issue 5: 5, doc. #1.

46. CWIHPB, Issue 5: 6–8, docs. #2–5.

47. *New York Times*, February 10, 1950, A1.

48. *New York Times*, March 8, 1950, A6.

49. See Goncharov, Lewis, and Xue 1995, 140.

50. Armstrong 2004, 238–39.

51. CWIHPB, Issue 4: 61.

52. Waltz 1970, 1979; Mearsheimer 1992. For summary and further references, see Copeland 2015, 21–22.

53. Copeland 2015, chap. 6.

54. CIA (HT), 223–32, doc. #45.

55. Painter 1986: 172–73.

56. "Memorandum for the President," July 27, 1950, HSTL, Papers of HST, PSF: Intelligence File, 1946–53, Central Intelligence Reports.

57. Painter 1986, 171.

58. The Importance of Iranian and Middle East Oil to Western Europe Under Peacetime Conditions, NIE-14, January 8, 1951, HSTL, Papers of HST, PSF: Intelligence File, 1946–53, Central Intelligence Reports.

59. Leffler 1992, 483.

60. Memorandum of Meeting at the White House between President Truman and General Eisenhower, November 18, 1952, HSTL, Student Research File (File B), Oil Crisis in Iran, 1951–53.

61. FRUS 1952–54, X: 526.

62. FRUS 1952–54, X: 529–34; Painter 1986, 189–90; and Rubin 1980, 77;

63. FRUS 1952–54, X: 533–34.

64. See Eisenhower 1963, 160–61.

65. See memoranda on March 1 and 2, 1953, in FRUS 1952–54, X: 689–92.

66. FRUS 1952–54, X: 692–701.

67. Kinzer 2005; Yergin 1991.

68. Given space limitations, I will not cover British decision-making during the crisis, but suffice it to say that declining trade expectations were a determinative force.

69. FRUS 1955–57, XIX: 123–25. Compare to NSC 5501 of January 1955, FRUS 1955–57, XIX: 24–38.

70. See FRUS 1955–57, XIX: 242–68, esp. 248–54 and 267–68, which stress the Soviet shift away from "reliance on violence" against the free world to "reliance on division, enticement, and duplicity."

71. Hahn 1991, 202–10.

72. FRUS 1955–57, XVI: 5–6.

73. Hahn 1991, 212; FRUS 1955–57, XVI: 9–10.

74. FRUS 1955–57, XVI: 11–12.

75. FRUS 1955–57, XVI: 11–12.

76. FRUS 1955–57, XVI: 16.

77. FRUS 1955–57, XVI: 26, 28.

78. Eisenhower 1965, 39.

79. FRUS 1955–57, XVI: 55–56.

80. FRUS 1955–57, XVI: 21.

81. FRUS 1955–57, XIV: 62–68.

82. FRUS 1955–57, XVI: 78–93.

83. FRUS 1955–57, XIV: 69–71; see also Eisenhower 1965, appendix B.

84. On August 9, for example, Dulles argued at an NSC meeting that the United States should not restrain the British and French if they attacked Egypt. Eisenhower rejected such a policy, and by mid-August Dulles was towing the president's line in discussions with London. The president also continually objected to the military's efforts to push him toward more hard-line action. See Hahn 1991, 214–15.

85. Fursenko and Naftali 2007, 104.

86. See Hahn 1991, 220–21.

87. Hahn 1991, 219.

88. Eisenhower 1965, 51.

89. The National Security Council document of April 1950, NSC 68, would become the basis for a new and more "expansive" containment policy after the North Korean attack in June. For the full document, see DAPS, 385–442.

# Chapter 9

1. Copeland 2000a, chap. 7.

2. In practice, of course, this did not mean Washington expected Soviet leaders to renounce their communist principles, but simply to show that they were willing to make concessions that would hurt ideological allies (e.g., North Vietnam in 1972) to secure Western trade and technology. Being willing to make such trade-offs is itself a signal of a change in character type.

3. Mastanduno 1992.

4. Quoted in Mastanduno 1992, 93.

5. See Mastanduno 1992, 93–118 and table on 112. The above discussion excludes the unique year of 1964, when U.S. exports to Russia suddenly jumped to $146 million. This jump reflected a one-time Soviet purchase of grain, and by 1965 exports were back to around $45 million.

6. FRUS 1955–57, XIX: 242–68.

7. Eisenhower 1965, 180–82.

8. Parrott 1983, 1985; Fursenko and Naftali 2007.

9. FRUS 1955–57, XIX: 621.

10. Ambrose 1984; Taubman 2003. Because the Soviets kept hiding the fact that they were not keeping up in second-generation strategic intercontinental missiles, Kennedy, as president, could not confirm the U.S. advantage until the deployment of satellites in the fall of 1961. But Khrushchev was very worried in early 1961 by JFK's acceleration of the successful missile buildup on land and sea started by Eisenhower, since it seemed that Kennedy was seeking a position of permanent superiority. Things would come to a head in the spring of 1962 when the president and his secretary of defense would talk of disarming Russia's missiles in the early stages of nuclear war (the "no cities" doctrine). See Copeland 2000a, chap. 7; and Copeland 2015, 300–304.

11. Fursenko and Naftali 2007; Parrott 1983, 1985; Zubok 2009.

12. Memorandum of Conversation, February 18, 1958, DDEL, U.S. Council on Foreign Economic Policy, Records, 1954–61, Policy Papers Series.

13. Quoted in a secretary of commerce memorandum to Clarence Randall, January 28, 1959, DDEL, CFEP, Records, 1954–61, Policy Papers Series.

14. Statement, March 3, 1958, DDEL, CFEP, Records, 1954–61, Policy Papers Series.

15. See letter with Dillon's cover note from June 4 in DDEL, U.S. CFEP, Records, 1954–61, Policy Paper Series.

16. See letter released by James Hagerty, Eisenhower's press secretary, July 14, 1958, DDEL, CFEP, Records, 1954–61, Policy Papers Series.

17. See "Control Status of Categories Mentioned in Khrushchev Letter of June 2, 1958," undated, in DDEL, CFEP, Records 1054–61, Policy Papers Series.

18. See FRUS 1958–60, III: 78–79 and 98–116.

19. For a summary of the evidence, see Copeland 1993 and 2000a.

20. Memorandum for Director of Central Intelligence, November 16, 1958, DDEL, Eisenhower Dwight D., Records as President, White House Central Files (Confidential File), 1953–61.

21. Jentleson 1986, 81–83.

22. "Soviet Attempts to Penetrate West European Oil Market," December 29, 1958, DDEL, CFEP, Records 1954–61, Policy Paper Series.

23. See Randall's Memorandum for Mr. Gordon Gray, December 16, 1956, DDEL, CFEP, Records 1954–61, Policy Papers Series.

24. Extended Minutes of CFEP Meeting of January 8, 1959, with attached letter of January 9, 1959, DDEL, CFEP Records 1954–61, Policy Paper Series. See also FRUS 1958–60, IV: 749–53.

25. "Outline for a Study on Peaceful Trade Relations," undated, DDEL, CFEP Records 1954–61, Policy Papers Series. The State Department in January also prepared a detailed series of briefing papers for Mikoyan's visit on everything from MFN and U.S. trade credits to Soviet policy toward developing states and protection against dumping and patent violations. See the various record files in CFEP Records 1954–61, Policy Papers Series.

26. See Memorandum of Conversation, January 19, 1959, attached to letter from Dillon to Randall, January 23, in DDEL, CFEP Records 1954–61, Policy Paper Series.

27. "Outline for a Study of the Advantages and Disadvantages to Be Derived by the United States from Peaceful Trade with the Soviet Bloc," March 5, 1959, DDEL, CFEP Records 1954–61, Policy Paper Series.

28. "Memorandum for Mr. Clarence B. Randall," March 23, 1959, DDEL, CFEP Records 1954–61, Policy Paper Series. The first four pages of this 20-page report can be found in FRUS 1958–60, IV: 764–68.

29. Ambrose 1984: 824–25.

30. "Major Themes of Khrushchev's Public and Private Statements and U.S. Counter-Arguments," September 8, 1959, DDEL, Eisenhower, Dwight D., Records as President, White House Central Files (Confidential File), 1953–61, Subject Series.

31. "U.S. Objective in Khrushchev Visit and Suggested Tactics for Conversation with Him," September 11, 1959, DDEL, Eisenhower, Dwight D., Records as President, White House Central Files (Confidential File), 1953–61, Subject Series.

32. This advice was reiterated in yet another briefing paper from the State Department that Eisenhower received the next day. "Economic Relations with the U.S.S.R.," September 12. 1959,

in DDEL, Eisenhower, Dwight D., Records as President, White House Central Files (Confidential File), 1953–61, Subject Series.

33. Ambrose 1984, 541–42; Eisenhower 1965, 435–37.

34. Taubman 2003, 437–38.

35. Memorandum of Conversation, September 27, 1959, in letter to Randall from Robert Brewster, October 8, 1959, DDEL, CFEP Records 1954–61, Policy Papers Series.

36. Fursenko and Naftali 2007, 241–42.

37. Quoted in Fursenko and Naftali 2007, 242–43.

38. Fursenko and Naftali 2007, 246–47; Montgomery 2006.

39. On Lend-Lease Negotiations, February 4, 1960, DDEL, CFEP Records 1954–61, Policy Papers Series.

40. My short summary of the crisis is based on Beschloss 1988; Fursenko and Naftali 2007; Ambrose 1984.

41. Quoted in Ambrose 1984, 580.

42. On the problem of adverse power oscillations in bipolarity, see Copeland 2000a, 25–27, 47–48, 186–206.

43. Prados 1986, 114.

44. Memorandum for Mr. Bundy, January 30, 1961, JFKL, NSF, Box 275, Folder "Department of Defense, Defense Budget FY 1963 1/61–10/61; Memorandum for the President, January 31, 1961, JFKL, NSF, Box 313, Folder 2; Record of Actions by the National Security Council, February 6, 1961, JFKL, NSF, Box 313, Folder 2.

45. A Comparison of Capital Investment in the U.S. and the U.S.S.R., 1950–59, February 1961, JFKL, NSF, Box 176.

46. Notes on Discussion of the Thinking of the Soviet Leadership, written by Bundy on February 13, NSA (BC).

47. Copeland 2000a, 181–86.

48. From Hope Harrison's summary of the documents, in Harrison 1993, 28; see also Harrison 2005.

49. Memorandum for the President, February 26, 1961, JFKL, NSF, Box 176, Folder: "U.S.S.R. General 2/21/61–3/1/61."

50. Funigiello 1988, 125–26.

51. Funigiello 1988, 129–33.

52. On July 9, Kennedy was given a new National Intelligence Estimate that noted that the pace of the Soviet ICBM program had increased, and that in a preemptive attack, Russia might soon be able to hit U.S. bases and still respond to a U.S. retaliation. Kennedy immediately asked that a special committee of key departments be formed to study the NIE's implications and report within a month. National Intelligence Estimate, 11-8-62, July 6, 1962, NSA (SE): doc. 372; FRUS, 1961–63, Vol. 8: 342–43. See also Copeland 2000a, chap. 7.

53. Memorandum for the National Security Council, July 10, 1962, JFKL, NSF, Box 313, Folder 35.

54. Memorandum for the National Security Council, July 16, 1962, JFKL, NSF, Box 313, Folder 35.

55. See Copeland 2000a, 186–208 and endnote 71 on page 297, as well as Copeland 1996.

56. Fursenko and Naftali 1997; Copeland 1996 and 2000a, endnote 71 on page 297.

57. See Aslund 1989, 15; Ericson 1990, 77.

58. See Hoffman and Laird 1982, chap. 1.

59. See Hoffman and Laird 1982, chap. 1.

60. Quoted in Parrott 1983, 186.

61. See Walker 1987, 38–39; Arbatov 1993, 154–55.

62. Quoted in Anderson 1993, 127. See also the 1967 argument by two Soviet analysts that the country could use trade within the growing international division of labor to improve economic performance (Hoffman and Laird 1982, 80–81).

63. Aslund 1989, 15; Hewitt 1988, 239.

64. Volten 1982, 64. On Soviet fears about being able to keep up in an extended arms race, given the West's technological superiority, see Parrott 1983, 243, 197–201; Hoffman and Laird 1982, 119 and chap. 6; Garthoff 1994a, 115.

65. Quoted in Volten 1982, 66–67. See also Parrott 1983, 248–49; Arbatov 1993, 206; Garthoff 1994a, 101; Jentleson 1986, 135.

66. Kissinger 1979, 1254–55, 152–53, 1203. See Garthoff 1994a, 33–34, 103–5, 346.

67. Kissinger's congressional testimony in 1975, cited in Garthoff 1994a, 33–34.

68. The recently released FRUS documents show the Americans were still anxious about offering trade and credits for the first year of the new administration. They did not see any real economic benefits for the United States and doubted the amount of leverage more open trade would buy in terms of better Soviet behavior. By 1970, as the Soviet need for trade became increasingly clear, the strategic value of using trade as "leverage" in U.S.-Soviet bargaining was solidified. See esp. FRUS 1969–76, IV: docs. nos. 290, 292, 294, 298, and 307 from 1969, compared to docs. nos. 312, 317, 320, and 321 from 1970.

69. Stevenson 1985, 155; FRUS 1969–76, IV: docs. nos. 349–52.

70. Jentleson 1986, 139.

71. Mastanduno 1992, 147.

72. U.S. firms were essential, since they possessed the most advanced drilling and extraction technology then available. See Jentleson 1986, 139–41, 147.

73. See Mastanduno 1992, tables 4 and 5 on pages 112 and 158.

74. Garthoff 1994a, 366–67.

75. Quoted in Garthoff 1994a, 389, from the now declassified July 1973 document.

76. Volten 1982, 112; Garthoff 1994a, 389.

77. The Kremlin simply couldn't understand how such an apparently minor domestic matter might bring down a president.

78. See Mastanduno 1992, 146 and table 5, 158. At the end of the June 1973 summit, the communiqué reiterated the gains in U.S.-Soviet economic relations, with both sides agreeing to shoot for $2–$3 billion of trade over the next three years. Stevenson 1985, 161.

79. Garthoff's words, based on information given to him by this official (1994a, 102n70).

80. Volten 1982, 108–9, 111, 234.

81. Parrott 1985, 38.

82. Nixon 1978, 884–86.

83. Kissinger 1982, 594. This was not just his retrospective view. At the end of October, Kissinger received an analysis by an associate that noted Brezhnev's conciliatory posture during the crisis was partly due to American firmness, and partly the result of "Brezhnev's

own stake in his détente policy" (Kissinger 1982, 600). See also Garthoff 1994a, 409–20, 434–41.

84. Israelyan 1995, 31, 2.

85. Quoted in Lebow and Stein 1994, 201.

86. See Israelyan 1995, chap. 11.

87. Kissinger 1982, 467–69. See also Lebow and Stein 1994, 210.

88. Kissinger 1982, 579, 584; see also Garthoff 1994a, 422–23 and KT: 155.

89. Kissinger would later admit to his colleagues in a private meeting on March 18, 1974, that recent Soviet behavior had been "fairly reasonable all across the board. . . . Even in the Middle East where our political strategy put them in an awful bind, they haven't really tried to screw us." (KT, 225).

90. See Jentleson 1986, 136–46.

91. Kissinger 1982, 249.

92. Garthoff 1994a, 506; Jentleson 1986, 143.

93. Kissinger's phrase in *Years of Upheaval* (1982, 996).

94. Garthoff 1994a, 509.

95. Garthoff 1994a, 512–13; Mastanduno 1992, 150; Njolstad 2010.

96. Kissinger's failure to prevent the congressional legislation, after having explicitly promised Brezhnev in late 1974 that he would do so, could only have underscored this weakness. See KT, 329–42 on the Kissinger-Brezhnev talks of October 24, which focused on U.S. domestic opposition to the trade treaty.

97. Garthoff 1994a, chap. 15.

98. See CWIHPB, Issues 8–9 (Winter 1996–97) for some initial documents.

99. Parrott 1985, 38–39. Jackson-Vanik upset Brezhnev's fragile domestic coalition in favor of peaceful relations with the United States. After 1974, opponents to détente and economic interdependence (the "traditionalists") gained the upper hand. Parrott 1983, 258–65; Volten 1982, 116–30, 238.

100. For scholars agreeing with this view, see Garthoff 1994a, 506 and passim; Njolstad 2010, 155–53; Jentleson 1986, chap. 5; George 1980, 22. Even Adam Ulam, an individual more inclined to blame aggressive Soviet intentions for the failure of détente, notes that with the undermining of the trade treaty, détente was not given a chance, and that by 1975 Soviet behavior was more assertive (Ulam 1983, 93–94, 134–35).

101. Putting particular stress on the former are constructivist scholars such as Wendt 1992; Risse-Kappen 1994; Koslowski and Kratochwil 1994; Lebow and Risse-Kappen 1995. For a decisive riposte, see Brooks and Wohlforth 2000–2001 (also Jervis 1996, 224–25). For a useful nonconstructivist view of how the narrowing of ideological distance helped reduce the U.S. perception of threat, facilitating a de-spiraling of tensions, see Haas 2005.

102. See Aslund 1989, 15; Doder 1986, 177–78; Gorbachev 1987, 18–19; Brooks and Wohlforth 2000–2001; Ellman and Kontorovich 1992.

103. Quoted in Kaiser 1991, 57, 59. For an argument that U.S. officials used the 1986 to 1991 period to exploit Soviet weakness and reduce it as a competitor, see Shifrinson 2018, chaps. 4–5. My position is that while keeping the Soviet Union weak was indeed part of the American logic, there was also a desire to use trade and technology to sustain Gorbachev in power and avoid a coup that would bring back hard-liners. Both Reagan and Bush felt strongly that Gorbachev was

the man who would moderate Soviet policy in ways conducive to overall U.S. security. Moreover, making sure the Russian *military* did not feel Washington was driving the Soviet Union
into the ground was part and parcel of the U.S. strategy for avoiding Soviet overreaction and
sustained Gorbachev's domestic position. For recent support for this position, see Service 2015
and Engel 2020.

104. Doder, 1986, 186–87, 169–70; Walker 1987, 47–48; Dobbs 1996, 88–89. A large number
of similar studies on Soviet economic problems were undertaken during 1983—according to
Gorbachev, over one hundred. See Oberdorfer 1991, 63.

105. Doder 1986, 182, 185.

106. Gorbachev 1987, 18–19, 135; Brown 2010, 248–49; Gorbachev 1996: 102–3.

107. Quoted in Walker 1987, 58–59. See also Brown 1997, 79–81; Doder 1986, 246.

108. Coleman's summary of the document, based on discussions with top Gorbachev advisor
Georgi Shakhnazarov, in Coleman 1996, 224.

109. Walker 1987, 51. Documents on Gorbachev's relations with Eastern Europe reveal an
additional power-driven reason for internal reform. In 1985–88 Gorbachev and his advisors
believed that without Soviet reform, Eastern Europe might very well fall into the American
orbit. The Eastern European states had already been turning to the West for loans that Moscow
could not provide and had been reorienting their exports westward to help pay the loans back.
Although the Soviets needed Eastern European trade with the West as a backdoor to Western
technology, they did not want their allies to go too far. Thus from 1985 to 1989 Gorbachev played
the risky game of encouraging Eastern European states to "reform socialism" in ways that would
enhance their trade with Russia while avoiding the kinds of changes that might lead to the collapse of socialism in Eastern Europe altogether. With hindsight, this policy only served to spur
Eastern Europe's ultimate defection from the Soviet bloc. But in the first years of Soviet reform,
and even by early 1989, the true risks of losing Eastern Europe could not be fully foreseen. See
WH, esp. docs. nos. 4, 5, 6, 8, and 9 on the 1985–86 period and docs. nos. 39, 41, 42, and 48 on the
late 1988/early 1989 period.

110. See docs. nos. 19, 25, 32, 40, and 52 from UECW (I thank Bill Wohlforth for alerting me
to these documents); Gorbachev 1996, 215, 401; Dobrynin 1995, 570; Matlock 1995, 77, 139–40.

111. On Gorbachev's obsession with countering the U.S. Strategic Defense Initiative ("Star
Wars"), see Gorbachev 1996, 407, 417–18, 455; Schultz 1993, 477–79, 577, 592, 768–69.

112. Gorbachev 1996, 217–18, 250; Dobbs 1996, 125 (quoting Gorbachev's recollection in
1993); and UECW docs. nos. 44 and 52.

113. Quoted in Oberdorfer 1991, 159–62.

114. Quoted in Schultz 1993, 530.

115. Garthoff 1994b, 218, 249.

116. Dobrynin 1995, 531, 518.

117. Mastanduno 1992, 300; Garthoff 1994b, 249, 198.

118. Quoted in Gorbachev 1987, 231n1.

119. Gorbachev 1987, 126, 222–23.

120. For the key documents revealing the depth of these suspicions, see RF, esp. 2–79,
176–284.

121. These were "costly signals" too hard for traditional Soviet leaders to make. Fearon 1995;
Kydd 2005; Glaser 2010; Copeland 1999–2000.

122. Arbatov 1993, 321–22.

123. Schultz 1993, chap. 36.

124. Schultz 1993, 1011–12.

125. See Gorbachev 1996. Unfortunately, oil prices by 1985–86 had plunged from their high in the early 1980s, greatly complicating Gorbachev's plan and forcing more radical reforms. For Reagan's recognition by late 1985 of Russia's economic problems and its need for U.S. trade and technology, see documents on pages 223–27 of Anderson and Anderson 2009.

126. Mastanduno 1992, 306; Garthoff 1994b, 342.

127. Gorbachev 1996, 456–57; Garthoff 1994b, 358; Oberdorfer 1991, 295.

128. Oberdorfer 1991, 316–18.

129. Gorbachev 1996, 608.

130. Mastanduno 1992, 308.

131. See Beschloss and Talbott 1993, 17–25. Ambassador in Moscow Matlock, however, made a push for increased trade in early 1989. Matlock 1995, 188.

132. Quoted in Baker 1995, 144–45. This followed up Shevardnadze's point to Baker in July that Soviet economic and social problems were "enormous," and that the financial system was in "very grave condition." Economic cooperation with the West would thus be helpful. Baker 1995, 138–39.

133. Garthoff 1994b, 384–85; Beschloss and Talbott 1993, 117–21.

134. See Oberdorfer 1991, 376; Matlock 1995, 271–72. The decision was no doubt influenced by a report earlier in the year noting that the Soviet need for Western technology could be used as leverage in any negotiations. See Bush and Scowcroft 1998, 41.

135. Garthoff 1994b, 386–87; Baker 1995, 156.

136. See MH: 619–46; Garthoff 1994b, 406–7; Beschloss and Talbott 1993, 151–55; Gorbachev 1996, 511–12; Bush and Scowcroft 1998, 162–63, 173. According to the Soviet transcript of the Malta meetings, Bush also told Gorbachev that after Jackson-Vanik was repealed, conditions would be favorable for eliminating restrictions on the granting of credit, allowing for the "development of effective cooperation on economic issues." Bush noted that his administration would send Moscow a document on this issue, detailing America's "serious plans in the areas of finance, statistics, market functions, etc." (MH: 622). With such language, the Americans were signaling their new commitment not just to more open trade, but to the financing needed to allow a cash-strapped Soviet state to exploit the new opportunity.

137. Quoted in Garthoff 1994b, 408.

138. Quoted in Dobrynin 1995, 634. According to Dobrynin, Gorbachev saw U.S. support for perestroika as the most significant result of the summit (Dobrynin 1995).

139. Oberdorfer 191, 418–19; Zelikow and Rice 1997, 279; Beschloss and Talbott 1993, 210–22.

140. Bush and Scowcroft 1998, 283–84; Oberdorfer 1991, 419–20.

141. Baker 1995, 254; Zelikow and Rice 1997, 279–80; Bush and Scowcroft 1998, 285.

142. Beschloss and Talbott 1993, 223; Zelikow and Rice, 1997, 280–81.

143. Gorbachev 1996, 542.

144. Quoted in Oberdorfer 1991, 423. As Secretary of State Baker recounts, the signing of the agreements on June 1 had an immediate effect on the willingness to cooperate over Third World issues. "It was almost as if Gorbachev's acceptance of Germany in NATO, and the President's

decision on the trade agreement, had moved our relations to a higher, more cooperative and personal plane." Baker 1995, 254.

145. Gorbachev 1996, 612.

146. Gorbachev 1996, 613–14 (Gorbachev's paraphrases from his actual speech).

147. Gorbachev 1996, 617.

148. See Buzan 1984 for references and summaries.

149. Here domestic politics played a constraining role on executive decision-making, even if dynamic realist factors were propelling Nixon and Kissinger.

## Chapter 10

1. These figures are drawn from a variety of sources, including World Bank and IMF data, and represent the broad consensus of China scholars. See *inter alia* Doshi 2021; Gill 2022; Economy 2022; Blustein 2019; Khan 2018; Hillman 2021; Shambaugh 2013; Ye 2020. Relative GDP is measured by exchange rates. China was already number one in terms of purchasing power parity by the late 2010s, although this measure is less useful for geopolitical analysis since it overstates a state's ability to project power around the world.

2. Prominent pessimists include Aaron Friedberg (2011, 2022); John Mearsheimer (2014, 2021); Michael Pillsbury (2015); Graham Allison (2017); Oriana Mastro (2014); Elizabeth Economy (2022); and Christopher Layne (2008). My use of the terms pessimists and optimists is drawn from two important papers by Brandon Yoder (2019a, 2020).

3. Jervis 1976, chap. 3.

4. More precisely, they argue that Beijing will be moderate as long as China's sense of national identity is not unnecessarily provoked over such issues as Taiwanese independence. And since such provocations are within the control of the American state, spirals of hostility are not inevitable. A list of prominent optimists (with caveats) would include Alistair Iain Johnston (2004, 2013); Michael Swaine (2011); Avery Goldstein (2005); Thomas Christensen (2011, 2015); G. John Ikenberry (2008); Susan Shirk (2007, 2023); David Shambaugh (2013); M. Taylor Fravel (2008); and David Kang (2007).

5. There are, of course, many who adopt a position somewhere between these extremes, including those who believe China has already started peaking and acting aggressively (Brands and Beckley 2022, 2021). I will address such alternatives in more detail below.

6. While this chapter does cover some of the key events of the post-1989 period, since this is a book about great power conflicts or regional struggles that risk such conflicts, it does not examine the two U.S. wars with Iraq (in 1991 and 2003). Suffice it to say that the vast majority of scholarship on the First Gulf War, as well as the partial release of documents from the George H. W. Bush Library, has essentially confirmed Bob Woodward's initial reporting—namely, that by early August 1991 President Bush felt he had to respond to Saddam Hussein's attack on Kuwait or risk Saddam expanding farther into northern Saudi Arabia and then using his control of 40 percent of the world's oil reserves to devastate the U.S. and allied economies (Woodward 1991). The Iraq War of 2003 was driven by a mix of factors. The prospect of Saddam acquiring weapons of mass destruction (WMD) and again threatening a critical oil-producing region clearly hung over key U.S. officials—many of whom, such as Colin Powell and Dick Cheney, were holdovers from the first Bush presidency. But it seems that most participants were

primarily driven by the belief that Saddam might indeed give WMD technology to terrorist groups, perhaps leading to a replay of the 9/11 attacks, this time with much more devastating results (see Leffler 2023).

7. Brands and Sullivan 2020. The Belt and Road Initiative (or BRI) is China's massive plan, announced by President Xi Jinping in 2013, to lend to or invest in countries around the world to increase their production capabilities, particularly with regard to the resources and food that China so desperately needs to sustain its GDP growth and internal stability. At present, over one hundred countries are involved in the BRI, and close to a trillion dollars has been spent or allocated for projects ranging from investment in raw material extraction, port and railway construction, power plants, and housing.

8. It is fair to say that China has not done anything that parallels what the United States did from 1898 to 1930 as the latter feared a potential slowdown in its growth and the intrusion of European powers into its core trading realm: namely, putting boots on the ground in Central America and the Caribbean over twenty-five times to secure the area for American economic growth. This restraint on China's part does not, of course, reflect a superior moral outlook, but simply the fact that in the multipolar world system of 1890 to 1930 where great power imperialism was the norm, the United States could get away with frequent military interventions in its "backyard." China after 1991, by contrast, was operating in a unipolar world that was moving toward bipolarity as China rose, and it would have instantly created a full-scale balancing response if it had tried landing troops in neighboring countries. For more on this, see Copeland 2019, 2003, 2015, 440–41.

9. Shambaugh 2013.

10. See figures 2.1 and 2.2 of chapter 2.

11. This discussion is drawn from, but extends, my earlier analysis of power trends in bipolarity versus multipolarity and the problems of states anticipating their own or the other's peaking and decline in relative power (Copeland 2000a, chap. 1).

12. Brands and Beckley 2021, 2022; Copeland 1996, 2000a, 2019.

13. See Xi's speeches in GOC, vols. 1 and 2. By the end of the 2010s, he was regularly speaking to Party members of the "great challenges of the new era" given both the natural slowing of China's GDP growth and the increasing efforts of U.S. administrations to put restraints on China developing its high-tech sectors. See GOC, vols. 3 and 4.

14. See Mastro 2022. Reading Brands and Beckley (2022) carefully, we see that their prediction of conflict due to China's supposed peaking is derived from a mistaken fusion of work on "power transitions" by scholars such as Organski and Kugler and Copeland's earlier work on states that have passed their peak and are in deep decline. The former argues that rising states are filled with pathological non-security drives such as status and glory. The latter indicates that states weak in potential power (especially territorial land mass and relative population) such as Germany after 1910 are inclined to start big conflicts when they believe they are no longer rising but rather declining deeply and inevitably. Brands and Beckley thus believe that China will be highly aggressive over the next decade because it is both an authoritarian state needing expansion to justify domestic oppression and because such a state will naturally fear deep decline against a liberal state. Yet currently there is no way of knowing if either of these core premises—that China is peaking and inevitably declining and that it is convinced it cannot exist with a democratic West—is true. Taking these premises *as* true could lead to a self-fulfilling prophecy,

whereby Washington starts to panic and seeks to deter China through a massive show of power and through economic coercion, thereby causing China to fear its inevitable decline. We must therefore be very careful about adopting the Brands-Beckley perspective until we have more information about its empirical veracity.

15. To maintain consistency with the externalist approach of the theoretical chapters, I continue to assume that the United States is itself a rational security-maximizing actor responding to changes outside the state, not to changes in domestic-level pressures and non-security objectives. I assume that periods such as the Trump administration, with Trump's clear obsession with his own self-image and status sometimes getting in the way of a fully rational national security policy (e.g., in negotiations with North Korea), will not be repeated. This allows the dynamic realist theory to predict U.S. policy responses as external circumstances change.

16. Anne-Marie Slaughter, head of the State Department's Policy Planning Staff during Obama's first term, told a gathering at the University of Virginia's Miller Center in 2014 that the primary motivation behind the pivot was the administration's uncertainty about China's long-term intentions should it catch up to the United States in relative power (author's meeting notes). Given that uncertainty, it made sense in 2011 to pre-position the United States in Asia to discourage Chinese leaders from entertaining any ideas of expansion in the Indo-Pacific.

17. Doshi 2021.

18. While many scholars such as Mearsheimer (2021) and Friedberg (2022) castigate U.S. officials for the second assumption—that trade would cause China to "liberalize" its political system—it is quite clear from the evidence that few policy makers thought any liberalization would go very far, and almost no one hung their hat on the hope that China would become less authoritarian. What *did* change is that, under Xi, China became *more* repressive and authoritarian. And this was partly a function of Xi's desire to make sure that liberal ideology did not gain momentum within China. After all, as recent polls show, individuals in the middle and upper classes have indeed absorbed the Western values of individual freedom, whether through studying abroad, tourism, or what they can glean from the internet. In short, one way to look at the increasing use of arbitrary arrests and surveillance is to see it as the endogenous result of the fear of a return to the chaos of 1989, precisely due to the *potential attractiveness* of liberalism and to U.S. efforts to spread the word!

19. See Campbell and Ratner 2018.

20. On Tiananmen's impact on CCP thinking, see esp. Vogel 2011; Doshi 2021; Khan 2018; Dingxin Zhao 2004; and Pantsov 2015. See also Premier Zhao Ziyang's secret journal (Zhao 2009), written in the decade after July 1989 when under house arrest, and the documents in TP.

21. Shirk 2007.

22. See Xi Jinping's speeches in volumes 3 and 4 of his published speeches covering 2017 to 2021 (GOC: 3 and 4).

23. If one wants to start with the idea that China since 2012 has already been shifting away from being a largely RSM actor given Xi's status-glory needs, this is not a problem for the analysis. As we will see with figure 10.3, this is simply to suggest that China is already on a particularly dangerous pathway (pathway E) and that the situation could get worse as these trends continue.

24. And as mentioned, this is what Brands and Beckley (2022) assume is already going on. See above for my critique.

25. On the former, see Blanchette 2019.

26. Given their low probability, I will not deal with variations of the four scenarios in which a Gorbachev-like reformer comes to power within China over the next two decades. Suffice it to say that we can expect a significant lessening of U.S.-China tension should such a happy turn of events come to pass.

27. And as the advent of Gorbachev in the mid-1980s demonstrates, authoritarian actors do not always move only in one direction internally—they can indeed become more pathological in ends and rationality, but they can also become more security-driven and reasonable.

28. Note that this is equivalent to the dotted line of rising C's peaking and subsequent decline in stage two of figure 10.1, but it is the endogenous result of the predominant state's economic policies.

29. This could happen either through both states growing absolutely but China simply having a higher percentage growth rate over time, or through modest GDP growth by China coupled with near-zero or declining growth by the United States.

30. The Trump administration achieved this objective in 2020—the Dutch company ASML stopped shipping to China its lithography machines that use extreme ultraviolet (EUV) light to manufacture semiconductor chips with transistors under 10 nanometers in size—and Biden has convinced the Dutch to continue the ban.

31. See Copeland 2022.

32. Consider declining A's view of rising C in figure 10.1 in stages one and two if it believes C will indeed reach dominance in stage three and then fear decline against a then-rising A whose future type is uncertain. For more on this problem, see Copeland 2000a, chap. 1.

33. Part of the U.S. advantage here is Asian states have China on or near their borders, while the United States is across an ocean. Even independently of China's regime type, this increases the sense that China is a threat and America is not (Walt 1987).

34. See Copeland 2000a and 2015, and Brands and Beckley 2022.

35. Mearsheimer has been arguing this for years. See Mearsheimer 2001 (and its updated edition of 2014) plus 2021.

36. Consider how in early August 2022, in response to Speaker Nancy Pelosi's visit, Xi was not only careful not to interrupt shipping through the Taiwan Strait, but he imposed sanctions only on some insignificant Taiwanese agricultural exports (less than one percent of Taiwan-China trade). He avoided restrictions on Taiwanese semiconductor exports and made no moves to punish the United States economically.

37. Their evidence is primarily "objective"—that is, an analysis of what appears to be happening within China—rather than based on documents on internal thinking at the highest level. While the secrecy of the CCP makes the latter hard to come by, this lacuna of direct evidence of Chinese perceptions of deep and inevitable decline means that Brands and Beckley cannot use Chinese hard-line rhetoric and behavior as evidence for their causal argument. There are many good competing arguments for why China has been, for example, more aggressive over Taiwan and the South China Sea over the last decade and a half. These competing arguments, however, are never tested.

38. There is a parallel here to how the Soviet belief in the superiority of Marxist-Leninist ideology during the Cold War gave Russian leaders the confidence needed to accept declining trends in the short term, knowing that over the long term the Soviet Union would triumph

over the West. It is hard to read Xi's hundreds of speeches to Party stalwarts since 2013 and not conclude that he does truly believe that the China Dream of equality with the United States by 2035–49 is China's future, regardless of "challenges of the present era." See GOC, vols. 1–4.

39. For overview and analysis, see especially Vogel 2011; Dingxin Zhao 2004.

40. Potter and Wang 2022.

41. Doshi 2021, 51–52.

42. Doshi 2021 and Khan 2018. See Potter and Wang (2019, 2022) for an extension of the "stability-is-everything" argument made by Chinese leaders after 1989 to the question of internal terrorism.

43. It did not help that this view was widely believed and promoted in Washington since the mid-1980s as both the Soviets and Chinese turned to increased economic openness as a way to reenergize their stagnating economies. Doshi (2021) notes a third shock of the 1989–91 period: the American success in the Gulf War of 1991 against Saddam Hussein. The United States showed that smart weaponry and air superiority could win wars quickly and at low cost; a lesson, along with the humiliating backdown of the Taiwan Straits crisis of 1995–96, that convinced Beijing that China needed to equalize both the strategic and regional balances of military power to increase its leverage over neighboring states, especially Taiwan.

44. Vogel 2011.

45. See discussion in chapter 1 with regard to figures 1.1 and 1.2.

46. Chubb 2020; Doshi 2021; Shirk 2023.

47. Ye 2020.

48. Paul Blustein (2019) shows that Chinese officials were very worried about the implications of reduced tariffs on Western penetration into the China market.

49. GOC, vols. 1–2.

50. Gilpin 1981.

51. The Americans were also lucky in that their westward expansion ended with an ocean, meaning fewer adversarial border states and access to a whole new set of markets, including of course the fabled markets of East Asia.

52. See Copeland 2015, 337–47 on the First Opium War and chaps. 3–5 on the 1890s to 1930s.

53. There may never have been signs outside the parks in the British and French sections of Shanghai stating "No Dogs or Chinese Allowed"—a line that is now part of the Chinese consciousness—but there were posted notices that made the basic point. One sign from 1917 that survives lists as its first rule that entry to the park was "reserved for the foreign community," while the fourth states that dogs and bicycles were not to be admitted. (See photo on Wikipedia entry for Huangpu Park.)

54. Boys 2015; Tyler 1999.

55. Gill 2022.

56. In this sense, Xi's vision is very much akin to Plato's in *The Republic*, with a small elite class acting for the good of the nation, while the many are allowed to pursue their more selfish drives, provided they accept the "noble lie" that, being metals of the earth (gold, silver, and bronze), they are united in the corporate whole.

57. Quoted in Bougon 2018, 39.

58. Bourgon 2018, 39–40.

59. There is of course a growing internal divide within the United States between religious Americans and those who do not identify with any organized religion or are explicitly atheistic.

60. Snyder 2000.

61. Source: U.N. Population Division. A similar psychological roadblock to the renewal of the working-age population is found in Japan, whose ratio of workers to retirees was already 3:1 in 2000 and is now below 2:1. The United States, by comparison, finds itself constantly renewed in its demographic base through its relatively open immigration system since 1965.

62. This is even before we consider the historical lesson that the study of Chinese history teaches: that when past dynasties had large armies abroad, the cost and the reduction of forces at home often led to domestic rebellion and the overthrow of the leaders in power.

63. On this point, I have benefited immensely from discussions with Mark Schwartz. We already see this phenomenon happening: through loopholes and corrupt payoffs, many wealthy Chinese citizens have been able to flee to Canada, the United States, Australia, and other appealing countries. But the CCP has sought to close the loopholes and punish the corruption that surrounds this behavior, including going after family members that have remained behind, regardless of whether they facilitated the initial flights.

64. Beijing has tried to create digital currencies that can act like cryptocurrencies on the world stage. Not surprisingly, given the inherent lack of credibility of such currencies, this strategy has not solved the fundamental problem.

65. This has also reduced the appeal of Huawei's 5G systems, since the smartphones that go with them are now incompatible, being only 4G.

66. Copeland 2022.

67. Ironically, despite the currently cozy relationship between Beijing and Moscow, the biggest threat of actual invasion, as it was in the late 1960s, still comes from China's neighbor to the north: Russia. But of course, this is one reason for any Chinese leader to *keep* the cozy relationship going.

68. Haas 2005.

69. Figures for first half of 2022 show exports growing by 15 percent versus the first half of 2021, indicating that construction and infrastructure are still basically flat or negative, since GDP growth was only 3 percent, and trade is still close to 40 percent of GDP. All of the above quarterly statistics are drawn from a series of online "China Briefings" by Dezan Shira Associates.

70. Although again, I should stress, reaching a semblance of the "great rejuvenation of the Chinese nation" can itself be seen as a means toward greater national security rather than simply as glory or status ends in themselves.

71. Ye 2020.

72. Robinson 2021.

73. Systemic theories such as dynamic realism should not try to explain what motivated Trump, but rather accept that in this particular case their variables acted more as constraining factors on his behavior, rather than as propelling factors.

74. This of course led to his impeachment by the House of Representatives. Other presidents that did seem to sacrifice America's position in the world to improve their own domestic positions might include the presidents from the mid-1870s to the 1880s such as Rutherford Hayes, James Garfield, and Chester Arthur. But because the severity of the external threat environment

was so much lower during this time, largely due to the distraction of Germany's rise, they could get away with such behavior without major damage to U.S. security.

75. In the language of Thomas Schelling (1966), Washington must simultaneously deter Beijing from attacking Taiwan by threatening to punish China economically if it does *and* reassure CCP leaders that if they do the right thing and act peacefully, they will receive the benefits of continued trade. I thank Thomas Christensen and Todd Sechser for reminding me of this dual aspect of Schelling's deterrence logic.

76. At the time of writing (April 2023), the Biden administration was wisely signaling that decoupling was a bad idea and would not be pursued as policy.

77. Remember that tanks of the PLA were called onto the streets in Zhengzhou, Henan, in July 2022 to restore order after the street protests of those pushing to have lost bank deposits restored seemed to be getting out of hand and spreading to neighboring cities. The local police, as in May–June 1989, were not seen as able to do the job alone.

78. Goldstein 2005.

79. Doshi 2021.

80. See in particular Morrissey 2014; Bjornstad 2021; Mansel 2020; Oresko, Gibbs, and Scott 1997.

81. By comparison, the United States has only four cities over two million, and the largest city, New York at 8.5 million, is one-third the size of Shanghai (26 million).

# REFERENCES

Abdelal, Rawi, and Jonathan Kirshner. 1999–2000. "Strategy, Economic Relations, and the Definition of National Interests." *Security Studies* 9, nos. 1–2.

Allison, Graham. 2017. *Destined for War: Can the United States and China Escape Thucydides' Trap?* Boston: Mariner Books.

Allison, Graham, and Philip Zelikow. 1999. *Essence of Decision: Explaining the Cuban Missile Crisis.* 2nd ed. London: Longman.

Alvord, Clarence Walworth. 1917. *The Mississippi Valley in British Politics.* 2 vols. Cleveland, OH: Arthur H. Clark.

Ambrose, Stephen E. 1984. *Eisenhower the President, 1952–1969.* London: George Allen.

Ammon, Harry. 1994. *James Monroe: The Quest for National Identity.* Charlottesville: University of Virginia Press.

Anderson, Martin, and Annelise Anderson. 2009. *Reagan's Secret War.* New York: Three Rivers.

Anderson, Richard D. 1993. *Public Policy in an Authoritarian State.* Ithaca, NY: Cornell University Press.

Andrews, Charles M. 1938. *The Colonial Period of American History: England's Commercial and Colonial Policy.* Vol. 4. New Haven, CT: Yale University Press.

Arbatov, Georgi. 1993. *The System: An Insider's Life in Soviet Politics.* New York: Random House.

Armstrong, Charles K. 2004. *The North Korean Revolution, 1945–1950.* Ithaca, NY: Cornell University Press.

Aslund, Anders. 1989. *Gorbachev's Struggle for Economic Reform.* Ithaca, NY: Cornell University Press.

Bailyn, Bernard. 1965. *The Ideological Origins of the American Revolution.* Cambridge, MA: Harvard University Press.

Baker, James A. III. 1995. *The Politics of Diplomacy: Revolution, War, and Peace, 1989–1992.* New York: Putnam's Sons.

Balzacq, Thierry, and Ronald R. Krebs. 2021. *The Oxford Handbook of Grand Strategy.* Oxford: Oxford University Press.

Beale, Howard K. 1984. *Theodore Roosevelt and the Rise of America to World Power.* Baltimore: Johns Hopkins University Press.

Beer, George Louis. 1907. *British Colonial Policy, 1754–1765.* New York: MacMillan.

Bemis, Samuel Flagg. 1949. *John Quincy Adams and the Foundations of American Foreign Policy.* New York: Random House.

Bemis, Samuel Flagg. 1962. *Jay's Treaty: A Study of Commerce and Diplomacy.* 2nd ed. New Haven, CT: Yale University Press.

Berg, A. Scott. 2013. *Wilson*. New York: Putnam's Sons.

Beschloss, Michael R. 1988. *Mayday: Eisenhower, Khrushchev, and the U2 Affair*. New York: Harper and Row.

Beschloss, Michael R., and Strobe Talbott. 1993. *At the Highest Levels: The Inside Story of the End of the Cold War*. Boston: Little Brown.

Binder, Frederik. 1994. *James Buchanan and the American Empire*. Selinsgrove, PA: Susquehanna University Press.

Bjornstad, Hall. 2021. *The Dream of Absolutism: Louis XIV and the Logic of Modernity*. Chicago: University of Chicago Press.

Blainey, Geoffrey. (1973) 1988. *The Causes of War*, 3rd ed. New York: Free Press.

Blanchette, Jude. 2019. *China's New Red Guards: The Return of Radicalism and the Rebirth of Mao Zedong*. Oxford: Oxford University Press.

Blum, Howard. 2014. *Dark Invasion: 1915, Germany's Secret War, and the Hunt for the First Terrorist Cell*. New York: Harper.

Blustein, Paul. 2019. *Schism: China, America, and the Fracturing of the Global Trading System*. Waterloo, ON: Centre for International Governance Innovation.

Boll, Michael M. 1984. *Cold War in the Balkans: American Foreign Policy and the Emergence of Communist Bulgaria, 1943–1947*. Lexington: University of Kentucky Press.

Booth, Ken, and Nicholas J. Wheeler. 2008. *The Security Dilemma: Fear, Cooperation, and Trust in World Politics*. New York: Palgrave.

Bougon, Francois. 2018. *Inside the Mind of Xi Jinping*. London: Hurst.

Boys, James D. 2015. *Clinton's Grand Strategy: U.S. Foreign Policy in a Post-Cold War World*. New York: Bloomsbury.

Braisted, William R. 1971. *The United States Navy in the Pacific, 1909–1922*. Austin: University of Texas Press.

Brands, Hal, and Michael Beckley. 2021. "China is a Declining Power—And That's the Problem." *Foreign Policy* 24.

Brands, Hal, and Michael Beckley. 2022. *Danger Zone: The Coming Conflict with China*. New York: Norton.

Brands, Hal, and Jake Sullivan. 2020. "China's Two Paths to Global Domination." *Foreign Policy* 23.

Brant, Irving. 1970. *The Fourth President: A Life of James Madison*. Norwalk, CT: Easton Press.

Breen, T. H. 2004. *The Marketplace of Revolution: How Consumer Politics Shaped American Independence*. Oxford: Oxford University Press.

Bourne, Kenneth. 1967. *Britain and the Balance of Power in North America, 1815–1908*. Berkeley: University of California Press.

Brooks, Stephen G. 1997. "Dueling Realisms." *International Organization* 51, no. 3.

Brooks, Stephen G., and William C. Wohlforth. 2000–2001. "Power, Globalization, and the End of the Cold War: Reevaluating a Landmark Case for Ideas." *International Security* 25, no. 3.

Brown, Archie. 1997. *The Gorbachev Factor*. Oxford: Oxford University Press.

Brown, Archie. 2010. "The Gorbachev Revolution and the End of the Cold War." In *The Cold War*, vol. 3, *Endings*, edited by Melvyn P. Leffler and Odd Arne Westad. Cambridge: Cambridge University Press.

Brown, Roger H. 1971. *The Republic in Peril: 1812*. New York: Norton.

Burstein, Andrew, and Nancy Isenberg. 2010. *Madison and Jefferson*. New York: Random House

Bush, George, and Brent Scowcroft. 1998. *A World Transformed*. New York: Knopf.

Buzan, Barry. 1984. "Economic Structure and International Security." *International Organization* 38, no. 4.

Calhoun, Frederick S. 1986. *Power and Principle: Armed Intervention in Wilsonian Foreign Policy*. Kent, OH: Kent State University Press.

Calvert, Peter. 1968. *The Mexican Revolution, 1910–1914: The Diplomacy of Anglo-American Conflict*. Cambridge: Cambridge University Press.

Campbell, Charles S. 1976. *The Transformation of American Foreign Relations, 1865–1900*. New York: Harper and Row.

Campbell, Kurt M., and Ely Ratner. 2018. "The China Reckoning: How Beijing Defied American Expectations." *Foreign Affairs* 97.

Carter, Ralph G., and James M. Scott. 2012. "Congress." In *Routledge Handbook of American Foreign Policy*, edited by Steven W. Hook and Christopher M. Jones. New York: Routledge.

Cashman, Greg. 2013. *What Causes War?* 2nd ed. Lanham, MD: Rowman and Littlefield.

Cerami, Charles. 2004. *Jefferson's Great Gamble*. Naperville, IL: Sourcebooks.

Chace, James, and Caleb Carr. 1988. *America Invulnerable: The Quest for Absolute Security from 1812 to Star Wars*. New York: Summit Books.

Chaffin, Tom. 2002. *Pathfinder: John Charles Frémont and the Course of American Empire*. Norman: University of Oklahoma Press.

Christensen, Thomas J. 2011. *Worse than a Monolith: Alliance Politics and Problems of Coercive Diplomacy in Asia*. Princeton, NJ: Princeton University Press.

Christensen, Thomas J. 2015. *The China Challenge: Shaping the Choices of a Rising Power*. New York: Norton.

Chubb, Andrew. 2020. "PRC Assertiveness in the South China Sea: Measuring Continuity and Change, 1970–2015." *International Security* 45, no. 3.

Cogliano, Francis D. 2014. *Emperor of Liberty: Thomas Jefferson's Foreign Policy*. New Haven, CT: Yale University Press.

Cohen, Warren I. 1980. *America's Response to China*. 2nd ed. New York: Wiley.

Colaresi, Michael P., Karen Rasler, and William R. Thompson. 2008. *Strategic Rivalries in World Politics*. Cambridge: Cambridge University Press.

Coleman, Fred. 1996. *The Decline and the Fall of the Soviet Empire*. New York: St. Martin's Griffin.

Collins, Alan. 1997. *The Security Dilemma and the End of the Cold War*. Keele, UK: Keele University Press.

Cooper, John Milton Jr. 1977. *Walter Hines Page*. Chapel Hill: University of North Carolina Press.

Cooper, John Milton Jr. 2009. *Woodrow Wilson*. New York: Knopf.

Copeland, Dale C. 1993. *Realism and the Origins of Major War*. Ph.D. dissertation, University of Chicago, Department of Political Science.

Copeland, Dale C. 1996. "Neorealism and the Myth of Bipolar Stability: Toward a New Dynamic Realist Theory of Major War." *Security Studies* 5, no. 3.

Copeland, Dale C. 1997. "Do Reputations Matter?" *Security Studies* 7, no. 1.

Copeland, Dale C. 1999–2000. "Trade Expectations and the Outbreak of Peace: Détente 1970–74 and the End of the Cold War 1985–91." *Security Studies* 9, nos. 1–2.

Copeland, Dale C. 2000a. *The Origins of Major War*. Ithaca, NY: Cornell University Press.

Copeland, Dale C. 2000b. "The Constructivist Challenge to Structural Realism." *International Security* 25, no. 2.

Copeland, Dale C. 2003. "Economic Interdependence and the Future of U.S.-Chinese Relations." In *International Relations Theory and the Asia-Pacific*, edited by G. John Ikenberry and Michael Mastanduno. New York: Columbia University Press.

Copeland, Dale C. 2011. "Rationalist Theories of International Politics and the Problem of the Future." *Security Studies* 20, no.5.

Copeland, Dale C. 2012a. "Realism and Neorealism in the Study of Regional Conflict." In *International Relations Theory and Regional Transformation*, edited by T. V. Paul. Cambridge: Cambridge University Press.

Copeland, Dale C. 2012b. "Trade Expectations and the Grand Strategies of Germany and Japan in the Interwar Era." In *The Grand Strategies of the Great Powers in the Interwar Era*, edited by Steven Lobell, Norrin Ripsman, and Jeffrey Taliaferro. Cambridge: Cambridge University Press.

Copeland, Dale C. 2015. *Economic Interdependence and War*. Princeton, NJ: Princeton University Press.

Copeland, Dale C. 2018a. "Introduction to Study of Rare-Events." *Qualitative and Mixed-Methods Research* 2.

Copeland, Dale C. 2018b. "Reply to Critics." *Qualitative and Mixed-Methods Research* 2.

Copeland, Dale C. 2019. "Grappling with the Rise of China: A New Model for Thinking about Sino-American Relations." In *Chinese Strategic Intentions: A Deep Dive into China's Worldwide Activities*. White Paper of Department of Defense, Strategic Multilateral Assessment, online publication, December.

Copeland, Dale C. 2022. "When Trade Leads to War: China, Russia, and the Limits of Interdependence." *Foreign Affairs*, August (online).

Costigliola, Frank, 2016. "Reading for Emotion." In *Explaining the History of American Foreign Relations*, edited by Frank Costigliola and Michael J. Hogan. 3rd ed. Cambridge: Cambridge University Press.

Costigliola, Frank, and Michael J. Hogan. 2016. *Explaining the History of American Foreign Relations*. 3rd ed. Cambridge: Cambridge University Press.

Cox, Eric. 2010. *Why Enduring Rivalries Do—or Don't—End*. Boulder, CO: Lynne Rienner.

Crabb, Cecil V. 1982. *The Doctrines of American Foreign Policy*. New Orleans: Louisiana State University Press.

Crawford, Neta. 2000. "The Passion of World Politics: Propositions on Emotion and Emotional Relationships." *International Security* 24, no. 4.

Cumings, Bruce. 1981. *The Origins of the Korean War*. Vol. 1. Princeton, NJ: Princeton University Press.

Cumings, Bruce. 1990. *The Origins of the Korean War*. Vol. 2. Princeton, NJ: Princeton University Press.

Dallek, Robert. 1979. *Franklin D. Roosevelt and American Foreign Policy, 1932–1945*. Oxford: Oxford University Press.

Debs, Alexandre, and Nuno Montiero. 2014. "Known Unknowns: Power Shifts, Uncertainty, and War." *International Organization* 68, no. 1.

DeConde, Alexander. 1966. *The Quasi-War: The Politics and Diplomacy of the Undeclared War with France, 1797–1801*. New York: Scribner.

Destler, I. M. 2012. "The Foreign Economic Bureaucracy." In *Routledge Handbook of American Foreign Policy*, edited by Steven W. Hook and Christopher M. Jones. New York: Routledge.

Diehl, Paul, ed. 1998. *The Dynamics of Enduring Rivalries*. Champaign: University of Illinois Press.

Dobbs, Charles. 1982. *The Unwanted Symbol: American Foreign Policy, the Cold War, and Korea*. Kent, OH: Kent State University Press.

Dobbs, Michael. 1996. *Down with Big Brother: The Fall of the Soviet Empire*. New York: Vintage.

Dobrynin, Anatoly. 1995. *In Confidence*. New York: Random House.

Dobson, John M. 1988. *Reticent Expansionism: The Foreign Policy of William McKinley*. Pittsburgh, PA: Duquesne University Press.

Doder, Dusko. 1986. *Shadows and Whispers: Power Politics Inside the Kremlin from Brezhnev to Gorbachev*. Harmondsworth, UK: Penguin.

Doenecke, Justus D. 2011. *Nothing Less Than War: A New History of America's Entry into World War I*. Lawrence: University Press of Kentucky.

Doshi, Rush. 2021. *The Long Game: China's Grand Strategy to Displace American Order*. Oxford: Oxford University Press.

Doyle, Michael W. 1997. *Ways of War and Peace: Realism, Liberalism, and Socialism*. New York: Norton.

Draper, Theodore. 1996. *A Struggle for Power: The American Revolution*. New York: Vintage.

Dueck, Colin. 2006. *Reluctant Crusaders: Power, Culture, and Change in American Grand Strategy*. Princeton, NJ: Princeton University Press, 2006.

Economy, Elizabeth C. 2022. *The World According to China*. Cambridge: Polity.

Edelson, Max S. 2017. *The New Map of Empire: How Britain Imagined America before Independence*. Cambridge, MA: Harvard University Press.

Edelstein, David M. 2017. *Over the Horizon*. Ithaca, NY: Cornell University Press.

Egnal, Marc. 1988. *A Mighty Empire: The Origins of the American Revolution*. Ithaca, NY: Cornell University Press.

Eisenberg, Carolyn Woods. 1996. *Drawing the Line: The American Decision to Divide Germany, 1944–1949*. Cambridge: Cambridge University Press.

Eisenhower, Dwight D. 1963. *Mandate for Change, 1953–1956*. Garden City, NY: Doubleday.

Eisenhower, Dwight D. 1965. *Waging Peace, 1956–1961*. Garden City, NY: Doubleday.

Elkins, Stanley, and Eric McKitrick. 1993. *The Age of Federalism: The Early American Republic, 1788–1800*. Oxford: Oxford University Press.

Ellman, Michael, and Vladimir Kontorovich, eds. 1992. *The Disintegration of the Soviet Economic System*. London: Routledge.

Ellsberg, Daniel. 1968. *The Theory and Practice of Blackmail*. Santa Monica, CA: Rand.

Ellwood, David W. 1992. *Rebuilding Europe: Western Europe, America, and Postwar Reconstruction*. New York: Longman.

Elman, Colin. 2004. "Extending Offensive Realism: The Louisiana Purchase and America's Rise to Regional Hegemony." *American Political Science Review* 98, no. 4.

Engel, Jeffrey. 2020. *When the World Seemed New: George H. W. Bush and the End of the Cold War*. Boston: Houghton Mifflin.

Engel, Jeffrey. 2015. *The Four Freedoms: Franklin D. Roosevelt and the Evolution of an American Idea*. Oxford: Oxford University Press.

Englund, Will. 2017. *March 1917: On the Brink of War and Revolution*. New York: Norton.

Ericson, Richard E. 1990. "The Soviet Statistical Debate: Khanin vs. TsSu." In *The Impoverished Superpower*, edited by Henry S. Rowen and Charles Wolf, Jr. San Francisco: Institute for Contemporary Studies.

Fearon, James D. 1992. *Threats to Use Force*. Ph.D. dissertation. University of California–Berkeley, Department of Political Science.

Fearon, James D. 1995. "Rationalist Explanations for War." *International Organization* 49, no. 3.

Fearon, James D. 1997. "Signaling Foreign Policy Interests: Tying Hands versus Sinking Costs." *Journal of Conflict Resolution* 41, no. 1.

Fearon, James D. 1998. "Bargaining, Enforcement, and International Cooperation." *International Organization* 52, no. 2.

Feis, Herbert. 1967. *Churchill, Roosevelt, Stalin: The War They Waged and the Peace They Sought*. 2nd ed. Princeton, NJ: Princeton University Press.

Findlay, Ronald, and Kevin O'Rourke. 2007. *Power and Plenty: Trade, War, and the World Economy in the Second Millennium*. Princeton, NJ: Princeton University Press.

Flexner, James. 1972. *George Washington: Anguish and Farewell 1793–1799*. Boston: Little, Brown.

Foyle, Douglas C. 2012. "Public Opinion." In *Routledge Handbook of American Foreign Policy*, edited by Steven W. Hook and Christopher M. Jones. New York: Routledge.

Fordham, Benjamin O. 1998. *Building the Cold War Consensus: The Political Economy of US National Security Policy, 1949–51*. Ann Arbor: University of Michigan Press.

Fordham, Benjamin O. 2007. "Revisionism Reconsidered: Exports and American Intervention in World War I." *International Organization* 61, no. 2.

Fordham, Benjamin O. 2008. "Power or Plenty? Economic Interests, Security Concerns, and American Intervention." *International Studies Quarterly* 52, no. 4.

Fravel, M. Taylor. 2008. *Strong Borders, Secure Nation: Cooperation and Conflict in China's Territorial Disputes*. Princeton, NJ: Princeton University Press.

Friedberg, Aaron L. 2011. *A Contest for Supremacy: China, America, and the Struggle for Mastery in Asia*. New York: Norton.

Friedberg, Aaron L. 2022. *Getting China Wrong*. New York: Polity Press.

Frieden, Jeffry A. 1988. "Sectoral Conflicts and U.S. Foreign Economic Policy, 1914–1940." *International Organization* 42, no. 1.

Fukuyama, Francis. 1989. "The End of History?" *The National Interest* 16.

Funigiello, Philip J. 1988. *American-Soviet Trade in the Cold War*. Chapel Hill: University of North Carolina Press.

Fursenko, Aleksandr, and Timothy Naftali. 1997. *"One Hell of a Gamble": Khrushchev, Castro, and Kennedy, 1958–1964*. New York: Norton.

Fursenko, Aleksandr, and Timothy Naftali. 2007. *Khrushchev's Cold War*. New York: Norton.

Gaddis, John Lewis. 1982. *Strategies of Containment*. Oxford: Oxford University Press.

Gaddis, John Lewis. 1983. "The Emerging Post-Revisionist Synthesis on the Origins of the Cold War." *Diplomatic History* 7, no. 3.

Galloway, Colin G. 2006. *The Scratch of a Pen: 1763 and the Transformation of North America.* Oxford: Oxford University Press.

Gardner, Lloyd C. 1964. *Economic Aspects of New Deal Diplomacy.* Madison: University of Wisconsin Press.

Gardner, Lloyd C. 1993. *Spheres of Influence: The Great Powers Partition Europe from Munich to Yalta.* Chicago: Ivan Dee.

Gardner, Lloyd C. 2009. *Three Kings: The Rise of an American Empire in the Middle East After World War II.* New York: New Press.

Garthoff, Raymond L. 1994a. *Détente and Confrontation.* Rev. ed. Washington, DC: Brookings.

Garthoff, Raymond L. 1994b. *The Great Transition: American-Soviet Relations and the End of the Cold War.* Washington, DC: Brookings.

Gellner, Ernest. 2008. *Nations and Nationalism.* Ithaca, NY: Cornell University Press.

George, Alexander L. 1980. *Presidential Decision-making in Foreign Policy.* Boulder, CO: Westview.

George, Alexander L., and Richard Smoke. 1974. *Deterrence in American Foreign Policy.* New York: Columbia University Press.

Gibson, Alan. 2009. *Interpreting the Founding: Guide to the Enduring Debates over the Origins and Foundations of the American Republic.* 2nd ed. Lawrence: University of Kansas Press.

Gilderhus, Mark T. 1977. *Diplomacy and Revolution: U.S.-Mexican Relations under Wilson and Carranza.* Tucson: University of Arizona Press.

Gilderhus, Mark T. 1986. *Pan-American Visions: Woodrow Wilson in the Western Hemisphere, 1913–1921.* Tucson: University of Arizona Press.

Gill, Bates. 2022. *Daring to Struggle: China's Global Ambitions Under Xi Jinping.* Oxford: Oxford University Press.

Gilpin, Robert. 1975. *U.S. Power and Multinational Corporations.* New York: Basic Books.

Gilpin, Robert. 1977. "Economic Interdependence and National Security in Historical Perspective." In *Economic Issues and National Security,* edited by Klaus Knorr and Frank N. Trager. Lawrence, KS: Allen.

Gilpin, Robert. 1981. *War and Change in World Politics.* Cambridge: Cambridge University Press.

Gipson, Lawrence Henry. 1967. *The Triumphant Empire: The Empire Beyond the Storm.* Vol. 13. New York: Knopf.

Glaser, Charles L. 1992. "Political Consequences of Military Strategy: Expanding and Refining the Spiral and Deterrence Models." *World Politics* 44, no. 4.

Glaser, Charles. 1994–95. "Realists as Optimists." *International Security* 19, no. 3.

Glaser, Charles. 1997. "The Security Dilemma Revisited." *World Politics* 50, no. 1.

Glaser, Charles. 2010. *Rationalist Theory of International Politics.* Princeton, NJ: Princeton University Press.

Goddard, Stacie. 2018. *When Right Makes Might: Rising Powers and World Order.* Ithaca, NY: Cornell University Press.

Goertz, Gary, and James Mahoney. 2012. *A Tale of Two Cultures.* Princeton, NJ: Princeton University Press.

Goldstein, Avery. 2005. *Rising to the Challenge: China's Grand Strategy and International Security.* Stanford, CA: Stanford University Press.

Goncharov, Sergei, John Lewis, and Litai Xue. 1995. *Uncertain Partners: Stalin, Mao, and the Korean War.* Stanford, CA: Stanford University Press.

Gorbachev, Mikhail. 1987. *Perestroika.* New York: Harper and Row.

Gorbachev, Mikhail. 1996. *Memoirs.* New York: Doubleday.

Gould, Lewis L. 1981. *The Presidency of William McKinley.* Lawrence: University of Kansas Press.

Gowa, Joanne S. 1994. *Allies, Adversaries, and International Trade.* Princeton, NJ: Princeton University Press.

Graebner, Norman. 1983. *Empire on the Pacific.* New York: Regina Books.

Graebner, Norman. 1985. *Foundations of American Foreign Policy: A Realistic Appraisal from Franklin to McKinley.* New York: Rowman and Littlefield.

Greene, Jack P. 1970. *Great Britain and the American Colonies, 1606–1763.* Columbia: University of South Carolina Press.

Greene, Jack P. 1990. *Peripheries and Center: Constitutional Development in the Extended Polities of the British Empire and the United States 1607–1788.* New York: Norton.

Greene, Jack P. 1995. *Understanding the American Revolution.* Charlottesville: University of Virginia Press.

Greene, Jack P. 2010. *The Constitutional Origins of the American Revolution.* Cambridge: Cambridge University Press.

Greene, Jack P., and Philip D. Morgan, eds. 2008. *Atlantic History: A Critical Appraisal.* Oxford: Oxford University Press.

Greenfeld, Leah. 1992. *Nationalism: Five Roads to Modernity.* Cambridge, MA: Harvard University Press.

Grieb, Kenneth J. 1969. *The United States and Huerta.* Lincoln: University of Nebraska Press.

Grieco, Joseph. 1988. "Anarchy and the Limits of Cooperation: A Realist Critique." *International Organization* 42, no. 2.

Haas, Mark. 2005. *The Ideological Origins of Great Power Politics.* Ithaca, NY: Cornell University Press.

Haglund, David G. 1984. *The Battle of Latin America: Franklin D. Roosevelt and the End of Isolation, 1936–41.* Baltimore: Johns Hopkins University Press.

Hahn, Peter L. 1991. *The United States, Great Britain, and Egypt, 1945–1956.* Chapel Hill: University of North Carolina Press.

Hancy, Patrick J. 2012. "Interest Groups." In *Routledge Handbook of American Foreign Policy,* edited by Steven W. Hook and Christopher M. Jones. New York: Routledge.

Hane, Mikiso. 1972. *Japan: A Historical Survey.* New York: Scribner.

Harbutt, Fraser J. 2010. *Yalta 1945: Europe and America at the Crossroads.* Cambridge: Cambridge University Press.

Harriman, Averell, and Elie Abel. 1975. *Special Envoy to Churchill and Stalin, 1941–1946.* New York: Random House.

Harrison, Hope M. 1993. "Ulbricht and the Concrete 'Rose': New Archival Evidence on the Dynamics of Soviet-East German Relations and the Berlin Crisis." Cold War International History Project, Washington DC, working paper no. 5.

Harrison, Hope M. 2005. *Driving the Soviets Up the Wall: Soviet-East German Relations, 1953–61.* Princeton, NJ: Princeton University Press.

Haynes, Kyle, and Brandon Yoder. 2020. "Offsetting Uncertainty: Reassurance with Two-Sided Incomplete Information." *American Journal of Political Science* 64, no. 1.

Hearden, Patrick J. 1987. *Roosevelt Confronts Hitler: America's Entry into World War II*. Dekalb: Northern Illinois University Press.

Hearden, Patrick J. 2002. *Architects of Globalism: Building a New World Order during World War II*. Fayetteville: University of Arkansas Press.

Heckscher, August. 1991. *Woodrow Wilson*. New York: Charles Scribner's Sons.

Herring, George C. 1973. *Aid to Russia, 1941–1946: Strategy, Diplomacy, the Origins of the Cold War*. New York: Columbia University Press.

Herring, George C. 2002. *America's Longest War: The United States and Vietnam, 1950–1975*. 4th ed. New York: McGraw-Hill.

Herring, George C. 2008. *From Colony to Superpower: U.S. Foreign Relations since 1776*. Oxford: Oxford University Press

Hewitt, Ed A. 1988. *Reforming the Soviet Economy*. Washington, DC: Brookings.

Hietala, Thomas R. 1985. *Manifest Design: Anxious Aggrandizement in Late Jacksonian America*. Ithaca, NY: Cornell University Press.

Hill, Peter P. 2005. *Napoleon's "Troublesome Americans": Franco-American Relations, 1804–1815*. Potomac Books.

Hirschman, Albert O. 1980. *National Power and the Structure of Foreign Trade*. Exp. ed. Berkeley: University of California Press.

Hixson, Walter L. 2016. *American Foreign Relations: A New Diplomatic History*. London: Routledge.

Hoffman, Erik P., and Robbin F. Laird. 1982a. *"The Scientific-Technological Revolution" and Soviet Foreign Policy*. New York: Pergamon.

Hoffman, Erik P., and Robbin F. Laird. 1982b. *The Politics of Economic Modernization in the Soviet Union*. Ithaca, NY: Cornell University Press.

Hogan, Michael J., and Thomas G. Paterson, eds. 1991. *Explaining the History of American Foreign Relations*. Cambridge: Cambridge University Press.

Holton, Woody. 1999. *Indians, Debtors, Slaves, and the Making of the American Revolution in Virginia*. Chapel Hill: University of North Carolina Press.

Hook, Steven W., and Christopher M. Jones, eds. 2012. *Routledge Handbook of American Foreign Policy*. New York: Routledge.

Horne, Gerald. 2014. *The Counter-Revolution of 1776: Slave Resistance and the Origins of the United States*. New York: New York University Press.

Horsman, Reginald. 1962. *The Causes of the War of 1812*. Philadelphia: University of Pennsylvania Press.

Howe, Daniel Walker. 2009. *What Hath God Wrought: The Transformation of America, 1815–1848*. Oxford: Oxford University Press.

Hunt, Michael H. 2009. *Ideology and American Foreign Policy*. New Haven, CT: Yale University Press.

Hunt, Michael H., and Steven Levine. 2012. *Arc of Empire: America's Wars in Asia from the Philippines to Vietnam*. Chapel Hill: University of North Carolina Press.

Ikenberry, G. John. 2008. "The Rise of China and the Future of the West." *Foreign Affairs* 87, no. 1.

Ikenberry, G. John. 2011. *Liberal Leviathan: The Origins, Crisis, and Transformation of the American World Order*. Princeton, NJ: Princeton University Press.

Ikenberry, G. John, ed. 2014. *Power, Order, and Change*. Cambridge: Cambridge University Press.

Ikenberry, G. John. 2020. *A World Safe for Democracy: Liberal Internationalism and the Crises of the Global Order*. New Haven, CT: Yale University Press.

Immerman, Richard. 2012. *Empire for Liberty: A History of American Imperialism from Benjamin Franklin to Paul Wolfowitz*. Princeton, NJ: Princeton University Press.

Israelyan, Victor. 1995. *Inside the Kremlin During the Yom Kippur War*. University Park: Pennsylvania State University Press.

Janis, Irving. 1982. *Groupthink: Psychological Studies of Policy Decisions and Fiascos*. 2nd ed. New York: Houghton Mifflin.

Jentleson, Bruce. 1986. *Pipeline Politics: The Complex Political Economy of East-West Energy Trade*. Ithaca, NY: Cornell University Press.

Jervis, Robert. 1968. "Hypotheses on Misperception." *World Politics* 20, no. 3.

Jervis, Robert. 1976. *Perception and Misperception in International Politics*. Princeton, NJ: Princeton University Press.

Jervis, Robert. 1978. "Cooperation under the Security Dilemma." *World Politics* 30, no. 2.

Jervis, Robert. 1982. "Security Regimes." *International Organization* 36, no. 2.

Jervis, Robert. 1991. "Domino Beliefs and Strategic Behavior." In *Dominos and Bandwagons*, edited by Robert Jervis and Jack Snyder. New York: Columbia University Press.

Jervis, Robert. 1996. "Perception, Misperception, and the End of the Cold War." In *Witnesses to the End of the Cold War*, edited by William C. Wohlforth. Baltimore: Johns Hopkins University Press.

Jervis, Robert. 1997. *System Effects*. Princeton, NJ: Princeton University Press.

Johnston, Alistair Iain. 2004. "Beijing's Security Behavior in the Asia-Pacific: Is China a Satisfied Power?" In *Rethinking Security in East Asia*, edited by J. J. Suh, P. J. Katzenstein, and A. Carlson. Stanford, CA: Stanford University Press.

Johnston, Alistair Iain. 2013. "How New and Assertive is China's New Assertiveness?" *International Security* 37, no. 4.

Jones, Christopher M. 2012. "Bureaucratic Politics." In *Routledge Handbook of American Foreign Policy*, edited by Steven W. Hook and Christopher M. Jones. New York: Routledge.

Jones, Howard, and Donald A. Rakestraw. 1997. *Prologue to Manifest Destiny: Anglo-American Relations in the 1840s*. Rowman and Littlefield.

Jones, Howard, and Randall B. Woods. 1993. "Origins of the Cold War in Europe and the Near East." *Diplomatic History*. 17, no.2.

Jones, Joseph Marion. 1965. *Fifteen Weeks: An Inside Account of the Genesis of the Marshall Plan*. New York: Mariner.

Joseph, Michael F. 2021. "A Little Bit of Cheap Talk Is a Dangerous Thing: States Can Communicate Intentions Persuasively and Raise the Risk of War." *Journal of Politics* 83, no. 1.

Kagan, Robert. 2006. *Dangerous Nation*. New York: Vintage.

Kagan, Robert. 2023. *The Ghost at the Feast: America and the Collapse of the World Order, 1900–1941*. New York: Knopf.

Kaiser, David. 2000. *American Tragedy: Kennedy, Johnson, and the Origins of the Vietnam War*. Cambridge, MA: Harvard University Press.

Kaiser, Robert G. 1991. *Why Gorbachev Happened*. New York: Simon and Schuster.

Kang, David C. 2007. *China Rising: Peace, Power, and Order in East Asia*. New York: Columbia University Press.

Kapstein, Ethan B. 1990. *The Insecure Alliance: Energy Crises and Western Politics since 1944*. New York: Oxford University Press.

Karp, Walter. 2010. *Politics of War*. New York: Franklin Square Press.

Katz, Friedrich. 1981. *The Secret War in Mexico: Europe, the United States, and the Mexican Revolution*. Chicago: University of Chicago Press.

Kaufmann, Burton I. 1974. *Efficiency and Expansion: Foreign Trade Organization in the Wilson Administration, 1913–1921*. Westport, CT: Greenwood.

Kearn, David. 2014. *Great Power Security Competition: Arms Control and the Challenge of Technological Change*. Lanham, MD: Lexington Books.

Kennan, George F. 1984. *American Diplomacy*. Exp. ed. Chicago: University of Chicago Press.

Kennedy, Ross A. 2009. *The Will to Believe: Woodrow Wilson, World War I, and America's Strategy for Peace and Security*. Kent, OH: Kent State University Press.

Keohane, Robert O. 1993. "Institutional Theory and the Realist Challenge after the Cold War." In *Neorealism and Neoliberalism*, edited by David A. Baldwin. New York: Columbia University Press.

Ketcham, Ralph. 1990. *James Madison*. Charlottesville: University of Virginia Press.

Khan, Sulmann Wasif. 2018. *Haunted by Chaos: China's Grand Strategy from Mao Zedong to Xi Jinping*. Cambridge, MA: Harvard University Press.

Kim, Woosang, and James Morrow. 1992. "When Do Power Shifts Lead to War?" *American Journal of Political Science* 36, no. 2.

Kimball, Warren F. 1991. *The Juggler: Franklin D. Roosevelt as Wartime Statesman*. Princeton, NJ: Princeton University Press.

Kimball, Warren F. 1997. *Forged in War: Roosevelt, Churchill, and the Second World War*. New York: William Morrow.

Kinzer, Stephen. 2005. *All the Shah's Men: An American Coup and the Roots of Middle East Terror*. Hoboken, NJ: John Wiley and Sons.

Kirshner, Jonathan. 2007. *Appeasing Bankers: Financial Caution on the Road to War*. Princeton, NJ: Princeton University Press.

Kirshner, Jonathan. 2022. *An Unwritten Future: Realism and Uncertainty in World Politics*. Princeton, NJ: Princeton University Press.

Kissinger, Henry A. 1979. *White House Years*. Boston: Little, Brown.

Kissinger, Henry A. 1982. *Years of Upheaval*. Boston: Little, Brown.

Knock, Thomas. J. 1992. *To End All Wars: Woodrow Wilson and the Quest for a New World Order*. Princeton, NJ: Princeton University Press.

Knollenberg, Bernhard. 2002. *The Origin of the American Revolution, 1759–1766*. Indianapolis, IN: Liberty Fund.

Knorr, Klaus E. 1944. *British Colonial Theories, 1570–1850*. Toronto, ON: Toronto University Press.

Knorr, Klaus E. 1973. *Power and Wealth: The Political Economy of International Power*. New York: Basic Books.

Knorr, Klaus E. 1975. *The Power of Nations: The Political Economy of International Relations*. New York: Basic Books.

Kolko, Gabriel. 1990. *The Politics of War*. New York: Pantheon.

Koslowski, Rey, and Friedrich V. Kratochwil. 1994. "Understanding Change in International Politics: The Soviet Empire's Demise and the International System." *International Organization* 48, no. 2.

Krasner, Stephen D. 1978. *Defending the National Interest: Raw Materials and U.S. Foreign Policy*. Princeton, NJ: Princeton University Press.

Kupchan, Charles A., and Clifford A. Kupchan. 1991. "Concerts, Collective Security, and the Future of Europe." *International Security* 16, no. 1.

Kydd, Andrew. 1997a. "Game Theory and the Spiral Model." *World Politics* 49, no. 3.

Kydd, Andrew. 1997b. "Sheep in Sheep's Clothing: Why Security Seekers Do Not Fight Each Other." *Security Studies* 7, no. 1.

Kydd, Andrew, 2000. "Trust, Reassurance, and Cooperation." *International Organization* 54, no. 2.

Kydd, Andrew. 2005. *Trust and Mistrust in International Politics*. Princeton, NJ: Princeton University Press.

Labs, Eric. 1997. "Beyond Victory: Offensive Realism and the Expansion of War Aims." *Security Studies* 6, no. 4.

Lacouture, Jean. 1992. *De Gaulle: The Ruler, 1945–1970*. New York: Norton.

LaFeber, Walter. 1965a. *John Quincy Adams and the Foundations of American Foreign Policy*.

LaFeber, Walter. 1965b. *The New Empire: An Interpretation of American Expansion, 1869–1898*. Ithaca, NY: Cornell University Press.

LaFeber, Walter. 1989. *The Panama Canal*. Oxford: Oxford University Press.

LaFeber, Walter. 1994. *The American Age: U.S. Foreign Policy at Home and Abroad, 1750 to the Present*. 2nd ed. New York: Norton.

LaFeber, Walter. 1998. *The Clash: U.S.-Japanese Relations Throughout History*. New York: Norton.

Lake, David A. 1999. *Entangling Relations: American Foreign Policy and Its Century*. Princeton, NJ: Princeton University Press.

Langer, William L. 1951. *The Diplomacy of Imperialism, 1890–1902*. 2nd ed. New York: Knopf.

Lansing, Robert. 1935. *War Memoirs of Robert Lansing, Secretary of State*. New York: Bobbs-Merrill.

Lascurettes, Kyle M. 2020. *Orders of Exclusion: Great Powers and the Strategic Sources of Foundational Rules in International Relations*. Oxford: Oxford University Press.

Lawson, Philip. 1989. *The Imperial Challenge: Quebec and Britain in the Age of the American Revolution*. Montreal: McGill-Queen's University Press.

Layne, Christopher. 1994. "Kant or Cant: The Myth of the Democratic Peace." *International Security* 19, no. 2.

Layne, Christopher. 2002. "The 'Poster Child for Offensive Realism': America as a Global Hegemon." *Security Studies* 12, no. 2.

Layne, Christopher. 2006. *The Peace of Illusions: American Grand Strategy from 1940 to the Present*. Ithaca, NY: Cornell University Press.

Lebow, Richard Ned. 1981. *Between Peace and War*. Baltimore: Johns Hopkins University Press.

Lebow, Richard Ned, and Janice Gross Stein. 1994. *We All Lost the Cold War*. Princeton, NJ: Princeton University Press.

Lebow, Richard Ned, and Thomas Risse-Kappen, eds. 1995. *International Relations Theory and the End of the Cold War*. New York: Columbia University Press.

Lee, Steven Hugh. 1995. *Outposts of Empire: Korea, Vietnam, and the Origins of the Cold War in Asia, 1949–1954*. Montreal, QC: McGill-Queens University Press.

Leffler, Melvyn P. 1979. *The Elusive Quest: America's Pursuit of European Stability and French Security, 1939–1945*. Chapel Hill: University of North Carolina Press.

Leffler, Melvyn P. 1984. "The American Conception of National Security and the Beginnings of the Cold War." *American Historical Review* 89, no. 2.

Leffler, Melvyn P. 1986. "Adherence to Agreements: Yalta and the Experiences of the Early Cold War." *International Security* 11, no. 1.

Leffler, Melvyn P. 1992. *A Preponderance of Power: National Security, the Truman Administration and the Cold War*. Stanford, CA: Stanford University Press.

Leffler, Melvyn P. 1994a. "Interpretive Wars over the Cold War, 1945–50." In *American Foreign Relations Reconsidered, 1890–1993*, edited by Gordon Martel. London: Routledge.

Leffler, Melvyn P. 1994b. *The Specter of Communism*. New York: Hill and Wang.

Leffler, Melvyn P. 1996. *The Struggle for Germany and the Origins of the Cold War*. Occasional paper no. 16 (German Historical Institute).

Leffler, Melvyn P. 2007. *For the Soul of Mankind: The United States, the Soviet Union, and the Cold War*. New York: Hill and Wang.

Leffler, Melvyn P. 2019. *Safeguarding Democratic Capitalism: U.S. Foreign Policy and National Security, 1920–2015*. Princeton, NJ: Princeton University Press.

Leffler, Melvyn P. 2023. *Confronting Saddam Hussein: George W. Bush and the Invasion of Iraq*. Oxford: Oxford University Press.

Leonard, Thomas M. 2001. *James K. Polk: A Clear and Unquestionable Destiny*. Wilmington, DE: Scholarly Resources.

Levy, Jack S. 1986. "Organizational Routines and the Causes of War." *International Studies Quarterly* 30, no. 2.

Levy, Jack S. 1987. "Declining Power and the Preventive Motivation for War." *World Politics* 40, no. 1.

Levy, Jack S. 1997. "Prospect Theory, Rational Choice, and International Relations." *International Studies Quarterly* 41, no. 1.

Levy, Jack S., and William R. Thompson. 2010. *Causes of War*. New York: Wiley-Blackwell.

Lewis, James E. 1998. *The American Union and the Problem of Neighborhood*. Chapel Hill: University of North Carolina Press

Lieven, Anatol. 2012. *America Right or Wrong*. Oxford: Oxford University Press.

Link, Arthur S. 1960. *Wilson: The Struggle for Neutrality, 1914–1915*. Princeton, NJ: Princeton University Press.

Link, Arthur S. 1964. *Wilson: Confusions and Crises, 1915–1916*. Princeton, NJ: Princeton University Press.

Link, Arthur S. 1965. *Wilson: Campaigns for Progressivism and Peace, 1916–1917*. Princeton, NJ: Princeton University Press.

Lipset, Seymour Martin. 1996. *American Exceptionalism: A Double-Edged Sword*. New York: Norton.

Lobell, Steven, Norrin Ripsman, and Jeffrey Talliaferro. 2009. *Neoclassical Realism, the State, and Foreign Policy*. Cambridge: Cambridge University Press.

Logevall, Fredrik. 2001. *Choosing War: The Lost Chance for Peace and the Escalation of War in Vietnam*. Berkeley: University of California Press.

Logevall, Fredrik. 2012. *Embers of War: The Fall of an Empire and the Making of America's Vietnam*. New York: Random House.

Love, Robert W. 1992. *History of the U.S. Navy*. Vol. 1. Mechanicsburg, VA: Stackpole Books.

Lovejoy, David S. 1987. *The Glorious Revolution in America*. Middletown, VT: Wesleyan University Press.

Lyon, Alynna J. 2012. "Liberalism." In *Routledge Handbook of American Foreign Policy*, edited by Steven W. Hook and Christopher M. Jones. London: Routledge.

Maass, Richard. 2019. *The Picky Eagle: How Democracy and Xenophobia Limited American Expansionism*. Ithaca, NY: Cornell University Press.

MacDonald, Douglas J. 1995–96. "Communist Bloc Expansion in the East Cold War: Challenging Realism, Refuting Revisionism." *International Security* 20, no. 3.

Mackie, John L. 1980. *Cement of the Universe*. Oxford: Clarendon Press, 1980.

Maddox, Robert James. 1988. *From War to Cold War*. Boulder, CO: Westview.

Mahan, Alfred T. 1890. *The Influence of Sea Power Upon History, 1660–1783*. Boston: Little, Brown.

Maier, Pauline. 1991. *From Resistance to Revolution: Colonial Radicals and the Development of American Opposition to Britain, 1765–1776*. New York: Norton.

Malone, Dumas. 1962. *Jefferson and His Times: The Ordeal of Liberty*. Boston: Little, Brown.

Mansel, Philip. 2020. *The King of the World: The Life of Louis XIV*. Chicago: University of Chicago Press.

Maoz, Zeev, and Ben D. Mor. 2002. *Bound by Struggle: The Strategic Evolution of Enduring International Rivalries*. Ann Arbor: University of Michigan Press.

Marks, Frederick W. 1986. *Independence on Trial: Foreign Affairs and the Making of the Constitution*. Wilmington, DE: Scholarly Resources.

Martel, Gordon, ed. 1994. *American Foreign Relations Reconsidered, 1890–1993*. London: Routledge.

Martel, Leon. 1979. *Lend-Lease, Loans, and the Coming of the Cold War*. Boulder, CO: Westview.

Mastanduno, Michael. 1988. "Trade as a Strategic Weapon: American and Alliance Export Control Policy in the Early Postwar Period." *International Organization* 42, no. 1.

Mastanduno, Michael. 1992. *Economic Containment: CoCom and the Politics of East-West Trade*. Ithaca, NY: Cornell University Press.

Mastro, Oriana Skylar. 2014. "Why Chinese Assertiveness Is Here to Stay." *Washington Quarterly* 37, no. 4.

Mastro, Oriana Skylar, and Derek Scissors. 2022. "China Hasn't Reached the Peak of its Power: Why Beijing Can Afford to Bide Its Time." *Foreign Affairs* August (online).

Matlock, Jack F. 1995. *Autopsy of an Empire*. New York: Random House.

Mayers, David. 2007. *Dissenting Voices in America's Rise to Power*. Cambridge: Cambridge University Press.

McCormick, James M., ed. 2012. *The Domestic Sources of American Foreign Policy*, 6th ed. Lanham, MD: Rowman and Littlefield.

McCormick, Thomas J. 1967. *China Market: America's Quest for Informal Empire, 1893–1901*. Chicago: Quadrangle.

McCullough, David. 1979. *The Path Between the Seas: The Creation of the Panama Canal, 1870–1914*. New York: Simon and Schuster.

McCusker, John J., and Russell R. Menard. 1991. *The Economy of British America, 1607–1787*. Chapel Hill: University of North Carolina Press.

McDermott, Rose. 1998. *Risk-Taking in International Politics: Prospect Theory in American Foreign Policy*. Ann Arbor: University of Michigan Press.

McJimsey, George. 1987. *Harry Hopkins*. Cambridge, MA: Harvard University Press.

McLellan, David S. 1976. *Dean Acheson*. New York: Dodd, Mead.

Mead, Walter Russell. 2001. *Special Providence: American Foreign Policy and How It Changed the World*. New York: Knopf.

Mead, Walter Russell. 2007. *God and Gold: Britain, America, and the Making of the Modern World*. New York: Vintage.

Mearsheimer, John. J. 1990. "Back to the Future: Instability in Europe after the Cold War." *International Security* 15, no. 1.

Mearsheimer, John. J. 1992. "Disorder Restored." In *Rethinking America's Security*, edited by Graham Allison and Gregory F. Treverton. New York: Norton.

Mearsheimer, John. J. 1994–95. "The False Promise of International Institutions." *International Security* 19, no. 3.

Mearsheimer, John. J. 2001. *The Tragedy of Great Power Politics*. New York: Norton.

Mearsheimer, John. J. 2014. *The Tragedy of Great Power Politics*. Updated ed. New York: Norton.

Mearsheimer, John. J. 2018. *The Great Delusion: Liberal Dreams and International Realities*. New Haven, CT: Yale University Press.

Mearsheimer, John. J. 2021. "The Inevitable Rivalry: American, China, and the Tragedy of Great Power Politics." *Foreign Affairs* 100.

Mearsheimer, John J., and Stephen M. Walt. 2007. *The Israel Lobby and U.S. Foreign Policy*. New York: Farrar, Straus, and Giroux.

Mee, Charles L. 1975. *Meeting at Potsdam*. New York: M. Evans.

Mercer, Jonathan. 1995. "Anarchy and Identity." *International Organization* 49, no. 2.

Mercer, Jonathan. 1996. *Reputation and International Politics*. Ithaca, NY: Cornell University Press.

Merk, Frederick. 1966. *The Monroe Doctrine and American Expansionism, 1843–1849*. New York: Knopf.

Merk, Frederick. 1978. *History of the Westward Movement*. New York: Knopf.

Merk, Frederick. 1995. *Manifest Destiny and Mission in American History*. Cambridge, MA: Harvard University Press.

Metzger, Charles H. 1936. *The Quebec Act: A Primary Cause of the American Revolution*. New York: U.S. Catholic Historical Society.

Miller, Benjamin. 2021. *Grand Strategy from Truman to Trump*. Chicago: University of Chicago Press.

Milner, Helen, and Dustin Tingley. 2015. *Sailing the Water's Edge: The Domestic Politics of American Foreign Policy*. Princeton, NJ: Princeton University Press.

Mitchell, Nancy. 1999. *The Danger of Dreams: German and American Imperialism in Latin America*. Chapel Hill: University of North Carolina.

Montgomery, Evan Braden. 2006. "Breaking Out of the Security Dilemma: Realism, Reassurance, and the Problem of Uncertainty." *International Security* 31, no. 2.

Moravcsik, Andrew. 1997. "Taking Preferences Seriously: A Liberal Theory of International Politics." *International Organization* 51, no. 4.

Morrissey, Robert. 2014. *The Economy of Glory: From Ancien Regime France to the Fall of Napoleon*. Oxford: Oxford University Press.

Munro, Dana G. 1964. *The United States and the Caribbean Republics, 1921–1933*. Princeton, NJ: Princeton University Press.

Musicant, Ivan. 1998. *Empire by Default: The Spanish-American War and the Dawn of the American Century*. New York: Henry Holt.

Narizny, Kevin. 2007. *The Political Economy of Grand Strategy*. Ithaca, NY: Cornell University Press.

Narizny, Kevin. 2017. "On Systemic Paradigms and Domestic Politics: A Critique of the Newest Realism." *International Security* 42, no. 2.

Nash, Gary B. 1979. *The Urban Crucible: Social Change, Political Consciousness, and the Origins of the American Revolution*. Cambridge, MA: Harvard University Press.

Nau, Henry R. 2002. *At Home Abroad: Identity and Power in American Foreign Policy*. Ithaca, NY: Cornell University Press.

Nau, Henry R. 2013. *Conservative Internationalism*. Princeton, NJ: Princeton University Press.

Nelson, Eric. 2017. *The Royalist Revolution: Monarchy and the American Founding*. Cambridge, MA: Harvard University Press.

Newell, Margaret Ellen. 1998. *From Dependency to Independence: Economic Revolution in Colonial New England*. Ithaca, NY: Cornell University Press.

Niebuhr, Reinhold. (1953) 2010. *The Irony of American History*. Chicago: University of Chicago Press.

Ninkovich, Frank. 1994. *Modernity and Power: A History of Domino Theory in the Twentieth Century*. Chicago: University of Chicago Press.

Nixon, Richard. 1978. *RN: The Memoirs of Richard Nixon*. New York: Grosset and Dunlap.

Njolstad, Olav. 2010. "The Collapse of Superpower Détente, 1975–1980." In *The Cold War*, vol. 3, *Endings*, edited by Melvyn P. Leffler and Odd Arne Westad. Cambridge: Cambridge University Press.

Oberdorfer, Don. 1991. *The Turn: From Cold War to a New Era*. New York: Poseidon.

Offner, John L. 1992. *An Unwanted War: The Diplomacy of the United States and Spain over Cuba, 1895–1898*. Chapel Hill: University of North Carolina.

Onuf, Peter S. 2000. *Jefferson's Empire: The Language of American Nationhood*. Charlottesville: University of Virginia Press.

Oren, Ido. 1995. "The Subjectivity of the 'Democratic' Peace: Changing U.S. Perceptions of Imperial Germany." *International Security* 20, no. 2.

Oresko, Robert, G. C. Gibbs, and H. M. Scott. 1997. *Royal and Republican Sovereignty in Early Modern Europe*. Cambridge: Cambridge University Press.

Osgood, Robert E. 1953. *Ideals and Self-Interest in America's Foreign Relations*. Chicago: University of Chicago Press.

O'Sullivan, Christopher D. 2008. *Sumner Welles, Postwar Planning, and the Quest for a New World Order, 1937–1943*. New York: Columbia University Press.

Owen, John M. 1994. "How Liberalism Produces the Democratic Peace." *International Security* 20, no. 2.

Owen, John M. 1997. *Liberal Peace, Liberal War*. Ithaca, NY: Cornell University Press.

Owen, John M. 2010. *The Clash of Ideas in World Politics*. Princeton, NJ: Princeton University Press.

Painter, David S. 1986. *Oil and the American Century: The Political Economy of U.S. Foreign Oil Policy, 1941–1954*. Baltimore: Johns Hopkins University Press.

Pantsov, Alexander V. 2015. *Deng Xiaoping: A Revolutionary Life*. Oxford: Oxford University Press.

Parrott, Bruce. 1983. *Politics and Technology in the Soviet Union*. Cambridge, MA: MIT Press.

Parrott, Bruce. 1985. "Soviet Foreign Policy, Internal Politics, and Trade with the West." In *Trade, Technology, and Soviet-American Relations*, edited by Bruce Parrott. Bloomington: Indiana University Press.

Paterson, Thomas G. 1973. *Soviet-American Confrontation: Postwar Reconstruction and the Origins of the Cold War*. Baltimore: Johns Hopkins University Press.

Pechatnov, Vladimir O. 1995. "The Big Three After World War II: New Documents on Soviet Thinking about Post-War Relations with the United States and Great Britain." Cold War International History Project, Washington, DC, working paper no. 13.

Pechatnov, Vladimir O. 1999. "'The Allies Are Pressing on You to Break Your Will . . .': Foreign Policy Correspondence between Stalin and Molotov and Other Politburo Members, September 1945–December 1946." Cold War in International History Project, Washington, DC, working paper no. 26.

Perez, Louis A. Jr. 1998. *The War of 1898: The United States and Cuba in History and Historiography*. Durham: University of North Carolina Press.

Perkins, Bradford. 1961. *Prologue to War, 1805–1812*. Berkeley: University of California Press.

Peterson, Paul E. 1994. *The President, the Congress, and the Making of Foreign Policy*. Norman: University of Oklahoma Press.

Philpott, Daniel. 2010. *Revolutions in Sovereignty*. Princeton, NJ: Princeton University Press.

Pincus, Steve. 2005. *1688: The First Modern Revolution*. New Haven, CT: Yale University Press.

Pletcher, David M. 1973. *The Diplomacy of Annexation: Texas, Oregon, and the Mexican War*. Columbia: University of Missouri Press.

Pletcher, David M. 1998. *The Diplomacy of Trade and Investment: American Economic Expansion in the Hemisphere, 1865–1900*. Columbia: University of Missouri Press.

Pletcher, David M. 2001. *The Diplomacy of Involvement: American Economic Expansion across the Pacific, 1784–1900*. Columbia: University of Missouri Press.

Plokhy, S. M. 2010. *Yalta: The Price of Peace*. New York: Vintage.

Plummer, Brenda Gayle. 1988. *Haiti and the Great Powers, 1902–1915*. Baton Rouge: Louisiana State University Press.

Poast, Paul. 2019. "Beyond the 'Sinew of War': The Political Economy of Security as a Subfield." *Annual Review of Political Science*.

Posen, Barry R. 1984. *The Sources of Military Doctrine*. Ithaca, NY: Cornell University Press.

Posen, Barry R. 2014. *Restraint*. Ithaca, NY: Cornell University Press.

Potter, Philip, and Chen Wang. 2019. "Governmental Responses to Terrorism in Autocracies: Evidence from China." *British Journal of Political Science* 52, no. 1.

Potter, Philip, and Chen Wang. 2022. *Zero Tolerance: Repression and Violence on China's New Silk Road*. Cambridge: Cambridge University Press.

Powell, Robert. 2006. "War as a Commitment Problem." *International Organization* 60, no. 1.

Prados, John. 1986. *The Soviet Estimate: U.S. Intelligence Analysis and Soviet Strategic Forces.* Princeton, NJ: Princeton University Press.

Pratt, Julius W. 1964. *Expansionists of 1898: The Acquisition of Hawaii and the Spanish Islands.* Chicago: Quadrangle.

Pratt, Julius W., Vincent P. DeSantis, and Joseph M. Siracusa. 1979. *A History of United States Foreign Policy.* 4th ed. Englewood Cliffs, NJ: Prentice-Hall.

Preston, Andrew. 2016. "The Religious Turn in American Diplomatic History." In *Explaining the History of American Foreign Relations,* edited by Frank Costigliola and Michael J. Hogan. 3rd ed. Cambridge: Cambridge University Press.

Ralph, J. G. 1999. "Security Dilemmas and the End of the Cold War." *Review of International Studies* 25, no. 4.

Restad, Hilde Eliassen. 2015. *American Exceptionalism.* London: Routledge.

Ripsman, Norrin, Jeffrey W. Talliaferro, and Steven Lobell. 2016. *Neoclassical Realist Theory of International Politics.* Oxford: Oxford University Press.

Robinson, John. 2021. *The Great Red Fleet: China's Port Call Diplomacy.* PhD Dissertation, University of Virginia, Department of Politics.

Rosato, Sebastian. 2021. *Intentions in Great Power Politics: Uncertainty and the Roots of Conflict.* New Haven, CT: Yale University Press.

Rose, Gideon. 1998. "Neoclassical Realism and Theories of Foreign Policy." *World Politics* 51, no. 1.

Rosecrance, Richard, and Arthur Stein. 1993. *The Domestic Sources of Grand Strategy.* Ithaca, NY: Cornell University Press.

Rotter, Andrew J. 1987. *The Path to Vietnam: Origins of the American Commitment to Southeast Asia.* Ithaca, NY: Cornell University Press.

Rubin, Barry. 1980. *Paved with Good Intentions: The American Experience and Iran.* Oxford: Oxford University Press.

Russett, Bruce. 1993. *Grasping the Democratic Peace.* Princeton, NJ: Princeton University Press.

Russett, Bruce, John R. Oneal, and David R. Davis. 1998. "The Third Leg of the Kantian Tripod for Peace: International Organizations and Militarized Disputes, 1950–85." *International Organization* 52, no. 3.

Schaffer, Mark. 2012. "Individual and Group Decision Making." In *Routledge Handbook of American Foreign Policy,* edited by Steven W. Hook and Christopher M. Jones. New York: Routledge.

Schaller, Michael. 1985. *The American Occupation of Japan: The Origins of Cold War in Asia.* Oxford: Oxford University Press.

Schelling, Thomas. 1966. *Arms and Influence.* New Haven, CT: Yale University Press.

Schlesinger, Arthur. 1918. *The Colonial Merchants and the American Revolution.* London: P. S. King and Sons.

Schoonover, Thomas D. 2003. *Uncle Sam's War of 1898 and the Origins of Globalization.* Lawrence: University Press of Kansas.

Schultz, George. 1993. *Turmoil and Triumph.* New York: Scribner's Sons.

Selverstone, Marc J. 2022. *The Kennedy Withdrawal: Camelot and the American Commitment to Vietnam.* Cambridge, MA: Harvard University Press.

Service, Robert. 2015. *The End of the Cold War: 1985–1999.* New York: PublicAffairs.

Shambaugh, David. 2013. *China Goes Global: The Partial Power.* Oxford: Oxford University Press.

Sherman, Martin J. 1987. *A World Destroyed: Hiroshima and the Origins of the Arms Race.* New York: Vintage.

Sherry, Michael S. 1977. *Preparing for the Next War.* New Haven, CT: Yale University Press.

Shifrinson, Joshua R. Itzkowitz. 2018. *Rising Titans, Falling Giants: How Great Powers Exploit Power Shifts.* Ithaca, NY: Cornell University Press.

Shirk, Susan L. 2007. *China: Fragile Superpower.* New York: Oxford University Press.

Shirk, Susan L. 2023. *Overreach: How China Derailed Its Peaceful Rise.* Oxford: Oxford University Press.

Shoup, Lawrence, and William Minter. 2004. *Imperial Brain Trust: The Council on Foreign Relations and United States Foreign Policy.* New York: Author's Choice.

Silverstone, Scott. 2004. *Divided Union: The Politics of War in the Early American Republic.* Ithaca, NY: Cornell University Press.

Simms, Brendan. 2008. *Three Victories and a Defeat: The Rise and Fall of the First British Empire, 1714–1783.* New York: Basic.

Skocpol, Theda. 1979. *States and Social Revolutions.* Cambridge: Cambridge University Press.

Smith, John Edward. 2007. *FDR.* New York: Random House.

Smith, Page. 1962. *John Adams.* 2 vols. New York: Doubleday.

Smith, Peter H. 2012. *Talons of the Eagle: Latin America, the United States and the World.* Oxford: Oxford University Press.

Smith, Tony. 2017. *Why Wilson Matters: The Origins of American Liberal Internationalism and Its Crisis Today.* Princeton, NJ: Princeton University Press.

Snyder, Jack. 1991. *Myths of Empire: Domestic Politics and International Ambition.* Ithaca, NY: Cornell University Press.

Snyder, Jack. 2000. *From Voting to Violence: Democratization and Nationalist Conflict.* New York: Norton.

Spaniel, William, and Michael Poznansky. 2020. "Bad-Faith Cooperation." *International Interactions* 46, no. 4.

Spykman, Nicolas. (1942) 2007. *America's Strategy in World Politics: The United States and the Balance of Power.* Abingdon, UK: Routledge.

Spykman, Nicolas. (1943) 1969. *The Geography of Peace.* North Haven, CT: Archon Books.

Stern, Philip, and Carl Wennerlind. 2013. *Mercantilism Reimagined: Political Economy in Early Modern Britain and Its Empire.* Oxford: Oxford University Press.

Stevenson, Richard W. 1985. *The Rise and Fall of Détente.* Urbana: University of Illinois Press.

Stoll, Ira. 2008. *Samuel Adams: A Life.* New York: Free Press.

Stourzh, Gerard. 1969. *Benjamin Franklin and American Foreign Policy.* 2nd ed. Chicago: University of Chicago Press.

Swaine, Michael D. 2011. *America's Challenge: Engaging a Rising China in the Twenty-First Century.* Washington, DC: Carnegie Endowment for International Peace.

Tang, Shiping. 2010. *A Theory of Security Strategy for Our Time: Defensive Realism.* London: Palgrave Macmillan.

Taubman, William. 2003. *Khrushchev: The Man and his Era.* New York: Norton.

Thomas, Evan. 2010. *The War Lovers: Roosevelt, Lodge, Hearst, and the Rush to Empire, 1898*. Boston: Little, Brown.

Toll, Ian W. 2008. *Six Frigates: The Epic Founding of the U.S. Navy*. New York: Norton.

Tombs, Robert, and Isabelle Tombs. 2007. *That Sweet Enemy: The French and the British from the Sun King to the Present*. New York: Knopf.

Trachtenberg, Marc. 1999. *A Constructed Peace: The Making of the European Settlement, 1945–1963*. Princeton, NJ: Princeton University Press.

Trachtenberg, Marc. 2006. *The Craft of International History*. Princeton, NJ: Princeton University Press.

Trager, Robert. 2011. "Multidimensional Diplomacy." *International Organization* 65, no.3.

Trager, Robert. 2017. *Diplomacy: Communication and the Origins of International Order*. Cambridge: Cambridge University Press.

Trubowitz, Peter. 1998. *Defining the National Interest: Conflict and Change in American Foreign Policy*. Chicago: University of Chicago Press.

Trubowitz, Peter. 2011. *Politics and Strategy: Partisan Ambition and American Statecraft*. Princeton, NJ: Princeton University Press.

Truman, Harry S. 1955. *Year of Decisions*. Garden City, NY: Doubleday.

Tuchman, Barbara. 1958. *The Zimmermann Telegram*. New York: Macmillan.

Tuchman, Barbara. 1985. *March of Folly: From Troy to Vietnam*. New York: Random House.

Tucker, Robert W. 2007. *Woodrow Wilson and the Great War*. Charlottesville: University of Virginia Press.

Tucker, Robert W., and David C. Hendrickson. 1982. *The Fall of the First British Empire: Origins of the Wars of American Independence*. Baltimore: John Hopkins University Press.

Tucker, Robert W., and David C. Hendrickson. 1990. *Empire of Liberty: The Statecraft of Thomas Jefferson*. Oxford: Oxford University Press.

Tumulty, Joseph P. 1921. *Woodrow Wilson as I Know Him*. Ann Arbor: University of Michigan Press.

Tyler, Patrick. 1999. *The Great Wall: Six Presidents and China*. New York: Public Affairs.

Ulam, Adam. 1983. *Dangerous Relations: The Soviet Union in World Politics, 1970–1982*. New York: Oxford University Press.

Van Alstyne, Richard W. 1965. *The Rising American Empire*. Chicago: Quadrangle.

Van Evera, Stephen. 1999. *Causes of War*. Ithaca, NY: Cornell University Press.

Vaughn, James M. 2019. *The Politics of Empire at the Accession of George III: The East India Company and the Crisis and Transformation of Britain's Imperial State*. New Haven, CT: Yale University Press.

Vogel, Ezra F. 2011. *Deng Xiaoping and the Transformation of China*. Cambridge, MA: Harvard University Press.

Volten, Peter. 1982. *Brezhnev's Peace Program*. Boulder, CO: Westview.

Walker, Martin. 1987. *The Waking Giant: The Soviet Union under Gorbachev*. London: Abacus.

Walt, Stephen M. 1987. *The Origins of Alliances*. Ithaca, NY: Cornell University Press.

Walt, Stephen M. 1996. *Revolutions and War*. Ithaca, NY: Cornell University Press.

Walt, Stephen M. 2018. *The Hell of Good Intentions*. New York: Farrar, Straus and Giroux.

Waltz, Kenneth. 1970. "The Myth of Interdependence." In *The Multinational Corporation*, edited by Charles P. Kindleberger. Cambridge: Cambridge University Press.

Waltz, Kenneth. 1979. *Theory of International Politics*. New York: Random House.

Warden, G. B. 1970. *Boston, 1689–1776*. Boston: Little, Brown.

Weeks, Jessica. 2014. *Dictators at War and Peace*. Ithaca, NY: Cornell University Press.

Weeks, William Earl. 1992. *John Quincy Adams and American Global Empire*. Lexington: University of Kentucky Press.

Weinberg, Albert K. (1935) 1963. *Manifest Destiny: A Study of Nationalist Expansionism in American History*. Chicago: Quadrangle.

Weisiger, Alex. 2013. *Logics of War: Explanations for Limited and Unlimited Conflicts*. Ithaca, NY: Cornell University Press.

Welch, Richard E. Jr. 1979. *Response to Imperialism: The United States and the Philippine-American War, 1899–1902*. Chapel Hill: University of North Carolina.

Wertheim, Stephen. 2020. *Tomorrow the World: The Birth of U.S. Global Supremacy*. Cambridge, MA: Belknap Press.

Wheelan, Joseph. 2003. *Jefferson's War: American First War on Terror, 1801–1805*. New York: Carroll and Graf.

Widenor, Willam C. 1980. *Henry Cabot Lodge and the Search for an American Foreign Policy*. Berkeley: University of California Press.

William, Ian. 2005. *Rum: A Social and Social History of the Real Spirit of 1776*. New York: Nation.

Williams, William Appleman. 1962. *The Tragedy of American Diplomacy*. Rev. ed. New York: Dell.

Wohlforth, William C., ed. 2003. *Cold War Endgame: Oral History, Analysis, and Debates*. University Park: Pennsylvania State University Press.

Wolford, Scott, Dan Reiter, and Clifford J. Carrubba. 2011. "Information, Commitment, and War." *Journal of Conflict Resolution* 55, no. 4.

Wood, Gordon S. (1969) 1998. *The Creation of the American Republic, 1776–1787*. Chapel Hill: University of North Carolina Press.

Wood, Gordon S. 1991. *The Radicalism of the American Revolution*. New York: Vintage.

Wood, Gordon S. 2011. *Empire of Liberty: A History of the Early Republic, 1789–1815*. Oxford: Oxford University Press.

Wright, Esmond. 1986. *Franklin of Philadelphia*. Cambridge, MA: Harvard University Press.

Yarhi-Milo, Keren. 2014. *Knowing the Adversary*. Princeton, NJ: Princeton University Press.

Yarhi-Milo, Keren. 2018. *Who Fights for Reputation? The Psychology of Leaders in International Conflict*. Princeton, NJ: Princeton University Press.

Ye, Min. 2020. *The Belt Road and Beyond: State-Mobilized Globalization in China, 1998–2018*. Cambridge: Cambridge University Press.

Yegorova, Natalia I. 1996. "The 'Iran Crisis' of 1945–46: A View from the Russian Archives." Cold War International History Project, Washington, DC, working paper no.15.

Yergin, Daniel. 1991. *The Prize: The Epic Quest for Oil, Money, and Power*. New York: Simon and Schuster.

Yoder, Brandon K. 2019a. "Uncertainty, Shifting Power and Credible Signals in U.S.-China Relations: Why the 'Thucydides Trap' is Real, but Limited." *Journal of Chinese Political Science* 24, no. 1.

Yoder, Brandon K. 2019b. "Retrenchment as a Screening Mechanism: Power Shifts, Strategic Withdrawal, and Credible Signals." *American Journal of Political Science* 63, no. 1.

Yoder, Brandon K., 2019c. "Hedging for Better Bets: Power Shifts, Credible Signals, and Preventive Conflict." *Journal of Conflict Resolution* 63, no. 4.

Yoder, Brandon K. 2020. "How Credible Are China's Foreign Policy Signals? IR Theory and the Debate about China's Intentions." *Chinese Journal of International Politics* 13, no. 4.

Yoder, Brandon K., and William Spaniel. 2022. "Costly Concealment: Secret Foreign Policymaking, Transparency, and Credible Reassurance." *International Organization* 76, no. 4.

Zakaria, Fareed. 1998. *From Wealth to Power: The Unusual Origins of America's World Role*. Princeton, NJ: Princeton University Press.

Zelikow, Philip, and Condoleezza Rice. 1997. *Germany Unified and Europe Transformed*. Cambridge, MA: Harvard University Press.

Zhao, Dingxin. 2004. *The Power of Tiananmen: State-Society Relations and the 1989 Beijing Student Movement*. Chicago: University of Chicago Press.

Zhao, Ziyang 2009. *Prisoner of the State: The Secret Journal of Zhao Ziyang*. New York: Simon and Schuster.

Zimmermann, Warren. 2004. *The First Great Triumph*. New York: Farrar, Straus and Giroux.

Zoellick, Robert. 2021. *America in the World: A History of U.S. Diplomacy*. New York: Hachette.

Zubok, Vladislav. 2009. *A Failed Empire: The Soviet Union in the Cold War from Stalin to Gorbachev*. Chapel Hill: University of North Carolina Press.

# INDEX

Abdelal, Rawi, 149–50, 415n19

Adams, John, 67, 72, 83, 91, 109

Adams, John Quincy, 109, 114–16, 146, 172

Adams, Sam, 65–69, 81–85, 88, 90

alliances, 9, 12, 17, 24, 30, 39, 50, 58–59, 60, 88, 100, 111, 116–17, 146, 190, 193, 217, 219, 221, 225–27, 229, 233–34, 238, 241, 289, 300–301, 309, 350, 384, 387, 423n122, 424n8, 430n38

American Revolution. *See* War of Colonial Independence

Andropov, Yuri, 345–47. *See also* Gorbachev, Mikhail

Arbatov, Georgi, 347–48

arms buildups and arms racing, 3, 17, 20, 39, 49–50, 199, 201, 210, 219, 224, 226, 243, 286, 310–12, 319, 324–25, 330–34, 339–40, 346–49, 351, 435n64

Austria, 8, 26, 96, 104, 202, 225, 229, 276, 278, 415n13, 423n111

Bailyn, Bernard, 64; recognition of role of power (1763–76), 406n8

Baker, James A., 349–50, 424n129, 438n132, 438n144

Ball, George, 335

Barbary War, First, 96, 409n5

bargaining model of war, 402n37, 404n48. *See also* Fearon, James; Kydd, Andrew; Yoder, Brandon

Beckley, Michael, 359–60, 372–73, 439n5, 440n14, 441n24, 442n37

Belt and Road Initiative, ix, 2, 31, 43, 234, 355, 361, 364, 370, 376, 382–83, 387, 389–90, 440n7. *See also* China (2007–present)

Berlin Crisis (1948–49), 288–89, 292–94

Berlin Crisis (1958–61), 333–37

bipolarity. *See* polarity

Braisted, William, 211

Brands, Hal, 359–60, 372–73, 439n5, 440n14, 441n24, 442n37

Brezhnev, Leonid, 336, 339–42, 346–47, 435n83, 436n96, 436n99

Britain (1708–1815), 6, 20, 12–13, 63–93, 94–114, 367, 406n4, 406n6, 406nn8–10, 407nn16–17, 407n24, 408nn35–36, 408n48, 409n53, 409n10. *See also* War of Colonial independence; War of 1812

Britain (1816–95), 6, 12, 30–31, 37, 45, 96, 114–41, 402n27, 404n50, 409n7, 409n10, 411n42, 411n59. *See also* Civil War (1861–65), American; Mexico-American War; Venezuela

Britain (1896–1913), 7, 24–25, 28, 37, 45, 145–62, 416n61, 419n6, 419n11. *See also* Germany (1896–1917)

Britain (1914–18), 191–94, 196–98, 200–211, 218–31, 419n11, 419n21, 420nn30–31, 422n95. *See also* Wilson, Woodrow; Germany (1896–1917)

Britain (1919–42), 8, 18, 232–42, 249–52, 257, 261, 265–66, 274–81, 290–93, 443n54. *See also* Second World War, Europe

Britain (1943–56), 305–17, 330, 368, 382, 425n38, 428n111, 431n68, 432n84. *See also* Churchill, Winston; Iranian Crisis, 1953; Suez Crisis, 1956

Britain (pre-1707 England), 6, 19–20, 22

Britain (1957–91), 36, 323, 330–31, 356

Brooks, Stephen, 436n101

Brown, Roger, 112–13

Buchanan, James, 131–38, 146, 413n104, 414n119

Bulgaria, 246, 268–80, 428n122

Bullitt, William, 250–51

Bush, George H.W., 321, 347–52, 372, 378–79, 436n103, 438n136, 439n6. *See also* Gulf War

Bush, George W., 439n6. *See also* Iraq War

Buzan, Barry, 425n28

Byrnes, James, 265–66, 275–78, 283–84, 290, 427n95

Campbell, Charles, 162

Canada, 5, 12, 63, 73–75, 89, 96, 104, 110–14, 119, 140–41, 150, 222, 224, 368, 398n32, 407n26, 412n61, 444n63. *See also* War of 1812

Chamberlain, Neville, 18, 38, 237, 295

Cheney, Dick, 439n6

Chiang, Kai-shek, 253, 296, 376, 426n51

China (1830–1911), 6–7, 31, 69, 71, 95, 120, 128–29, 144–47, 157–58, 161, 164, 167–68, 186, 188; Opium War and, 378; Taiping Rebellion, 380

China (1912–49), 200, 210, 212, 223, 227, 234, 238, 240, 242, 244–47, 254, 273, 419n10, 425n38, 426n51; Truman-Stalin secret trade deal on (1945), 273, 284, 426n51

China (1949–76), 19–20, 24, 26, 42, 295–99, 301–3, 312, 321, 430n41. *See also* Mao Zedong

China (1977–90), 21, 360, 362–374. *See also* Tiananmen Square Crisis

China (1991–2006), 17, 26, 356, 360–61; post-1997 "going abroad," 378–79

China (2007–present), ix, 1–3, 6, 10, 13, 15, 21, 24–25, 31, 39, 41–44, 53, 64, 92, 234, 321, 352–53, 351–52; China Dream, 363, 372, 375, 442n38; dependence on semiconductors, 355, 360, 367–68, 384–86, 389–90,
393, 442n36; diminishing marginal returns and tie to Belt and Road Initiative, 26, 31, 36, 43, 234, 356, 358, 361, 366–67, 377, 387, 389–90, 440n7; end of "hide and bide," 53, 391; explanations for the collapse of Soviet Union, 379–80; "FDR's legacy" and, 356, 368, 382, 387, 390; fear of domestic instability, 355, 372–75, 380, 391–93, 443n42; goals of glory, question of, 441n23; Han control and, 381; lack of allies and, 382–83; naval buildup, 376–77; Obama "pivot" to Asia and, 355, 361, 368, 384, 441n16; oil dependence, 389; parallels with 1750–76 period, 63–64, 92–93; parallels with Far East 1931–41, 2, 22, 25–26, 39, 51, 370, 378, 389; parallels with Louis XIV's France, 391–92; population concentration, problem of, 393; recent tension with Japan, 376, 378, 384–85, 390; Renminbi as global currency, problems with, 383–84; technological catch-up for, 384–85; South China Sea and, 376–77, 387–81; Taiwan and, 442nn36–37, 443n43, 445n75; Trump and, 398n32; whether already peaking and declining, 359–60, 372–75, 439n5, 440n14, 441n24, 442n37. *See also* Beckley, Michael; Belt and Road Initiative; Brands, Hal; Hu, Jintao; Obama, Barack; Trump, Donald; Xi, Jinping

chips, computer. *See* semiconductors

Chubb, Andrew, 376

Churchill, Winston, 240, 263–64, 273–81, 322, 427n91, 428n109, 428n122

Civil War (1861–65), American, 141, 143, 148, 152, 159, 402n28, 405n61; dynamic realism and origins of, 415n13

Cold War, x, 2, 4, 9, 12–13, 353–53; ending of, 10, 20, 319–22, 345–53; ideological underpinnings of, 9, 19–20, 42, 45, 47–48, 243, 245, 255, 271, 283, 287–88, 292, 295, 320–21, 326, 345, 442n38; lessons of, for U.S.-China relations, 2, 355–56, 362, 370, 380–82, 387–93; origins of, 9, 232–35,

242–85; Roosevelt's bases around the Soviet Union, 251–53; seeking détente within, 9–10, 322–44; William Bullitt's 1943 analysis, 250–51. See also *individual cases and specific U.S. presidents*

collective security, 7, 190–91, 193, 204, 222–24, 227, 229–30, 241, 283, 422n100. *See also* League of Nations; Wilson, Woodrow

commercial liberalism. *See* liberalism

commitment problems, 50, 224, 256, 398n24, 404n48, 409n53. *See also* defensive realism; signaling arguments

common knowledge assumption, weakness of, 38–39

crisis escalation, 2, 15, 50, 56, 58, 65, 76, 85, 90–91, 94, 100–103, 108, 115–20, 126, 131, 135, 137–139, 144–45, 162–64, 172–74, 197–98, 206, 215, 219, 284, 289, 291–95, 300–301, 305–8, 316–17, 333–37, 353, 356, 367, 369, 387, 403n37, 429n132, 429n5

Cuban Missile Crisis, 2, 56, 319, 333–37, 432n10, 434n52

cultural distance, 35, 42–48, 95, 141, 245, 271, 283, 318, 380–81, 392

Czechoslovakia, 18, 256–57, 269, 271, 295, 310–11, 400n6

Dallek, Robert, 248

Daniels, Josephus, 198, 211, 221–22, 228

defensive realism, ix, 3–4, 10, 14–17, 21–22; character type, use of, 36; common knowledge assumption, use of, 39, 401n20; dependent variables, failure to explain extremes of, 53, 403n40, 404n49; First World War and, 422n100; Gorbachev and, 400n8; insights of, ix, 3, 10–17, 31, 34, 39, 42, 49; irrationality of adversary, need to include potential, 39–40, 401n20; weaknesses of, 3, 17, 35, 37, 39, 42, 49, 49, 53, 398n23, 401n20, 403n42, 404n49; static nature of, 403n42; uncertainty about the future, downplaying of, 42. *See also*

crisis escalation; "isms," rejection of; security dilemma; signaling arguments; spiraling, problems of

Deng, Xiaoping, 21, 25, 27, 53, 374–75, 378–79, 391. *See also* China (1977–90); China (1991–2006)

deterrence model, 355, 370, 374. *See also* Jervis, Robert

Dillon, Douglas, 325, 328–32, 433n15, 433n26

diminishing marginal returns, 26, 29–31, 33, 51; China and, 356, 358, 377, 390. *See also* dynamic realism

diversionary motives, 55, 59, 405n56

dollar diplomacy, 194

Dominican Republic, 429n5

domino logic, 9, 289, 295–97. *See also* resolve

Doshi, Rush, 375, 443n43

dynamic realism: assumptions of, x, 35, 38, 44, 52, 54–55, 397n18, 398n34, 399nn1–2, 400n4, 400n6, 400n14, 401n21, 402n37, 404n47, 406n7, 441n15; definition of security as about both invasion and external subversion of social order, 2, 6, 15, 19–20, 27–29, 33, 42, 50, 112, 124, 234, 267, 363, 380, 388, 395n3, 401n16; diminishing marginal returns and, 26, 29–31, 33, 51; economies of scale and, 25, 29–30, 33, 43–44, 51–52; expected probability of survival as metric for state ends, 40; feedback loops in, 10, 14–15, 21–22, 31, 48–55, 246, 327, 403n43; as fusion of offensive and defensive realisms, 3, 14–15, 49–54, 60; leaning of states, given external situation, 15, 41, 50, 52–55, 155–56, 409n1; offensive realist baseline in, 18, 40, 96, 115, 144, 153, 249, 395n2, 403n45; rationality and, ix–x, 10, 17, 21–22, 24, 31, 33–44, 47–55, 61, 356–57, 362–65, 367–71, 386, 388, 391, 398n34, 399n1, 400n14, 401n16, 401nn18–19, 402n37, 403n43, 404n49, 441n15, 442n27; tensions and, inherent, vii, 2, 15, 25, 32, 53–54, 94, 155, 357;

dynamic realism (*continued*)
trade-off logic within, viii, 3, 7, 15, 18, 25,
31–32, 34, 40–41, 48–54; variation in
other's motives, importance of, 39, 42. *See also*
arms buildups and arms racing; crisis
escalation; economic power spheres;
feedback loops; "isms," rejection of;
signaling arguments; spiraling, problems of;
trade expectations; trade-security dilemma

economic power spheres, ix–x, 2–5, 8–11, 15,
19–33, 40, 44–45, 47, 50–52, 54–55, 68,
94–95, 98, 114–16, 118, 141–44, 149, 153–57,
1612, 162, 186, 191–96, 1999–207, 209–10,
212–13, 215–17, 219, 222–25, 229–30, 233–40,
242–52, 255, 258, 262–63, 269, 273, 276,
22–84, 287–89, 291–92, 294–99, 304–5,
317–18, 320–23, 325–27, 347, 349, 255–57,
361, 364, 367–68, 370–72, 376–79, 382–85,
387, 389, 395n3, 398n34, 399n1, 409n10,
416n54, 419n7, 419n21, 421n60, 424n5,
425n38, 426n46. *See also* dynamic realism;
realms of trade, three
economies of scale, 25, 29–30, 33, 43–44,
51–52; China and, 387. *See also* dynamic
realism
Edelstein, David, 403n42
Eden, Anthony, 251, 275, 278, 310, 312–15
Egypt, 46, 238, 280, 282, 305–6, 310–17,
341–43, 432n84
Eisenhower, Dwight D., 9, 289, 298–99,
305–18, 320–38, 389, 432n84, 432n10,
433n32. *See also* Berlin Crisis (1958–61);
Cold War
Elman, Colin, 410n24
externalist approach, 15–16, 46, 60, 396n14,
396n16; dynamic realism as, 16, 46, 60.
*See also* defensive realism; dynamic
realism; offensive realism

Fearon, James, 398n24, 402n37, 404n48,
409n53
feedback loops, 10, 21–22, 31–32, 34, 48–53,
327, 403n43, 442n28. *See also* arms

buildups and arms racing; crisis
escalation; security dilemma; spiraling,
problems of; trade-security dilemma
Fillmore, Millard, 146–47
First World War, U.S. entry into. *See* Wilson,
Woodrow
Fordham, Benjamin, 229, 424n130
France, 19, 25, 67, 70–78, 89, 91, 96, 98–103,
104–13, 116–18, 127–31, 133, 138–40, 149,
153, 155, 157–61, 172, 192–93, 205, 218–19,
221, 228–30, 238–39, 246, 251, 256–58,
263–64, 269, 279, 281–82, 293, 305, 310,
316, 331, 392, 407n31, 409n9, 410n16,
411n57, 414n119, 420n30, 424n8. *See also*
Napoleon I

Garthoff, Raymond, 340, 344
George, Alexander, 430n34
Germany (1870–95), 7, 144–45, 149–50, 155–57,
161, 164, 415n24, 444n74
Germany (1896–1917), 8, 12, 25, 28, 189–92,
193–212, 213–31, 386–87, 405n56, 419n6,
419n21, 420n33, 422n87, 422n91, 423n111,
424n127, 424n129, 440n14
Germany (1918–32), 37, 400n11
Germany (1933–44), 8, 18, 29, 37, 41, 232–42,
246–50, 264, 267, 282, 285, 369, 371, 387,
391, 400n6, 424n8. *See also* Second World
War, Europe
Germany (1944–45), 246, 263–58, 263–67,
269, 273–77, 281–82, 369–69
Germany (1946–50), 288–89, 292–94.
*See also* Berlin Crisis (1948–49)
Germany (1951–89), 296, 333–37, 425n29.
*See also* Berlin Crisis (1958–61)
Germany (1990–present), 349–51, 438n144.
*See also* Gorbachev, Mikhail
Gilpin, Robert, 21, 377
Glaser, Charles, 34, 400n14, 401n18
Gorbachev, Mikhail, 20, 47, 320–31, 331,
345–52, 365, 370, 372, 379–80, 391, 400n8,
436n103, 437n104, 437n109, 437n112,
438n125, 438n138, 438n144, 442nn26–27
Gowa, Joanne, 399n43, 404n50

Graebner, Norman, 130

Greece, 116, 246, 275–76, 284, 292, 382, 428n109

greed as a motive for war, 13, 17, 28, 37, 39, 49, 51, 82, 97, 103, 111, 122, 195, 400n14, 401n18

Greene, Jack, 406n8

Grew, Joseph, 260–62, 270–71, 427n74, 427n83

Grey, Lord, 197, 202, 204–5, 219, 420n31, 420n44

Gulf War, 350; origins of, 439n6

Haas, Mark, 19, 34–35, 45, 399n3, 402nn27–29

Haiti, 73, 80, 101–2, 148, 205, 207–8, 421n55

Hamilton, Alexander, 14, 20–21, 98, 112, 409n2, 409n10

Harriman, Averell, 251, 254–55, 257–58, 261–62, 269–290, 308, 427n78

Harrison, Benjamin, 152, 156, 415n24

Hawaii, 12, 128, 144, 148–56, 161–63, 165, 169, 186, 415n22, 417n76

Hearden, Patrick, 238

Herring, George, 261

Hietala, Thomas, 127, 129, 412n67

Hitler, Adolf, 8, 18, 38, 41, 60, 232–33, 236–37, 241–42, 246–50, 261, 267, 282, 371, 381, 391, 400n11, 400n14, 401n19

Hixson, Walter, 396n8

House, Edward, 190, 196–207, 215–16, 219–28. See also Wilson, Woodrow

Hu, Jintao, 387

Hu, Yaobang, 374

Hull, Cordell, 238, 242, 244, 252, 255

Hungary, 271, 275–76, 279–81, 428n122

Hunt, Michael, 396n8

India, 69, 71–73, 79, 83–88, 240, 297, 307, 311, 378, 389, 413n103

internalist approach, 16, 59–60, 66, 396n14, 396n16. See also liberalism

Iranian Crisis (1944), 252–53, 290

Iranian Crisis (1946), 253, 284, 290–92

Iranian Crisis (1953), 289, 304–10, 316–17, 431n58

Iraq War (2003), 185; origins of, 439n6. See also Bush, George W.

"isms," rejection of, 396n16

Israel, 305, 310–12, 316, 341–43

Italy, 1, 199, 220, 228, 246, 253, 257, 263, 275–76, 279, 282, 354, 428n122, 429n17

Jackson, Andrew, 14, 115, 119–121, 125, 412n85

Jackson-Vanik Amendment, 343, 347, 436n99, 438n136

Japan (1840–1918), 7, 25, 28, 31, 39, 128, 145, 147, 152–53, 156–57, 161–62, 169, 186, 416n57, 423n104

Japan (1919–44), 2, 7–8, 22, 29, 192–95, 200, 210–15, 217, 220–27, 218, 232, 236, 240, 242, 245–46, 249, 252–53. See also Second World War, Pacific

Japan (1945–90), 9, 20, 29, 31, 60, 260–62, 282–84; role in origins of U.S. involvement in Korean War, 299–303; role in origins of U.S. involvement in Vietnam, 9, 289–90, 295–299, 430n30.

Japan (1991–present), 376, 378, 382–85, 390, 444n61. See also China (2007–present)

Jefferson, Thomas, 96, 98, 101–3, 104–6, 107–8, 111–13, 115, 409n9, 410n27, 410n24, 411n36

Jentleson, Bruce, 328

Jervis, Robert, 34, 50, 355, 422n100. See also security dilemma; spiraling, problems of

Johnson, Andrew, 148

Johnson, Lyndon B., 296, 298. See also Vietnam War

Kagan, Robert, 396n8

Kaufman, Burton, 209, 421n60

Kearn, David, 399n2

Kennan, George, 291–92, 296

Kennedy, John F., 9, 296, 298–99, 320–21, 324, 334–37, 432n10, 434n52. *See also* Berlin Crisis (1958–61), Cuban Missile Crisis

Kennedy, Ross, 422n82

Keohane, Robert, 399n43, 404n50

Khan, Sulmann Wasif, 375

Khrushchev, Nikita, 26, 47, 310–11, 320–27, 230–36, 252, 432n10

Kim, Il-sung, 300, 303

Kimball, William, 163

Kissinger, Henry, 321, 327, 337, 339–47, 398n31, 424n3, 435n83, 436n89, 436n96, 439n149

Knorr, Klaus, 21

Korean War, 288–89, 294–96, 299–304

Kosygin, Alexei, 336, 339

Krasner, Stephen, 421n65, 424n5, 429n5

Kydd, Andrew, 34, 398n23, 402n37

LaFeber, Walter, 151, 159

Lansing, Robert, 191, 203, 206–8, 216, 218, 419n21, 422n100

Lascurettes, Kyle, 418n4

Layne, Christopher, 395n2, 395n7, 401n15, 405n58, 425n31

League of Nations, 18, 204, 223–24, 235–36, 420n44

Leffler, Melvyn, 292, 398n34, 425n29, 429n130

Levy, Jack, 396n12, 397n22

liberalism, x, 3–4, 7–9, 37, 44–46, 48; commercial liberalism, 120–21, 153, 187, 244, 288–89, 294–95, 299–300, 310, 320, 344, 383–84, 388–92, 418n122, 429n2; critics of, 18; democratic peace, evidence against, 163, 186–88, 205, 361; failure to explain sweep of American foreign policy, 14, 396n8; as internalist approach, 15–16, 60, 110–11, 113, 141, 243, 306, 310, 352, 396n16, 400n4; liberal hegemony after 1991, 4, 395n7; liberal international economic order, 20, 238, 240; liberal internationalism, vii,

14, 213, 229–36, 421n51; liberal states as threats to China, 362–63, 375–80, 441n18; liberal theories of American foreign policy, various, 60–62, 243, 247; liberal values in history, 67, 95, 97, 110–11, 113, 119, 141, 144–45, 187, 190, 205, 219, 232, 306, 316, 319, 345, 347, 402n27; spreading, 4, 7, 60, 224, 229, 375, 379–82, 388, 395n2, 441n18; trade and China's hoped-for liberalization, 441n18; Woodrow Wilson and, 190–91, 205. *See also* internalist approach; "isms," rejection of; *individual cases as tests of*

Lieven, Anatol, 396n8

Linkage, 258, 277, 321, 327, 332, 337, 339, 344, 386

Lodge, Henry Cabot, 145, 154, 158–65, 417n76

Louisiana Purchase, 101–3, 106, 112–13, 120, 140, 154

Louisiana Territory, 96, 101, 172

Mackie, John, 404n54

Madison, James, 6, 96–98, 102–4, 116–17, 410n29, 411n36, 411n42, 411n47

Mahan, Alfred Thayer, 7, 20–21, 128, 145, 156, 162–63, 183, 187, 211, 252, 387, 398n31, 416n37

Manchuria, 157, 164, 242, 253–54, 282, 284, 426n51

Mao Zedong, 19, 25, 27, 254, 295–96, 297–98, 300–303, 364, 374, 378–79, 385

Marks, Frederick, 409n10

McCloy, John, 256, 258

McKinley, William, 7, 144–47, 152, 154–88, 417n76. *See also* Spanish-American War (1898)

Mead, Walter Russell, 14

Mearsheimer, John, xi, 13, 16, 18–19, 24–25, 37, 395n2, 395n7, 397n20, 397n21, 398n34, 399n2, 401n15, 403n42, 442n35. *See also* offensive realism; worst-case assumption

Mercantilism, 7, 21, 67, 73–74, 98–99, 217, 219, 237–38, 248, 271, 284, 320, 338, 380, 387, 392, 402n27, 406n9, 407n29; market-based, 67, 73, 407n24; staples-based, 67, 73–76, 82, 86, 407n29. *See also* economic power spheres

Merk, Frederick, 145

methodology, 5, 11, 15, 36, 56–60; causal roles played by different factors, 57; INJS (individually necessary, jointly sufficient) bundles of factors, 57–59; Mackie on INUS research, 404n54; rare events research and, 55–56

Mexico, 6, 12, 60, 87, 97, 114–15, 121, 139, 145, 148, 192–93, 194–217, 223–27, 368, 398n32, 411n57, 413n88, 415n14, 419n6, 422n82. *See also* Polk, James K.; Tyler, John; Wilson, Woodrow

Mexico-American War, 6, 12, 60, 97, 114–16, 120, 127–41. *See also* Polk, James K.; Tyler, John

Mikoyan, Anatos, 328–29, 433n25

military-security dilemma, 51. *See also* arms buildups and arms racing; crisis escalation; security dilemma; spiraling, problems of

Miller, Benjamin, 395n7

Minter, William, 238, 430n27

Molotov, Vyacheslav, 254, 259, 267, 275–80, 290, 301–3

Monroe, James, 96–97, 102, 106–118, 128, 132, 191, 410n33, 411n42, 411n47

Monroe Doctrine, 96, 117–18, 128, 132, 149–51, 153, 191, 194, 196, 1999, 203, 210–11, 222, 224, 234, 419n21, 421n55

Morgenthau, Henry, 253, 255

Mossadeq, Mohammed, 306–10

multipolarity. *See* polarity

Napoleon I, 16, 98, 101–9, 140, 200, 229, 237, 411n40

Nasser, Gamal Abdel, 303, 306, 310–17

Nau, Henry, 14

Nelson, Eric, 406n6

neoclassical realism, 142, 395n7, 397n18, 404n51, 405n58, 425n29; dynamic realism as systemic framework for, 397n18, 404n51; limitations of, 395n7, 397n18; tie to liberalism, 425n29. *See also* defensive realism; "isms," rejection of; offensive realism

Nixon, Richard M., 321, 327, 337, 339–44, 439n149

North Atlantic Treaty Organization (NATO), 24, 60, 350; expansion, post-1991, 31, 398n25; unification of Germany (1990–91) and, 350, 438n144

Obama, Barack, 361, 368, 384, 441n16

offensive-defensive balance, 2, 55, 401n21, 403n40

offensive realism, ix, xi, 3–4, 10, 14–17; American foreign policy, view of, 4, 395n7; backsliding and character in, 38, 400n11; character type of adversary, downplaying of, 32–39; China, problems explaining, 53, 397n20, 441n18; commerce, discounting of, 18–19, 24–25; democratic peace, curious acceptance of, 400n11; dependent variables, failure to explain extremes of, 53, 404n49; insights of, 3, 15, 17–18, 21, 37, 115, 142, 398n24, 403n45; limited-aims revisionists, ignoring of, 403n45; military power, focus on, 17, 22; security dilemma and spiraling issues, downplaying of, 7, 21–22, 34; shared rationality, problematic assumption of, 38–39; as "special case" of dynamic realism, xi, 60, 115–16, 405n57; static nature of, 403n42; "stopping power of water" assumption, error of, 395n2; on trade's link to war, 320; vulnerability versus relative gains, failure to see tension between, 19, 24–25; worst case assumption of, problem with, 16–17, 37–39, 369, 397n21, 398n34, 399n2, 403n42, 403n45. *See also* defensive realism; dynamic realism; "isms," rejection of; Mearsheimer, John; neoclassical realism offensive realist baseline, 18, 40, 96, 115–16, 144, 395n2, 403n45

Offner, John, 417n76

Oren, Ido, 419n6

Ostend Manifesto, 414n9

Owen, John, 46, 61

Pacific War 1941–45. *See* Second World War, Pacific

Page, Walter, 200, 202–3, 219–20

Palmerston, Lord, 119–20

Panama Canal, 7, 12, 146, 151, 163, 187, 196–97, 208, 211, 223, 278, 416n61, 424n129

Parrott, Bruce, 344

Peel, Robert, 130, 134

Pincus, Steve, 406n10

Pitt, William, 73, 75–76, 81–82, 86, 88, 89, 92, 407n24, 407n26, 408n36

Pletcher, David, 412n67, 414n114

Poland, 237, 256–61, 268–71, 274, 277, 281, 285, 312, 427n66. *See also* Cold War; Second World War, Europe

polarity, viii, 1, 55, 153, 233–34, 239, 358, 411n59, 434n42, 440n8, 440n11; bipolarity, concerns within, 233, 239, 243, 282, 358, 434n42, 440n11; China's worry about emerging bipolarity, 440n8; historical multipolar Europe as benefit for United States, 153, 192, 197, 204, 234, 238–39, 411n59, 419n7, 440n8, 440n11; multipolarity as spur to trade, 399n43. *See also* dynamic realism

Polk, James K., 6–7, 97, 115, 121–40, 146, 167, 412n67, 413n88, 413n95, 413nn103–104, 414n106

Posen, Barry, 395n7

Potter, Philip, 443n42

Powell, Colin, 439n6

Preston, Andrew, 396n8

preventive war, viii, 46, 56, 59, 220, 285, 310, 337, 372, 396n12, 397n22, 403n42, 405n56

problem of the future, 50, 403n41

propelling factors, role of, 5, 11, 12, 16, 19, 36, 39, 55–59, 61–62, 66, 92, 95, 97, 101, 103, 111, 120, 133, 144, 154, 160, 186, 188, 230, 232, 294, 389, 406n7, 421n60, 444n73. *See also* methodology

Prussia, 19, 104, 153

Putin, Vladimir, 354, 386, 388

Quasi-War (1798–1800), 96, 101, 140

Quebec, 73–75, 82, 408n47

Quebec Act (1774), 88–89, 408n47

realms of trade, three, 22–34, 42, 50–54, 62–63, 68, 92, 94–95, 140, 144, 186, 230, 233, 246, 282, 287, 293, 294, 304, 317, 323, 329, 356, 384, 399n1. *See also* dynamic realism; economic power spheres

resolve, 34, 36, 48, 89, 92, 119, 226, 265, 296, 300, 339, 351, 356, 320, 374, 393, 400n7, 404n48. *See also* defensive realism; domino logic; Fearon, James; signaling arguments

revisionism, neo-Marxist, 4, 6, 13, 28, 160, 187, 229, 232–33, 243, 287, 395n3, 424n4

revisionist powers, 18–19, 37–39, 337, 392. *See also* dynamic realism; offensive realism; offensive realist baseline

Romania, 246, 268–80, 428n122

Roosevelt, Franklin D., 5, 8, 12, 60, 232–38, 241–58, 282–84, 368; "FDR's legacy," 356, 368, 382, 387, 390. *See also* Cold War; Second World War, Europe

Roosevelt, Theodore, 145, 154, 158–65, 204, 230. *See also* Panama Canal; Spanish-American War (1898)

Rosato, Sebastian, 19, 399n2, 403n42. *See also* offensive realism

Rotter, Andrew, 296, 298

Rush, Doshi, 335–37

Sadat, Anwar, 242. *See also* Egypt; Nixon, Richard M.; Yom Kippur War (1973)

Schaller, Michael, 296

Schelling, Thomas, 445n75

Schlesinger, Arthur (Sr.), 86–87

Schultz, George, 347–48. *See also* Cold War

Second World War, Europe, 8, 232–34, 235–42. *See also* Germany (1933–44); Hitler, Adolf; Roosevelt, Franklin D.

Second World War, Pacific, 2, 8, 232–33, 236, 240–42. *See also* Japan (1919–44)

security dilemma, 10, 17, 21–22, 34–35, 40, 48–53, 119, 322, 371, 397n21, 398n34. *See also* arms buildups and arms racing; crisis escalation; defensive realism; dynamic realism; Glaser, Charles; Jervis, Robert; Kydd, Andrew; military-security dilemma; spiraling, problems of; trade-security dilemma

semiconductors, 355, 360, 367–68, 384–86, 389–90, 393, 442n36. *See also* China (2007–present)

Shifrinson, Joshua, 436n103

Shirk, Susan, 376

Shoup, Lawrence, 238, 430n27

signaling arguments, 37, 39, 42, 321, 332, 339, 347, 352, 356, 386–87, 389, 398n23, 401n20, 402n37, 432n2, 437n121, 438n136, 445n76. *See also* defensive realism; Glaser, Charles; Jervis, Robert; Kydd, Andrew; Yoder, Brandon

Skocpol, Theda, 396n10

Spain, 7, 12, 19, 83, 95–96, 101–3, 115–16, 140, 143, 152, 155, 158–60, 162–88, 274–75, 409n3. *See also* Louisiana Purchase; Monroe Doctrine; Spanish-American War (1898)

Spanish-American War (1898), 7, 94, 142–45, 152, 154–88, 416n52, 417n81, 417n90; as evidence against democratic peace, 163, 186–88. *See also* Lodge, Henry Cabot; Mahan, Alfred Thayer; McKinley, William; Roosevelt, Theodore

spheres of influence, economic. *See* economic power spheres

spheres of influence, traditional, 10, 12, 19, 114, 116, 203, 217, 234, 244–45, 249–50, 252–53, 272, 283, 287, 295, 298–99, 307, 311, 322, 341, 361, 384, 416n54, 425n38, 428n109. *See also* alliances; economic power spheres

spiraling, problems of, ix, 2–3, 15, 17–18, 21–22, 27, 31, 34–37, 40–41, 43, 48–57, 54, 66, 68, 74, 85, 92, 94–95, 100–101, 115–19, 199, 201, 216, 221–22, 235, 240, 242, 248, 253, 259, 273, 284, 311, 319–21, 333, 352–53, 355–56, 367, 369, 371, 374, 387, 389, 393, 397n21, 398n34, 404n49, 405n57, 436n101, 439n4. *See also* crisis escalation; feedback loops; Jervis, Robert; security dilemma; trade-security dilemma

spiral model, 201, 355, 374. *See also* defensive realism; Glaser, Charles; Jervis, Robert; Kydd, Andrew; signaling arguments; spiraling, problems of

Spykman, Nicolas, 238

Stalin, Joseph, 8, 42, 48, 233, 241–44, 247–64, 267–85, 289–90, 294–96, 299–304, 310, 317, 322, 371, 381, 391, 426n51, 428n109, 428n122, 429n133. *See also* Berlin Crisis (1948–49); Cold War; Roosevelt, Franklin D.; Truman, Harry S.

Stimson, Henry, 256, 258, 260, 263–64, 276

Suez Canal (pre-1946), 151, 280

Suez Crisis (1956), 289, 304–6, 310–17. *See also* Eden, Anthony; Egypt; Eisenhower, Dwight D.; Nasser, Gamal Abdel

Taft, William Howard, 191, 194, 204, 233–34. *See also* dollar diplomacy

Taylor, Zachary, 136–38, 146, 413n103

tensions, vii, 2, 15, 25, 32, 53–54, 94, 199. *See also* trade-offs

Texas, struggle over (1836–45), 120–27. *See also* Jackson, Andrew; Polk, James K.; Tyler, John

Tiananmen Square Crisis (1989), 362, 372–75, 378–80, 391–92, 441n20

Trachtenberg, Marc, 424n1, 425n29

trade expectations, viii, x, 3, 5–6, 9–10, 14–15, 21, 27, 32, 34, 36, 42–44, 51–54, 59; empirical examples of, 85, 94–95, 97–98, 101–3, 110–13, 116–18, 120, 140–41, 152–53, 168, 244–46, 249, 252, 256, 260, 272, 276, 282–85, 286–90, 292, 295, 304–5, 310, 316–17, 319–22, 329, 337–41, 343–45, 349–53; U.S.-China relations and, 352–53, 366–67, 371–72, 386–87, 393, 399n1, 403n43, 406n10, 409n5, 429n4, 431n68. See also dynamic realism; signaling arguments; uncertainty regarding future

trade-offs, viii, 3, 7, 15, 18, 25, 31–32, 34, 40–41, 48–54; empirical examples of, prominent, 23, 235, 336, 357, 374, 388, 391, 406n9; as signal of character type, 432n2. See also dynamic realism; tensions

trade-security dilemma, 22, 35, 36, 51–52, 322, 352, 369. See also dynamic realism; feedback loops

Trubowitz, Peter, 396n8

Truman, Harry S., 5, 9, 233–34, 244–45, 247–48, 258–67, 270, 272–86, 290–93, 297–99, 301–9, 427n66, 427n78, 427n91, 428n122, 428n125, 429n133. See also Cold War

Truman Doctrine, 247, 292–93, 317

Trump, Donald, 368–69, 373, 384, 388, 442n30; as anomaly for realist theories, 388, 441n15, 444n73; economic restrictions of, on China, 368, 384, 398n32

Tumulty, Joseph, 198, 217

Turkey, 278–79, 281, 292

Tyler, John, 121–29, 139–40, 412n67; extension of Monroe Doctrine, 128

uncertainty regarding future, xi, 3, 15, 17–18, 21, 27, 35–37, 42–43, 48–49, 141, 144, 204, 219, 221, 224, 245, 327, 333, 357–59, 398n23, 399n2, 403n42, 404nn48–49. See also dynamic realism; offensive realism; trade expectations

Venezuela, 161, 414n2

Vietnam War, 5, 9, 20; origins of U.S. involvement in, 289, 294–99; origins of escalation in 1964–65, 289, 295–96, 299. See also domino logic; Korean War

Walt, Stephen, 35, 395n7, 401n21. See also defensive realism

Waltz, Kenneth, vii–viii, xi, 25, 399n3, 403n42

Wang, Chen, 443n42

War of 1812, 6–8, 94, 96, 97–114, 119, 122, 135, 140–41, 167, 2000, 202, 229, 411n40, 411n42, 420n25

War of Colonial Independence, 6, 13, 63–93

Washington, George, 90, 100–101, 106–07, 114

Weeks, Jessica, 46

Wertheim, Stephen, 238, 248

Wilson, Woodrow, vii, 5, 7–8, 234, 248, 251, 282, 418n4, 419n7, 421n55, 424n127, 424n129; Austria-Hungary, effort to keep it intact (1917), 8, 225, 229, 423n111; influence on Franklin D. Roosevelt, 232, 234, 238–39; Japanese threat, perception of, 7, 192–95, 200, 210–15, 217, 220–27, 423n104; and Mexico, 192–97, 205–210, 214, 216–18, 223–26, 230, 419n6, 419n11, 419n21; origins of entry into First World War, 5, 189–231; positive pre-war view of Germany, 422n91; possible war with Britain (1916), 220–22; South America and, 191, 203–04, 208–11, 215, 224, 420n38, 420n40; struggle with Britain for post-war dominance, 192, 217–22; supposed interest in democracy promotion, 421n51, 423n104, 423n122; Versailles Conference (1919), 8, 190, 235; and War of 1812, 200, 203, 229, 420n25. See also House, Edward; liberalism; Page, Walter; Tumulty, Joseph

Wilsonianism, 14, 60, 232, 241, 244, 248, 418n4

Wohlforth, William, 436n101, 437n110
Wood, Gordon, 64, 66
Woodford, Stewart, 158, 168–84, 417n81, 417n84
Worst-case assumption, 16, 37–39, 369, 397n21, 398n34, 399n2, 403n42, 403n45. *See also* Mearsheimer, John; offensive realism

Xi, Jinping, 41, 355–56, 36–64, 370, 374–81, 385–87, 391–92, 440n7, 441n23, 441n18, 442n38, 443n56. *See also* China (2007–present)

Yarhi-Milo, Keren, 405n71
Ye, Min, 376, 387
Yegorava, Natalia, 241
Yoder, Brandon, 439n2
Yom Kippur War (1973), 341–43. *See also* Israel; Kissinger, Henry

Zakaria, Fareed, 142–43, 148–49, 155, 395n7
Zhao, Ziyang, 374, 441n20. *See also* China (1977–90); Tiananmen Square Crisis (1989)
Zimmermann telegram, 193, 226–27, 230

## A NOTE ON THE TYPE

This book has been composed in Arno, an Old-style serif typeface in the classic Venetian tradition, designed by Robert Slimbach at Adobe.